CH00923993

Henry Parry Liddon

The Divinity of Our Lord and Saviour Jesus Christ

Elibron Classics
www.elibron.com

Elibron Classics series.

ISBN 1-4212-7253-9 (paperback)
ISBN 1-4212-7252-0 (hardcover)

This Elibron Classics Replica Edition is an unabridged facsimile of the edition published in 1885 by Rivingtons, London.

THE
DIVINITY OF OUR LORD

Works by the same Author.

Cheap Edition, Revised. Small 8vo., 2s. 6d.; or, in Cover, 1s. 6d.

Some Elements of Religion. Lent Lectures.

The Crown 8vo. (Fourth) Edition, 5s., may still be had.

Eighth Edition, Revised. Crown 8vo. 5s.

Sermons Preached before the University of Oxford. First Series, 1859—1868.

Third Edition. Crown 8vo. 5s.

Sermons Preached before the University of Oxford. Second Series, 1868—1882.

Crown 8vo. 7s. 6d.

Of the Five Wounds of the Holy Church. By ANTONIO ROSMINI. Edited, with an Introduction, by H. P. LIDDON.

Crown 8vo. 3s. 6d.

Report of Proceedings at the Reunion Conference, held at Bonn, September, 1874. With a Preface by H. P. LIDDON.

Crown 8vo. 3s. 6d.

Report of Proceedings at the Reunion Conference of 1875, with Preface by H. P. LIDDON. [London: B. M. PICKERING.]

Second Edition. 8vo. 2s. 6d.

Walter Kerr Hamilton, Bishop of Salisbury. A Sketch.

Fourth Edition. With Portrait. Large Type. 24mo. 2s. 6d.

A Manual for the Sick; with other Devotions. By LANCELOT ANDREWES, D.D., sometime Lord Bishop of Winchester.

Second Edition. Royal 32mo. 2s. 6d.

Private Prayers. By the Rev. E. B. PUSEY, D.D. Edited, with a Preface, by H. P. LIDDON.

Second Edition. Large Type. 24mo. 1s.

Prayers for a Young Schoolboy. By the Rev. E. B. PUSEY, D.D. Edited, with a Preface, by H. P. LIDDON.

The Divinity of Our Lord and Saviour Jesus Christ.

EIGHT LECTURES PREACHED BEFORE
THE UNIVERSITY OF OXFORD IN THE YEAR 1866

ON THE FOUNDATION OF THE LATE REV. JOHN BAMPTON, M.A.
CANON OF SALISBURY

BY

H. P. LIDDON, D.D.
CANON RESIDENTIARY OF ST. PAUL'S, AND LATE IRELAND PROFESSOR AT OXFORD

'Deus Verbum non accepit personam hominis, sed naturam, et in æternam Personam Divinitatis accepit temporalem substantiam carnis.'
S. Fulg. de Fide ad Petrum, c. 17.

ELEVENTH EDITION, REVISED

RIVINGTONS
WATERLOO PLACE, LONDON
MDCCCLXXXV

'Wenn Christus nicht wahrer Gott ist, die mahometanische Religion eine unstreitige Verbesserung der christlichen war, und Mahomet selbst ein ungleich grössrer und würdigerer Mann gewesen ist als Christus.'

Lessing, Sämmtl. Schriften, Bd. 9, *p.* 291.

'Simul quoque cum beatis videamus
Glorianter vultum Tuum, Christe Deus,
Gaudium quod est immensum atque probum,
Sæcula per infinita sæculorum.'

Rhythm. Eccl.

EXTRACT

FROM THE LAST WILL AND TESTAMENT

OF THE LATE

REV. JOHN BAMPTON,

CANON OF SALISBURY.

—— "I give and bequeath my Lands and Estates to the "Chancellor, Masters, and Scholars of the University of Oxford "for ever, to have and to hold all and singular the said Lands or "Estates upon trust, and to the intents and purposes hereinafter "mentioned; that is to say, I will and appoint that the Vice-"Chancellor of the University of Oxford for the time being shall "take and receive all the rents, issues, and profits thereof, and "(after all taxes, reparations, and necessary deductions made) "that he pay all the remainder to the endowment of eight "Divinity Lecture Sermons, to be established for ever in the "said University, and to be performed in the manner following:

"I direct and appoint, that, upon the first Tuesday in Easter "Term, a Lecturer may be yearly chosen by the Heads of Col-"leges only, and by no others, in the room adjoining to the "Printing-House, between the hours of ten in the morning and "two in the afternoon, to preach eight Divinity Lecture "Sermons, the year following, at St. Mary's in Oxford, between "the commencement of the last month in Lent Term, and the "end of the third week in Act Term.

"Also I direct and appoint, that the eight Divinity Lecture "Sermons shall be preached upon either of the following "Subjects—to confirm and establish the Christian Faith, and "to confute all heretics and schismatics—upon the divine "authority of the holy Scriptures—upon the authority of the "writings of the primitive Fathers, as to the faith and practice "of the primitive Church—upon the Divinity of our Lord and "Saviour Jesus Christ—upon the Divinity of the Holy Ghost— "upon the Articles of the Christian Faith, as comprehended in "the Apostles' and Nicene Creed.

"Also I direct, that thirty copies of the eight Divinity Lec-"ture Sermons shall be always printed, within two months after "they are preached; and one copy shall be given to the Chan-"cellor of the University, and one copy to the Head of every "College, and one copy to the Mayor of the city of Oxford, and "one copy to be put into the Bodleian Library; and the "expense of printing them shall be paid out of the revenue of "the Land or Estates given for establishing the Divinity Lecture "Sermons; and the Preacher shall not be paid, nor be entitled "to the revenue, before they are printed.

"Also I direct and appoint, that no person shall be qualified "to preach the Divinity Lecture Sermons, unless he hath taken "the degree of Master of Arts at least, in one of the two Uni-"versities of Oxford or Cambridge; and that the same person "shall never preach the Divinity Lecture Sermons twice."

PREFACE

TO THE FIRST EDITION.

PERHAPS an apology may be due to the University for the delay which has occurred in the appearance of this volume. If so, the writer would venture to plead that he undertook the duties of the Bampton Lecturer at a very short notice, and, it may be, without sufficiently considering what they involved. When, however, the accomplished Clergyman whom the University had chosen to lecture in the year 1866 was obliged by a serious illness to seek a release from his engagement, the vacant post was offered to the present writer with a kindness and generosity which, as he thought, obliged him, although entirely unprepared, to accept it and to meet its requirements as well as he could.

Under such circumstances, the materials which were made ready in some haste for use in the pulpit seemed to require a close revision before publication. In making this revision—which has been somewhat seriously interrupted by other duties—the writer has not felt at liberty to introduce alterations except in the way of phrase and illustration. He has, however, availed himself of the customary licence to print at length some considerable paragraphs, the sense of which, in order to save time, was only summarily given when the lectures were delivered. And he has subjoined the Greek text of the more important passages of the New Testament to which he has had occasion to refer; as experience seems to prove that very many readers do not verify quotations from Holy Scripture for themselves, or at least that they content themselves with examining the few which are generally thought to be of most importance. Whereas, the force of the argument for our Lord's Divinity, as indeed is the case with other truths of the New Testament, is eminently cumulative. Such an argument is to be appreciated, not by studying the comparatively few texts which expressly assert the doctrine, but that large number of passages which indirectly, but most vividly, imply it.

It is perhaps superfluous to observe that eight lectures can deal with little beyond the outskirts of a vast, or to speak more accurately, of an exhaustless subject. The present volume attempts only to notice, more or less directly, some of those assaults upon the doctrine of our Lord's Divinity which have been prominent or popular of late years, and which have, unhappily, had a certain weight among persons with whom the writer is acquainted.

Whatever disturbing influence the modern destructive criticism may have exerted upon the form of the old argument for the Divinity of Christ, the main features of that argument remain substantially unchanged. The writer will have deep reason for thankfulness, if any of those whose inclination or duty leads them to pursue the subject, should be guided by his references to the pages of those great theologians whose names, whether in our own country or in the wider field of Catholic Christendom, are for ever associated with the vindication of this most fundamental truth of the Faith.

In passing the sheets of this work through the press, the writer has been more largely indebted than he can well say to the invigorating sympathy and varied learning of the Rev. W. Bright, Fellow of University College; while the Index is due to the friendly interest of another Fellow of that College, the Rev. P. G. Medd.

That in so wide and so mysterious a subject all errors have been avoided, is much more than the writer dares to hope.

But at least he has not intentionally contravened the clear sense of Holy Scripture, or any formal decision whether of the Undivided Church or of the Church of England. May He to the honour of Whose Person this volume is devoted, vouchsafe to pardon in it all that is not calculated to promote His truth and His glory! And for the rest, 'quisquis hæc legit, ubi pariter certus est, pergat mecum; ubi pariter hæsitat, quærat mecum; ubi errorem suum cognoscit, redeat ad me; ubi meum, revocet me. Ita ingrediamur simul charitatis viam, tendentes ad Eum de Quo dictum est, Quærite Faciem Ejus semper[a].'

CHRIST CHURCH,
Ascension Day, 1867.

[a] S. Aug. de Trin. i. 5.

PREFACE

TO THE SECOND EDITION.

The kindly welcome given to this volume, both at home and in America, has led to a demand for another edition, which has taken the writer somewhat by surprise. He has, however, availed himself of the opportunity to make what use he could of the criticisms which have come, from whatever quarter, under his notice. Some textual errors have been corrected. Some ill-considered or misunderstood expressions have been modified. References to authorities and sources of information, which were accidentally omitted, have been supplied. To a few of the notes there has been added fresh matter, of an explanatory or justificatory character. The index, too, has been remodelled and enlarged. But the book remains, it is needless to say, substantially unchanged. And if it is now offered to the public in a somewhat altered guise, this has been done in order to meet the views of friends, who have urged, not perhaps altogether without reason, that 'in the Church of England, books on Divinity are so largely adapted to the taste and means of the wealthier classes, as to imply that the most interesting of all subjects can possess no attractions for the intelligence and heart of persons who enjoy only a moderate income.'

Of the topics discussed in this book, there is one which has invited a larger share of attention than others, both from those who share and from those who reject the Faith of the Church. It is that central argument for our Saviour's Deity, which is based on His persistent self-assertion, taken in conjunction with the sublimity of His Human character. The supreme importance of this consideration is indeed obvious. Certainly, in the order of historical treatment, the inferences which may be deduced from Prophecy, and from Christ's supernatural design to found the 'Kingdom of Heaven,' naturally precede that which arises from His language about Himself. But, in the order of the formation of conviction, the latter argument must claim precedence. It is, in truth, more fundamental. It is the heart of the entire subject, from which a vital strength flows into the accessory although important topics grouped around it. Apart from Our Lord's personal claims, the language of prophecy would have been only a record of unfulfilled anticipations, and the lofty Christology of the Apostles only a sample of their misguided enthusiasms; whereas the argument which appeals to Christ's claims, taken in conjunction with His character, is independent of the collateral arguments which in truth it supports. If the argument from prophecy could be discredited, by assigning new dates to the prophetical books, and by theories of a cultured political foresight; if the faith of the Apostles could be accounted for upon grounds which referred it to their individual peculiarities of thought and temper; there would still remain the unique phenomenon of the sublimest of characters inseparably linked, in the Person of Jesus, to the most energetic proclamation of self.

In this inmost shrine of Christian Truth, there are two courses open to the negative criticism. It may indeed endeavour to explain away Our Lord's self-assertion in the interests, as it conceives, of His Human Character. The impossibility of really doing this has been insisted upon in these lectures. For Christ's self-assertion is not merely embodied in statements which would be blasphemy in the mouth of a created being; it underlies and explains His entire attitude towards His disciples, towards His countrymen, towards the human race, towards the religion of Israel. Nor is Christ's self-assertion confined to the records of one Evangelist, or to a particular period in His ministry. The three first Evangelists bear witness to it, in different terms, yet not less significantly than does St. John; and it belongs as truly, though not perhaps so patently, to Our Lord's first great discourse as to His last. From first to last He asserts, He insists upon the acceptance of Himself. But when this is acknowledged, a man must either base such self-assertion on its one sufficient justification, by accepting the Church's faith in the Deity of Christ; or he must regard it as fatal to the moral beauty of Christ's Human character.—*Christus, si non Deus, non bonus.*

It is urged by persons whose opinions are entitled to great respect that, however valid this argument may be, its religious expediency must be open to serious question. And undoubtedly such like arguments cannot at any time be put forward without involving those who do so in grave responsibility. Of this the writer, as he trusts, has not been unmindful. He has not used a dangerous weapon gratuitously, nor, so far as he knows his own motives, with any purpose so miserable as that of producing a rhetorical effect.

What, then, are the religious circumstances which appear to warrant the employment of such an argument at present?

Speaking roughly, men's minds may be grouped into three classes with reference to the vital question which is discussed in these lectures.

1. There are those who, by God's mercy, have no doubt on the subject of Our Lord's Godhead. To mere dialecticians their case may appear to be one of sheer intellectual stagnation. But the fact is, that they possess, or at least that they have altogether within their reach, a far higher measure of real 'life' than is even suspected by their critics. They are not seeking truth; they are enjoying it. They are not like Alpine climbers still making their way up the mountain side; they have gained the summit, and are gazing on the panorama which is spread around and beneath them. It is even painful to them to think of 'proving' a truth which is now the very life of their souls. In their whole spiritual activity, in their prayers, in their regular meditations, in their study of Holy Scripture, in their habitual thoughts

respecting the eternal Future, they take Christ's Divinity for granted; and it never occurs to them to question a reality from which they know themselves to be continually gaining new streams of light and warmth and power.

To such as these, this book may or may not be of service. To some Christians, who are filled with joy and peace in believing, a review of the grounds of any portion of their faith may be even distressing. To others such a process may be bracing and helpful. But in any case it should be observed that the foot-notes contain passages from unbelieving writers, which are necessary to shew that the statements of the text are not aimed at imaginary phantoms, but which also are not unlikely to shock and distress religious and believing minds very seriously. In such a matter to be forewarned is to be forearmed.

2. There are others, and, it is to be feared, a larger class than is often supposed, who have made up their minds against the claims of Divine Revelation altogether. They may admit the existence of a Supreme Being, in some shadowy sense, as an Infinite Mind, or as a resistless Force. They may deny that there is any satisfactory reason for holding that any such Being exists at all. But whether they are Theists or Atheists, they resent the idea of any interference from on high in this human world, and accordingly they denounce the supernatural, on *à priori* grounds. The trustworthiness of Scripture as an historical record is to their minds sufficiently disproved by the undoubted fact, that its claim to credit is staked upon the possibility of certain extraordinary miracles. When that possibility is denied, Jesus Christ must either be pronounced to be a charlatan, or a person of whose real words and actions no trustworthy account has been transmitted to us.

Whichever conclusion be accepted by those who belong to the class in question, it is plain that this book cannot hope to assist them. For it treats as certain, facts of which they deny even the possibility. It must of necessity appear to them to be guilty of a continuous *petitio principii;* since they dispute its fundamental premises. If any such should ever chance to examine it, they would probably see in it 'only another illustration of the hopelessness of getting "orthodox" believers even to appreciate the nature and range of the difficulties which are felt by liberal thinkers.'

It may be replied that something should have been done towards meeting those particular 'difficulties.' But, in point of fact, this would have been to choose another subject for the lectures of 1866. A few lectures, after all, can only deal with some aspects of a great Doctrine; and every treatise on a question of Divinity cannot be expected to begin *ab ovo*, and to discuss the Existence and the Personality of God. However little may be assumed, there will always be persons eager to complain of the minimized 'assumption' as altogether unjustifiable; because there are always persons who deny the most elementary Theistic truth. This being the case, the practical question to be determined is this:—How much is it advisable to take for granted in a given condition of faith and opinion, with a view to dealing with the doubts and difficulties of the largest number? The existence and personality of God, and the possibility and reality of the Christian Revelation, have been often discussed; while the truth and evidential force of miracles were defended in the year 1865 by a Bampton Lecturer of distinguished ability. Under these circumstances, the present writer deliberately assumed a great deal which is denied in our day and country by many active minds, with a view to meeting the case, as it appeared to him, of a much larger number, who would not dispute his premises, but who fail to see, or hesitate to acknowledge, the conclusion which they really warrant.

3. For, in truth, the vast majority of our countrymen still shrink with sincere dread from anything like an explicit rejection of Christianity. Yet no one who hears what goes on in daily conversation, and who is moderately conversant with the tone of some of the leading organs of public opinion, can doubt the existence of a wide-spread unsettlement of religious

belief. People have a notion that the present is, in the hackneyed phrase, 'a transitional period,' and that they ought to be keeping pace with the general movement. Whither indeed they are going, they probably cannot say, and have never very seriously asked themselves. Their most definite impression is that the age is turning its back on dogmas and creeds, and is moving in a negative direction under the banner of 'freedom.' They are, indeed, sometimes told by their guides that they are hurrying forward to a chaos in which all existing beliefs, even the fundamental axioms of morality, will be ultimately submerged. Sometimes, too, they are encouraged to look hopefully forward beyond the immediate foreground of conflict and confusion, to an intellectual and moral Elysium, which will be reached when Science has divested Religion of all its superstitious incumbrances, and in which 'thought' and 'feeling,' after their long misunderstanding, are to embrace under the supervision of a philosophy higher than any which has yet been elaborated. But these visions are seen only by a few, and they are not easily popularized. The general tendency is to avoid speculations, whether hopeful or discouraging, about the future, yet to acquiesce in the theory so constantly suggested, that there is some sort of necessary opposition between dogma and goodness, and to recognise the consequent duty of promoting goodness by the depreciation and destruction of dogma. Thus, the movement, although negative in one sense, believes itself to be eminently positive in another. With regard to dogma, it is negative. But it sincerely affects a particular care for morality; and in purifying and enforcing moral truth, it endeavours to make its positive character most distinctly apparent.

It is easy to understand the bearing of such a habit of mind when placed face to face with the Person of Our Lord. It tends to issue practically (although, in its earlier stages, not with any very intelligent consciousness) in Socinianism. It regards the great statements whereby Christ's Godhead is taught or guarded in Scripture and the Creeds, if not with impatience and contempt, at least with real although silent aversion. Church formularies appear to it simply in the light of an incubus upon true religious thought and feeling; for it is insensible to the preciousness of the truths which they guard. Hence as its aims and actions become more and more defined, it tends with increasing decision to become Humanitarian. Its dislike of the language of Nicæa hardens into an explicit denial of the truth which that language guards. Yet, if it exults in being unorthodox, and therefore is hostile to the Creed, it is ambitious to be pre-eminently moral, and therefore it lays especial emphasis upon the beauty and perfection of Christ's Human character. It aspires to analyse, to study, to imitate that character in a degree which was, it thinks, impossible during those ages of dogma which it professes to have closed. It thus relieves its desire to be still loyal in some sense to Jesus Christ, although under new conditions: if it discards ancient formularies, it maintains that this rejection takes place only and really in the interest of moral truth.

Now it is to such a general habit of mind that this book as a whole, and the argument from Our Lord's self-assertion in particular, ventures to address itself. Believing that the cause of dogma is none other than the cause of morality,—that the perfect moral character of Jesus Christ is really compatible only with the Nicene assertion of His absolute Divinity,—the writer has endeavoured to say so. He has not been at pains to disguise his earnest conviction, that the hopes and sympathies, which have been raised in many sincerely religious minds by the so-called Liberal-religious movement of our day, are destined to a rude and bitter disappointment. However long the final decision between 'some faith' and 'no faith' may be deferred, it must be made at last. Already advanced rationalistic thought agrees with Catholic believers in maintaining that Christ is not altogether a good man, if He is not altogether Superhuman. And if this be so, surely it is prudent as well as honest to say so. They who do not wish to break with Christ Our Lord, and to cast out His very Name as evil, in the years to come, will be thankful to have recognised the real tendencies of an anti-dogmatic teaching which for the moment may have won their sympathies. It is of the last importance in religious thinking, not less than in religious practice, that the question, Whither am I going? should be asked and answered. Such a question is not the less important because for the present all is smooth and reassuring, combining the reality of religious change with the avoidance of any violent shock to old convictions. It has been said that there is a peculiar fascination in the movement of a boat which is gliding softly and swiftly down the rapids above Niagara. But a man must be strangely constituted to be able, under such circumstances, so to abandon himself to the sense of present satisfaction as to forget the fate which is immediately before him.

The argument from Christ's character to His Divinity which is here put forward can make no pretence to originality. To the present writer, it was suggested in its entirety, some years ago, upon a perusal of Mr. F. W. Newman's 'Phases of Faith.' The seventh chapter of that remarkable but saddening work yielded the analysis which has been expanded in these lectures, and which the lecturer had found, on more than one occasion, to be serviceable in assisting Socinians to understand the real basis of the Church's faith respecting the dignity of her Head. It agrees, moreover, even in detail, with the work of the great preacher of the Church of France, to whose earnestness and genius the present writer has elsewhere professed himself to be, and always must feel, sincerely indebted.

The real justification of such arguments lies in a fact which liberal thinkers will not be slow to recognise [a]. If the moral

[a] Do we not however find a sanction for this class of arguments in appeals such as the following? St. John vii. 42: 'If God were your Father, ye would have loved Me.' St. John v. 38: 'And ye have not His Word abiding in you: for, whom He hath sent, Him ye believe not.' And is not this summarized in the apostolical teaching? 1 St. John ii. 23: 'Whosoever denieth the Son, the same hath not the Father.' Such passages

sense of man be impaired by the Fall, it is not so entirely disabled as to be incapable of discerning moral beauty. If it may err when it attempts to determine, on purely *à priori* human grounds, what should be the conduct and dispensations of God in dealing with His creatures, it is not therefore likely to be in error when it stands face to face with human sincerity, and humility, and love. At the feet of the Christ of the Gospels, the moral sense may be trusted to protest against an intellectual aberration which condemns Him as vain and false and selfish, only that it may rob Him of His aureole of Divinity. 'In the seventh chapter of the "Phases of Faith,"' I quote the words of a thoughtful friend, 'there is the satisfaction of feeling that one has reached the very floor of Pandemonium, and that a rebound has become almost inevitable. Anything is better than to be sinking still, one knows not how deeply, into the abyss.'

It may be said that other alternatives have been put forward, with a view of forcing orthodox members of the Church of England into a position analogous to that in which the argument of these lectures might place a certain section of Latitudinarian thinkers. For example, some Roman Catholic and some sceptical writers unite in urging that either all orthodox Christianity is false, or the exclusive claims of the Church of Rome must be admitted to be valid. Every such alternative must be considered honestly, and in view of the particular evidence which can be produced in its support. But to propound the present alternative between Rome and unbelief, is practically to forget that the acceptance of the dogmatic principle, or of any principle, does not commit those who accept it to its exaggerations or corruptions; and that the promises of Our Lord to His people in regard alike to Unity and to Holiness, are, in His mysterious providence, permitted to be

appear to shew, that to press an inference, whether it be moral or doctrinal, from an admitted truth, by insisting that the truth itself is virtually rejected if the inference be declined, is not accurately described as a trick of modern orthodoxy.

traversed by the misuse of man's free-will. In a word, the dilemma between Roman Catholicism and infidelity is, as a matter of fact, very far from being obviously exhaustive: but it is difficult to see that any intermediate position can be really made good between the denial of Christ's Human perfection and the admission that He is a Superhuman Person. And when this admission is once fairly made, it leads by easy and necessary steps to belief in His true Divinity.

The great question of our day is, whether Christ our Lord is only the author and founder of a religion, of which another Being, altogether separate from Him, namely, God, is the object; or whether Jesus Christ Himself, true God and true Man, is, with the Father and the Holy Ghost, the Object of Christian faith and love as truly as, in history, He was the Founder of Christendom. Come what may, the latter belief has been, is, and will be to the end, the Faith of His Church.

May those who are tempted to exchange it for its modern rival reflect that the choice before them does not lie between a creed with one dogma more, and a creed with one dogma less, nor yet between a mediæval and a modern rendering of the Gospel history. It is really a choice between a phantom and a reality; between the implied falsehood and the eternal truth of Christianity; between the interest which may cling to a discredited and evanescent memory of the past, and the worship of a living, ever-present, and immaculate Redeemer.

CHRIST CHURCH,
Whitsuntide, 1868.

PREFACE

TO THE NINTH EDITION.

MORE than thirteen years have elapsed since any alteration was made in the text or notes of this volume; but some criticisms, more or less direct, have appeared, of which the writer has long been anxious to take advantage, by correcting proved inaccuracies or by the addition of explanatory matter. In doing this he has found reason to regret that it is not possible to reconstruct the book, on a larger scale, without destroying its identity, and thus forfeiting its place in the series to which it belongs. If he has left some objections unnoticed, this is because he could not afford, on the score of space, to notice any but such as have enabled him to improve his work. Thus an objection that passages of the New Testament which assert our Lord's Humanity had been overlooked will be found to be answered incidentally by the more complete Index of texts, for which this edition is indebted to the Rev. J. O. Johnston, M.A., of Keble College. Criticisms which imply a difference of fundamental principle could not be adequately considered without entering upon discussions, any one of which might furnish matter for a separate treatise[a].

CHRIST CHURCH,
Advent, 1881

[a] See Note H, p. 548.

ANALYSIS OF THE LECTURES.

LECTURE I.

THE QUESTION BEFORE US.

St. Matt. xvi. 13.

LECTURE II.

ANTICIPATIONS OF CHRIST'S DIVINITY IN THE OLD TESTAMENT.

Gal. iii. 8.

LECTURE III.

OUR LORD'S WORK IN THE WORLD A WITNESS TO HIS DIVINITY.

St. Matt. xiii. 54–56.

LECTURE IV.

OUR LORD'S DIVINITY AS WITNESSED BY HIS CONSCIOUSNESS.

St. John x. 33.

LECTURE V.

THE DOCTRINE OF CHRIST'S DIVINITY IN THE WRITINGS OF ST. JOHN.

1 St. John i. 1–3.

LECTURE VI.

OUR LORD'S DIVINITY AS TAUGHT BY ST. JAMES, ST. PETER, AND ST. PAUL.

Gal. ii. 9.

LECTURE VII.

THE HOMOOUSION.

Tit. i. 9.

LECTURE VIII.

SOME CONSEQUENCES OF THE DOCTRINE OF OUR LORD'S DIVINITY.

Rom. viii. 32.

THE LECTURES.

LECTURE I.

THE QUESTION BEFORE US.

When Jesus came into the coasts of Cæsarea Philippi, He asked His disciples, saying, Whom do men say that I the Son of Man am? And they said, Some say that Thou art John the Baptist: some, Elias; and others, Jeremias, or one of the Prophets. He saith unto them, But whom say ye that I am?—ST. MATT. xvi. 13.

THUS did our Lord propose to His first followers the momentous question, which for eighteen centuries has riveted the eye of thinking and adoring Christendom. The material setting, if we may so term it, of a great intellectual or moral event ever attracts the interest and lives in the memory of men; and the Evangelist is careful to note that the question of our Lord was asked in the neighbourhood of Cæsarea Philippi. Jesus Christ had reached the northernmost point of His journeyings. He was close to the upper source of the Jordan, and at the base of the majestic mountain which forms a natural barrier to the Holy Land at its northern extremity. His eye rested upon a scenery in the more immediate foreground, which from its richness and variety has been compared by travellers to the Italian Tivoli [a]. Yet there belonged to this spot a higher interest than any which the beauty of merely inanimate or irrational nature can furnish; it bore visible traces of the hopes, the errors, and the struggles of the human soul. Around a grotto which Greek settlers had assigned to the worship of the sylvan Pan, a Pagan settlement had gradually formed itself. Herod the Great had adorned the spot with a temple of white marble, dedicated to his patron Augustus; and more recently, the rising city, enlarged and beautified by Philip the tetrarch, had received a new name

[a] Stanley, Sinai and Palestine, p. 397.

which combined the memory of the Cæsar Tiberius with that of the local potentate. It is probable that our Lord at least had the city in view [b], even if He did not enter it. He was standing on the geographical frontier of Judaism and Heathendom. Paganism was visibly before Him in each of its two most typical forms of perpetual and world-wide degradation. It was burying its scant but not utterly lost idea of an Eternal Power and Divinity [c] beneath a gross materialistic nature-worship; and it was prostituting the sanctities of the human conscience to the lowest purposes of an unholy and tyrannical statecraft. And behind and around our Lord was that peculiar people, of whom, as concerning the flesh, He came Himself [d], and to which His first followers belonged. Israel too was there; alone in her memory of a past history such as no other race could boast; alone in her sense of a present degradation, political and moral, such as no other people could feel; alone in her strong expectation of a Deliverance which to men who were 'aliens from' her sacred 'commonwealth' seemed but the most chimerical of delusions. On such a spot does Jesus Christ raise the great question which is before us in the text, and this, as we may surely believe, not without a reference to the several wants and hopes and efforts of mankind thus visibly pictured around Him. How was the human conscience to escape from that political violence and from that degrading sensualism which had riveted the yoke of Pagan superstition? How was Israel to learn the true drift and purpose of her marvellous past? How was she to be really relieved of her burden of social and moral misery? How were her high anticipations of a brighter future to be explained and justified? And although that 'middle wall of partition,' which so sharply divided off her inward and outward life from that of Gentile humanity, had been built up for such high and necessary ends by her great inspired lawgiver, did not such isolation also involve manifest counterbalancing risks and loss? was it to be eternal? could it, might it be 'broken down'? These questions could only be answered by some further Revelation, larger and clearer than that already possessed by Israel, and absolutely new to Heathendom. They demanded some nearer, fuller, more persuasive self-unveiling than any

[b] Dean Stanley surmises that the rock on which was placed the Temple of Augustus may possibly have determined the form of our Lord's promise to St. Peter in St. Matt. xvi. 18. Sinai and Palestine, p. 399.

[c] Rom. i. 20.

[d] Ibid. ix. 5.

which the Merciful and Almighty God had as yet vouchsafed to His reasonable creatures. May not then the suggestive scenery of Cæsarea Philippi have been chosen by our Lord, as well fitted to witness that solemn enquiry in the full answer to which Jew and Gentile were alike to find a rich inheritance of light, peace and freedom? Jesus 'asked His disciples, saying, Whom do men say that I the Son of Man am?'

Let us pause to mark the significance of the fact that our Lord Himself proposes this consideration to His disciples and to His Church.

It has been often maintained of late that the teaching of Jesus Christ Himself differs from that of His Apostles and of their successors, in that He only taught religion, while they have taught dogmatic theology[e].

This statement appears to proceed upon a presumption that religion and theology can be separated, not merely in idea and for the moment, by some process of definition, but permanently and in the world of fact. What then is religion? If you say that religion is essentially thought whereby man unites himself to the Eternal and Unchangeable Being[f], it is at least plain that the object-matter of such a religious activity as this is exactly identical with the object-matter of theology. Nay more, it would seem to follow that a religious life is simply a life of theological speculation. If you make religion to consist in 'the knowledge of our practical duties considered as God's commandments[g],' your definition irresistibly suggests God in His capacity of universal Legislator, and it thus carries the earnestly and honestly religious man into the heart of theology. If you protest that religion

[e] Baur more cautiously says: 'Wenn wir mit der Lehre Jesu die Lehre des Apostels Paulus zusammenhalten, so fällt sogleich der grosse Unterschied in die Augen, welcher hier stattfindet zwischen einer noch *in der Form eines allgemeinen Princips sich aussprechenden Lehre*, und einem schon zur Bestimmtheit des Dogma's gestalteten Lehrbegriff.' Vorlesungen über N. T. Theologie, p. 123. But it would be difficult to shew that the 'Universal Principle' does not involve and embody a number of definite dogmas. Baur would not admit that St. John xiv., xv., xvi. contain words really spoken by Jesus Christ: but the Sermon on the Mount itself is sufficiently dogmatic. Cf. St. Matt. vi. 4, 6, 14, 26, 30; vii. 21, 22.

[f] So Fichte, quoted by Klee, Dogmatik, c. 2. With this definition those of Schelling and Hegel substantially concur. It is unnecessary to remark that thought is only one element of true religion.

[g] So Kant, ibid. This definition (1) reduces religion to being merely an affair of the understanding, and (2) identifies its substance with that of morality.

has nothing to do with intellectual skill in projecting definitions, and that it is at bottom a feeling of tranquil dependence upon some higher Power [h], you cannot altogether set aside the capital question which arises as to the nature of that Power upon which religion thus depends. Even if you should contend that feeling is the essential element in religion, still you cannot seriously maintain that the reality of that to which such feeling relates is altogether a matter of indifference [i]. For the adequate satisfaction of this religious feeling lies not in itself but in its object; and therefore it is impossible to represent religion as indifferent to the absolute truth of that object, and in a purely æsthetical spirit, concerned only with the beauty of the idea before it, even in a case where the reflective understanding may have condemned that idea as logically false. Religion, to support itself, must rest consciously on its object: the intellectual apprehension of that object as true is an integral element of religion. In other words, religion is practically inseparable from theology. The religious Mahommedan sees in Allah a being to whose absolute decrees he must implicitly resign himself; a theological dogma then is the basis of the specific Mahommedan form of religion. A child reads in the Sermon on the Mount that our Heavenly Father takes care of the sparrows, and of the lilies of the field [j], and the child prays to Him accordingly. The truth upon which the child rests is the dogma of the Divine Providence, which encourages trust, and warrants prayer, and lies at the root of the child's religion. In short, religion cannot exist without some view of its object, namely, God; but no sooner do you introduce any intellectual aspect whatever of God, nay, the bare idea that such a Being exists, than you have before you not merely a religion, but at least, in some sense, a theology [k].

[h] 'Abhängigkeitsgefühl.' Schleiermacher's account of religion has been widely adopted in our own day and country. But (1) it ignores the active side of true religion, (2) it loses sight of man's freedom no less than of God's, and (3) it may imply nothing better than a passive submission to the laws of the Universe, without any belief whatever as to their Author.

[i] Dorner gives an account of this extreme theory as maintained by De Wette in his Religion und Theologie, 1815. De Wette appears to have followed out some hints of Herder's, while applying Jacobi's doctrine of feeling, as 'the immediate perception of the Divine,' and the substitute for the practical reason, to theology. Cf. Dorner, Person Christi, Zw. Th. p. 996, sqq.

[j] St. Matt. vi. 25–30.

[k] Religion includes in its complete idea the knowledge and the worship of God. (S. Aug. de Util. Cred. c. 12. n. 27.) Cicero gives the limited

Had our Lord revealed no one truth except the Parental character of God, while at the same time He insisted upon a certain morality and posture of the soul as proper to man's reception of this revelation, He would have been the Author of a theology as well as of a religion. In point of fact, besides teaching various truths concerning God, which were unknown before, or at most only guessed at, He did that which in a merely human teacher of high purpose would have been morally intolerable. He drew the eyes of men towards Himself. He claimed to be something more than the Founder of a new religious spirit, or than the authoritative promulgator of a higher truth than men had yet known. He taught true religion indeed as no man had yet taught it, but He bent the religious spirit which He had summoned into life to do homage to Himself, as being its lawful and adequate Object. He taught the highest theology, but He also placed Himself at the very centre of His doctrine, and He announced Himself as sharing the very throne of that God Whom He so clearly unveiled. If He was the organ and author of a new and final revelation, He also claimed to be the very substance and material of His own message; His most startling revelation was Himself.

These are statements which will be justified, it is hoped, hereafter[1]; and, if some later portions of our subject are for a moment anticipated, it is only that we may note the true and extreme significance of our Lord's question in the text. But let us also ask ourselves what would be the duty of a merely human teacher of the highest moral aim, entrusted with a great spiritual mission and lesson for the benefit of mankind? The example of St. John Baptist is an answer to this enquiry. Such a teacher would represent himself as a mere 'voice' crying aloud in the moral wilderness around him, and anxious, beyond aught else, to shroud his own insignificant person beneath the majesty of his message. Not to do this would be to proclaim his own moral degradation; it would be a public confession that he

sense which Pagan Rome attached to the word: 'Qui omnia quæ ad cultum deorum pertinerent, diligenter retractarent et tanquam relegerent, sunt dicti religiosi, ex relegendo.' (De Nat. Deorum, ii. 28.) Lactantius gives the Christian form of the idea, whatever may be thought of his etymology: 'Vinculo pietatis obstricti Deo, et religati sumus, unde ipsa religio nomen accepit.' (Inst. Div. iv. 24.) Religion is the bond between God and man's whole nature: in God the heart finds its happiness, the reason its rule of truth, the will its freedom.

[1] See Lecture IV.

could only regard a great spiritual work for others as furnishing an opportunity for adding to his own social capital, or to his official reputation. When then Jesus Christ so urgently draws the attention of men to His Personal Self, He places us in a dilemma. We must either say that He was unworthy of His own words in the Sermon on the Mount[m], or we must confess that He has some right, and is under the pressure of some necessity, to do that which would be morally insupportable in a merely human teacher. Now if this right and necessity exist, it follows that when our Lord bids us to consider His Personal rank in the hierarchy of beings, He challenges an answer. Remark moreover that in the popular sense of the term the answer is not less a theological answer if it be that of the Ebionitic heresy than if it be the language of the Nicene Creed. The Christology of the Church is in reality an integral part of its theology; and Jesus Christ raises the central question of Christian theology when He asks, 'Whom do men say that I the Son of Man am?'

It may be urged that our Lord is inviting attention, not to His essential Personality, but to His assumed office as the Jewish Messiah; that He is, in fact, asking for a confession of His Messiahship.

Now observe the exact form of our Lord's question, as given in St. Matthew's Gospel; which, as Olshausen has remarked, is manifestly here the leading narrative: 'Whom do men say that I the Son of Man am?' This question involves an assertion, namely, that the Speaker is the Son of Man. What did He mean by that designation? It is important to remember that with two exceptions[n] the title is only applied to our Lord in the New Testament by His own lips. It was His self-chosen Name: why did He choose it?

First, then, it was in itself, to Jewish ears, a clear assertion of Messiahship. In the vision of Daniel 'One like unto the Son of Man[o] had come with the clouds of heaven, ... and there was given Him dominion and glory and a kingdom.' This kingdom succeeded in the prophet's vision to four inhuman kingdoms, correspondent to the four typical beasts; it was the kingdom of a prince, human indeed, and yet from heaven. In consequence

[m] Observe the principle involved in St. Matt. vi. 1–8.

[n] Acts vii. 56; Rev. i. 13, xiv. 14.

[o] כבר אנש—ὡς υἱὸς ἀνθρώπου, LXX. Dan. vii. 13, sqq. Cf. Ezek. i. 26, and J. B. Carpzovii, Diss. de Filio Hominis ad Dan. vii., in Thesaurus Theologico-Philologicus, p. 887, sqq.

of this prophecy, the 'Son of Man' became a popular and official title of the Messiah. In the Book of Enoch, which is assigned with the highest probability by recent criticism to the second century before our era [p], this and kindred titles are continually applied to Messiah. Our Lord in His prophecy over Jerusalem predicted that at the last day 'they shall see the Son of Man coming in the clouds with power and great glory [q].' And when standing at the tribunal of Caiaphas He thus addressed His judges: 'I say unto you, hereafter shall ye see the Son of Man sitting at the right hand of power, and coming in the clouds of heaven [r].' In these passages there is absolutely no room for doubting either His distinct reference to the vision in Daniel, or the claim which the title Son of Man was intended to assert. As habitually used by our Lord, it was a constant setting forth of His Messianic dignity, in the face of the people of Israel [s].

Why indeed He chose this one, out of the many titles of Messiah, is a further question, a brief consideration of which lies in the track of the subject before us.

It would not appear to be sufficient to reply that the title Son of Man is the most unpresuming, the least glorious of the titles of Messiah, and was adopted by our Lord as such. For if such a title claimed, as it did claim, Messiahship, the precise etymological force of the word could not neutralize its current and recognised value in the estimation of the Jewish people. The claim thus advanced was independent of any analysis of the exact sense of the title which asserted it. The title derived its popular force from the office with which it was associated. To adopt the title, however humble might be its strict and intrinsic meaning, was to claim the great office to which in the minds of men it was indissolubly attached.

[p] Cf. Dillmann, Das Buch Enoch, 1853, p. 157. Dillmann places the book in the time of John Hyrcanus, B.C. 130-109. Dr. Pusey would assign to it a still earlier date. Cf. Daniel the Prophet, p. 390, note 2, and 391, note 3.

[q] St. Matt. xxiv. 30.

[r] Ibid. xxvi. 64.

[s] 'Den Namen des υἱὸς τοῦ ἀνθρώπου gebraucht Jesus Selbst auf eine so eigenthümliche Weise von Sich, dass man nur annehmen kann, Er habe mit jenem Namen, wie man auch seine Bedeutung genauer bestimmen mag, irgend eine Beziehung auf die Messiasidee ausdrücken wollen.' Baur, Das Christenthum, p. 37. Cf. also the same author's Vorlesungen über Neutestamentliche Theologie, p. 76, sqq. In St. Matt. x. 23, xiii. 37-41, the official force of the title is obvious. That it was a simple periphrasis for the personal pronoun, without any reference to the office or Person of the Speaker, is inconsistent with Acts vii. 56, and St. Matt. xvi. 13.

As it had been addressed to the prophet Ezekiel [t], the title Son of Man seemed to contrast the frail and shortlived life of men with the boundless strength and the eternal years of the Infinite God. And as applied to Himself by Jesus, it doubtless expresses a real Humanity, a perfect and penetrating community of nature and feeling with the lot of human kind. Thus, when our Lord says that authority was given Him to execute judgment because He is the Son of Man, it is plain that the point of the reason lies, not in His being Messiah, but in His being Human. He displays a genuine Humanity which could deem nothing human strange, and could be touched with a feeling of the infirmities of the race which He was to judge [u]. But the title Son of Man means more than this in its application to our Lord. It does not merely assert His real incorporation with our kind; it exalts Him indefinitely above us all as the representative, the ideal, the pattern Man [x]. He is, in a special sense, the Son of Mankind, the genuine offspring of the race. His is the Human Life which does justice to the idea of Humanity. All human history tends to Him or radiates from Him. He is the point in which humanity finds its unity; as St. Irenæus says, He 'recapitulates' it [y]. He closes the earlier history of our race; He inaugurates its future. Nothing local, transient, individualizing, national, sectarian, dwarfs the proportions of His world-embracing Character; He rises above the parentage, the blood, the narrow horizon which bounded, as it seemed, His Human Life; He is the Archetypal Man in Whose presence distinctions of race, intervals of ages, types of civilization, degrees of mental culture are as nothing. This sense of the title seems to be implied in such passages as that in which He contrasts 'the foxes which have holes, and the birds of the air which have nests,' with 'the Son of Man Who hath not where to lay His Head [z].' It is not the official Messiah, as

[t] בן־אדם i.e. 'mortal.' (Cf. Gesen. in voc. אדם.) It is so used eighty-nine times in Ezekiel. Compare Num. xxiii. 19; Job xxv. 6, xxxv. 8. In this sense it occurs frequently in the plural. In Ps. viii. 4, 5 and lxxx. 17 it refers, at least ultimately, to our Lord.

[u] St. John v. 27; Heb. iv. 15.

[x] 'Urbild der Menscheit.' Neander, Das Leben Jesu Christi, p. 130, sqq. Mr. Keble draws out the remedial force of the title as 'signifying that Jesus was the very seed of the woman, the Second Adam promised to undo what the first had done.' Eucharistical Adoration, pp. 31-33.

[y] Adv. Hær. III. 18. 1. 'Longam hominum expositionem in Se Ipso recapitulavit, in compendio nobis salutem præstans.'

[z] St. Matt. viii. 20; St. Luke ix. 58.

such; but 'the fairest among the children of men,' the natural Prince and Leader, the very prime and flower of human kind, Whose lot is thus harder than that of the lower creatures, and in Whose humiliation humanity itself is humbled below the level of its natural dignity.

As the Son of Man then, our Lord is the Messiah; He is a true member of our human race, and He is moreover its Pattern and Representative; since He fulfils and exhausts that moral Ideal to which man's highest and best aspirations have ever pointed onward. Of these senses of the term the first was the more popular and obvious; the last would be discerned as latent in it by the devout reflection of His servants. For the disciples the term Son of Man implied first of all the Messiahship of their Master, and next, though less prominently, His true Humanity. When then our Lord enquires 'Whom do men say that I the Son of Man am?' He is not merely asking whether men admit what the title Son of Man itself imports, that is to say, the truth of His Humanity or the truth of His Messiahship. The point of His question is *this*:—what is He besides being the Son of Man? As the Son of Man, He *is* Messiah; but what is the Personality which sustains the Messianic office? As the Son of Man, He *is* truly Human; but what is the Higher Nature with which this emphatic claim to Humanity is in tacit, but manifest contrast? What is He in the seat and root of His Being? Is His Manhood a robe which He has thrown around a Higher form of pre-existent Life, or is it His all? Has He been in existence some thirty years at most, or are the august proportions of His Life only to be meted out by the days of eternity? 'Whom say men that I the Son of Man am?'

The disciples reply, that at that time, in the public opinion of Galilee, our Lord was, at the least, a preternatural personage. On this point there was, it would seem, a general consent. The cry of a petty local envy which had been raised at Nazareth, 'Is not this the Carpenter's Son?' did not fairly represent the matured or prevalent opinion of the people. The people did not suppose that Jesus was in truth merely one of themselves, only endued with larger powers and with a finer religious instinct. They thought that His Personality reached back somehow into the past of their own wonderful history. They took Him for a saint of ancient days, who had been re-invested with a bodily form. He was the great expected miracle-working Elijah; or He was the disappointed prophet who had followed

His country to its grave at the Captivity; or He was the recently-martyred preacher and ascetic John the Baptist; or He was, at any rate, one of the order which for four hundred years had been lost to Israel; He was one of the Prophets.

Our Lord turns from these public misconceptions to the judgment of that little Body which was already the nucleus of His future Church: 'But whom say ye that I am?' St. Peter replies, in the name of the other disciples [a], 'Thou art the Christ, the Son of the Living God.' In marked contrast to the popular hesitation which refused to recognise explicitly the justice of the claim so plainly put forward by the assumption of the title 'Son of Man,' the Apostle confesses, 'Thou art the Christ.' But St. Peter advances a step beyond this confession, and replies to the original question of our Lord, when he adds 'The Son of the Living God.' In the first three Evangelists, as well as in St. John, this solemn designation expresses something more than a merely theocratic or ethical relationship to God [b]. If St. Peter had meant that Christ was the Son of God solely in virtue of His membership in the old Theocracy, or by reason of His consummate moral glory [c], the confession would have

[a] St. Chrysostom, in loc., calls St. Peter τὸ στόμα τῶν ἀποστόλων, ὁ πανταχοῦ θερμός.

[b] See Lect. V. p. 246, sqq.

[c] The title of 'sons' is used in the Old Testament to express three relations to God. (1) God has entered into the relation of Father to all Israel (Deut. xxxii. 6; Isa. lxiii. 16), whence he entitles Israel 'My son,' 'My firstborn' (Exod. iv. 22, 23), when claiming the people from Pharaoh; and Ephraim, 'My dear son, a pleasant child' (Jer. xxxi. 20), as an earnest of restoration to Divine favour. Thus the title is used as a motive to obedience (Deut. xiv. 1); or in reproach for ingratitude (Ibid. xxxii. 5; Isa. i. 2, xxx. 1, 9; Jer. iii. 14); or especially of such as were God's sons, not in name only, but in truth (Ps. lxxiii. 15; Prov. xiv. 26; and perhaps Isa. xliii. 6). (2) The title is applied once to judges in the Theocracy (Ps. lxxxii. 6), 'I *have said*, Ye are gods, and all of you are children of the Most High.' Here the title refers to the name Elohim, given to the judges as representing God in the Theocracy, and as judging in His Name and by His Authority. Accordingly to go to them for judgment is spoken of as going to Elohim (Deut. xvii. 9). (3) The exact phrase 'sons of God' is, with perhaps one exception (Gen. vi. 2), used of superhuman beings, who until the Incarnation were more nearly like God than were any of the family of men (Job i. 6, ii. 1, xxxviii. 7). The singular, 'My Son,' 'The Son,' is used only in prophecy of the Messiah (Ps. ii. 7, 12; and Acts xiii. 33; Heb. i. 5, v. 5), and in what is believed to have been a Divine manifestation, very probably of God the Son (Dan. iii. 25). The line of David being the line of the Messiah, culminating in the Messiah, as in David's One perfect Son, it was said in a lower sense of each member of that line, but in its

involved nothing distinctive with respect to Jesus Christ, nothing that was not in a measure true of every good Jew, and that may not be truer far of every good Christian. If St. Peter had intended only to repeat another and a practically equivalent title of the Messiah, he would not have equalled the earlier confession of a Nathanael[d], or have surpassed the subsequent admission of a Caiaphas[e]. If we are to construe his language thus, it is altogether impossible to conceive why 'flesh and blood' could not have 'revealed' to him so obvious and trivial an inference from his previous knowledge, or why either the Apostle or his confession should have been solemnly designated as the selected Rock on which the Redeemer would build His imperishable Church.

Leaving however a fuller discussion of the interpretation of this particular text, let us note that the question raised at Cæsarea Philippi is still the great question before the modern world. Whom do men say now that Jesus, the Son of Man, is?

I. No serious and thoughtful man can treat such a subject with indifference. I merely do you justice, my brethren, when I defy you to murmur that we are entering upon a merely abstract discussion, which has nothing in common with modern human interests, congenial as it may have been to those whom some writers have learnt to describe as the professional word-warriors of the fourth and fifth centuries. You would not be guilty of including the question of our Lord's Divinity in your catalogue of *tolerabiles ineptiæ*. There is that in the Form of the Son of Man which prevails to command something more than attention, even in an age so conspicuous for its boisterous self-assertion as our own, and in intellectual atmospheres as far as possible removed from the mind of His believing and adoring Church. Never since He ascended to His Throne was He the object of a more passionate adoration than now; never did He encounter the glare of a hatred more intense and more defiant: and between these, the poles of a contemplation incessantly directed upon His Person, there are shades and levels of thought and feeling, many and graduated, here detracting from the highest

full sense only of Messiah, 'I will be to Him a Father, and He shall be to Me a Son' (2 Sam. vii. 14; Heb. i. 5; Ps. lxxxix. 27). The application of the title to collective Israel in Hos. xi. 1, is connected by St. Matthew (ii. 15) with its deeper force as used of Israel's One true Heir and Representative. Cf. Mill, Myth. Interp. p. 330. Compare too the mysterious intimations of Prov. xxx. 4, Ecclus. li. 10, of a Divine Sonship internal to the Being of God.

[d] St. John i. 49.

[e] St. Matt. xxvi. 63.

expressions of faith, there shrinking from the most violent extremities of blasphemy. A real indifference to the claims of Jesus Christ upon the thoughts and hearts of men is scarcely less condemned by some of the erroneous tendencies of our age than by its characteristic excellences. An age which has a genuine love of historical truth must needs fix its eye on that august Personality which is to our European world, in point of creative influence, what no other has been or can be. An age which is distinguished by a keen æsthetic appreciation, if not by any very earnest practical culture of moral beauty, cannot but be enthusiastic when it has once caught sight of that incomparable Life which is recorded in the Gospels. But also, an anti-dogmatic age is nervously anxious to attack dogma in its central stronghold, and to force the Human Character and Work of the Saviour, though at the cost of whatever violence of critical manipulation, to detach themselves from the great belief with which they are indissolubly associated in the mind of Christendom. And an age, so impatient of the supernatural as our own, is irritated to the highest possible point of disguised irritability by the spectacle of a Life which is supernatural throughout, which positively bristles with the supernatural, which begins with a supernatural birth, and ends in a supernatural ascent to heaven, which is prolific of physical miracle, and of which the moral wonders are more startling than the physical. Thus it is that the interest of modern physical enquiries into the laws of the Cosmos or into the origin of Man is immediately heightened when these enquiries are suspected to have a bearing, however indirect, upon Christ's Sacred Person. Thus your study of the mental sciences, aye, and of philology, ministers whether it will or no to His praise or His dishonour, and your ethical speculations cannot complete themselves without raising the whole question of His Authority. And such is Christ's place in history, that a line of demarcation between its civil and its ecclesiastical elements seems to be practically impossible; your ecclesiastical historians are prone to range over the annals of the world, while your professors of secular history habitually deal with the central problems and interests of theology.

If Christ could have been ignored, He would have been ignored in Protestant Germany, when Christian Faith had been eaten out of the heart of that country by the older Rationalism. Yet scarcely any German 'thinker' of note can be named who has not projected what is termed a Christology. The Christ of Kant is the Ideal of Moral Perfection, and as such, we are told, he is to be carefully distinguished from the historical Jesus, since of this Ideal alone, and in a transcendental sense, can the statements of the orthodox creed be predicated [f]. The Christ of Jacobi is a Religious Ideal, and worship addressed to the historical Jesus is denounced as sheer idolatry, unless beneath the recorded manifestation the Ideal itself be discerned and honoured [g]. According to Fichte, on the contrary, the real interest of philosophy in Jesus is historical and not metaphysical; Jesus first possessed an insight into the absolute unity of the being of man with that of God, and in revealing this insight He communicated the highest knowledge which man can possess [h]. Of the later Pantheistic philosophers, Schelling proclaims that the Christian theology is hopelessly in error, when it teaches that at a particular moment of time God became Incarnate, since God is 'external to' all time, and the Incarnation of God is an eternal fact. But Schelling contends that the man Christ Jesus is the highest point or effort of this eternal incarnation, and the beginning of its real manifestation to men: 'none before Him after such a manner has revealed to man the Infinite [i].' And the Christ of Hegel is not the actual Incarnation of God in Jesus of Nazareth, but the symbol of His incarnation in humanity at large [j]. Fundamentally differing, as do these conceptions, in various ways, from the creed of the Church of Christ, they nevertheless represent so many efforts of non-

[f] Religion innerhalb der Grenzen der blossen Vernunft. Werke, Bd. x. p. 73, esp. p. 142.

[g] Schrift von den Göttl. Dingen, p. 62, sqq.

[h] Anweisung zum seligen Leben Vorl. 6. Werke, Bd. v. p. 482.

[i] Vorlesungen über die methode des Akad. Studien. Werke, Bd. v. p. 298, sqq.

[j] Rel. Phil. Bd. ii. p. 263. This idea is developed by Strauss. See his Glaubenslehre, ii. 209, sqq.; and Leben Jesu, Auf. 2, Bd. ii. p. 739, sqq. 'Der Schlüssel der ganzen Christologie ist, das als Subject der Prädikate, welche die Kirche Christo beilegt, statt eines Individuums eine Idee, aber eine reale, nicht Kantisch unwirkliche gesetzt wird. . . . Die Menscheit ist die Vereinigung der beiden Naturen, der Menschgewordene Gott . . . Durch den Glauben an diesen Christus, namentlich an Seinen Tod und seine Auferstehung wird der Mensch vor Gott gerecht, d. h., durch die Belebung der Idee der Menscheit in sich,' &c. Feuerbach has carried this forward into pure materialism, and he openly scorns and denounces Christianity: Strauss has more recently described Feuerbach as 'the man who put the dot upon the i which we had found,' and he too insists upon the moral necessity of rejecting Christianity; Lebens und Characterbild Marklins, pp. 124, 125, sqq., quoted by Luthardt, Apolog. p. 301. Other disciples of Hegel, such as Marheinecke, Rosenkranz, and Göschel, have endeavoured to give to their master's teaching a more positive direction.

Christian thought to do such homage as is possible to its great Object; they are so many proofs of the interest which Jesus Christ necessarily provokes in the modern world, even when it is least disposed to own His true supremacy.

Nor is the direction which this interest has taken of late years in the sphere of unbelieving theological criticism less noteworthy in its bearings on our present subject. The earlier Rationalism concerned itself chiefly with the Apostolical age. It was occupied with a perpetual analysis and recombination of the various influences which were supposed to have created the Catholic Church and the orthodox creed. St. Paul was the most prominent person in the long series of hypotheses by which Rationalism professed to account for the existence of Catholic Christianity. St. Paul was said to be the 'author' of that idea of a universal religion which was deemed to be the most fundamental and creative element in the Christian creed: St. Paul's was the vivid imagination which had thrown around the life and death of the Prophet of Nazareth a halo of superhuman glory, and had fired an obscure Jewish sect with the ambition of founding a spiritual empire able to control and embrace the world. St. Paul, in short, was held to be the real creator of Christianity; and our Lord was thrown into the background, whether from a surviving instinct of awe, or on the ground of His being relatively insignificant. This studied silence of active critical speculation with respect to Jesus Christ might indeed have been the instinct of reverence, but it was at least susceptible of a widely different interpretation.

In our day this equivocal reserve is no longer possible. The passion for reality, for fact, which is so characteristic of the thought of recent years, has carried critical enquiry backwards from the consciousness of the Apostle to that on which it reposed. The interest of modern criticism centres in Him Who is ever most prominently and uninterruptedly present to the eye of faith. The popular controversies around us tend more and more to merge in the one great question respecting our Lord's Person: that question, it is felt, is bound up with the very existence of Christianity. And a discussion respecting Christ's Person obliges us to consider the mode of His historical manifestation; so that His Life was probably never studied before by those who practically or avowedly reject Him so eagerly as it is at this moment. For Strauss He may be no more than a leading illustration of the applicability of the Hegelian philosophy to purposes of historical analysis; for Schenkel He may be a sacred impersonation of the anti-hierarchical and democratic temper, which aims at revolutionizing Germany. Ewald may see in Him the altogether human source of the highest spiritual life of humanity; and Renan, the semi-fabulous and somewhat immoral hero of an oriental story, fashioned to the taste of a modern Parisian public. And what if you yourselves are even now eagerly reading an anonymous writer, of far nobler aim and finer moral insight than these, who has endeavoured, by a brilliant analysis of one side of Christ's moral action, to represent Him as embodying and originating all that is best and most hopeful in the spirit of modern philanthropy, but who seems not indisposed to substitute for the creed of His Church, only the impatient proclamation of His Roman judge. Aye, though you salute your Saviour in Pilate's words, Behold the Man! at least you cannot ignore Him; you cannot resist the moral and intellectual forces which converge in our day with an ever-increasing intensity upon His Sacred Person; you cannot turn a deaf ear to the question which He asks of His followers in each generation, and which He never asked more solemnly than now: 'Whom say men that I the Son of Man am[k]?'

II. Now all serious Theists, who believe that God is a Personal Being essentially distinct from the work of His hands, must make one of three answers, whether in terms or in substance, to the question of the text.

1. The Ebionite of old, and the Socinian now, assert that Jesus Christ is merely man, whether (as Faustus Socinus himself teaches) supernaturally born of a Virgin[l], or (as modern Rationalists generally maintain) in all respects subject to ordinary natural laws[m], although of such remarkable moral eminence, that He may, in the enthusiastic language of ethical admiration, be said to be 'Divine.' And when Sabellianism would escape from the manifold self-contradictions of Patripassianism[n], it too becomes no less Humanitarian in its doctrine as to the Person of our Lord, than Ebionitism itself. The Monarchianism of Praxeas or of Noetus, which denied the

[k] On recent 'Lives' of our Lord, see Appendix, Note A.

[l] Chr. Rel. Brevissima Inst. i. 654: 'De Christi essentiâ ita statue: Illum esse hominem in virginis utero, et sic sine viri ope Divini Spiritûs vi conceptum.'

[m] Wegscheider, Instit. § 120, sqq.

[n] Cf. Tertull. adv. Prax. c. 2.

distinct Personality of Christ[o] while proclaiming His Divinity in the highest terms, was practically coincident in its popular result with the coarse assertions of Theodotus and Artemon[p]. And in modern days, the phenomenon of practical Humanitarianism, disguised but not proscribed by very vehement protestations apparently condemning it, is reproduced in the case of such well-known writers as Schleiermacher or Ewald. They use language at times which seems to do the utmost justice to the truth of Christ's Divinity: they recognise in Him the perfect Revelation of God, the true Head and Lord of human kind; but they deny the existence of an immanent Trinity in the Godhead; they recognise in God no pre-existent Personal Form as the basis of His Self-Manifestation to man; they are really Monarchianists in the sense of Praxeas; and their keen appreciation of the ethical glory of Christ's Person cannot save them from consequences with which it is ultimately inconsistent, but which are on other grounds logically too inevitable to be permanently eluded[q]. A Christ who is 'the perfect Revelation of God,' yet who 'is not personally God,' does not really differ from the altogether human Christ of Socinus; and the assertion of the Personal Godhead of Christ can only escape from the profane absurdities of Patripassianism, when it presupposes the eternal and necessary existence in God of a Threefold Personality.

2. The Arian maintains that our Lord Jesus Christ existed before His Incarnation, that by Him, as by an instrument, the Supreme God made the worlds, and that, as being the most ancient and the highest of created beings, He is to be worshipped; that, however, Christ had a beginning of existence (*ἀρχὴν ὑπάρξεως*), that there was a time when He did not exist (*ἦν ὅτε οὐκ ἦν*); that He has His subsistence from what once was not (*ἐξ οὐκ ὄντων ἔχει τὴν ὑπόστασιν*[r]), and cannot therefore

[o] 'Hæc perversitas, quæ se existimat meram veritatem possidere, dum *unicum* Deum non aliàs putat credendum quam si *ipsum eundemque* et Patrem et Filium et Spiritum Sanctum dicat. Quasi non sic quoque unus sit omnia, dum ex uno omnia, *per substantiæ scilicet unitatem*, et nihilominùs custodiatur *οἰκονομίας* sacramentum, quæ unitatem in trinitatem disponit, tres dirigens, Patrem et Filium, et Spiritum Sanctum.' Adv. Prax. c. 2.

[p] Euseb. Hist. Eccl. v. 28: *ψιλὸν ἄνθρωπον γενέσθαι τὸν Σωτῆρα.* Tert. de Præscr. Hær. c. 53. App.; Theodoret, Hær. Fab. lib. ii. init.

[q] Cf. Dorner, Pers. Christi, Band ii. p. 153. Schleiermacher, although agreeing with Schelling and Hegel in denying an immanent Trinity in the Godhead, did not (Dorner earnestly pleads) agree in the Pantheistic basis of that denial. P. C. ii. p. 1212. Compare Ewald, Geschichte Christus', p. 447, quoted by Dorner.

[r] Socrates, i. 5.

be called God in the sense in which that term is applied by Theists to the Supreme Being[s].

3. In contrast with these two leading forms of heresy stands that which has ever been and is the faith of the whole Catholic Church of Christ: 'I believe in One Lord Jesus Christ, the Only-begotten Son of God, Begotten of His Father before all worlds, God of God, Light of Light, Very God of Very God, Begotten not made, Being OF ONE SUBSTANCE WITH the Father; By Whom all things were made; Who for us men and for our salvation came down from heaven, and was incarnate by the Holy Ghost of the Virgin Mary, and was made Man.'

Practically indeed these three answers may be still further reduced to two, the first and the third; for Arianism, no less than Sabellianism, is really a form of the Humanitarian or naturalist reply to the question. Arianism does indeed admit the existence of a pre-existent being who became incarnate in Jesus, but it parts company with the Catholic belief, by asserting that this being is himself a creature, and not of the very Substance of the Supreme God. Thus Arianism is weighted with the intellectual difficulties of a purely supernatural Christology, while yet it forfeits all hold upon the Great Truth which to a Catholic believer sustains and justifies the remainder of his creed. The real question at issue is not merely whether Christ is only a man; it is whether or not He is only a created being. When the question is thus stated, Arianism must really take its place side by side with the most naked Deism; while at the same time it suggests, by its incarnation of a created Logos, the most difficult among the problems which meet a believer in the Hypostatic Union of our Lord's Two Natures. In order to escape from this position, it virtually teaches the existence of two Gods, each of whom is an object of worship, one of whom has been created by the Other; One of whom might, if He willed, annihilate the other[t]. Thus in Arianism reason and faith are equally

[s] Cf. further Waterland, Defence of Some Queries, Works (ed. Van-Mildert), vol. i. pp. 402, 403.

[t] Waterland, Works, vol. i. p. 78, note f. Bp. Van-Mildert quotes from Mr. Charles Butler's Historical Account of Confessions of Faith, chap. x. sect. 2, a remarkable report of Dr. Clarke's conference with Dr. Hawarden in the presence of Queen Caroline. After Dr. Clarke had stated his system at great length and in very guarded terms, Dr. Hawarden asked his permission to put one simple question, and Dr. Clarke assented. 'Then,' said Dr. Hawarden, 'I ask, Can God the Father annihilate the Son and the Holy Ghost? Answer me Yes or No.' Dr. Clarke continued for some time in deep thought, and then said, 'It was a question which he had never

disappointed: the largest demands are made upon faith, yet the Arian Christ after all is but a fellow-creature; and reason is encouraged to assail the mysteries of the Catholic creed in behalf of a theory which admits of being reduced to an irrational absurdity. Arianism therefore is really at most a resting-point for minds which are sinking from the Catholic creed downwards to pure Humanitarianism; or which are feeling their way upwards from the depths of Ebionitism, or Socinianism, towards the Church. This intermediate, transient, and essentially unsubstantial character of the Arian position was indeed made plain, in theory, by the vigorous analysis to which the heresy was subjected on its first appearance by St. Athanasius[u], and again in the last century, when, at its endeavour to make a home for itself in the Church of England, in the person of Dr. Samuel Clarke, it was crushed out, under God, mainly by the genius and energy of the great Waterland. And history has verified the anticipations of argument. Arianism at this day has a very shadowy, if any real, existence; and the Church of Christ, holding in her hands the Creed of Nicæa, stands face to face with sheer Humanitarianism, more or less disguised, according to circumstances, by the thin varnish of an admiration yielded to our Lord on æsthetic or ethical grounds.

III. At the risk of partial repetition, but for the sake of clearness, let us here pause to make two observations respecting that complete assertion of the Divinity of our Lord for which His Church is responsible at the bar of human opinion.

1. The Catholic doctrine, then, of Christ's Divinity in no degree interferes with or overshadows the complemental truth of His perfect Manhood. It is perhaps natural that a greater emphasis should be laid upon the higher truth which could be apprehended only by faith than on the lower one which, during the years of our Lord's earthly Life, was patent to the senses of men. And Holy Scripture might antecedently be supposed to take for granted the reality of Christ's Manhood, on the ground of there being no adequate occasion for full, precise, and reiterated assertions of so obvious a fact. But nothing is more remarkable in Scripture than its provision for the moral and intellectual needs of ages far removed from those which are traversed by the books included in the Sacred

considered.' Mahomed had done so: Rodwell's Korân, p. 541. On the '*precarious*' existence of God the Son, according to the Arian hypothesis, see Waterland's Farther Vindication of Christ's Divinity, ch. iii. sect. 19.

[u] See Lect. VII.

Canon. In the present instance, by a series of incidental although most significant statements, the Gospels guard us with nothing less than an exhaustive precaution against the fictions of a Docetic or of an Apollinarian Christ. We are told that the Eternal Word *σὰρξ ἐγένετο* [x], that He took human nature upon Him in its reality and completeness [y]. The Gospel narrative, after the pattern of His own words in the text, exhibits Jesus as the Son of Man, while yet it draws us on by an irresistible attraction to contemplate that Higher Nature which was the seat of His eternal Personality. The superhuman character of some most important details of the Gospel history does not disturb the broad scope of that history as being the record of a Human Life, with Its physical and mental affinities to our own daily experience.

The great Subject of the Gospel narratives has a true human Body. He is conceived in the womb of a human Mother [z]. He is by her brought forth into the world [a]; He is fed at her breast during infancy [b]. As an Infant, He is made to undergo the painful rite of circumcision [c]. He is a Babe in swaddling-clothes lying in a manger [d]. He is nursed in the arms of the aged Simeon [e]. His bodily growth is traced up to His attaining the age of twelve [f], and from that point to manhood [g]. His presence at the marriage-feast in Cana [h], at the great entertainment in the house of Levi [i], and at the table of Simon the Pharisee [k]; the supper which He shared at Bethany with the friend whom He had raised from the grave [l], the Paschal festival which He desired so earnestly to eat before He suf-

[x] St. John i. 14. Cf. Meyer in loc. for a refutation of Zeller's attempt to limit σὰρξ in this passage to the bodily organism, as exclusive of the anima rationalis.

[y] St. John viii. 40; 1 Tim. ii. 5.

[z] συλλήψῃ ἐν γαστρὶ, St. Luke i. 31. πρὸ τοῦ συλληφθῆναι αὐτὸν ἐν τῇ κοιλίᾳ, Ibid. ii. 21. εὑρέθη ἐν γαστρὶ ἔχουσα ἐκ Πνεύματός Ἁγίου, St. Matt. i. 18. τὸ γὰρ ἐν αὐτῇ γεννηθὲν ἐκ Πνεύματός ἐστιν Ἁγίου, Ibid. i. 20; Isa. vii. 14.

[a] St. Matt. i. 25; St. Luke ii. 7, 11; Gal. iv. 4: ἐξαπέστειλεν ὁ Θεὸς τὸν Υἱὸν αὐτοῦ, γενόμενον ἐκ γυναικός.

[b] St. Luke xi. 27: μάστοι οὓς ἐθήλασας.

[c] Ibid. ii. 21.

[d] Ibid. ii. 12: Βρέφος ἐσπαργανωμένον, κείμενον ἐν τῇ φάτνῃ.

[e] Ibid. ii. 28: καὶ αὐτὸς ἐδέξατο αὐτὸ εἰς τὰς ἀγκάλας αὐτοῦ.

[f] Ibid. ii. 40: τὸ δὲ παιδίον ηὔξανε.

[g] Ibid. ii. 52: Ἰησοῦς προέκοπτε . . . ἡλικίᾳ.

[h] St. John ii. 2.

[i] St. Luke v. 29: δοχὴν μεγάλην.

[k] St. Luke vii. 36.

[l] St. John xii. 2.

fered[m], the bread and fish of which He partook before the eyes of His disciples in the early dawn on the shore of the Lake of Galilee, even after His Resurrection[n],—are witnesses that He came, like one of ourselves, 'eating and drinking[o].' When He is recorded to have taken no food during the forty days of the Temptation, this implies the contrast presented by His ordinary habit[p]. Indeed, He seemed to the men of His day much more dependent on the physical supports of life than the great ascetic who had preceded Him[q]. He knew, by experience, what are the pangs of hunger, after the forty days' fast in the wilderness[r], and in a lesser degree, as may be supposed, when walking into Jerusalem on the Monday before His Passion[s]. The profound spiritual sense of His redemptive cry, 'I thirst,' uttered while He was hanging on the Cross, is not obscured, when its primary literal meaning, that while dying He actually endured that wellnigh sharpest form of bodily suffering, is explicitly recognised[t]. His deep sleep on the Sea of Galilee in a little bark which the waves threatened momentarily to engulf[u], and His sitting down at the well of Jacob, through great exhaustion produced by a long journey on foot from Judæa[x], proved that He was subject at times to the depression of extreme fatigue. And, not to dwell at length upon those particular references to the several parts of His bodily frame which occur in Holy Scripture[y], it is obvious to note that the evangelical account of His physical Sufferings, of His Death[z], of His Burial[a], and of the Wounds in His Hands and Feet and Side after His Resur-

[m] St. Luke xxii. 8, 15.

[n] St. John xxi. 12, 13.

[o] St. Luke vii. 34: *ἐλήλυθεν ὁ Υἱὸς τοῦ ἀνθρώπου ἐσθίων καὶ πίνων.*

[p] Ibid. iv. 2: *οὐκ ἔφαγεν οὐδὲν ἐν ταῖς ἡμέραις ἐκείναις.*

[q] Ibid. vii. 34: *ἰδοὺ, ἄνθρωπος φάγος καὶ οἰνοπότης.*

[r] St. Matt. iv. 2: *ὕστερον ἐπείνασε.*

[s] Ibid. xxi. 18: *ἐπανάγων εἰς τὴν πόλιν, ἐπείνασε.*

[t] St. John xix. 28: *διψῶ.*

[u] St. Matt. viii. 24: *αὐτὸς δὲ ἐκάθευδε.*

[x] St. John iv. 6: *ὁ οὖν Ἰησοῦς κεκοπιακὼς ἐκ τῆς ὁδοιπορίας ἐκαθέζετο οὕτως ἐπὶ τῇ πηγῇ.*

[y] *τὴν κεφαλὴν*, St. Luke vii. 46; St. Matt. xxvii. 29, 30; St. John xix. 30; *τοὺς πόδας*, St. Luke vii. 38; *τὰς χεῖρας*, St. Luke xxiv. 40; *τῷ δακτύλῳ*, St. John viii. 6; *τὰ σκέλη*, St. John xix. 33; *τὰ γόνατα*, St. Luke xxii. 41; *τὴν πλευρὰν*, St. John xix. 34; *τὸ σῶμα*, St. Luke xxii. 19, &c.

[z] St. Luke xxii. 44, &c., xxiii.; St. Matt. xxvi., xxvii.; St. Mark xiv. 32, seq., xv.

[a] St. John xix. 39, 40: *ἔλαβον οὖν τὸ σῶμα τοῦ Ἰησοῦ καὶ ἔδησαν αὐτὸ ὀθονίοις μετὰ τῶν ἀρωμάτων*: cf. ver. 42.

rection[b], are so many emphatic attestations to the fact of His true and full participation in the material side of our common nature.

Equally explicit and vivid is the witness which Scripture affords to the true Human Soul of our Blessed Lord[c]. Its general movements are not less spontaneous, nor do Its affections flow less freely, because no sinful impulse finds a place in It, and each pulse of Its moral and mental Life is in conscious harmony with, and subjection to, an all-holy Will. Jesus rejoices in spirit on hearing of the spread of the kingdom of heaven among the simple and the poor[d]: He beholds the young ruler, and forthwith loves him[e]. He loves Martha and her sister and Lazarus with a common, yet, as seems to be implied, with a discriminating affection[f]. His Eye on one occasion betrays a sudden movement of deliberate anger at the hardness of heart which could steel itself against truth by maintaining a dogged silence[g]. The scattered and fainting multitude melts Him to compassion[h]: He sheds tears of sorrow at the grave of Lazarus[i], and at the sight of the city which has rejected His Love[k]. In contemplating His approaching Passion[l] and the ingratitude of the traitor-Apostle[m], His Soul is shaken by a vehement agitation which He does not conceal from His disciples. In the garden of Gethsemane He wills to enter into an agony of amazement and dejection. His mental sufferings are so keen and piercing that His tender frame gives way beneath the trial, and He sheds

[b] St. John xx. 27; St. Luke xxiv. 39: ἴδετε τὰς χεῖράς μου καὶ τοὺς πόδας μου, ὅτι αὐτὸς ἐγώ εἰμι· ψηλαφήσατέ με καὶ ἴδετε· ὅτι πνεῦμα σάρκα καὶ ὀστέα οὐκ ἔχει καθὼς ἐμὲ θεωρεῖτε ἔχοντα.

[c] 1 St. Pet. iii. 18: θανατωθεὶς μὲν σαρκὶ, ζωοποιηθεὶς δὲ πνεύματι ἐν ᾧ καὶ τοῖς ἐν φυλακῇ πνεύμασιν πορευθεὶς ἐκήρυξεν. The τῷ before πνεύματι in the Textus Receptus being only an insertion by a copyist, πνεῦμα here means our Lord's Human Soul. The clause ἐν ᾧ . . . ἐκήρυξεν forbids here the sense of πνεῦμα at Rom. i. 3. Cf. p. 317, note [t]; p. 334, note [x].

[d] St. Luke x. 21: ἠγαλλιάσατο τῷ πνεύματι.

[e] St. Mark x. 21: ὁ δὲ Ἰησοῦς ἐμβλέψας αὐτῷ ἠγάπησεν αὐτόν.

[f] St. Mark xi. 5.

[g] St. Mark iii. 5: περιβλεψάμενος αὐτοὺς μετ' ὀργῆς, συλλυπούμενος ἐπὶ τῇ πωρώσει τῆς καρδίας αὐτῶν.

[h] St. Matt. ix. 36: ἐσπλαγχνίσθη περὶ αὐτῶν.

[i] St. John xi. 33–35: Ἰησοῦς οὖν ὡς εἶδεν αὐτὴν κλαίουσαν καὶ τοὺς συνελθόντας αὐτῇ Ἰουδαίους κλαίοντας, ἐνεβριμήσατο τῷ πνεύματι, καὶ ἐτάραξεν ἑαυτόν. . . . Ἐδάκρυσεν ὁ Ἰησοῦς.

[k] St. Luke xix. 41: Ἰδὼν τὴν πόλιν, ἔκλαυσεν ἐπ' αὐτῇ.

[l] St. John xii. 27: νῦν ἡ ψυχή μου τετάρακται.

[m] Ibid. xiii. 21: ὁ Ἰησοῦς ἐταράχθη τῷ πνεύματι καὶ ἐμαρτύρησε.

His Blood before they nail Him to the Cross[n]. His Human Will consciously submits itself to a Higher Will[o], and He learns obedience by the discipline of pain[p]. He carries His dependence still further, He is habitually subject to His parents[q]; He recognises the fiscal regulations of a pagan state[r]; He places Himself in the hands of His enemies[s]; He is crucified through weakness[t]. If an Apostle teaches that all the treasures of wisdom and knowledge are hidden in Him[u], an Evangelist records that He increases in wisdom as He increases in stature[x]. Conformably with these representations, we find Him as Man expressing creaturely dependence upon God by prayer. He rises up a great while before day at Capernaum, and departs into a solitary place, that He may pass the hours in uninterrupted devotion[y]. He makes intercession for His whole redeemed Church in the Paschal supper-room[z]; He offers to Heaven strong crying with tears in Gethsemane[a]; He asks pardon for His Jewish and Gentile murderers at the very moment of His Crucifixion[b]; He resigns His departing Spirit into His Father's Hands[c].

Thus, as one Apostle teaches, He took a Body of Flesh[d], and His whole Humanity both of Soul and Body shared in the sinless infirmities which belong to our common nature[e]. To deny

[n] St. Mark xiv. 33: *ἤρξατο ἐκθαμβεῖσθαι καὶ ἀδημονεῖν, καὶ λέγει αὐτοῖς, 'Περίλυπός ἐστιν ἡ ψυχή μου ἕως θανάτου.'* St. Luke xxii. 44: *γενόμενος ἐν ἀγωνίᾳ ἐκτενέστερον προσηύχετο, ἐγένετο δὲ ὁ ἱδρὼς αὐτοῦ ὡσεὶ θρόμβοι αἵματος καταβαίνοντες ἐπὶ τὴν γῆν.* Cf. Heb. v. 7.

[o] St. Luke xxii. 42: *μὴ τὸ θέλημά μου, ἀλλὰ τὸ σὸν γενέσθω.*

[p] Heb. v. 8: *ἔμαθεν ἀφ' ὧν ἔπαθε τὴν ὑπακοήν.* Cf. especially St. Matt. xxvii. 46.

[q] St. Luke ii. 51: *ἦν ὑποτασσόμενος αὐτοῖς.*

[r] St. Matt. xxii. 21. For our Lord's payment of the Temple tribute, cf. Ibid. xvii. 25, 27.

[s] Ibid. xvii. 22; St. John x. 18: *οὐδεὶς αἴρει αὐτὴν* [sc. *τὴν ψυχήν μου*] *ἀπ' ἐμοῦ, ἀλλ' ἐγὼ τίθημι αὐτὴν ἀπ' ἐμαυτοῦ.*

[t] 2 Cor. xiii. 4: *ἐσταυρώθη ἐξ ἀσθενείας.*

[u] Col. ii. 3: *ἐν ᾧ εἰσι πάντες οἱ θησαυροὶ τῆς σοφίας καὶ τῆς γνώσεως ἀπόκρυφοι.*

[x] St. Luke ii. 40: *ἐκραταιοῦτο πνεύματι.* ver. 52: *προέκοπτε σοφίᾳ.* See Lect. VIII.

[y] St. Mark i. 35.

[z] St. John xvii. 1: *ἐπῆρε τοὺς ὀφθαλμοὺς αὐτοῦ εἰς τὸν οὐρανὸν, καὶ εἶπε.*

[a] Heb. v. 7: *ἐν ταῖς ἡμέραις τῆς σαρκὸς αὐτοῦ, δεήσεις τε καὶ ἱκετηρίας . . . . μετὰ κραυγῆς ἰσχυρᾶς καὶ δακρύων προσενέγκας.* St. Luke xxii. 42-44.

[b] St. Luke xxiii. 34: *πάτερ, ἄφες αὐτοῖς· οὐ γὰρ οἴδασι τί ποιοῦσι.* That this prayer referred to the Jews, as well as the Roman soldiers, is clear from Acts iii. 17.

[c] St. Luke xxiii. 46.

[d] Col. i. 22: *σώματι τῆς σαρκός.*

[e] Heb. ii. 11: *ὅ τε γὰρ ἁγιάζων καὶ οἱ ἁγιαζόμενοι ἐξ ἑνὸς πάντες.* Ver. 14: *μετέσχε σαρκὸς καὶ αἵματος.* Ver. 17: *ὤφειλε κατὰ πάντα τοῖς ἀδελφοῖς ὁμοιωθῆναι.* Ibid. iv. 15: *πεπειρασμένον δὲ κατὰ πάντα καθ' ὁμοιότητα.*

this fundamental truth, 'that Jesus Christ is come in the Flesh,' is, in the judgment of another Apostle, the mark of the Deceiver, of the Antichrist[f]. Nor do the prerogatives of our Lord's Manhood destroy Its perfection and reality, although they do undoubtedly invest It with a robe of mystery, which Faith must acknowledge, but which she cannot hope to penetrate. Christ's Manhood is not unreal because It is impersonal; because in Him the place of any created individuality at the root of thought and feeling and will is supplied by the Person of the Eternal Word, Who has wrapped around His Being a created Nature through which, in its unmutilated perfection, He acts upon humankind[g]. Christ's Manhood is not unreal, because It is sinless; because the entail of any taint of transmitted sin is in Him cut off by a supernatural birth of a Virgin Mother; and because His whole life of thought, feeling, will, and action is in unfaltering harmony with the law of absolute Truth[h]. Nor is the reality of His Manhood impaired by any exceptional beauty whether of outward form or of mental endowment, such as might become One 'fairer than the children of men[i],' and taking precedence of them in all things[k]; since in Him our nature does but resume

[f] 1 St. John iv. 2: *πᾶν πνεῦμα ὃ ὁμολογεῖ Ἰησοῦν Χριστὸν ἐν σαρκὶ ἐληλυθότα, ἐκ τοῦ Θεοῦ ἐστι.* 2 St. John 7: *πολλοὶ πλάνοι εἰσῆλθον εἰς τὸν κόσμον, οἱ μὴ ὁμολογοῦντες Ἰησοῦν Χριστὸν ἐρχόμενον ἐν σαρκί· οὗτος ἐστιν ὁ πλάνος καὶ ὁ Ἀντίχριστος.*

[g] The *ἀνυποστασία* of our Lord's Humanity is a result of the Hypostatic Union. To deny it is to assert that there are Two Persons in Christ, or else it is to deny that He is more that Man. Compare Hooker, Eccl. Pol. v. 52. 3, who appeals against Nestorius to Heb. ii. 16, *οὐ γὰρ δήπου ἀγγέλων ἐπιλαμβάνεται, ἀλλὰ σπέρματος Ἀβραὰμ ἐπιλαμβάνεται* At His Incarnation the Eternal Word took on Him Human Nature, not a Human Personality. Luther appears to have denied the Impersonality of our Lord's Manhood. But see Dorner, Person Christi, Bd. ii. p. 540.

[h] The Sinlessness of our Lord's Manhood is implied in St. Luke i. 35. Thus He is *ὃν ὁ Πατὴρ ἡγίασε καὶ ἀπέστειλεν εἰς τὸν κόσμον*, St. John x. 36; and He could challenge His enemies to convict Him of sin, St. John viii. 46. In St. Mark x. 18, St. Luke xviii. 19, He is not denying that He is good; but He insists that none should call Him so who did not believe Him to be God. St. Paul describes Him as *τὸν μὴ γνόντα ἁμαρτίαν*, 2 Cor. v. 21; and Christ is expressly said to be *χωρὶς ἁμαρτίας*, Heb. iv. 15; *ὅσιος, ἄκακος, ἀμίαντος, κεχωρισμένος ἀπὸ τῶν ἁμαρτωλῶν*, Heb. vii. 26; *ἀμνὸς ἄμωμος καὶ ἄσπιλος*, 1 St. Pet. i. 19; *ὁ ἅγιος καὶ δίκαιος*, Acts iii. 14. Still more emphatically we are told that *ἁμαρτία ἐν αὐτῷ οὐκ ἔστι*, 1 St. John iii. 5; while the same truth is indirectly taught, when St. Paul speaks of our Lord as sent *ἐν ὁμοιώματι σαρκὸς ἁμαρτίας*, Rom. viii. 3. Mr. F. W. Newman does justice to the significance of a Sinless Manhood, although, unhappily, he disbelieves in It; Phases of Faith, p. 141, sqq. Cf. Lect IV. p. 167.

[i] Ps. xlv. 3.

[k] Col. i. 18: *ἐν πᾶσι πρωτεύων.*

its true and typical excellence as the crowning glory of the visible creation of God[l].

This reality and perfection of our Lord's Manhood has been not less jealously maintained by the Church than it is clearly asserted in the pages of Scripture. From the first the Church has taught that Jesus Christ is 'Perfect Man, of a reasonable Soul and Human Flesh subsisting.' It is sometimes hinted that believers in our Saviour's Godhead must necessarily entertain some prejudice against those passages of Scripture which expressly assert the truth of His Manhood. It is presumed that such passages must be regarded by them as so many difficulties[m] to be surmounted or evaded by a theory which is supposed to be conscious of their hostilty to itself. Whereas, in truth, to a Catholic instinct, each declaration of Scripture, whatever be its apparent bearing, is welcome as being an unveiling of the Mind of God, and therefore as certainly reconcileable with other sides of truth, whether or no the method of such reconciliation be immediately obvious. As a matter of fact, our Lord's Humanity has been insisted upon by the great Church teachers of antiquity not less earnestly than His Godhead. They habitually argue that it belonged to His essential Truth to be in reality what He seemed to be. He seemed to be human; therefore He was Human[n]. Yet His Manhood, so they proceed to maintain,

[l] Ps. viii. 6-8. Cp. Heb. ii. 6-10.

[m] Thus 'Examination of Bampton Lectures,' p. 250. The writer thinks that our Lord's words in St. Luke iv. 18, 19; St. Matt. xx. 23; xxiii. 53; St. John xiv. 28, etc., are as little to be reconciled with our Lord's true Godhead, as are the passages in which He claims to have existed before Abraham or to be the Judge of all men, with true human goodness, if, after all, He be only Man. (See Lect. IV.) Yet surely a discussion of the properties or liabilities of the human body, which should take no account of the endowments of the human mind, does not necessarily deny their existence. Nor is it to be placed on the same moral level with the language of an adventurer, who should claim rights by hinting that he possessed powers and accomplishments, to which nothing corresponded in sober fact.

[n] St. Irenæus, Adv. Hær. v. 1. 2: εἰ δὲ μὴ ὢν ἄνθρωπος ἐφαίνετο ἄνθρωπος, οὔτε ὃ ἦν ἐπ' ἀληθείας, ἔμεινε πνεῦμα Θεοῦ, ἐπεὶ ἀόρατον τὸ πνεῦμα, οὔτε ἀλήθειά τις ἦν ἐν αὐτῷ, οὐ γὰρ ἦν ἐκεῖνα ἅπερ ἐφαίνετο. Tert. De Carne Christi, cap. 5: 'Si caro cum passionibus ficta, et spiritus ergo cum virtutibus falsus. Quid dimidias mendacio Christum? Totus Veritas est. Maluit crede [non] nasci quam ex aliquâ parte mentiri, et quidem in Semet ipsum, ut carnem gestaret sine ossibus duram, sine musculis solidam, sine sanguine cruentam, sine tunicâ vestitam, sine fame esurientem, sine dentibus edentem, sine linguâ loquentem, ut phantasma auribus fuit sermo ejus per imaginem vocis.' St. Aug. De Div. Qu. 83. qu. 14: 'Si phantasma fuit corpus Christi, fefellit Christus, et si fefellit, Veritas non est. Est autem Veritas Christus.

[LECT

would have been fictitious, if any one faculty or element of human nature had been wanting to It. Therefore His Reasonable Soul was as essential as His Bodily Frame[o]. Without a Reasonable Soul His Humanity would have been but an animal existence[p]; and the intellectual side of man's nature would have been unredeemed[q]. Nor did the Church in her collective capacity ever so insist on Christ's Godhead as to lose sight of the truth of His Perfect Manhood. Whether by the silent force of the belief of her children, or by her representative writers on behalf of the faith, or by the formal decisions of her councils, she has ever resisted the disposition to sacrifice the confession of Christ's created nature to that of His uncreated Godhead[r]. She kept at bay intellectual temptations and impulses which might have easily overmastered the mind of a merely human society. When Ebionites were abroad, she maintained against the Docetæ that our Saviour's body was not fictitious or apparitional. When the mutterings of that Humanitarian movement which culminated in the great scandal of Paulus of Samosata were distinctly audible, she asserted the truth of our Lord's Human Soul against Beryllus of Bostra[s]. When Arianism had not as yet ceased to be formidable, she was not tempted by Apollinaris to admit that the Logos in Christ took the place of the rational element in man. While Nestorianism was still vigorous, she condemned the Monophysite formula which practically made Christ an unincarnate God: nor did she rest until the Monothelite echo of the more signal error had been silenced by her assertion of the reality of His Human Will.

Nor is the Manhood of our Saviour prized by the Church only as a revealed dogma intellectually essential to the formal

Non ergo phantasma fuit Corpus Ejus.' Docetism struck at the very basis of truth, by sanctioning Pyrrhonism. St. Iren. Adv. Hær. iv. 33.

[o] St. Aug. Ep. 187, ad Dardan. n. 4: 'Non est Homo Perfectus, si vel anima carni, vel animæ ipsi mens humana defuerit.' Confess. vii. c. 19.

[p] St. Aug. De Div. Qu. 83, qu. 80. n. 1.

[q] St. Cyr. Alex. De Inc. c. 15.

[r] It may suffice to quote the language of the Council of Chalcedon, A.D. 451: *τέλειον τὸν αὐτὸν ἐν Θεότητι καὶ τέλειον τὸν αὐτὸν ἐν ἀνθρωπότητι, Θεὸν ἀληθῶς καὶ ἄνθρωπον ἀληθῶς, τὸν αὐτὸν ἐκ ψυχῆς λογικῆς καὶ σώματος, ὁμοούσιον τῷ Πατρὶ κατὰ τὴν Θεότητα καὶ ὁμοούσιον τὸν αὐτὸν ἡμῖν κατὰ τὴν ἀνθρωπότητα, κατὰ πάντα ὅμοιον ἡμῖν χωρὶς ἁμαρτίας.* Routh, Opusc. ii. 78. When these words were spoken, the cycle of possible controversy on the subject was complete. The Monothelite question had virtually been settled by anticipation.

[s] Socr. H. E. iii. 7: *ἔμψυχον εἶναι τὸν ἐνανθρωπήσαντα.* Syn. Bost. anno 244.

integrity of the Creed. Every believing Christian knows that it touches the very heart of his inner life. What becomes of the one Mediator between God and man, if the Manhood whereby He places Himself in contact with us men is but unreal and fictitious? What becomes of His Human Example, of His genuine Sympathy, of His agonizing and world-redeeming Death, of His plenary representation of our race in heaven, of the recreative virtue of His Sacraments, of the 'touch of nature' which makes Him, most holy as He is, in very deed kin with us? All is forthwith uncertain, evanescent, unreal. If Christ be not truly Man, the chasm which parted earth and heaven has not been bridged over. God, as before the Incarnation, is still awful, remote, inaccessible. Tertullian's inference is no exaggeration: 'Cum mendacium deprehenditur Christi Caro. . . . omnia quæ per Carnem Christi gesta sunt, mendacio gesta sunt. . . . . Eversum est totum Dei opus[t].' Or, as St. Cyril of Jerusalem tersely presses the solemn argument: εἰ φάντασμα ἦν ἡ ἐνανθρώπησις, φάντασμα καὶ ἡ σωτηρία[u].

2. Let it be observed, on the other hand, that the Nicene assertion of our Blessed Lord's Divinity does not involve any tacit mutilation or degradation of the idea conveyed by the sacred Name of God. When Jesus Christ is said by His Church to be God, that word is used in its natural, its absolute, its incommunicable sense. This must be constantly borne in mind, if we would escape from equivocations which might again and again obscure the true point before us. For Arianism will confess Christ's Divinity, if, when it terms Him God, it may really mean that He is only a being of an inferior and created nature. Socinianism will confess Christ's Divinity, if this confession involves nothing more emphatic than an acknowledgement of the fact that certain moral features of God's character shone forth from the Human Life of Christ with an absolutely unrivalled splendour. Pantheism will confess Christ's Divinity, but then it is a Divinity which He must share with the universe. Christ may well be divine, when all is divine, although Pantheism too may admit that Christ is divine in a higher sense than any other man, because He has more clearly recognised or exhibited 'the eternal oneness of the finite and the Infinite, of God and humanity.' The coarsest forms of unbelief will confess our Lord's Divinity, if they may proceed to add, by way of explanation, that such language is but the echo of

[t] Adv. Marc. iii. 8.

[u] Catech. iv. 9.

an apotheosis, informally decreed to the prophet of Nazareth by the fervid but uncritical enthusiasm of His Church.

No: the Divinity of Jesus Christ is not to be thus emptied of its most solemn and true significance. It is no mere titular distinction, such as the hollow or unthinking flattery of a multitude might yield to a political chief, or to a distinguished philanthropist. Indeed Jesus Christ Himself, by His own teaching, had made such an apotheosis of Himself morally impossible. He had, as no teacher before Him, raised, expanded, spiritualized man's idea of the Being and Nature of the Great Creator. Baur has remarked that this higher exhibition of the solitary and incommunicable Life of God is nowhere so apparent as in that very Gospel the special object of which is to exhibit Christ Himself as the eternal Word made Flesh [x]. Indeed God was too vividly felt to be a living Presence by the early Christians, to be transformed by them upon occasion into a decoration which might wreathe the brow of any, though it were the highest human virtue. In heathendom this was naturally otherwise. Yet animal indulgence and intellectual scepticism must have killed out the sense of primary truths which nature and conscience had originally taught, before imperial Rome could feel no difficulty in decreeing temples and altars to such samples of our race as were not a few of the men who successively filled the throne of the Cæsars [y]. The Church, with her eye upon the King Eternal, Immortal, Invisible [z], could never have raised Jesus to the full honours of Divinity, had He been merely Man. And Christianity from the first has proclaimed herself, not the authoress of an apotheosis, but the child and the product of an Incarnation.

She could not have been both. Speaking historically, an apotheosis belongs to the Greek world; while half-mimicries

[x] Vorlesungen über N. T. Theologie, p. 354.

[y] See Döllinger, Heidenthum und Judenthum, bk. viii. pt. 2. § 2. The city of Cyzicus was deprived of its freedom for being unwilling to worship Augustus (Tac. Ann. iv. 36). Thrasea Pætus was held guilty of treason for refusing to believe in the deification of Poppæa (Tac. Ann. xvi. 22). Caligula insisted on being worshipped as a god during his lifetime (Suetonius, Caius, xxi. 22). On the number of cattle sacrificed to Domitian, see Pliny, Panegyr. xi. The worship of Antinous, who had lived on terms of criminal intercourse with Hadrian, was earnestly promoted by that Emperor. Döllinger reckons fifty-three apotheoses between Cæsar and Diocletian, fifteen of which were of ladies belonging to the Imperial family. For the discredit into which the Imperial apotheosis fell among the literary classes, see Boissier, Religion Romaine, i. 175, sqq.

[z] 1 Tim. i. 17.

of the Incarnation are characteristically oriental. Speaking philosophically, the god of an apotheosis is a creation of human thought or of human fancy; the God of an incarnation is presupposed as an objectively existing Being, Who manifests Himself by it in the sphere of sense. Speaking religiously, belief in an apotheosis must be fatal to the primary movements of piety towards its object, whenever men are capable of earnest and honest reflection; while it is incontestable that the doctrine of an incarnation stimulates piety in a degree precisely proportioned to the sincerity of the faith which welcomes it. Thus the ideas of an apotheosis and an incarnation stand towards each other in historical, philosophical, and religious contrast. Need I add that religiously, philosophically, and historically, Christianity is linked to the one, and is simply incompatible with the other?

No: the Divinity of Jesus is not such divinity as Pantheism might ascribe to Him. In the belief of the Church Jesus stands alone among the sons of men as He of Whom it can be said without impiety, that He is not merely divine, but God. Such a restriction in favour of a Single Personality, contradicts the very vital principle of Pantheistic thought. Schelling appropriately contends that the Indians with their many incarnations shew more intelligence respecting the real relations of God and the world than is implied by the doctrine of a solitary incarnation, as taught in the Creed of Christendom. Upon Pantheistic grounds, this is perfectly reasonable; although it might be added that any limited number of incarnations, however considerable, would only approximate to the real demands of the theory which teaches that God is incarnate in everything. But then, such divinity as Pantheism can ascribe to Christ is, in point of fact, no divinity at all. When God is nature, and nature is God, everything indeed is divine, but also nothing is Divine; and Christ shares this phantom-divinity with the universe, nay with the agencies of moral evil itself. In truth, our God does not exist in the apprehension of Pantheistic thinkers; since, when such truths as creation and personality are denied, the very idea of God is fundamentally sapped, and although the prevailing belief of mankind may still be humoured by a discreet retention of its conventional language, the broad practical result is in reality neither more nor less than Atheism.

You may indeed remind me of an ingenious distinction, by which it is suggested that the idea of God is not thus sacrificed in Pantheistic systems, and on the ground that although God and the universe are *substantially* identical, they are not *logically* so. Logically speaking, then, you proceed to distinguish between God and the universe. You look out upon the universe, and you arrive at the idea of God by a double process, by a process of abstraction, and by a process of synthesis. In the visible world you come into sensible contact with the finite, the contingent, the relative, the imperfect, the individual. Then, by a necessary operation of your reason, you disengage from these ideas their correlatives; you ascend to a contemplation of infinity, of necessity, of the absolute, the perfect, the universal. Here abstraction has done its work, and synthesis begins. By synthesis you combine the general ideas which have been previously reached through abstraction. These general ideas are made to converge in your brain under the presidency of one central and unifying idea, which you call God. You are careful to insist that this god is not a real but an ideal being; indeed it appears that he is so ideal, that he would cease to be god if he could be supposed to become real. God, you say, is the 'Idea' of the universe; the universe is the 'realization' of God. The god who is enthroned in your thought *must* have abandoned all contact with reality; let him re-enter but for a moment upon the domain of reality, and, such are the exigencies of your doctrine, that he must forthwith be compelled to abdicate his throne [a]. But meanwhile, as you contend, he is logically distinct from the universe; and you repel with some warmth the orthodox allegation, that to identify him *substantially* with the universe, amounts to a practical denial of his existence.

Yet after all, let us ask what is really gained by thus distinguishing between a logical and a substantial identity? What is this god, who is to be thus rescued from the religious ruins which mark the track of Pantheistic thought? Is he, by the terms of your own distinction, anything more than an 'Idea'; and must he not vary in point of perfection with the accuracy and exhaustiveness of those processes of abstraction and synthesis by which you undertake to construct him? And if this be so, is it worth our while to discuss the question whether or not so precarious an 'Idea' was or was not incarnate in Jesus Christ? Upon the terms of the theory, would not an incarnation of God be fatal to His

[a] Cf. M. Caro's notice of Vacherot's La Métaphysique et la Science, Idée de Dieu, p. 265, sqq.; especially p. 289, sqq.

'logical,' that is to His only admitted mode of existence? or would such divinity, if we could ascribe it to Jesus Christ, be anything higher than the fleeting and more or less imperfect speculation of a finite brain?

Certainly Pantheism would never have attained to so strong a position as that which it actually holds in European as well as in Asiatic thought, unless it had embodied a great element of truth, which is too often ignored by some arid Theistic systems. To that element of truth we Christians do justice, when we confess the Omnipresence and Incomprehensibility of God; and still more, when we trace the gracious consequences of His actual Incarnation in Jesus Christ. But we Christians know also that the Great Creator is essentially distinct from the work of His Hands, and that He is What He is, in utter independence of the feeble thought whereby He enables us to apprehend His Existence. We know that all which is not Himself, is upheld in being from moment to moment by the fiat of His Almighty Will. We know that His Existence is, strictly and in the highest sense, Personal. Could we deny these truths, it would be as easy to confess the Divinity of Christ, as it would be impossible to deny the divinity of any created being. If we are asked to believe in an impersonal God, who has no real existence apart from creation or from created thought, in order that we may experience fewer philosophical difficulties in acknowledging our Lord's Divinity, we reply that our faith cannot consent thus '*propter vitam vivendi perdere causas*.' We cannot thus sacrifice the substance of the first truth of the Creed that we may retain the phraseology of the second. We dare not thus degrade, or rather annihilate, the very idea of God, even for the sake of securing a semblance (more it could not be) of those precious consolations which the Christian heart seeks and finds at the Manger of the Divine Child in Bethlehem, or before the Cross of the Lord of Glory on Mount Calvary.

No: the Divinity of Jesus is not divinity in the sense of Socinianism. It is no mere manifestation whether of the highest human goodness, or of the noblest of divine gifts. It is not merely a divine presence vouchsafed to the soul; it is not merely an intercommunion of the soul and God, albeit maintained even ceaselessly—maintained in its fulness from moment to moment. Such indeed was the high grace of our Lord's sinless Humanity, but that grace was not itself His Divinity. For a work of grace, however beautiful and perfect, is one thing;

an Uncreated Divine Essence is another. In the Socinian sense of the term, you all, my Christian brethren, are, or may be, divine; you may shew forth God's moral glory, if less fully, yet not less truly, than did Jesus. By adoption, you too are sons of God; and the Church teaches that each of you was made a partaker of the Divine Nature at his baptism. But suppose that neither by act, nor word, nor thought, you have done aught to forfeit that blessed gift, do I forthwith proceed to profess my belief in your divinity? And why not? Is it not because I may not thus risk a perilous confusion of thought, issuing in a degradation of the Most Holy Name? Your life of grace is as much a gift as your natural life; but however glorious may be the gift, aye, though it raise you from the dust to the very steps of God's Throne, the gift is a free gift after all, and its greatness does but suggest the interval which parts the recipient from the inexhaustible and boundless Life of the Giver.

Most true indeed it is that the perfect holiness which shone forth from our Lord's Human Life has led thousands of souls to perceive the truth of His essential Godhead. When once it is seen that His moral greatness is really unique, it is natural to seek and to accept, as a basis of this greatness, His possession of a unique relationship to the Fountain of all goodness[b]. Thus the Sermon on the Mount leads us naturally on to those dis-

[b] 'Je mehr sich so dem erkennenden Glauben die Ueberzeugung von der Einzigkeit der sittlichen Hoheit Christi erschliesst, desto natürlicher ja nothwendiger muss es nun auch von diesem festen Punkte aus demselben Glauben werden, mit Verständniss Christo in das Gebiet Seiner Reden zu folgen, wo Er Seiner eigenthümlichen und einzigen Beziehung zu dem Vater gedenkt. Jesu Heiligkeit und Weisheit, durch die Er unter den sündigen, vielirrenden Menschen einzig dasteht, weiset so, *da sie nicht kann noch will als rein subjektives, menschliches Produkt angesehen werden, auf einen übernatürlichen Ursprung Seiner Person.* Diese muss, um inmitten der Sünderwelt begreiflich zu sein, aus einer eigenthümlichen und wunderbar schöpferischen That Gottes abgeleitet, ja es muss in Christus, wenn doch Gott nicht deistisch von der Welt getrennt sondern in Liebe ihr nahe und wesentlich als Liebe zu denken ist, von Gott aus betrachtet eine Incarnation göttlicher Liebe, *also göttlichen Wesens* gesehen werden, was Ihn als den Punkt erscheinen lässt, wo Gott und die Menscheit einzig und innigst geeinigt sind. Freilich, man lässt sich in diesem Stücke noch so oft durch einen abstracten, subjectiven Moralismus irre machen, der die Tiefe des Ethischen nicht erfasst. Aber wer tiefer blickend auch *von einer ontologischen und metaphysischen Bedeutung des Ethischen weiss,* dem muss die Einzigkeit der Heiligkeit und Liebe Christi ihren Grund *in einer Einzigkeit auch Seines Wesens* haben, diese aber in Gottes Sich mittheilender, offenbarender Liebe.' (Dorner, Person Christi, Bd. ii. pp. 1211, 1212.)

courses in St. John's Gospel in which Christ unveils His Essential Oneness with the Father. But the ethical premiss is not to be confused with the ontological conclusion. It is true that a boundless love of man shone forth from the Life of Christ; it is true that each of the Divine attributes is commensurate with the Divine Essence. It is true that 'he that dwelleth in love dwelleth in God, and God in him.' But it is not true that every moral being which God blesses by His Presence is God. The Divine Presence, as vouchsafed to Christian men, is a gift superadded to and distinct from the created personality to which it is accorded: there was a time when it had not been given, and a time may come when it will be withdrawn. Such a Presence may indeed in a certain secondary sense 'divinize' a created person[c], robing him with so much of moral beauty and force of deity as a creature can bear. But this blessed gift does not justify us in treating the creature to whom it is vouchsafed as the Infinite and Eternal God. When Socinianism deliberately names God, it means equally with ourselves, not merely a Perfect Moral Being, not merely Perfect Love and Perfect Justice, but One Whose Knowledge and Whose Power are as boundless as His Love. It does not mean that Christ is God in this, the natural sense of the word, when it confesses His moral divinity; yet, beyond all controversy, this full and natural sense of the term is the sense of the Nicene Creed.

No: Jesus Christ is not divine in the sense of Arius. He is not the most eminent and ancient of the creatures, decorated by the necessities of a theological controversy with That Name which a serious piety can dare to yield to One Being alone. Ascribe to the Christ of Arius an antiquity as remote as you will from the age of the Incarnation, place him at a height as high as any you can conceive, above the highest archangel; still what, after all, is this ancient, this super-angelic being but a creature who had a beginning, and who, if the Author of his existence should so will, may yet cease to be? Such a being, however exalted, is parted from the Divine Essence by a fathomless chasm; whereas the Christ of Catholic Christendom is internal to That Essence; He is of one Substance with the Father—*ὁμοούσιος τῷ Πατρί*: and in this sense, as distinct from any other, He is properly and literally Divine.

This assertion of the Divinity of Jesus Christ depends on

[c] 2 St. Peter i. 4: *ἵνα διὰ τούτων* [sc. *ἐπαγγελμάτων*] *γένησθε θείας κοινωνοὶ φύσεως.*

a truth beyond itself. It postulates the existence in God of certain real distinctions having their necessary basis in the Essence of the Godhead. That Three such distinctions exist is a matter of Revelation. In the common language of the Western Church these distinct forms of Being are named Persons. Yet that term cannot be employed to denote Them, without considerable intellectual caution. As applied to men, Person implies the antecedent conception of a species, which is determined for the moment, and by the force of the expression, into a single incommunicable modification of being[d]. But the conception of species is utterly inapplicable to That One Supreme Essence Which we name God; and, according to the terms of the Catholic doctrine, the same Essence belongs to Each of the Divine Persons. Not however that we are therefore to suppose nothing more to be intended by the revealed doctrine than three varying relations of God in His dealings with the world. On the contrary, His Self-Revelation has for its basis certain eternal distinctions in His Nature, which are themselves altogether anterior to and independent of any relation to created life. Apart from

[d] So runs the definition of Boethius. 'Persona est naturæ rationalis individua substantia.' (De Pers. et Duabus Naturis, c. 3.) Upon which St. Thomas observes: 'Conveniens est ut hoc nomen (persona) de Deo dicatur; non tamen eodem modo quo dicitur de creaturis, sed excellentiori modo.' (Sum. Th., 1[a]. qu. 29. a. 3.) When the present use of *οὐσία* and *ὑπόστασις* had become fixed in the East, St. Gregory Nazianzen tells us that in the formula '*μία οὐσία, τρεῖς ὑποστάσεις*,' *οὐσία* signifies *τὴν φύσιν τῆς θειότητος*, while *ὑποστάσεις* points to *τὰς τῶν τριῶν ἰδιότητας*. He observes that with this sense the Westerns were in perfect agreement; but he deplores the poverty of their theological language. They had no expression really equivalent to *ὑπόστασις*, as contrasted with *οὐσία*, and they were therefore obliged to employ the Latin translation of *πρόσωπον* that they might avoid the appearance of believing in three *οὐσίαι*. (Orat. xxi. 46.) St. Augustine laments the necessity of having to say '*quid* Tria sint, Quæ Tria esse fides vera pronuntiat.' (De Trin. vii. n. 7.) 'Cum ergo quæritur quid Tria, vel quid Tres, conferimus nos ad inveniendum aliquod speciale vel generale nomen, quo complectamur hæc Tria: *neque occurrit animo, quia excedit supereminentia Divinitatis usitati eloquii facultatem*.' (Ibid.) 'Cum conaretur humana inopia loquendo proferre ad hominum sensus, quod in secretario mentis pro captu tenet de Domino Deo Creatore suo, sive per piam fidem, sive per qualemcunque intelligentiam, *timuit dicere tres essentias, ne intelligeretur in Illâ Summâ Æqualitate ulla diversitas*. Rursus non esse tria quædam non poterat dicere, quod Sabellius quia dixit, in hæresim lapsus est. . . . Quæsivit *quid* Tria diceret, et dixit *substantias sive personas, quibus nominibus non diversitatem intelligi voluit, sed singularitatem noluit*.' (De Trin. vii. n. 9.) Cf. Serm. cxvii. 7, ccxv. 3, ccxliv. 4. On the term Person, see further St. Athan. Treatises, i. 155, note f. (Lib. Fath.)

1] D

these distinctions, the Christian Revelation of an Eternal Fatherhood, of a true Incarnation of God, and of a real communication of His Spirit, is but the baseless fabric of a dream [e]. These three distinct 'Subsistences [f],' which we name Father, Son, and Spirit, while they enable us the better to understand the mystery of the Self-sufficing and Blessed Life of God before He surrounded Himself with created beings, are also strictly compatible with the truth of the Divine Unity [g]. And when we say that Jesus Christ is God, we mean that in the Man Christ Jesus, the second of these Persons or Subsistences, One in Essence with the First and with the Third, vouchsafed to become Incarnate.

IV. The position then which is before us in these lectures is briefly the following: Our Lord Jesus Christ, being truly and perfectly Man, is also, according to His Higher Pre-existent Nature, Very and Eternal God; since it was the Second Person of the Ever Blessed Trinity, Who, at the Incarnation, robed Himself with a Human Body and a Human Soul. Such explicit language will of course encounter objections in more than one quarter of the modern world; and if of these objections one or two prominent samples be rapidly noticed, it is possible that, at least in the case of certain minds, the path of our future discussion will be cleared of difficulties which are at present more or less distinctly supposed to obstruct it.

(*a*) One objection to our attempt in these lectures may be expected to proceed from that graceful species of literary activity which may be termed, without our discrediting it, Historical Æstheticism. The protest will take the form of an appeal to the sense of beauty. True beauty, it will be argued, is a creation of nature; it is not improved by being meddled with. The rocky hill-side is no longer beautiful when it has been quarried; nor is the river-course, when it has been straightened and deepened for purposes of navigation; nor is the forest which

[e] Cf. Wilberforce on the Incarnation, p. 152.

[f] 'Subsistentiæ, relationes subsistentes.' Sum. Th. 1ª. qu. 29. a. 2; and qu. 40. a. 2.

[g] This compatibility is expressed by the doctrine of the περιχώρησις—the safeguard and witness of the Divine Unity; St. John xiv. 11; 1 Cor. ii. 11: the force of which is not impaired by St. John xiv. 20, xvii. 21, 23; 1 St. John iv. 15, 16, v. 20. This doctrine, as 'protecting the Unity of God, without entrenching on the perfections of the Son and the Spirit, may even be called the characteristic of Catholic Trinitarianism, as opposed to all counterfeits, whether philosophical, Arian, or oriental.' Newman's 'Arians,' p. 190, 1st ed. Cf. Athan. Treatises, ii. 403. note i.

[LECT.

has been fenced and planted, and made to assume the disciplined air of a symmetrical plantation. In like manner, you urge, that incomparable Figure whom we meet in the pages of the New Testament, has suffered in the apprehensions of orthodox Christians, from the officious handling of a too inquisitive Scholasticism. As cultivation robs wild nature of its beauty, even so, you maintain, is 'definition' the enemy of the fairest creations of our sacred literature. You represent 'definition' as ruthlessly invading regions which have been beautified by the freshness and originality of the moral sentiment, and as substituting for the indefinable graces of a living movement, the grim and stiff artificialities of a heartless logic. You wonder at the bad taste of men who can bring the decisions of Nicæa and Chalcedon into contact with the story of the Gospels. What is there in common, you ask, between these dead metaphysical formulæ and the ever-living tenderness of that matchless Life? You protest that you would as readily essay to throw the text of Homer or of Milton into a series of syllogisms, that you would with as little scruple scratch the paint from a masterpiece of Raffaelle with the intention of subjecting it to a chemical analysis, as go hand in hand with those Church-doctors who force Jesus of Nazareth into rude juxtaposition with a world of formal thought, from which, as you conceive, He is severed by the intervention of three centuries of disputation, and still more by all which raises the highest forms of natural beauty above the awkward pedantry of debased art.

Well, my brethren, if the object of the Gospel be attained when it has added one more chapter to the poetry of human history, when it has contributed one more Figure to the world's gallery of historical portraits, upon which a few educated persons may periodically expend some spare thought and feeling;—if this be so, you are probably right. Plainly you are in pursuit of that which may nourish sentiment, rather than of that which can support moral vigour or permanently satisfy the instinct of truth. Certainly your sentiment of beauty may be occasionally shocked by those direct questions and rude processes, which are necessary to the investigation of intellectual truth and to the sustenance of moral life. You would repress these processes; you would silence these questions; or at least you would not explicitly state your own answer to them. Whether, for instance, the stupendous miracle of the Resurrection be or be not as certain as any event of public interest which has taken place in Europe during the present year, is a point which does not affect, as it seems, the worth or the completeness of your Christology. Your Christ is an Epic; and you will suffer no prosaic scholiast to try his hand upon its pages. Your Christ is a portrait; and, as we are all agreed, a portrait is a thing to admire, and not to touch.

But there is a solemn question which must be asked, and which, if a man is in earnest, he will inevitably ask; and that question will at once carry him beyond the narrow horizon of a literary æstheticism in his treatment of the matter before us. . . . My brethren, where is Jesus Christ now? and what is He? Does He only speak to us from the pages which were traced by His followers eighteen centuries ago? Is He no more than the first of the shadows of the past, the first of memories, the first of biographies, the most perfect of human ideals? Is He only an Ideal, after all? Does He reign, only in virtue of a mighty tradition of human thought and feeling in His favour, which creates and supports His imaginary throne? Is He at this moment a really living Being? And if living, is He a human ghost, flitting we know not where in the unseen world, and Himself awaiting an award at the hands of the Everlasting? or is He a super-angelic Intelligence, sinless and invested with judicial and creative powers, but as far separated from the inaccessible Life of God as must be even the first of creatures from the everlasting Creator? Does He reign, in any true sense, either on earth or in heaven? or is His Regal Government in any degree independent of the submission or the resistance which His subjects may offer to it? Is He present personally as a living Power in this our world? Has He any certain relations to you? Does He think of you, care for you, act upon you? Can He help you? Can He save you from your sins, can He blot out their stains and crush their power, can He deliver you in your death-agony from the terrors of dissolution, and bid you live with Him in a brighter world for ever? Can you approach Him now, commune with Him now, cling to Him now, become one with Him now, not by an unsubstantial act of your own imaginations, but by an actual objective transaction, making you incorporate with His Life? Or is the Christian answer to these most pressing questions a weakly delusion, or at any rate too definite a statement; and must we content ourselves with the analysis of an historical Character, while we confess that the Living Personality which once created and animated It may or may not be God, may or may not be able to hear us and help us, may or may not be in distinct conscious existence at this moment, may or may not have been altogether annihilated some eighteen hundred years ago? Do you urge that it is idle to ask these questions, since we have no adequate materials at hand for dealing with them? That is a point which it is hoped may be more or less cleared up during the progress of our present enquiry. But if such questions are to remain unanswered, do not shut your eyes to the certain consequence. A Christ who is conceived of as only pictured in an ancient literature may indeed furnish you with the theme of a magnificent poetry, but he cannot be the present object of your religious life. A religion must have for its object an actually Living Person: and the purpose of the definitions which you deprecate, is to exhibit and assert the exact force of the revealed statements respecting the Eternal Life of Christ, and so to place Him as a Living Person in all His Divine Majesty and all His Human Tenderness before the eye of the soul which seeks Him. When you fairly commit yourself to the assertion that Christ is at this moment living at all, you leave the strictly historical and æsthetical treatment of the Gospel record of His Life and character, and you enter, whether it be in a Catholic or in an heretical spirit, upon the territory of Church definitions. In your little private sphere, you bow to that practical necessity which obliged great Fathers and Councils, often much against their will, to take counsel of the Spirit Who illuminated the collective Church, and to give point and strength to Christian faith by authoritative elucidations of Christian doctrine. Nor are you therefore rendered insensible to the beauty of the Gospel narrative, because you have discovered that thus to ascertain and bear in mind, so far as Revelation warrants your effort, what is the exact Personal dignity and what the enduring prerogatives of Him in Whom you have believed, is in truth a matter of the utmost practical importance to your religious life.

(β) But the present enquiry may be objected to, on higher grounds than those of literary and æsthetic taste. 'Are there not,' it will be pleaded, 'moral reasons for deprecating such discussions? Surely the dogmatic and theological temper is sufficiently distinct from the temper which aims, beyond everything else, at moral improvement. Surely good men may be indifferent divines, while accomplished divines may be false or impure at heart. Nay more, are not morality and theology, not merely distinct, but also more or less antagonistic interests? Does not the enthusiastic consideration of dogmatic problems tend to divert men's minds from that attention which is due to the practical obligations of life? Is not the dogmatic temper, you ask, rightly regarded as a species of "intellectual ritualism" which lulls men into the belief that they have true religion at heart, when in point of fact they are merely gratifying a private taste and losing sight of honesty and sober living in the intoxicating study of the abstractions of controversy? On the other hand, will not a high morality shrink with an instinctive reverence from the clamorous and positive assertions of the theologians? In particular, did Jesus Christ Himself require at the hands of His disciples a dogmatic confession of belief in His Divinity[h]? Was He not content if they acted upon His moral teaching, if they embraced that particular aspect of moral obligations which is of the highest importance to the well-being of society, and which we have lately termed the Enthusiasm of Humanity?' This is what is urged; and then it is added, 'Shall we not best succeed in doing our duty if we try better to understand Christ's Human Character, while we are careful to keep clear of those abstract and transcendental questions about Him, which at any rate have not promoted the cause of moral progress?'

This language is notoriously popular in our day; but the substantial objection which it embodies has been already stated by a writer whom it is impossible to name without mingled admiration and sorrow,—admiration for his pure and lofty humanity, —sorrow for the profound errors which parted him in life and in death from the Church of Jesus Christ. 'Love to Jesus Christ,' says William Channing, 'depends very little on our conception of His rank in the scale of being. On no other topic have Christians contended so earnestly, and yet it is of secondary importance. To know Jesus Christ is not to know the precise place He occupies in the Universe; it is something more: it is to look into His mind; it is to approach His soul; to comprehend His spirit, to see how He thought and felt and purposed and loved. . . I am persuaded,' he continues, 'that controversies about Christ's Person have in one way done great injury. They have turned attention from His character. Suppose that, as Americans, we should employ ourselves in debating the questions, where Washington was born, and from what spot he came when he appeared at the head of our armies; and that in the fervour of these contentions we should overlook the character of his mind, the spirit that moved within

[h] Ecce Homo, p. 69, sqq.

him, . . . how unprofitably should we be employed? Who is it that understands Washington? Is it he that can settle his rank in the creation, his early history, his present condition? or he to whom the soul of that good man is laid open, who comprehends and sympathizes with his generous purposes [i]?'

Channing's illustration of his position in this passage is important. It unconsciously but irresistibly suggests that indifference to the clear statement of our Lord's Divinity is linked to a fundamental assumption of its falsehood. Doubtless Washington's birthplace and present destiny is for the Americans an altogether unpractical consideration, when placed side by side with the study of his character. But the question had never been raised whether the first of religious duties which a creature should pay to the Author and End of his existence was or was not due to Washington. Nobody has ever asserted that mankind owes to the founder of the American Republic the tribute of a prostrate adoration in spirit and in truth. Had it occurred to Channing's mind as even possible that Jesus Christ was more than a mere man who lived and died eighteen centuries ago, he could not have permitted himself to make use of such an illustration. To do justice to Channing, he had much too clear and fine an intellect to imagine that the fundamental question of Christianity could be ignored on moral grounds. Those who know anything of his works are aware that his own opinion on the subject was a very definite one, and that he has stated the usual arguments on behalf of the Socinian heresy with characteristic earnestness and precision.

My brethren, all are agreed as to the importance of studying and copying the Human Character of Jesus Christ. Whether it be really possible to have a sincere admiration for the Character of Jesus Christ without believing in His Divinity, is a question which I shall not shrink from considering hereafter [j]. Whether a true morality does not embrace, as one part of it, an honest acceptance and profession of all attainable religious Truth, is a question which men can decide without being theologians. As for reverence, there is a time to keep silence, and a time to speak. Reverence will assuredly speak, and that plainly, when silence would dishonour its Object: the reverence which is always silent as to matters of belief may be but the drapery of a profound scepticism, which lacks the courage to unveil itself before the eyes of men. Certainly our Lord did not

[i] Works, vol. ii. p. 145.

[j] See Lecture IV.

Himself exact from His first followers, as an indispensable condition of discipleship, any profession of belief in His Godhead. But why? Simply because His requirements are proportioned to the opportunities of mankind. He had taught as men were able to bear His teaching[k]. Although His precepts, His miracles, His character, His express language, all pointed to the Truth of His Godhead, the conscience of mankind was not laid under a formal obligation to acknowledge It until at length He had been 'defined'[l] to be 'the Son of God with power, according to the Spirit of Holiness, by the Resurrection from the dead.' Our present moral relation, then, to the truth of Christ's Divinity differs altogether from that in which His first disciples were placed. It is a simple matter of history that Christendom has believed the doctrine for eighteen centuries; but, besides this, the doctrine challenges at our hands, as I have already intimated, a moral duty as its necessary expression both in the sanctuary of our own thought and before the eyes of men.

Let us face this aspect of the subject in its concrete and every-day form. Those whom I now see around me are without exception, or almost without exception, members of the Church of England. If any here have not the happiness to be communicants, yet, at least, my brethren, you all attend the ordinary Sunday morning service of our Church. In the course of doing so, you sing the Te Deum, you repeat several times the Gloria Patri; but you also kneel down, or profess to kneel down, as joining before God and man in the Litany. Now the second petition in the Litany runs thus: 'O God the Son, Redeemer of the world, have mercy upon us miserable sinners.' What do you seriously mean to do when you join in that petition? Whom are you really addressing? What is the basis and ground of your act? What is its morality? If Jesus Christ is merely a creature, is He in a position to have mercy upon you? Are you doing dishonour to the Most High by addressing Christ in these terms at all? Channing has said that the petition, 'By Thine agony and bloody sweat, by Thy cross and passion, Good Lord, deliver us,' is *appalling*[m]. On the Socinian hypothesis, Channing's language is no exaggeration: the Litany is an 'appalling' prayer, as the Gloria Patri is an 'appalling' doxology. Nor would you escape from this moral difficulty,

k St. John xvi. 12.

l Rom. i. 4: τοῦ ὁρισθέντος υἱοῦ Θεοῦ.

m Unitarian Christianity, Works, vol. ii. p. 541.

[LECT.

if unhappily you should refuse to join in the services of the Church. Your conscience cannot decline to decide in favour of the general duty of adoring Jesus Christ, or against it. And this decision presupposes the resolution, in one sense or the other, of the dogmatic question on which it depends. Christ either is, or He is not God. The worship which is paid to Christ either ought to be paid to Him, or it ought to be, not merely withheld, but denounced. It is either rigorously due from all Christians to our Lord, or it is an outrage on the rights of God. In any case to take part in a service which, like our Litany, involves the prostrate adoration of Jesus Christ, without explicitly recognising His right to receive such adoration, is itself immoral. If to be true and honest in our dealings with each other is a part of mere natural virtue, surely to mean what we say when we are dealing with Heaven is not less an integral part of morality [n]. I say nothing of that vast unseen world of thought and feeling which in the soul of a Christian believer has our Blessed Saviour for its Object, and the whole moral justification of which depends upon the conception which we form of Christ's 'rank in the scale of being.' It is enough to point out to you that the discussion in hand has a practical, present, and eminently a moral interest, unless it be consistent with morality to use in the presence of God and man, a language which we do not believe, or as to the meaning of which we are content to be indifferent.

(γ) Once more. It may be urged, from a widely different quarter, that our enquiry is dangerous, if not to literary or moral interests, yet to the spirit of simple Christian piety. 'Take care,' so the warning may run, 'lest, instead of preaching the Gospel, you should be merely building up a theological pyramid. Beware of sacrificing spiritual objects to intellectual ones. Surely the great question for a sinner to consider is whether or not he be justified before God: do not then let us bury the simple Gospel beneath a heap of metaphysics.'

Now the matter to be considered is whether this absolute

[n] Bp. Butler, Analogy, ii. 1. p. 157. 'Christianity, even what is peculiarly so called, as distinguished from natural religion, has yet somewhat very important, even of a moral nature. For, the office of our Lord being made known, and the relation He stands in to us, the obligation of religious regards to Him is plainly moral, as much as charity to mankind is; since this obligation arises, before external commands, immediately out of that His office and relation itself.'

separation between what is assumed to be the 'simple Gospel' and what is called 'metaphysics' is really possible. In point of fact the simple Gospel, when we come to examine it, is necessarily on one side metaphysical. Educated men, at least, will not be scared by a term, which a scarcely pardonable ignorance may suppose to denote nothing more than the trackless region of intellectual failure. If the Gospel is real to you; if you believe it to be true, and possess it spiritually and intellectually; you cannot but see that it leads you on to the frontier of a world of thought which you may yourselves shrink from entering, but which it is not prudent to depreciate. You say that the main question is to know that you are justified? Very well; but, omitting all other considerations, let me ask you one question: Who is the Justifier? Can He really justify if He is only Man? Does not His power to 'save to the uttermost those that come unto God by Him' depend upon the fact that He is Himself Divine? Yet when, with St. John, you confess that He is the Eternal Logos, you are dealing quite as distinctly with a question of 'metaphysics,' as if you should discuss the value of *οὐσία* and *ὑπόστασις* in primitive Christian Theology. It is true that such discussions will carry you beyond the region of Scripture terminology; but, at least to a sober and thoughtful mind, can it really matter whether a term, such as 'Trinity,' be or be not in Scripture, if the area of thought which it covers be identical with that contained in the Scripture statements [o]? And, to undervalue those portions of truth which cannot be made rhetorically or privately available to excite religious feeling, is to accept a principle which, in the long run, is destructive of the Faith. In Germany, Spener the Pietist held no mean place among the intellectual ancestors of Paulus and of Strauss. In England, a gifted intellect has traced the 'phases' of its progressive disbelief; and if, in its downward course, it has gone so far as to deny that Jesus Christ was even a morally righteous Man, its starting-point was as nearly as possible that of the earnest but shortsighted piety, which imagines that it can dare actively to exercise thought on the Christian Revelation, and withal to ignore those ripe decisions which we owe to the illuminated mind of Primitive Christendom.

[o] Sum. Th. 1[a]. qu. 29. a. 3. Waterland, Works, iii. 652. Importance of Doctrine of H. Trin. c. 7. 'The sense of Scripture *is* Scripture.' Dr. Mill's Letter on Dr. Hampden's Bampton Lectures, p. 14. See Lect. VIII.

[LECT.

There is no question between us, my brethren, as to the supreme importance of a personal understanding and contract between the single soul and the Eternal Being Who made and Who has redeemed it. But this understanding must depend upon ascertained Truths, foremost among which is that of the Godhead of Jesus Christ. And in these lectures an attempt will be made to lay bare and to re-assert some few of the bases upon which that cardinal Truth itself reposes in the consciousness of the Church, and to kindle perchance, in some souls, a fresh sense of its unspeakable importance. It will be our object to examine such anticipations of this doctrine as are found in the Old Testament[p], to note how it is implied in the work of Jesus Christ[q], and how inseparable it is from His recorded Consciousness of His Personality and Mission[r], to trace its distinct, although varying assertion in the writings of His great Apostles[s], and in the earliest ages of His Church[t], and finally to shew how intimate and important are its relations to all that is dearest to the heart and faith of a Christian[u].

It must be a ground of rejoicing that throughout these lectures we shall keep thus close to the Sacred Person of our Lord Himself. And if, indeed, none of us as yet believed in His Godhead, it might be an impertinence on the part of the preacher to suggest any spiritual advice which takes for granted the conclusion of his argument. But you who, thank God, are Christians by living conviction as well as by baptismal privilege, must already possess too strong and too clear a faith in the truth before us, to be in any sense dependent on the success or the failure of a feeble human effort to exhibit it. You at least will endeavour, as we proceed, to bear steadily in mind, that He of Whom we speak and think is no mere tale or portrait of the ancient world, no dead abstraction of modern or of mediæval thought, but a living Being, Who is an observant witness alike of the words spoken in His Name and of the mental and moral response which they elicit. If we must needs pass in review the erring thoughts and words of men, let us be sure that our final object is not a criticism of error, but the clearer apprehension and possession of truth. They who believe, may by reason of the very loyalty and fervour of their devotion, so anxiously

[p] Lect. II. [q] Lect. III. [r] Lect. IV.
[s] Lect. V, VI. [t] Lect. VII. [u] Lect VIII.

and eagerly watch the fleeting, earth-born mists which for a moment have threatened to veil the Face of the Sun of Righteousness, as to forget that the true weal and safety of the soul is only assured while her eye is persistently fixed on His imperishable glory. They who have known the aching misery of earnest doubt, may perchance be encouraged, like the once sceptical Apostle, to probe the wounds with which from age to age error has lacerated Christ's sacred form, and thus to draw from a nearer contact with the Divine Redeemer the springs of a fresh and deathless faith, that shall win and own in Him to all eternity the unclouded Presence of its Lord and God.

LECTURE II.

ANTICIPATIONS OF THE DOCTRINE IN THE OLD TESTAMENT.

The Scripture, foreseeing that God would justify the heathen through faith, preached before the Gospel unto Abraham, saying, In thee shall all nations be blessed.—GAL. iii. 8.

IF we endeavour to discover how often, and by what modes of statement, such a doctrine as that of our Lord's Divinity is anticipated in the Old Testament, our conclusion will be materially affected by the belief which we entertain respecting the nature and the structure of Scripture itself. At first sight, and judged by an ordinary literary estimate, the Bible presents an appearance of being merely a large collection of heterogeneous writings. Historical records, ranging over many centuries, biographies, dialogues, anecdotes, catalogues of moral maxims, and accounts of social experiences, poetry, the most touchingly plaintive and the most buoyantly triumphant, predictions, exhortations, warnings, varying in style, in authorship, in date, in dialect, are thrown, as it seems, somewhat arbitrarily into a single volume. No stronger tie is supposed to have bound together materials so various and so ill-assorted, than the interested or the too credulous industry of some clerical caste in a distant antiquity, or at best than such uniformity in the general type of thought and feeling as may naturally be expected to characterize the literature of a nation or of a race. But beneath the differences of style, of language, and of method, which are undeniably prominent in the Sacred Books, and which appear so entirely to absorb the attention of a merely literary observer, a deeper insight will discover in Scripture such manifest unity of drift and purpose, both moral and intellectual, as to imply the continuous action of a Single Mind. To this unity Scripture itself bears witness, and nowhere more emphatically than in the text before us. Observe that St. Paul does not treat the Old Testament as being to him what Hesiod, for instance, became to the later Greek world. He does not regard it as a great repertorium or storehouse of quotations, which might be accidentally or fancifully employed to illustrate the events or the theories of a later age, and to which accordingly he had recourse for purposes of literary ornamentation. On the contrary, St. Paul's is the exact inverse of this point of view. According to St. Paul, the great doctrines and events of the Gospel dispensation were directly anticipated in the Old Testament. If the sense of the Old Testament became patent in the New, it was because the New Testament was already latent in the Old [a]. *Προϊδοῦσα δὲ ἡ γραφὴ ὅτι ἐκ πίστεως δικαιοῖ τὰ ἔθνη ὁ Θεὸς, προευηγγελίσατο τῷ Ἀβραάμ.* Scripture is thus boldly identified with the Mind Which inspires it; Scripture is a living Providence. The Promise to Abraham anticipates the work of the Apostle; the earliest of the Books of Moses determines the argument of the Epistle to the Galatians. Such a position is only intelligible when placed in the light of a belief in the fundamental Unity of all Revelation, underlying, and strictly compatible with its superficial variety. And this true, internal Unity of Scripture, even when the exact canonical limits of Scripture were still unfixed, was a common article of belief to all Christian antiquity. It was common ground to the sub-apostolic and to the Nicene age; to the East and to the West; to the School of Antioch and to the School of Alexandria; to mystical interpreters like St. Ambrose, and to literalists like St. Chrysostom; to cold reasoners, such as Theodoret, and to fervid poets such as Ephrem the Syrian; to those who, with Origen, conceded much to reason, and to those who, with St. Cyril or St. Leo, claimed much for faith. Nay, this belief in the organic oneness of Scripture was not merely shared by schools and writers of divergent tendencies within the Church; it was shared by the Church herself with her most vehement heretical opponents. Between St. Athanasius and the Arians there was no question as to the relevancy of the reference in the book of Proverbs [b] to the pre-existent Person of our Lord, although there was a vital difference between them as to the true sense and force of that reference. Scripture was believed to contain an harmonious and integral body of Sacred Truth, and each

[a] St. Aug. Quæst. in Ex. qu. 73: 'quanquam et in Vetere Novum lateat, et in Novo Vetus pateat.'

[b] Prov. viii. 22. Cf. St. Athan. Orat. c. Arian. ii. 44. p. 113, ed. Bright.

[LECT.

part of that body was treated as being more or less directly, more or less ascertainably, in correspondence with the rest. This belief expressed itself in the world-wide practice of quoting from any one book of Scripture in illustration of the mind of any other book. Instead of illustrating the sense of each writer only from other passages in his own works, the existence of a sense common to all the Sacred Writers was recognised, and each writer was accordingly interpreted by the language of the others. To a modern naturalistic critic it might seem a culpable, or at least an undiscriminating procedure, when a Father illustrates the Apostolical Epistles by a reference to the Pentateuch, or even one Evangelist by another, or the dogmatic sense of St. Paul by that of St. John. And unquestionably, in a merely human literature, such attempts at illustration would be misleading. The different intellectual horizons, modes of thought, shades and turns of feeling, which constitute the peculiarities of different writers, debar us from ascertaining, under ordinary circumstances, the exact sense of any one writer, except from himself. In an uninspired literature, such as the Greek or the English, it would be absurd to appeal to a primitive annalist or poet with a view to determining the meaning of an author of some later age. We do not suppose that Hesiod 'foresaw' the political doctrines of Thucydides, or the moral speculations of Aristotle. We do not expect to find in Chaucer or in Clarendon a clue to or a forecast of the true sense of Macaulay or of Tennyson. No one has ever imagined that either the Greek or the English literature is a whole in such sense that any common purpose runs persistently throughout it, or that we can presume upon the existence of a common responsibility to some one line of thought in the several authors who have created it, or that each portion is under any kind of obligation to be in some profound moral and intellectual conformity with the rest. But the Church of Christ has ever believed her Bible to be throughout and so emphatically the handiwork of the Eternal Spirit, that it is no absurdity in Christians to cite Moses as foreshadowing the teaching of St. Paul and of St. John. According to the tenor of Christian belief, Moses, St. Paul, and St. John are severally regarded as free yet docile organs of One Infallible Intelligence, Who places them at different points along the line of His action in human history; Who through them and others, as the ages pass before Him, slowly unveils His Mind; Who anticipates the fulness of later revelations by the hints contained in His earlier disclosures; Who in the compass of His boundless Wisdom 'reacheth from one end to another mightily, and sweetly ordereth all things[c].'

Such a belief in the organic unity of Scripture is not fatal to a recognition of those differences between its several portions, upon which some modern critics would lay an exaggerated emphasis. When St. Paul recognises an organic connection between the distant extremities of the records of Revelation, he does not debar himself from recognising differences in form, in matter, in immediate purpose, which part the Law of Moses from the writings of the New Testament[d]. The unlikeness which subsists between the head and the lower limbs of an animal is not fatal to their common share in its nervous system and in the circulation of its blood. Nay more, this oneness of Scripture is a truth compatible with the existence within its compass of different measures and levels of Revelation. The unity of consciousness in a human life is not forfeited by growth of knowledge, or by difference of circumstances, or by varieties of experience. Novatian compares the unfolding of the mind of God in Revelation to the gradual breaking of the dawn, attempered as it is to the human eye, which after long hours of darkness could not endure a sudden outflash of noonday sunlight[e]. The Fathers trace in detail the application of this principle to successive revelations in Scripture, first, of the absolute Unity of God, and afterwards, of Persons internal to that Unity[f]. The Sermon on the Mount contrasts its own higher moral level with that of the earlier dispensation[g]. Ethically and dogmatically the New Testament is an advance upon the Old, yet both are within the Unity of Inspiration. Different degrees of light do not imply any intrinsic contrariety. If the Epistle to the Galatians points out the moral incapacity of the Mosaic Law, the Epistle to the Hebrews teaches us its typical and unfailing significance. If Christian converts from Judaism had been 'called out of

[c] Wisd. viii. 1.

[d] e.g. cf. Gal. iii. 23-25; Rom. x. 4; Heb. viii. 13.

[e] Novatian, de Trin. c. 26: 'Gradatim enim et per incrementa fragilitas humana nutriri debet, . . periculosa enim sunt quæ magna sunt, si repentina sunt. Nam etiam lux solis subita post tenebras splendore nimio insuetis oculis non ostendet diem, sed potius faciet cæcitatem.'

[f] St. Epiphanius, Hæres. 74. 10; St. Gregor. Nazianzen, Orat. xxxi. n. 26: *ἐκήρυσσε φανερῶς ἡ Παλαιὰ τὸν Πατέρα, τὸν Υἱὸν ἀμυδρότερον.* Cf. Kuhn, Dogmatik, Band ii. p. 5.

[g] St. Matt. v. 21, 22, 27, 28, 33, 34; comp. Ibid. xii. 5-8.

[LECT.

darkness into God's marvellous light[h],' yet still 'whatsoever things were written aforetime,' in the Jewish Scriptures, 'were written for the learning' of Christians[i].

You will have anticipated, my brethren, the bearing of these remarks upon the question before us. There are explicit references to the doctrine of our Lord's Divinity in the Old Testament, which we can only deny by discrediting the historical value of the documents which contain them. But there are also occult references to this doctrine which we are not likely to detect, unless, while seeking them, we are furnished with an exegetical principle, such as was that of the organic unity of Scripture, as understood by the Ancient Church. The geologist can inform us from surface indications, where and at what depths to find the coal-field or the granite; but we can all recognise granite or coal when we see them in the sunlight. Let us then first place ourselves under the guidance of the great minds of antiquity, with a view to discovering some of those more hidden allusions to the doctrine which are found in earlier portions of the Old Testament Scriptures; and let us afterwards trace, however hastily, those clearer intimations of it which abound in the later Messianic prophecies, and which are indeed so plain, that 'whoso runs may read them.'

I. (*a*) At the beginning of the Bock of Genesis there appear to be intimations of the existence of a plurality of Persons within the One Essence of God. It is indeed somewhat remarkable that the full significance of the two words[j], by which Moses describes the primal creative act of God, was not insisted upon by the primitive Church teachers. It attracted attention in the middle ages, and it was more particularly noticed after the revival of Hebrew Letters. When Moses is describing this Divine action, he joins a singular verb to a plural noun. Language, it would seem, thus submits to a violent anomaly, that she may the better hint at the presence of Several Powers or Persons, Who not merely act together, but Who constitute a Single Agent. We are indeed told that this Name of God, Elohim, was borrowed from Polytheistic sources, that it was retained in its plural form in order to express majesty or magnificence, and that it was then united to singular verbs and adjectives in order to make it do the work of a Monotheistic Creed[k]. But on the other hand, it is confessed on all sides that the promulgation and protection of a belief in the Unity of God was the central

[h] 1 St. Pet. ii. 9. [i] Rom. xv. 4. [j] Gen. i. 1, ברא אלהים.
[k] Herder, Geist der Hebr. Poësie, Bd. i. p. 48.

and dominant object of the Mosaic literature and of the Mosaic legislation. Surely such an object would not have been imperilled for no higher purpose than that of amplification. There must have been a truth at stake which demanded the risk. The Hebrew language could have described God by singular forms such as El, Eloah, and no question would have been raised as to the strictly Monotheistic force of those words. The Hebrew language might have 'amplified' the idea of God thus conveyed by less dangerous processes than the employment of a plural form. Would it not have done so, unless the plural form had been really necessary, in order to suggest some complex mystery of God's inner Life, until that mystery should be more clearly unveiled by the explicit Revelations of a later day? The analogies of the language may indeed prove that the plural form of the word had a majestic force; but the risk of misunderstanding would surely have counterbalanced this motive for using it, unless a vital need had demanded its retention. Nor will the theory that the plural noun is merely expressive of majesty in ברא אלהים, avail to account for the plural verb in the words, 'Let Us make man[l].' In these words, which precede the final act and climax of the Creation, the early Fathers detected a clear intimation of a Plurality of Persons in the Godhead[m]. The supposition that in these words a Single Person is in a dramatic colloquy with Himself, is less reasonable than the opinion that a Divine Speaker is addressing a multitude of inferior beings, such as the Angels. But apart from other considerations, we may well ask, what would be the 'likeness' or 'image' common to God and to the Angels, in which man was to be created[n]? or why should created essences such as the Angels be invited to take part in a Creative Act at all? Each of the foregoing explanations is really weighted with greater difficulties than the Patristic doctrine, to the effect that the verb, 'Let Us make,' points to a Plurality of Persons within the Unity of the One Agent, while the 'Likeness,' common to All These Persons and itself One, suggests very pointedly Their participation in an Undivided Nature. And in such sayings as 'Behold the man

[l] Gen. i. 26. Cp. Drach, Deuxième Lettre d'un Rabbin Converti aux Israelites ses Pères, Paris, 1827, p. 26.

[m] Cf. the references in Petavius, de Trinitate, ii. 7. 6.

[n] 'Non raro etiam veteres recentioresque interpretes, ut אלהים de angelis intelligerent, theologicis potius quam exegeticis argumentis permoti esse videntur; cf. . . . Gen. i. 26, 27, ex quo Samaritani cum Abenezra hominem ad angelorum, non ad Dei, similitudinem creatum esse probant.' Gesenius, Thesaur. in voc. אלהים, 2.

is become like One of Us[o],' used with reference to the Fall, or 'Go to; let Us go down and there confound their language[p],' uttered on the eve of the dispersion of Babel, it is clear that an equality of rank is distinctly assumed between the Speaker and Those Whom He is addressing. The only adequate alternative to that interpretation of these texts which is furnished by the Trinitarian doctrine, and which sees in them a preparation for the disclosures of a later age, is the violent supposition of some kind of pre-Mosaic Olympus, the many deities of which are upon a level of strict equality with each other[q]. But if this supposition be admitted, how are we to account for the presence of such language in the Pentateuch at all? How can a people, confessedly religious and intelligent, such as were the Hebrews, have thus stultified their whole religious history and literature, by welcoming or retaining, in a document of the highest possible authority, a nomenclature which contained so explicit a denial of the first Article of the Hebrew Faith?

The true sense of the comparatively indeterminate language which occurs at the beginning of Genesis, is more fully explained by the Priestly Blessing which we find to be prescribed for ritual usage in the Book of Numbers[r]. This blessing is spoken of as a putting the *Name* of God[s], that is to say, a symbol unveiling His Nature[t], upon the children of Israel. Here then we discover a distinct limit to the number of the Persons Who are hinted at in Genesis, as being internal to the Unity of God. The Priest is to repeat the Most Holy Name Three times. The Hebrew accentuation, whatever be its date, shews that the Jews themselves saw in this repetition the declaration of a mystery in the Divine Nature. Unless such a repetition had been designed to secure the assertion of some important truth, a single mention of the Sacred Name would have been more natural in a system, the object of which was to impress belief in the Divine Unity upon an entire people. This significant repetition, suggesting

[o] Gen. iii. 22. כאחד ממנו. LXX. ὡς εἷς ἐξ ἡμῶν.

[p] Gen. xi. 7.

[q] Klose, De polytheismi vestigiis apud Hebræos ante Mosen, Gotting. 1830, referred to by Kuhn, Dogmatik, Bd. ii. p. 10.

[r] Num. vi. 23–26.

[s] Ibid. ver. 27.

[t] 'Nach der biblischen Anschauung und inbesondere des A. T. ist überhaupt der Zusammenhang zwischen Name und Sache ein sehr enger, und ein ganz anderer als im modernen Bewusstein, wo sich der Name meist zu einem bloss conventionellen Zeichen abgeschwächt hat; der Name ist die Sache selbst, sofern diese in die Erscheinung tritt und erkannt wird, der ins Wort gefasste Ausdruck des Wesens.' König, Theologie der Psalmen, p. 266.

without distinctly asserting a Trinity in the Being of God, did its work in the mind of Israel. It is impossible not to be struck with the recurrence of the Threefold rhythm of prayer or praise, again and again, in the Psalter [u]. Again and again the poetical parallelism is sacrificed to the practical and theological object of making the sacred songs of Israel contain an exact acknowledgment of that inner law of God's Nature, which had been shadowed out in the Pentateuch. And to omit traces of this influence of the priestly blessing which are discoverable in Jeremiah and Ezekiel [x], let us observe the crowning significance of the vision of Isaiah [y]. In that adoration of the Most Holy Three, Who yet are One [z], by the veiled and mysterious Seraphim; in that deep self-abasement and misery of the Prophet, who, though a man of unclean lips, had yet seen with his eyes the King, the Lord of Hosts [a]; in that last enquiry on the part of the Divine Speaker, the very terms of which reveal Him as One and yet more than One [b],—what a flood of almost Gospel light [c] is poured upon the intelligence of the elder Church! If we cannot altogether assert with the opponents of the Lutheran Calixtus, that the doctrine of the Trinity is so clearly contained in the Old Testament as to admit of being deduced from it without the aid of the Apostles and Evangelists; enough at least has been said to shew that the Old Testament presents us with a doctrine of the Divine Unity which is very far removed from the hard and sterile Monotheism of the Koran. Within the Uncreated and Unapproachable Essence, Israel could plainly distinguish the shadows of a Truth which we Christians fully express at this hour, when we 'acknowledge the glory of the Eternal Trinity, and in the power of the Divine Majesty worship the Unity.'

(β) From these adumbrations of Personal Distinctions within the Being of God, we pass naturally to consider that series of remarkable apparitions which are commonly known as the Theophanies, and which form so prominent a feature in the early history of the Old Testament Scriptures. When we are told that God spoke to our fallen parents in Paradise [d], and appeared

[u] Cf. Ps. xxix. 4, 5, and 7, 8; xcvi. 1, 2, and 7, 8; cxv. 9, 10, 11; cxviii. 2-4, and 10-12, and 15, 16.
[x] On this subject, see Dr. Pusey's Letter to the Bishop of London, p. 131.
[y] Isaiah vi. 2-8. [z] Ibid. ver. 3. [a] Ibid. ver. 5.
[b] Ibid. ver. 8. [c] Heb. i. 1.
[d] Gen. iii. 8: 'They heard the voice of the Lord God walking in the garden in the cool of the day.'

to Abram in his ninety-ninth year[e], there is no distinct intimation of the mode of the Divine manifestation. But when 'Jehovah appeared' to the great Patriarch by the oak of Mamre[f], Abraham 'lift up his eyes and looked, and lo, Three Men stood by him[g].' Abraham bows himself to the ground; he offers hospitality; he waits by his Visitors under the tree, and they eat[h]. One of the Three is the spokesman; he appears to bear the Sacred Name Jehovah[i]; he is seemingly distinguished from the 'two angels' who went first to Sodom[j]; he promises that the aged Sarah shall have a son, and that 'all the nations of the earth shall be blessed in Abraham[k].' With him Abraham intercedes for Sodom[l]; by him judgment is afterwards executed upon the guilty city. When it is said that 'Jehovah rained upon Sodom and Gomorrah brimstone and fire from Jehovah out of heaven[m],' a sharp distinction is established between a visible and an Invisible Person, each bearing the Most Holy Name. This distinction introduces us to the Mosaic and later representations of that very exalted and mysterious being, the מלאך יהוה or Angel of the Lord. The Angel of the Lord is certainly distinguished from Jehovah; yet the names by which he is called, the powers which he assumes to wield, the honour which is paid to him, shew that in him there was at least a special Presence of God. He seems to speak sometimes in his own name, and sometimes as if he were not a created personality, but only a veil or organ of the Higher Nature That spoke and acted through him. Thus he assures Hagar, as if speaking in the character of an ambassador from God, that 'the Lord had heard her affliction[n].' Yet he promises her, 'I will multiply thy seed exceedingly[o],' and she in return 'called the Name of the Lord that spake unto her, Thou God seest me[p].' He arrests Abraham's arm, when the Patriarch is on the point of carrying out God's bidding by offering Isaac as a sacrifice[q]; yet he associates himself with Him from Whom 'Abraham had not withheld his son, his only son.' He accepts for himself Abraham's obedience as rendered to God, and he subsequently at a second appearance adds the promise, 'In thy seed shall all the nations of

[e] Gen. xvii. 1-3: 'The Lord appeared to Abram, and said unto him, I am the Almighty God. . . . And Abram fell on his face: and God talked with him.'

[f] Ibid. xviii. 1.

[g] Ibid. ver. 2.

[h] Ibid. ver. 8.

[i] Ibid. ver. 17.

[j] Compare Gen. xviii. 22 and xix. 1. LXX. ἦλθον δὲ οἱ δύο ἄγγελοι.

[k] Gen. xviii. 10, 18.

[l] Ibid. vers. 23-33.

[m] Ibid. xix. 24; cf. St. Justin, Dial. Tryp. c. 56.

[n] Gen. xvi. 11.

[o] Ibid. ver. 10.

[p] Ibid. ver. 13.

[q] Ibid. xxii. 11, 12.

the earth be blessed; because thou hast obeyed My voice [r].' He appears to Jacob in a dream, he announces himself as 'the God of Bethel, where thou anointedst the pillar, and where thou vowedst a vow unto Me [s].' Thus he was 'the Lord' who in Jacob's vision at Bethel had stood above the ladder and said, 'I am the Lord God of Abraham thy father, and the God of Isaac [t].' He was, as it seems, the Chief of that angel-host whom Jacob met at Mahanaim [u]; with him Jacob wrestled for a blessing at Peniel; of him Jacob says, 'I have seen God face to face, and my life is preserved.' When blessing the sons of Joseph, the dying Patriarch invokes not only 'the God Which fed me all my life long unto this day,' but also 'the Angel which redeemed me from all evil [x].' In the desert of Midian, the Angel of the Lord appears to Moses 'in a flame of fire out of the midst of a bush.' The bush remains miraculously unconsumed [y]. 'Jehovah' sees that Moses turns aside to see, and 'Elohim' calls to Moses out of the midst of the bush [z]. The very ground on which Moses stands is holy; and the Lawgiver hides his face, 'for he was afraid to look upon God [a].' The Speaker from the midst of the bush announces Himself as the God of Abraham, the God of Isaac, and the God of Jacob [a]. His are the Mercy, the Wisdom, the Providence, the Power, the Authority of the Most High [b]; nay, all the Divine attributes [c]. When the children of Israel are making their escape from Egypt, the Angel of the Lord leads them; in the hour of danger he places himself between the camp of Israel and the host of Pharaoh [d]. How deeply Israel felt the value of his protecting care, we may learn from the terms of the message to the King of Edom [e]. God promises that the Angel shall keep Israel in the way, and bring the people to Canaan [f]; his presence is a guarantee that the Amorites and other idolatrous races shall be cut off [g]. Israel is to obey this Angel, and to provoke him not; for the Holy 'Name is in him [h].' Even after the sin of the Golden Calf, the promised guardianship of the Angel is not forfeited; while a distinction is clearly drawn between the Angel and Jehovah Himself [i]. Yet the Angel is

r Gen. xxii. 18; cf. Heb. vi. 13, 14.
s Gen. xxxi. 11, 13.
t Ibid. xxviii. 13.
u Ibid. xxxii. 1.
x Ibid. xlviii. 15, 16.
y Exod. iii. 1, 2.
z Ibid. ver. 4.
a Ibid. ver. 6.
b Ibid. vers. 7-14.
c Ibid. vers. 14-16.
d Ibid. xiv. 19.
e Num. xx. 16.
f Exod. xxiii. 20; compare xxxii. 34.
g Ibid. xxiii. 23; cf. Joshua v. 13-15.
h Exod. xxiii. 21, כי שמי בקרבו.
i Ibid. xxxiii. 2, 3: 'I will send an angel before thee . . . for I will not go up in the midst of thee; for thou art a stiff-necked people.'

expressly called the Angel of God's Presence[k]; he fully represents God. God must in some way have been present in him. No merely created being, speaking and acting in his own right, could have spoken to men, or have allowed men to act towards himself, as did the Angel of the Lord. Thus he withstands Balaam, on his faithless errand, and bids him go with the messengers of Balak; but adds, 'Only the word that I shall speak unto thee, that thou shalt speak.' As 'Captain of the host of the Lord,' he appears to Joshua in the plain of Jericho. Joshua worships God in him[l]; and the Angel asks of the conqueror of Canaan the same tokens of reverence as had been exacted from Moses[m]. Besides the reference in the Song of Deborah[n] to the curse pronounced against Meroz by the Angel of the Lord, the Book of Judges contains accounts of three appearances, in each of which we are scarcely sensible of the action of a created personality, so completely is the language and bearing that of the Higher Nature present in the Angel. At Bochim he expostulates with the assembled people for their breach of the covenant in failing to exterminate the Canaanites. God speaks by him as in His own Name; He refers to the covenant which He had made with Israel, and to His bringing the people out of Egypt; He declares that, on account of their disobedience He will not drive the heathen nations out of the land[o]. In the account of his appearance to Gideon, the Angel is called sometimes the Angel of the Lord, sometimes the Lord, or Jehovah. He bids Gideon attack the Midianite oppressors of Israel, and adds the promise, 'I will be with thee.' Gideon places an offering before the Angel, that he may, if he wills, manifest his character by some sign. The Angel touches the offering with the end of his staff, whereupon fire rises up out of the rock and consumes the offering. The Angel disappears, and Gideon fears that he will die because he has seen 'the Angel of the Lord face to face[p].' When the wife of Manoah is reporting the Angel's first appearance to herself, she says that 'A man of God came' to her, 'and his countenance was like the countenance of the Angel of God, very terrible.' She thus speaks of the Angel as of a Being already

[k] Exod. xxxiii. 14; compare Isaiah lxiii. 9.

[l] In Josh. vi. 2 the captain of the Lord's Host (cf. ch. v. 14) *appears* to be called Jehovah. But cf. Mill, Myth. Int. p. 354.

[m] Josh. v. 13-15; Exod. iii. 5; compare Exod. xxiii. 23.

[n] Judges v. 23.

[o] Ibid. ii. 1-5. See Keil, Comm. in loc.

[p] Judg. vi. 11-22. Keil, Comm. in loc. See Hengstenberg, Christol. O. Test. vol. iv. append. iii. p. 292.

known to Israel. At his second appearance the Angel bids Manoah, who 'knew not that he was an Angel of the Lord,' and offered him common food, to offer sacrifice unto the Lord. The Angel refuses to disclose his Name, which is 'wonderful[q].' When Manoah offers a kid with a meat-offering upon a rock unto the Lord, the Angel mounts visibly up to heaven in the flame of the sacrifice. Like Gideon, Manoah fears death after such near contact with so exalted a Being of the other world. 'We shall surely die,' he exclaims to his wife, 'because we have seen God[r].'

But you ask, Who was this Angel? The Jewish interpreters vary in their explanations[s]. The earliest Fathers answer with general unanimity that he was the Word or Son of God Himself. For example, in the Dialogue with Trypho, St. Justin proves against his Jewish opponent, that God did not appear to Abraham by the oak of Mamre, *before* the appearance of the 'three men,' but that He was One of the Three[t]. Trypho admits this, but he objects that it did not prove that there was any God besides Him Who had appeared to the Patriarchs. Justin replies that a Divine Being, personally although not substantially distinct from the supreme God, is clearly implied in the statement that 'the Lord rained upon Sodom and upon Gomorrah, brimstone and fire from the Lord out of heaven[u].' Trypho yields the point. Here it is plain that St. Justin did not suppose that a created being was called God on account of his mission; St. Justin believes that One Who was of the substance of God appeared to Abraham[x]. Again, the Fathers of the first Synod at Antioch, in the letter which was sent to Paulus of Samosata before his deposition, state that the 'Angel of the

[q] פלאי, cf. Is. ix. 6.

[r] Judges xiii. 6-22. Cf. Keil, Comm. in loc. Hengst. ubi supra. Vitringa de Angelo Sacerdote, obs. vi. 14.

[s] Cf. the authorities quoted by Drach, Lettres d'un Rabbin Converti, Lettre ii. p. 169. On the other side, Abenezra, in Exod. iii. 2.

[t] With St. Justin's belief that the Son and two Angels appeared to Abraham, cf. Tertullian. adv. Marc. ii. 27, iii. 9; St. Hil. de Trin. iv. 27. That three created Angels appeared to Abraham was the opinion of St. Augustine (De Civ. Dei, x. 8, xvi. 29). St. Ambrose sees in the 'three men' an adumbration of the Blessed Trinity: 'Tres vidit et unum Dominum appellavit.' De Abraham, i. c. 5; Prudent. Apotheosis, 28. This seems to be the sense of the English Church. See First Lesson for Evensong on Trinity Sunday.

[u] Gen. xix. 24.

[x] Dial. cum Tryph. § 56, sqq. On the appearance in the burning bush, cf. Ibid. § 59-61; cf. too ch. 127. Comp. St. Justin, Apol. i. c. 63.

Father being Himself Lord and God, μεγάλης βουλῆς ἄγγελος [y], appeared to Abraham, and to Jacob, and to Moses in the burning bush [z].' It is unnecessary to multiply quotations in proof of a fact which is beyond dispute [a].

The Arian controversy led to a modification of that estimate of the Theophanies which had prevailed in the earlier Church. The earlier Church teachers had clearly distinguished, as Scripture distinguishes, between the Angel of the Lord, Himself, as they believed, Divine, and the Father. But the Arians endeavoured to widen this personal distinctness into a deeper difference, a difference of Natures. Appealing to the often-assigned ground [b] of the belief respecting the Theophanies which had prevailed in the ante-Nicene Church, the Arians argued that the Son had been seen by the Patriarchs, while the Father had not been seen, and that an Invisible Nature was distinct from and higher than a nature which was cognizable by the senses [c]. St. Augustine boldly faced this difficulty, and his great work on the Trinity gave the chief impulse to another current of interpretation in the Church. St. Augustine strenuously insists upon the Scriptural truth [d] of the Invisibility of God as God [e]. The Son,

[y] This gloss of the LXX. in Is. ix. 6 was a main ground of the early Patristic application of the title of the Angel to God the Son. 'Although Malachi foretells our Lord's coming in the Flesh under the titles of "the Lord," "the Angel," or "Messenger of the Covenant," (chap. iii. 1) there is no proof that He is anywhere spoken of absolutely as "the Angel," or that His Divine Nature is so entitled.' Dr. Pusey, Daniel the Prophet, p. 516, note 1.

[z] Mansi, Conc. i. p. 1035.

[a] Compare however St. Irenæus adv. Hær. iv. 7. § 4; Clem. Alex. Pæd. i. 7; Theophilus ad Autol. ii. 31; Constit. Apostol. v. 20; Tertullian. adv. Prax. cap. 13, 14, and 15; St. Cyprian. adv. Judæos, ii. c. 5, 6; St. Cyr. Hieros. Catech. 10; St. Hil. de Trin. lib. 4 and 5; St. Chrysost. Hom. in Genes. 42, 48; Theodoret, Interr. v. in Exod. (Op. i. p. 121), on Exod. iii. 2. Cf. some additional authorities given by P. Vandenbroeck, De Theophaniis, sub Vet. Testamento, p. 17, sqq; Bull, Def. Fid. Nic. lib. i. c. 1.

[b] e. g. cf. Tertullian. adv. Marc. ii. c. 27.

[c] St. Aug. Serm. vii. n. 4. The Arian criticism ran thus: 'Filius visus est patribus, Pater non est visus: invisibilis autem et visibilis diversa natura est.'

[d] St. John i. 18, &c.

[e] 'Ipsa enim natura vel substantia vel essentia, vel quolibet alio nomine appellandum est id ipsum, quod Deus est, quidquid illud est *corporaliter videri non potest.*' De Trin. ii. c. 18, n. 35. The Scotists, who opposed the general Thomist doctrine to the effect that a created angel was the instrument of the Theophanies, carefully guarded against the ideas that the substance of God could be seen by man in the body, or that the bodily form which they believed to have been assumed was *personally* united to the Eternal Word, since this was peculiar to the Divine Incarnation. (Scotus in lib. ii. sent. dist. 8.) Scotus explains that the being who

therefore, as being truly God, was by nature as invisible as the Father. If the Son appeared to the Patriarchs, He appeared through the intermediate agency of a created being, who represented Him, and through whom He spoke and acted[f]. If the Angel who represented Him spoke and acted with a Divine authority, and received Divine honours, we are referred to the force of the general law whereby, in things earthly and heavenly, an ambassador is temporarily put in the place of the Master who accredits him[g]. But Augustine further warns us against attempting to say positively, Which of the Divine Persons manifested Himself, in this or that instance, to Patriarchs or Prophets, except where some remarkable indications determine our conclusion very decisively[h]. The general doctrine of this great teacher, that the Theophanies were not direct appearances of a Person in the Godhead, but Self-manifestations of God through a created being, had been hinted at by some earlier Fathers[i],

assumes a bodily form, need only be 'intrinsecus motor corporis; nam tunc assumit, id est ad se sumit, quia ad operationes proprias sibi explendas utitur illo sicut instrumento.' (Ibid. Scholion i.)

[f] 'Proinde illa omnia, quæ Patribus visa sunt, cum Deus illis secundum suam dispensationem temporibus congruam præsentaretur, per creaturam facta esse, manifestum est . . . Sed jam satis quantum existimo . . . demonstratum est, . . . quod antiquis patribus nostris ante Incarnationem Salvatoris, cum Deus apparere dicebatur, voces illæ ac species corporales per angelos factæ sunt, *sive* ipsis loquentibus vel agentibus aliquid ex personâ Dei, sicut etiam prophetas solere ostendimus, *sive assumentibus ex creaturâ quod ipsi non essent,* ubi Deus figuratè demonstraretur hominibus; quod genus significationum nec Prophetas omisisse, multis exemplis docet Scriptura.' De Trin. iii. 11, n. 22, 27.

[g] 'Sed ait aliquis: cur ergo Scriptum est, Dixit Dominus ad Moysen; et non potiùs, Dixit angelus ad Moysen? Quia *cum verba judicis præco pronuntiat,* non scribitur in Gestis, ille præco dixit; sed ille judex; sic etiam loquente prophetâ sancto, etsi dicamus Propheta dixit, nihil aliud quam Dominum dixisse intelligi volumus. Et si dicamus, Dominus dixit; prophetam non subtrahimus, sed quis per eum dixerit admonemus.' De Trin. iii. c. 11, n. 23.

[h] 'Nihil aliud, quantum existimo, divinorum sacramentorum modesta et cauta consideratio persuadet, nisi ut temerè non dicamus, Quænam ex Trinitate Persona cuilibet Patrum et Prophetarum in aliquo corpore vel similitudine corporis apparuerit, nisi cum continentia lectionis aliqua probabilia circumponit indicia. . . . Per subjectam creaturam non solum Filium vel Spiritum Sanctum, sed etiam Patrem corporali specie sive similitudine mortalibus sensibus significationem Sui dare potuisse credendum est.' De Trin. ii. c. 18, n. 35.

[i] Compare St. Irenæus adv. Hær. iv. 20, n. 7 and 24: 'Verbum naturaliter quidem invisibile, palpabile in hominibus factum.' Origen (Hom. xvi. in Jerem.) speaking of the vision in Exod. iii. says, 'God was here beheld in the Angel.'

[LECT.

and was insisted on by contemporary and later writers of the highest authority [k]. This explanation has since become the predominant although by no means the exclusive judgment of the Church [l]; and if it is not unaccompanied by considerable difficulties when we apply it to the sacred text, it certainly seems to relieve us of greater embarrassments than any which it creates [m].

But whether the ante-Nicene (so to term it) or the Augustinian line of interpretation be adopted with respect to the Theophanies, no sincere believer in the historical trustworthiness of Holy Scripture can mistake the importance of their relation to the doctrine of our Lord's Divinity. If the Theophanies were not, as has been pretended, mythical legends, the natural product of the Jewish mind at a particular stage of its development, but actual matter-of-fact occurrences in the history of ancient Israel, must we not see in them a deep Providential meaning? Whether in them the Word or Son actually appeared, or whether God made a created angel the absolutely perfect exponent of His Thought and Will, do they not point in either case to a purpose in the Divine Mind which would only be realized when man had been admitted to a nearer and more palpable contact with God than was possible under the Patriarchal or Jewish dispensations? Do they not suggest, as their natural climax and explanation, some Personal Self-unveiling of God before the eyes of His creatures? Would not God appear to have been training His people, by this long and mysterious series of communications, at length to recognise and to worship Him when hidden under, and indissolubly one with a created nature? Apart from the specific circumstances which may seem to have explained each Theophany at the time of its taking place, and considering them as a series of phenomena, is there any other account of them so much in

[k] St. Jerome (ed. Vall.) in Galat. iii. 19: 'Quod in omni Veteri Testamento ubi angelus primum visus refertur et postea quasi Deus loquens inducitur, angelus quidem verè ex ministris pluribus quicunque est visus, sed in illo Mediator loquatur, Qui dicit; Ego sum Deus Abraham, etc. Nec mirum si Deus loquatur in angelis, cum etiam per angelos, qui in hominibus sunt, loquatur Deus in prophetis, dicente Zachariâ: et ait angelus, qui loquebatur in me, ac deinceps inferente; hæc dicit Deus Omnipotens.' Cf. St. Greg. Magn. Mag. Moral. xxviii. 2; St. Athan. Or. iii. c. Arian. § 14.

[l] The earlier interpretation has been more generally advocated by English divines. P. Vandenbroeck's treatise already referred to shews that it still has adherents in other parts of the Western Church.

[m] See especially Dr. Pusey, Daniel the Prophet, p. 515, note 20; p. 516, sqq.

harmony with the general scope of Holy Scripture, as that they were successive lessons addressed to the eye and to the ear of ancient piety, in anticipation of a coming Incarnation of God?

(γ) This preparatory service, if we may venture so to term it, which had been rendered to the doctrine of our Lord's Divinity by the Theophanies in the world of sense, was seconded by the upgrowth and development of a belief respecting the Divine Kochmah or Wisdom in the region of inspired ideas.

1. The 'Wisdom' of the Jewish Scriptures is certainly more than a human endowment [n], and even, as it would seem, more than an Attribute of God. It may naturally remind us of the Archetypal Ideas of Plato, but the resemblance is scarcely more than superficial. The 'Wisdom' is hinted at in the Book of Job. In a well-known passage of majestic beauty, Job replies to his own question, Where shall the Wisdom [o] be found? He represents Wisdom as it exists in God, and as it is communicated in the highest form to man. In God 'the Wisdom' is that Eternal Thought, in which the Divine Architect ever beheld His future creation [p]. In man, Wisdom is seen in moral growth; it is 'the fear of the Lord,' and 'to depart from evil [q].' The Wisdom is here only revealed as underlying, on the one side, the laws of the physical universe, on the other, those of man's moral nature. Certainly as yet, 'Wisdom' is not in any way represented as personal; but we make a great step in passing to the Book of Proverbs. In the Book of Proverbs the Wisdom is co-eternal with Jehovah; Wisdom assists Him in the work of Creation; Wisdom reigns, as one specially honoured, in the palace of the King of Heaven; Wisdom is the adequate object of the eternal joy of God; God possesses Wisdom, Wisdom delights in God.

[n] The word חכמה is, of course, used in this lower sense. It is applied to an inspired skill in making priestly vestments (Exod. xxviii. 3), or sacred furniture generally (Ibid. xxxi. 6 and xxxvi. 1, 2); to fidelity to known truth (Deut. iv. 6; cf. xxxii. 6); to great intellectual accomplishments (Dan. i. 17). Solomon was typically חכם: his 'Wisdom' was exhibited in moral penetration and judgment (1 Kings iii. 28, x. 4, sqq.); in the knowledge of many subjects, specially of the works of God in the natural world (Ibid. iv. 33, 34); in the knowledge of various poems and maxims, which he had either composed or which he remembered (Ibid. iv. 32; Prov. i. 1). Wisdom, as communicated to men, included sometimes supernatural powers (Dan. v. 11), but specially moral virtue (Ps. xxxvii. 30, li. 6; Prov. x. 31); and piety to God (Ps. cxi. 10). In God החכמה is higher than any of these; He alone originally possesses It (Job xii. 12, 13, xxviii. 12, sqq.).

[o] Job xxviii. 12. החכמה. [p] Ibid. vers. 23-27. [q] Ibid. ver. 28.

'Jehovah (says Wisdom) possessed Me in the beginning of His way,
Before His works of old.
I was set up from everlasting,
From the beginning, or ever the earth was.
When there were no depths, I was brought forth;
When there were no fountains abounding with water.
Before the mountains were settled,
Before the hills was I brought forth:
While as yet He had not made the earth, nor the fields,
Nor the highest part of the dust of the world.
When He prepared the heavens, I was there:
When He set a compass upon the face of the depth:
When He established the clouds above:
When He strengthened the fountains of the deep:
When He gave to the sea His decree,
That the waters should not pass His commandment:
When He appointed the foundations of the earth:
Then I was by Him, as One brought up with Him:
And I was daily His Delight, rejoicing always before Him;
Rejoicing in the habitable part of His earth;
And My delights were with the sons of men [r].'

Are we listening to the language of a real Person or only of a poetic personification? A group of critics defends each hypothesis; and those who maintain the latter, point to the picture of Folly in the succeeding chapter [s]. But may not a study of that picture lead to a very opposite conclusion? Folly is there no mere abstraction, she is a sinful woman of impure life, 'whose guests are in the depths of hell.' The work of Folly is the very work of the Evil One, the real antagonist of the Divine Kochmah. Folly is the principle of absolute Unwisdom, of consummate moral Evil. Folly, by the force of the antithesis, enhances our impression that 'the Wisdom' is personal. The Arians understood the word [t] which is rendered 'possessed' in our English Bible, to mean 'created,' and they thus degraded the Wisdom to the level of a creature. But they did not doubt that this created Wisdom was a real being or person [u]. Modern critics

[r] Prov. viii. 22-31. For Patristic expositions of this passage, see Petavius, de Trin. ii. 1.

[s] Prov. ix. 13-18.

[t] The Arians appealed to the LXX. reading ἔκτισε (not ἐκτήσατο). On κτίζειν as meaning any kind of production, see Bull, Def. Fid. Nic. lib. ii. c. 6, sec. 8. In a note on Athan. Treatises, ii. 342, Dr. Newman cites Aquila, St. Basil, St. Gregory Nyss. and St. Jerome, for the sense ἐκτήσατο.

[u] As Kuhn summarily observes: 'Das war überhaupt nicht die Frage in christlichen Alterthum, ob hier von einem Wesen die Rede sei, das war allgemein anerkannt, sondern von welcher Art, in welchem Verhältniss zu Gott es gedacht sei.' Dogmatik, ii. p. 29, note (2).

know that if we are to be guided by the clear certain sense of the Hebrew root [x], we shall read 'possessed,' and not 'created,' and they admit without difficulty that the Wisdom is uncreated by, and co-eternal with the Lord Jehovah. But they resolve Wisdom into an impersonal and abstract idea or quality. The true interpretation is probably related to these opposite mistakes, as was the Faith of the Church to the conflicting theories of the Arians and the Sabellians. Each error contributes something to the cause of truth; the more ancient may teach us that the Wisdom is personal; the more modern, that it is uncreated and co-eternal with God.

2. But even if it should be thought, that 'the personified idea of the Mind of God in Creation,' rather than the presence of 'a distinct Hypostasis [y],' is all that can with certainty be discovered in the text of the Book of Proverbs; yet no one, looking to the contents of those sacred Sapiential Books, which lie outside the precincts of the Hebrew Canon, can well doubt that something more had been inferred by the most active religious thought in the Jewish Church. The Son of Sirach, for instance, opens his great treatise with a dissertation on the source of Wisdom. Wisdom is from all eternity with God; Wisdom proceeds from God before any finite thing, and is poured out upon all His Works [z]. But Wisdom, 'thus created from the beginning before the world,' and having an unfailing existence [a], is bidden by God to make her 'dwelling in Jacob, and her inheritance in Israel [b].' Wisdom is thus the prolific mother of all forms of moral beauty [c]; she is given to all of God's true children [d]; but she is specially resident in the holy Law, 'which Moses commanded for an heritage unto the congregations of Jacob [e].' In that beautiful chapter which contains this passage, Wisdom is conceived of as all-operative, yet as limited by nothing; as a physical yet also as a spiritual power; as eternal, and yet having definite relations to time; above all, as perpetually extending the range of her fruitful

[x] This both in Hebrew and (with one exception) in Arabic. Cf. Gesenius, Thesaurus, in קָנָה and قنا. So, too, the Syr. ܩܢܐ. Neither Gen. xiv. 19 nor Deut. xxxii. 6 *require* that קָנָה should be translated 'created,' still less Ps. cxxxix. 13, where it means 'to have rights over.' Gesenius quotes no other examples. The current meaning of the word is 'to acquire' or 'possess,' as is proved by its certain sense in the great majority of cases where it is used.

[y] So apparently Döllinger, Heidenthum und Judenthum, bk. x. part iii. sec. 2.

[z] Ecclus. i. 1–10. [a] Ibid. xxiv. 9. [b] Ibid. vers. 8–12. [c] Ibid. vers. 13–18. [d] Ibid. [e] Ibid. ver. 23.

self-manifestation[f]. Not to dwell upon language to the same effect in Baruch[g], we may observe that in the Book of Wisdom the Sophia is more distinctly personal[h]. If this Book is less prominently theocratic than Ecclesiasticus, it is even more explicit as to the supreme dignity of Wisdom, as seen in its unique relation to God. Wisdom is a pure stream flowing from the glory of the Almighty[i]; Wisdom is that spotless mirror which reflects the operations of God, and upon which He gazes as He works[k]; Wisdom is the Brightness of the Everlasting Light[l]; Wisdom is the very Image of the Goodness of God[m]. Material symbols are unequal to doing justice to so spiritual an essence: 'Wisdom is more beautiful than the sun, and above all the order of the stars; being compared with the light she is found before it[n].' 'Wisdom is more moving than any motion: she passeth and goeth through all things by reason of her pureness[o].' Her sphere is not merely Palestine, but the world, not this or that age, but the history of humanity. All that is good and true in human thought is due to her: 'in all ages entering into holy souls she maketh them friends of God and prophets[p].' Is there not here, in an Alexandrian dress, a precious and vital truth sufficiently familiar to believing Christians? Do we not already seem to catch the accents of those weighty formulæ by which Apostles will presently define the pre-existent glory of their Majestic Lord? Yet are we not steadily continuing, with no very considerable measure of expansion, in that very line of sacred thought, to which the patient servant of God in the desert, and the wisest of kings in Jerusalem, have already, and so authoritatively, introduced us?

3. The doctrine may be traced at a stage beyond, in the writings of Philo Judæus. We at once observe that its form is altered; instead of the Wisdom or Sophia we have the Logos or Word. Philo indeed might have justified the change of phraseology by an appeal even to the Hebrew Scriptures. In the Hebrew Books, the Word of Jehovah manifests the energy of

[f] Cf. especially Ecclus. xxiv. 5–8, 10–18, 25–28, and i. 14–17.

[g] Compare Baruch iii. 14, 15, 29–32, 35, 36, and the remarkable verse 37.

[h] Lücke, who holds that in the Book of Proverbs and in Ecclesiasticus there is merely a personification, sees a 'dogmatic hypostatizing' in Wisd. vii. 22, sqq. Cf. too Dähne, Alexandrinische Religionsphilosophie, ii. 134, &c.

[i] Wisd. vii. 25.

[k] Ibid. 26: ἔσοπτρον ἀκηλίδωτον τῆς τοῦ Θεοῦ ἐνεργείας.

[l] Ibid. ἀπαύγασμα φωτὸς ἀϊδίου, compare Heb. i. 3.

[m] Ibid. εἰκὼν τῆς ἀγαθότητος τοῦ Θεοῦ, compare 2 Cor. iv. 4, Col. i. 15.

[n] Ibid. ver. 29. [o] Ibid. ver. 24, compare ver. 27. [p] Ibid. ver. 27.

God: He creates the heavens[q]; He governs the world[r]. Accordingly, among the Palestinian Jews, the Chaldee paraphrasts almost always represent God as acting, not immediately, but through the mediation of the Memra[s] or Word. In the Greek Sapiential Books, the Word is apparently identical with the Wisdom[t]; but the Wisdom is always prominent, the Word is rarely mentioned[u]. Yet the Logos of Ecclesiasticus is the organ of creation[v], while in the Book of Wisdom the Logos is clearly personified, and is a minister of the Divine Judgment[x].

[q] Ps. xxxiii. 6. דבר יהוה.

[r] Ps. cxlvii. 15; Isa. lv. 11.

[s] מימרא or דבור. Thus on Hosea i. 7, 'I will save them by the Lord their God,' the Chald. Paraphr. runs, 'I will redeem them by *the Word* Jehovah their God.'

[t] Thus in Ecclus. xxiv. 3 the *σοφία Θεοῦ* uses the language which might be expected of the *λόγος Θεοῦ*, in saying that she came forth from the Mouth of the Most High. In chap. i. 5 *πηγὴ σοφίας λόγος Θεοῦ* (om Tisch.) is probably spurious. In the Book of Wisdom *σοφία* is identified on the one side with the *ἅγιον πνεῦμα παιδείας* (chap. i. 4, 5), and the *πνεῦμα Κυρίου* (ver. 7); *πνεῦμα* and *σοφία* are united in the expression *πνεῦμα σοφίας* (vii. 7; compare ix. 17). On the other side *σοφία* and the *λόγος* are both instruments of creation (Wisd. ix. 1, 2; for the *πνεῦμα*, cf. Gen. i. 2, and Ps. xxxiii. 6), they both 'come down from heaven' (Ibid. ver. 10, and xviii. 15, and the *πνεῦμα*, ix. 17), and achieve the deliverance of Israel from Egypt (cf. xviii. 15 with x. 15-20). The representation seems to suggest no mere ascription of identical functions to altogether distinct conceptions or Beings, but a real inner essential unity of the Spirit, the Word, and the Wisdom. 'Es ist an sich eine und dieselbe göttliche Kraft, die nach aussen wirksam ist, aber es sind verschiedene Beziehungen und Arten dieser Wirksamkeit, wornach sie Wort, Geist, Weisheit Gottes gennant wird.' Kuhn, p. 27. That the *πνεῦμα* really pointed to a distinct Hypostasis in God became plain only at a later time to the mind of His people. On the relations of the רוח יהוה, the הכמה, and the דבר יהוה to each other, see Kuhn, p. 24.

[u] Kuhn has stated the relation of the 'Wisdom,' 'Word,' and 'Spirit' to God and to each other, in the Sapiential Books, as follows: 'Die Unterscheidung Gottes und Seiner Offenbarung in der Welt ist die Folie, auf der sich ein innerer Unterschied in Gott abspiegelt, der Unterschied Gottes nämlich von Seinem Worte, Seiner Weisheit. Diese, wiewohl sie zunächst blosse Eigenschaften und somit Sein an Sich seiendes Wesen, oder Kräfte und Wirksamkeiten Gottes nach aussen, somit dasselbe Wesen, sofern Es Sich in der Welt manifestirt, ausdrücken, erscheinen sofort tiefer gefasst als etwas für sich, unter dem Gesichtspunkt eines eigenen göttlichen Wesens, einer göttlichen Person. Unter einander verhalten sie sich aber so, dass einerseits Wort und Geist, desgleichen andrerseits Wort und Weisheit Gottes theils unterschieden, theils aber auch wieder wesentlich gleichbedeutend genommen sind, so dass ausser dem Hauptunterschiede Gottes von Seinem Andern noch ein weiterer, der Unterschied dieses Andern von einem Dritten hinzuzukommen, zugleich aber auch die Identität des ihnen (unter Sich und mit Gott) gemeinsamen Wesens angedeutet zu sein scheint.' Lehre von Gottl. Dreieinigkeit, p. 23.

[v] Ecclus. xliii. 26.

[x] Wisd. xviii. 15.

In Philo, however, the Sophia falls into the background [y], and the Logos is the symbol of the general doctrine, for other reasons perhaps, but mainly as a natural result of Philo's profound sympathy with Stoic and Platonic thought. If the Book of Wisdom adopts Platonic phraseology, its fundamental ideas are continuous with those of the Hebrew Scriptures [z]. Philo, on the contrary, is a hearty Platonist; his Platonism enters into the very marrow of his thought. It is true that in Philo Platonism and the Jewish Revelation are made to converge. But the process of their attempted assimilation is an awkward and violent one, and it involves the great Alexandrian in much involuntary self-contradiction. Philo indeed is in perpetual embarrassment between the pressure of his intellectual Hellenic instincts on the one side, and the dictates of his religious conscience as a Jewish believer on the other. He constantly abandons himself to the currents of Greek thought around him, and then he endeavours to set himself right with the Creed of Sinai, by throwing his Greek ideas into Jewish forms. If his Logos is apparently moulded after the pattern of the νοῦς βασιλικὸς ἐν τῇ τοῦ Διὸς φύσει—the Regal Principle of Intelligence in the Nature of Zeus—with which we meet in the Philebus of Plato [a], Philo doubtless would fain be translating and explaining the דבר יהוה of the Hebrew Canon, in perfect loyalty to the Faith of Israel. The Logos of Philo evidently presupposes the Platonic doctrine of Ideas; but then, with Philo, these Ideas are something more than the

[y] Philo distinguishes between Wisdom and Philosophy: Philosophy or wise living is the slave of Wisdom or Science; σοφία is ἐπιστήμη θείων καὶ ἀνθρωπίνων καὶ τῶν τούτων αἰτιῶν (Cong. Qu. Erud. Grat. § 14, ed. Mangey, tom. i. p. 530). Philo explains Exod. xxiv. 6 allegorically, as the basis of a distinction between Wisdom as it exists in men and in God, τὸ θεῖον γένος ἀμιγὲς καὶ ἄκρατον (Quis Rer. Div. Hær. § 38, i. p. 498). Wisdom is the mother of the world (Quod Det. Potiori Insid. § 16, i. p. 202); her wealth is without limits, she is like a deep well, a perennial fountain, &c. But Philo does not in any case seem to personify Wisdom; his doctrine of Wisdom is eclipsed by that of the Logos.

[z] Vacherot (École d'Alexandrie, vol. i. p. 134, Introd.) says of Wisdom and Ecclesiasticus: 'Ces monumens renferment peu de traces des idées Grècques dont ils semblent avoir précédé l'invasion en Orient.' Ecclesiasticus was written in Hebrew under the High-Priesthood of Simon I, B.C. 303–284, by Jesus the Son of Sirach, and translated into Greek by his grandson, who came to reside at Alexandria under Ptolemy Euergetes.

[a] Plat. Philebus, p. 30. 'There is not,' says Professor Mansel, 'the slightest evidence that the Divine Reason was represented by Plato as having a distinct personality, or as being anything more than an attribute of the Divine Mind.' Cf. art. Philosophy, in Kitto's Cycl. of Bibl. Literature, new ed.

models after which creation is fashioned, or than the seals which are impressed upon concrete forms of existence [b]. The Ideas of Philo are energizing powers or causes whereby God carries out His plan of creation [c]. Of these energetic forces, the Logos, according to Philo, is the compendium, the concentration. Philo's Logos is a necessary complement of his philosophical doctrine concerning God. Philo indeed, as the devout Jew, believes in God as a Personal Being Who has constant and certain dealings with mankind; Philo, in his Greek moods, conceives of God not merely as a single simple Essence, but as beyond Personality, beyond any definite form of existence, infinitely distant from all relations to created life, incapable of any contact even with a spiritual creation, subtilized into an abstraction altogether transcending the most abstract conceptions of impersonal being. It might even seem as if Philo had chosen for his master, not Plato the theologian of the Timæus, but Plato the pure dialectician of the Republic. But how is such an abstract God as this to be also the Creator and the Providence of the Hebrew Bible? Certainly, according to Philo, matter existed before Creation [d]; but how did God mould matter into created forms of life? This, Philo will reply, was the work of the Logos, that is to say, of the ideas collectively. The Philonian Logos is the Idea of ideas [e]; he is the shadow of God by which as by an instrument He made the worlds [f]; he is himself the intelligible or Ideal World, the Archetypal Type of all creation [g]. The Logos of Philo is the most ancient and most general of created things [h];

[b] Cf. Philo, de Mundi Opif. § 44, tom. i. p. 30; Legis Allegor. i. § 9, tom. i. p. 47.

[c] De Monarchiâ, i. § 6, tom. ii. p. 219: *ὀνομάζουσι δὲ αὐτὰς οὐκ ἀπὸ σκοποῦ τινὲς τῶν παρ' ὑμῖν ἰδέας, ἐπειδὴ ἕκαστον τῶν ὄντων ἰδιοποιοῦσι, τὰ ἄτακτα τάττουσαι, καὶ τὰ ἄπειρα καὶ ἀόριστα καὶ ἀσχημάτιστα περατοῦσαι καὶ περιορίζουσαι καὶ σχηματίζουσαι καὶ συνόλως τὸ χεῖρον εἰς τὸ ἄμεινον μεθαρμοζόμεναι.* Comp. the remarkable passage in De Vict. Offer. § 13, tom. ii. p. 261.

[d] In one passage only does Philo appear to ascribe to God the creation of matter. De Somn. i. § 13, tom. i. 632. If so, for once his Jewish conscience is too strong for his Platonism. But even here his meaning is at best doubtful. Cf. Döllinger, Heid. und Judenth. bk. x. pt. 3, § 5.

[e] De Mundi Opif. § 6; i. p. 5: *ἰδέα τῶν ἰδεῶν ὁ Θεοῦ λόγος.*

[f] Legis Allegor. iii. 31; i. p. 106: *σκιὰ Θεοῦ δὲ ὁ λόγος αὐτοῦ ἐστιν ᾧ καθάπερ ὀργάνῳ προσχρησάμενος ἐκοσμοποίει.* De Monarch. ii. § 5; tom. ii. 225; De Cherub. § 35, tom. i. p. 162.

[g] De Mundi Opif. § 6, i. p. 5: *ἡ ἀρχέτυπος σφραγὶς, ὅν φαμεν εἶναι κόσμον νοητὸν, αὐτὸς ἂν εἴη τὸ ἀρχέτυπον παράδειγμα . . . ὁ Θεοῦ λόγος.* The *λόγος* is dissociated from the *παράδειγμα* in De Conf. Ling. c. xiv. i. 414.

[h] Legis Allegor. iii. 61, i. p. 121: *καὶ ὁ λόγος δὲ τοῦ Θεοῦ ὑπεράνω παντός ἐστι τοῦ κόσμου, καὶ πρεσβύτατος καὶ γενικώτατος τῶν ὅσα γέγονε.*

he is the Eternal Image of God[i]; he is the band whereby all things are held together[k]; he fills all things, he sustains all things[l]. Through the Logos, God, the abstract, the intangible, the inaccessible God, deals with the world, with men. Thus the Logos is mediator as well as creator[m]; he is a high-priest and intercessor with God; he interprets God to man; he is an ambassador from heaven[n]. He is the god of imperfect men, who cannot ascend by an ecstatic intuition to a knowledge of the supreme God[o]; he is thus the nutriment of human souls, and a source of spiritual delights[p]. The Logos is the eldest angel or the archangel[q]; he is God's Eldest, His Firstborn Son[r]; and we almost seem to touch upon the apprehension of that sublime, that very highest form of communicated life, which is exclusive of the ideas of inferiority and of time, and which was afterwards so happily and authoritatively expressed by the doctrinal formula of an eternal generation. But, as we listen, we ask ourselves one capital and inevitable question: Is Philo's Logos a personal being, or is he after all a pure abstraction? Philo is silent; for on such a point as this the Greek and the Jew in him are hope-

[i] De Conf. Ling. § 28, i. 427. 'Although,' says Philo, 'we are not in a position to be considered the Sons of God, yet we may be the children τῆς ἀϊδίου εἰκόνος αὐτοῦ, λόγου τοῦ ἱερωτάτου.

[k] De Plantat. § 2, i. 331: δεσμὸν γὰρ αὐτὸν ἄῤῥηκτον τοῦ παντὸς ὁ γεννήσας ἐποίει πατήρ.

[l] De Mundo, § 2, ii. p. 604: τὸ ὀχυρώτατον καὶ βεβαιότατον ἔρεισμα τῶν ὅλων ἐστίν. Οὗτος ἀπὸ τῶν μέσων ἐπὶ τὰ πέρατα καὶ ἀπὸ τῶν ἄκρων εἰς μέσα ταθεὶς δολιχεύει τὸν τῆς φύσεως δρόμον ἀήττητον, συνάγων πάντα τὰ μέρη καὶ σφίγγων.

[m] Quis Rer. Div. Hær. § 42, i. p. 501: τῷ δὲ ἀρχαγγέλῳ καὶ πρεσβυτάτῳ λόγῳ δωρεὰν ἐξαίρετον ἔδωκεν ὁ τὰ ὅλα γεννήσας πατὴρ, ἵνα μεθόριος στὰς τὸ γενόμενον διακρίνῃ τοῦ πεποιηκότος.

[n] Ibid.: ὁ δ' αὐτὸς ἱκέτης μέν ἐστι τοῦ θνητοῦ κηραίνοντος ἀεὶ πρὸς τὸ ἄφθαρτον, πρεσβυτὴς δὲ τοῦ ἡγεμόνος πρὸς τὸ ὑπήκοον. Cf. De Somniis, § 37, i. 653; De Migr. Abraham. § 18, i. 452. De Gigant. § 11: ὁ ἀρχιερεὺς λόγος.

[o] Legis Allegor. iii. § 73, i. 128: οὗτος [sc. ὁ λόγος] γὰρ ἡμῶν τῶν ἀτελῶν ἂν εἴη θεὸς, τῶν δὲ σοφῶν καὶ τελείων, ὁ πρῶτος, i.e. God Himself. Cf. § 32 and § 33, i. 107.

[p] Legis Allegor. iii. § 59, i. 120: Ὁρᾷς τῆς ψυχῆς τροφὴν οἵα ἐστί; Λόγος Θεοῦ συνεχὴς, ἐοικὼς δρόσῳ. Cf. also § 62. De Somniis, § 37, i. 691: τῷ γὰρ ὄντι τοῦ θείου λόγου ῥύμη συνεχὴς μεθ' ὁρμῆς καὶ τάξεως φερομένη, πάντα διὰ πάντων ἀναχεῖται καὶ εὐφραίνει.

[q] De Conf. Ling. § 28, i. 427: κἂν μηδέπω μέντοι τυγχάνῃ τις ἀξιόχρεως ὢν υἱὸς Θεοῦ προσαγορεύεσθαι, σπουδαζέτω κοσμεῖσθαι κατὰ τὸν πρωτόγονον αὐτοῦ Λόγον, τὸν ἄγγελον πρεσβύτατον ὡς ἀρχάγγελον πολυώνυμον ὑπάρχοντα.

[r] De Conf. Ling. § 14, i. 414: τοῦτον μὲν γὰρ πρεσβύτατον υἱὸν ὁ τῶν ὄντων ἀνέτειλε Πατὴρ, ὃν ἑτέρωθι πρωτόγονον ὠνόμασε.

lessly at issue. Philo's whole system and drift of thought must have inclined him to personify the Logos; but was the personified Logos to be a second God, or was he to be nothing more than a created angel? If the latter, then he would lose all those lofty prerogatives and characteristics, which, platonically speaking, as well as for the purposes of mediation and creation, were so entirely essential to him. If the former, then Philo must break with the very first article of the Mosaic creed; he must renounce his Monotheism. Confronted with this difficulty, the Alexandrian wavers in piteous indecision; he really recoils before it. In one passage indeed he even goes so far as to call the Logos a 'second God[s],' and he is accordingly ranked by Petavius among the forerunners of Arius. But on the whole he appears to fall back upon a position which, however fatal to the completeness of his system, yet has the recommendation of relieving him from an overwhelming difficulty. After all that he has said, his Logos is really resolved into a mere group of Divine ideas, into a purely impersonal quality included in the Divine Being[t]. That advance

[s] Fragment quoted from Euseb. Præp. Evang. lib. vii. c. 13 in Phil. Oper. ii. 625: *θνητὸν γὰρ οὐδὲν ἀπεικονισθῆναι πρὸς τὸν ἀνωτάτω καὶ πατέρα τῶν ὅλων ἐδύνατο, ἀλλὰ πρὸς τὸν δεύτερον θεὸν, ὅς ἐστιν ἐκείνου Λόγος.* But the Logos is called *θεός* only *ἐν καταχρήσει.* Op. i. 655.

[t] That Philo's Logos is *not* a distinct Person is maintained by Dorner, Person Christi, Einleitung, p. 23, note i. 44, sqq. note 40; by Döllinger, Heid. und Judenthum, bk. x. p. iii. § 5; and by Burton, Bampton Lectures, note 93. The opposite opinion is that of Gfrörer (see his Philo und die Jüdisch-Alexandrinische Theologie), and of Lücke (see Professor Mansel, in Kitto's Encycl., art. Philosophy, p. 526, note). Professor Jowett, at one time, following Gfrörer, appears to find in Philo 'the complete personification of the Logos,' although he also admits that Philo's idea of the Logos 'leaves us in doubt at last whether it is not a quality only, or mode of operation in the Divine Being.' (Ep. of St. Paul, i. p. 510, 2nd ed.) He hesitates indeed to decide the question, on the ground that 'the word "person" has now a distinctness and unity which belongs not to that age.' (p. 485.) Surely the idea (at any rate) of personality, whether distinctly analyzed or no, is a primary element of all human thought. It is due to Professor Jowett to call attention to the extent (would that it were wider and more radical!) to which he disavows Gfrörer's conclusions. (Ibid. p. 454, note.) And I quote the following words with sincere pleasure: 'The object of the Gospel is real, present, substantial,—an object such as men may see with their eyes and hold in their hands. . . . But in Philo the object is shadowy, distant, indistinct; whether an idea or a fact we scarcely know. . . . Were we to come nearer to it, it would vanish away.' (Ibid. p. 413, 1st ed.; p. 509, 2nd ed., in which there are a few variations.) A study of the passages referred to in Mangey's index will, it is believed, convince any unprejudiced reader that Philo did not know his own mind; that his Logos was sometimes impersonal and sometimes not, or that he sometimes *thought* of a personal Logos, and never *believed* in one.

toward the recognition of a real Hypostasis,—so steady, as it seemed, so promising, so fruitful,—is but a play upon language, or an intellectual field-sport, or at best, the effort which precedes or the mask which covers a speculative failure. We were tempted perchance for a moment to believe that we were listening to the master from whom Apostles were presently to draw their inspirations; but, in truth, we have before us in Philo Judæus only a thoughtful, not insincere, but half-heathenized believer in the Revelation of Sinai, groping in a twilight which he has made darker by his Hellenic tastes, after a truth which was only to be disclosed in its fulness by another Revelation, the Revelation of Pentecost.

This hesitation as to the capital question of the Personality of the Logos, would alone suffice to establish a fundamental difference between the vacillating, tentative speculation of the Alexandrian, and the clear, compact, majestic doctrine concerning our Lord's Pre-existent Godhead, which meets us under a somewhat similar phraseological form [u] in the pages of the New Testament. When it is assumed that the Logos of St. John is but a reproduction of the Logos of Philo the Jew, this assumption overlooks fundamental discrepancies of thought, and rests its case upon occasional coincidences of language [v]. For besides the contrast between the abstract ideal Logos of Philo, and the concrete Personal Logos of the fourth Evangelist, which has already been noticed, there are even deeper differences, which would have made it impossible that an Apostle should have sat in spirit as a pupil at the feet of the Alexandrian, or that he should have allowed himself to breathe the same general religious atmosphere. Philo is everywhere too little alive to the presence and to the consequences of moral evil [w]. The history

[u] On the general question of the phraseological coincidences between Philo and the writers in the New Testament, see the passages quoted in Professor Mansel's article 'Philosophy' (Kitto's Encycl.), already referred to. I could sincerely wish that I had had the advantage of reading that article before writing the text of these pages.

[v] 'Gfrörer,' Professor Jowett admits, 'has exaggerated the resemblances between Philo and the New Testament, making them, I think, more real and less verbal than they are in fact.' (Ep. of St. Paul, i. 454, note.) 'Il est douteux,' says M. E. Vacherot, 'que Saint Jean, qui n'a jamais visité Alexandrie, ait connu les livres du philosophe juif.' Histoire Critique de l'école d'Alexandrie, i. p. 201. And the limited circulation of the writings of the theosophical Alexandrians would appear from the fact that Philo himself appears never to have read those of his master Aristobulus. Cf. Valkenaer, de Aristobulo, p. 95.

[w] See the remarks of M. E. de Pressensé, Jésus-Christ, p. 112.

of Israel, instead of displaying a long, earnest struggle between the Goodness of God and the wickedness of men, interests Philo only as a complex allegory, which, by a versatile exposition, may be made to illustrate various ontological problems. The priesthood, and the sacrificial system, instead of pointing to man's profound need of pardon and expiation, are resolved by him into the symbols of certain cosmical facts or theosophic theories. Philo therefore scarcely hints at the Messiah, although he says much concerning Jewish expectations of a brighter future; he knows no means of reconciliation, of redemption; he sees not the need of them. According to Philo, salvation is to be worked out by a perpetual speculation upon the eternal order of things; and asceticism is of value in assisting man to ascend into an ecstatic philosophical reverie. The profound opposition between such a view of man's moral state, and that stern appeal to the humbling realities of human life which is inseparable from the teaching of Christ and His Apostles, would alone have made it improbable that the writers of the New Testament are under serious intellectual obligations to Philo. Unless the preaching which could rouse the conscience to a keen agonizing sense of guilt is in harmony with a lassitude which ignores the moral misery that is in the world; unless the proclamation of an Atoning Victim crucified for the sins of men be reconcilable with an indifference to the existence of any true expiation for sin whatever; it will not be easy to believe that Philo is the real author of the creed of Christendom. And this moral discrepancy does but tally with a like doctrinal antagonism. According to Philo, the Divinity cannot touch that which is material: how can Philo then have been the teacher of an Apostle whose whole teaching expands the truth that the Word, Himself essentially Divine, was made flesh and dwelt among us? Philo's real spiritual progeny must be sought elsewhere. Philo's method of interpretation may have passed into the Church; he is quoted by Clement and by Origen, often and respectfully. Yet Philo's doctrine, it has been well observed, if naturally developed, would have led to Docetism rather than to Christianity[x]; and we trace its influence in forms of theosophic Gnosticism, which only agree in substituting the wildest licence of the metaphysical fancy, for simple submission to that historical fact of the Incarnation of God, which is the basis of the Gospel.

[x] Dorner, Person Christi, i. 57 (Einleit.).

But if Philo was not St. John's master, it is probable that his writings, or rather the general theosophic movement of which they are the most representative sample, may have supplied some contemporary heresies with their stock of metaphysical material, and in this way may have determined, by an indirect antagonism, the providential form of St. John's doctrine. Nor can the general positive value of Philo's labours be mistaken, if he is viewed apart from the use that modern scepticism has attempted to make of particular speculations to which he gave such shape and impulse. In making a way for some leading currents of Greek thought into the heart of the Jewish Revelation, hitherto wellnigh altogether closed to it, Philo was not indeed teaching positive truth, but he was breaking down some intellectual barriers against its reception, in the most thoughtful portion of the human family. In Philo, Greek Philosophy almost stood at the door of the Catholic Church; but it was Greek Philosophy endeavouring to base itself, however precariously, upon the authority of the Hebrew Scriptures. The Logos of Philo, though a shifting and incomplete speculation, may well have served as a guide to thoughtful minds from that region of unsettled enquiry that surrounds the Platonic doctrine of a Divine Reason, to the clear and strong faith which welcomes the full Gospel Revelation of the Word made Flesh. Philo's Logos, while embodying elements foreign to the Hebrew Scriptures, is nevertheless in a direct line of descent from the Inspired doctrine of the Wisdom in the Book of Proverbs; and it thus illustrates the comprehensive vigour of the Jewish Revelation, which could countenance and direct, if it could not absolutely satisfy, those fitful guesses at and gropings after truth which were current in Heathendom. If Philo could never have created the Christian Doctrine which has been so freely ascribed to him, he could do much, however unconsciously, to prepare the soil of Alexandrian thought for its reception; and from this point of view, his Logos must appear of considerably higher importance than the parallel speculations as to the Memra, the Shekinah, the doctrine of the hidden and the revealed God, which in that and later ages belonged to the tradition of Palestinian Judaism [y].

[y] Compare Dorner, Person Christi, Einleit. p. 59, on the Adam Kadmon, and p. 60, on the Memra, Shekinah, and Metatron. 'Zu der Idee einer Incarnation des wirklich Göttlichen aber haben es alle diese Theologumene insgesammt nie gebracht.' They only involve a parastatic appearance of God, are symbols of His Presence, and are altogether impersonal; or if personal (as the Metatron), they are clearly conceived of as created

'Providence,' says the accurate Neander, 'had so ordered it, that in the intellectual world in which Christianity made its first appearance, many ideas should be in circulation, which at least seemed to be closely related to it, and in which Christianity could find a point of connection with external thought, on which to base the doctrine of a God revealed in Christ[z].' Of these ideas we may well believe that the most generally diffused and the most instrumental was the Logos of Alexandria, if not the exact Logos of Philo.

It is possible that such considerations as some of the foregoing, when viewed relatively to the great and vital doctrine which is before us in these lectures, may be objected to on the score of being 'fanciful.' Nor am I insensible, my brethren, to the severity of such a condemnation when awarded by the practical intelligence of Englishmen. Still it is possible that such a criticism would betoken on the part of those who make it some lack of wise and generous thought. 'Fanciful,' after all, is a relative term; what is solid in one field of study may seem fanciful in another. Before we condemn a particular line of thought as 'fanciful,' we do well to enquire whether a penetration, a subtlety, a versatility, I might add, a spirituality of intelligence, greater than our own, might not convict the condemnation itself of an opposite demerit, which need not be more particularly described. Especially in sacred literature, the imputation of fancifulness is a rash one; since a sacred subject-matter is not likely, *à priori*, to be fairly amenable to the coarser tests and narrower views of a secular judgment. It may be that the review of those adumbrations of the doctrine of our Lord's Divinity, in which we have been engaged, is rather calculated to reassure a believer than to convince a sceptic. Christ's Divinity illuminates the Hebrew Scriptures, but to read them as a whole by this light we must already have recognised the truth from which it radiates. Yet it would be an error to suppose that the Old Testament has no relations of a more independent character to the doctrine of Christ's Godhead. The Old Testament witnesses to the existence of a great national belief, the importance of which cannot be ignored by any man who would do justice to the history of human thought. And

personalities. This helps to explain the fact that during the first three centuries the main attacks on our Lord's Godhead were of Jewish origin. Cf. Dorner, ubi sup. note 14. On the Rabbinical ascription of Divine attributes to the Metatron, as higher than all angels, see Drach, Harmonie, ii. p. 417.

[z] Kirchen Geschichte, i. 3, p. 989.

we proceed to ask whether that belief has any, and what, bearing upon the faith of Catholic Christendom as to the Person of her Lord.

II. There is then one element, or condition of national life, with which no nation can dispense. A nation must have its eye upon a future, more or less defined, but fairly within the apparent scope of its grasp. Hope is the soul of moral vitality; and any man, or society of men, who would live, in the moral sense of life, must be looking forward to something. You will scarcely suspect me, my brethren, of seeking to disparage the great principle of tradition;—that principle to which the Christian Church owes her sacred volume itself, no less than her treasure of formulated doctrine, and the structural conditions and sacramental sources of her life;—that principle to which each generation of human society is deeply and inevitably indebted for the accumulated social and political experiences of the generations before it. Precious indeed, to every wise man, to every association of true-hearted and generous men, must ever be the inheritance of the past. Yet what is the past without the future? What is memory when unaccompanied by hope? Look at the case of the single soul. Is it not certain that a life of high earnest purpose will die outright, if it is permitted to sink into the placid reverie of perpetual retrospect, if the man of action becomes the mere 'laudator temporis acti'? How is the force of moral life developed and strengthened? Is it not by successive conscious efforts to act and to suffer at the call of duty? Must not any moral life dwindle and fade away if it be not reaching forward to a standard higher, truer, purer, stronger than its own? Will not the struggles, the sacrifices, the self-conquests even of a great character in bygone years, if they now occupy its whole field of vision, only serve to consummate its ruin? As it doatingly fondles them in memory, will it not be stiffened by conceit into a moral petrifaction, or consigned by sloth to the successive processes of moral decomposition? Has not the Author of our life so bound up its deepest instincts and yearnings with His own eternity, that no blessings in the past would be blessings to us, if they were utterly unconnected with the future? So it is also in the case of a society. The greatest of all societies among men at this moment is the Church of Jesus Christ. Is she sustained only by the deeds and writings of her saints and martyrs in a distant past, or only by her reverent trustful sense of the Divine Presence which blesses her in the actual present? Does she not resolutely pierce the gloom of the future, and confidently reckon upon new struggles and triumphs on earth, and, beyond these, upon a home in Heaven, wherein she will enjoy rest and victory,—a rest that no trouble can disturb, a victory that no reverse can forfeit? Is not the same law familiar to us in this place, as it affects the well-being of a great educational institution? Here in Oxford we feel that we cannot rest upon the varied efforts and the accumulated credit even of ten centuries. We too have hopes embarked in the years or in the centuries before us; we have duties towards them. We differ, it may be, even radically, among ourselves as to the direction in which to look for our academical future. The hopes of some of us are the fears of others. This project would fain banish from our system whatever proclaims that God had really spoken, and that it is man's duty and happiness gladly and submissively to welcome His message; while that scheme would endeavour, if possible, to fashion each one of our intellectual workmen more and more strictly after the type of a believing and fervent Christian. The practical difference is indeed profound; but we are entirely agreed as to the general necessity for looking forward. On both sides it is understood that an institution which is not struggling upwards towards a higher future, must resign itself to the conviction that it is already in its decadence, and must expect to die.

Nor is it otherwise with that association of men which we call a nation, the product of race, or the product of circumstances, the product in any case of a Providential Will, Which welds into a common whole, for the purposes of united action and of reciprocal influence, a larger or smaller number of human beings. A nation must have a future before it; a future which can rebuke its despondency and can direct its enthusiasm; a future for which it will prepare itself; a future which it will aspire to create or to control. Unless it would barter away the vigorous nerve of true patriotism for the feeble pedantry of a soulless archæology, a nation cannot fall back altogether upon the centuries which have flattered its ambition, or which have developed its material well-being. Something it must propose to itself as an object to be compassed in the coming time; something which is as yet beyond it. It will enlarge its frontier; or it will develope its commercial resources; or it will extend its schemes of colonization; or it will erect its overgrown colonies into independent and friendly states; or it will bind the severed sections of a divided race into one gigantic nationality that shall awe, if it do not subdue, the nations around. Or perchance its attention will be concentrated on the improvement of its social life, and on the details of its internal legislation. It will extend the range of civil privileges; it will broaden the basis of government; it will provide additional encouragements to and safeguards for public morality; it will steadily aim at bettering the condition of the classes who are forced, beyond others, to work and to suffer. Thankful it may well be to the Author of all goodness for the enjoyment of past blessings; but the spirit of a true thankfulness is ever and very nearly allied to the energy of hope. Self-complacent a nation cannot be, unless it would perish. Woe indeed to the country which dares to assume that it has reached its zenith, and that it can achieve or attempt no more!

Now Israel as a nation was not withdrawn from the operation of this law, which makes the anticipation of a better future of such vital importance to the common life of a people. Israel indeed had been cradled in an atmosphere of physical and political miracle. Her great lawgiver could point to the event which gave her national existence as to an event unique in human history[a]. No subsequent vicissitudes would obliterate the memory of the story which Israel treasured in her inmost memory, the story of the stern Egyptian bondage followed by the triumphant Exodus. How retrospective throughout is the sacred literature of Israel! It is not enough that the great deliverance should be accurately chronicled; it must be expanded, applied, insisted on in each of its many bearings and aspects by the lawgiver who directed and who described it; it must be echoed on from age to age, in the stern expostulations of Prophets and in the plaintive or jubilant songs of Psalmists. Certainly the greater portion of the Old Testament is history. Israel was guided by the contents of her sacred books to live in much grateful reflection upon the past. Certainly, it was often her sin and her condemnation that she practically lost sight of all that had been done for her. Yet if ever it were permissible to forget the future, Israel, it should seem, might have forgotten it. She might have closed her eyes against the dangers which threatened her from beyond the Lebanon, from beyond the Eastern and the Southern desert, from beyond the Western sea, from within her own borders, from the streets and the palaces of her capital. She might have abandoned herself in an

[a] Deut. iv. 34.

ecstasy of perpetuated triumph to the voices of her poets and to the rolls of her historians. But there was One Who had loved Israel as a child, and had called His infant people out of Egypt, and had endowed it with His Name and His Law, and had so fenced its life around by protective institutions, that, as the ages passed, neither strange manners nor hostile thought should avail to corrupt what He had so bountifully given to it. Was He forgetful to provide for and to direct that instinct of expectation, without which as a nation it could not live? Had He indeed not thus provided, Israel might have struggled with vain energy after ideals such as were those of the nations around her. She might have spent herself, like the Tyrian or Sidonian merchant, for a large commerce; she might have watched eagerly, and fiercely, like the Cilician pirate or like the wild sons of the desert, for the spoils of adjacent civilizations; she might have essayed to combine, after the Greek pattern, a discreet measure of sensuality with a great activity of the speculative intellect; she might have fared as did the Babylonian, or the Persian, or the Roman; at least, she might have attempted the establishment of a world-wide tyranny around the throne of a Hebrew Belshazzar or of a Hebrew Nero. Nor is her history altogether free from the disturbing influence of such ideals as were these; we do not forget the brigandage of the days of the Judges, or the imperial state and prowess of Solomon, or the commercial enterprise of Jehoshaphat, or the union of much intellectual activity with low moral effort which marked more than one of the Rabbinical schools. But the life and energy of the nation was not really embarked, at least in its best days, in the pursuit of these objects; their attractive influence was intermittent, transient, accidental. The expectation of Israel was steadily directed towards a future, the lustre of which would in some real sense more than eclipse her glorious past. That future was not sketched by the vain imaginings of popular aspirations; it was unveiled to the mind of the people by a long series of authoritative announcements. These announcements did not merely point to the introduction of a new state of things; they centred very remarkably upon a coming Person. God Himself vouchsafed to satisfy the instinct of hope which sustained the national life of His own chosen people; and Israel lived for the expected Messiah.

But Israel, besides being a civil polity, was a theocracy;

she was not merely a nation, she was a Church. In Israel religion was not, as with the peoples of pagan antiquity, a mere attribute or function of the national life. Religion was the very soul and substance of the life of Israel; Israel was a Church encased, embodied in a political constitution. Hence it was that the most truly national aspirations in Israel were her religious aspirations. Even the modern naturalist critics cannot fail to observe, as they read the Hebrew Scriptures, that the mind of Israel was governed by two dominant convictions, the like of which were unknown to any other ancient people. God was the first thought in the mind of Israel. The existence, the presence of One Supreme, Living, Personal Being, Who alone exists necessarily, and of Himself; Who sustains the life of all besides Himself; before Whom, all that is not Himself is but a shadow and vanity; from Whose sanctity there streams forth upon the conscience of man that moral law which is the light of human life; and in Whose mercy all men, especially the afflicted, the suffering, the poor, may, if they will, find a gracious and long-suffering Patron,—this was the substance of the first great conviction of the people of Israel. Dependent on that conviction was another. The eye of Israel was not merely opened towards the heavens; it was alive to the facts of the moral human world. Israel was conscious of the presence and power of sin. The 'healthy sensuality,' as Strauss has admiringly termed it[b], which pervaded the whole fabric of life among the Greeks, had closed up the eye of that gifted race to a perception which was so familiar to the Hebrews. We may trace indeed throughout the best Greek poetry a vein of deep suppressed melancholy[c]; but the secret

[b] See Luthardt, Apologetische Vorträge, vorl. vii. note 6. The expression occurs in Schubart's Leben, ii. 461. Luthardt quotes a very characteristic passage from Goethe (vol. xxx. Winckelmann, Antikes Heidnisches, pp. 10–13) to the same effect: 'If the modern, at almost every reflection, casts himself into the Infinite, to return at last, if he can, to a limited point; the ancients feel themselves at once, and without further wanderings, at ease only within the limits of this beautiful world. Here were they placed, to this were they called, here their activity has found scope, and their passions objects and nourishment.' The 'heathen mind,' he says, produced 'such a condition of human existence, a condition intended by nature,' that 'both in the moment of highest enjoyment and in that of deepest sacrifice, nay, of absolute ruin, we recognise the indestructibly healthy tone of their thought.' Similarly in Strauss' Leben Märklin's, 1851, p. 127, Märklin says, 'I would with all my heart be a heathen, for here I find truth, nature, greatness.'

[c] See the beautiful passage quoted from Lasaulx, Abhandlung über den Sinn der Œdipus-sage, p. 10, by Luthardt, ubi supra, note 7. Cf. also

of this subtle, of this inextinguishable sadness was unknown to the accomplished artists who gave to it an involuntary expression, and who lavished their choicest resources upon the oft-repeated effort to veil it beneath the bright and graceful drapery of a versatile light-heartedness peculiarly their own. But the Jew knew that sin was the secret of human sorrow. He could not forget sin if he would; for before his eyes, the importunate existence and the destructive force of sin were inexorably pictured in the ritual. He witnessed daily sacrifices for sin; he witnessed the sacrifice of sacrifices which was offered on the Day of Atonement, and by which the 'nation of religion,' impersonated in its High Priest, solemnly laid its sins upon the sacrificial victim, and bore the blood of atonement into the Presence-chamber of God. Then the moral law sounded in his ears; he knew that he had not obeyed it. If the Jew could not be sure that the blood of bulls and goats really effected his reconciliation with God; if his own prophets told him that moral obedience was more precious in God's sight than sacrificial oblations; if the ritual, interpreted as it was by the Decalogue, created yearnings within him which it could not satisfy, and deepened a sense of pollution which of itself it could not relieve; yet at least the Jew could not ignore sin, or think lightly of it, or essay to gild it over with the levities of raillery. He could not screen from his sight its native blackness, and justify it to himself by a philosophical theory which should represent it as inevitable, or as being something else than what it is. The ritual forced sin in upon his daily thoughts; the ritual inflicted it upon his imagination as being a terrible and present fact; and so it entered into and coloured his whole conception alike of national and of individual life. Thus was it that this sense of sin moulded all true Jewish hopes, all earnest Jewish anticipations of the national future. A future which promised political victory or deliverance, but which offered no relief to the sense of sin, would have failed to meet the better aspirations, and to cheer the real heart of a people which, amid whatever unfaithfulness to its measure of light, yet had a true knowledge of God, and was keenly alive to the fact and to the effects of moral evil. And He Who, by His earlier revelations, had Himself made the moral needs of Israel so deep, and had bidden the

Döllinger, Heid. und Jud. bk. v. pt. 1, § 2: Abp. Trench, Huls. Lectures, ed. 3, p. 305; also Comp. Il. xvii. 446; Od. xi. 489, xviii. 130; Eurip. Hippol. 190, Med. 1224, Fragm. No. 454, 808.

hopes of Israel rise so high, vouchsafed to meet the one, and to offer a plenary satisfaction to the other, in the doctrine of an expected Messiah.

It is then a shallow misapprehension which represents the Messianic belief as a sort of outlying prejudice or superstition, incidental to the later thought of Israel, and to which Christianity has attributed an exaggerated importance, that it may the better find a basis in Jewish history for the Person of its Founder. The Messianic belief was in truth interwoven with the deepest life of the people. The promises which formed and fed this belief are distributed along nearly the whole range of the Jewish annals; while the belief rests originally upon sacred traditions, which carry us up to the very cradle of the human family, although they are preserved in the sacred Hebrew Books. It is of importance to inquire whether this general Messianic belief included any definite convictions respecting the personal rank of the Being Who was its object.

In the gradual unfolding of the Messianic doctrine, three stages of development may be noted within the limits of the Hebrew Canon, and a fourth beyond it. (*a*) Of these the first appears to end with Moses. The Protevangelium contains a broad indeterminate prediction of a victory of humanity[d] over the Evil Principle that had seduced man to his fall. The 'Seed of the woman' is to bruise the serpent's head[e]. With the lapse of years this blessing, at first so general and indefinite, is narrowed down to something in store for the posterity of Shem[f], and subsequently for the descendants of Abraham[g]. In Abraham's Seed all the families of the earth are to be blessed. Already within this bright but generally indefinite prospect of deliverance and blessing, we begin to discern the advent of a Personal Deliverer. St. Paul argues, in accordance with the Jewish interpretation, that 'the Seed' is here a personal Messiah[h]; the singular form of the word denoting His individuality, while its collective force suggests the representative

[d] So two of the Targums, which nevertheless refer the fulfilment of the promise to the days of the King Messiah. The singular form of the collective noun would here, as in Gen. xxii. 18, have been intended to suggest an individual descendant.

[e] Gen. iii. 15; cf. Rom. xvi. 20; Gal. iv. 4; Heb. ii. 14; 1 St. John iii. 8.

[f] Gen. ix. 26.

[g] Ibid. xxii. 18.

[h] Gal. iii. 16. See the Rabbinical authorities quoted by Wetstein, in loc. On the objection raised from the collective force of σπέρμα, cf. Bishop Ellicott, in loc.

character of His Human Nature. The characteristics of this personal Messiah emerge gradually in successive predictions. The dying Jacob looks forward to a Shiloh as One to Whom of right belongs the regal and legislative authority[i], and to Whom the obedient nations will be gathered. Balaam sings of the Star That will come out of Jacob and the Sceptre That will rise out of Israel[k]. This is something more than an anticipation of the reign of David: it manifestly points to the glory and power of a Higher Royalty. Moses[l] foretells a Prophet Who would in a later age be raised up from among the Israelites, like unto himself. This Prophet accordingly was to be the Lawgiver, the Teacher, the Ruler, the Deliverer of Israel. If the prophetic order at large is included in this prediction[m], it is only as being personified in the Last and the Greatest of the Prophets, in the One Prophet Who was to reveal perfectly the mind of God, and Whose words were to be implicitly obeyed. During this primary period we do not find explicit assertions of the Divinity of Messiah. But in that predicted victory over the Evil One; in that blessing which is to be shed on all the families of the earth; in that rightful sway over the gathered peoples; in the absolute and perfect teaching of that Prophet Who is to be like the great Lawgiver while yet He transcends him,—must we not trace a predicted destiny which reaches higher than the known limits of the highest human energy? Is not this early prophetic language only redeemed from the imputation of exaggeration or vagueness, by the point and justification which are secured to it through the more explicit disclosures of a succeeding age?

(β) The second stage of the Messianic doctrine centres in the reigns of David and Solomon. The form of the prophecy here as elsewhere is suggested by the period at which it is uttered. When mankind was limited to a single family, the Hope of the future had lain in the seed of the woman: the Patriarchal age had looked forward to a descendant of Abraham; the Mosaic to a Prophet and a Legislator. In like manner the age of the

[i] Gen. xlix. 10. On the reading שלה see Pusey, Daniel the Prophet, p. 252. The sense given in the text is supported by Targum Onkelos, Jerusalem Targum, the Syr. and Arab. versions, possibly by those of Aquila and Symmachus (but see Field, Orig. Hexapl. tom. i. p. 70); while LXX. ἕως ἂν ἔλθῃ τὰ ἀποκείμενα αὐτῷ, Vulg. 'donec veniat Qui mittendus est.'

[k] Num. xxiv. 17. See J. H. Willemeri Diss. in Thesaur. Theol. Philolog., p. 362.

[l] Deut. xviii. 18, 19; see Hengstenberg's Christologie des A. T. vol. i. p. 90; Acts iii. 22, vii. 37; St. John i. 21, vi. 14, xii. 48, 49.

[m] Cf. Deut. xviii. 15.

Jewish monarchy in its bloom of youth and prowess, was bidden fix its eye upon an Ideal David Who was to be the King of the future of the world. Not that the colouring or form of the prophetic announcement lowered its scope to the level of a Jewish or of a human monarchy. The promise of a kingdom to David and to his house *for ever*[n], a promise on which, we know, the great Psalmist rested at the hour of his death[o], could not be fulfilled by any mere continuation of his dynasty on the throne of Jerusalem. It implied, as both David and Solomon saw, some Superhuman Royalty. Of this Royalty the Messianic Psalms present us with a series of pictures, each of which illustrates a distinct aspect of its dignity, while all either imply or assert the Divinity of the King. In the second Psalm, for instance, Messiah is associated with the Lord of Israel as His Anointed Son[p], while against the authority of Both the heathen nations are rising in rebellion[q]. Messiah's inheritance is to include all heathendom[r]; His Sonship is not merely theocratic or ethical, but Divine[s]. All who trust in Him are blessed; all who incur His wrath must perish with a sharp and swift destruction[t]. In the first recorded prayer of the Church of

[n] 2 Sam. vii. 16 (Ps. lxxxix. 36, 37; St. John xii. 34). 'From David's address to God, after receiving the message by Nathan, it is plain that David understood the Son promised to be the Messiah in Whom his house was to be established for ever. But the words which seem most expressive of this are in this verse now rendered very unintelligibly "and is this the manner of man?" whereas the words וזאת תורת האדם literally signify "and this is (or must be) the law of the man, or of the Adam," i.e. this promise must relate to the law, or ordinance, made by God to Adam concerning the Seed of the woman, the Man, or the Second Adam, as the Messiah is expressly called by St. Paul, 1 Cor. xv. 45-47.'—Kennicott, Remarks on the Old Testament, p. 115. He confirms this interpretation by comparing 1 Chron. xvii. 17 with Rom. v. 14.

[o] 2 Sam. xxiii. 5.

[p] Ps. ii. 7. See J. Frischmuthi Dissert. de Messiâ Dei Filio ad Ps. ii. in Thesaur. Theol.-Philolog. p. 571.

[q] Ps. ii. 2.

[r] Ps. ii. 8, 9. Cf. St. Aug. cont. Faustum Man. xiii. 7: 'Dabo Tibi gentes hæreditatem Tuam . . Quod genti Judæorum in quâ regnavit David non esse concessum, Christi autem nomine longe lateque omnes gentes occupante, nemo dubitat esse completum.'

[s] Ps. ii. 7.

[t] Ps. ii. 12. See Dr. Pusey's note on St. Jerome's rendering of נשקו בר, Daniel the Prophet, p. 478, note 2: 'It seems to me that St. Jerome preferred the rendering "the Son," since he adopted it where he could explain it [viz. in the brief commentary], but gave way to prejudice in rendering "adore purely."' Cf. also Replies to Essays and Reviews, p. 98. Also Delitzsch Psalmen, i. p. 15, note. 'Dass בר den Artikel nicht verträgt, dient auch im Hebr. öfter die Indetermination *ad amplificandum* (s. Fleischer zu Zamachschari's Gold. Halsbändern Anm. 2. S. 1. f.) indem sie

Christ[u], in St. Paul's sermon at Antioch of Pisidia[v], in the argument which opens the Epistle to the Hebrews[x], this Psalm is quoted in such senses, that if we had no Rabbinical text-books at hand, we could not doubt the belief of the Jewish Church respecting it[y]. The forty-fifth Psalm is a picture of the peaceful and glorious union of the King Messiah with His mystical bride, the Church of redeemed humanity. Messiah is introduced as a Divine King reigning among men. His form is of more than human beauty; His lips overflow with grace; God has blessed Him for ever, and has anointed Him with the oil of gladness above His fellows. But Messiah is also directly addressed as God; He is seated upon an everlasting throne[z]. Neither of these Psalms can be adapted without exegetical violence to the circumstances of Solomon or of any other king of

durch die in ihr liegende Unbegrenztheit die Einbildungskraft zur Vergrösserung des so ausgedrückten Begriffs auffordert. Ein arab. Ausleger würde an u. St. erklären: "Küsset einen Sohn, und was für einen Sohn!"' See J. H. Willemeri de Osculo Filii ad Ps. ii. Diss. in Thesaur. Theol.-Philolog., p. 582.

[u] Acts iv. 25, 26. [v] Ibid. xiii. 33. [x] Heb. i. 5; cf. Rom. i. 4.

[y] The Chaldee Targum refers this Psalm to the Messiah. So the Bereshith Rabba Aben-Ezra, D. Kimchi, Talm. Tr. Succah. fol. 52, &c. The interpretation was changed with a view to avoiding the pressure of the Christian arguments. 'Our masters,' says R. Solomon Jarchi, 'have expounded [this Psalm] of King Messiah; but, according to the letter, and for furnishing answer to the Minim [i.e. the Christian "heretics"], it is better to interpret it of David himself.' Quoted by Pearson on art. 2, notes; Chandler, Defence of Christianity, p. 212; Pocock, Porta Mosis, note, p. 307. See too Dr. Pye Smith, Messiah, vol. i. p. 197.

[z] Dr. Pusey observes that of those who have endeavoured to evade the literal sense of the words addressed to King Messiah (ver. 6), 'Thy throne, O God, is for ever and ever,' 'no one who thought he could so construct the sentence that the word *Elohim* need not designate the being addressed, doubted that *Elohim* signified God; and no one who thought that he could make out for the word *Elohim* any other meaning than that of "God," doubted that it designated the being addressed. A right instinct prevented each class from doing more violence to grammar or to idiom than he needed, in order to escape the truth which he disliked. If people thought that they might paraphrase "Thy throne, O Judge" or "Prince," or "image of God," or "who art as a God to Pharaoh," they hesitated not to render with us "Thy throne is for ever and ever." If men think that they may assume such an idiom as "Thy throne of God" meaning "Thy Divine throne," or "Thy throne is God" meaning "Thy throne is the throne of God," they doubt not that *Elohim* means purely and simply God. . . . If people could persuade themselves that the words were a parenthetic address to God, no one would hesitate to own their meaning to be "Thy throne, O God, is for ever and ever."' Daniel the Prophet, pp. 470, 471, and note 8. Rev. v. 13. Cf. Delitzsch in loc.

ancient Israel; and the New Testament interprets the picture of the Royal Epithalamium, no less than that of the Royal triumph over the insurgent heathen, of the one true King Messiah[a]. In another Psalm the character and extent of this Messianic Sovereignty are more distinctly pictured[b]. Solomon, when at the height of his power, sketches a Superhuman King, ruling an empire which in its character and in its compass altogether transcends his own. The extremest boundaries of the kingdom of Israel melt away before the gaze of the Psalmist. The new kingdom reaches 'from sea to sea, and from the flood unto the world's end[c].' It reaches from each frontier of the Promised Land, to the remotest regions of the known world, in the opposite quarter. From the Mediterranean it extends to the ocean that washes the shores of Eastern Asia; from the Euphrates to the utmost West. At the feet of its mighty Monarch, all who are most inaccessible to the arms or to the influence of Israel hasten to tender their voluntary submission. The wild sons of the desert[d], the merchants of Tarshish in the then distant Spain[e], the islanders of the Mediterranean[f], the Arab chiefs[g], the wealthy Nubians[h], are foremost in proffering their homage and fealty. But all kings are at last to fall down in submission before the Ruler of the new kingdom; all nations are to do Him service[i]. His empire is to be co-extensive with the world: it is also to be co-enduring with time[k]. His empire is to be spiritual; it is to confer peace on the world, but by righteousness[l]. The King will Himself secure righteous judgment[m], salvation[n], deliverance[o], redemption[p], to His subjects. The needy, the afflicted, the friendless, will be the especial objects of His tender care[q]. His appearance in the world will be like the descent of 'the rain upon the mown grass[r];' the true life of man seems to have been killed out, but it is yet capable of being restored by Him. He Himself, it is hinted, will be out of sight; but His *Name* will endure for ever; His Name will 'propagate[s];' and men shall be blessed in Him[t], to the end of time. This King is immortal; He is also all-knowing and all-mighty. 'Omniscience alone can hear the cry of every human

[a] Heb. i. 8.
[b] Ps. lxxii.
[c] Ibid. ver. 8.
[d] Ps. lxxii. 9, ציים.
[e] Ibid. ver. 10.
[f] Ibid.
[g] Ibid.
[h] Ibid. סבא.
[i] Ibid. ver. 11.
[k] Ibid. ver. 17.
[l] Ibid. ver. 3.
[m] Ibid. vers. 2, 4.
[n] Ibid. vers. 4, 13.
[o] Ibid. ver. 12.
[p] Ibid. ver. 14.
[q] Ibid. vers. 12, 13.
[r] Ibid. ver. 6; cf. 2 Sam. xxiii. 4.
[s] Ps. lxxii. 17.
[t] Ibid.

heart; Omnipotence alone can bring deliverance to every human sufferer[u].' Look at one more representation of this Royalty, that to which our Lord Himself referred, in dealing with his Jewish adversaries[x]. David describes his Great Descendant Messiah as his 'Lord[y].' Messiah is sitting on the right hand of Jehovah, as the partner of His dignity. Messiah reigns upon a throne which impiety alone could assign to any human monarch; He is to reign until His enemies are made His footstool[z]; He is ruler now, even among His unsubdued opponents[a]. In the day of His power, His people offer themselves willingly to His service; they are clad not in earthly armour, but 'in the beauties of holiness[b].' Messiah is Priest as well as King[c]; He is an everlasting Priest of that older order which had been honoured by the father of the faithful. Who is this everlasting Priest, this resistless King, reigning thus amid His enemies and commanding the inmost hearts of His servants? He is David's Descendant; the Pharisees knew that truth. But He is also David's Lord. How could He be both, if He was merely human? The belief of Christendom can alone answer the question which our Lord addressed to the Pharisees. The Son of David is David's Lord, because He is God; the Lord of David is David's Son, because He is God Incarnate[d].

(γ) These are but samples of that rich store of Messianic prophecy which belongs to the second or Davidic period, and much more of which has an important bearing on our present subject. The third period extends from the reign of Uzziah to the close of the Hebrew Canon in Malachi. Here Messianic prophecy reaches its climax: it expands into the fullest particularity of detail respecting Messiah's Human life; it mounts to the highest assertions of His Divinity. Isaiah is the richest mine of Messianic prophecy in the Old Testament[e]. Messiah,

[u] Daniel the Prophet, p. 479.

[x] St. Matt. xxii. 41-45; Ps. cx. 1. [y] Ps. cx. 1. [z] Ibid.

[a] Ps. cx. 2. [b] Ibid. ver. 3. [c] Ibid. ver. 4.

[d] On Ps. cx. see Pusey on Daniel, p. 466, sqq. Delitzsch, Psalmen ii. p. 639. Martini, Pugio Fidei, p. iii. c. 3, sqq. For evidence of later Jewish attempts to parry the Christian argument by interpreting the psalm of Hezekiah, see St. Just. Mart. Dial. cum Tryph. 33, 83; Tertull. adv. Marcion. v. 9: of Zerubbabel, St. Chrysos. Expos. in Ps. cix.

[e] With reference to the modern theory (Renan, Vie de Jésus, p. 37, &c. &c.) of a 'later Isaiah,' or 'Great Unknown,' living at the time of the Babylonish Captivity, and the assumed author of Is. xl.-lxvi., it may suffice to refer to Dean Payne Smith's valuable volume of University Sermons on the subject. When it is taken for granted on *à priori* grounds that *bonâ*

especially designated as 'the Servant of God,' is the central figure in the prophecies of Isaiah. Both in Isaiah and in Jeremiah, the titles of Messiah are often and pointedly expressive of His true Humanity. He is the Fruit of the earth [f]; He is the Rod out of the stem of Jesse [g]; He is the Branch or Sprout of David, the Zemach [h]. He is called by God from His mother's womb [i]; God has put His Spirit upon Him [j]. He is anointed to preach good tidings to the meek, to bind up the broken-hearted, to proclaim liberty to the captive [k]. He is a Prophet; His work is greater than that of any prophet of Israel. Not merely will He come as a Redeemer to them that turn from transgression in Jacob [l], and to restore the preserved of Israel [m]; He is also given as a Light to the Gentiles, as the Salvation of God unto the end of the earth [n]. Such is His Spiritual Power as Prophet and Legislator that He will write the law of the Lord, not upon tables of stone, but on the heart and conscience of the true Israel [o]. In Zechariah as in David He is an enthroned Priest [p], but it is the Kingly glory of Messiah which predominates throughout the prophetic representations of this period [q], and in which His Superhuman Nature is most distinctly suggested. According to Jeremiah, the Branch

fide prediction of strictly future events is impossible, the Bible predictions must either be resolved into the far-sighted anticipations of genius, or, if their accuracy is too detailed to admit of this explanation, they must be treated as being only historical accounts of the events referred to, thrown with whatever design into the form of prophecy. The predictions respecting Cyrus in the latter part of Isaiah are too explicit to be reasonably regarded as the results of natural foresight; hence the modern assumption of a 'later Isaiah' as their real author. 'Supposing this assumption,' says Bishop Ollivant, 'to be true, this later Isaiah was not only a deceiver, but also a witness to his own fraud; for he constantly appeals to prophetic power as a test of truth, making it, and specifically the prediction respecting the deliverance of the Jews by Cyrus, an evidence of the foreknowledge of Jehovah, as distinguished from the nothingness of heathen idols. And yet we are to suppose that when this fraud was first palmed upon the Jewish nation, they were so simple as not to have perceived that out of his own mouth this false prophet was condemned!'—Charge of Bishop of Llandaff, 1866, p. 99, note b. Comp. Delitzsch, Der Prophet Jesaia, p. 23, and his discussion of the question in the introduction to chapters xl-lxvi. Smith's Dict. Bible, art. 'Isaiah.'

[f] Isa. iv. 2.

[g] Ibid. xi. 1.

[h] Jer. xxiii. 5; xxxiii. 15, Zech. iii. 8, vi. 12.

[i] Isa. xlix. 1.

[j] Ibid. xlii. 1.

[k] Ibid. lxi. 1.

[l] Ibid. lix. 20; cf. xii. 3.

[m] Isa. xlix. 6.

[n] Ibid.

[o] Jer. xxxi. 31–35. See J. Frischmuthi de Fœdere Novo ad Jer. xxxi. Dis. in Thesaur. Theol.-Philolog. p. 855, 860.

[p] Zech. vi. 13.

[q] See Ezek. xxxiv. 23, 24; Hos. iii. 5, &c.

of Righteousness, who is to be raised up among the posterity of David, is a King who will reign and prosper and execute judgment and justice in the earth [r]. According to Isaiah, this expected King, the Root of Jesse, 'will stand for an ensign of the people;' the Gentiles will seek Him; He will be the rallying-point of the world's hopes, the true centre of its government [s]. 'Kings will see and arise, princes also will worship [t];' in deep religious awe, 'kings will shut their mouths at Him [u].' Righteousness, equity, swift justice, strict faithfulness, will mark His administration [v]; He will not be dependent like a human magistrate upon the evidence of His senses; He will not judge after the sight of His eyes, nor reprove after the hearing of His ears [w]; He will rely upon the infallibility of a perfect moral insight. Beneath the shadow of His throne, all that is by nature savage, proud, and cruel among the sons of men will learn the habits of tenderness, humility, and love [x]. 'The wolf also shall dwell with the lamb, and the leopard shall lie down with the kid; and the calf and the young lion and the fatling together; and a little child shall lead them.' The reign of moral light [y], of spiritual graces, of innocence, of simplicity, will succeed to the reign of physical and brute force [z]. The old sources of moral danger will become harmless through His protecting presence and blessing; 'the sucking child shall play on the hole of the asp, and the weaned child shall put his hand on the cockatrice' den [a];' and in the end 'the earth shall be full of the knowledge of the Lord, as the waters cover the sea [b].' Daniel is taught that at the 'anointing of the Most Holy'—after a defined period—God will 'finish the transgressions,' and 'make an end of sins,' and 'make reconciliation for iniquity,' and 'bring in everlasting righteousness [c].' Zechariah too especially points out the moral and spiritual characteristics of the reign of King Messiah. The founder of an eastern dynasty must ordinarily wade through blood and slaughter to the steps of his throne, and must maintain his authority by force. But the daughter of Jerusalem beholds her King coming to her, 'Just and having salvation, lowly and riding upon an ass.' 'The chariots are cut off from Ephraim, and the horse from Jerusalem;' the King 'speaks peace unto the heathen;' the 'battle-bow is broken;'

[r] Jer. xxiii. 5; xxx. 8, 9.
[s] Isa. xi. 10.
[t] Ibid. xlix. 7.
[u] Isa. lii. 15.
[v] Ibid. xi. 4, 5.
[w] Ibid. ver. 3.
[x] Ibid. vers. 6-8.
[y] Ibid. lx. 1, 2, 19, 20.
[z] Ibid. lxv. 16.
[a] Ibid. xi. 8.
[b] Ibid. ver. 9.
[c] Dan. ix. 24.

and yet His dominion extends 'from sea to sea, and from the river to the ends of the earth [d].'

In harsh and utter contrast, as it seems, to this representation of Messiah as a Jewish King, the moral conqueror and ruler of the world, there is another representation of Him which belongs to the Davidic period as well as to that of Isaiah. Messiah had been typified in David persecuted by Saul and humbled by Absalom, no less truly than He had been typified in Solomon surrounded by all the glory of his imperial court. If Messiah reigns in the forty-fifth or in the seventy-second Psalms, He suffers, nay He is pre-eminent among the suffering, in the twenty-second. We might suppose that the suffering Just One who is described by David, reaches the climax of anguish; but the portrait of an archetypal Sorrow has been even more minutely touched by the hand of Isaiah. In both writers, however, the deepest humiliations and woes are confidently treated as the prelude to an assured victory. The Psalmist passes, from what is little less than an elaborate programme of the historical circumstances of the Crucifixion, to an announcement that by these unexampled sufferings the heathen will be converted, and all the kindreds of the Gentiles will be brought to adore the true God [e]. The Prophet describes the Servant of God as 'despised and rejected of men [f];' His sorrows are viewed with general satisfaction; they are accounted a just punishment for His own supposed crimes [g]. Yet in reality He bears our infirmities, and carries our sorrows [h]; His wounds are due to our transgressions; His stripes have a healing virtue for us [i]. His sufferings and death are a trespass-offering [j]; on Him is laid the iniquity of all [k]. If in Isaiah the inner meaning of the tragedy is more fully insisted on, the picture itself is not less vivid than that of the Psalter. The suffering Servant stands before His judges; 'His Visage is so marred more than any man, and His Form more than the sons of men [l];' like a lamb [m], innocent, defenceless, dumb, He is led forth to the slaughter; 'He is cut off from the land of the living [n].' Yet the Prophet

[d] Zech. ix. 9, 10. J. Frischmuthi, De Messiâ Rege Sionis Diss. in Thesaur. Theol.-Philolog. p. 1016.

[e] Ps. xxii. 1–21, and 27. Phillips, on Ps. xxii., argues that the Messianic sense is 'the true and only true' sense of it. See J. Frischmuthi, De Messiæ manuum et pedum perforatione ad Ps. xxii. 17, Diss. in Thesaur. Theol.-Philolog., p. 611.

[f] Isa. liii. 3.
[g] Ibid. ver. 4.
[h] Ibid.
[i] Ibid. ver. 5.
[j] Ibid. ver. 12.
[k] Ibid. ver. 6.
[l] Ibid. lii. 14.
[m] Ibid. liii. 7.
[n] Ibid. ver. 8.

pauses at His grave to note that He 'shall see of the travail of His soul and shall be satisfied [o],' that God 'will divide Him a portion with the great,' and that He will Himself 'divide the spoil with the strong.' And all this is to follow 'because He hath poured out His soul unto death [p].' His death is to be the condition of His victory; His death is the destined instrument whereby He will achieve His mediatorial reign of glory.

Place yourselves, brethren, by an effort of intellectual sympathy in the position of the men who heard this language while its historical fulfilment, so familiar to us Christians, was as yet future. How self-contradictory must it have appeared to them, how inexplicable, how full of paradox! How strong must have been the temptation to anticipate that invention of a double Messiah, to which the later Jewish doctors had recourse, that they might escape the manifest cogency of the Christian argument [q]. That our Lord should actually have submitted Himself to the laws and agencies of disgrace and discomfiture, and should have turned His deepest humiliation into the very weapon of His victory, is not the least among the evidences of His Divine power and mission. And the prophecy which so paradoxically dared to say that He would in such fashion both suffer and reign, assuredly and implicitly contained within itself another and a higher truth. Such majestic control over the ordinary conditions of failure betokened something more than an extraordinary man, something not less than a distinctly Superhuman Personality. Taken in connection with the redemptive powers, the world-wide sway, the spiritual, heart-controlling teaching, so distinctly ascribed to Him, this prediction that the Christ would die, and would convert the whole world by death, prepares us for the most explicit statements of the prophets respecting His Person. It is no surprise to a mind which has dwelt steadily on the destiny which prophecy thus assigns to Messiah, that Isaiah and Zechariah should speak of Him as Divine. We will not lay stress upon the fact, that in

[o] Isa. liii. 11. [p] Ibid. ver. 12. Compare also Isa. lxiii. 1.

[q] See Hengstenberg's account of the Jewish interpretations of Isaiah lii. 13-liii. 12, Christolog. vol. ii. pp. 310-319 (Clarke's trans.), and 'The Fifty-third Chapter of Isaiah according to the Jewish Interpreters: by Driver and Neubauer, with Introduction by E. B. Pusey, D.D. Oxford and Leipzig, 1876.' Dr. Payne Smith on Isaiah, p. 172. The theory of a second Messiah was elaborated later than the second century, but before the fifth. Pusey, Univ. Serm. p. 144.

[LECT.

Isaiah the Redeemer of Israel and of men is constantly asserted to be the Creator [r], Who by Himself will save His people [s]. Significant as such language is as to the bent of the Divine Mind, it is not properly Messianic. But in that great prophecy [t], the full and true sense of which is so happily suggested to us by its place in the Church services for Christmas Day, the 'Son' who is given to Israel receives a fourfold Name. He is a Wonder-Counsellor, or Wonderful, above all earthly beings; He possesses a Nature which man cannot fathom; and He thus shares and unfolds the Divine Mind [u]. He is the Father of the Everlasting Age or of Eternity [v]. He is the Prince of Peace. Above all, He is expressly named, the Mighty God [w]. Conformably with this Jeremiah calls Him Jehovah Tsidkenu [x],

[r] Isa. xliv. 6; xlviii. 12, 13, 17.

[s] Ibid. xlv. 21–24; Hos. i. 7: cf. Rom. xiv. 11; Phil. ii. 10; Isa. xxxv. 4, xl. 3, 9, 10.

[t] Isa. ix. 6.

[u] פלא יועץ. These two words must clearly be connected, although they do not stand in the relation of the *status constructus*. Gen. xvi. 12. יועץ designated the attribute here concerned, פלא the superhuman Possessor of it.

[v] אבי־עד, Bp. Lowth's Transl. of Isaiah in loc.

[w] This is the plain literal sense of the words. The habit of construing אל־גבור as 'strong hero,' which was common to Gesenius and the older rationalists, has been abandoned by later writers, such as Hitzig and Knobel. Hitzig observes that to render אל־גבור by 'strong hero' is contrary to the *usus loquendi*. 'אל,' he argues, 'is always, even in such passages as Gen. xxxi. 29, to be rendered "God." In all the passages which are quoted to prove that it means "princeps," "potens," the forms are,' he says, 'to be derived not from אל, but from איל, which properly means "ram," then "leader," or "prince" of the flock of men.' (See the quot. in Hengst. Christ. ii. p. 88, Clarke's transl.). But while these later rationalists recognise the true meaning of the phrase, they endeavour to represent it as a mere name of Messiah, indicating nothing as to His possessing a Divine Nature. Hitzig contends that it is applied to Messiah 'by way of exaggeration, in so far as He possesses divine qualities;' and Knobel, that it belongs to Him as a hero, who in His wars with the Gentiles will shew that He possesses divine strength. But does the word 'El' admit of being applied to a merely human hero? 'El,' says Dr. Pusey, 'the name of God, is nowhere used *absolutely* of any but God. The word is used once relatively, in its first appellative sense, *the mighty of the nations* (Ezek. xxxi. 11), in regard to Nebuchadnezzar. Also once in the plural (Ezek. xxxii. 21). It occurs absolutely in Hebrew 225 times, and in every place is used of God.' Daniel. p. 483. Can we then doubt its true force in the present passage, especially when we compare Isa. x. 21, where אל־גבור is applied indisputably to the Most High God? Cf. Delitzsch, Jesaia, p. 155. On the whole passage see J. Frischmuthi, De Prosopographiâ Messiæ ad Esai. ix. 6, Diss. in Thesaur. Theol.-Philolog. p. 754.

[x] Jer. xxiii. 5, 6. This title is also applied by Jeremiah to Jerusalem in the Messianic age, in other words, to the Christian Church. Jer. xxxiii. 16.

II]

as Isaiah had called Him Emmanuel[y]. Micah speaks of His eternal pre-existence[z], as Isaiah had spoken of His endless reign[a]. Daniel predicts that His dominion is an everlasting dominion that shall not pass away[b]. Zechariah terms Him the Fellow or Equal of the Lord of Hosts[c]; and refers to His

15, 16. The reason is not merely to be found in the close fellowship of Christ with His Church as taught by St. Paul (Eph. v. 23, 30), who even calls the Church, Christ (1 Cor. xii. 12). Jehovah Tsidkenu expresses the great fact of which our Lord is the author, and Christendom the result. That fact is the actual gift of God's justifying, sanctifying righteousness to our weak sinful humanity. As applied to the Church then, the title draws attention to the reality of the gift; as applied to Christ, to the Person of Him through Whom it is given. It cannot be paralleled with names given to inanimate objects such as Jehovah Nissi, nor even with such personal names as Jehoram, Jehoshaphat, and the like. In these cases there is no ground for identifying the kings in question with the Exalted Jehovah, or with Jehovah the Judge. The title before us, *of itself*, may not necessarily imply the Divinity of Christ; it was indeed given in another form to Zedekiah. Its real force, as applied to our Lord, is however shewn by other prophetic statements about Him, just as He is called Jesus, in a fundamentally distinct sense from that which the word bore in its earlier applications. But cf. Pye Smith, Messiah, i. 271, sqq. Hengst. Christ. ii. 415, sqq. Reinke, Messianischen Weissagungen, iii. 510, sqq. Critici Sacri, vol. 4, p. 5638. J. Frischmuthi de Nomine Messiæ glorioso ad Jer. xxiii. 6, Diss. in Thesaur. Theol.-Philolog. p. 832. D. Kimchi in loc., Talm. in Tr. Baba Batra, fol. 79; Midrash. Thehillim in Ps. xxi. Pearson on Creed, ii. 181, ed. 1833.

[y] Isa. vii. 14; St. Matt. i. 23. Like Jehovah Tsidkenu, Emmanuel does really suggest our Lord's Divine Person, as Isa. ix. 6, would alone imply. That עלמה means a literal virgin, that the fulfilment of this prophecy is to be sought for *only* in the birth of our Lord, and that this announcement of God's mighty Salvation in the future, might well have satisfied Ahaz that the lesser help against the two kings in the immediate present would not be wanting, are points well discussed by Hengstenberg, Christ. ii. 43-66. Reinke, Weissagung von der Jungfrau und von Immanuel, Münster, 1848. Even if it were certain that the Name Emmanuel was in the first instance given to a child born in the days of Ahaz, it would still be true that 'then did God in the highest sense become with us, when He was seen upon earth.' St. Chrys. in Isa. ch. vii. s. 6, quoted by Hengst. Christol. ubi supra. See too, Smith's Dict. of Bible, art. 'Isaiah,' i. p. 879; Dr. Payne Smith, Proph. of Isaiah, pp. 21-27. C. Lochner, De loco classico ad Esai. vii. 14. Diss. in Thesaur. Theol.-Philolog., p. 691.

[z] Mic. v. 2, cf. verse 4. See Chandler's Defence of Christianity, p. 124; Mill on Mythical Interpr. p. 318; Pusey, Minor Prophets, in loc.

[a] Isa. ix. 6. But see also Mic. iv. 7.

[b] Dan. vii. 14.

[c] Zech. xiii. 7. עמיתי does not mean only an associate of any kind, or a neighbour. 'The word rendered "My fellow" was revived by Zechariah from the language of the Pentateuch. It was used eleven times in Leviticus, and then was disused. There is no doubt then that the word, being

[LECT.

Incarnation and still more clearly to His Passion as being that of Jehovah Himself[d]. Haggai implies His Divinity by foretelling that His presence will make the glory of the second temple greater than the glory of the first[e]. Malachi points to Him as the Angel of the Covenant, as Jehovah, Whom Israel was seeking, and Who would suddenly come to His temple[f], as the Sun of Righteousness[g].

Read this language as a whole; read it by the light of the great doctrine which it attests, and which in turn illuminates it, the doctrine of a Messiah, Divine as well as Human;—all is natural, consistent, full of point and meaning. But divorce it from that doctrine in obedience to a foregone and arbitrary placitum of the negative criticism, to the effect that Jesus Christ shall be banished at any cost from the scroll of prophecy;—how full of difficulties does such language forthwith become, how overstrained and exaggerated, how insipid and disappointing! Doubtless it is possible to bid defiance alike to Jewish and to Christian interpreters, and to resolve upon seeing in the prophets only such a sense as may be consistent with the theoretical exigencies of Naturalism. It is possible to suggest that what looks like supernatural prediction is only a clever or chance farsightedness, and that expressions which literally anticipate a distant history are but the exuberance of poetry, which, from its very vagueness, happens to coincide with some feature, real or imagined, of the remote future.

revived out of Leviticus, is to be understood as in Leviticus; but in Leviticus it is used strictly of a fellow-man, one who is as himself. Lev. vi. 2, xviii. 20, xix. 11, 15, 17, xxiv. 19, xxv. 14, 15, 17. . . The name designates not one joined by friendship or covenant, or by any voluntary act, but one united indissolubly by common bonds of nature, which a man may violate, but cannot annihilate. . . . When then this title is applied to the relation of an individual to God, it is clear that That Individual can be no mere man, but must be one united with God by an Unity of Being. The "Fellow" of the Lord is no other than He who said in the Gospel, "I and My Father are One."' Pusey, Daniel, pp. 487, 488. Hengst. Christ. iv. pp. 108-112.

[d] Zech. ii. 10-13, xi. 12. 13, xii. 10; St. John xix. 34, 37; Rev. i. 7. See Frischmuth's Dissertations, 'De vili et abjecto xxx argenteorum pretio quo Salvator noster Messias a Judæis æstimatus fuit,' and 'De Messiâ Confixo,' in Thesaur. Theol.-Philolog. p. 1031, 1042. Pusey, Univ. Serm. 1859-1872, p. 143.

[e] Hag. ii. 7, 9. See J. Frischmuthi de Gloriâ Templi secundi. Diss. in Thesaur. Theol.-Philolog. p. 994.

[f] Mal. iii. 1. See J. Frischmuthi, De Angelo Fœderis. Diss. in Thesaur. Theol.-Philolog. p. 1058.

[g] Mal. iv. 2.

It is possible to avoid any frank acknowledgment of the imposing spectacle presented by converging and consentient lines of prophecy, and to refuse to consider the prophetic utterances, except in detail and one by one; as if forsooth Messianic prophecy were an intellectual enemy whose forces must be divided by the criticism that would conquer it. It is possible, alas! even for accomplished scholarship so fretfully to carp at each instance of pure prediction in the Bible, to nibble away the beauty and dim the lustre of each leading utterance with such persevering industry, as at length to persuade itself that the predictive element in Scripture is insignificantly small, or even that it does not exist at all. That modern criticism of this temper should refuse to accept the prophetic witness to the Divinity of the Messiah, is more to be regretted than to be wondered at. And yet, if it were seriously supposed that such criticism had succeeded in blotting out all reference to the Godhead of Christ from the pages of the Old Testament, we should still have to encounter and to explain that massive testimony to the Messianic belief[h] which lives on in the Rabbinical literature; since that literature, whatever be the date of particular existing treatises, contains traditions, neither few nor indistinct, of indisputable antiquity. From that literature it is clear that the ancient Jews believed the expected Messiah to be a Divine Person[i]. It cannot be pretended that this belief came from without, from the schools of Alexandria, or from the teaching of Zoroaster. It was notoriously based upon the language of the Prophets and Psalmists. And we of today, even with our improved but strictly mechanical apparatus of grammar and dictionary, can scarcely undertake to correct the early unprejudiced interpretation of men who read the Old Testament with at least as much instinctive insight into the meaning of its archaic language, and of its older forms of thought and of feeling, as an Englishman in this generation

[h] If however the Book of Baruch was expanded into its present form at Alexandria from an earlier Hebrew document, written probably by Baruch himself, this statement must be partly qualified. Baruch iii. 35–37; cf. St. John i. 14.

[i] For the Rabbinical conception of the Person of Messiah, see Martini, Pugio Fidei, Pars iii. Dist. 3, cap. 1; 2. § 6 ad fin. § 8. With reference to some recent attacks upon the value of Martini's citations from Jewish writers, consult 'The Book of Tobit,' ed. by A. Neubauer, Oxf. 1878, pp. xviii–xxiv. Compare also Schöttgen, Horæ Hebraicæ, tom ii. lib. 1, c. 1, 2; lib. 3, Thesis 3; Drach, Harmonie, &c., pt. 2, c. 1. tom. ii. 385, sqq.

can command when he applies himself to the study of Shakespeare or of Milton.

(δ) The last stage of the Messianic doctrine begins only after the close of the Hebrew Canon. Among the Jews of Alexandria, the hope of a Messiah seems to have fallen into the background. This may have been due to the larger attractions which doctrines such as those of the Sophia and the Logos would have possessed for Hellenized populations, or to a somewhat diminished interest in the future of Jewish nationality caused by long absence from Palestine, or to a cowardly unwillingness to avow startling religous beliefs in the face of keen heathen critics [k]. The two latter motives may explain the partial or total absence of Messianic allusions from the writings of Philo and Josephus; the former will account for the significant silence of the Book of Wisdom. Among the peasantry, and in the schools of Palestine, the Messianic doctrine lived on. The literary or learned form of the doctrine, being based on and renewed by the letter of Scripture, was higher and purer than the impaired and debased belief which gradually established itself among the masses of the people. The popular degradation of the doctrine may be traced to the later political circumstances of the Jews, acting upon the secular and materialized element in the national character. The Messianic belief, as has been shewn, had two aspects, corresponding respectively to the political and to the religious yearnings of the people of Israel. If such a faith was a relief to a personal or national sense of sin, it was also a relief to a sense of political disappointment or degradation. And keen consciousness of political favour became a dominant sentiment among the Jewish people during the centuries immediately preceding our Lord's Incarnation. With some fitful glimpses of national life, as under the Asmoneans, the Jews of the Restoration passed from the yoke of one heathen tyranny to that of another. As in succession they served the Persian monarchs, the Syrian Greeks, the Idumæan king, and the Roman magistrate, the Jewish people cast an eye more and more wistfully to the political hopes which might be extracted from their ancient and accepted Messianic belief. They learned to pass more and more lightly over the prophetic pictures of a Messiah robed in moral majesty, of a Messiah relieving the woes of the whole human family, of a

[k] Yet in Tobit xiv. 6, 7, the reference to the conversion of the heathen world belongs to the highest religious hopes of Messianic prophecy. Ps. xxii. 27. The book is placed by Ewald at B.C. 350, and may be earlier.

Messiah suffering torture and shame in the cause of truth. They dwelt more and more eagerly upon the pictures of His world-wide conquest and imperial sway, and they construed those promises of coming triumph in the most earthly and secular sense; they looked for a Jewish Alexander or for a Jewish Cæsar. The New Testament exhibits the popular form of the Messianic doctrine, as it lay in the minds of Galileans, of Samaritans, of the men of Jerusalem. It is plain how deeply, when our Lord appeared, the hope of a Deliverer had sunk into the heart both of peasant and townsman; yet it is equally plain how earthly was the taint which had passed over the popular apprehension of this glorious hope, since its first full proclamation in the days of the Prophets. Doubtless there were saints like the aged Simeon, whose eyes longed sore for the Divine Christ foretold in the great age of Hebrew prophecy. But generally speaking, the piety of the enslaved Jew had become little else than a wrong-headed patriotism. His religious expectations had been taken possession of by his civic passions, and were liable at any moment to be placed at the service of a purely political agitation. Israel as a theocracy was sacrificed in his thought to Israel as a state; and he was willing to follow any adventurer into the wilderness or across the Jordan, if only there was a remote prospect of bringing the Messianic predictions to bear against the hated soldiery and police of Rome. A religious creed is always impoverished when it is degraded to serve political purposes; and belief in the Divinity of Messiah naturally waned and died away, when the highest functions attributed to Him were merely those of a successful general or of an able statesman. The Apostles themselves, at one time, looked mainly or only for a temporal prince; and the people who were willing to hail Jesus as King Messiah, and to conduct Him in royal pomp to the gates of the holy city, had so lost sight of the real eminence which Messiahship involved, that when He claimed to be God, they endeavoured to stone Him for blasphemy, and this claim of His was in point of fact the crime for which their leaders persecuted Him to death[1].

And yet when Jesus Christ presented Himself to the Jewish people, He did not condescend to sanction the misbelief of the time, or to swerve from the tenor of the ancient revelation. He claimed to satisfy the national hopes of Israel by a prospect which would identify the future of Israel with that of the world.

[1] Cf. Lect. IV. pp. 193, 194.

He professed to answer to the full, unmutilated, spiritual expectations of prophets and of righteous men. They had desired to see and had not seen Him, to hear and had not heard Him. Long ages had passed, and the hope of Israel was still unfulfilled. Psalmists had turned back in accents wellnigh of despair to the great deliverance from the Egyptian bondage, when the Lord brake the heads of the dragons in the waters, and brought fountains out of the hard rock. Prophets had been assured that at last the vision of ages should 'speak and not lie,' and had been bidden 'though it tarry, wait for it, because it will surely come, it will not tarry.' Each victory, each deliverance, prefigured Messiah's work; each saint, each hero, foreshadowed some separate ray of His personal glory; each disaster gave strength to the mighty cry for His intervention: He was the true soul of the history, as well as of the poetry and prophecy of Israel. And so much was demanded of Him, so superhuman were the proportions of His expected actions, that He would have disappointed the poetry and history no less than the prophecy of Israel had He been merely one of the sons of men. Yet when at last in the fulness of time He came, that He might satisfy the desire of the nations, He was rejected by a stiff-necked generation, because He was true to the highest and brightest anticipations of His Advent. A Christ who had contented himself with the debased Messianic idea of the Herodian period, might have precipitated an insurrection against the Roman rule, and might have antedated, after whatever intermediate struggles, the fall of Jerusalem. Jesus of Nazareth claimed to be the Divine Messiah of David and of Isaiah; and therefore He died upon the cross, to achieve, not the political enfranchisement of Palestine, but the spiritual redemption of humanity.

1. Permit me to repeat an observation which has already been hinted at. The several lines of teaching by which the Old Testament leads up to the doctrine of our Lord's Divinity, are at first sight apparently at issue with that primary truth of which the Jewish people and the Jewish Scriptures were the appointed guardians. 'Hear, O Israel, the Lord our God is one Lord[m].' That was the fundamental law of the Jewish belief and polity. How copious are the warnings against the surrounding idolatries in the Jewish Scriptures[n]! With what

[m] Deut. vi. 4; cf. ibid. iv. 35, xxxii. 39; Ps. xcvi. 5; Isa. xlii. 8, xliii. 10-13, xliv. 6, 8, xlv. 5, 6, 18, 21, 22, xlviii. 11, 12; Wisd. xii. 13; Ecclus. i. 8.

[n] Deut. iv. 16-18.

varied, what delicate, what incisive irony do the sacred writers lash the pretensions of the most gorgeous idol-worships, while guarding the solitary Majesty and the unshared prerogatives of the God of Israel[o]! 'The specific distinction of Judaism,' says Baur, 'marking it off from all forms of heathen religious belief whatever, is its purer, more refined, and monotheistic conception of God. From the earliest antiquity downwards, this was the essential basis of the Old Testament religion[p].' And yet this discriminating and fundamental truth does but throw out into sharper outline and relief those suggestions of personal distinctions in the Godhead; that personification of the Wisdom, if indeed the Wisdom be not a Person; those visions in which a Divine Being is so closely identified with the Angel who represents Him; those successive predictions of a Messiah personally distinct from Jehovah, yet also the Saviour of men, the Lord and Ruler of all, the Judge of the nations, Almighty, Everlasting, nay, One Whom prophecy designates as God. How was the Old Testament consistent with itself, how was it loyal to its leading purpose, to its very central and animating idea, unless it was in truth entrusted with a double charge; unless, besides teaching explicitly the Creed of Sinai, it was designed to teach implicitly a fuller revelation, and to prepare men for the Creed of the day of Pentecost? If indeed the Old Testament had been a semi-polytheistic literature; if in Israel the Divine Unity had been only a philosophical speculation, shrouded from the popular eye by the various forms with which some imaginative antiquity had peopled its national heaven; if the line of demarcation between such angel ministers and guardians as we read of in Daniel and Zechariah, and the High and Holy One Who inhabiteth eternity, had been indistinct or uncertain; if the Most Holy Name had been really lavished upon created beings with an indiscriminate profusion that deprived it of its awful, of its incommunicable value[q],—then these intimations which we have been reviewing would have been less startling than they are. As it is, they receive prominence from the sharp, unrelieved antagonism in which they seem to stand to the main scope of the books which contain them. And thus they are a perpetual witness that the Jewish Revelation is not to be final; they irresistibly suggest a deeper truth

[o] Ps. cxv. 4-8; Isa. xxxvii. 19, xliv. 9-20, xlvi. 5 sq.; Jer. ii. 27, 28, x. 3-6, 8-10, 14, 16; Hab. ii. 18, 19; Wisd. xiii. xiv.

[p] Christenthum, p. 17; cf. Lect. I. 26.

[q] On the senses of *Elohim* in the Old Testament, see Appendix, Note B.

[LECT.

which is to break forth from the pregnant simplicity of God's earlier message to mankind; they point, as we know, to the Prologue of St. John's Gospel and to the Council chamber of Nicæa, in which the absolute Unity of the Supreme Being will be fully exhibited as harmonizing with the true Divinity of Him Who was thus announced in His distinct Personality to the Church of Israel.

2. It may be urged that the Old Testament might conceivably have set forth the doctrine of Christ's Godhead in other and more energetic terms than those which it actually employs. Even if this should be granted, let us carefully bear in mind that the witness of the Old Testament to this truth is not confined to the texts which expressly assert that Messiah should be Divine. The Human Life of Messiah, His supernatural birth, His character, His death, His triumph, are predicted in the Old Testament with a minuteness which utterly defies the rationalistic insinuation, that the argument from prophecy in favour of Christ's claims may after all be resolved into an adroit manipulation of sundry more or less irrelevant quotations. No amount of captious ingenuity will destroy the substantial fact that the leading features of our Lord's Human manifestation were announced to the world some centuries before He actually came among us. Do I say that to be the subject of prophecy is of itself a proof of Divinity? Certainly not. But at least when prophecy is so copious and elaborate, and yet withal so true to the facts of history which it predicts, its higher utterances, which lie beyond the verification of the human senses, acquire corresponding significance and credit. If the circumstances of Christ's Human Life were actually chronicled by prophecy, prophecy is entitled to submissive attention when she proceeds to assert, in whatever terms, that the Christ Whom she has described is more than Man.

It must be a robust and somewhat coarse scepticism which can treat those early glimpses into the laws of God's inner being, those mysterious apparitions to Patriarchs and Lawgivers, those hypostatized representations of Divine Attributes, above all, that Divinity repeatedly and explicitly ascribed to the predicted Restorer of Israel, only as illustrations of the exuberance of Hebrew imagination, only as redundant tropes and moods of Eastern poetry. For when the destructive critics have done their worst, we are still confronted by the fact of a considerable literature, indisputably anterior to the age of Christianity, and foretelling in explicit terms the coming of a Divine and

Human Saviour. We cannot be insensible to the significance of this broad and patent fact. Those who in modern days have endeavoured to establish an absolute power over the conduct and lives of their fellow-men have found it necessary to spare no pains in one department of political effort. They have endeavoured to 'inspire,' if they could not suppress, that powerful agency, which both for good and for evil moulds and informs popular thought. The control of the press from day to day is held in our times to be among the highest exercises of despotic power over a civilized community; and yet the sternest despotism will in vain endeavour to recast in its own favour the verdict of history. History, as she points to the irrevocable and unchanging past, can be won neither by violence nor by blandishments to silence her condemnations, or to lavish her approvals, or in any degree to unsay the evidence of her chronicles, that she may subserve the purpose and establish the claim of some aspiring potentate. But He Who came to reign by love as by omnipotence, needed not to put force upon the thought and speech of His contemporaries, even could He have willed to do so [o]. For already the literature of fifteen centuries had been enlisted in His service; and the annals and the hopes of an entire people, to say nothing of the yearnings and guesses of the world, had been moulded into one long anticipation of Himself. Even He could not create or change the past; but He could point to its unchanging voice as the herald of His own claims and destiny. His language would have been folly on the lips of the greatest of the sons of men, but it does no more than simple justice to the true mind and constant drift of the Old Testament. With His Hand upon the Jewish Canon, Jesus Christ could look opponents or disciples in the face, and bid them 'Search the Scriptures, for in them ye think ye have eternal life, and they are they which testify of Me.'

[o] Lacordaire.

LECTURE III.

OUR LORD'S WORK IN THE WORLD A WITNESS TO HIS DIVINITY.

Whence hath This Man this Wisdom, and these mighty works? Is not This the carpenter's Son? is not His mother called Mary? and His brethren, James, and Joses, and Simon, and Judas? And His sisters, are they not all with us? Whence then hath This Man all these things?

St. Matt. xiii. 54-56.

A sceptical prince once asked his chaplain to give him some clear evidence of the truth of Christianity, but to do so in a few words, because a king had not much time to spare for such matters. The chaplain tersely replied, 'The Jews, your majesty.' The chaplain meant to say that the whole Jewish history was a witness to Christ. In the ages before the Incarnation Israel witnessed to His work and to His Person, by its Messianic belief, by its Scriptures, by its ritual, by its rabbinical schools. In the ages which have followed the Incarnation, Israel has witnessed to Him no less powerfully as the people of the dispersion. In all the continents, amid all the races of the world, we meet with the nation to which there clings an unexpiated, self-imprecated guilt. This nation dwells among us and around us Englishmen; it shares largely in our material prosperity; its social and civil life are shaped by our national institutions; it sends its representatives to our tribunals of justice and to the benches of our senate: yet its heart, its home, its future, are elsewhere. It still hopes for Him Whom we Christians have found; it still witnesses, by its accumulating despair, to the truth of the creed which it so doggedly rejects. Our rapid survey then of those anticipations of our Lord's Divinity which are furnished by the Old Testament, and by the literature more immediately dependent on it, has left untouched a district of history fruitful in considerations which bear upon our subject. But it must suffice to have hinted at the testimony which is thus indirectly yielded by the later Judaism; and we pass to-day to a topic which is in some sense continuous with that of our last lecture. We have seen how the appearance of a Divine Person, as the Saviour of men, was anticipated by the Old Testament; let us enquire how far Christ's Divinity is attested by the phenomenon which we encounter in the formation and continuity of the Christian Church.

I. When modern writers examine and discuss the proportions and character of our Lord's 'plan,' a Christian believer may rightly feel that such a term can only be used in such a connection with some mental caution. He may urge that in forming an estimate of strictly human action, we can distinguish between a plan and its realization; but that this distinction is obviously inapplicable to Him with Whom resolve means achievement, and Who completes His action, really if not visibly, when He simply wills to act. It might further be maintained, and with great truth, that the pretension to exhibit our Lord's entire design in His Life and Death proceeds upon a misapprehension. It is far from being true that our Lord has really laid bare to the eyes of men the whole purpose of the Eternal Mind in respect of His Incarnation. Indeed nothing is plainer, or more upon the very face of the New Testament, than the limitations and reserve of His disclosures on this head. We see enough for faith and for practical purposes, but we see no more. Amid the glimpses which are offered us respecting the scope and range of the Incarnation, the obvious shades off continually into mystery, the visible commingles with the unseen. We Christians know just enough to take the measure of our ignorance; we feel ourselves hovering intellectually on the outskirts of a vast economy of mercy, the complete extent and the inner harmonies of which One Eye alone can survey.

If however we have before us only a part of the plan which our Lord meant to carry out by His Incarnation and Death, assuredly we do know something and that from His Own Lips. If it is true that success can never be really doubtful to Omnipotence, and that no period of suspense can be presumed to intervene between a resolve and its accomplishment in the Eternal Mind; yet, on the other hand, it is a part of our Lord's gracious condescension that He has, if we may so speak, entered into the lists of history. He has come among us as one of ourselves; He has made Himself of no reputation, and has been found in fashion as a man. He has despoiled Himself of His advantages; He has actually stated what He proposed to do in the world, and has thus submitted Himself to the verdict of man's experience. His own Words are our warrant for comparing them with His Work; and He has interposed the struggles of centuries between His Words and their fulfilment. He has so shrouded His Hand of might as at times to seem as if He would court at least the possibilities of failure. Putting aside then for the moment any recorded intimations of Christ's Will in respect of other spheres of being, with all their mighty issues of life and death, let us enquire what it was that He purposed to effect within the province of human action and history.

Now the answer to this question is simply, that He proclaimed Himself the Founder of a world-wide and imperishable Society. He did not propose to act powerfully upon the convictions and the characters of individual men, and then to leave to them, when they believed and felt alike, the liberty of voluntarily forming themselves into an association, with a view to reciprocal sympathy and united action. From the first, the formation of a society was not less an essential feature of Christ's plan, than was His redemptive action upon single souls. This society was not to be a school of thinkers, nor a self-associated company of enterprising fellow-workers; it was to be a Kingdom, the kingdom of heaven, or, as it is also called, the kingdom of God[a]. For ages indeed the Jewish theocracy had been a kingdom of God upon earth[b]. God was the one true King of ancient Israel. He was felt to be present in Israel as a Monarch living among His subjects. The temple was His palace; its sacrifices and ritual were the public acknowledgment of His present but invisible Majesty. But the Jewish polity, considered as a system, was an external rather than an internal kingdom of God. Doubtless there were great saints in ancient Israel; doubtless Israel had prayers and hymns such as may be found in the Psalter, than which nothing more searching and more spiritual has been since produced in Christendom. Looking however to the popular working of the Jewish theocratic system, and to what is implied as to its character in Jeremiah's prophecy of a profoundly spiritual kingdom which was to succeed it[c], may we not conclude that the Royalty of God was represented rather to

[a] *βασιλεία τῶν οὐρανῶν* occurs thirty-two times in St. Matthew's Gospel, to which it is peculiar; *βασιλεία τοῦ Θεοῦ* five times. The latter term occurs fifteen times in St. Mark, thirty-three times in St. Luke, twice in St. John, seven times in the Acts of the Apostles. In St. Matt. xiii. 43, xxvi. 29, we find *ἡ βασιλεία τοῦ Πατρός*. Our Lord speaks of *ἡ βασιλεία ἡ ἐμὴ* three times, St. John xviii. 36.

[b] St. Matt. xxi. 43.

[c] Jer. xxxi. 31–34, quoted in Heb. viii. 8-11.

the senses than to the heart and intelligence of at least the mass of His ancient subjects? Jesus Christ our Lord announced a new kingdom of God; and, by terming it *the* Kingdom of God, He implied that it would first fully deserve that sacred name, as corresponding with Daniel's prophecy of a fifth empire[d]. Let us moreover note, in passing, that when using the word 'kingdom,' our Lord did not announce a republic. Writers who carry into their interpretation of the Gospels ideas which have been gained from a study of the Platonic dialogues or of the recent history of France, may permit themselves to describe our Lord as Founder of the Christian republic. And certainly St. Paul, when accommodating himself to political traditions and aspirations which still prevailed largely throughout the Roman world, represents and recommends the Church of Christ as the source and home of the highest moral and mental liberty, by speaking freely of our Christian 'citizenship,' and of our coming at baptism to the 'city' of the living God[e]. Not that the Apostle would press the metaphor to the extent of implying that the new society was to be a spiritual democracy; since he very earnestly taught that even the inmost thoughts of its members were to be ruled by their Invisible King[f]. This indeed had been the claim of the Founder of the kingdom Himself[g]; He willed to be King, absolutely and without a rival, in the new society; and the nature and extent of His legislation plainly shews us in what sense He meant to reign.

The original laws of the new kingdom are for the most part set forth by its Founder in His Sermon on the Mount. After a preliminary statement of the distinctive character which was to mark the life and bearing of those who would fully correspond to His Mind and Will[h], and a further sketch of the nature and depth of the influence which His subjects were to exert upon other men[i], He proceeds to define the general relation of the new law which He is promulgating to the law that had preceded it[k]. The vital principle of His legislation, namely, that moral obedience shall be enforced, not merely in the performance of or in the abstinence from outward acts, but in the deepest and most

[d] Dan. vii. 9–15.

[e] Phil. iii. 20: *ἡμῶν γὰρ τὸ πολίτευμα ἐν οὐρανοῖς ὑπάρχει.* Cf. Acts xxiii. 1: *πεπολίτευμαι τῷ Θεῷ.* Phil. i. 27: *ἀξίως τοῦ εὐαγγελίου πολιτεύεσθε.* Heb. xiii. 14. In Heb. xi. 10, xii. 22, *πόλις* apparently embraces the whole Church of Christ, visible and invisible; in Heb. xi. 16, xiii. 14, it is restricted to the latter.

[f] 2 Cor. x. 5.

[g] St. Matt. xxiii. 8.

[h] Ibid. v. 1–12.

[i] Ibid. vers. 13–16.

[k] Ibid. vers. 17–20.

secret springs of thought and motive, is traced in its application to certain specific prescriptions of the older Law[l]; while other ancient enactments are modified or set aside by the stricter purity[m], the genuine simplicity of motive and character[n], the entire unselfishness[o], and the superiority to personal prejudices and exclusiveness[p] which the New Lawgiver insisted on. The required life of the new kingdom is then exhibited in detail; the duties of almsgiving[q], of prayer[r], and of fasting[s], are successively enforced; but the rectification of the ruling motive is chiefly insisted on as essential. In performing religious duties, God's Will, and not any conventional standard of human opinion, is to be kept steadily before the eye of the soul. The Legislator insists upon the need of a single, supreme, unrivalled motive in thought and action, unless all is to be lost. The uncorruptible treasure must be in heaven; the body of the moral life will only be full of light if 'the eye is single;' no man can serve two masters[t]. The birds and the flowers suggest the lesson of trust in and devotion to the One Source and End of life; all will really be well with those who in very deed seek His kingdom and His righteousness[u]. Charity in judgment of other men[x], circumspection in communicating sacred truth[y], confidence and constancy in prayer[z], perfect consideration for the wishes of others[a], yet also a determination to seek the paths of difficulty and sacrifice, rather than the broad easy ways trodden by the mass of mankind[b];—these features will mark the conduct of loyal subjects of the kingdom. They will beware too of false prophets, that is, of the movers of spiritual sedition, of teachers who are false to the truths upon which the kingdom is based and to the temper which is required of its real children. The false prophets will be known by their moral unfruitfulness[c], rather than by any lack of popularity or success. Finally, obedience to the law of the kingdom is insisted on as the one condition of safety; obedience[d],—as distinct from professions of loyalty; obedience,—which will be found to have really based a man's life upon the immoveable rock at that solemn moment when all that stands upon the sand must utterly perish[e].

Such a proclamation of the law of the kingdom as was the

[l] St. Matt. v. 21–30. [m] Ibid. vers. 31, 32. [n] Ibid. vers. 33-37. [o] Ibid. vers. 38-42. [p] Ibid. vers. 43-47. [q] Ibid. vi. 1-4. [r] Ibid. vers. 5-8. [s] Ibid. vers. 16-18. [t] Ibid. ver. 24. [u] Ibid. vers. 25-34. [x] Ibid. vii. 1-5. [y] Ibid. ver. 6. [z] Ibid. vers. 7-11. [a] Ibid. ver. 12. [b] Ibid. vers. 13, 14. [c] Ibid. vers. 15-20. [d] Ibid. vers. 21-23. [e] Ibid. vers. 24-27.

Sermon on the Mount, already implied that the kingdom would be at once visible and invisible. On the one hand certain outward duties, such as the use of the Lord's Prayer and fasting, are prescribed [f]; on the other, the new law urgently pushes its claim of jurisdiction far beyond the range of material acts into the invisible world of thought and motive. The visibility of the kingdom lay already in the fact of its being a society of men, and not a society solely made up of incorporeal beings such as the angels. The King never professes that He will be satisfied with a measure of obedience which sloth or timidity might confine to the region of inoperative feelings and convictions; He insists with great emphasis upon the payment of homage to His Invisible Majesty, outwardly, and before the eyes of men. Not to confess Him before men is to break with Him for ever [g]; it is to forfeit His blessing and protection when these would most be needed. The consistent bearing, then, of His loyal subjects will bring the reality of His rule before the sight of men; but, besides this, He provides His realm with a visible government, deriving its authority from Himself, and entitled on this account to deferential and entire obedience on the part of His subjects. To the first members of this government His commission runs thus:—'He that receiveth you, receiveth Me [h].' It is the King Who will Himself reign throughout all history on the thrones of His representatives; it is He Who, in their persons, will be acknowledged or rejected. In this way His empire will have an external and political side; nor is its visibility to be limited to its governmental organization. The form of prayer [i] which the King enjoins on His subjects, and the outward visible actions by which, according to His appointment, membership in His kingdom is to be begun [j] and maintained [k], make the very life and movement of the new society, up to a certain point, visible. But undoubtedly the real strength of the kingdom, its deepest life, its truest action, are veiled from sight. At bottom it is to be a moral, not a material empire; it is to be a realm not merely of bodies but of souls, of souls instinct with intelligence and love. Its seat of power will be the conscience of mankind. Not 'here' or 'there' in outward signs of establishment and supremacy, but in the free conformity of the thought and heart of its members to the Will of their Unseen Sovereign, shall its power be most

f St. Matt. vi. 9-13, 16.
g Ibid. x. 32; St. Luke xii. 8.
h St. Matt. x. 40; comp. St. Luke x. 16.
i St. Matt. vi. 9-13.
j Ibid. xxviii. 19; St. John iii. 5.
k St. Luke xxii. 19; 1 Cor. xi. 24; St. John vi. 53.

clearly recognised. Not as an oppressive outward code, but as an inward buoyant exhilarating motive, will the King's Law mould the life of His subjects. Thus the kingdom of God will be found to be 'within' men[l]; it will be set up, not like an earthly empire by military conquest or by violent revolution, but noiselessly and 'not with observation[m].' It will be maintained by weapons more spiritual than the sword. 'If,' said the Monarch, 'My kingdom were of this world, then would My servants fight, but now is My kingdom not from hence[n].'

The charge to the twelve Apostles exhibits the outward agency by which the kingdom would be established[o]; and the discourse in the supper-room unveils yet more fully the secret sources of its strength and the nature of its influence[p]. But the 'plan' of its Founder with reference to its establishment in the world is perhaps most fully developed in that series of parables, which, from their common object and from their juxtaposition in St. Matthew's Gospel, are commonly termed Parables of the Kingdom.

How various would be the attitudes of the human heart towards the 'word of the kingdom,' that is, towards the authoritative announcement of its establishment upon the earth, is pointed out in the Parable of the Sower. The seed of truth would fall from His Hand throughout all time by the wayside, upon stony places, and among thorns, as well as upon the good ground[q]. It might be antecedently supposed that within the limits of the new kingdom none were to be looked for save the holy and the faithful. But the Parable of the Tares corrects this too idealistic anticipation; the kingdom is to be a field in which until the final harvest the tares must grow side by side with the wheat[r]. The astonishing expansion of the kingdom throughout the world is illustrated by 'the grain of mustard seed, which indeed is the least of

[l] St. Luke xvii. 21. [m] Ibid. ver. 20. [n] St. John xviii. 36.

[o] St. Matt. x. 5-42. [p] St. John xiv. xv. xvi.

[q] St. Matt. xiii. 3-8, 19-23.

[r] St. Matt. xiii. 24-30, 36-43. 'In catholicâ enim ecclesiâ, quæ non in solâ Africâ sicut pars Donati, sed per omnes gentes, sicut promissa est, dilatatur atque diffunditur, in universo mundo, sicut dicit Apostolus, fructificans et crescens, et boni sunt et mali.' St. Aug. Ep. 208, n. 6. 'Si boni sumus in ecclesiâ Christi, frumenta sumus; si mali sumus in ecclesiâ Christi, palea sumus, tamen ab areâ non recedimus. Tu qui vento tentationis foris volasti, quid es? Triticum non tollit ventus ex areâ. Ex eo ergo, ubi es, agnosce quid es.' In Ps. lxx. (Vulg.) Serm. ii. n. 12. Civ. Dei, i. 35, and especially Retract. ii. 18.

all seeds, but when it is grown it is the greatest among herbs[s].' The principle and method of that expansion are to be observed in the action of 'the leaven hid in the three measures of meal[t].' A secret invisible influence, a soul-attracting, soul-subduing enthusiasm for the King and His work, would presently penetrate the dull, dense, dead mass of human society, and its hard heart and stagnant thought would expand, in virtue of this inward impulse, into a new life of light and love. Thus the kingdom is not merely represented as a mighty whole, of which each subject soul is a fractional part. It is exhibited as an attractive influence, acting energetically upon the inner personal life of individuals. It is itself the great intellectual and moral prize of which each truth-seeking soul is in quest, and to obtain which all else may wisely and well be left behind. The kingdom is a treasure hid in a field[u], that is, in a line of thought and enquiry, or in a particular discipline and mode of life; and the wise man will gladly part with all that he has to buy that field. Or the kingdom is like a merchant-man seeking 'goodly pearls[v];' he sells all his possessions that he may buy the 'one pearl of great price.' Here it is hinted that entrance into the kingdom is a costly conquest and mastery of truth, of that one absolute and highest Truth, which is contrasted with the lower and relative truths current among men. The preciousness of membership in the kingdom is only to be completely realized by an unreserved submission to the law of sacrifice; the kingdom flashes forth in its full moral beauty before the eye of the soul, as the merchant-man resigns his all in favour of the one priceless pearl. In these two parables, then, the individual soul is represented as seeking the kingdom; and it is suggested how tragic in many cases would be the incidents, how excessive the sacrifices, attendant upon 'pressing into it.' But a last parable is added in which the kingdom is pictured, not as a prize which can be seized by separate souls, but as a vast imperial system, as a world-wide home of all the races of mankind[w]. Like a net[x] thrown into the Galilean lake, so would the kingdom extend its toils around entire tribes and nations of men; the vast struggling multitude would be drawn nearer and nearer to the eternal shore; until at last the awful and final

[s] St. Matt. xiii. 31, 32. [t] Ibid. ver. 33. [u] Ibid. ver. 44.
[v] Ibid. vers. 45, 46.
[w] So in Rev. xi. 15: *ἐγένετο ἡ βασιλεία τοῦ κόσμου τοῦ Κυρίου ἡμῶν καὶ τοῦ Χριστοῦ αὐτοῦ.* [x] St. Matt. xiii. 47–50.

[LECT.

separation would take place beneath the eye of Absolute Justice; the good would be gathered into vessels, but the bad would be cast away.

The proclamation of this kingdom was termed the Gospel, that is, the good news of God. It was good news for mankind, Jewish as well as Pagan, that a society was set up on earth wherein the human soul might rise to the height of its original destiny, might practically understand the blessedness and the awfulness of life, and might hold constant communion in a free, trustful, joyous, childlike spirit with the Author and the End of its existence. The ministerial work of our Lord was one long proclamation of this kingdom. He was perpetually defining its outline, or promulgating and codifying its laws, or instituting and explaining the channels of its organic and individual life, or gathering new subjects into it by His words of wisdom or by His deeds of power, or perfecting and refining the temper and cast of character which was to distinguish them. When at length He had Himself overcome the sharpness of death, He opened this kingdom of heaven to all believers on the Day of Pentecost. His ministry had begun with the words, 'Repent ye, for the kingdom of heaven is at hand [y];' He left the world, bidding His followers carry forward the frontier of His kingdom to the utmost limits of the human family [z], and promising them that His presence within it would be nothing less than co-enduring with time [a].

Let us note more especially two features in the 'plan' of our Blessed Lord.

(a) And, first, its originality. Need I say, brethren, that real originality is rare? In this place many of us spend our time very largely in imitating, recombining, reproducing existing thought. Conscious as we are that for the most part we are only passing on under a new form that which in its substance has come to us from others, we honestly say so; yet it may chance to us at some time to imagine that in our brain an idea or a design has taken shape, which is originally and in truth our own creation—

> 'Libera per vacuum posui vestigia princeps;
> Non aliena meo pressi pede [b].'

Those few, rapid, decisive moments in which genius consciously enjoys the exhilarating sense of wielding creative power, may

[y] St. Matt. iv. 17. [z] Ibid. xxviii. 19; St. Luke xxiv. 47; Acts i. 8.
[a] St. Matt. xxviii. 20. [b] Hor. Ep. i. 19. 21.

naturally be treasured in memory; and yet, even in these, how hard must it be to verify the assumed fact of an absolute originality! We of this day find the atmosphere of human thought, even more than the surface of the earth, preoccupied and thronged with the results of man's activity in times past and present. In proportion to our consciousness of our real obligations to this general stock of mental wealth, must we not hesitate to presume that any one idea, the immediate origin of which we cannot trace, is in reality our own? Suppose that in this or that instance we do believe ourselves, in perfect good faith, to have produced an idea which is really entitled to the merit of originality. May it not be, that if at the right moment we could have examined the intellectual air around us with a sufficiently powerful microscope, we should have detected the germ of our idea 'floating in upon our personal thought from without[c]?' We only imagine ourselves to have created the idea because, at the time of our inhaling it, we were not conscious of doing so. The idea perhaps was suggested indirectly; it came to us along with some other idea upon which our attention was mainly fixed; it came to us so disguised or so undeveloped, that we cannot recognise it, so as to trace the history of its growth. It came to us during the course of a casual conversation; or from a book the very name of which we have forgotten; and our relationship towards it has been after all that of a nurse, not that of a parent. We have protected it, cherished it, warmed it, and at length it has grown within the chambers of our mind, until we have recognised its value and led it forth into the sunlight, shaping it, colouring it, expressing it after a manner strictly our own, and believing in good faith that because we have so entirely determined its form, we are the creators of its substance[d]. At any rate, my brethren, genius herself has not been slow to confess how difficult it is to say that any one of her triumphs is certainly due to a true originality. In one of his later recorded conversations Goethe was endeavouring to decide what are the real obligations of genius to the influences which inevitably affect it. 'Much,' said he, 'is talked about originality; but what does originality mean? We are no sooner born than the world around begins to act upon us; its action lasts to the end of our lives and enters into everything. All that we

[c] This illustration was suggested to me, some years ago, by a well-known Oxford tutor. It is developed, with his usual force, by Félix, Jésus-Christ, p. 128.

[d] Bautain, Étude sur l'art de parler en public.

can truly call our own is our energy, our vigour, our will. If I,' he continued, 'could enumerate all that I really owe to the great men who have preceded me, and to those of my own day, it would be seen that very little is really my own. It is a point of capital importance to observe at what time of life the influence of a great character is brought to bear on us. Lessing, Winkelmann, and Kant, were older than I, and it has been of the greatest consequence to me that the two first powerfully influenced my youth and the last my old age[e].' On such a subject, Goethe may be deemed a high authority, and he certainly was not likely to do an injustice to genius, or to be guilty of a false humility when speaking of himself.

But our Lord's design to establish upon the earth a kingdom of souls was an original design. Remark, as bearing upon this originality, our Lord's isolation in His early life. His social obscurity is, in the eyes of thoughtful men, the safeguard and guarantee of His originality. It is not seriously pretended, on any side, that Jesus Christ was enriched with one single ray of His thought from Athens, from Alexandria, from the mystics of the Ganges or of the Indus, from the disciples of Zoroaster or of Confucius. The centurion whose servant He healed, the Greeks whom He met at the instance of St. Philip, the Syro-phœnician woman, the judge who condemned and the soldiers who crucified Him, are the few Gentiles with whom He is recorded to have had dealings during His earthly life. But was our Lord equally isolated from the world of Jewish speculation? M. Renan, indeed, impatient at the spectacle of an unrivalled originality, suggests, not without some hesitation, that Hillel was the real teacher of Jesus[f]. But Dr. Schenkel

[e] Conversations de Goethe, trad. Delerot, tom. ii. p. 342, quoted in the Rev. des Deux Mondes, 15 Oct. 1865.

[f] 'Hillel fut le vrai maître de Jésus, s'il est permis de parler de maître quand il s'agit d'une si haute originalité.' Vie de Jésus, p. 35. As an instance of our Lord's real independence of Hillel, a single example may suffice. A recent writer on 'the Talmud' gives the following story. 'One day a heathen went to Shammai, the head of the rival academy, and asked him mockingly to convert him to the law while he stood on one leg. The irate master turned him from the door. He then went to Hillel, who gave him that reply—*since so widely propagated*—"Do not unto another what thou wouldest not have another do unto thee. This is the whole law: the rest is mere commentary."' Quarterly Review, Oct. 1867, p. 441. art. 'The Talmud.' Or, as Hillel's words are rendered by Lightfoot: 'Quod tibi ipsi odiosum est, proximo ne feceris: nam hæc est tota lex.' Hor. Hebr. in Matt. p. 129. The writer in the Quarterly Review appears to assume the identity of Hillel's saying with the precept of our Blessed Lord,

will tell us that this suggestion rests on no historical basis whatever[g], while we may remark in passing that it is at issue with a theory which you would not care to notice at length, but which M. Renan cherishes with much fondness, and which represents our Lord's 'tone of thought' as a psychological result of the scenery of north-eastern Palestine[h]. The kindred assumption that when making His yearly visits to Jerusalem for the Feast of the Passover, or at other times, Jesus must have become the pupil of some of the leading Jewish doctors of the day, is altogether gratuitous. Once indeed, when He was twelve years old, He was found in a synagogue, hard by the temple, in close intellectual contact with aged teachers of the Law. But all who hear Him, even then, in His early Boyhood, are astonished at His understanding and answers; and the narrative of the Evangelist implies that the occurrence was not repeated. Moreover there was no teaching in Judæa at that era, which had not, in the true sense of the expression, a sectarian colouring. But what is there in the doctrine or in the character of Jesus that connects Him with a Pharisee or a Sadducee, or an Herodian, or an Essene[i] type of education? Is it not significant that, as Schleiermacher remarks, 'of all the sects then in vogue none ever claimed Jesus as representing

St. Matt. vii. 12; St. Luke vi. 31. Yet in truth how wide is the interval between the merely *negative* rule of the Jewish President (which had already been given in Tobit iv. 15), and the *positive* precept—ὅσα ἂν θέλητε ἵνα ποιῶσιν ὑμῖν οἱ ἄνθρωποι, οὕτω καὶ ὑμεῖς ποιεῖτε αὐτοῖς—of the Divine Master. On Gibbon's citation from Isocrates of a precept equivalent to Hillel's, see Archbishop Trench, Huls. Lect. p. 157. Hillel said that there would be no Messiah, since the promise and its fulfilment belonged to the time of Hezekiah; Westcott, Introd. p. 123.

[g] 'Ganz unbewiesen ist es,' Schenkel, Charakterbild Jesu, p. 39, note. When however Dr. Schenkel himself says, 'Den Einblick, den Er [sc. Jesus] in das Wesen und Treiben der religiösen Richtungen und Parteiungen seines Volkes in so hohem Masse befass, hat Er aus persönlicher Wahrnehmung und unmittelbarem Verkehr mit den Häuptern und Vertretern der verschiedenen Parteistandpunkte gewonnen' (ibid.), where is the justification of this assertion, except in the Humanitarian and Naturalistic theory of the writer, which makes some such assumption necessary?

[h] Vie de Jésus, p. 64: 'Une nature ravissante contribuait à former cet esprit.' Then follows a description of the flowers, the animals, the insects, and the mountains (p. 65), the farms, the fruit-gardens, and the vintage (p. 66), of Northern Galilee. M. Renan concludes, 'cette vie contente et facilement satisfaite . . se spiritualisait en rêves éthérés, en une sorte de mysticisme poétique confondant le ciel et la terre. . . . Toute l'histoire du Christianisme naissant est devenue de la sorte une délicieuse pastorale.' p. 67.

[i] Milman, Hist. Christ. i. p. 153, note x.

it, none branded Him with the reproach of apostasy from its tenets[j]?' Even if we lend an ear to the precarious conjecture that He may have attended some elementary school at Nazareth, it is plain that the people believed Him to have gone through no formal course of theological training. 'How knoweth This Man letters, having never learned[k]?' was a question which betrayed the popular surprise created by a Teacher Who spoke with the highest authority, and Who yet had never sat at the feet of an accredited doctor. It was the homage of public enthusiasm which honoured Him with the title of Rabbi; since this title did not then imply that one who bore it had been qualified by any intellectual exercises for an official teaching position. Isolated, as it seemed, obscure, uncultivated, illiterate, the Son of Mary did not concern Himself to struggle against or to reverse what man would deem the crushing disadvantages of His lot. He did not, like philosophers of antiquity, or like the active spirits of the middle ages, spend His Life in perpetual transit between one lecturer of reputation and another, between this and that focus of earnest and progressive thought. He was not a Goethe, continually enriching and refining his conceptions by contact with a long succession of intellectual friends, reaching from Lavater to Eckermann. Still less did He, during His early Manhood, live in any such atmosphere as that of this place, where interpenetrating all our differences of age and occupation, and even of conviction, there is the magnificent inheritance of a common fund of thought, to which, whether we know it or not, we are all constantly and inevitably debtors. He mingled neither with great thinkers who could mould educated opinion, nor with men of gentle blood who could give its tone to society; He passed those thirty years as an under-workman in a carpenter's shop; He lived in what might have seemed the depths of mental solitude and of social obscurity; and then He went forth, not to foment a political revolution, nor yet to found a local school of evanescent sentiment, but to proclaim an enduring and world-wide Kingdom of souls, based upon the culture of a common moral character, and upon intellectual submission to a common creed.

Christ's isolation, then, is the guarantee of His originality; yet had He lived as much in public as He lived in obscurity, where, let me ask, is the kingdom of heaven anticipated as a practical project in the ancient world? What, beyond the inter-

[j] Leben Jesu, vorl. xvi.

[k] St. John vii. 15.

change of thought on moral subjects, has the kingdom proclaimed by our Lord in common with the philosophical schools or coteries which grouped themselves around Socrates and other teachers of classical Greece[l]? These schools, indeed, differed from the kingdom of heaven, not merely in their lack of any pretensions to supernatural aims or powers, but yet more, in that they only existed for the sake of a temporary convenience, and that their members were bound to each other by no necessary ties[m]. Again, what was there in any of the sects of Judaism that could have suggested such a conception as the kingdom of heaven? Each and all they differ from it, I will not say in organization and structure, but in range and compass, in life and action, in spirit and aim. Or was the kingdom of heaven even traced in outline by the vague yearnings and aspirations after a better time, which entered so mysteriously into the popular thought of the heathen populations in the Augustan age[n]? Certainly it was an answer, complete yet unexpected, to these aspirations. They did not originate it; they could not have originated it; they primarily pointed to a material rather than to a moral Utopia, to an idea of improvement which did not enter into the plan of

[l] Mr. Lecky makes an observation upon the originality of our Lord's moral teaching, considered generally, which is well worthy of attention. Rationalism in Europe, i. p. 338. 'Nothing too, can, as I conceive, be more erroneous or superficial than the reasonings of those who maintain that the moral element in Christianity has in it nothing distinctive or peculiar. The method of this school, of which Bolingbroke may be regarded as the type, is to collect from the writings of different heathen writers, certain isolated passages embodying precepts that were inculcated by Christianity; and when the collection had become very large the task was supposed to be accomplished. But the true originality of a system of moral teaching depends not so much upon the elements of which it is composed, as upon the manner in which they are fused into a symmetrical whole, upon the proportionate value that is attached to different qualities, or, to state the same thing by a single word, upon the type of character that is formed. Now it is quite certain that the Christian type differs, not only in degree, but in kind from the Pagan one.' This general observation might legitimately include the vital differences which sever all merely human schemes of moral association and co-operation from that of the Founder of the Christian Church. See also Tulloch on The Christ of the Gospels, p. 190.

[m] This point is well stated in Ecce Homo, p. 91, sqq. The writer observes that if Socrates were to appear at the present day, he would form no society, as the invention of printing would have rendered it unnecessary. But the formation of an organized society was of the very essence of the work of Christ. It is a pleasure to recognise the fulness with which this vital truth is set forth by one from whom serious Churchmen must feel themselves to be separated by some deep differences of belief and principle.

[n] Virgil, Ecl. iv., Æn. vi. 793, and Suetonius, Vespasianus, iv. 5.

the Founder of the new kingdom. But you ask if the announcement of the kingdom of heaven by our Lord was not really a continuation of the announcement of the kingdom of heaven by St. John the Baptist? You might go further, and enquire, whether this proclamation of the kingdom of heaven is not to be traced up to the prophecy of Daniel respecting a fifth empire? For the present of course I waive the question which an Apostle [o] would have raised, as to whether the Spirit That spoke in St. John and in Daniel was not the Spirit of the Christ Himself. But let us enquire whether Daniel or St. John do anticipate our Lord's plan in such a sense as to rob it of its immediate originality. The Baptist and the prophet foretell the kingdom of heaven. Be it so. But a name is one thing, and the vivid complete grasp of an idea is another. We are accustomed to distinguish with some wholesome severity between originality of phrase and originality of thought. An intrinsic poverty of thought may at times succeed in formulating an original expression; while a true originality will often, nay generally, welcome a time-honoured and conventional phraseology, if it can thus secure currency and acceptance for the truth which it has brought to light and which it desires to set forth [p]. The originality of our Lord's plan lay not in its name, but in its substance. When St. John said that the kingdom of heaven was at hand [q], when Daniel represented it as a world-wide and imperishable empire, neither prophet nor Baptist had really anticipated the idea; one

[o] 1 St. Peter i. 11.

[p] Pascal, Pensées, art. vii. 9 (ed. Havet. p. 123): 'Qu'on ne dise pas que je n'ai rien dit de nouveau; la disposition des matières est nouvelle. Quand on joue à la paume, c'est une même balle dont on joue l'un et l'autre; mais l'un la place mieux. J'aimerais autant qu'on me dît que je me suis servi des mots anciens. Et comme si les mêmes pensées ne formaient pas un autre corps de discours par une disposition différente, aussi bien que les mêmes mots forment d'autres pensées par leur différente disposition.'

[q] The teaching of St. John Baptist centred around three points: (1) the call to penitence (St. Matt. iii. 2, 8–10; St. Mark i. 4; St. Luke iii. 3, 10–14); (2) the relative greatness of Christ (St. Matt. iii. 11–14; St. Mark i. 7; St. Luke iii. 16; St. John i. 15, 26, 27, 30–34); (3) the Judicial (*οὗ τὸ πτύον ἐν τῇ χειρὶ αὐτοῦ*, St. Matt. iii. 12; St. Luke iii. 17) and Atoning (*ἴδε ὁ ἀμνὸς τοῦ Θεοῦ, ὁ αἴρων τὴν ἁμαρτίαν τοῦ κόσμου*, St. John i. 29, 36) Work of Christ. In this way St. John corresponded to prophecy as preparing the way of the Lord (St. Matt. iii. 3; St. Mark i. 3; St. Luke iii. 4; St. John i. 23; Isa. xl. 3); but beyond naming the kingdom, the nature of the preparation required for entering it, the supernatural greatness, and two of the functions of the King, St. John did *not* anticipate our Lord's disclosures. St. John's teaching left men quite uninformed as to what the kingdom of heaven was to be in itself.

furnished the name of a coming system, the other a measure of its greatness. But what was the new institution to be in itself; what were to be its controlling laws and principles; what the animating spirit of its inhabitants; what the sources of its life; what the vicissitudes of its establishment and triumph? These and other elements of His plan are exhibited by our Lord Himself, in His discourses, His parables, His institutions. That which had been more or less vague, He made definite; that which had been abstract, He threw into a concrete form; that which had been ideal, He clothed with the properties of working reality; that which had been scattered over many books and ages, He brought into a focus. If prophecy supplied Him with some of the materials which He employed, prophecy could not have enabled Him to succeed in combining them. He combined them because He was Himself; His Person supplied the secret of their combination. His originality is indeed seen in the reality and life with which He lighted up the language used by men who had been sent in earlier ages to prepare His way; but if His creative thought employed these older materials, it did not depend on them. He actually gave a practical and energetic form to the idea of a strictly independent society of spiritual beings, with enlightened and purified consciences, cramped by no national or local bounds of privilege, and destined to spread throughout earth and heaven[r]. When He did this,

[r] Guizot, Essence de la Religion chrétienne, p. 307: 'Je reprends ces deux grands principes, ces deux grandes actes de Jésus-Christ, l'abolition de tout privilège dans les rapports des hommes avec Dieu, et la distinction de la vie religieuse, et de la vie civile; je les place en regard de tous les faits, de tous les états sociaux antérieurs à la venue de Jésus-Christ, et *je ne puis découvrir à ces caractères essentiels de la religion chrétienne, aucune filiation, aucune origine humaine.* Partout, avant Jésus-Christ, les religions étaient nationales, locales, établissant entre les peuples, les classes, les individus, des distances et des inégalités énormes. Partout aussi avant Jésus-Christ, la vie civile et la vie religieuse étaient confondues et s'opprimaient mutuellement; la religion ou les religions étaient des institutions incorporées dans l'état, et que l'état réglait ou réprimait selon son intérêt. Dans l'universalité de la foi religieuse, et l'indépendance de la société religieuse, je suis constraint de voir des nouveautés sublimes, des éclairs de la lumière divine!' Even Channing, who understates our Lord's 'plan,' is alive to the originality and greatness of that part of it which he recognises; Works, ii. 57. 'The plans and labours of statesmen sink into the sports of children, when compared with the work which Jesus announced. . . . . . The idea of changing the moral aspect of the whole earth, of recovering all nations to the pure and inward worship of the one God, and to a Spirit of Divine and fraternal love (our Lord proposed much more than this), was one of which we meet not a trace in philosopher or legislator before Him. The human

prophets were not His masters; they had only foreshadowed His work. His plan can be traced in that masterful completeness and symmetry, which is the seal of its intrinsic originality, to no source beyond Himself. Well might we ask with His astonished countrymen the question which was indeed prompted by their jealous curiosity, but which is natural to a very different temper, 'Whence hath this Man this wisdom?'[s]

(β) And this opens upon us the second characteristic of our Lord's plan, I mean that which in any merely human plan, we should call its audacity. This audacity is observable, first of all, in the fact that the plan is originally proposed to the world with what might appear to us to be such hazardous completeness. The idea of the kingdom of God issues almost 'as if in a single jet[t]' and with a fully developed body from the thought of Jesus Christ. Put together the Sermon on the Mount, the Charge to the Twelve Apostles, the Parables of the Kingdom, the Discourse in the Supper-room, and the institution of the two great Sacraments, and the plan of our Saviour is before you. And it is enunciated with an accent of calm unfaltering conviction that it will be realized in human history.

This is a phenomenon which we can only appreciate by contrasting it with the law to which it is so signal an exception. Generally speaking, an ambitious idea appears at first as a mere outline, and it challenges attention in a tentative way. It is put forward enquiringly, timidly, that it may be completed by the suggestions of friends or modified by the criticism of opponents. The highest genius is always most keenly alive to the vicissitudes which may await its own creations; it knows with what difficulty a promising project is launched safely and unimpaired out of the domain of abstract speculation into the region of practical human life. Even in art, where the materials to be moulded are, as compared with the subjects of moral or political endeavour, so much under command, it is not prudent to presume that a design or a conception will be carried out without additions or without

mind had given no promise of this extent of view. . . . . . We witness a vastness of purpose, a grandeur of thought and feeling, so original, so superior to the workings of all other minds, that nothing but our familiarity can prevent our contemplation of it with wonder and profound awe.'

[s] See Félix, Jésus-Christ et la Critique Nouvelle, pp. 127-133; Bushnell, Nature and the Supernatural, pp. 237-8. Keim has exaggerated the influence of Pharisaism upon the language and teaching of our Lord, which only resembled Pharisaism as being addressed to the Jewish mind in terms which it understood. Geschichtliche Christus, pp. 18-22.

[t] Pressensé, Jésus-Christ, p. 325.

curtailments. In this place we all have heard that between the θεωρία and the γένεσις of art there may be a fatal interval. The few bold strokes by which a Raffaelle has suggested a new form of power or of beauty, may never be filled up upon his canvas. The working-drawings of a Phidias or a Michael Angelo may never be copied in stone or in marble. As has been said of S. T. Coleridge, art is perpetually throwing out designs which remain designs for ever; and yet the artist possesses over his material, and even over his hand and his eye, a control which is altogether wanting to the man who would reconstruct or regenerate human society. For human society is an aggregate of human intelligences and of human wills, that is to say, of profound and mysterious forces, upon the direction of which under absolutely new circumstances it is impossible for man to calculate. Accordingly, social reformers tell us despondingly that facts make sad havoc of their fairest theories; and that schemes which were designed to brighten and to beautify the life of nations are either forgotten altogether, or, like the Republic of Plato, are remembered only as famous samples of the impracticable. For whenever a great idea, affecting the well-being of society, is permitted to force its way into the world of facts, it is liable to be carried out of its course, to be thrust hither and thither, to be compressed, exaggerated, disfigured, mutilated, degraded, caricatured. It may encounter currents of hostile opinion and of incompatible facts, upon which its projector had never reckoned; its course may be forced into a direction the exact reverse of that which he most earnestly desired. In the first French Revolution some of the most humane sociological projects were distorted into becoming the very animating principles of wholesale and extraordinary barbarities. In England we are fond of repeating the political maxim that 'constitutions are not made, but grow;' we have a proverbial dread of the paper-schemes of government which from time to time are popular among our gifted and volatile neighbours. It is not that we English cannot admire the creations of political genius; but we hold that in the domain of human life genius must submit herself to the dictation of circumstances, and that she herself seems to shade off into erratic folly when she cannot clearly recognise the true limits of her power.

Now Jesus Christ our Lord was in the true and very highest sense of the term a social reformer; yet He fully proclaimed the whole of His social plan before He began to realize it. Had He been merely a 'great man,' He would have been more prudent. He would have conditioned His design; He would have tested it; He would have developed it gradually; He would have made trial of its working power; and then He would have re-fashioned, or contracted, or expanded it, before finally proposing it to the consideration of the world. But His actual course must have seemed one of utter and reckless folly, unless the event had shewn it to be the dictate of a more than human wisdom. He speaks as One Who is sure of the compactness and faultlessness of His design; He is certain that no human obstacle can baulk its realization. He produces it simply without effort, without reserve, without exaggeration; He is calm, because He is in possession of the future, and sees His way clearly through its tangled maze. There is no proof, no distant intimation of a change or of a modification of His plan. He did not, for instance, first aim at a political success, and then cover His failure by giving a religious turn or interpretation to His previous manifestoes; He did not begin as a religious teacher, and afterwards aspire to convert His increasing religious influence into political capital. No attempts to demonstrate any such vacillation in His purpose have reached even a moderate measure of success [u]. Certainly, with the lapse of time, He enters upon a larger and larger area of ministerial action; He developes with majestic assurance, with decisive rapidity, the integral features of His work; His teaching centres more and more upon Himself as its central subject; but He nowhere retracts, or modifies, or speaks or acts as would one who feels that he is dependent upon events or agencies which he cannot control [x]. A poor woman pays Him

[u] Dr. Schenkel, in his Charakterbild Jesu, represents our Lord as a pious Jew, who did not assume to be the Messiah before the scene at Cæsarea Philippi. Kap. xii. § 4, p. 138: 'Dadurch, dass Jesus Sich nun wirklich zu dem Bekenntnisse des Simon bekannte, trat er mit einem Schlage aus der verworrenen und verwirrenden Läge heraus, in welche Er, durch die Unklarheit seiner Jünger und den Meinungstreit in seiner Umgebung gebracht war. Ein Stichwort war jetzt gesprochen.' This theory is obliged to reject the evangelical accounts of our Lord's Baptism and Temptation, and to distort from their plain meaning the narratives of our Lord's sermon in the synagogue at Nazareth (St. Luke iv. 16), of His call of the twelve Apostles, and of His claim to forgive sin. See the excellent remarks of M. Pressensé, Jésus-Christ, pp. 326, 327.

[x] Channing, Works, ii. 55. 'We feel that a new Being, of a new order of mind, is taking part in human affairs. There is a native tone of grandeur and authority in His teaching. He speaks as a Being related to the whole human race. A narrower sphere than the world never enters His thoughts. He speaks in a natural spontaneous style of accomplishing the most arduous and important change in human affairs. This unlaboured manner of expressing great thoughts is particularly worthy of attention. You never hear from Jesus that swelling, pompous, ostentatious language, which

ceremonial respect at a feast, and He simply announces that the act will be told as a memorial of her throughout the world [y]; He bids His Apostles do all things whatsoever He had commanded them [z]; He promises them His Spirit as a Guide into all necessary truth [a]: but He invests them with no such discretionary powers, as might imply that His design would need revision under possible circumstances, or could be capable of improvement. He calmly turns the glance of His thought upon the long and chequered future which lies clearly displayed before Him, and in the immediate foreground of which is his own humiliating Death [b]. Other founders of systems or of societies have thanked a kindly Providence for shrouding from their gaze the vicissitudes of coming time;

> 'Prudens futuri temporis exitum
> Caliginosâ nocte premit deus [c];'

but the Son of Man speaks as One Who sees beyond the most distant possibilities, and Who knows full well that His work is indestructible. 'The gates of hell,' He calmly observes, 'shall not prevail against it [d];' 'Heaven and earth shall pass away, but My words shall not pass away [e].'

Nor is the boldness of Christ's plan less observable in its actual substance, than in the fact of its original production in such completeness. Look at it, for the moment, from a political point of view. Here is, as it seems, a Galilean peasant, surrounded by a few followers taken like Himself from the lowest orders of society; yet He deliberately proposes to rule all human thought, to make Himself the Centre of all human affections, to be the Lawgiver of humanity, and the Object of man's adoration [f]. He founds a spiritual society, the thought

almost necessarily springs from an attempt to sustain a character above our powers. He talks of His glories, as one to whom they were familiar. . . . He speaks of saving and judging the world, of drawing all men to Himself, and of giving everlasting life, as we speak of the ordinary powers which we exert.'

[y] St. Matt. xxvi. 13; St. Mark xiv. 9.

[z] St. Matt. xxviii. 20.

[a] St. John xvi. 13.

[b] St. Matt. xx. 19; St. Mark viii. 31.

[c] Hor. Od. iii. 29. 29.

[d] St. Matt. xvi. 18.

[e] Ibid. xxiv. 35.

[f] Bushnell, Nature and the Supernatural, p. 232. 'To Jesus alone, the simple Galilean carpenter, it happens . . . that, having never seen a map of the world in His whole life, or heard the name of half the great nations on it, He undertakes, coming out of His shop, a scheme as much vaster and more difficult than that of Alexander, as it proposes more, and what is more Divinely benevolent.'

[LECT.

and heart and activity of which are to converge upon His Person, and He tells His followers that this society which He is forming is the real explanation of the highest visions of seers and prophets, that it will embrace all races and extend throughout all time. He places Himself before the world as the true goal of its expectations, and He points to His proposed work as the one hope for its future. There was to be a universal religion, and He would found it. A universal religion was just as foreign an idea to heathenism[g] as to Judaism. Heathenism held that the state was the highest form of social life; religious life, like family life, was deemed subordinate to political interests. Morality was pretty nearly dwarfed down to the measure of common political virtue; sin was little else than political misdemeanour; religion was but a subordinate function of national life, differing in different countries according to the varying genius of the people, and rightly liable to being created or controlled by the government. A century and a half after the Incarnation, in his attack upon the Church, Celsus ridicules the idea of a universal religion as a manifest folly[h]; yet Jesus Christ has staked His whole claim to respect and confidence upon announcing it. Jesus Christ made no concessions to the passions or to the prejudices of mankind. The laws and maxims of His kingdom are for the most part in entire contradiction to the instincts of average human nature; yet He predicts that His Gospel will be preached in all the world, and that finally there will be one flock and One Shepherd of men[i]. 'Go,' He says to His Apostles, 'make disciples of all nations, baptizing them in the Name of the Father, and of the Son, and of the Holy Ghost; teaching them to observe all things whatsoever I have commanded you; and, lo, I am with you alway, even unto the end of the world[k].' He founds a world-wide religion, and He promises to be the present invigorating force of that religion to the end of time. Are we not too accustomed to this language to feel the full force of its original meaning? How startlingly must it not have fallen upon the ears of Apostles! Words like these are not accounted for by any difference between the East and

[g] The Stoic 'cosmopolitanism' (Sir A. Grant's Ethics of Aristotle, vol. i. 255; Merivale on Conversion of Roman Empire, p. 60) did not amount to a religion.

[h] Origen. contr. Celsum, ii. 46.

[i] St. John x. 16. Christ and His Apostles were to *begin* to preach to Israel. St. Matt. xv. 24, x. 5, 6.

[k] St. Matt. xxviii. 19, 20.

the West, between ancient and modern modes of speech. They will not bear honest translation into any modern phrase that would enable good men to use them now. Can we imagine such a command as that of our Lord upon the lips of the best, of the wisest of men whom we have ever known? Would it not be simply to imagine that goodness or wisdom had been exchanged for the folly of an intolerable presumption? Such language as that before us is indeed folly, unless it be something else; unless it be proved by the event to have been the highest wisdom, the wisdom of One, Whose ways are not our ways, nor His thoughts our thoughts[l].

II. But has the plan of Jesus Christ been carried out? Does the kingdom of heaven exist on earth?

(1.) The Church of Christ is the living answer to that question. Boileau says somewhere that the Church is a great thought which every man ought to study. It would be more practical to say that the Church is a great fact which every man ought to measure. Probably we Christians are too familiarized with the blessed presence of the Church to do justice to her as a world-embracing institution, and as the nurse and guardian of our moral and mental life. Like the air we breathe, she bathes our whole being with influences which we do not analyse; and we hold her cheap in proportion to the magnitude of her unostentatious service. The sun rises on us day by day in the heavens, and we heed not his surpassing beauty until our languid sense is roused by some observant astronomer or artist. The Christian Church pours even upon those of us who love her least, floods of intellectual and moral light; and yet it is only by an occasional intellectual effort that we detach ourselves sufficiently from the tender monotony of her influences, to understand how intrinsically extraordinary is the double fact of her perpetuated existence and of her continuous expansion.

Glance for a moment at the history of the Christian Church from the days of the Apostles until now. What is it but a history of the gradual, unceasing self-expansion of an institution which, from the first hour of its existence, deliberately aimed, as it is aiming even now, at the conquest of the world[m]? Compare the Church which sought refuge and which prayed in the upper chamber at Jerusalem, with the Church of which St. Paul

[l] Isa. lv. 8. Cf. Bushnell, Nature and the Supernatural, pp. 231–233; Félix, ubi supra, pp. 134–139.

[m] St. Luke xxiv. 47; Acts i. 8, ix. 15; St. Mark xvi. 20.

is the pioneer and champion in the latter portion of the Acts of the Apostles, or with the Church to which he refers, as already making its way throughout the world, in his Apostolical Epistles[n]. Compare again the Church of the Apostolical age with the Church of the age of Tertullian. Christianity had then already penetrated, at least in some degree, into all classes of Roman society[o], and was even pursuing its missionary course in regions far beyond the frontiers of the empire[p], in the forests of Germany, in the wilds of Scythia, in the deserts of Africa, and among the unsubdued and barbarous tribes who inhabited the northern extremity of our own island. Again, how nobly conscious is the Church of the age of St. Augustine of her world-wide mission, and of her ever-widening area! how sharply is this consciousness contrasted with the attempt of Donatism to dwarf down the realization of the plan of Jesus Christ to the narrow proportions of a national or provincial enterprise[q]! In the writings of Augustine especially, we see the Church of Christ tenaciously grasping the deposit of revealed unchanging doctrine, while liturgies the most dissimilar, and teachers of many tongues[r], and a large variety of ecclesiastical cus-

[n] Rom. i. 8, x. 18, xv. 18–21; Col. i. 6, 23; cf. 1 St. Peter i. 1, &c.

[o] Tert. Apol. 37: 'Hesterni sumus, et vestra omnia implevimus, urbes, insulas, castella, municipia, conciliabula, castra ipsa, tribus, decurias, palatium, senatum, forum, sola vobis relinquimus templa.' Cf. de Rossi, Roma Sotteranea, i. p. 309.

[p] Tert. adv. Judæos, c. 7: 'Jam Getulorum varietates, et Maurorum multi fines, Hispaniarum omnes termini, et Galliarum diversæ nationes, et *Britannorum inaccessa Romanis loca*, Christo vero subdita et Sarmatarum, et Dacorum, et Germanorum, et Scytharum, et abditarum multarum gentium et provinciarum, et insularum multarum nobis ignotarum, et quæ enumerare minus possumus. In quibus omnibus locis, Christi nomen, Qui jam venit, regnat, utpote ante Quem omnium civitatum portæ sunt apertæ.'

[q] St. Aug. Ep. xlix. n. 3: 'Quærimus ergo, ut nobis respondere non graveris, quam causam forte noveris quâ factum est, ut Christus amitteret hæreditatem Suam per orbem terrarum diffusam, et subito in solis Afris, nec ipsis omnibus remaneret. Etenim ecclesia Catholica est etiam in Africâ quia per omnes terras eam Deus esse voluit et prædixit. Pars autem vestra, quæ Donati dicitur, non est in omnibus illis locis, in quibus et literæ et sermo et facta apostolica cucurrerunt.' In Ps. lxxxv. n. 14: 'Christo enim tales maledicunt, qui dicunt, quia periit ecclesia de orbe terrarum, et remansit in solâ Africâ.' Compare S. Hieron. adv. Lucifer. tom. iv. pt. ii. p. 298: 'Si in Sardiniâ tantum habet [ecclesiam Christus] nimium pauper factus est.' And St. Chrys. in Col. Hom. i. n. 2; in 1 Cor. Hom. xxxii. n. 1.

[r] In Ps. xliv. (Vulg.) Enarr. n. 24: 'Sacramenta doctrinæ in linguis omnibus variis. Alia lingua Afra, alia Syra, alia Græca, alia Hebræa, alia illa et illa; faciunt istæ linguæ varietatem vestis reginæ hujus; quomodo autem omnis varietatis vestis in unitate concordat, sic et omnes linguæ ad unam fidem.'

toms [s], find an equal welcome within her comprehensive bosom. Yet contrast the Church of the fourth and fifth centuries with the Church of the middle ages, or with the Church of our own day. In the fourth and even in the fifth century, whatever may have been the activity of individual missionaries, the Church was still for the most part contained within the limits of the empire; and of parts of the empire she had scarcely as yet taken possession. She was still confronted by powerful sections of the population, passionately attached for various reasons to the ancient superstition: nobles such as the powerful Symmachus, and orators like the accomplished Libanius, were among her most earnest opponents. But it is now scarcely less than a thousand years since Jesus Christ received at least the outward submission of the whole of Europe; and from that time to this His empire has been continually expanding. The newly-discovered continents of Australia and America have successively acknowledged His sway. He is shedding the light of His doctrine first upon one and then upon another of the islands of the Pacific. He has beleagured the vast African continent on either side with various forms of missionary enterprise. And although in Asia there are vast, ancient, and highly organized religions which are still permitted to bid Him defiance, yet India, China, Tartary, and Kamtchatka have within the last few years witnessed heroic labours and sacrifices for the spread of His kingdom, which would not have been unworthy of the purest and noblest enthusiasms of the Primitive Church. Nor are these efforts so fruitless as the ruling prejudices or the lack of trustworthy information on such subjects, which are so common in Western Europe, might occasionally suggest [t].

Already the kingdom of the Redeemer may be said to embrace three continents; but what are its prospects, even if we

[s] Ep. liv. ad Januar. n. 2: 'Alia vero [sunt] quæ per loca terrarum regionesque variantur, sicuti est quod alii jejunant sabbato, alii non; alii quotidiè communicant Corpori et Sanguini Domini, alii certis diebus accipiunt; alibi nullus dies prætermittitur, quo non offeratur, alibi sabbato tantum et dominico, alibi tantum dominico; et si quid aliud hujusmodi animadverti potest, *totum hoc genus rerum liberas habet observationes:* nec disciplina ulla est in his melior gravi prudentique Christiano, quam ut *eo modo agat, quo agere viderit ecclesiam, ad quam forte devenerit.* Quod enim neque contra fidem, neque bonos mores esse convincitur, indifferenter est habendum et propter eorum, inter quos vivitur, societatem servandum est.'

[t] As to the Russian Missions, see Boissard, Église de Russie, tom. i. pp. 100-104; Voices from the East, by Rev. J. M. Neale, London, Masters, 1859, pp. 81-113.

measure them by a strictly human estimate? Is it not a simple matter of fact that at this moment the progress of the human race is entirely identified with the spread of the influence of the nations of Christendom? What Buddhist, or Mohammedan, or Pagan nation is believed by others, or believes itself, to be able to affect for good the future destinies of the human race? The idea of a continuous progress of humanity, whatever perversions that idea may have undergone, is really a creation of the Christian faith. The nations of Christendom, in exact proportion to the strength, point, and fervour of their Christianity, seriously believe that they can command the future, and instinctively associate themselves with the Church's aspirations for a world-wide empire. Such a confidence, by the mere fact of its existence, is already on the road to justifying itself by success. It never was stronger, on the whole, than it is in our own day. If in certain districts of European opinion it may seem to be waning, this is only because such sections of opinion have for the moment rejected the empire of Christ. Their aberrations do not set aside, they rather act as a foil to that general belief in a moral and social progress of mankind which at bottom is so intimately associated with the belief of Christian men in the coming triumph of the Church.

(2.) But long ere this, my brethren, as I am well aware, you have been prepared to interrupt me with a group of objections. Surely, you will say, this representation of the past, of the present, and of the future of the Church may suffice for an ideal picture, but it is not history. Is not the verdict of history a different and a less encouraging one? First of all, do Church annals present this spectacle of an ever-widening extension of the kingdom of Christ? What then is to be said of the spread of great and vital heresies, such as the mediæval Nestorianism, through countries which once believed with the Church in the One Person and two Natures of her Lord[u]? Again, is it not a matter of historical fact that the Church has lost entire provinces both in Africa and in the East, since the rise of Mohammedanism? And are her losses only to be measured by the territorial area which she once occupied, and from which she has been beaten back by the armies of the alien? Has she not, by the controversies of the tenth and of the sixteenth centuries, been herself splintered into three great sections, which still continue to act in outward separation from each other, to their own

[u] See Gibbon, Decl. and Fall, ch. xlvii.

extreme mutual loss and discouragement, and to the immense and undisguised satisfaction of all enemies of the Christian name? Are not large bodies of active and earnest Christians living in separation from her communion? Do not our missionary associations perpetually lament their failures to achieve any large permanent conquests for Christ? Once more, is it not a matter of notoriety that the leading nations of Christian Europe are themselves honeycombed by a deadly rationalism, which gives no quarter in its contemptuous yet passionate onslaughts on the faith of Christians, and which never calculated more confidently than it does at the present time upon achieving the total destruction of the empire of Jesus Christ?

My brethren, you do a service to my argument in stating these apparent objections to its force. The substance of your plea cannot be ignored by any who would honestly apprehend the matter before us. You point, for instance, to the territorial losses which the Church has sustained at the hands of heretical Christians or of Moslem invaders. True: the Church of Christ has sustained such losses. But has she not more than redressed them in other directions? Is she not now, in India and in Africa, carrying the banner of the Cross into the territory of the Crescent? You insist upon the grave differences which form a barrier at this moment between the Eastern and the Western Churches, and between the two great divisions of the Western Church itself. Your estimate of those differences may be a somewhat exaggerated one. The renewed harmony and co-operation of the separated portions of the family of Christ may not be so entirely remote as you would suggest. Yet we must undoubtedly acknowledge that existing divisions, like all habitual sin within the sacred precincts of the Church, are a standing and very serious violation of the law of its Founder. Nor is this disorder summarily to be remedied by our ceding to the unwarrantable pretensions of one section of the Church, which may endeavour to persuade the rest of Christendom, that it is itself co-extensive with the whole kingdom of the Saviour. The divisions of Christ's family, lamentable and in many ways disastrous as they are, must be ended, if at all, by the warmer charity and more fervent prayers of believing Christians. But meanwhile, do not these very divisions afford an indirect illustration of the extraordinary vitality of the new kingdom? Has the kingdom ceased to enlarge its territory since the troubled times of the sixteenth century? On the contrary, it is simply a matter of fact that, since that date, its ratio of extension has been greater than at any previous period. The philosopher who supposes that the Church is on the point of dying out because of her divisions must be strangely insensible to the higher convictions which are increasingly prevailing in the minds of men. And the confessions of failure on the part of some of our missionaries are certainly balanced by many and thankful narratives of great results accomplished under circumstances of the utmost discouragement.

But you insist most emphatically upon the spread and upon the strength of modern rationalism. You say that rationalism is enthroned in the midst of civilizations which the Church herself has formed and nursed. You urge that rationalism, like the rottenness which has seized upon the heart of the forest oak, must sooner or later arrest the growth of branch and foliage, and bring the tree which it is destroying to the ground. Now we cannot deny, what is indeed a patent and melancholy fact, that some of the most energetic of the intellectual movements in modern Europe frankly avow and enthusiastically advocate an explicit and total rejection of the Christian creed. Yet it is possible to overrate the importance and to mistake the true significance of this recent advance of unbelief. Of course Christian faith can be daunted or surprised by no form or intensity of opposition to truth, when there are always so many reasons for opposing it. We Christians know what we have to expect from the human heart in its natural state; while on the other hand we have been told that the gates of hell shall not prevail against the Church of the Redeemer. But, in speculating on the future destinies of the Church, as they are affected by rationalism, this hopeful confidence of a sound faith may be seconded by the calm estimate of the reflective reason. For, first, it may fairly be questioned whether the publicly proclaimed unbelief of modern times is really more general or more pronounced than the secret but active and deeply penetrating scepticism which during considerable portions of the middle ages laid such hold upon the intellect of Europe [v]. Yet the mediæval sceptics cannot be said to have permanently hampered the progress of the Church. Again, modern unbelief may be deemed less formidable when we steadily observe its moral impotence for all constructive purposes. Its strength and genius lie only in the direction of destruction. It has shewn no sort of power to build up any spiritual fabric or system which, as a shelter and a

[v] Cf. Newman, Lectures on University Subjects, pp. 296, 297; Milman, Latin Christianity, vi. 444. See too St. Anselm, Cur Deus Homo, i. 4.

discipline for the hearts and lives of men, can take the place of that which it seeks to destroy. Leaving some of the deepest, most legitimate, and most ineradicable needs of the human soul utterly unsatisfied, modern unbelief can never really hope permanently to establish a popular 'religion of humanity[x].' Thus the force of its intellectual onset upon revealed dogma is continually being broken by the consciousness, that it cannot long maintain the ground which it may seem to itself for the moment to have won. Its highest speculative energy is more than counterbalanced by the moral power of some humble teacher of a positive creed for whom possibly it entertains nothing less than a sovereign contempt. Thirdly, unbelief resembles social or political persecution in this, that, indirectly, it does an inevitable service to the Faith which it attacks. It forces earnest believers in Jesus Christ to minimize all differences which are less than fundamental. It compels Christian men to repress with a strong hand all exaggeration of existing motives for a divided action. It obliges Christians, sometimes in spite of themselves, to work side by side for their insulted Lord. Thus it not only creates freshened sympathies between temporarily severed branches of the Church; it draws toward the Church herself, with an increasingly powerful and comprehensive attraction, many of those earnestly believing men, who, as is the case with numbers among our nonconformist brethren in this country, already belong, in St. Augustine's language, to the soul, although not to the body, of the Catholic Communion. Lastly, it unwittingly contributes to augment the evidential strength of Christianity, at the very moment of its assault upon Christian doctrine. The fierceness of man turns to the praise of Jesus Christ, by demonstrating, each day, each year, each decade of years, each century, the indestructibility of His work in the world; and unbelief voluntarily condemns itself to the task of maintaining before the eyes of men that enduring tradition of an implacable hostility to the kingdom of heaven, which it is the glory of our Saviour so explicitly to have predicted, and so consistently and triumphantly to have defied.

[x] The attempt of M. Auguste Comte, in his later life, to elaborate a kind of ritual as a devotional and æsthetical appendage to the Positivist Philosophy, implies a sense of this truth. M. Comte however does not appear to have carried any large section of the Positivist school with him in this singular enterprise. But a like poverty of moral and spiritual provision for the soul of man is observable in rationalistic systems which stop very far short of the literal godlessness of the Positive Philosophy.

(3.) For these and other reasons, modern unbelief, although formidable, will not be deemed so full of menace to the future of the kingdom of our Lord as may sometimes be apprehended by the nervous timidity of Christian piety. This will appear more certain if from considering the extent of Christ's realm we turn to the intensive side of His work among men. For indeed the depth of our Lord's work in the soul of man has ever been more wonderful than its breadth. The moral intensity of the life of a sincere Christian is a more signal illustration[y] of the reality of the reign of Christ, and of the success of His plan, than is the territorial range of the Christian empire. 'The King's daughter is all glorious within.' Christianity may have conferred a new sanction upon civil and domestic relationships among men; and it certainly infused a new life into the most degraded society that the world has yet seen[z]. Still this was not its primary aim; its primary efforts were directed not to this world, but to the next[a]. Christianity has changed many of the outward aspects of human existence; it has created a new religious language, a new type of worship, a new calendar of time. It has furnished new ideals to art; it has opened nothing less than a new world of literature; it has invested the forms of social intercourse among men with new graces of refinement and mutual consideration. Yet these are but some of the superficial symptoms of its real work. It has achieved these changes in the outward life of Christian nations, because it has penetrated to the very depths of man's heart and thought; because it has revolutionized his convictions and tamed his will, and then expressed its triumph in the altered social system of that section of the human race which has generally received it. How

[y] 2 Thess. i. 11, 12, where the Apostle's prayers for the moral and spiritual growth of the Thessalonians are offered ὅπως ἐνδοξάσθῃ τὸ ὄνομα τοῦ Κυρίου ἡμῶν Ἰησοῦ ἐν ὑμῖν.

[z] St. Aug. Ep. cxxxviii. ad Marcellin. n. 15: 'Qui doctrinam Christi adversam dicunt esse reipublicæ, dent exercitum talem, quales doctrina Christi esse milites jussit, dent tales provinciales, tales maritos, tales conjuges, tales parentes, tales filios, tales dominos, tales servos, tales reges, tales judices, tales denique debitorum ipsius fisci redditores et exactores, quales esse præcipit doctrina Christiana, et audeant eam dicere adversam esse reipublicæ, immò verò non dubitent eam confiteri magnam, si obtemperetur, salutem esse reipublicæ.'

[a] St. Hieronymus adv. Jovin. lib. ii. tom. iv. pars ii. p. 200, ed. Martian: 'Nostra religio non πυκτὴν, non athletam (St. Jerome might almost have in his eye a certain well-known modern theory) non nautas, non milites, non fossores, sed sapientiæ erudit sectatorem, qui se Dei cultui dedicavit, et scit cur creatus sit, cur versetur in mundo, quo abire festinet.'

complete at this moment is the reign of Christ in the soul of a sincere Christian! Christ is not a limited, He is emphatically an absolute Monarch. Yet His rule is welcomed by His subjects with more than that enthusiasm which a free people can feel for its elected magistracy. Every sincere Christian bows to Jesus Christ as to an Intellectual Master. Our Lord is not merely listened to as a Teacher of Truth; He is contemplated as the absolute Truth itself. Accordingly no portion of His teaching is received by true Christians merely as a 'view,' or as a 'tentative system,' or as a 'theory,' which may be entertained, discussed, partially adopted, and partially set aside. Those who deal thus with Him are understood to have broken with Christianity, at least as a practical religion. For a Christian, the Words of Christ constitute the highest criterion and rule of truth. All that Christ has authorized is simply accepted, all that He has condemned is simply rejected, with the whole energy of the Christian reason. Christ's Thought is reflected, it is reproduced, in the thought of the true Christian. Christ's authority in the sphere of speculative truth is thankfully acknowledged by the Christian's voluntary and unreserved submission to the slightest known intimations of his Master's judgment. High above the claims of human teachers, the tremendous self-assertion of Jesus Christ echoes on from age to age,—'I am the Truth[b].' And from age to age the Christian mind responds by a life-long endeavour 'to bring every thought into captivity unto the obedience of Christ[c].' But if Jesus Christ is Lord of the Christian's thought, He is also Lord of the Christian's affections. Beauty it is which provokes love; and Christ is the highest Moral Beauty. He does not merely rank as an exponent of the purest morality. He is absolute Virtue, embodied in a human life, and vividly, energetically set forth before our eyes in the story of the Gospels. As such, He claims to reign over the inmost affections of men. As such, He secures the first place in the heart of every true Christian. To have taken the measure of His Beauty, and yet not to love Him, is, in a Christian's judgment, to be self-condemned. 'If any man love not the Lord Jesus Christ, let him be Anathema Maranatha[d].' And ruling the affections of the Christian, Christ is also King of the sovereign faculty in the Christianized soul; He is Master of the Christian will. When He has tamed its native stubbornness, He teaches it day by day a more and more pliant accuracy of

[b] St. John xiv. 6. [c] 2 Cor. x. 5. [d] 1 Cor. xvi. 22.

movement in obedience to Himself. Nay, He is not merely its rule of action, but its very motive power; each act of devotion and self-sacrifice of which it is capable is but an extension of the energy of Christ's Own moral Life. 'Without Me,' he says to His servants, 'ye can do nothing[e];' and with St. Paul His servants reply, 'I can do all things through Christ Which strengtheneth Me[f].'

This may be expressed in other terms by saying that, both intellectually and morally, Christ is Christianity[g]. Christianity is not related to our Lord as a philosophy might be to a philosopher, that is, as a moral or intellectual system thrown off from his mind, resting thenceforward on its own merits, and implying no necessary relation towards its author on the part of those who receive it, beyond a certain sympathy with what was at one time a portion of his thought[h]. A philosophy may be thus abstracted altogether from the person of its originator, with entire impunity. Platonic thought would not have been damaged, if Plato had been annihilated; and in our day men are Hegelians or Comtists, without believing that the respective authors of those systems are in existence at this moment, nay rather, in the majority of cases, while deliberately holding that they have ceased to be. The utmost stretch of personal allegiance, on the part of the disciple of a philosophy to its founder, consists, ordinarily speaking, in a sentiment of devotion 'to his memory.' But detach Christianity from Christ, and it vanishes before your eyes into intellectual vapour. For it is of the essence of Christianity that, day by day, hour by hour, the Christian should live in conscious, felt, sustained relationship to the Ever-living Author of his creed and of his life. Christianity is non-existent apart from Christ; it centres in Christ; it radiates, now as at the first, from Christ. It is not a mere doctrine bequeathed by Him to a world with which He has ceased to have dealings; it perishes outright when men attempt to abstract it from the Living Person of its Founder. He is felt by His people to be their Living Lord, really present with them now, and even unto the end of the world. The Christian life springs from and is sustained by the apprehension of Christ present in His Church, present in and with His members as a πνεῦμα ζωοποιοῦν[i]. Christ is the quickening Spirit of Christian

[e] St. John xv. 5.

[f] Phil. iv. 13; cf. i. 19.

[g] See Newman, Grammar of Assent, p. 457.

[h] Luthardt, Grundwahrheiten des Christenthums, p. 227: 'Er ist der Inhalt seiner Lehre.'

[i] 1 Cor. xv. 45.

humanity; He lives in Christians; He thinks in Christians; He acts through Christians and with Christians; He is indissolubly associated with every movement of the Christian's deepest life. 'I live,' exclaims the Apostle, 'yet not I, but Christ liveth in me[j].' This felt presence of Christ it is, which gives both its form and its force to the sincere Christian life. That life is a loyal homage of the intellect, of the heart, and of the will, to a Divine King, with Whom will, heart, and intellect are in close and constant communion, and from Whom there flows forth, through the Spirit and the Sacraments, that supply of light, of love, and of resolve, which enriches and ennobles the Christian soul. My brethren, I am not theorizing or describing any merely ideal state of things; I am but putting into words the inner experience of every true Christian among you; I am but exhibiting a set of spiritual circumstances which, as a matter of course, every true Christian endeavours to realize and make his own, and which, as a matter of fact, blessed be God! very many Christians do realize, to their present peace, and to their eternal welfare.

Certainly it is not uncommon in our day to be informed, that 'the Sermon on the Mount is a dead letter in Christendom.' In consequence (so men speak) of the engrossing interest which Christians have wrongly attached to the discussion of dogmatic questions, that original draught of essential Christianity, the Sermon on the Mount, has been wellnigh altogether lost sight of. Perhaps you yourselves, my brethren, ere now have repeated some of the current commonplaces on this topic. But have you endeavoured to ascertain whether it is indeed as you say? You remark that you at least have not met with Christians who seemed to be making any sincere efforts to turn the Sermon on the Mount into practice. It may be so. But the question is, where have you looked for them? Do you expect to meet them rushing hurriedly along the great highways of life, with the keen, eager, self-asserting multitude? Do you expect, that with their eye upon the Beatitudes and upon the Cross, they will throng the roads which lead to worldly success, to earthly wealth, to temporal honour? Be assured that those who know where moral beauty, aye, the highest, is to be found, are not disappointed, even at this hour, in their search for it. Until you have looked more carefully, more anxiously than has probably been the case, for the triumphs of our Lord's work in

[j] Gal. ii. 20.

Christian souls, you may do well to take upon trust the testimony of others. You may at least be sufficiently generous, aye, and sufficiently reasonable, to believe in the existence at this present time of the very highest types of Christian virtue. It is a simple matter of fact that in our day, multitudes of men and women do lead the life of the Beatitudes; they pray, they fast, they do alms to their Father Which seeth in secret. These are Christians who take no thought for the morrow. These are Christians whose righteousness does exceed that worldly and conventional standard of religion, which knows no law save the corrupt public opinion of the hour, and which inherits in every generation the essential spirit of the Scribes and Pharisees. These are Christians who shew forth the moral creativeness of Jesus Christ in their own deeds and words; they are living witnesses to His solitary and supreme power of changing the human heart. They were naturally proud; He has enabled them to be sincerely humble. They were, by the inherited taint of their nature, impure; He has in them shed honour upon the highest forms of chastity. They too were, as in his natural state man ever is, suspicious of and hostile to their fellow-men, unless connected with them by blood, or by country, or by interest. But Jesus Christ has taught them the tenderest and most practical forms of love for man viewed simply as man; He has inspired them with the only true, that is, the Christian, humanitarianism. Think not that the moral energy of the Christian life was confined to the Church of the first centuries. At this moment, there are millions of souls in the world, that are pure, humble, and loving. But for Jesus Christ our Lord, these millions would have been proud, sensual, selfish. At this very day, and even in atmospheres where the taint of scepticism dulls the brightness of Christian thought, and enfeebles the strength of Christian resolution, there are to be found men, whose intelligence gazes on Jesus with a faith so clear and strong, whose affection clings to Him with so trustful and so warm an embrace, whose resolution has been so disciplined and braced to serve Him by a persevering obedience, that, beyond a doubt, they would joyfully die for Him, if by shedding their blood they could better express their devotion to His Person, or lead others to know and to love Him more. Blessed be God, that portion of His one Fold in which He has placed us, the Church of England, has not lacked the lustre of such lives as these. Such assuredly was Ken; such was Bishop Wilson; such have been many whose names have never appeared in the page of history. Has not one indeed quite lately passed from among us, the boast and glory of this our University, great as a poet, greater still, it may be, as a scholar and a theologian, greatest of all as a Christian saint? Certainly to know him, even slightly, was inevitably to know that he led a life distinct from, and higher than, that of common men. To know him well, was to revere and to love in him the manifested beauty of his Lord's presence; it was to trace the sensibly perpetuated power of the Life, of the Teaching, of the Cross of Jesus[k].

4. On the other hand, look at certain palpable effects of our Lord's work which lie on the very face of human society. If society, apart from the Church, is more kindly and humane than in heathen times, this is due to the work of Christ on the hearts of men. The era of 'humanity' is the era of the Incarnation. The sense of human brotherhood, the acknowledgment of the sacredness of human rights, the recognition of that particular stock of rights which appertains to every human being, is a creation of Christian dogma. It has radiated from the heart of the Christian Church into the society of the outer world. Christianity is the power which first gradually softened slavery, and is now finally abolishing it. Christianity has proclaimed the dignity of poverty, and has insisted upon the claims of the poor, with a success proportioned to the sincerity which has welcomed her doctrines among the different peoples of Christendom. The hospital is an invention of Christian philanthropy[l]; the active charity of the Church of the fourth century forced into the Greek language a word for which Paganism had had no occasion. The degradation of woman in the Pagan world has been exchanged for a position of special privilege and honour, accorded to her by the Christian nations. The sensualism which Pagans mistook for love has been placed under the ban of all true Christian feeling; and in Christendom, love is now the purest of moral impulses; it is the tenderest, the noblest, the most refined of the movements of the soul. The old, the universal, the natural feeling of bitter hostility between races, nations, and classes of men is denounced by Christianity. The spread of Christian truth inevitably breaks down the ferocities of national prejudice, and prepares the world for that cosmopolitanism which, we are told, is its most probable future. International law had no real

[k] The author of the Christian Year had passed to his rest during the interval that elapsed between the delivery of the second and the third of these lectures, on March 30, 1866.

[l] Hallam's Middle Ages, chap. ix. part i. vol. ii. p. 365.

existence until the nations, taught by Christ, had begun to feel the bond of brotherhood. International law is now each year becoming more and more powerful in regulating the affairs of the civilized world. And if we are sorrowfully reminded that the prophecy of a world-wide peace within the limits of Christ's kingdom has not yet been realized; if Christian lands, in our day as before, are reddened by streams of Christian blood; yet the utter disdain of the plea of right, the high-handed and barbarous savagery, which marked the wars of heathendom, have given way to sentiments in which justice can at least obtain a hearing, and which compassion and generosity, drawing their inspirations from the Cross, have at times raised to the level of chivalry.

But neither would any improvements in man's social life, nor even the regenerate lives of individual Christians, of themselves, have realized our Lord's 'plan' in its completeness [m]. His design was to found a society or Church; individual sanctity and social amelioration are only effects radiating from the Church. The Church herself is the true proof of His success. After the lapse of eighteen centuries the kingdom of Christ is here, and it is still expanding. How fares it generally with a human undertaking when exposed to the action of a long period of time? The idea which was its very soul is thrown into the shade by some other idea; or it is warped, or distorted, or diverted from its true direction, or changed by some radical corruption. In the end it dies out from among the living thoughts of men, and takes its place in the tomb of so much forgotten speculation, on the shelves of a library. Within a short lifetime we may follow

[m] A reviewer, who naturally must dissent from parts of the teaching of these lectures, but of whose generosity and fairness the lecturer is deeply sensible, reminds him that 'Our Lord came to carry out the counsel of the Eternal Father; and that counsel was, primarily, to establish, through His sacrificial death, an economy of mercy, under which justification and spiritual and eternal life should be realized by all who should penitently rely on Him.' St. John iii. 16, vi. 38-40. Undoubtedly. But this 'economy of mercy' included the establishment of a world-embracing church, within which it was to be dispensed. Col. i. 10-14. Our Lord founded His Church, not by way of achieving a vast social feat or victory, but with a view to the needs of the human soul, which He came from heaven to save. Nevertheless the Church is not related to our Lord's design as an 'inseparable accident.' It is that design itself, viewed on its historical and social side; it is the form which, so far as we know, His redemptive work necessarily took, and which He Himself founded as being the imperishable result of His Incarnation and Death. St. Matt. xvi. 18. Cf. *Wesleyan-Methodist Magazine*, Dec. 1867, p. 1086.

many a popular moral impulse from its cradle to its grave From the era of its young enthusiasm, we mark its gradual entry upon the stage of fixed habit; from this again we pass to its day of lifeless formalism, and to the rapid progress of its decline. But the Society founded by Jesus Christ is here, still animated by its original idea, still carried forward by the moral impulse which sustained it in its infancy. If Christian doctrine has, in particular branches of the Church, been overlaid by an encrustation of foreign and earthly elements, its body and substance is untouched in each great division of the Catholic Society; and much of it, we rejoice to know, is retained by communities external to the Holy Fold. If intimate union with the worldly power of the State (as especially in England during the last century) has sometimes seemed to chill the warmth of Christian love, and to substitute a heartless externalism for the spiritual life of a Christian brotherhood; yet again and again the flame of that Spirit Whom the Son of Man sent to 'glorify' Himself, has burst up from the depths of the living heart of the Church, and has kindled among a generation of sceptics or sensualists a pure and keen enthusiasm which confessors and martyrs might have recognised as their own. The Church of Christ in sooth carries within herself the secret forces which renew her moral vigour, and which will, in God's good time, visibly reassert her essential unity. Her perpetuated existence among ourselves at this hour bears a witness to the superhuman powers of her Founder, not less significant than that afforded by the intensity of the individual Christian life, or by the territorial range of the Christian empire.

III. The work of Jesus Christ in the world is a patent fact, and it is still in full progress before our eyes. The question remains, How are we to account for its success?

1. If this question is asked with respect to the ascendancy of such a national religion as the popular Paganism of Greece, it is obvious to refer to the doctrine of the prehistoric mythus. The Greek religious creed was, at least in the main, a creation of the national imagination at a period when reflection and experience could scarcely have existed. It was recommended to subsequent generations, not merely by the indefinable charm of poetry which was thrown around it, not merely by the antiquity which shrouded its actual origin, but by its accurate sympathy with the genius as with the degradations of the gifted race which had produced it. But of late years we have heard less of the attempt to apply the doctrine of the mythus to a series of well-

ascertained historical events, occurring in the mid-day light of history, and open to the hostile criticism of an entire people. The historical imagination, steadily applied to the problem, refuses to picture the unimaginable process by which such stupendous 'myths' as those of the Gospel could have been festooned around the simple history of a humble preacher of righteousness [n]. The early Christian Church does not supply the intellectual agencies that could have been equal to any such task. As Rousseau has observed, the inventor of such a history would have been not less wonderful than its Subject [o]; and the utter reversal of the ordinary laws of a people's mental development would have been itself a miracle. Nor was it to be anticipated that a religion which was, as the mythical school asserts, the 'creation of the Jewish race,' would have made itself a home, at the very beginning of its existence, among the Greek and the Roman peoples of the Western world. If however we are referred to the upgrowth and spread of Buddhism, as to a phenomenon which may rival and explain the triumph of Christianity, it may be sufficient to reply that the writers who insist upon this parallel are themselves eminently successful in analysing the purely natural causes of the success of Çakya-Mouni. They dwell among other points on the rare delicacy and fertility of the Aryan imagination [p], and on the absence of any strong counter-attraction to arrest the course of the new doctrine in Central and South-eastern Asia. Nor need we fear to admit, that, mingled with the darkest errors, Buddhism contained elements of truth so undeniably powerful as to appeal with great force to some of the noblest aspirations of the soul of man [q]. But Buddhism, vast as is the population which professes it, has not yet made its way into a second continent; while the religion of Jesus Christ is to be found in every quarter of the globe. As for the rapid and widespread growth of the religion of the False Prophet, it may be explained, partly by the practical

[n] Luthardt, Grundwahrheiten des Christenthums, p. 234.

[o] The well-known words of the Émile are these: 'Jamais des auteurs juifs n'eussent trouvé ce ton ni cette morale; et l'Évangile a des caractères de vérité si grands, si frappants, si parfaitement inimitables, que l'inventeur en serait plus étonnant que le héros.'

[p] Cf. on this point the interesting Essay of M. Taine, Études Critiques, p. 321.

[q] Cf. Saint-Hilaire, Le Bouddha et sa Religion, pp. 142–148. Yet M. St. Hilaire describes Buddhism as presenting 'un spiritualisme sans âme, une vertu sans devoir, une morale sans liberté, une charité sans amour, un monde sans nature et sans Dieu.' Ib. p. 182.

genius of Mohammed, partly by the rare qualities of the Arab race. If it had not claimed to be a new revelation, Mohammedanism might have passed for a heresy adroitly constructed out of the Jewish and Christian Scriptures. Its doctrine respecting Jesus Christ reaches the level of Socinianism [r]; and, as against Polytheism, its speculative force lay in its insistance upon the truth of the Divine Unity. A religion which consecrated sensual indulgence could bid high for an Asiatic popularity against the Church of Christ; and Mohammed delivered the scymetar, as the instrument of his apostolate, into the hands of a people whose earlier poetry shews it to have been gifted with intellectual fire and strength of purpose of the highest order. But it has not yet been asserted that the Church fought her way, sword in hand, to the throne of Constantine; nor were the first Christians naturally calculated to impose their will forcibly upon the civilized world, had they ever desired to do so. Still less is a parallel to the work of Jesus Christ to be found in that of Confucius. Confucius indeed was not a warrior like Mohammed, nor a mystic like Çakya-Mouni; he appealed neither to superior knowledge nor to miraculous power. Confucius collected, codified, enforced, reiterated all that was most elevated in the moral traditions of China; he was himself deeply penetrated with the best ethical sentiments of Chinese antiquity [s]. His success was that of an earnest patriot who was also, as a patriot, an antiquarian moralist. But he succeeded only in China, nor could his work roll back that invasion of Buddhism which took place in the first century of the Christian era. Confucianism is more purely national than Buddhism and Mohammedanism; and in this respect it contrasts more sharply with the world-wide presence of Christianity. Yet if Confucianism is unknown beyond the frontiers of China, it is equally true that neither Buddhism nor Mohammedanism have done more than spread themselves over territories contiguous to their original homes. Whereas, almost within the first century of her existence, the Church had her missionaries in Spain on one hand, and, as it seems, in India on the other; and her Apostle proclaimed that his Master's cause was utterly independent of all distinctions of race and nation [t]. In our own day, Christian charity is freely spending its energies and its blood in efforts to

[r] See Korân, sura 3. The family of Imran. ed. Rodwell, pp. 428-9.
[s] Cf. Max Müller, Chips from a German Workshop, vol. i. p. 308.
[t] Col. iii. 11; Rom. i. 14.

carry the work of Jesus Christ into regions where He has been so stoutly resisted by these ancient and highly organized forms of error. Yet in the streets of London or of Paris we do not hear of the labours of Moslem or Buddhist missionaries, instinct with any such sense of a duty and mission to all the world in the name of truth, as that which animates, at this very hour, those heroic pioneers of Christendom whom Europe has sent to Delhi or to Pekin [u].

2. From the earliest ages of the Church, the rapid progress of Christianity in the face of apparently insurmountable difficulties, has attracted attention, on the score of its high evidential value [v]. The accomplished but unbelieving historian of the Decline and Fall of the Roman Empire undertook to furnish the scepticism of the last century with a systematized and altogether *natural* account of the spread of Christianity [w]. The five 'causes' which he instances as sufficient to explain the work of Jesus Christ in the world are, the 'zeal' of the early Christians, the 'doctrine of a future life,' the 'miraculous powers ascribed to the primitive Church,' the 'pure and austere morals of the first Christians,' and 'the union and discipline of the Christian republic.' But surely each of these causes points at once and irresistibly to a cause beyond itself [x]. If the zeal of the first Christians was, as Gibbon will have it, a fanatical habit of mind inherited from Judaism, how came it not merely to survive, but to acquire a new intensity, when the narrow nationalism which provoked it in the Jew had been wholly renounced? What was it that made the first Christians so zealous amid surrounding lassitude, so holy amid encompassing pollution? Why should the doctrine of a life to come have had a totally different effect

[u] We are indeed told that 'if we were to judge from the history of the last thousand years, it would appear to shew that the permanent area of Christianity is conterminous with that of Western civilization, and that its doctrines could find acceptance only among those who, by incorporation into the Greek and Latin races, have adopted their system of life and morals.' International Policy, p. 508. The Anglo-Positivist school however is careful to explain that it altogether excludes Russia from any share in 'Western civilization;' Russia, it appears, is quite external to 'the West.' Ibid. pp. 14-17, 58, 95, &c.

[v] St. Justin. Dialog. cum Tryph. 117, 121; St. Irenæus, adv. Hær. i. c. 10, § 2; Tertull. adv. Judæos, vii; Apolog. 37; Orig. contr. Celsum, i. 26, ii. 79. Cf. Freppel, Examen Critique, p. 110.

[w] No reader of Gibbon will be misled by the sarcasm of the opening paragraphs of Decl. and Fall, c. xv. Would that Gibbon had really supposed himself to be describing only the 'secondary causes' of the progress of Christianity.

[x] Eclipse of Faith, p. 186.

when proclaimed by the Apostles from any which it had had when taught by Socrates or by Plato, or by other thinkers of the Pagan world? How came it that a few peasants and tradesmen could erect a world-wide organization, sufficiently elastic to adapt itself to the genius of races the most various, sufficiently uniform to be everywhere visibly conservative of its unbroken identity? If the miracles of the early Church, or any one of them, were genuine, how can they avail to explain the *naturalness* of the spread of Christianity? If they were all false, how extraordinary is this spectacle of a moral triumph, such as even Gibbon acknowledges that of Christianity to be, brought about by means of a vast and odious imposition! Gibbon's argument would have been more conclusive if the 'causes' to which he points could themselves have been satisfactorily accounted for in a *natural* way. As it was, the historian of Lausanne did an indirect service to Christendom, of that kind for which England has sometimes been indebted to the threatening preparations of a great military neighbour. Gibbon indicated very clearly the direction which would be taken by modern assailants of the faith; but he is not singular in having strengthened the cause which he sought to ruin, by furnishing an indirect demonstration of the essentially supernatural character of the spread of the Gospel.

3. But you remind me that if the sceptical artillery of Gibbon is out of date, yet the 'higher criticism' of our day has a more delicate, and, as is presumed, a more effective method of stating the naturalistic explanation of the work of Jesus Christ in the world. Jesus Christ, you say, was born at a time when the world itself forced victory upon Him, or at least ensured for Him an easy triumph[y]. The wants and aspirations of a worn-out civilization, the dim but almost universal presentiment of a coming Restorer of mankind, the completed organization of a great world-empire, combined to do this. You urge that it is possible so to correspond to the moral and intellectual drift of a particular period, that nothing but a perverse stupidity can escape a success which is all but inevitable. You add that Jesus Christ 'had this chance' of appearing at a critical moment in

[y] Renan, Les Apôtres, pp. 302, 303. M. Renan is of opinion that 'la conversion du monde aux idées juives (!) et chrétiennes était inévitable:' his only astonishment is that 'cette conversion se soit fait si lentement et si tard.' On the other hand, the new faith is said to have made 'de proche en proche *d'étonnantes* progrès' (Ibid. p. 215); and, with reference to Antioch, 'on *s'étonne* des progrès accomplis en si peu de temps.' Ibid. p. 236.

the history of humanity; and that when the world was ripe for His religion, He and His Apostles had just adroitness enough not to be wholly unequal to the opportunity. The report of His teaching and of His Person was carried on the crest of one of those waves of strange mystic enthusiasm, which so often during the age of the Cæsars rolled westward from Asia towards the capital of the world; and though the Founder of Christianity, it is true, had perished in the surf, His work, you hold, in the nature of things, could not but survive Him.

(*a*) In this representation, my brethren, there is a partial truth which I proceed to recognise. It is true that the world was weary and expectant; it is true that the political fabric of the great empire afforded to the Gospel the same facilities for self-extension as those which it offered to the religion of Osiris, or to the fable of Apollonius Tyanæus. But those favourable circumstances are only what we should look for at the hands of a Divine Providence, when the true religion was to be introduced into the world; and they are altogether unequal to account for the success of Christianity. It is alleged that Christianity corresponded to the dominant moral and mental tendencies [z] of the time so perfectly, that those tendencies secured its triumph. But is this accurate? Christianity was cradled in Judaism; but was the later Judaism so entirely in harmony with the temper and aim of Christianity? Was the age of the Zealots, of Judas the Gaulonite, of Theudas, likely to welcome the spiritual empire of such a teacher as our Lord [a]? Were the moral dispositions of the Jews, their longings for a political Messiah, their fierce legalism, their passionate jealousy for the prerogatives of their race, calculated—I do not say to further the triumph of the Church, but—to enter even distantly into her distinctive spirit and doctrines? Did not the Synagogue persecute Jesus to death, when it had once discerned the real character of His teaching? It may be argued that the favourable dispositions in question which made the success of Christianity practically inevitable were to be found among the Hellenistic Jews [b]. The Hellenistic Jews were less cramped by national prejudices, less strictly observant of the Mosaic ceremonies, more willing to welcome Gentile proselytes than was the case with the Jews of Palestine. Be it so. But the Hellenistic Jews were just as

[z] Renan, Les Apôtres, c. 19, pp. 366, sqq.
[a] Freppel, Examen Critique, p. 114.
[b] Renan, Les Apôtres, c. 6, p. 113.

opposed as the Jews of Palestine to the capital truths of Christianity. A crucified Messiah, for instance, was not a more welcome doctrine in the synagogues of Corinth or of Thessalonica than in those of Jerusalem. Never was Judaism broader, more elastic, more sympathetic with external thought, more disposed to make concessions, than in Philo Judæus, the most representative of Hellenistic Jews. Yet Philo insists as stoutly as any Palestinian Rabbi upon the perpetuity of the law of Moses. As long, he says, as the human race shall endure, men shall carry their offerings to the temple of Jerusalem [c]. Indeed in the first age of Christianity the Jews, both Palestinian and Hellenistic, illustrate, unintentionally of course, but very remarkably, the supernatural law of the expansion of the Church. They persecute Christ in His members, and yet they submit to Him; they are foremost in enriching the Church with converts, after enriching her with martyrs. Wherever the preachers of the Gospel appear, it is the Jews who are their fiercest persecutors [d]; the Jews rouse against them the passions of the Pagan mob, or appeal to the prejudice of the Pagan magistrate [e]. Yet the synagogue is the mission-station from which the Church's action originally radiates; the synagogue, as a rule, yields their first spiritual conquests to the soldiers ot the Cross. In the Acts of the Apostles we remark on the one hand the hatred and opposition with which the Jew met the advancing Gospel, on the other, the signal and rapid conquests of the Gospel among the ranks of the Jewish population [f]. The former fact determines the true significance of the latter. Men do not persecute systems which answer to their real sympathies; St. Paul was not a Christian

[c] De Monarchiâ, lib. ii. § 3, ii. 224: *ἐφ' ὅσον γὰρ τὸ ἀνθρώπων γένος διαμενεῖ, ἀεὶ καὶ αἱ πρόσοδοι τοῦ ἱεροῦ φυλαχθήσονται συνδιαιωνίζουσαι παντὶ τῷ κόσμῳ*: quoted by Freppel.

[d] How far St. Paul thought that Judaism contributed to the triumph of the Church might appear from 1 Thess. ii. 15, 16. Compare Acts xiii. 50, xiv. 5, 19, xvii. 5, 13, xviii. 12, xix. 9, xxii. 21, 22.

[e] Renan, Les Apôtres, p. 143: 'Ce qu'il importe, en tout cas, de remarquer, c'est qu'à l'époque où nous sommes, les persécuteurs du Christianisme ne sont pas les Romains; ce sont les Juifs orthodoxes. . . C'était Rome, ainsi que nous l'avons déjà plusieurs fois remarqué, qui empêchait le Judaïsme de se livrer pleinement à ses instincts d'intolérance, et d'étouffer les développements libres qui se produisaient dans son sein. Toute diminution de l'autorité juive était un bienfait pour la secte naissante.' (p. 251.) See Martyr. St. Polyc. c. 13.

[f] Acts vi. 7. This one text disposes of M. Renan's assertion as to the growth of the Church, that 'les orthodoxes rigides s'y prêtaient peu.' Apôtres, p. 113.

at heart, and without intending it, before his conversion. The Church triumphed in spite of the dominant tendencies and the fierce opposition of Judaism, both in Palestine and elsewhere; she triumphed by the force of her inherent and Divine vitality. The process whereby the Gospel won its way among the Jewish people was typified in St. Paul's experience; the passage from the traditions of the synagogue to the faith of Pentecost cost nothing less than a violent moral and intellectual wrench, such as could be achieved only by a supernatural force, interrupting the old stream of thought and feeling and introducing a new one.

(β) But if success was not forced upon the Christian Church by the dispositions and attitude of Judaism; can it be said that Paganism supplies us with the true explanation of the triumph of the Gospel? What then were those intellectual currents, those moral ideals, those movements, those aspirations, discoverable in the Paganism of the age of the Cæsars, which were in such effective alliance with the doctrine and morality of the New Testament? What was the general temper of Pagan intellect, but a self-asserting, cynical scepticism? Pagan intellect speaks in orators like Cicero [g], publicly deriding the idea of rewards and punishments hereafter, and denying the intervention of a higher Power in the affairs of men [h]; or it speaks in statesmen like Cæsar, proclaiming from his place in the Roman senate that the soul does not exist after death [i]; or in historians like Tacitus, repudiating with self-confident disdain the idea of a providential government of the world [j]; or in poets like Horace, making profession of the practical Atheism of the school of Epicurus, it is hard to say, whether in jest or in earnest [k]; or in men of science like Strabo [l] and Pliny [m], maintaining that religion is a governmental device for keeping the passions of the lower orders under restraint, and that the soul's immortality is a mere dream or nursery-story. 'Unbelief in the official religion,' says

[g] Cicero however, in his speculative moods, was the 'only Roman who undertook to rest a real individual existence of souls after death on philosophical grounds.' Döllinger, Heidenthum und Judenthum, bk. viii. § 3.

[h] Cic. pro Cluentio, c. 61; De Nat. Deor. iii. 32; De Off. iii. 28; De Divin. ii. 17.

[i] Sallust. Catilin. 50-52.

[j] Tacitus, Ann. xvi. 33, vi. 22. Yet see Hist. i. 3, iv. 78.

[k] Hor. Sat. i. 5, 100, sq.; cf. Lucret. v. 83, vi. 57, sq.; Milman, Hist. Christ. i. 41.

[l] Geogr. i. c. 2; cf. Polyb. Hist. Gen. vi. 56.

[m] Plin. vii. 55.

M. Renan, 'was prevalent throughout the educated class. The very statesman who most ostentatiously upheld the public worship of the empire made very amusing epigrams at its expense[n].' What was the moral and social condition of Roman Paganism? Modern unbelief complains that St. Paul has characterized the social morality of the Pagan world in terms of undue severity[o]. Yet St. Paul does not exceed the specific charges of Tacitus, of Suetonius, of Juvenal, of Seneca, that is to say, of writers who, at least, had no theological interest in misrepresenting or exaggerating the facts which they deplore[p]. When Tacitus summarizes the moral condition of Paganism by his exhaustive phrase '*corrumpere et corrumpi*,' he more than covers the sorrowing invective of the Apostle. Indeed our modern historian of the Apostolic age, who sees nothing miraculous in the success of the Gospel[q], has himself characterized the moral condition of the Pagan world in terms yet more severe than those of the Apostle whom he condemns. According to M. Renan, Rome under the Cæsars 'became a school of immorality and cruelty[r];' it was a 'very hell[s];' 'the reproach that Rome had poisoned the world at large, the Apocalyptic comparison of Pagan Rome to a prosti-

[n] Renan, Les Apôtres, pp. 340, 341.

[o] Ibid. p. 309, note 1: 'L'opinion beaucoup trop sévère de Saint Paul (Rom. i. 24 et suiv.) s'explique de la même manière. Saint Paul *ne connaissait pas la haute société Romaine.* Ce sont là, d'ailleurs, de ces invectives comme en font les prédicateurs, et qu'il ne faut jamais prendre à la lettre.' Do the Satires of Juvenal lead us to suppose that if St. Paul had 'known the high society of Rome,' he would have used a less emphatic language? And is it a rule with preachers, whether Apostolic or post-Apostolic, not to mean what they say?

[p] Juvenal, Sat. i. 87, ii. 37, iii. 62, vi. 293. Seneca, Epist. xcvii.; De Benefic. i. 9, iii. 16. Tacitus, Hist. i. 2; Germ. xix. See other quotations in Wetstein, Nov. Test. in loc. It may be that Tacitus, in his affection for the old régime of the republic, was tempted to exaggerate the sins of the empire, and that Juvenal dwelt upon the vices of the capital with somewhat of the narrow prejudice of provincialism. Still, after allowing for this, there is a groundwork of fact in these representations which amply justifies St. Paul.

[q] Renan, Les Apôtres, p. 366: 'Tel était le monde que les missionaires chrétiens entreprirent de convertir. On doit voir maintenant, ce me semble, qu'une telle entreprise ne fut pas une folie, et que sa réussite ne fut pas un miracle.'

[r] Ibid. p. 305.

[s] Ibid. p. 310: 'L'esprit de vertige et de cruauté débordait alors, et faisait de Rome un véritable enfer.' P. 317: 'A Rome, il est vrai, tous les vices s'affichaient avec un cynisme révoltant; les spectacles surtout avaient introduit une affreuse corruption.' This statement is not an exaggeration. See Döllinger, Heidenthum und Judenthum, bk. ix. pt. ii. § 3, 4, pp. 704-721.

tute who had poured forth upon the earth the wine of her immoralities, was in many respects a just comparison[t].' Nor was the moral degradation of Paganism confined to the capital of the great empire. The provinces were scarcely purer than the capital. Each province poured its separate contribution of moral filth into the great store which the increasing centralization of the empire had accumulated in the main reservoir at Rome; each province in turn received its share of this reciprocated corruption[u]. In particular, the East, that very portion of the empire in which the Gospel took its rise, was the main source of the common infection[v]. Antioch was itself a centre of moral putrefaction[w]. Egypt was one of the most corrupt countries in the world; and the same account might be given generally of those districts and cities of the empire in which the Church first made her way, of Greece, and Asia Minor, and Roman Africa, of Ephesus and Corinth, of Alexandria and Carthage. 'The middle of the first century of our era was, in point of fact, one of the worst epochs of ancient history[x].'

But was such an epoch, such a world, such a 'civilization' as this calculated to 'force success' on an institution like 'the kingdom of heaven,' or on a doctrine such as that of the New Testament? If indeed Christianity had been an 'idyll' or 'pastoral,' the product of the simple peasant life and of the bright sky of Galilee, there is no reason why it should

[t] Les Apôtres, p. 325: 'Le reproche d'avoir empoisonné la terre, l'assimilation de Rome à une courtisane qui a versé au monde le vin de son immoralité était juste à beaucoup d'égards.' Yet M. Renan is so little careful about contradicting himself that he elsewhere says, 'Le monde, à l'époque Romaine, accomplit un progrès de moralité et subit une décadence scientifique.' (p. 326.) The nature of this progress seems to have been somewhat Epicurean: 'Le monde s'assouplissait, perdait sa rigeur antique, acquérait *de la mollesse*, et de la sensibilité.' (p. 318.)

[u] Ibid. p. 326: 'La province valait mieux que Rome, ou plutôt les éléments impurs qui de toutes parts s'amassaient à Rome, comme en un égoût, avaient formé là *un foyer d'infection*.'

[v] Ibid. p. 305: 'Le mal venait surtout de l'Orient, de ces flatteurs de bas étage, de ces hommes infâmes que l'Égypte et la Syrie envoyaient à Rome.' P. 306: 'Les plus choquantes ignominies de l'empire, telles que l'apothéose de l'empereur, sa divinisation de son vivant, venaient de l'Orient, et surtout de l'Égypte, qui était alors un des pays les plus corrumpus de l'univers.'

[w] Ibid. p. 218: 'La légèreté Syrienne, le charlatanisme Babylonien, toutes les impostures de l'Asie, se confondant à cette limite des deux mondes avaient fait d'Antioche la capitale du mensonge, la sentine de toutes les infamies.' P. 219: 'L'avilissement des âmes y était effroyable. *Le propre de ces foyers de putréfaction morale, c'est d'amener toutes les races au même niveau.*'

[x] Ibid. p. 343.

not have attracted a momentary interest in literary circles, although it certainly would have escaped from any more serious trial at the hands of statesmen than an unaffected indifference to its popularity. But what was the Gospel as it met the eye and fell upon the ear of Roman Paganism? 'We preach,' said the Apostle, 'Christ Crucified, to the Jews an offence, and to the Greeks a folly [y].' 'I determined not to know anything among you Corinthians, save Jesus Christ, and Him Crucified [z].' Here was a truth linked inextricably with other truths equally 'foolish' in the apprehension of Pagan intellect, equally condemnatory of the moral degradation of Pagan life. In the preaching of the Apostles, Jesus Crucified confronted the intellectual cynicism, the social selfishness, and the sensualist degradation of the Pagan world. To its intellect He said, 'I am the truth [a];' He bade its proud self-confidence bow before His intellectual Royalty. To its selfish, heartless society, careful only for bread and amusement, careless of the agonies which gave interest to the amphitheatre, He said, 'A new commandment give I unto you, that ye love one another, as I have loved you [b].' Disinterested love of slaves, of barbarians, of political enemies, of social rivals, love of man as man, was to be a test of true discipleship. And to the sensuality, so gross, and yet often so polished, which was the very law of individual Pagan life, He said, 'If any man will come after Me, let him deny himself, and take up his cross daily, and follow Me [c];' 'If thine eye offend thee, pluck it out and cast it from thee; it is better for thee that one of thy members should perish, and not that thy whole body should be cast into hell [d].' Sensuality was to be dethroned, not by the negative action of a prudential abstinence from indulgence, but by the strong positive force of self-mortification. Was such a doctrine likely, of its own weight and without any assistance from on high, to win its way to acceptance [e]? Is it not certain that debased souls are so far from aspiring naturally towards that which is holy, elevated and pure, that

[y] 1 Cor. i. 23: *ἡμεῖς δὲ κηρύσσομεν Χριστὸν ἐσταυρουμένον, Ἰουδαίοις μὲν σκάνδαλον, Ἕλλησι δὲ μωρίαν.*

[z] 1 Cor. ii. 2: *οὐ γὰρ ἔκρινα τοῦ εἰδέναι τι ἐν ὑμῖν, εἰ μὴ Ἰησοῦν Χριστὸν, καὶ τοῦτον ἐσταυρωμένον.*

[a] St. John xiv. 6.

[b] Ibid. xiii. 34.

[c] St. Matt. xvi. 24; St. Mark viii. 34.

[d] St. Matt. xviii. 9; St. Mark ix. 47.

[e] M. Renan himself observes that 'la dégradation des âmes en Égypte y rendait rares, d'ailleurs, les aspirations qui ouvririent partout (!) au christianisme de si faciles accès.' Les Apôtres, p. 284.

they feel towards it only hatred and repulsion? Certainly Rome was unsatisfied with her old national idolatries; but if she turned her eyes towards the East, it was not to welcome the religion of Jesus, but the impure rites of Isis and Serapis, of Mithra and Astarte. The Gospel came to her unbidden, in obedience to no assignable attraction in Roman society, but simply in virtue of its own expansive, world-embracing force. Certainly Christianity answered to the moral wants of the world, as it really answers at this moment to the true moral wants of all human beings, however unbelieving or immoral they may be. The question is, whether the world so clearly recognised its real wants as forthwith to embrace Christianity. The Physician was there; but did the patient know the nature of his own malady sufficiently well not to view the presence of the Physician as an intrusion? Was it likely that the old Roman society, with its intellectual pride, its social heartlessness, and its unbounded personal self-indulgence, should be enthusiastically in love with a religion which made intellectual submission, social unselfishness, and personal mortification, its very fundamental laws? The history of the three first centuries is the answer to that question. The kingdom of God was no sooner set up in the Pagan world than it found itself surrounded by all that combines to make the progress of a doctrine or of a system impossible. The thinkers were opposed to it: they denounced it as a dream of folly[f]. The habits and passions of the people were opposed to it: it threatened somewhat rudely to interfere with them. There were venerable institutions, coming down from a distant antiquity, and gathering around them the stable and thoughtful elements of society: these were opposed to it, as to an audacious innovation, as well as from an instinctive perception that it might modify or destroy themselves. National feeling was opposed to it: it flattered no national self-love; it was to be the home of human kind; it was to embrace the world; and as yet the nation was the highest conception of associated life to which humanity had reached. Nay, religious feeling itself was opposed to it; for religious feeling had been enslaved by ancient falsehoods. There were worships, priesthoods, beliefs,

[f] Tac. Ann. xv. 44: 'Repressa in præsens exitiabilis superstitio rursus erumpebat.' Suetonius, Claudius, xxv.; Nero, xvi.: 'Christiani, genus hominum superstitionis novæ ac maleficæ.' Celsus apud Origenem, iii. 17. Celsus compared the Church's worship of our Lord with the Egyptian worship of cats, crocodiles, &c.

in long-established possession; and they were not likely to yield without a struggle. Picture to yourselves the days when the temple of the Capitoline Jupiter was still thronged with worshippers, while often the Eucharist could only be celebrated in the depths of the Catacombs. It was a time when all the administrative power of the empire was steadily concentrated upon the extinction of the Name of Christ. What were then to a human eye the future prospects of the kingdom of God? It had no allies, like the sword of the Mahommedan, or like the congenial mysticism which welcomed the Buddhist, or like the politicians who strove to uphold the falling Paganism of Rome. It found no countenance even in the Stoic moralists[g]; they were indeed among its fiercest enemies. If, as M. Renan maintains, it ever was identified by Pagan opinion, with the *cœtus illiciti*, with the *collegia illicita*, with the burial-clubs of the imperial epoch; this would only have rendered it more than ever an object of suspicion to the government[h]. Between the new doctrine and the old Paganism there was a deadly feud; and the question for the Church was simply whether she could suffer as long as her enemies could persecute. Before she could triumph in the western world, the soil of the empire had to be reddened by Christian blood. Ignatius of Antioch given to the lions at Rome[i]; Polycarp of Smyrna

[g] Döllinger, Heidenth. und Judenth., bk. ix. pt. 2. § 6. has some very interesting remarks on the characteristics of the later Stoicism. It was a recoil from the corruption of the time. 'Wie die Aerzte in Zeiten grosser Krankheiten ihre besten Studien machen, so hatten auch die Stoiker in dem allgemein herrschenden Sittenverderben ihren moralischen Blick geschärft.' p. 729. Seneca's knowledge of the human heart, the pathos and solemnity of M. Aurelius, the self-control, patience, and self-denying courage preached by Epictetus and Arrian, are fully acknowledged. But Stoicism was virtue upon paper, unrealized except in the instance of a few coteries of educated people. It was virtue, affecting Divine strength in the midst of human weakness. Nothing could really be done for humanity by 'diesen selbstgefälligen Tugendstolz, der alles nur sich selbst verdanken wollte, der sich der Gottheit gleich setzte, und bei aller menschlichen Gebrechlichkeit doch die Sicherheit der Gottheit für sich in Anspruch nahm.' (Sen. Ep. 53.) Stoicism had no lever with which to raise man as man from his degradations: and its earlier expositors even prescribed suicide as a means of escape from the miseries of life, and from a sense of moral failure. (Döll. ubi supra, p. 728; comp. Sir A. Grant's Ethics of Arist. vol. i. p. 272.) Who can marvel at its instinctive hatred of a religion which proclaimed a higher code of Ethics than its own, and which, moreover, possessed the secret of teaching that code practically to all classes of mankind?

[h] Les Apôtres, pp. 355, 361, 362.

[i] A. D. 107.

condemned to the flames[j]; the martyrs of Lyons and Vienne, and among them the tender Blandina[k], extorting by her fortitude the admiration of the very heathen; Perpetua and Felicitas at Carthage[l] conquering a mother's love by a stronger love for Christ[m];—these are but samples of the 'noble army' which vanquished heathendom. 'Plures efficimur,' cries Tertullian, spokesman of the Church in her exultation and in her agony, 'quoties metimur a vobis; semen est sanguis Christianorum[n].' To the heathen it seems a senseless obstinacy; but with a presentiment of the coming victory, the Apologist exclaims, 'Illa ipsa obstinatio quam exprobatis, magistra est[o].'

Who was He That had thus created a moral force which could embrace three centuries of a protracted agony, in the confidence that victory would come at last[p]? What was it in Him, so fascinating and sustaining to the thought of His followers, that for Him men and women of all ages and ranks in life gladly sacrificed all that is dearest to man's heart and nature? Was it only His miracles? But the evidential force of miracle may be easily evaded. St. John's Gospel appears to have been written with a view to furnishing, among other things, an authoritative explanation of the moral causes which actually prevented the Jews from recognising the significance of our Lord's miracles. Was it simply His character? But to understand a perfect character you must be attracted to it, and have some strong sympathies with it. And the language of human nature in the presence of superior goodness is often that of the Epicurean in the Book of Wisdom: 'Let us lie in wait for the righteous, because he is not for our turn, and he is clean contrary to our doings. . . . . . He was made to reprove our thoughts; he is grievous unto us even to behold; for his life is not like other men's, his ways are of another fashion[q].' Was it His teaching? True, never man spake like this Man; but taken alone, the highest and holiest teaching might have seemed to humanity to be no more than 'the sound of one that had a pleasant voice,

[j] A. D. 169. [k] A. D. 177.
[l] A. D. 202. [m] So Dionysia in Alexandria; Eus. H. E. vi. 41.
[n] Apol. c. 50. [o] Ibid.
[p] M. Renan observes scornfully, 'Il n'y a pas eu beaucoup de martyrs très-intelligents.' Apôtres, p. 382. Possibly not, if intelligence is but another name for scepticism. Certain it is that martyrdom requires other and higher qualities than any which mere intelligence can supply.
[q] Wisd. ii. 12, 15.

and could play well upon an instrument.' His Death? Certainly He predicted that in dying He would draw all men unto Him; but Who was He That could thus turn the instrument of His humiliation into the certificate of His glory? His Resurrection? His Resurrection indeed was emphatically to be the reversal of a false impression, but it was to witness to a truth beyond itself; our Lord had expressly predicted that He would rise from the grave, and that His Resurrection would attest His claims[r]. None of these things taken separately will account for the power of Christ in history. In the convergence of all these; of these majestic miracles; of that Character, which commands at once our love and our reverence; of that teaching, so startling, so awful, so searching, so tender; of that Death of agony, encircled with such a halo of moral glory; of that deserted tomb, and the majestic splendour of the Risen One;—a deeper truth, underlying all, justifying all, explaining all, is seen to reveal itself. We discern, as did the first Christians, beneath and beyond all that meets the eye of sense and the eye of conscience, the Eternal Person of our Lord Himself. It is not the miracles, but the Worker; not the character, but its living Subject; not the teaching, but the Master; not even the Death or the Resurrection, but He Who died and rose, upon Whom Christian thought, Christian love, Christian resolution ultimately rest. The truth which really and only accounts for the establishment in this our human world of such a religion as Christianity, and of such an institution as the Church, is the truth that Jesus Christ was believed to be more than Man, the truth that Jesus Christ is what men believed Him to be, the truth that Jesus Christ is God[s].

It is here that we are enabled duly to estimate one broad feature of the criticism of Strauss. Both in his earlier and scientific work, published some thirty years ago for scholars, and in his more recent publication addressed to the German people, that writer strips Jesus Christ our Lord of all that makes Him superhuman. Strauss eliminates from the Gospel most of Christ's discourses, all of His miracles, His supernatural Birth, and His Resurrection from the grave. The so-termed 'historical' residuum might easily be compressed within the limits of a newspaper paragraph, and it retains nothing that can rouse a moderate measure, I do not say of enthusiasm, but even of interest. And

[r] St. Matt. xii. 39; Rom. i. 4.
[s] Cf. Milman, Hist. Christ. i. 50; Pusey, Univ. Sermons, 1859–1872, p. 28.

[LECT

yet few minds on laying down either of these unhappy books can escape the rising question: 'Is this hero of a baseless legend, this impotent, fallible, erring Christ of the "higher criticism," in very deed the Founder of the Christian Church?' The difficulty of accounting for the phenomenon presented by the Church, on the supposition that the 'historical' account of its Founder is that of Dr. Strauss, does not present itself forcibly to an Hegelian, who loses himself in *à priori* theories as to the necessary development of a thought, and is thus entranced in a sublime forgetfulness of the actual facts and laws of human life and history. But here M. Renan is unwittingly a witness against the writer to whom he is mainly indebted for his own critical apparatus. The finer political instinct, the truer sense of the necessary proportions between causes and effects in human history, which might be expected to characterize a thoughtful Frenchman, will account for those points in which M. Renan has departed from the path traced by his master. He feels that there is an impassable chasm between the life of Jesus according to Strauss, and the actual history of Christendom. He is keenly alive to the absurdity of supposing that such an impoverished Christ as the Christ of Strauss, can have created Christendom. Although therefore, as we have seen, he subsequently[t] endeavours to account for the growth of the Church in a naturalistic way, his native sense of the fitting proportions of things impels him to retouch the picture traced by the German, and to ascribe to Jesus of Nazareth, if not the reality, yet some shadowy semblance of Divinity[u]. Hence such features of M. Renan's work as his concessions in respect of St. John's Gospel. In making these concessions, he is for the moment impressed with the political absurdity of ascribing Christendom to the thought and will of a merely human Christ. Although his unbelief is too radical to allow him to do adequate justice to such a consideration, his indirect admission of its force has a value, to which Christian believers will not be insensible.

But a greater than M. Renan is said to have expressed the common-sense of mankind in respect of the Agency which alone can account for the existence of the Christian Church. If the first Napoleon was not a theologian, he was at least a man whom vast experience had taught what kind of forces can really produce a lasting effect upon mankind, and under what conditions they may be expected to do so. A time came when the good Provi-

[t] In his later work, Les Apôtres. [u] Vie de Jésus, pp. 250, 426, 457.

dence of God had chained down that great but ambitious spirit to the rock of St. Helena; and the conqueror of civilized Europe had leisure to gather up the results of his unparalleled life, and to ascertain with an accuracy, not often attainable by monarchs or warriors, his own true place in history. When conversing, as was his habit, about the great men of the ancient world, and comparing himself with them, he turned, it is said, to Count Montholon with the enquiry, 'Can you tell me who Jesus Christ was?' The question was declined, and Napoleon proceeded, 'Well, then, I will tell you. Alexander, Cæsar, Charlemagne, and I myself have founded great empires; but upon what did these creations of our genius depend? Upon force. Jesus alone founded His empire upon love, and to this very day millions would die for Him. . . . . I think I understand something of human nature; and I tell you, all these were men, and I am a man: none else is like Him; Jesus Christ was more than man. . . I have inspired multitudes with such an enthusiastic devotion that they would have died for me, . . but to do this it was necessary that I should be *visibly* present with the electric influence of my looks, of my words, of my voice. When I saw men and spoke to them, I lighted up the flame of self-devotion in their hearts. . . . Christ alone has succeeded in so raising the mind of man towards the Unseen, that it becomes insensible to the barriers of time and space. Across a chasm of eighteen hundred years, Jesus Christ makes a demand which is beyond all others difficult to satisfy; He asks for that which a philosopher may often seek in vain at the hands of his friends, or a father of his children, or a bride of her spouse, or a man of his brother. He asks for the human heart; He will have it entirely to Himself. He demands it unconditionally; and forthwith His demand is granted. Wonderful! In defiance of time and space, the soul of man, with all its powers and faculties, becomes an annexation to the empire of Christ. All who sincerely believe in Him, experience that remarkable supernatural love towards Him. This phenomenon is unaccountable; it is altogether beyond the scope of man's creative powers. Time, the great destroyer, is powerless to extinguish this sacred flame; time can neither exhaust its strength nor put a limit to its range. This is it which strikes me most; I have often thought of it. This it is which proves to me quite convincingly the Divinity of Jesus Christ [v].'

[v] This is freely translated from the passages quoted by Luthardt, Apologetische Vorträge, pp. 234, 293; and Bersier, Serm. p. 334. The same conversation is given substantially by Chauvelot, Divinité du Christ, pp. 11–13,

Here surely is the common-sense of humanity. The victory of Christianity is the great standing miracle which Christ has wrought. Its significance is enhanced if the miracles of the New Testament are rejected[x], and if the Apostles are held to have received no illumination from on high[y]. Let those in our day who believe seriously that the work of Christ may be accounted for on natural and human grounds, say who among themselves will endeavour to rival it. Who of our contemporaries will dare to predict that eighteen hundred years hence his ideas, his maxims, his institutions, however noble or philanthropic they may be, will still survive in their completeness and in their vigour? Who can dream that his own name and history will be the rallying-point of a world-wide interest and enthusiasm in some distant age? Who can suppose that beyond the political, the social, the intellectual revolutions which lie in the future of humanity, he will himself still survive in the memory of men, not as a trivial fact of archæology, but as a moral power, as the object of a devoted and passionate affection?

Paris 1863; in a small brochure attributed to M. le Pasteur Bersier, and published by the Religious Tract Society, Napoléon, Meyrueis, Paris, 1859; by M. Auguste Nicolas, in his Études Philosophiques sur le Christianisme, Bruxelles, 1849, tom. ii. pp. 352–356; and by the Chevalier de Beauterne in his Sentiment de Napoléon sur le Christianisme, édit. par M. Bathild Bouniol, Paris 1864, pp. 87–118. In the preface to General Bertrand's Campagnes d'Égypte et de Syrie, there is an allusion to some reported conversations of Napoleon on the questions of the existence of God and of our Lord's Divinity, which, the General says, never took place at all. But M. de Montholon, who with General Bertrand was present at the conversations which are recorded by the Chevalier de Beauterne, writes from Ham on May 30, 1841, to that author: 'J'ai lu avec un vif intérêt votre brochure; *Sentiment de Napoléon sur la Divinité de Jésus-Christ*, et je ne pense pas qu'il soit possible de mieux exprimer les croyances religieuses de l'empereur.' Sentiment de Napoléon, Avertissem. p. viii. Writing, as it would seem, in ignorance of this testimony, M. Nicolas says: 'Cité plusieurs fois et dans des circonstances solennelles, ce jugement passe généralement pour historique.' Études, ii. p. 352, note (1).

[x] 'Se il mondo si rivolse al cristianesmo
Diss' io, senza miracoli, quest' uno
È tal, che gli altri non sono il centesmo;
Che tu entrasti povero e digiuno
In campo, a seminar la buona pianta,
Che fu già vite, ed ora è fatta pruno.'
Dante, Paradiso, xxiv. 106–111.

[y] 'Apres la mort de Jésus-Christ, douze pauvres pêcheurs et artisans entreprirent d'instruire et de convertir le monde. . . . le succès fut prodigieux . . . . Tous les chrétiens couraient au martyre, tous les peuples couraient au baptême; l'histoire de ces premiers temps était *un prodige continuel*.' Rousseau, Réponse au Roi de Pologne, Paris, 1829, Discours, pp. 64, 65.

What man indeed that still retains, I will not say the faith of a Christian, but the modesty of a man of sense, must not feel that there is a literally infinite interval between himself and that Majestic One, Who, in the words of Jean Paul Richter, 'being the Holiest among the mighty, and the Mightiest among the holy, has lifted with His pierced Hand empires off their hinges, has turned the stream of centuries out of its channel, and still governs the ages[z]?'

The work of Jesus Christ is not merely a fact of history, it is a fact, blessed be God! of individual experience. If the world is one scene of His conquests, the soul of each true Christian is another. The soul is the microcosm within which, in all its strength, the kingdom of God is set up. Many of you know, from a witness that you can trust, Christ's power to restore to your inward life its original harmony. You are conscious that He is the fertilizing and elevating principle of your thought, the purifying principle of your affections, the invigorating principle of your wills. You need not to ask the question 'whence hath this Man this wisdom and these mighty works?' Man, you are well assured, cannot thus from age to age enlarge the realm of moral light, and make all things new; man cannot thus endow frail natures with determination, and rough natures with tenderness, and sluggish natures with keen energy, and restless natures with true and lasting peace. These every-day tokens of Christ's presence in His kingdom, of themselves answer the question of the text. If He Who could predict that by dying in shame He would secure the fulfilment of an extraordinary plan, and assure to Himself a world-wide empire, can be none other than the Lord of human history; so certainly the Friend, the Teacher, the Master Who has fathomed and controlled our deepest life of thought and passion, is welcomed by the Christian soul as something more than a student exploring its mysteries, or than a philanthropic experimentalist alleviating its sorrows. He is hailed, He is loved, He is worshipped, as One Who possesses a knowledge and a strength which human study and human skill fail to compass; it is felt that He is so manifestly the true Saviour of the soul, because He is none other than the Being Who made it.

[z] Jean Paul: 'Ueber den Gott in der Geschichte und im Leben.' Sämmtl. Werke, xxxiii. 6; Stirm. p. 194.

LECTURE IV.

OUR LORD'S DIVINITY AS WITNESSED BY HIS CONSCIOUSNESS.

The Jews answered Him, saying, For a good work we stone Thee not; but for blasphemy; and because that Thou, being a Man, makest Thyself God.—St. John x. 33.

It is common with some modern writers to represent the questions at issue between the Faith and its opponents, in respect of the Person of our Lord, as being substantially a question between the 'historical spirit' and the spirit of dogmatism. The dogmatic temper is painted by them as a baseless but still powerful superstition, closely pressed by the critical enquiries and negative conclusions of our day, but culpably shutting its eyes against the advancing truth, the power of which nevertheless it cannot but instinctively feel, and clinging with the wrong-headed obstinacy of despair to the cherished but already condemned formulæ of its time-honoured and worn-out metaphysics. Opposed to it, we are told, is the 'historical spirit,' young, vigorous, fearless, truthful, flushed with successes already achieved, assured of successes yet to come. The 'historical spirit' is thus said to represent the cause of an enlightened progress in conflict with a stupid and immoral conservatism. The 'historical spirit' is described as the love of sheer reality, as the longing for hard fact, determined to make away with all 'idols of the den,' however ancient, venerated, and influential, in the sphere of theology. The 'historical spirit' accordingly undertakes to 'disentangle the real Person of Jesus from the metaphysical envelope' within which theology is said to have 'encased' Him. The Christ is to be rescued from that cloud-land of abstract and fanciful speculation, to which He is stated to have been banished by the patristic and scholastic divines; He is to be restored to Christendom in manifest subjection to all the actual conditions and laws of human history. 'Look,' it is said, 'at that figure of the Christ which you see traced in mosaics in the apsis of a Byzantine church.

That Countenance upon which you gaze, with its rigid, unalterable outline, with its calm, strong mien of unassailable majesty; that Form from which there has been stripped all the historic circumstance of life, all that belongs to the changes and chances of our mortal condition; what is it but an artistic equivalent and symbol of the Catholic dogma? Elevated thus to a world of unfading glory, and throned in an imperturbable repose, the Byzantine Christos Pantocrator must be viewed as the expression of an idea, rather than as the transcript of a fact. A certain interest may be allowed to attach to such a representation, from its illustrating a particular stage in the development of religious thought. But the "historical spirit" must create what it can consider a really "historical" Christ, who will be to the Christ of St. Athanasius and St. John what a Rembrandt or a Rubens is to a Giotto or a Cimabue.' If the illustration be objected to, at any rate, my brethren, the aim of the so-termed 'historical' school is sufficiently plain. It proposes to fashion a Christ who is to be æsthetically graceful and majestic, but strictly natural and human. This Christ will be emancipated from the bandages which 'supernaturalism has wrapped around the Prophet of Nazareth.' He will be divorced from any idea of incarnating essential Godhead; but, as we are assured, He will still be something, aye more than the Christ of the Creed has ever been yet, to Christendom. He will be at once a living man, and the very ideal of humanity; at once a being who obeys the invincible laws of nature, like ourselves, yet of moral proportions so mighty and so unrivalled that his appearance among men shall adequately account for the phenomenon of an existing and still expanding Church.

Accordingly by this representation it is intended to place us in a dilemma. 'You must choose,' men seem to say, 'between history and dogma; you must choose between history which can be verified, and dogma which belongs to the sphere of inaccessible abstractions. You must make your choice; since the Catholic dogma of Christ's Divinity is pronounced by the higher criticism to be irreconcileable with the historical reality of the Life of Jesus.' And in answer to that challenge, let us proceed, my brethren, to choose history, and as a result of that choice, if it may be, to maintain that the Christ of history is either the God Whom we believers adore, or that He is far below the assumed moral level of the mere man, whose character rationalism still, at least generally, professes to respect in the pages of its mutilated Gospel.

For let us observe that the Catholic doctrine has thus much in its favour:—it takes for granted the only existing history of Jesus Christ. It is not compelled to mutilate or to enfeeble it, or to do it critical violence. It is in league with this history; it is at home, as is no other doctrine, in the pages of the Evangelists.

Consider, first of all, the general impression respecting our Lord's Person, which arises upon a survey of the miracles ascribed to Him in all the extant accounts of His Life. To a thoughtful Humanitarian, who believes in the preternatural elements of the Gospel history, our Lord's miracles, taken as a whole, must needs present an embarrassing difficulty. The miraculous cures indeed, which, more particularly in the earlier days of Christ's ministry, drew the eyes of men towards Him, as to the Healer of sickness and of pain, have been 'explained,' however unsatisfactorily, by the singular methods generally accepted among the older rationalists. A Teacher, it used to be argued, of such character as Jesus Christ, must have created a profound impression; He must have inspired an entire confidence; and the cures which He seemed to work were the immediate results of the impression which He created; they were the natural consequences of the confidence which He inspired. Now, apart from other and many obvious objections to this theory, let us observe that it is altogether inapplicable to the 'miracles of power,' as they are frequently termed, which are recorded by the three first Evangelists, no less than by St. John. 'Miracles of this class,' says a freethinking writer, 'are not cures which could have been effected by the influence of a striking sanctity acting upon a simple faith. They are prodigies; they are, as it seems, works which Omnipotence Alone could achieve. In the case of these miracles it may be said that the laws of nature are simply suspended. Jesus does not here merely exhibit the power of moral and mental superiority over common men; He upsets and goes beyond the rules and bounds of the order of the universe. A word from His mouth stills a tempest. A few loaves and fishes are fashioned by His Almighty hand into an abundant feast, which satisfies thousands of hungry men. At His bidding life returns to inanimate corpses. By His curse a fig-tree which had no fruit on it is withered up[a].' The writer

[a] Schenkel, Charakterbild Jesu, p. 21. Dr. Schenkel concludes: 'Sonst erscheint Jesus in den drei ersten Evangelien durchgängig als ein wahrer, innerhalb der Grenzen menschlicher Beschränkung sich bewegender Mensch; durch Seine Wunderthätigkeit werden diese Grenzen durchbrochen; Allmachtswunder sind menschlich nicht mehr begreiflich.'

proceeds to argue that such miracles must be expelled from any Life of Christ which 'criticism' will condescend to accept. They belong, he contends, to that 'torrent of legend,' with which, according to the rationalistic creed, Jesus was surrounded after His Death by the unthinking enthusiasm of His disciples [b]. But then a question arises as to how much is to be included within this legendary 'torrent.' In particular, and above all else, is the Resurrection of Jesus Christ from the grave to be regarded as a part of its contributions to the Life of Christ? Here there is a division among the rationalizing critics. There are writers who reject our Lord's miracles of power, His miraculous Conception, and even His Ascension into heaven, and who yet shrink from denying that very fundamental fact of all, the fact that on 'the third day He rose from the dead, according to the Scriptures [c].' A man must have made up his mind against Christianity more conclusively than men are generally willing to avow, if he is to speculate with M. Renan in the face of Christendom, as to the exact spot in which 'the worms consumed the lifeless body' of Jesus [d]. This explicit denial of the literal Resurrection of Jesus from the grave is not compensated for by some theory identical with, or analogous to, that of Hymenæus and Philetus [e] respecting the general Resurrection, whereby the essential subject of Christ's Resurrection is changed, and the idea of Christianity, or the soul of the converted Christian, as distinct from the Body of the Lord Jesus, is said to have been raised from the dead. For such a denial, let us mark it well, of the literal Resurrection of the Human Body of Jesus involves nothing less than an absolute and total rejection of Christianity. All orthodox Churches, all the great heresies, even Socinianism, have believed in the Resurrection of Jesus. The literal Resurrection of Jesus was the cardinal

[b] Schenkel, Charakterbild Jesu, p. 21: 'Dass ein Lebensbild, wie dasjenige des Erlösers, bald nach dessen irdischem Hinscheiden von einem reichen Sagenstrom umflossen wurde, liegt in der Natur der Sache.' It may be asked—Why? If these legendary decorations are the inevitable consequences of a life of devotion to moral truth and to philanthropy, how are we to explain their absence in the cases of so many moralists and philanthropists ancient and modern?

[c] Cf. Hase, Leben Jesu, p. 281, compared with p. 267.

[d] Les Apôtres, p. 38: 'Pendant que la conviction inébranlable des Apôtres se formait, et que la foi du monde se préparait, en quel endroit les vers consumaient-ils le corps inanimé qui avait été, le samedi soir, déposé au sépulcre? On ignorera toujours ce détail; car, naturellement, les traditions chrétiennes ne peuvent rien nous apprendre là-dessus.'

[e] 2 Tim. ii. 18: Ὑμέναιος καὶ Φίλητος, οἵτινες περὶ τὴν ἀλήθειαν ἠστόχησαν, λέγοντες τὴν ἀνάστασιν ἤδη γεγονέναι. 1 Tim. i. 20.

fact upon which the earliest preachers of Christianity based their appeal to the Jewish people[f]. St. Paul, writing to a Gentile Church, expressly makes Christianity answer with its life for the literal truth of the Resurrection. 'If Christ be not risen, then is our preaching vain, and your faith is also vain. . . Then they also which are fallen asleep in Christ are perished[g].' Some modern writers would possibly have reproached St. Paul with offering a harsh alternative instead of an argument. But St. Paul would have replied, first, that our Lord's honour and credit were entirely staked upon the issue, since He had foretold His Resurrection as the 'sign' which would justify His claims[h]; and secondly, that the fact of the Resurrection was attested by evidence which must outweigh everything except an *à priori* conviction of the impossibility of miracle, since it was attested by the word of more than two hundred and fifty living persons who had actually seen the Risen Jesus[i]. As to objections to miracle of an *à priori* character, St. Paul would have argued, as most Theists, and even the French philosopher, have argued, that such objections could not be urged by any man who believed seriously in a *living* God at all[j]. But on the other hand, if the Resur-

[f] Acts i. 22, ii. 24, 32, iii. 15, iv. 10, v. 30, x. 40, xiii. 30, 33, 34, xvii. 31.

[g] 1 Cor. xv. 14, 18.

[h] St. Matt. xii. 39, 40.

[i] 1 Cor. xv. 6: Ἔπειτα ὤφθη ἐπάνω πεντακοσίοις ἀδελφοῖς ἐφάπαξ, ἐξ ὧν οἱ πλείους μένουσιν ἕως ἄρτι, τινὲς δὲ καὶ ἐκοιμήθησαν. It is quite arbitrary to say that 'the Resurrection with Paul is by no means a human corporeal resurrection as with the Evangelists,' that 'his ὤφθη κἀμοί implies no more than a flash and a sound, which he interpreted as a presence of Christ.' (Westm. Rev. Oct. 1867, p. 529.) On this shewing, the ὤφθη Σίμωνι in St. Luke xxiv. 34 might similarly be resolved into an illusion. The ἑωράκαμεν of St. John xx. 25 might be as unreal as the ἑώρακα of 1 Cor. ix. 1. Contrast with the positive tone of 1 Cor. xv. 6 the measured hesitation of 2 Cor. xii. 2. It is also a mere assumption to say that a 'palpable body' could not be seen at once by 500 persons; and the suggestion that St. Paul's own belief in 'a continued celestial life of Christ,' and in the moral resurrection of Christians was 'afterwards materialized' into 'the history of a bodily resurrection of Christ, and the expectation of a bodily resurrection of mankind from the grave,' is nothing less than to fasten upon the Apostle the pseudo-spiritualistic error, against which in this chapter he so passionately contends. On this subject, see 'The Resurrection of Jesus Christ,' by R. Macpherson, D.D., pp. 127, 346; Pressensé, Jesus Christ, pp. 660–665.

[j] 'Dieu peut-Il faire des miracles, c'est à dire, peut-Il déroger aux lois, qu'Il a établies? Cette question sérieusement traitée serait impie, si elle n'était absurde. Ce serait faire trop d'honneur à celui, qui la resoudrait negativement, que de le punir; il suffirait de l'enfermer. Mais aussi, quel homme a jamais nié, que Dieu pût faire des miracles?' Rousseau, Lettres écrites de la Montagne, Lettre iii.

rection be admitted to be a fact, it is puerile to object to the other miracles of Jesus, or to any other Christian miracles, provided they be sufficiently attested. To have admitted the stupendous truth that Jesus, after predicting that He would be put to a violent death, and then rise from the dead, was actually so killed, and then did actually so rise, must incapacitate any thoughtful man for objecting to the supernatural Conception or to the Ascension into heaven, or to the more striking wonders wrought by Jesus, on any such ground as that of intrinsic improbability. The Resurrection has, as compared with the other miraculous occurrences narrated in the Gospels, all the force of an *à fortiori* argument; they follow, if we may use the term, naturally from it; they are fitly complemental incidents of a history in which the Resurrection has already made it plain, that we are dealing with One in Whose case our ordinary experience of the limits and conditions of human power is altogether at fault.

But if the miracles of Jesus be admitted in the block, as by a 'rational' believer in the Resurrection they must be admitted; they do point, as I have said, to the Catholic belief, as distinct from any lower conceptions respecting the Person of Jesus Christ. They differ from the miracles of prophets and Apostles in that, instead of being answers to prayer, granted by a Higher Power, they manifestly flow forth from the majestic Life resident in the Worker[k]. And instead of presenting so many 'difficulties' which have to be surmounted or set aside, they are in entire harmony with that representation of our Saviour's Personal glory which is embodied in the Creeds. St. John accordingly calls them Christ's 'works,' meaning that they were just such acts as might be expected from Him, being such as He was. For our Lord's miracles are something more than evidences that He was the organ of a Divine revelation. They do not merely secure a deferential attention to His disclosures respecting the nature of God, the duty and destiny of man, His own Person, mission, and work. Certainly they have this properly evidential force; He Himself appealed to them as having it[l]. But it would be difficult altogether to account for their form, or for their varieties, or for the times at which they were wrought, or for the motives which were actually assigned for working them, on the supposition that their value was only evidential. They are like the kind deeds of the wealthy, or the good advice of the

[k] Wilberforce on the Incarnation, p. 91, note 11. Christian Remembrancer, Oct. 1863, p. 274.

[l] St. John x. 38.

[LECT.

wise; they are like that debt of charity which is due from the possessors of great endowments to suffering humanity. Christ as Man owed this tribute of mercy which His Godhead had rendered it possible for Him to pay, to those whom (such was His love) He was not ashamed to call His brethren. But besides this, Christ's miracles are physical and symbolic representations of His redemptive action as the Divine Saviour of mankind. Their form is carefully adapted to express this action. By healing the palsied, the blind, the lame, Christ clothed with a visible form His plenary power to cure spiritual diseases, such as the weakness, the darkness, the deadly torpor of the soul. By casting out devils from the possessed, He pointed to His victory over the principalities and powers of evil, whereby man would be freed from their thraldom and restored to moral liberty[m]. By raising Lazarus from the corruption of the grave, He proclaimed Himself not merely a Revealer of the Resurrection, but the Resurrection and the Life itself. The drift and meaning of such a miracle as that in which our Lord's 'Ephphatha' brought hearing and speech to the deaf and dumb is at once apparent when we place it in the light of the Sacrament of baptism[n]. The feeding of the five thousand is remarkable as the one miracle which is narrated by all the Evangelists; and even the least careful among readers of the Gospel cannot fail to be struck with the solemn actions which precede the wonder-work, as well as by the startling magnificence of the result. Yet the permanent significance of that extraordinary scene at Bethsaida Julias is never really understood, until our Lord's great discourse in the synagogue of Capernaum, which immediately follows it, is read as the spiritual exposition of the physical miracle, which is thus seen to be a commentary, palpable to sense, upon the vital efficacy of the Holy Communion[o].

[m] St. Matt. xii. 28; St. Luke xi. 20.

[n] St. Mark viii. 34, 35.

[o] Compare St. John vi. 26–59; and observe the correspondence between the actions described in St. Matt. xiv. 19, and xxvi. 26. The deeper Lutheran commentators are noticeably distinguished from the Calvinistic ones in recognising the plain Sacramental reference of St. John vi. 53, sqq. See Stier, 'Reden Jesu,' in loc.; Olshausen, Comm. in loc.; Kahnis, H. Abendmahl, p. 104, sqq. For the ancient Church, see St. Chrys. Hom. in loc.; Tertull. De Orat. 6; Clem. Alex. Pædagog. I. vi. p. 123; St. Cyprian, De Oratione Dominicâ, p. 192; St. Hilary, De Trin. viii. 14, cited in Wilb. H. Euch. p. 199. The Church of England authoritatively adopts the sacramental interpretation of the passage by her use of it in the Exhortation at the time of the celebration of the Holy Communion. 'The benefit is great,

In our Lord's miracles then we have before us something more than a set of credentials; since they manifest forth His Mediatorial Glory. They exhibit various aspects of that redemptive power whereby He designed to save lost man from sin and death; and they lead us to study, from many separate points of view, Christ's majestic Personality, as the Source of the various wonders which radiate from it. And assuredly such a study can have but one result for those who honestly believe in the literal reality of the wonders described; it must force upon them a conviction of the Divinity of the worker [p].

if with a true penitent heart and lively faith we receive that Holy Sacrament: for *then* we spiritually eat the Flesh of Christ and drink His Blood; *then* we dwell in Christ and Christ in us; we are one with Christ and Christ with us.' Cf. too the 'Prayer of Humble Access.'

[p] It may be urged that Socinians have been earnest believers in the Resurrection and other preternatural facts of the Life of Christ, while explicitly denying His Godhead. This is true; but it is strictly true only of past times, or of those of our contemporaries who are more or less inaccessible, happily for themselves, to the intellectual influences of modern scepticism. It would be difficult to find a modern Socinian of high education who believed in the literal truth of all the miraculous incidents recorded in the Gospels. This is not merely a result of modern objections to miracle; it is a result of the connexion, more clearly felt, even by sceptics, than of old, between the admission of miracles and the obligation to admit attendant dogma. In his Essay on Channing, M. Renan has given expression to this instinct of modern sceptical thought. 'Il est certain,' he observes, 'que si l'esprit moderne a raison de vouloir une religion, qui, sans exclure le surnaturel, en diminue la dose autant que possible, la religion de Channing est la plus parfaite et la plus épurée qui ait paru jusqu'ici. Mais est-ce là tout, en vérité, et quand le symbole sera réduit à croire à Dieu et au Christ, qu'y aura-t-on gagné? Le scepticisme se tiendra-t'il pour satisfait? La formule de l'univers en sera-t-elle plus complète et plus claire? La destinée de l'homme et de l'humanité moins impénétrable? Avec son symbole épuré, Channing évite-t-il mieux que les théologiens catholiques les objections de l'incrédulité? Hélas! non. Il admet la résurrection de Jésus-Christ, et n'admet pas sa Divinité; il admet le Bible, et n'admet pas l'enfer. Il déploie toutes les susceptibilités d'un scholastique pour établir contre les Trinitaires, en quel sens le Christ est fils de Dieu, et en quel sens il ne l'est pas. Or, *si l'on accorde qu'il y a eu une Existence réelle et miraculeuse d'un bout à l'autre, pourquoi ne pas franchement l'appeler Divine?* L'un ne demande pas un plus grand effort de croyance que l'autre. En vérité, dans cette voie, il n'y a que le premier pas qui coute; il ne faut pas marchander avec le surnaturel; la foi va d'une seule pièce, et, le sacrifice accompli, il ne sied pas de réclamer en détail les droits dont on a fait une fois pour toutes l'entière cession.' Études d'Histoire Religieuse, pp. 377, 378. Who would not rather, a thousand times over, have been Channing than be M. Renan? Yet is it not clear that, half a century later, Channing must have believed much less, or, as we may well trust, much more, than was believed by the minister of Federal-street Chapel, Boston?

But the miracles which especially point to the Catholic doctrine as their justification, and which are simply incumbrances blocking up the way of a Humanitarian theorist, are those of which our Lord's Manhood is itself the subject. According to the Gospel narrative, Jesus enters this world by one miracle, and He leaves it by another. His human manifestation centres in that miracle of miracles, His Resurrection from the grave after death. The Resurrection is the central fact up to which all leads, and from which all radiates. Such wonders as Christ's Birth of a Virgin-mother, His Resurrection from the tomb, and His Ascension into heaven, are not merely the credentials of our redemption, they are distinct stages and processes of the redemptive work itself. Taken in their entirety, they interpose a measureless interval between the Life of Jesus and the lives of the greatest of prophets or of Apostles, even of those to whom it was given to still the elements and to raise the dead. To expel these miracles from the Life of Jesus is to destroy the identity of the Christ of the Gospels; it is to substitute a new Christ for the Christ of Christendom. Who would recognise the true Christ in the natural son of a human father, or in the crucified prophet whose body has rotted in an earthly grave? Yet on the other hand, who will not admit that He Who was conceived of the Holy Ghost and born of a Virgin-mother, Who, after being crucified, dead, and buried, rose again the third day from the dead, and then went up into heaven before the eyes of His Apostles, must needs be an altogether superhuman Being? The Catholic doctrine then is at home among the facts of the Gospel narrative by the mere fact of its proclaiming a superhuman Christ, while the modern Humanitarian theories are ill at ease among those facts. The four Evangelists, amid their distinguishing peculiarities, concur in representing a Christ Whose Life is encased in a setting of miracles. The Catholic doctrine meets these representations more than half-way; they are in sympathy with, if they are not admitted to anticipate, its assertion. The Gospel miracles point at the very least to a Christ Who is altogether above the range of human experience; and the Creeds recognise and confirm this indication by saying that He is Divine. Thus the Christ of dogma is the Christ of history: He is the Christ of the only extant history which describes the Founder of Christendom at all. He may not be the Christ of some modern commentators upon that history; but these commentators do not affect to take the history as it has come down to us. As the Gospel narratives stand, they present a block of difficulties to Humanitarian theories; and these difficulties can only be removed by mutilations of the narratives so wholesale and radical as to destroy their substantial interest, besides rendering the retention of the fragments which may be retained, a purely arbitrary procedure. The Gospel narratives describe the Author of Christianity as the Worker and the subject of extraordinary miracles; and these miracles are such as to afford a natural lodgment for, nay, to demand as their correlative, the doctrine of the Creed. That doctrine must be admitted to be, if not the divinely authorized explanation, at least the best intellectual conception and *résumé* of the evangelical history. A man need not be a believer in order to admit, that in asserting Christ's Divinity we make a fair translation of the Gospel story into the language of abstract thought; and that we have the best key to that story when we see in it the doctrine that Christ is God, unfolding itself in a series of occurrences which on any other supposition seem to wear an air of nothing less than legendary extravagance.

It may—it probably will—be objected to all this, that a large number of men and women at the present day are on the one hand strongly prepossessed against the credibility of all miracles whatever, while on the other they are sincere 'admirers' of the moral character of Jesus Christ. They may not wish explicitly and in terms to reject the miraculous history recorded in the Gospels; but still less do they desire to commit themselves to an unreserved acceptance of it. Whether from indifference to miraculous occurrences, or because their judgment is altogether in suspense, they would rather keep the preternatural element in our Lord's Life out of sight, or shut their eyes to it. But they are open to the impressions which may be produced by the spectacle of high ethical beauty, if only the character of Christ can be disentangled from a series of wonders, which, as transcending all ordinary human experience, do not touch the motives that compel their assent to religious truth. Accordingly we are warned, that if it is not a piece of spiritual thoughtlessness, and even cruelty, it is at any rate a rhetorical mistake to insist upon a consideration so opposed to the intellectual temper of the time.

This is what may be urged: but let it be observed, that the objector assumes a point which should rather have been proved. He assumes the possibility of putting forward an honest picture of the Life of Jesus, which shall uphold the beauty, and even the perfection of His moral character, while denying the historical reality of His miracles, or at any rate while ignoring them. Whereas, if the only records which we possess of the Life of Jesus are to be believed at all, they make it certain that Jesus Christ did claim to work, and was Himself the embodiment of, startling miracles[q]. How can this fact be dealt with by a modern disbeliever in the miraculous? Was Christ then the ignorant victim and promoter of a crude superstition? Or was He, as M. Renan considers, passive and unresisting, while credited with working wonders which He knew to be merely thaumaturgic tricks[r]? On either supposition, is it possible to uphold Him as 'the moral ideal of humanity,' or indeed as the worthy object of any true moral enthusiasm? We cannot decline this question; it is forced upon us by the subject-matter. A neutral attitude towards the miraculous element in the Gospel history is impossible. The claim to work miracles is not the least prominent element of our Lord's teaching; nor are the miracles which are said to have been wrought by Him a fanciful or ornamental appendage to His action. The miraculous is inextricably interwoven with the whole Life of Christ. The ethical beauty, nay the moral integrity of our Lord's character is dependent, whether we will it or not, upon the reality of His miracles. It may be very desirable to defer as far as possible to the mental prepossessions of our time; but it is not practicable to put asunder two things which God has joined together, namely, the beauty of Christ's character and the *bonâ fide* reality of the miracles which He professed to work.

But let us nevertheless follow the lead of this objection by turning to consider what is the real bearing of our Lord's moral character upon the question of His Divinity. In order to do this, it is necessary to ask a previous question. What position did Jesus Christ, either tacitly or explicitly, claim to occupy in His intercourse with men? What allusions did He make to the subject of His Personality? You will feel, my brethren, that it

[q] Ecce Homo, p. 43: 'On the whole, miracles play so important a part in Christ's scheme, that any theory which would represent them as due entirely to the imagination of His followers or of a later age, destroys the credibility of the documents, not partially, but wholly, and leaves Christ a personage as mythical as Hercules.'

[r] Cf. Vie de Jésus, p. 265: 'Il est donc permis de croire qu'on lui imposa sa réputation de thaumaturge, *qu'il n'y résista pas beaucoup*, mais qu'il ne fit rien non plus pour y aider, et qu'en tout cas, il sentait la vanité de l'opinion à cet égard. Ce serait manquer à la bonne méthode historique d'écouter trop ici nos répugnances.' See M. Renan's account of the raising of Lazarus, ibid. pp. 361, 362.

is impossible to overrate the solemn importance of such a point as this. We are here touching the very heart of our great subject: we have penetrated to the inmost shrine of Christian truth, when we thus proceed to examine those words of the Gospels which exhibit the consciousness of the Founder of Christianity respecting His rank in the scale of being. With what awe, yet with what loving eagerness, must not a Christian enter on such an examination!

No reader of the Gospels can fail to see that, speaking generally, and without reference to any presumed order of the events and sayings in the Gospel history, there are two distinct stages or levels in the teaching of Jesus Christ our Lord.

I. Of these the first is mainly concerned with primary fundamental moral truth. It is in substance a call to repentance, and the proclamation of a new life. It is summarized in the words, 'Repent ye, for the kingdom of heaven is at hand[s].' A change of mind, both respecting self, and respecting God, was necessary before a man could lead the new life of the kingdom of heaven. In a previous lecture we have had occasion to consider the kingdom of heaven as the outline or plan of a world-wide institution which was to take its place in history. But viewed in its relation to the life of the soul, the kingdom of heaven is the home and the native atmosphere of a new and higher order of spiritual existence. This new life is not merely active thought, such as might be stimulated by the cross-questioning of a Socrates; nor is it moral force, the play of which was limited to the single soul that possessed it. It is moral and mental life, having God and men for its objects, and accordingly lived in an organized society, as the necessary counterpart of its energetic action. Of this stage of our Lord's preaching, the Sermon on the Mount is the most representative document. The Sermon on the Mount preaches penitence by laying down the highest law of holiness. It contrasts the externalized devotion, the conventional and worldly religion of the time, created and sanctioned by the leading currents of public opinion, and described as the righteousness of the Scribes and Pharisees, with a new and severe ideal of morality, embodied in the new law of Christian perfection. It stimulates and regulates penitence, by proposing a new conception of blessedness; by contrasting the spirit of the new law with the literalism of the old; by exhibiting the devotional duties, the ruling motives, the characteristic temper, and the special dangers

[s] St. Matt. iv. 17.

of the new life. Incidentally the Sermon on the Mount states certain doctrines, such as that of the Divine Providence, with great explicitness[t]; but, throughout it, the moral element is predominant. This great discourse quickens and deepens a sense of sin by presenting the highest ideal of an inward holiness. In the Sermon on the Mount our Lord is laying broad and deep the foundations of His spiritual edifice. A pure and loving heart; an open and trustful conscience; a freedom of communion with the Father of spirits; a love of man as man, the measure of which is to be nothing less than a man's love of himself; above all a stern determination, at any cost, to be true, true with God, true with men, true with self;—such are the pre-requisites for genuine discipleship; such the spiritual and subjective bases of the new and Absolute Religion; such the moral material of the first stage of our Lord's public teaching.

In this first stage of our Lord's teaching let us moreover note two characteristics.

(*a*) And first, that our Lord's recorded language is absolutely wanting in a feature, which, on the supposition of His being merely human, would seem to have been practically indispensable. Our Lord does not place before us any relative or lower standard of morals. He proposes the highest standard; He enforces the absolute morality. 'Be ye therefore perfect,' He says, 'even as your Father Which is in Heaven is perfect[u].' Now in the case of a human teacher of high moral and spiritual attainments, what should we expect to be a necessary accompaniment of this teaching? Surely we should expect some confession of personal unworthiness thus to teach. We should look for some trace of a feeling (so inevitable in this pulpit) that the message which must be spoken is the rebuke, if not the condemnation, of the man who must speak it. Conscious of many shortcomings, a human teacher must at some time relieve his natural sense of honesty, his fundamental instinct of justice, by noting the discrepancy between his weak, imperfect, perhaps miserable self, and his sublime and awful message. He must draw a line, if I may so speak, between his official and his personal self; and in his personal capacity he must honestly, anxiously, persistently associate himself with his hearers, as being before God, like each one of themselves, a learning, struggling, erring soul. But Jesus Christ makes no approach to such a distinction between Himself

[t] St. Matt. vi. 25–33. [u] Ibid. v. 48.

and His message. He bids men be like God, and He gives not the faintest hint that any trace of unlikeness to God in Himself obliges Him to accompany the delivery of that precept with a protestation of His own personal unworthiness. Do you say that this is only a rhetorical style or mood derived by tradition from the Hebrew prophets, and natural in any Semitic teacher who aspired to succeed them? I answer, that nothing is plainer in the Hebrew prophets than the clear distinction which is constantly maintained between the moral level of the teacher and the moral level of His message. The prophetic ambassador represents the Invisible King of Israel; but the holiness of the King is never measured, never compromised by the imperfections of His representative. The prophetic writings abound in confessions of weakness, in confessions of shortcomings, in confessions of sin. The greatest of the prophets is permitted to see the glory of the Lord, and he forthwith exclaims in agony, 'Woe is me! for I am undone; because I am a man of unclean lips, and I dwell in the midst of a people of unclean lips: for mine eyes have seen the King, the Lord of Hosts [v].'

But the silence of Jesus respecting any such sense of personal unworthiness has been accounted for by the unrivalled closeness of His life-long communion with God. Is it then certain that the holiest souls are least alive to personal sin? Do they whose life of thought is little less than the breath of a perpetual prayer, and who dwell continuously in the presence-chamber of the King of kings, profess themselves insensible to that taint of sin, from which none are altogether free? Is this the lesson which we learn from the language of the best of the servants of God? My brethren, the very reverse is the case. Those who have lived nearest to God, and have known most about Him, and have been most visibly irradiated by the light of His countenance, have been foremost to acknowledge that the 'burden' of remaining imperfection in themselves was truly 'intolerable.' Their eager protestations have often seemed to the world to be either the exaggerations of fanaticism, or else the proof of a more than ordinary wickedness. For blemishes which might have passed unobserved in a spiritual twilight, are lighted up with torturing clearness by those searching, scorching rays of moral truth, that stream from the bright Sanctity of God upon the soul that beholds It. In that Presence the holiest of creatures must own with the Psalmist, 'Thou hast set our misdeeds before Thee, and

[v] Isa. vi. 5.

our secret sins in the light of Thy countenance [x].' Such self-accusing, broken-hearted confessions of sin have been the utterances of men the most conspicuous in Christendom for holiness of life; and no true saint of God ever supposed that by a constant spiritual sight of God the soul would lose its keen truthful sense of personal sinfulness. No man could presume that this sense of sinfulness, as distinct from the sense of unpardoned guilt, would be banished by close communion with God, unless his moral standard was low, and his creed imperfect. Any such presumption is utterly inconsistent with a true sight of Him Whose severe and stainless beauty casts the shadow of failure upon all that is not Himself, and Who charges His very angels with moral folly.

Yet Jesus Christ never once confesses sin; He never once asks for pardon. Is it not He, Who so sharply rebukes the self-righteousness of the Pharisee? Might He not seem to ignore all human piety that is not based upon a broken heart? Does He not deal with human nature at large as the true prodigal, who must penitently return to a Father's love as the one condition of its peace and bliss? Yet He Himself never lets fall a hint, He Himself never breathes a prayer, which implies any, the slightest trace, of a personal remorse [y]. From no casual admission do we gather that any, the most venial sin, has ever been His. Never for one moment does He associate Himself with any passing experience of that anxious dread of the penal future with which His own awful words must needs fill the sinner's heart. If His Soul is troubled, at least His moral sorrows are not His own, they are a burden laid on Him by His love for others. Nay, He challenges His enemies to convince Him of sin. He declares positively that He does always the will of the Father [z]. Even when speaking of Himself as Man, He always refers to eternal life as His inalienable possession. It might, so perchance we think, be the illusion of a moral dulness, if only He did not penetrate the sins of others with such relentless analysis. It might, we imagine, be a subtle pride, if we did not know Him to be so unrivalled in His great humility [a]. This consciousness

[x] Ps. xc. 8. Perowne observes that no New Testament writer ever applies Old Testament confessions of sinfulness to Jesus Christ. Psalms, i. p. 54. Cf. Mozley, Lectures, p. 125.

[y] Heb. vii. 27, where τοῦτο can only refer to ὑπὲρ τῶν τοῦ λαοῦ ἀναφέρειν: cf. ὅσιος, ἄκακος, κ.τ.λ., ver. 26.

[z] St. John viii. 46, ibid. ver. 29, cf. ver. 26; cf. Lect. I. p. 23. note h.

[a] Hollard, Caractère de Jésus-Christ, p. 150. Cf. also Ullmann, Sündlosigkeit, Th. I. Kap. 3. § 4. The frivolous objections to our Lord's

of an absolute sinlessness in such a Soul as that of Jesus Christ, points to a moral elevation unknown to our actual human experience. It is, at the very least, suggestive of a relation to the Perfect Moral Being altogether unique in human history[b].

sinlessness which are urged from St. Luke ii. 41–52, St. Matt. xxi. 12–17, and 17–22, and from His relation to Judas, are discussed in this work, Th. III. Kap. 1. § 4. This interesting writer however, while asserting *non peccâsse* of our Lord, falls short of Catholic truth in denying to Him the '*non posse peccare.*' The objections advanced by M. F. Pecant in his *Le Christ et la Conscience*, 1859, are plainly a result of that writer's Humanitarianism. Our Lord's answers to His Mother, His cursing the barren fig-tree, His sending the devils into the herd of swine, His driving the money-changers from the temple, and His last denunciations against the Pharisees, present no difficulty to those who see in Him the Lord, as well as the Son of Mary, the Maker and Owner of the world of nature, the Searcher and Judge of human hearts. Cf. also note C.

[b] Cf. Mr. F. W. Newman, in his Phases of Faith, p. 143: 'We have a very imperfect history of the Apostle James; and I do not know that I could adduce any fact specifically recorded concerning him in disproof of his absolute moral perfection, if any of his Jerusalem disciples had chosen to set up this as a dogma of religion. Yet no one would blame me as morose, or indisposed to acknowledge genius and greatness, if I insisted on believing James to be frail and imperfect, while admitting that I knew almost nothing about him. And why? Singly and surely, because we know him to be *a man*: that suffices. To set up James or John or Daniel as my model and my Lord; to be swallowed up in him, and press him upon others as a universal standard, would be despised as a self-degrading idolatry, and resented as an obtrusive favouritism. Now why does not the same equally apply if the name Jesus be substituted for these? Why, in defect of all other knowledge than the bare fact of his manhood, are we not unhesitatingly to take for granted that he does *not* exhaust all perfection, and is at best only one amongst many brethren and equals?' The answer is that we have to choose between believing in Christ's moral perfection, and condemning Him of being guilty either of spiritual blindness or hypocrisy (see Ullmann, ubi sup.); and that His teaching, His actions, and (Mr. Newman will allow us to add) His supernatural credentials, taken together, make believing Him to be sinless the easier alternative. But Mr. Newman's remarks are of substantial value, as indirectly shewing, from a point of view much further removed from Catholic belief than Socinianism itself, how steadily a recognition of our Lord's moral perfection as Man tends to promote an acceptance of the truth that He is GOD. 'If,' says Mr. Newman, 'I were already convinced that this person [he means our Lord] was a great Unique, separated from all other men by an impassable chasm in regard to his physical origin, I (for one) should be much readier to believe *that he was unique and unapproachable in other respects*; for all God's works have an internal harmony. It could not be for nothing that this exceptional personage was sent into the world. That he was intended for head of the human race in one or more senses, would be a plausible opinion; nor should I feel any incredulous repugnance against believing his morality to be, if not divinely perfect, yet separated from that of common men so far *that he might be a God to us*, just as every parent is to a young child.' Ibid. p. 142.

(β) The other characteristic of this stage of our Lord's teaching is the attitude which He at once and, if I may so say, naturally assumes, not merely towards the teachers of His time, but towards the letter of that older, divinely-given Revelation which they preserved and interpreted. The people early remarked that Jesus 'taught as One having authority, and not as the Scribes[c].' The Scribes reasoned, they explained, they balanced argument against argument, they appealed to the critical or verifying faculty of their hearers. But here is a Teacher, Who sees truth intuitively, and announces it simply, without condescending to recommend it by argument. He is a Teacher, moreover, not of truth obvious to all, but of truth which might have seemed to the men who first heard it to be what we should call paradoxical. He condemns in the severest language the doctrine and the practice of the most influential religious authorities among His countrymen. He takes up instinctively a higher position than He assigns to any who had preceded Him in Israel. He passes in review, and accepts or abrogates not merely the traditional doctrines of the Jewish schools, but the Mosaic law itself. His style runs thus: 'It was said *to* them of old time, . . . but I say unto you[d].'

Here too it is necessary to protest against statements which imply that this authoritative teaching of Jesus was merely a continuation of the received prophetical style. It is true that the prophets gave prominence to the moral element in the teaching of the Pentateuch, that they expanded it, and that so far they anticipated one side of the ministry of Jesus Himself. But the prophets always appealed to a higher sanction; the prophetic argument addressed to the conscience of Israel was ever, 'Thus saith the Lord.' How significant, how full of import as to His consciousness respecting Himself is our Lord's customary phrase, 'Verily, I say unto you[e].' What prophet ever set himself above the great Legislator, above the Law written by the finger of God on Sinai? What prophet ever undertook to ratify the Pentateuch as a whole, to contrast his own higher morality with some of its precepts in detail, to imply even remotely that he was competent to revise that which every Israelite knew to be the handiwork of God? What prophet ever

[c] St. Matt. vii. 29.

[d] Ibid. v. 27. For the translation of τοῖς ἀρχαίοις, see Archbishop Trench on Auth. Vers. of New Testament, p. 79.

[e] ἀμὴν λέγω, κ.τ.λ. occurs forty-nine times in the Synoptic Gospels; in St. John ἀμὴν, ἀμὴν, twenty-five times.

thus implicitly placed himself on a line of equality, not with Moses, not with Abraham, but with the Lord God Himself? So momentous a claim requires explanation if the claimant be only human. This impersonation of the source of moral law must rest upon some basis: what is the basis on which it rests?

In the Sermon on the Mount Jesus Christ does not deign to justify His lofty critical and revisionary attitude towards the ancient Law. He neither explains nor exaggerates His power to review the older revelation, and to reveal new truth. He simply teaches; He abrogates, He establishes, He sanctions, He unfolds, as the case may be, and in a tone which implies that His right to teach is not a matter for discussion.

It was inevitable that the question should be asked, anxiously, earnestly, fiercely, 'Who is This Teacher?' I say, it was inevitable, for if you teach the lowest moral truth, in the humblest sphere, your right to do so will sooner or later be called in question. To teach moral truth is to throw down a challenge to human nature, human nature being such as it actually is, that is to say, conscious of more or less disloyalty to the moral light which it already possesses, and indisposed to become responsible for knowledge of a yet higher standard of moral truth, the existence of which it may already suspect. Accordingly the challenge which is thus made is generally met by a sharp counter-scrutiny into the claims, be they personal or official, of the teacher who dares to make it. This penalty of teaching can only be escaped either in certain rare and primitive conditions of society, or else when the teacher fails to do his duty. Missionaries have described savage tribes whose sense of ignorance was too sincere, and who were too grateful for knowledge, to take umbrage at the practical bearings of a new doctrine. Poets have sung of ancestors

> 'Qui præceptorem sancti voluere parentis
> Esse loco[f].'

Generally speaking, however, an immunity from criticism is to be secured by signal inefficiency, feebleness, or disloyalty to principle, on the part of the teacher. A teacher of morals may have persuaded his conscience that the ruling worldly opinion of his time can safely be regarded as its court of final appeal. He may have forced his thought to shape itself with prudent docility into those precise conventionalities of expression which are understood to mean nothing, or which have lost their power. In such a

[f] Juv. vii. 209.

case too it may happen that the total failure to achieve moral and spiritual victories will not necessarily entail on the teacher complete social or professional obscurity, while it will certainly protect him against any serious liability to hostile interference.

Picture to yourselves, on the contrary, a teacher who is not merely under the official obligation to say something, but who is morally convinced that he has something to say. Imagine one who believes alike in the truth of his message and in the reality of his mission to deliver it. Let his message combine those moral contrasts which give permanency and true force to a doctrine, and which the Gospel alone has combined in their perfection. Let this teacher be tender, yet searching; let him win the hearts of men by his kindly humanity, while he probes, aye to the quick, their moral sores. Let him be uniformly calm, yet manifestly moved by the fire of repressed passion. Let him be stern yet not unloving, and resolute without sacrificing the elasticity of his sympathy, and genial without condescending to be the weakly accomplice of moral mischief. Let him pursue and expose the latent evil of the human heart through all the mazes of its unrivalled deceitfulness, without sullying his own purity, and without forfeiting his strong belief in the present capacity of every human being for goodness. Let him 'know what is in man,' and yet, with this knowledge clearly before him, let him not only not despair of humanity, but respect it, nay love it, even enthusiastically. Above all, let this teacher be perfectly independent. Let him be independent of the voice of the multitude; independent of the enthusiasm and promptings of his disciples; independent even when face to face with the bitter criticism and scorn of his antagonists; independent of all save God and his conscience. In a word, conceive a case in which moral authority and moral beauty combine to elicit a simultaneous tribute of reverence and of love. Clearly such a teacher must be a moral power; and as a consequence, his claim to teach must be scrutinized with a severity proportioned to the interest which he excites, and to the hostility which he cannot hope to escape provoking. And such a Teacher, or rather much more than this, was Jesus Christ our Lord.

Nor is this all. The scrutiny which our Lord thus necessarily encountered from without was responded to, or rather it was anticipated, by self-discovery from within. 'The soul,' it has been said, 'like the body, has its pores;' and in a sincere soul the pores of its life are always open. Instinctively, unconsciously, and whether a man will or not, the insignificance or the greatness of the inner life always reveals itself. In our Lord this self-revelation was not involuntary, or accidental, or forced; it was in the highest degree deliberate. He knew the thoughts of those about Him, and He anticipated their expression. He placed beyond a doubt, by the most explicit statements, that which might have been more than suspected, if He had only preached the Sermon on the Mount.

II. It is characteristic then of what may be termed the second stage of our Lord's public teaching, that He distinctly, repeatedly, energetically preaches Himself. He does not leave men to draw inferences about Himself from the power of His moral teaching, or from the awe-inspiring nature of His miracles. He does not content Himself with teaching primary moral truths concerning God and our duties towards God and towards one another. He does not bequeath to His Apostles the task of elaborating a theory respecting the Personal rank of their Master in the scale of being. On the contrary, He Himself persistently asserts the real character of His position relatively to God and man, and of His consequent claims upon the thought and heart of mankind. Whether He employs metaphor, or plain unmetaphorical assertion, His meaning is too clear to be mistaken. He speaks of Himself as the Light of a darkened world[g], as the Way by which man may ascend to heaven[h], as the Truth which can really satisfy the cravings of the soul[i], as the Life which must be imparted to all who would live in very deed, to all who would really live for ever[j]. Life is resident in Him in virtue of an undefined and eternal communication of it from the Father[k]. He is the Bread of Life[l]. He is the Living Bread That came down from heaven[m]; believers in Him will feed on Him and will have eternal life[n]. He points to a living water of the Spirit, which He can give, and which will quench the thirst

[g] St. John viii. 12: Ἐγώ εἰμι τὸ φῶς τοῦ κόσμου· ὁ ἀκολουθῶν ἐμοὶ οὐ μὴ περιπατήσει ἐν τῇ σκοτίᾳ, ἀλλ' ἕξει τὸ φῶς τῆς ζωῆς.

[h] Ibid. xiv. 6: Ἐγώ εἰμι ἡ ὁδός.

[i] Ibid.: Ἐγώ εἰμι . . . ἡ ἀλήθεια. Mark xiii. 31: ὁ οὐρανὸς καὶ ἡ γῆ παρελεύσονται· οἱ δὲ λόγοι μου οὐ μὴ παρέλθωσι. [παρελεύσονται, Tisch.]

[j] St. John xiv. 6: Ἐγώ εἰμι . . . . ἡ ζωή.

[k] Ibid. v. 26: ὥσπερ γὰρ ὁ Πατὴρ ἔχει ζωὴν ἐν ἑαυτῷ, οὕτως ἔδωκε καὶ τῷ υἱῷ ζωὴν ἔχειν ἐν ἑαυτῷ.

[l] Ibid. vi. 35: Ἐγώ εἰμι ὁ ἄρτος τῆς ζωῆς. Ibid. ver. 48.

[m] Ibid. ver. 51: Ἐγώ εἰμι ὁ ἄρτος ὁ ζῶν ὁ ἐκ τοῦ οὐρανοῦ καταβάς.

[n] Ibid. ver. 47: ἀμὴν ἀμὴν λέγω ὑμῖν, ὁ πιστεύων εἰς ἐμὲ, ἔχει ζωὴν αἰώνιον. Ibid. v. 40: οὐ θέλετε ἐλθεῖν πρός με, ἵνα ζωὴν ἔχητε.

of souls that drink it[o]. All who came before Him He characterizes as having been, by comparison with Himself, the thieves and robbers of mankind[p]. He is Himself the One Good Shepherd of the souls of men[q]; He knows and He is known of His true sheep[r]. Not only is He the Shepherd, He is the very Door of the sheepfold; to enter through Him is to be safe[s]. He is the Vine, the Life-tree of regenerate humanity[t]. All that is truly fruitful and lovely in the human family must branch forth from Him[u]; all spiritual life must wither and die, if it be severed from His[x]. He stands consciously between earth and heaven. He claims to be the One Means of a real approach to the Invisible God: no soul of man can come to the Father but through Him[y]. He promises that all prayer offered in His Name shall be answered: 'If ye ask anything in my Name *I* will do it[z].' He contrasts Himself with a group of His countrymen as follows: 'Ye are from beneath, I am from above; ye are of this world, I am not of this world[a].' He anticipates His Death, and foretells its consequences: 'I, if I be lifted up from the earth, will draw all men unto Myself[b].' He claims to be the Lord of the realm of death; He will Himself wake the sleeping dead; all that are in the graves shall hear His voice[c]; nay, He will raise Himself from the dead[d]. He proclaims, 'I am the Resurrection and the Life[e].' He encourages men to trust

[o] St. John iv. 14: ὃς δ' ἂν πίῃ ἐκ τοῦ ὕδατος οὗ ἐγὼ δώσω αὐτῷ, οὐ μὴ διψήσει εἰς τὸν αἰῶνα.

[p] Ibid. x. 8: πάντες ὅσοι πρὸ ἐμοῦ ἦλθον, κλέπται εἰσὶ καὶ λῃσταί.

[q] Ibid. ver. 11: Ἐγώ εἰμι ὁ ποιμὴν ὁ καλός. Ibid. ver. 14.

[r] Ibid. ver. 14: γινώσκω τὰ ἐμὰ, καὶ γινώσκομαι ὑπὸ τῶν ἐμῶν.

[s] Ibid. ver. 9: Ἐγώ εἰμι ἡ θύρα· δι' ἐμοῦ ἐάν τις εἰσέλθῃ, σωθήσεται.

[t] Ibid. xv. 1: Ἐγώ εἰμι ἡ ἄμπελος ἡ ἀληθινή.

[u] Ibid. ver. 5: ὁ μένων ἐν ἐμοὶ κἀγὼ ἐν αὐτῷ, οὗτος φέρει καρπὸν πολύν· ὅτι χωρὶς ἐμοῦ οὐ δύνασθε ποιεῖν οὐδέν.

[x] Ibid. ver. 6: ἐὰν μή τις μείνῃ ἐν ἐμοὶ, ἐβλήθη ἔξω ὡς τὸ κλῆμα, καὶ ἐξηράνθη.

[y] Ibid. xiv. 6: οὐδεὶς ἔρχεται πρὸς τὸν Πατέρα, εἰ μὴ δι' ἐμοῦ.

[z] Ibid. ver. 14: ἐάν τι αἰτήσητε ἐν τῷ ὀνόματί μου, ἐγὼ ποιήσω.

[a] Ibid. viii. 23: ὑμεῖς ἐκ τῶν κάτω ἐστὲ, ἐγὼ ἐκ τῶν ἄνω εἰμί· ὑμεῖς ἐκ τοῦ κόσμου τούτου ἐστὲ, ἐγὼ οὐκ εἰμὶ ἐκ τοῦ κόσμου τούτου.

[b] Ibid. xii. 32: κἀγὼ ἐὰν ὑψωθῶ ἐκ τῆς γῆς, πάντας ἑλκύσω πρὸς ἐμαυτόν.

[c] Ibid. v. 28, 29: ἔρχεται ὥρα, ἐν ᾗ πάντες οἱ ἐν τοῖς μνημείοις ἀκούσονται τῆς φωνῆς αὐτοῦ, καὶ ἐκπορεύσονται. Ibid. vi. 39, xi. 25.

[d] Ibid. ii. 19: λύσατε τὸν ναὸν τοῦτον, καὶ ἐν τρισὶν ἡμέραις ἐγερῶ αὐτόν. Ibid. x. 18: ἐξουσίαν ἔχω θεῖναι αὐτὴν [τὴν ψυχήν μου], καὶ ἐξουσίαν ἔχω πάλιν λαβεῖν αὐτήν.

[e] Ibid. xi. 25: Ἐγώ εἰμι ἡ ἀνάστασις καὶ ἡ ζωή.

in Him as they trust in God[f]; to make Him an object of faith just as they believe in God[g]; to honour Him as they honour the Father[h]. To love Him is a necessary mark of the children of God: 'If God were your Father, ye would have loved Me[i].' It is not possible, He rules, to love God, and yet to hate Himself: 'He that hateth Me, hateth My Father also[j].' The proof of a true love to Him lies in doing His bidding: 'If ye love Me, keep *My* commandments[k].'

Of this second stage of our Lord's teaching the most representative document is the Discourse in the supper-room. How great is the contrast between that discourse and the Sermon on the Mount! In the Sermon on the Mount, which deals with questions of human character and of moral obligation, the reference to our Lord's Person is comparatively indirect. It lies, not in explicit statements, but in the authority of His tone, in the attitude which He tacitly assumes towards the teachers of the Jewish people, and towards the ancient Law. In the last discourse it is His Person rather than His teaching which is especially prominent; His subject in that discourse is Himself. Certainly He preaches Himself in His relationship to His redeemed; but still He preaches above all and in all, Himself. All radiates from Himself, all converges towards Himself. The sorrows and perplexities of His disciples, the mission and work of the Paraclete, the mingling predictions of suffering and of glory, are all bound up with the Person of Jesus, as manifested by Himself. In those matchless words all centres so consistently in Jesus, that it might seem that Jesus alone is before

[f] St. John xiv. 1: *μὴ ταρασσέσθω ὑμῶν ἡ καρδία· πιστεύετε εἰς τὸν Θεὸν, καὶ εἰς ἐμὲ πιστεύετε.* St. Aug. Tr. 67. in Joann.: 'Consequens est enim ut si in Deum creditis, et in Me credere debeatis, quod non esset consequens, si Christus non esset Deus.' St. John xvi. 33: *ταῦτα λελάληκα ὑμῖν, ἵνα ἐν ἐμοὶ εἰρήνην ἔχητε. ἐν τῷ κόσμῳ θλίψιν ἕξετε·* [*ἔχετε*, Tisch.] *ἀλλὰ θαρσεῖτε, ἐγὼ νενίκηκα τὸν κόσμον.*

[g] Ibid. vi. 29: *τοῦτό ἐστι τὸ ἔργον τοῦ Θεοῦ, ἵνα πιστεύσητε εἰς ὃν ἀπέστειλεν ἐκεῖνος.* Ibid. ver. 40: *τοῦτο γάρ ἐστιν τὸ θέλημα τοῦ Πατρός μου· ἵνα πᾶς ὁ θεωρῶν τὸν Υἱὸν καὶ πιστεύων εἰς αὐτὸν, ἔχῃ ζωὴν αἰώνιον.* Ibid. ver. 47: *ὁ πιστεύων εἰς ἐμὲ, ἔχει ζωὴν αἰώνιον.* Cf. Acts xxvi. 18: *τοῦ λαβεῖν αὐτοὺς ἄφεσιν ἁμαρτιῶν, καὶ κλῆρον ἐν τοῖς ἡγιασμένοις, πίστει τῇ εἰς ἐμέ.*

[h] St. John v. 23: *ἵνα πάντες τιμῶσι τὸν Υἱὸν, καθὼς τιμῶσι τὸν Πατέρα.*

[i] Ibid. viii. 42: *εἰ ὁ Θεὸς πατὴρ ὑμῶν ἦν, ἠγαπᾶτε ἂν ἐμέ.* Cf. Ibid. xvi. 27.

[j] Ibid. xv. 23: *ὁ ἐμὲ μισῶν, καὶ τὸν Πατέρα μου μισεῖ.*

[k] Ibid. xiv. 15: *ἐὰν ἀγαπᾶτέ με, τὰς ἐντολὰς τὰς ἐμὰς τηρήσατε.* 2 St. John 6: *καὶ αὕτη ἐστὶν ἡ ἀγάπη, ἵνα περιπατῶμεν κατὰ τὰς ἐντολὰς αὐτοῦ.*

[LECT.

us; alone in the greatness of His supramundane glory; alone in bearing His burden of an awful, fathomless sorrow.

It will naturally occur to us that language such as that which has just been quoted is mainly characteristic of the fourth Gospel; and you will permit me, my brethren, to consider the objection which may underlie that observation somewhat at length in a future lecture[l]. For the present the author of 'Ecce Homo' may remind those who, for whatever reasons, refuse to believe Christ to have used these words, that 'we cannot deny that He used words which have substantially the same meaning. We cannot deny that He called Himself King, Master, and Judge of men; that He promised to give rest to the weary and the heavy-laden; that He instructed His followers to hope for life from feeding on His Body and His Blood[m].'

Indeed so entirely is our Lord's recorded teaching penetrated by His Self-assertion, that in order to represent Him as simply teaching moral truth, while keeping Himself strictly in the background of His doctrine, it would be necessary to deny the trustworthiness of all the accounts of His teaching which we possess. To recognise the difference which has been noticed between the two phases of His teaching merely amounts to saying that in the former His Self-proclamation is implied, while it is avowed in the latter. For even in that phase of Christ's teaching which the three first Evangelists more particularly record, the public assumption of titles and functions such as those of King, Teacher, and Judge of the human race, implies those statements about Himself which are preserved in the fourth Gospel.

Consider, for instance, what is really involved in a claim to judge the world. That Jesus Christ did put forward this claim must be conceded by those who admit that we have in our hands any true records of Him whatever. Some who reject that account of the four Gospels which is given us by the Catholic Church, may perhaps consent to listen to the opinion of Mr. Francis W. Newman. 'I believe,' says that writer, 'that Jesus habitually spoke of Himself by the title Son of Man, [and] that in assuming that title He tacitly alluded to the seventh chapter of Daniel, and claimed for Himself the throne of judgment over all mankind. I know no reason to doubt that He actually delivered in substance the discourse in the twenty-fifth chapter of St. Matthew[n].'

[l] See Lecture V.

[m] Ecce Homo, p. 177. Cf. also Mill, Myth. Interpret. p. 59.

[n] Phases of Faith, p. 149; cf. St. Matt. xxv. 31-46.

That our Lord advanced this tremendous claim to be the Judge of all mankind is equally the conviction of foreign critics, who are as widely removed as possible from any respect whatever for the witness of the Church of Christ to Holy Writ [o]. But let us reflect steadily on what Christ is thus admitted to have said about Himself by the most advanced representatives of the destructive criticism. Christ says that He will return to earth as Judge of all mankind. He will sit upon a throne of glory, and will be attended by bands of obedient angels. Before Him will be gathered all the nations of the world, and He will judge them. In other words, He will proceed to discharge an office involving such spiritual insight, such discernment of the thoughts and intents of the heart of each one of the millions at His feet, such awful, unshared supremacy in the moral world, that the imagination recoils in sheer agony from the task of seriously contemplating the assumption of these duties by any created intelligence. He will draw a sharp trenchant line of eternal separation through the dense throng of all the assembled races and generations of men. He will force every individual human being into one of the two distinct classes respectively destined for endless happiness and endless woe. He will reserve no cases as involving complex moral problems beyond His own power of decision. He will sanction no intermediate class of awards, to meet the neutral morality of souls whom men might deem 'too bad for heaven, yet too good for hell.' If it should be urged that our Lord is teaching truth in the garb of parable, and that His words must not be taken too literally, it may be answered that, supposing this to be the case (a supposition by no means to be conceded), the main features, the purport and drift of the entire representation cannot be mistaken. The Speaker claims to be Judge of all the world. Whenever, or however, you understand Him to exercise His function, Christ claims in that discourse to be nothing less than the Universal Judge. You cannot honestly translate His language into any modern and prosaic equivalent, that does not carry with it this tremendous claim. Nor is it relevant to observe that

[o] Baur, Vorlesungen über N. T. Theologie, p. 109: 'Dass Jesus Sich Selbst als den künftigen Richter betrachtete, und ankündigte, lässt sich auch nach dem Evangelium Matthäus nicht in Zweifel ziehen. Fasst man die Lehre und Wirksamkeit Jesu auch nur nach dem sittlichen Gesichtspunkt auf, unter welchen sie der Bergrede und den Parabeln zufolge zu stellen ist, so gehört dazu wesentlich auch die Bestimmung, *dass sie der absolute Maasstab zur Beurtheilung des sittlichen Werthes des Thuns und Verhaltens der Menschen ist.*'

Messiah had been pictured in prophecy as the Universal Judge, and that in assuming to judge the world Jesus Christ was only claiming an official consequence of the character which He had previously assumed. Surely this does not alter the nature of the claim. It does indeed shew what was involved in the original assertion that He was the Messiah; but it does not shew that the title of Universal Judge was a mere idealist decoration having no practical duties attached to it. On the contrary, Jesus Christ asserts the practical value of the title very deliberately; He insists on and expands its significance; He draws out what it implies into a vivid picture. It cannot be denied that He literally and deliberately put Himself forward as Judge of all the world; and the moral significance of this Self-exaltation is not affected by the fact that He made it as a part of His general Messianic claim. If He could not claim to be Messiah without making it, He ought not to have claimed to be Messiah unless He had a right to make it. It may be pleaded that He Himself said that the Father had given Him authority to execute judgment because He is the Son of Man[p]. But this, as has already been shewn, means simply that He is the Universal Judge because He is Messiah. True, the chosen title of Messiahship implies His real Humanity; and His Human Nature invests Him with special fitness for this as for the rest of His mediatorial work. But then the title Son of Man, as implying His Humanity, is in felt contrast to a higher Nature which it suggests. He is more than human; but He is to judge us, because He is also Man. On the whole it is impossible to reflect steadily on this claim of Jesus Christ without feeling that either such a claim ought never to have been made, or that it carries us forward irresistibly to a truth beyond and above itself.

In dealing with separate souls our Lord's tone and language are not less significant. We will not here dwell on the fact of His forgiving sins[q], and of transmitting to His Church the power of forgiving them[r]. But it is clear that He treats those who come to Him as literally belonging to Himself, in virtue of an existing right. He commands, He does not invite, discipleship.

[p] St. John v. 27.

[q] St. Matt. ix. 6; St. Mark ii. 10. M. Salvador represents in our own day the Jewish feeling respecting this claim of our Lord. 'Voilà pourquoi les docteurs se recrièrent de nouveau en entendant le Fils de Marie s'arroger à lui-même, et transmettre à ses délégués le droit du pardon: ils y voyaient une autre manière de prendre la place de Dieu.' Jésus-Christ, tom. ii. p. 83.

[r] St. Matt. xvi. 19; St. John xx. 23.

To Philip, to the sons of Zebedee, to the rich young man, He says simply, 'Follow Me[s].' In the same spirit His Apostles are bidden to resent resistance to their Master's doctrine: 'When ye come into an house, salute it. And if the house be worthy, let your peace come upon it: but if it be not worthy, let your peace return to you. And whosoever shall not receive you, nor hear your words, when ye depart out of that house or city, shake off the dust of your feet. Verily I say unto you, It shall be more tolerable for the land of Sodom and Gomorrha in the day of judgment, than for that city[t].' And as His message is to be received upon pain of eternal loss, so in receiving it, men are to give themselves up to Him simply and unreservedly. No rival claim, however strong, no natural affection, however legitimate and sacred, may interpose between Himself and the soul of His follower. 'He that loveth father or mother more than Me is not worthy of Me; and he that loveth son or daughter more than Me is not worthy of Me[u];' 'If any man come to Me, and hate not his father, and mother, and wife, and children, and brethren, and sisters, yea, and his own life also, he cannot be My disciple[x].' Accordingly He predicts the painful severance between near relations which would accompany the advance of the Gospel: 'Suppose ye that I am come to give peace on earth? I tell you, Nay; but rather division: for from henceforth there shall be five in one house divided, three against two, and two against three. The father shall be divided against the son, and the son against the father; the mother against the daughter, and the daughter against the mother; the mother in law against her daughter in law, and the daughter in law against her mother in law[y].' And the Gospel narrative itself furnishes us with a remarkable illustration of our Lord's application of His claim. 'He said unto another, Follow Me. But he said, Lord, suffer me first to go and bury my father. Jesus said unto him, Let the dead bury their dead: but go thou and preach the kingdom of God. And another also said, Lord, I will follow Thee; but let me first go bid them farewell, which are at home at my house. And Jesus said unto him, No man, having put his hand to the plough, and looking back, is fit for the kingdom of God[z].'

It is impossible to ignore this imperious claim on the part of Jesus to rule the whole soul of man. Other masters may

[s] St. Matt. iv. 19, viii. 22, ix. 9, xix. 21; St. Mark ii. 14; St. Luke v. 27; St. John i. 43, x. 27. [t] St. Matt. x. 12-15. [u] Ibid. 37. [x] St. Luke xiv. 26. [y] Ibid. xii. 51-53. [z] Ibid. ix. 59-62.

demand a man's active energies, or his time, or his purse, or his thought, or some large share in his affections. But here is a claim on the whole man, on his very inmost self, on the sanctities of his deepest life. Here is a claim which altogether sets aside the dearest ties of family and kindred, if perchance they interfere with it. Does any who is merely man dare to advance such a claim as this? If so, is it possible that, believing him to be only a fellow-creature, we can listen to the claim with respect, with patience, without earnest indignation? Do not our souls belong only and wholly to Him Who made them? Can we not bury ourselves out of the sight and reach of every fellow-creature, in the hidden recesses of the spirit which we carry within? Can we not escape, if we will, from all eyes save One, from all wills save One, from all voices save One, from all beings excepting Him Who gave us life? How then can we listen to the demand which is advanced by Jesus of Nazareth? Is it tolerable if He is only man? If He does indeed share with ourselves the great debt of creation at the hand of God; if He exists, like ourselves, from moment to moment merely upon sufferance; or rather, if He is upheld in being in virtue of a continuous and gratuitous ministration of life, supplied to Him by the Author of all life; is it endurable that He should thus assume to deal with us as His own creatures, as beings who have no rights before Him, and whom He may command at will? Doubtless He speaks of certain souls as given Him by His Father [a]; but then He claims the fealty, the submission of all. And even if souls are only 'given' to Christ, how are we to account for this absolute gift of an immortal soul to a human Lord? What, in short, is the real moral justification of a claim, than which no larger could be urged by the Creator? How can Christ bid men live for Himself as for the very End of their existence? How can He rightly draw towards Himself the whole thought and love, I do not say, of a world, but of one single human being, with this imperious urgency, if He be indeed only the Christ of the Humanitarian teachers, if He be anything else or less than the supreme Lord of life?

It is then not merely an easy transition, it is a positive moral relief, to pass from considering these statements and claims to the declarations in which Jesus Christ explains them by explicitly asserting His Divinity. For although the solemn sentences in which He makes that supreme revelation are com-

[a] St. John x. 29.

paratively few, it is clear that the truth is latent, in the entire moral and intellectual posture which we have been considering, unless we are prepared to fall back upon a fearful alternative which it will be my duty presently to notice.

Every man who takes a public or stirring part in life may assume that he has to deal with three different classes of men. He must face 'his personal friends, his declared opponents, and a large neutral body which is swayed by turns in the opposite directions of friendliness and opposition.' Towards each of these classes he has varying obligations; and from their different points of view they form their estimate of his character and action. Now our Lord, entering as He did perfectly into the actual conditions of our human and social existence, exposed Himself to this triple scrutiny, and met it by a correspondingly threefold revelation. He revealed His Divinity to His disciples, to the Jewish people, and to His embittered opponents, the chief priests and Pharisees.

Bearing in mind His acceptance of the confessions of Nathanael [b] and of St. Peter [c], as well as His solemn words to Nicodemus [d], let us consider His language in the supper-room to St. Philip. It may have been Philip's restlessness of mind, taking pleasure, as men will, in the mere starting a religious difficulty for its own sake; it may have been an instinctive wish to find some excuse for escaping from those sterner obligations which, on the eve of the Passion, discipleship would threaten presently to impose. However this was, Philip preferred to our Lord the peremptory request, 'Lord, shew us the Father, and it sufficeth us.' Well might the answer have thrilled those who heard it. 'Have I been so long time with you, and yet thou hast not known Me, Philip? He that hath seen Me hath seen the Father; and how sayest thou then, Shew us the Father? Believest thou not that I am in the Father, and the Father in Me [e]?' Now what this indwelling really implied is seen in our Lord's answer to a question of St. Jude. St. Jude had asked how it was that Christ would manifest Himself to His servants, and not to the world. Our Lord replies that the heavenly revelation is made to love; but the form in which this answer is couched is of the highest significance. 'If a Man love Me, he will keep My words; and My Father will love him, and We will come unto him, and make Our abode with him [f].' '*We* will come unto him and

[b] St. John i. 49. [c] St. Matt. xvi. 16. [d] St. John iii. 18.
[e] St. John xiv. 9, 10; Williams on Study of the Gospels, p. 403.
[f] St. John xiv. 23.

make *Our* abode!' Reflect: Who is This Speaker That promises to dwell in the soul of man? And with Whom does He associate Himself? It may be true of any eminent saint, that 'God speaks not to him, as to one outside Himself; that God is in him; that he feels himself with God; that he draws from his own heart what he tells us of the Father; that he lives in the bosom of God by the intercommunion of every moment[g].' But such an one could not forget that, favoured as he is by the Divine Presence illuminating his whole inner life, he still lives at an immeasurable distance beneath the Being Whose condescension has so enriched him. In virtue of his sanctity, he would surely shrink with horror from associating himself with God; from promising, along with God, to make a dwelling-place of the souls that love himself; from representing his presence with men as a blessing co-ordinate with the presence of the Father; from attributing to himself oneness of will with the Will of God; from implying that side by side with the Father of spirits, he was himself equally a ruler and a helper of the life of the souls of men.

The most prominent statements however which our Lord made on the subject of His Divinity occur in those conversations with the Jews which are specially recorded in the fourth Gospel. Our Lord discovers this great truth to the Jewish people by three distinct methods of statement.

(*a*) In the first place, He distinctly places Himself on terms of equality with the Father, by a double claim. He claims a parity of working power, and He claims an equal right to the homage of mankind. Of these claims the former is implicitly contained in passages to which allusion has been already made. We have seen that it is contained in the assumption of a *judicial authority* equal to the task of deciding the final condition of every individual human being. Although this office is delegated to and exercised by our Lord as Man, yet so stupendous a task is obviously not less beyond the reach of any created intelligence than the providential government of the world. In like manner, this claim of an equality in working power with the Father is inseparable from our Lord's statements that He could confer

[g] Quoted in Dean Stanley's Lectures on the Jewish Church, part ii. p. 161, from Renan (Vie de Jésus, p. 75), who is speaking of our Lord. M. Renan, in using this language, is very careful to explain that he does not mean to assert that our Lord is God: 'Jésus n'énonce pas un moment l'idée sacrilège (!) qu'il soit Dieu.' Ibid.

animal life[h], and that the future restoration of the whole human race to life would be effected by an act of His will[i]. These statements were made by our Lord after healing the impotent man at the pool of Bethesda. They are in fact deductions from a previous and more comprehensive one. Our Lord had healed the impotent man on the Sabbath day and had bidden him take up his bed and walk. The Jews saw an infraction of the Sabbath, both in the command given to the impotent man, and in the act of healing him. They sought to slay our Lord; but He justified Himself by saying, 'My Father worketh hitherto, and I work[j].' 'Therefore,' continues the Evangelist, 'the Jews sought the more to kill Him, because He not only had broken the Sabbath, but said also that God was His Own Father, making Himself equal with God[k].' Now the Jews were not mistaken as to

[h] St. John v. 21: *ὁ Υἱὸς οὓς θέλει ζωοποιεῖ.* The quickening the dead is a special attribute of God (Deut. xxxii. 39; 1 Sam. ii. 6). If our Lord's power of quickening whom He would had referred only to the moral life of man, the statement would not have been less significant. To raise a soul from spiritual death is at least as great a miracle, and as strictly proper to God Almighty, as to raise a dead body. But the *ζωοποίησις* here in question, if moral in ver. 25, is physical in ver. 28; our Lord is alluding to His recently-performed miracle as an illustration of His power. Ibid. vers. 8, 9.

[i] St. John v. 28, 29: *ἔρχεται ὥρα, ἐν ᾗ πάντες οἱ ἐν τοῖς μνημείοις ἀκούσονται τῆς φωνῆς αὐτοῦ, καὶ ἐκπορεύσονται, οἱ τὰ ἀγαθὰ ποιήσαντες, εἰς ἀνάστασιν ζωῆς, οἱ δὲ τὰ φαῦλα πράξαντες, εἰς ἀνάστασιν κρίσεως.*

[j] St. John v. 17: *ὁ Πατήρ μου ἕως ἄρτι ἐργάζεται, κἀγὼ ἐργάζομαι.* 'Wie der Vater seit Anbeginn nicht aufgehört habe, zum Heil der Welt zu wirken, sondern immer fortwirke bis zur jetzigen Stunde, so mit Nothwendigkeit und Recht, ungeachtet des Sabbathsgesetzes, auch Er, als der Sohn, Welcher als Solcher in dieser Seiner Wirksamkeit nicht dem Sabbathsgesetze unterthan sein kann, sondern Herr des Sabbaths ist.' (St. Matt. xii. 8; St. Mark ii. 28.) Meyer in loc.

[k] St. John v. 18: *Πατέρα ἴδιον ἔλεγε τὸν Θεὸν, ἴσον ἑαυτὸν ποιῶν τῷ Θεῷ.* M. Salvador points out the abiding significance of our Lord's language in the opinion of his co-religionists. 'Si l'on ne s'attaquait qu'aux traditions et interprétations abusives, c'était s'en prendre à la jurisprudence du jour, aux docteurs, aux hommes; c'était user simplement du droit commun en Israël, et provoquer une réforme. Mais si l'on se mettait au dessus de l'institution en elle-même, si, comme Jésus devant les docteurs, on se proclamait le *Maître* absolu *du sabbath,* dans ce cas, entre circoncis, c'était attaquer à la loi, en renverser une des pierres angulaires; c'était imposer au grand Sacrificateur le devoir de faire entendre une voix accusatrice; enfin c'était s'élever au dessus du Dieu des Juifs, *ou tout-au-moins se prétendre son Égal.* Aussi un témoignage éclatant vient à l'appui de cette distinction, et ajoute une preuve à la conformité générale des quatres Évangiles. "Les Juifs," dit judicieusement l'apôtre et évangéliste Jean, "ne poursuivirent pas Jésus, par ce seul motif qu'il violait les ordonnances relatives au sabbath. On lui intenta une action par cette autre raison; qu'il se faisait égal à Dieu."' Salvador, Jésus-Christ, ii. pp. 80, 81.

our Lord's meaning. They knew that the Everlasting God 'neither rests nor is weary;' they knew that if He could slumber but for a moment the universe would collapse into the nothingness out of which He has summoned it. They knew that He 'rested on the seventh day' from the creation of new beings; but that in maintaining the life of those which already exist, He 'worketh hitherto.' They knew that none could associate himself as did Jesus with this world-sustaining energy of God, who was not himself God. They saw clearly that no one could cite God's example of an uninterrupted energy in nature and providence as a reason for setting aside God's positive law, without also and thereby claiming to be Divine. It did not occur to them that our Lord's words need have implied no more than a resemblance between His working and the working of the Father. If indeed our Lord had meant nothing more than this, He would not have met the objection urged by the Jews against His breaking the Sabbath. It would have been no argument against the Jews to have said, that because God's incessant activity is ever working in the universe, therefore a holy Jew might work on uninterruptedly, although he thereby violated the Sabbath day. With equal reason might it have been urged, that because God sees good to take the lives of His creatures, in His mercy no less than in His justice, therefore a religious man might rightfully put to death His tempted or afflicted brother. The Sabbath was a positive precept, but it rested on a moral basis. It had been given by God Himself. Our Lord claims a right to break the Sabbath, because God's ever active Providence is not suspended on that day. Our Lord thus places both His Will and His Power on the level of the Power and Will of the Father. He might have parried the Jewish attack by saying that the miracle of healing the impotent man was a work of God, and that He was Himself but the unresisting organ of a Higher Being. On the Socinian hypothesis He ought to have done so. But He represents the miracle as His own work. He claims distinctly to be Lord of nature, and thus to be equal with the Father in point of operative energy [l]. He makes the same assertion in saying that 'whatsoever things the Father doeth, those things the Son also doeth in like manner [m].' To narrow down these words so as to make them only refer to Christ's imitation of the moral nature

[l] St. Cyril. Alex. Thesaurus, p. 324.

[m] St. John v. 19: ἃ γὰρ ἂν ἐκεῖνος ποιῇ, ταῦτα καὶ ὁ Υἱὸς ὁμοίως ποιεῖ. Cf. viii. 28.

of God, is to take a liberty with the text for which it affords no warrant; it is to make void the plain meaning of Scripture by a sceptical tradition. Our Lord simply and directly asserts that the works of the Father, without any restriction, are, both as to their nature and mode of production, the works of the Son. Certainly our Lord insists very carefully upon the truth that the power which He wielded was derived originally from the Father. It is often difficult to say whether He is speaking, as Man, of the honour of union with Deity and of the graces which flowed from Deity, conferred upon His Manhood; or whether, as the Everlasting Son, He is describing those natural and eternal Gifts which are inherent in His Godhead, and which He receives from the Father, the Fountain or Source of Deity, not as a matter of grace or favour, but in virtue of His Eternal Generation. As God, 'the Son can do nothing of Himself,' and this, 'not from lack of power, but because His Being is inseparable from That of the Father [n].' It is true of Christ as God in one sense—it is true of Him as Man in another—that 'as the Father hath life in Himself, so hath He given to the Son to have life in Himself.' But neither is an absolute harmony of the works of Christ with the Mind and Will of the Father, nor a derivation of the Divine Nature of Christ Itself from the Being of the Father by an unbegun and unending Generation, destructive of the force of our Lord's representation of His operative energy as being on a par with that of the Father.

For, our Lord's real sense is made plain by His subsequent statement that 'the Father hath committed all judgment unto the Son; that all should honour the Son even as they honour the Father [o].' This claim is indeed no more than He had already advanced in bidding His followers trust Him and love Him. The obligation of honouring the Son is defined to be just

[n] Euthym.

[o] St. John v. 22, 23. Meyer in loc.: 'In dem richtenden Sohne erscheint der beauftragte *Stellvertreter* des Vaters, und er ist *in so fern* (also immer relativ) zu ehren *wie* der Vater.' But if the honour paid to the Son be merely relative, if He be merely honoured as an Ambassador or delegated Judge, then men do *not* honour Him *as* they honour the Father; they pay the Father one kind of honour, namely adoration, and they pay the Son a totally distinct kind of honour,—possibly respect. If this had been our Lord's meaning, would He not either have omitted καθὼς, or used two different verbs to express what is due from all men to the Father and to the Son respectively? Moses was 'as a GOD unto Pharaoh,' and GOD'S ambassador and judge among the children of Israel. Does he therefore claim that all men should honour Moses even as they honour Jehovah?

[LECT.

as stringent as the obligation of honouring the Father. Whatever form that honour may take, be it thought, or language, or outward act, or devotion of the affections, or submission of the will, or that union of thought and heart and will into one complex act of self-prostration before Infinite Greatness, which we of the present day usually mean by the term 'adoration,' such honour is due to the Son no less than to the Father. How fearful is such a claim if the Son be only human; how natural, how moderate, how just, if He is in very deed Divine!

(β) Beyond this assertion of an equal operative Power with the Father, and of an equal right to the homage of mankind, is our Lord's revelation of His absolute oneness of Essence with the Father. The Jews gathered around Him at the Feast of Dedication in the Porch of Solomon, and pressed Him to tell them whether He was the Christ or not[p]. Our Lord referred them to the teaching which they had heard, and to the miracles which they had witnessed in vain[q]; but He proceeded to say that there were docile and faithful souls whom He terms His 'sheep,' and whom He 'knew,' while they too understood and followed Him[r]. He goes on to insist upon the blessedness of these His true followers. With Him they were secure; no power on earth or in heaven could 'pluck them out of His Hand[s].' A second reason for the blessedness of His sheep follows: 'My Father which gave them Me is a Greater Power (μεῖζον) than all: and no man is able to pluck them out of My Father's Hand[t].' In these words our Lord repeats His previous assurance of the security of His sheep, but He gives a different reason for it. He had represented them as 'in His own Hand;' He now represents them as in the Hand of the Almighty Father. How does He consolidate these two reasons which together assure His 'sheep' of their security? By distinctly asserting His own oneness with the Father: 'I and My Father are One Thing[u].' Now what kind of unity is that which the context obliges us to see in this solemn statement? Is it such a unity as that which our Lord desired for His followers in His intercessory prayer; a unity of spiritual communion, of reciprocal love, of common participation in an imparted, heaven-sent

[p] St. John x. 22, 23.
[q] Ibid. ver. 25.
[r] Ibid. ver. 27.
[s] Ibid. ver. 28.
[t] Ibid. ver. 29.
[u] Ibid. ver. 30: Ἐγὼ καὶ ὁ Πατὴρ ἕν ἐσμεν. For a full explanation of this text see Bishop Beveridge's noble sermon on the Unity of Christ with God the Father, Works, vol. ii. Serm. xxv. See also note D.

Nature[v]? Is it a unity of design and co-operation, such as that which, in varying degrees, is shared by all true workers for God[w]? How would either of these lower unities sustain the full sense of the context, which represents the Hand of the Son as one with the Hand—that is, with the Love and Power—of the Father, securing to the souls of men an effectual preservation from eternal ruin? A unity like this must be a *dynamic* unity, as distinct from any mere moral and intellectual union, such as might exist in a real sense between a creature and its God. Deny this dynamic unity, and you destroy the internal connexion of the passage[x]. Admit this dynamic unity, and you admit, by necessary implication, a unity of Essence. The Power of the Son, which shields the redeemed from the foes of their salvation, is the very Power of the Father; and this identity of Power is itself the outflow and the manifestation of a Oneness of Nature. Not that at this height of contemplation the Person of the Son, so distinctly manifested just now in the work of guarding His redeemed, melts away into any mere aspect or relation of the Divine Being in His dealings with His creatures. As St. Augustine observes on this text, the 'unum' saves us from the Charybdis of Arianism; the 'sumus' is our safeguard against the Scylla of Sabellius. The Son, within the incommunicable unity of God, is still Himself; He is not the Father, but the Son. Yet this personal subsistence is in the mystery of the Divine Life strictly compatible with Unity of Essence;—the Father and the Son are one Thing.

'Intellexerunt Judæi, quod non intelligunt Ariani.' The Jews understood our Lord to assume Divine honours, and proceeded to execute the capital sentence decreed against blasphemy by

[v] As in St. John xvii. 11, 22, 23. [w] 1 Cor. iii. 8.

[x] Meyer in Joh. x. 29: 'Der Vater in dem Sohne ist und wirkt, und daher dieser, als Organ und Träger [He is, of course, much more than this] der gottlichen Thätigkeit bei Ausführung des Messianischen Werks, nicht geschieden von Gott [i.e. the Father] *nicht ein zweiter ausser und neben Gott ist*, sondern nach dem Wesen jener Gemeinschaft *Eins mit Gott*. *Gottes* Hand ist *daher* seine Hand in der Vollziehung des Werkes, bei welchem Er Gottes Macht, Liebe u. s. w. handhabt und zur Ausführung bringt. Die Einheit ist mithin die der dynamischen Gemeinschaft, wornach der Vater im Sohne ist, und doch grösser als der Sohn, [i.e. as man,] weil Er ihn geweiht und gesandt hat. Die Arianische Fassung *von der ethischen Harmonie* genügt nicht, da die Argumentation, ohne die Einheit der Macht (welche Chrys. Euth. Zig. u. V. auch Lücke mit Recht urgiren) zu verstehen, nicht zutreffen würde.' This interpretation is remarkable for its scholarly fairness in a writer who sits so loosely to the Catholic belief in our Lord's Godhead as Meyer.

the Mosaic law[y]. His words gave them a fair ground for saying that 'being Man, He made Himself God[z].' Now if our Lord had been in reality only Man, He might have been fairly expected to say so. Whereas He proceeds, as was often His wont, to reason with His opponents upon their own real or assumed grounds, and so to bring them back to a point at which they were forced to draw for themselves the very inference which had just roused their indignation. With this view our Lord points out the application of the word Elohim, to the wicked judges under the Jewish theocracy, in the eighty-second Psalm[a]. Surely, with this authoritative language before their eyes, His countrymen could not object to His calling Himself the Son of God. And yet He irresistibly implies that His title to Divinity is higher than, and indeed distinct in kind from, that of the Jewish magistrates. If the Jews could tolerate that ascription of a lower and relative divinity to the corrupt officials who, theocratically speaking, represented the Lord Jehovah; surely, looking to the witness of His works, Divinity could not be denied to One Who so manifestly wielded Divine power as did Jesus[b]. Our Lord's argument is thus *à minori ad majus;* and He arrives a second time at the assertion which had already given such offence to His countrymen, and which He now repeats in terms expressive of His sharing not merely a dynamical but an essential unity with the Father: 'The Father is in Me, and I in Him[c].' What the Father is to the Son, the Son is to the Father. The context again forbids us to compare this expression with the phrases which are often used to express the indwelling of God with holy souls, since no moral quality is here in question, but an identity of Power for the performance of superhuman works. Our Lord expresses this truth of His wielding the power of the Father, by asserting His identity of Nature with the Father, which involves His Omnipotence. And the Jews understood Him. He had not retracted what they accounted blasphemy, and they again endeavoured to take His life[d].

It will probably be said that the Church's interpretation of Christ's language in the Porch of Solomon is but an instance of that disposition to materialize spiritual truth, which seems to be

[y] St. John x. 31. [z] Ibid. ver. 33: Σὺ, ἄνθρωπος ὢν, ποιεῖς σεαυτὸν Θεόν.

[a] Ps. lxxxii. 6.

[b] St. John x. 37, 38. Cf. Perowne, Psalms, ii. 92.

[c] St. John x. 38: ἐν ἐμοὶ ὁ Πατὴρ, κἀγὼ ἐν αὐτῷ.

[d] Ibid. ver. 39: ἐζήτουν οὖν πάλιν αὐτὸν πιάσαι.

so unhappily natural to the mind of man. 'What grossness of apprehension,' it will be urged, 'is here! How can you thus confound language which merely asserts a sustained intercommunion between a holy soul and God, with those hard formal scholastic assertions of an identity of essence?' But it is obvious to rejoin that in cases like that before us, language must be morally held to mean what it is understood to mean by those to whom it is addressed. After all, language is designed to convey thought; and if a speaker perceives that his real mind has not been conveyed by one statement, he is bound to correct the deficiencies of that statement by another. Had our Lord been speaking to populations accustomed to Pantheistic modes of thinking, and insensible to the fundamental distinctness of the Uncreated from all forms of created life, His assertion of His oneness with the Father might perhaps have passed for nothing more than the rapture of a subjective ecstasy, in which the consciousness of the Speaker had been so raised above its ordinary level, that He could hyperbolically describe His sensations as Divine. Had our Lord been an Indian, or an Alexandrian, or a German mystic, some such interpretation might have been reasonably affixed to His language. Had Christ been a Christian instead of the Author of Christianity, we might, after carefully detaching His words from their context, have even supposed that He was describing the blessed experience of millions of believers; it being certain that, since the Incarnation, the soul of man is capable of a real union with the All-holy God. Undoubtedly writers like St. Augustine, and many of later date [e], do speak of the union between God and the Christian in terms which signally illustrate the loving condescension of God truly present in holy souls, of God's gift of Himself to His redeemed creatures. But the belief of these writers respecting the Nature of the Most High has placed the phrases of their mystical devotion beyond the reach of a possible misunderstanding. And our Lord was addressing earnest monotheists, keenly alive to the essential distinction between the Life of the Creator and the life of the creature, and religiously jealous of the Divine prerogatives. The Jews did not understand Christ's claim to be one with the Father in any merely moral, spiritual, or mystical sense. Christ did not

[e] e.g. Thomas à Kempis. Of his teaching respecting the union between GOD and the devout soul, there is a good summary in Ullmann's Reformers before the Reformation, vol. ii. pp. 139-149, Clarke's transl.

encourage them so to understand it. The motive of their indignation was not disowned by Him. They believed Him to mean that He was Himself a Divine Person; and He never repudiated that construction of His language.

(γ) In order however to determine the real sense of our Saviour's claim to be One with the Father, let us ask a simple question. Does it appear that He is recorded to have been conscious of having existed previously to His Human Life upon this earth? Suppose that He is only a good man enjoying the highest degree of constant spiritual intercommunion with God, no references to a Pre-existent Life can be anticipated. There is nothing to warrant such a belief in the Mosaic Revelation, and to have professed it on the soil of Palestine would simply have been taken by the current opinion of the people as a proof of mental derangement. But believe that Christ is the Only-begotten Son of God, manifested in the sphere of sense and time, and clothed in our human nature; and some references to a consciousness extending backwards through the past into a boundless eternity are only what would naturally be looked for at His hands.

Let us then listen to Him as He is proclaiming to His countrymen in the temple, 'If a man keep *My* saying, He shall never see death[f].' The Jews exclaim that by such an announcement He assumes to be greater than Abraham and the prophets. They indignantly ask, 'Whom makest Thou Thyself?' Here as elsewhere our Lord keeps both sides of His relation to the Eternal Father in full view: it is the Father that glorifies His Manhood, and the Jews would glorify Him too if they were the Father's true children. But it was not their Heavenly Father alone with whom the Jews were at variance. The earthly ancestor of the Jewish race might be invoked to rebuke his recreant posterity. 'Your father Abraham rejoiced to see My day, and he saw it and was glad.' Abraham had seen the day of Messiah by the light of prophecy, and accordingly this statement was a claim on the part of Jesus to be the true Messiah. Of itself such a claim would not have shocked the Jews; they would have discussed it on its merits. They had latterly looked for a political chief, victorious but human, in their expected Messiah; they would have welcomed any prospect of realizing their expectations. But they detected a deeper and to them a less welcome meaning in the words of Christ. He had meant,

[f] St. John viii. 52: *ἐάν τις τὸν λόγον τὸν ἐμὸν τηρήσῃ, θάνατον οὐ μὴ θεωρήσῃ εἰς τὸν αἰῶνα.*

they thought, by His 'Day' something more than the years of His Human Life. At any rate they would ask Him a question, which would at once justify their suspicions or enable Him to clear Himself. 'Thou,' they said to Him, 'art not yet fifty years old, and hast Thou seen Abraham?' Now if our Lord had only claimed to be a human Messiah, such as the Jews of later years had learned to look for, He must have earnestly disavowed any such inference from His words. He might have replied that if Abraham saw Him by the light of prophecy, this did not of itself imply that He was Abraham's contemporary, and so that He had Himself literally seen Abraham. But His actual answer more than justified the most extreme suspicions of His examiners as to His real meaning. 'Jesus said unto them, Verily, verily, I say unto you, Before Abraham was, *I am*.' In these tremendous words the Speaker institutes a double contrast, in respect both of the duration and of the mode of His existence, between Himself and the great ancestor of Israel. Πρὶν Ἀβραὰμ γενέσθαι. Abraham, then, had come into existence at some given point of time. Abraham did not exist until his parents gave him birth. But, Ἐγώ εἰμι. Here is simple existence, with no note of beginning or end[g]. Our Lord says not, 'Before Abraham was, I was,' but 'I am.' He claims pre-existence indeed, but He does not merely claim pre-existence; He unveils a consciousness of Eternal Being. He speaks as One on Whom time has no effect, and for Whom it has no meaning. He is the I AM of ancient Israel; He knows no past, as He knows no future; He is unbeginning, unending Being; He is the eternal 'Now.' This is the plain sense of His language[h], and perhaps the most instructive commentary upon its force is to be found in the violent expedients to which Humanitarian writers have been driven in order to evade it[i].

[g] St. John viii. 58. Meyer in loc.: 'Ehe Abraham ward, bin Ich, älter als Abraham's Werden ist meine Existenz.' Stier characterizes our Lord's words as 'a sudden [not to Himself] flash of revelation out of the depths of His own Eternal Consciousness.' That Christ should finally have spoken thus, is not, Stier urges, to be wondered at, on the supposition of this Eternal Consciousness ever abiding with Him. Rather is it wonderful, that He should ordinarily, and as a rule, have restrained it so much. Here too, indeed, He restrains Himself. He does not go on to say, as afterwards in the Great Intercession—πρὸ τοῦ τὸν κόσμον εἶναι (St. John xvii. 5).

[h] Milman, Hist. of Christianity, i. 249: 'The awful and significant words which identified Him, as it were, with Jehovah, the great self-existent Deity.' Why 'as it were'?

[i] Cf. Meyer on St. John viii. 58: 'Das ἐγώ εἰμι ist aber weder: Ich bin es (der Messias) zu deuten (*Faustus Socinus, Paulus*, ganz contextwidrig),

Here again the Jews understood our Lord, and attempted to kill Him; while He, instead of explaining Himself in any sense which would have disarmed their anger, simply withdrew from the temple[j].

With this statement we may compare Christ's references to His pre-existence in His two great sacramental Discourses. Conversing with Nicodemus He describes Himself as the Son of Man Who had come down from heaven, and Who while yet speaking was in heaven[k]. Preaching in the great synagogue of Capernaum, He calls Himself 'the Bread of Life Which had come down from heaven.' He repeats and expands this description of Himself. His pre-existence is the warrant of His life-giving power[l]. The Jews objected that they knew His father and mother, and did not understand His advancing any such claim as this to a pre-existent Life. Our Lord replied by saying that no man could come to Him unless taught of God to do so, and then proceeded to re-assert His pre-existence in the same terms as before[m]. He pursued His former statement into its mysterious consequences. Since He was the heaven-descended Bread of Life, His Flesh was meat indeed and His Blood was drink indeed[n]. They only would have life in them who should eat this Flesh and drink this Blood[o]. Life eternal, Resurrection at the last day[p], and His own Presence even now within the soul[q], would follow upon a due partaking of that heavenly food. When the disciples murmured at this doctrine as a 'hard saying[r],' our Lord met their objections by predicting His coming Ascension into Heaven as an event which would justify His allusions to His pre-existence, no less than to the life-giving virtue of His Manhood. 'What and if ye shall see the Son of Man ascend up where He was before[s]?' Again, the reality of our

noch in den *Rathschluss Gottes*, zu verlegen (*Sam. Crell, Grotius, Paulus, B. Crusius*), was schon durch das Praes. verboten wird. Nur noch geschichtlich bemerkenswerth ist die von Faustus Socinus auch in das Socinianische Bekenntniss (s. Catech. Racov. ed. Oeder, p. 144, f.) übergegangene Auslegung: "Ehe Abraham, Abraham, d. i. der Vater vieler Völker, wird, bin Ich es, nämlich der Messias, das Licht der Welt." Damit ermahne Er die Juden, an Ihn zu glauben, so lange es noch Zeit sei, ehe die Gnade von ihnen genommen und auf die Heiden übergetragen werde, wodurch dann Abraham der Vater vieler Völker werde.'

[j] St. John viii. 59. [k] Ibid. iii. 13. [l] Ibid. vi. 33.
[m] Ibid. vers. 44-51. [n] Ibid. ver. 55.
[o] Ibid. ver. 53. [p] Ibid. ver. 54.
[q] Ibid. ver. 56. [r] Ibid. ver. 60.
[s] Ibid. ver. 62. Strauss thinks it 'difficult but admissible' to interpret St. John viii. 58, with the Socinian Crell, of a purely ideal existence in the

Lord's pre-existence lightens up such mysterious sayings as the following: 'I know whence I came, and whither I go; but ye cannot tell whence I come, and whither I go [t];' 'I am from above: . . . I am not of this world [u];' 'If ye believe not that I am He, ye shall die in your sins [v];' 'I proceeded forth and came from God [w];' 'I came forth from the Father, and am come into the world: again, I leave the world, and go to the Father [x].' Once more, how full of solemn significance is that reference to 'the glory which I had with Thee before the world was [y]' in the great intercession which our Incarnate Saviour offered to the Eternal Father on the eve of His agony!

Certainly taken alone, our Lord's allusions to His pre-existence [z] need not imply His true Divinity. There is indeed no ground for the theory of a Palestinian doctrine of metempsychosis; and even Strauss shrinks from supposing that the fourth Evangelist makes Jesus the mouthpiece of Alexandrian theories of which a Jewish peasant would never have heard. Arianism however would argue, and with reason, that in some of the passages just referred to, though not in all, our Lord might conceivably have been speaking of a created, although pre-existent, life. Yet if we take these passages in connection with our Lord's assertion of His being One with the Father, each truth will be seen to support and complete the other. On the one hand, Christ asserts His substantial oneness with Deity, on the other, His distinct

predetermination of God. He considers it however 'scarcely possible to view the prayer to the Father (St. John xvii. 5) to confirm the δόξα which Jesus had with Him before the world was, as an entreaty for the communication of a glory predestined for Jesus from eternity.' He adds that the language of Jesus (St. John vi. 62) where He speaks of the Son of Man re-ascending where He was before, ἀναβαίνειν ὅπου ἦν τὸ πρότερον, is 'in its intrinsic meaning, as well as in that which is reflected on it from other passages, unequivocally significative of actual, not merely of ideal pre-existence.' Leben Jesu, pt. ii. kap. 4. § 65.

Here, as sometimes elsewhere, Strauss incidentally upholds the natural and Catholic interpretation of the text of the Gospels; nor are we now concerned with the theory to which he eventually applies it. It may be further observed, that Strauss might have at least interpreted St. John viii. 58 by the light of St. John vi. 62.

[t] St. John viii. 14. [u] Ibid. ver. 23. [v] Ibid. ver. 24.

[w] Ibid. ver. 42: ἐγὼ γὰρ ἐκ τοῦ Θεοῦ ἐξῆλθον καὶ ἥκω.

[x] Ibid. xvi. 28. [y] Ibid. xvii. 5.

[z] St. Luke x. 18 would be a weighty addition to these passages, if ἐκ τοῦ οὐρανοῦ could be pressed, against the apparent requirements of the context, so as to refer to the fall of the rebel angels. In that case ἐθεώρουν would be an act of the pre-existent Word. So many Fathers, and Hofmann, Schriftbew. i. p. 443, ed. 2.

[LECT.

pre-existent Personality. He might be an inferior and created Being, if He were not thus absolutely One with God. He might be only a saintly man, and, as such, described as an 'aspect,' a 'manifestation' of the Divine Life, if His language about His pre-existence did not clearly imply that before His birth of Mary He was already a living and superhuman Person.

If indeed, in His dealings with the multitude, our Lord had been really misunderstood, He had a last opportunity for explaining Himself when He was arraigned before the Sanhedrin. Nothing is more certain than that, whatever was the dominant motive that prompted our Lord's apprehension, the Sanhedrin condemned Him because He claimed Divinity. The members of the court stated this before Pilate. 'We have a law, and by our law He ought to die, because He made Himself the Son of God[a].' Their language would have been meaningless if they had understood by the 'Son of God' nothing more than the ethical or theocratic Sonship of their own ancient kings and saints. If the Jews held Christ to be a false Messiah, a false prophet, a blasphemer, it was because He claimed literal Divinity. True, the Messiah was to have been Divine. But the Jews had secularized the Messianic promises; and the Sanhedrin held Jesus Christ to be worthy of death under the terms of the Mosaic law, as expressed in Leviticus and Deuteronomy[b]. After the witnesses had delivered their various and inconsistent testimonies, the high priest arose and said, 'I adjure Thee by the living God, that Thou tell us whether Thou be the Christ, the Son of God. Jesus saith unto him, Thou hast said: nevertheless I say unto you, Hereafter shall ye see the Son of Man sitting on the right hand of power, and coming in the clouds of heaven. Then the high priest rent his clothes, saying, He hath spoken blasphemy[c].' The blasphemy did not consist, either in the assumption of the title Son of Man, or in the claim to be Messiah, or even, excepting indirectly, in that which by the terms of Daniel's prophecy was involved in Messiahship, namely, the commission to judge the world. It was the further claim[d] to be the Son of God,

[a] St. John xix. 7. 'Devant ce procurateur,' observes M. Salvador, 'chacune des parties émit une parole capitale. Telle fut celle du conseil ou de ses délégués: "Nous avons une loi; d'après cette loi il doit mourir," non parcequ'il s'est fait Fils de Dieu, selon l'expression familière à notre langue et à nos prophètes; mais parcequ'il se fait égal à Dieu, et Dieu même.' Salvador, Jésus-Christ, ii. p. 204.

[b] Lev. xxiv. 16; Deut. xiii. 5; cf. Wilson, Illustration of the Method of Explaining the New Testament, p. 26.

[c] St. Matt. xxvi. 63-65.

[d] Pressensé, Jésus-Christ, pp. 341, 615.

not in any moral or theocratic, but in the natural sense, at which the high priest and his coadjutors professed to be so deeply shocked. The Jews felt, as our Lord intended, that the Son of Man in Daniel's prophecy could not but be Divine; they knew what He meant by appropriating such words as applicable to Himself. Just as one body of Jews had endeavoured to destroy Jesus when He called God His Father in such sense as to claim Divinity [e]; and another when He contrasted His Eternal Being with the fleeting life of Abraham in a distant past [f]; and another when He termed Himself Son of God, and associated Himself with His Father as being dynamically and so substantially One [g]; —just as they murmured at His pretension to 'have come down from Heaven [h],' and detected blasphemy in His authoritative remission of sins [i];—so when, before His judges, He admitted that He claimed to be the Son of God, all further discussion was at an end. The high priest exclaimed 'Ye have heard His blasphemy;' and they all condemned Him to be guilty of death. And a very accomplished Jew of our own day, M. Salvador, has shewn that this question of our Lord's Divinity was the real point at issue in that momentous trial. He maintains that a Jew had no logical alternative to belief in the Godhead of Jesus Christ except the imperative duty of putting Him to death [k].

III. In order to do justice to the significance of our Lord's

[e] St. John v. 17, 18. [f] Ibid. viii. 58, 59. [g] Ibid. x. 30, 31, 39.
[h] Ibid. vi. 42. [i] St. Matt. ix. 3; St. Luke v. 20, 21.
[k] Salvador, Jésus-Christ, ii. pp. 132, 133, 195: 'La question avait un côté politique ou national juif: c'était la résistance du Fils de Marie, dans Jérusalem même, aux ordres et avertissements du grand Conseil. Au point de vue religieux, selon la loi, Jésus se trouvait en cause pour s'être déclaré égal à Dieu et Dieu lui-même.' See also the Rev. W. Wilson's Illustration of the Method of Explaining the New Testament, p. 77, sqq. Mr. Wilson shews that the Sanhedrin sincerely believed our Lord to be guilty of the crime of blasphemy, as inseparable, to a Jewish apprehension, from His claim to be Divine. This is argued (1) from the regularity of the proceedings of the Sanhedrin, the length of the trial, and the earnestness and unanimity of the judges. The false witnesses were considered as such by the Sanhedrin: our Lord was condemned on the strength of His Own confession; (2) from the language of the members of the Sanhedrin before Pilate: '*By our law* He ought to die, because He made Himself the Son of God;' (3) from the fact that the members of the Sanhedrin had no material object to gain by pronouncing Jesus guilty, without being persuaded of His criminality in claiming to be a Divine Person. Mr. Wilson fortifies these considerations by appealing to our Lord's silence, to St. Peter's address to his countrymen in Acts iii. 14-17, and to the general conduct of the Jewish people.

language about Himself, let us for a moment reflect on our very fundamental conceptions of His character. There is indeed a certain seeming impropriety in using that word 'character' with respect to Jesus Christ at all. For in modern language 'character' generally implies the predominance or the absence of some side or sides of that great whole, which we picture to ourselves in the background of each individual man as the true and complete ideal of human nature. This predominance or absence of particular traits or faculties, this precise combination of active or of passive qualities, determines the moral flavour of each individual life, and constitutes character. Character is that whereby the individual is marked off from the presumed standard or level of typical manhood. Yet the closest analysis of the actual Human Life of Jesus reveals a moral Portrait not only unlike any that men have witnessed before or since, but especially remarkable in that it presents an equally balanced and entirely harmonious representation of all the normal elements of our perfected moral nature[1]. Still, we may dare to ask the question: What are the features in that perfectly harmonious moral Life, upon which the reverence and the love of Christians dwells most constantly, most thankfully, most enthusiastically?

1. If then on such a subject I may utter a truism without irreverence, I say first of all that Jesus Christ was sincere. He possessed that one indispensable qualification for any teacher, specially for a teacher of religion: He believed in what He said, without reserve; and He said what He believed, without regard to consequences. Material error is very pardonable, if it be error which in good faith believes itself to be truth. But evident insincerity we cannot pardon; we cannot regard with any other sentiment than that of indignation the conscious propagation of what is known to be false, or even to be exaggerated. If however the sincerity of our Lord could be reasonably called in question, it might suffice, among the various facts which so irresistibly establish it, to point to His dealings with persons who followed and trusted Him. It is easy to denounce the errors of men who

[1] Young, Christ of History, p. 217: 'The difficulty which we chiefly feel in dealing with the character of Christ, as it unfolded itself before men, arises from its absolute perfection. On this very account it is less fitted to arrest observation. A single excellence unusually developed, though in the neighbourhood of great faults, is instantly and universally attractive. Perfect symmetry, on the other hand, does not startle, and is hidden from common and casual observers. But it is this which belongs emphatically to the Christ of the Gospels; and we distinguish in Him at each moment that precise manifestation which is most natural and most right.'

oppose us; but it is difficult to be always perfectly outspoken with those who love us, or who look up to us, or whose services may be of use to us, and who may be alienated by our outspokenness. Now Jesus Christ does not merely drag forth to the light of day the hidden motives of His powerful adversaries, that He may exhibit them with so mercifully implacable an accuracy, in all their baseness and pretension. He exposes, with equal impartiality, the weakness, or the unreality, or the self-deception of others who already regard Him with affection or who desire to espouse His cause. A disciple addresses him as 'Good Master.' The address was in itself sufficiently justifiable; but our Lord observed that the speaker had used it in an unreal and conventional manner. In order to mark His displeasure He solemnly asked, 'Why callest thou Me good? There is none good but One, that is, God [m].' A multitude which He has fed miraculously returns to seek Him on the following day; but instead of silently accepting this tacit proof of His popular power, He observes, 'Ye seek Me, not because ye saw the miracles, but because ye did eat of the loaves and were filled [n].' On another occasion, we are told, 'there went great multitudes with Him.' He turns, warns them that all human affections must be sacrificed to His service, and that none could be His disciple who does not take up the cross [o]. He solemnly bids men 'count the cost' before they 'build the tower' of discipleship [p]. He is on the point of being deserted by all, and an Apostle protests with fervid exaggeration that he is ready to go with Him to prison or to death. But our Lord, instead of at once welcoming the affection which dictated this protestation, pauses to shew Simon Peter how little he really knew of the weakness of his own heart [q]. With the woman of Samaria, with Simon the Pharisee, with the Jews in the temple, with the rich young man, it is ever the same; Christ cannot flatter, He cannot disguise, He cannot but set forth truth in its limpid purity [r]. Such was His moral attitude throughout: sincerity was the mainspring of His whole thought and action; and when He stood before His judges, He could exclaim, in this as in a wider sense, 'To this end was I born, and for this cause came I into the world, that I should bear witness unto the truth [s].' Surely this sincerity of our Holy Saviour is even at this hour a main secret of His attractive power. Men, we know, may

[m] St. Mark x. 18. [n] St. John vi. 26. [o] St. Luke xiv. 26, 27.
[p] Ibid. ver. 28. [q] St. John xiii. 37, 38.
[r] Cf. Newman, Parochial Sermons, vol. v. p. 37, serm. 3: 'Unreal Words.'
[s] St. John xviii. 37.

[LECT.

flatter and deceive, till at length the soul grows sick and weary of a world, which Truth in her stern simplicity might sometimes seem to have abandoned. But Jesus Christ, speaking to us from the Gospel pages, or speaking in the secret chambers of conscience, is a Monitor Whom we can trust to tell us the unwelcome but wholesome truth; and could we conceive of Him as false, He would no longer be Himself in our thought; He would not be changed; He would simply have disappeared [t].

2. A second moral truism: Jesus Christ was unselfish. His Life was a prolonged act of Self-sacrifice; and sacrifice of self is the practical expression and measure of unselfishness. It might have seemed that where there was no sin to be curbed or worn away by sorrow and pain, there room might have been found for a lawful measure of self-satisfaction. But 'even Christ pleased not Himself.' He 'sought not His own glory;' 'He came not to do His Own will [u].' His Body and His Soul, with all the faculties, the activities, the latent powers of each, were offered to the Divine Will. His friends, His relatives, His mother and His home, His pleasure, His reputation, His repose, were all abandoned for the glory of God and for the good of His brethren. His Self-sacrifice included the whole range of His human thought and affection and action; it lasted throughout His Life; its highest expression was His Death upon the Cross. Those who believe Him to have been merely a man endowed with the power of working miracles, or even only with the power of wielding vast moral influence over masses of men, cannot but recognise the rare loveliness and sublimity of a Life in which great powers were consciously possessed, yet were never exercised for those objects which the selfish instinct of ordinary men would naturally pursue. It is this disinterestedness; this devotion to the real interests of humankind; this radical antagonism of His whole character to that deepseated selfishness, which in our better moments we men hate in ourselves and which we always hate in others;—it is this complete

[t] Félix, Jésus-Christ, p. 316; Channing, Works, ii. 55: 'When I trace the unaffected majesty which runs through the life of Jesus, and see Him never falling below His sublime claims amidst poverty, and scorn, and in His last agony, I have a feeling of the reality of His character which I cannot express. I feel that the Jewish carpenter could no more have conceived and sustained this character under motives of imposture, than an infant's arm could repeat the deeds of Hercules, or his unawakened intellect comprehend and rival the matchless works of genius.'

[u] Rom. xv. 3; St. John v. 30, vi. 38; St. Matt. xxvi. 39.

renunciation of all that has no object beyond self, which has won to Jesus Christ the heart of mankind. In Jesus Christ we hail the One Friend Who loves perfectly; Who expresses perfect love by the utter surrender of Self; Who loves even unto death. In Jesus Christ we greet the Good Shepherd of humanity; He is the Good Shepherd under Whose care we can lack nothing, and Whose glory it is that He 'giveth His Life for the sheep[x].'

3. A third moral truism: Jesus Christ was humble. He might have appeared, even to human eyes, as 'One naturally contented with obscurity; wanting the restless desire for eminence and distinction which is so common in great men; hating to put forward personal claims; disliking competition and disputes who should be greatest; . . . fond of what is simple and homely, of children, and poor people[y].' It might have almost seemed as if His preternatural powers were a source of distress and embarrassment to Him; so eager was He to economize their exercise and to veil them from the eyes of men. He was particularly careful that His miracles should not add to His reputation[z]. Again and again He very earnestly enjoined silence on those who were the subjects of His miraculous cures[a]. He would not gratify persons whose motive in seeking His company was a vain curiosity to see the proofs of His power[b]. By this humility is Jesus Christ most emphatically distinguished from the philosophers of the ancient world. Whatever else they may have been, they were not humble. But Jesus Christ loses His individuality if you separate Him in thought for one moment from His 'great humility.' His humility is the key to His whole life; it is the measuring-line whereby His actions, His sufferings, His words, His very movements must be meted in order to be understood. 'Learn of Me,' He says, 'for I am meek and lowly of heart; and ye shall find rest unto your souls[c].'

But what becomes of these integral features of His character if, after considering the language which He actually used about Himself, we should go on to deny that He is God?

Is He, if He be not God, really humble? Is that reiterated Self-assertion, to the accents of which we have been listening this morning, consistent with any known form of creaturely humility? Can Jesus thus bid us believe in Him, love Him,

[x] St. John x. 11. [y] Ecce Homo, pp. 178, 179.

[z] St. Luke viii. 51.

[a] St. Matt. ix. 30: *ἐνεβριμήσατο*; xii. 16: *ἐπετίμησεν αὐτοῖς.*

[b] St. Mark viii. 11, 12; St. Matt. xvi. 1, 4; St. Luke xi. 16; St. John vi. 30. [c] St. Matt. xi. 29.

obey Him, live by Him, live for Him; can He thus claim to be the universal Teacher and the universal Judge, the Way, the Truth, the Life of humanity,—if He be indeed only man? What is humility but the honest recognition of truth respecting self? Could any mere man claim that place in thought, in society, in history, that authority over conscience, that relationship to the Most High; could he claim such powers and duties, such a position, and such prerogatives as are claimed by Jesus Christ, and yet be justly deemed 'meek and lowly of heart'? If Christ is God as well as Man, His language falls into its place, and all is intelligible; but if you deny His Divinity, you must conclude that some of the most precious sayings in the Gospel are but the outbreak of a preposterous self-laudation; they might well seem to breathe the very spirit of another Lucifer [d].

If Jesus Christ be not God, is He really unselfish? He bids men make Himself the centre of their affections and their thoughts; and when God does this He is but recalling man to that which is man's proper duty, to the true direction and law of man's being. But deny Christ's Divinity, and what will you say of the disinterestedness of His perpetual self-assertion [e]?

[d] Mr. F. W. Newman, Phases of Faith, p. 154: 'When I find his high satisfaction at all personal recognition and bowing before his individuality, I almost doubt whether, if one wished to draw the character of a *vain* and vacillating pretender, it would be possible to draw anything nearer to the purpose than this.' (p. 158), 'I can no longer give the same human reverence as before to one who has been seduced into vanity so egregious [as to claim to be the Son of Man].' So our Lord's parabolical sayings are said (p. 153) to 'indicate vanity and incipient sacerdotalism;' (p. 157), His tone, in dealing with the rich young man, is 'magisterial, decisive, and final,' so as to keep up 'his own ostentation of omniscience;' His precept bidding men receive those whom He sent (Matt. x. 40) suggests the observation that inasmuch as the disciples 'had no claims whatever, intrinsic or extrinsic, to reverence, it appears to me a very extravagant and fanatical sentiment thus to couple the favour or wrath of God with their reception or rejection' (p. 157). Compare Félix, Jésus-Christ, pp. 301–322.

[e] M. Renan accounts for our Lord's self-assertion in the following manner: 'Il ne prêchait pas ses opinions, il se prêchait lui-même. Souvent des âmes très-grandes et très-désintéressées présentent, associé à beaucoup d'élévation, ce caractère de perpétuelle attention à elles-mêmes, et *d'extrême susceptibilité personnelle, qui en général est le propre des femmes.* Leur persuasion que Dieu est en elles et s'occupe perpétuellement d'elles est si forte qu'elles ne craignent nullement de s'imposer aux autres.' (Vie de Jésus, p. 76.) Accordingly, we are told that 'Jésus ne doit pas être jugé sur la règle de nos petites convenances. L'admiration de ses disciples le débordait et l'entraînait. Il est évident que le titre de Rabbi, dont il s'était d'abord contenté, ne lui suffisait plus; le titre même de prophète ou d'envoyé de Dieu ne ré-

What matters it that He teaches the 'enthusiasm of humanity,' if that enthusiasm was after all to centre in a merely human self, and to surround His human presence with a tribute of superhuman honour? What avails it that He proclaims the law of self-renouncement, if He is Himself thus guilty of its signal infraction? Nay, for what generous purpose can He still be held to have died upon the Cross? The Cross is indeed for Christians the symbol and the throne of a boundless Love; but it is only such to those who believe in the Divinity of the Crucified. Deny the truth of Christ's account of Himself; deny the overwhelming moral necessity for His perpetual Self-assertion; and His Death may assume another aspect. For He plainly courted death by His last denunciations against the Pharisees, and by His presence at a critical moment in Jerusalem. That He was thus voluntarily slain and has redeemed us by His Blood is indeed the theme of the praises which Christians daily offer Him on earth and in paradise. But if He be not the Divine Victim freely offering Himself for men upon the altar of the Cross, may He not be what Christian lips cannot force themselves to utter? You urge that in any case He would be a man freely devoting himself for truth and goodness. But it is precisely here that His excessive self-assertion would impair our confidence in the purity of His motive. Is not self-sacrifice, even when pushed to the last extremity, a suspected and tainted thing, when it goes hand in hand with a consistent effort to give unwarranted prominence to self? Have not men ere now even risked death for the selfish, albeit unsubstantial, object of a posthumous renown[f]? If Jesus was merely man, and His death no more than the fitting close, the supreme effort of a life consistently devoted to the assertion of self, has He not 'succeeded beyond

pondait plus à sa pensée. La position qu'il s'attribuait était celle d'un être surhumain, et il voulait qu'on le regardât comme ayant avec Dieu un rapport plus élevé que celui des autres hommes.' (Vie de Jésus, p. 246.)

[f] Newman, Phases, p. 158: 'When he had resolved to claim Messiahship publicly, one of two results was inevitable, if that claim was ill-founded:—viz., either he must have become an impostor in order to screen his weakness; or he must have retracted his pretensions amid much humiliation and have retired into privacy to learn sober wisdom. *From these alternatives there was escape only by death,* and upon death Jesus purposely rushed.' (p. 161.) 'Does my friend deny that the death of Jesus was wilfully incurred? The "orthodox" not merely admit but maintain it. Their creed justifies it by the doctrine that his death was a "sacrifice" so pleasing to God as to expiate the sins of the world. This honestly meets the objections to self-destruction; for how better could life be used than by laying it down for such a prize.'

the dreams of the most delirious votary of fame? If the blood of a merely human Christ was the price which was deliberately paid for glory on Mount Calvary, then it is certain that the sufferer has had his reward. But at least he died, only as others have died, who have sought and found at the hands of their fellow-men, in death as in life, a tribute of sympathy, of admiration, of honour. And we owe to such a sufferer nothing beyond the compassionate silence wherewith charity would fain veil the violence of selfishness, robed in her garments, and seeking to share her glory and her power, while false to the very vital principle which makes her what she is[g].'

Once more, if Jesus Christ is not God, can we even say that He is sincere[h]? Let us suppose that it were granted, as it is by no means granted, that Jesus Christ nowhere asserts His literal Godhead[i]. Let us suppose that He was after all merely man, and had never meant to do more than describe, in the language of mysticism, the intertwining of His human Soul with the Spirit of God, in a communion so deep and absorbing as to obliterate His sense of distinct human personality. Let this, I say, be supposed to have been His meaning, and let His sincerity be taken for granted. Who then shall anticipate the horror of His soul or the fire of His words, when He is once made aware of the terrible misapprehension to which His language has given

[g] Félix, Jésus-Christ, p. 314; Young, The Christ of History, p. 229.

[h] Newman, Phases, p. 154: 'It sometimes seems to me the picture of a conscious and wilful impostor. His general character is too high for *this*; and I therefore make deductions from the account. Still I do not see how the present narrative could have grown up, if he had been really simple and straightforward and not perverted by his essentially false position.' Mr. Newman is complaining that our Lord 'does not honestly and plainly renounce pretension to miracle, as Mr. Martineau would,' but his language obviously suggests a wider application. (p. 158.) 'I feel assured, à priori, that such presumption [as that of claiming to be the Son of Man of Dan. vii.] *must have* entangled him into evasions and insincerities, which naturally end in crookedness of conscience and real imposture, however noble a man's commencement, and however unshrinking his sacrifice of goods and ease and life.'

[i] M. Renan indeed says, 'Jésus n'énonce pas un moment l'idée sacrilège qu'il soit Dieu.' (Vie de Jésus, p. 75.) Yet, 'on ne nie pas qu'il y eût dans les affirmations de Jésus *le germe de la doctrine* qui devait plus tard faire de lui une hypostase divine.' (Ibid. p. 247.) M. Renan even explains our Lord's language as to His Person on the ground that 'l'idéalisme transcendant de Jésus ne lui permit jamais d'avoir une notion bien claire de sa propre personnalité. *Il est son Père, son Père est lui.*' (p. 244.) In other words, our Lord did affirm His Divinity, but only because He was, unconsciously perhaps, a Pantheist!

rise in the minds around Him? 'Thou being a man, makest Thyself God.' The charge was literally true: being human, He did make Himself God. Christians believe that He only 'made' Himself that which He is. But if He is not God, where does He make any adequate repudiation of a construction of His words so utterly derogatory to the great Creator, so necessarily abhorrent to a good man's thought?

Is it urged that on one occasion He 'explained His claim to Divinity by a quotation which implied that He shared that claim with the chiefs of the theocracy?' It has already been shewn that by that quotation our Lord only deprecated immediate violence, and claimed a hearing for language which the Jews themselves regarded as not merely allowable, but sacred. The quotation justified His language only, and not His full meaning, which, upon gaining the ear of the people, He again proceeded to assert. Is it contended that in such sayings as that addressed to His disciples, 'My Father is greater than I[k],' He abandoned any pretension to be a Person internal to the Essential Life of God? It may suffice to reply, that this saying can have no such force, if its application be restricted, as the Latin Fathers do restrict it, and with great apparent probability, to our Lord's Manhood. But even if our Lord is here speaking, as the Greeks generally maintain, of His essential Deity, His Words still express very exactly a truth which is recognised and required by the Catholic doctrine. The Subordination of the Everlasting Son to the Everlasting Father is strictly compatible with the Son's absolute Divinity; it is abundantly implied in our Lord's language; and it is an integral element of the ancient doctrine which steadily represents the Father as Alone Unoriginate, the Fount of Deity in the Eternal Life of the Ever-blessed Trinity[l].

[k] St. John xiv. 28: *πορεύομαι πρὸς τὸν Πατέρα· ὅτι ὁ Πατήρ μου μείζων μου ἐστί.* For Patristic arguments against the Arian abuse of this text, see Suicer, Thes. ii. p. 1368. The *μειζονότης* of the Father is referred by St. Athanasius, St. Chrysostom, St. Basil (who, however, Ep. viii. gives the Latin int.), St. Hilary, to the Son's being the Only-begotten: cf. also Pearson on Cr. i. 243; Newman, Par. Serm. vi. 60. By St. Cyr. Alex. (de Rectâ Fide, 28; Thes. p. 91, and in loc.); St. Ambrose (in Conc. Aquil. § 36; de Fid. ii. 61); St. Augustine (in loc.; de Trin. i. 7; Enchir. x.); St. Leo (Ep. xxviii. ad Flav. c. 4; and in the Ath. Creed, to the Son's humiliation as incarnate. St. Augustine unites both explanations in De Fide et Symb. c. 9. St. Th. Aq. gives both: Summ. Theol. i. 33. 1; i. 43. 7.

[l] Bull, Def. Fid. Nic. iv. i. 1: 'Decretum illud Synodi Nicænæ, quo statuitur Filium Dei esse *Θεὸν ἐκ Θεοῦ*, Deum de Deo, suo calculo comprobârunt doctores Catholici, tum qui ante cum qui post Synodum illam

[LECT.

But surely an admission on the part of one in whom men saw nothing more than a fellow-creature, that the Everlasting God was 'greater' than himself, would fail to satisfy a thoughtful listener that no claim to Divinity was advanced by the speaker. Such an admission presupposes some assertion to which it stands in the relation of a necessary qualification. If any good man of our acquaintance should announce that God was 'greater' than himself, should we not hold him to be guilty of something worse than a stupid truism[m]? Would he not seem to imply that he was not really a creature of God's hand? Would not his words go to suggest that the notion of his absolute equality with God was not to be dismissed as altogether out of the question? Should we not peremptorily remind him that the life of man is related to the Life of God, not as the less to the greater, but as the created to the Uncreated, and that it is an impertinent irreverence to admit superiority of rank, where the real truth can only be expressed by an assertion of radical difference of natures? And assuredly a sane and honest man, who had been accused of associating himself with the Supreme Being, could not content himself with admitting that God was greater than himself. Knowing himself to be only human, would he not insist again and again, with passionate fervour, upon the incommunicable glory of the great Creator? Would not a purely human Christ have anticipated the burning words of the indignant Apostles at the gate of Lystra? Far more welcome to human virtue most surely it would have been to be accused of blasphemy for meaning what was never meant, than to be literally supposed to mean it. For indeed there are occasions when silence is impossible to a sincere soul[n]. Especially is this the case when acquiescence in falsehood is likely to gain personal reputation, when connivance at a

scripsêre. Nam illi omnes uno ore docuerunt naturam perfectionesque divinas, Patri Filioque competere non collateraliter aut coordinatè, sed subordinatè; hoc est, Filium eandem quidem naturam divinam cum Patre communem habere, sed à Patre communicatam; ita scilicet ut Pater solus naturam illam divinam a se habeat, sive à nullo alio, Filius autem à Patre; proinde *Pater, Divinitatis quæ in Filio est, fons, origo ac principium sit.*' See Bull's remarks on the error of calling the Son *αὐτόθεος*, as though He were not begotten of the Father, Ibid. iv. i. 7. Also Petavius, De Deo Deique proprietatibus, ii. 3, 6. Compare Hooker's Works, vol. i., Keble's Preface, p. lxxxi. When St. Athanasius calls our Lord *αὐτοσοφία* (Orat. ii. 78, iv. 24), *αὐτός* has the sense of 'full reality' as distinct from that of 'Self-origination;' the idea is excluded that He had only a measure of Wisdom or Divinity. See Petavius de Trin. vii. 11.

[m] Coleridge, Table-talk, p. 25.

[n] See Dean Alford on St. John xix. 9.

misapprehension may aggrandize self, ever so slightly, at the cost of others. How would the sincerity of a human teacher deserve the name, if, passively, without repudiation, without protest, he should allow language expressive whether of his moral elevation or of his mystical devotion to be popularly construed into a public claim to share the Rank and Name of the great God in heaven?

It is here that the so-termed historical Christ of M. Renan, who, as we are informed, is still the moral chief of humanity[o], would appear even to our natural English sense of honesty to be involved in serious moral difficulties. M. Renan indeed assures us, somewhat eagerly, that there are many standards of sincerity[p]; that is to say, that it is possible, under certain circumstances, to acquiesce knowingly in what is false, while yet being, in some

[o] Renan, Vie de Jésus, p. 457: 'Cette sublime personne, qui chaque jour préside encore au destin du monde, il est permis de l'appeler divine, non en ce sens que Jésus ait absorbé tout le divin, ou lui ait été adéquat (pour employer l'expression de la scolastique) mais en ce sens que Jésus est l'individu *qui a fait faire à son espèce le plus grand pas vers le divin.* L'humanité dans son ensemble offre un assemblage d'êtres bas, égoïstes, supérieurs à l'animal en cela seul que leur égoïsme est plus réfléchi. Mais, au milieu de cette uniforme vulgarité, des colonnes s'élèvent vers le ciel et attestent une plus noble destinée. Jésus est la plus haute de ces colonnes qui montrent à l'homme d'où il vient, et où il doit tendre. En lui s'est condensé tout ce qu'il y a de bon et d'élevé dans notre nature.' On the other hand, M. Renan is not quite consistent with himself, as he is of opinion that certain Pagans and unbelievers were in some respects superior to our Lord. 'L'honnête et suave Marc-Aurèle, l'humble et doux Spinoza, *n'ayant pas cru au miracle, ont été exempts de quelques erreurs que Jésus partagea.*' (Ibid. p. 451.) Moreover, this superiority to our Lord seems to be shared by that advanced school of sceptical enquirers to which M. Renan himself belongs. 'Par notre extrême délicatesse dans l'emploi des moyens de conviction, *par notre sincérité absolue et notre amour désintéressé de l'idée pure,* nous avons fondé, nous tous qui avons voué notre vie à la science, *un nouvel idéal de moralité.*' (Ibid.) Indeed, as regards our Lord, M. Renan suggests that 'il est probable que beaucoup de ses fautes ont été dissimulées.' (Ibid. p. 458.)

[p] Ibid. p. 252: 'Pour nous, races profondément sérieuses, la conviction signifie la sincérité avec soi-même. Mais la sincérité avec soi-même n'a pas beaucoup de sens chez les peuples orientaux, peu habitués aux délicatesses de l'esprit critique. Bonne foi et imposture sont des mots qui, dans notre conscience rigide, s'opposent comme deux termes inconciliables. En Orient, il y a de l'un à l'autre mille fuites et mille détours. Les auteurs de livres apocryphes (de "Daniel," d' "Hénoch," par exemple), hommes si exaltés, commettaient pour leur cause, et bien certainement sans ombre de scrupule, un acte que nous appellerions un faux. La vérité matérielle a très-peu de prix pour l'oriental; il voit tout à travers ses idées, ses intérêts, ses passions. L'histoire est impossible, si l'on n'admet hautement *qu'il y a pour la sincérité plusieurs mesures.*'

transcendental sense, sincere. Thus, just as the Christ of M. Renan can permit the raising of Lazarus to look like a miracle, while he must know that the whole episode has been a matter of previous arrangement[q], so he can apparently use language which is generally understood to claim Divinity, without being bound to explain that he is altogether human[r]. The 'ideal of humanity' contents himself, it appears, with a lower measure, so to call it, of sincerity; and while we are scarcely embarrassed by the enquiry whether such sincerity is sincere or not, we cannot hesitate to observe that it is certainly consistent neither with real humility nor with real unselfishness[s].

Thus our Lord's human glory fades before our eyes when we attempt to conceive of it apart from the truth of His Divinity. He is only perfect as Man, because He is truly God. If He is

[q] M. Renan introduces his account of the resurrection of Lazarus by observing that 'les amis de Jésus désiraient un grand miracle qui frappât vivement l'incrédulité hiérosolymite. La résurrection d'un homme connu à Jérusalem dut paraître ce qu'il y avait de plus convaincant. Il faut se rappeler ici que la condition essentielle de la vraie critique est de comprendre la diversité des temps, et de se dépouiller des répugnances instinctives qui sont le fruit d'une éducation purement raisonnable. Il faut se rappeler aussi que dans cette ville impure et pesante de Jérusalem *Jésus n'était plus lui-même. Sa conscience, par la faute des hommes et non par la sienne, avait perdu quelque chose de sa limpidité primordiale.*' (Vie de Jésus, p. 359.) Under these circumstances, 'il se passa à Béthanie quelque chose qui fut regardé comme une résurrection.' (p. 360.) '*Peut-être* Lazare, pâle encore de sa maladie, se fit-il entourer de bandelettes comme un mort, et enfermer dans son tombeau de famille. . . Jésus désira voir encore une fois celui qu'il avait aimé, et, la pierre ayant été écartée, Lazare sortit avec ses bandelettes et la tête entourée d'un suaire. Cette apparition dut naturellement être regardée par tout le monde comme une résurrection. La foi ne connaît d'autre loi que l'intérêt de ce qu'elle croit le vrai. . . . . Quant à Jésus, il n'était pas plus maître que saint Bernard, que saint François d'Assise de modérer l'avidité de la foule et de ses propres disciples pour le merveilleux. La mort, d'ailleurs, allait dans quelques jours lui rendre sa liberté divine, et *l'arracher aux fatales nécessités d'un rôle qui chaque jour devenait plus exigeant, plus difficile à soutenir.*' (p. 363.)

[r] Sometimes M. Renan endeavours to avoid this conclusion by representing our Lord's self-proclamation as being in truth the result of a vain self-surrender to the fanatical adulation of His followers, the reiteration of which in the end deceived Himself. (Vie de Jésus, p. 139): 'Naturellement, plus on croyait en lui, plus il croyait en lui-même.' Accordingly (p. 240) 'sa légende [i.e. the account given of Him in the Gospels and in the Apostles' Creed, and specially the doctrine of His Divinity] était le fruit d'une grande conspiration toute spontanée *et s'élaborait autour de lui de son vivant.*' Thus (p. 238) the Christ of M. Renan first allows himself to be falsely called the Son of David, and then 'il finit, ce semble, par y prendre plaisir.' Cf. p. 297, note.

[s] Félix, Jésus-Christ, p. 321.

not God, He is not a humble or an unselfish man. Nay, He is not even sincere; unless indeed we have recourse to a supposition upon which the most desperate of His modern opponents have not yet ventured, and say with His jealous kinsmen in the early days of His Ministry, that He was beside Himself[t]. Certainly it would seem that there must have been strange method in a madness which could command the adoration of the civilized world; nor would any such supposition be seriously entertained by those who know under what conditions the very lowest forms of moral influence are at all possible. The choice really lies between the hypothesis of conscious and culpable insincerity, and the belief that Jesus speaks literal truth and must be taken at His word[u].

You complain that this is one of those alternatives which orthodoxy is wont to substitute for less violent arguments, and from the exigencies of which you piously recoil? But under certain circumstances such alternatives are legitimate guides to truth, nay, they are the only guides available. Certainly we cannot create such alternatives by any process of dialectical manufacture, if they do not already exist. If they are not matters of fact, they can easily be convicted of inaccuracy. We who stand in this pulpit are not makers or masters of the eternal harmonies; we can but exhibit them as best we may. Truth, even in her severer moods, must ever be welcome to sincerity; and she does us a service by reminding us that it is not always possible to embrace within the range of our religious negations just so much dogma as we wish to deny, and to leave the rest really intact. It is no hardship to reason that we cannot deny the conclusion of a proposition of Euclid, without impugning the axioms which are the basis of its demonstration. It is no hardship to faith that we cannot deny the Divinity of Jesus, without casting a slur upon His Human Character. There are

[t] Channing, Works, ii. 56: 'The charge of an extravagant, self-deluding enthusiasm is the last to be fastened on Jesus. Where can we find traces of it in His history? Do we detect them in the calm authority of His precepts; in the mild, practical, beneficent spirit of His religion; in the unlaboured simplicity of the language in which He unfolds His high powers and the sublime truths of religion; or in the good sense, the knowledge of human nature which He always discovers in His estimate and treatment of the different classes of men with whom He acted? . . . . The truth is, that, remarkable as was the character of Jesus, it was distinguished by nothing more than by calmness and self-possession.'

[u] Cf. Guizot, Méditations sur l'Essence de la Religion Chrétienne. Paris, 1864, pp. 324-326.

fatal inclines in the world of religious thought; and even if men deem it courteous to ignore them, such courtesy is scarcely charitable. If our age does not guide anxious minds by its loyal adherence to God's Revelation, its very errors may have their uses; they may warn us off ground, on which Reason cannot rest, and where Faith is imperilled, by enacting before our eyes a *reductio ad absurdum* or a *reductio ad horribile.*

Of a truth the alternative before us is terrible; but can devout and earnest thought falter for a moment in the agony of its suspense? Surely it cannot. The moral Character of Christ, viewed in connection with the preternatural facts of His Human Life, will bear the strain which the argument puts upon it[1]. It is easier for a good man to believe that, in a world where he is encompassed by mysteries, where his own being itself is a consummate mystery, the Moral Author of the wonders around him should for great moral purposes have taken to Himself a created form, than that the one Human Life which realizes the idea of humanity, the one Man Who is at once perfect strength and perfect tenderness, the one Pattern of our race in Whom its virtues are combined, and from Whom its vices are eliminated, should have been guilty, when speaking about Himself, of an arrogance, of a self-seeking, and of an insincerity which, if admitted, must justly degrade Him far below the moral level of millions among His unhonoured worshippers. It is easier, in short, to believe that God has consummated His works of wonder and of mercy by a crowning Self-revelation in which mercy and beauty reach their climax, than to close the moral eye to the brightest spot that meets it in human history, and—since a bare Theism reproduces the main difficulties of Christianity without any of its compensations—to see at last in man's inexplicable destiny only the justification of his despair. Yet the true alternative to this frightful conclusion is in reality a frank acceptance of the doctrine which is under consideration in

[1] Channing, Works, ii. 61: 'I know not what can be added to heighten the wonder, reverence, and love, which are due to Jesus. When I consider Him, not only as possessed with the consciousness of an unexampled and unbounded majesty, but as recognising a kindred nature in all human beings, and living and dying to raise them to a participation of His divine glories; and when I see Him under these views allying Himself to men by the tenderest ties, embracing them with a spirit of humanity which no insult, injury, or pain could for a moment repel or overpower, I am filled with wonder as well as reverence and love. I feel that this character is not of human invention, that it was not assumed through fraud or struck out by enthusiasm; for it is infinitely above their reach.'

these lectures[y]. For Christianity, both as a creed and as a life, depends absolutely upon the Personal Character of its Founder. Unless His virtues were only apparent, unless His miracles were nothing better than a popular delusion, we must admit that His Self-assertion is justified, even in the full measure of its blessed and awful import. We must deny the antagonism which is said to exist between the doctrine of Christ's Divinity and the history of His human manifestation. We must believe and confess that the Christ of history is the Christ of the Catholic Creed.

Eternal Jesus! it is Thyself Who hast thus bidden us either despise Thee or worship Thee. Thou wouldest have us despise Thee as our fellow-man, if we will not worship Thee as our God. Gazing on Thy Human beauty, and listening to Thy words, we cannot deny that Thou art the Only Son of God Most High; disputing Thy Divinity, we could no longer clearly recognise Thy Human perfections. But if our ears hearken to Thy revelations of Thy greatness, our souls have already been won to Thee by Thy truthfulness, by Thy lowliness, and by Thy love. Convinced by these Thy moral glories, and by Thy majestic exercise of creative and healing power, we believe and are sure that Thou hast the words of eternal life. Although in unveiling Thyself before Thy creatures, Thou dost stand from age to age at the bar of hostile and sceptical opinion; yet assuredly from age to age, by the assaults of Thine enemies no less than in the faith of Thy believing Church, Thou art justified in Thy sayings and art clear when Thou art judged. Of a truth, Thou art the King of Glory, O Christ; Thou art the Everlasting Son of the Father.

[y] Channing might almost seem to have risen for a moment to the full faith of the Church of Christ in the following beautiful words; Works, ii. 57: 'I confess when I can escape the deadening power of habit, and can receive the full import of such passages as the following: "Come unto Me, all ye that labour and are heavy laden, and I will give you rest;" "I am come to seek and to save that which was lost;" "He that confesseth Me before men, him will I confess before My Father in Heaven;" "Whosoever shall be ashamed of Me before men, of him shall the Son of Man be ashamed when He cometh in the glory of the Father with the holy angels;" "In My Father's house are many mansions, I go to prepare a place for you;" I say, when I can succeed in realising the import of such passages, I feel myself listening to a being such as never before and never since spoke in human language. I am awed by the consciousness of greatness which these simple words express; and when I connect this greatness with the proofs of Christ's miracles, I am compelled to speak with the centurion, "Truly this was the Son of God."' Alas! that this language does not mean what we might hope, is too certain from other passages in his writings. See e.g. Works, ii. 510: 'Christ is a being distinct from the one GOD.'

LECTURE V.

THE DOCTRINE OF CHRIST'S DIVINITY IN THE WRITINGS OF ST. JOHN.

That Which was from the beginning, Which we have heard, Which we have seen with our eyes, Which we have looked upon, and our hands have handled, of the Word of Life; (for the Life was manifested, and we have seen It, and bear witness, and shew unto you that Eternal Life, Which was with the Father, and was manifested unto us;) That Which we have seen and heard declare we unto you.—ST. JOHN i. 1–3.

AN attempt was made last Sunday to determine, from the recorded language of Jesus Christ, what was the verdict of His Own consciousness, expressed as well as implied, respecting the momentous question of His higher and Eternal Nature. But we were incidentally brought face to face with a problem, the fuller consideration of which lies naturally in the course of the present discussion. It is undeniable that the most numerous and direct claims to Divinity on the part of our Lord are to be found in the Gospel of St. John. While this fact has a significance of a positive kind which will be noticed presently, it also involves the doctrine before us in the entanglement of a large critical question. To leave this question undiscussed would, under existing circumstances, be impossible. To discuss it, within the limits assigned to the lecturer, and even with a very moderate regard to the amount of details which it necessarily involves, must needs make a somewhat unwonted demand, as you will indulgently bear in mind, upon the patience and attention of the audience.

If the Book of Daniel has been recently described as the battle-field of the Old Testament, it is not less true that St. John's Gospel is the battle-field of the New. It is well understood on all sides that no question of mere *dilettante* criticism is at stake when the authenticity of St. John's Gospel is challenged. The point of this momentous enquiry lies close to the very heart of the creed of Christendom;

'Neque enim levia aut ludicra petuntur
Præmia; sed Turni de vitâ et sanguine certant[a].'

Strange and mournful it may well seem to a Christian that the pages of the Evangelist of Divine love should have been the object of an attack so energetic, so persevering, so inventive, so unsparing! Strange indeed such vehement hostility might be deemed, if only it were not in harmony with that deep instinct of our nature which forbids neutrality when we are face to face with high religious truth; which forces us to take really, if not avowedly, a side respecting it; which constrains us to hate or to love, to resist or to obey, to accept or to reject it. If St. John's Gospel had been the documentary illustration of some extinct superstition, or the title-deed of some suppressed foundation, at best capable of attracting the placid interest of studious antiquarianism, the attacks which have been made on it might well have provoked our marvel. As it is, there is no room for legitimate wonder, that the words of the Evangelist, like the Person of the Master, should be a stone of stumbling and a rock of offence. For St. John's Gospel is the most conspicuous written attestation to the Godhead of Him Whose claims upon mankind can hardly be surveyed without passion, whether it be the passion of adoring love, or the passion of vehement and determined enmity.

I. From the disappearance of the obscure heretics called Alogi, in the later sub-apostolic age[b], until the end of the seventeenth century, the authenticity of St. John's Gospel was not questioned. The earliest modern objections to it seem to have been put forward in this country, and to have been based on the assumption of a discrepancy between the narrative of St. John and those of the first three Gospels. These objections were combated by the learned Leclerc; and for well-nigh a century the point was thought to have been decided[c]. The brilliant reputation of Herder secured attention for his characteristic theory that St. John's Gospel describes, not the historical, but an ideal Christ. Herder was followed by several German writers,

[a] Virg. Æn. xii. 764, 765.

[b] That the Alogi had no idea of a *recent* origin of St. John's Gospel is clear from their ascribing it to Cerinthus. Dorner, Person Christi, i. p. 501, note. S. Epiph. Hær. li.

[c] It ought perhaps to have been added that Evanson's attack upon St. John in 1792 was answered by Dr. Priestley.

[LECT.

who accepted conclusions which he had implied, and who expressly rejected the authenticity of the fourth Gospel [d]. But these negative criticisms were met in turn by the arguments of Roman Catholic divines like Hug, and of critics who were by no means loyal even to Lutheran orthodoxy, such as Eichhorn and Kuinoel. By their labours the question was again held to have been set at rest in the higher regions of German scholarship and free-thinking. This second settlement was rudely disturbed by the publication of the famous 'Probabilia' of Bretschneider, the learned superintendent of Gotha, in the year 1820 [e]. Reproducing the arguments which had been advanced by the earlier negative speculation, and adding others of his own, Bretschneider rekindled the discussion. He exaggerated the contrast between the representation of our Lord's Person in St. John and that in the synoptists into a positive contradiction. Protestant Germany was then fascinated by the school of Schleiermacher, which, by the aid of a combination of criticism and mysticism [f], was groping its way back towards the creeds of the Catholic Church. Schleiermacher, as is well known, not only accepted the Church-belief respecting the fourth Gospel, but he found in that Gospel the reason for his somewhat reckless estimate of the other three. The sharp controversy which followed resulted in Bretschneider's retractation of his thesis, and the impression produced by this retractation was not violently interfered with until 1835, when Dr. Strauss shocked the conscience of all that was Christian in Europe by the publication of his first 'Life of Jesus.' Dr. Strauss' position in respect of St. John's Gospel was a purely negative one. He confined himself to asserting that St. John's Gospel was not what the Church had always believed it to be, that it was not the work of the son of Zebedee. The school of Tübingen aspired to supplement this negative criticism of Strauss by a positive hypothesis. St. John's Gospel was held to represent a highly-developed stage of an orthodox gnosis, the growth of which presupposed the lapse of at least a century since the age of the Apostles. It was decided by the

[d] Especially by Dr. Ammon, preacher and professor of theology at Erlangen and Dresden successively.

[e] Probabilia de Evangelii et Epistolarum Johannis Apostoli indole et origine. Lipsiæ, 1820.

[f] See more especially Schleiermacher's *Glaubenslehre*, and compare Professor Auberlen's account of the process through which, at Tübingen, he 'was led back, among other things, mainly by Schleiermacher's mysticism, so full of life and spirit, to the sanctuary of religion, and learnt to sit again at the feet of the Redeemer.' On Divine Revelation, pref.

leading writers of the school of Tübingen, by Drs. Baur, Schwegler, and Zeller, that the fourth Gospel was not composed until after the year A.D. 160. And, although this opinion may have been slightly modified by later representatives of the Tübingen school, such as Hilgenfeld; the general position, that the fourth Gospel was not written before the middle of the second century, is held by disciples of that school as one of its very fundamental tenets.

Here then it is necessary to enquire, what was the belief of the second century itself, as to the date and authenticity of St. John's Gospel[g].

Now it is scarcely too much to assert that every decade of the second century furnishes its share of proof that the four Gospels as a whole, and St. John's in particular, were to the Church of that age what they are to the Church of the present. Beginning at the end of the century, we may observe how general at that date was the reception of the four Gospels throughout the Catholic Church. Writing at Lyons, in the last decade of the century, St. Irenæus discourses on various cosmical and spiritual analogies to the fourfold form of the Gospel narrative (*εὐαγγέλιον τετράμορφον*) in a strain of mystical reflection which implies that the co-ordinate authority of the four Gospels had been already long established[h]. St. Irenæus, it is well known, had sat at the feet of St. Polycarp, who was himself a disciple of St. John. St. Irenæus, in his letter to the erring Florinus, records with reverent affection what Polycarp had told him of the lessons which he had personally learnt from John and the other disciples of Jesus[i]. Now is it barely probable that Irenæus should have

[g] For a recent and complete discussion of this subject see Prof. Westcott, St. John's Gospel, Intr. pp. xxviii–xxxii, London, Murray. [1881.]

[h] St. Irenæus, adv. Hær. iii. 11. 8: *ἐξ ὧν φανερὸν, ὅτι ὁ τῶν ἁπάντων τεχνίτης Λόγος, ὁ καθήμενος ἐπὶ τῶν Χερουβὶμ καὶ συνέχων τὰ πάντα, φανερωθεὶς τοῖς ἀνθρώποις, ἔδωκεν ἡμῖν τετράμορφον τὸ εὐαγγέλιον, ἑνὶ δὲ πνεύματι συνεχόμενον. . . . Καὶ γὰρ τὰ Χερουβὶμ τετραπρόσωπα· καὶ τὰ πρόσωπα αὐτῶν, εἰκόνες τῆς πραγματείας τοῦ Υἱοῦ τοῦ Θεοῦ. . . Καὶ τὰ εὐαγγέλια οὖν τούτοις σύμφωνα, ἐν οἷς ἐγκαθέζεται Χριστός. Τὸ μὲν γὰρ κατὰ Ἰωάννην, τὴν ἀπὸ τοῦ Πατρὸς ἡγεμονικὴν αὐτοῦ . . . . . καὶ ἔνδοξον γενεὰν διηγεῖται, λέγων· ἐν ἀρχῇ ἦν ὁ Λόγος.*

[i] St. Irenæus, fragment, vol. i. p. 822, ed. Stieren.: *εἶδον γάρ σε, παῖς ὢν ἔτι ἐν τῇ κάτω Ἀσίᾳ παρὰ τῷ Πολυκάρπῳ, λαμπρῶς πράττοντα ἐν τῇ βασιλικῇ αὐλῇ, καὶ πειρώμενον εὐδοκιμεῖν παρ' αὐτῷ· μᾶλλον γὰρ τὰ τότε διαμνημονεύω τῶν ἔναγχος γινομένων· (αἱ γὰρ ἐκ παίδων μαθήσεις, συναύξουσαι τῇ ψυχῇ, ἑνοῦνται αὐτῇ) ὥστε με δύνασθαι εἰπεῖν καὶ τὸν τόπον, ἐν ᾧ καθεζόμενος διελέγετο ὁ μακάριος Πολύκαρπος, καὶ τὰς προσόδους αὐτοῦ καὶ τὰς εἰσόδους καὶ τὸν χαρακτῆρα τοῦ βίου καὶ τὴν τοῦ σώματος ἰδέαν καὶ τὰς διαλέξεις ἃς ἐποιεῖτο πρὸς τὸ πλῆθος, καὶ τὴν μετὰ Ἰωάννου συναναστροφὴν ὡς ἀπήγγελλε, καὶ τὴν*

imagined that a literary forgery, which is asserted to have been produced at a date when he was himself a boy of twelve or fourteen years of age, was actually the work of the Apostle John[j]? At Carthage, about the same time, Tertullian wrote his great work against the heretic Marcion[k]. Tertullian brought to the discussion of critical questions great natural acuteness, which had been sharpened during his early life by his practice at the African bar. Tertullian distinguishes between the primary, or actually apostolical rank of St. Matthew and St. John, and the lower standing of St. Mark and St. Luke, as being apostolical men of a secondary degree[l]; but he treats all four as inspired writers of an authority beyond discussion[m]. Against Marcion's mutilations of the sacred text Tertullian fearlessly appeals to the witness of the most ancient apostolical Churches. Tertullian's famous canon runs thus: 'Si constat id verius quod prius, id prius quod et ab initio, id ab initio quod ab apostolis, pariter ubique constabit, id esse ab apostolis traditum, quod apud ecclesias apostolorum fuerit sacrosanctum[n].' But what would have been the worth of this appeal if it could have been even suspected that the last Gospel was really written when Tertullian was a boy or even a young man? At Alexandria, almost contemporaneously with Tertullian, St. Clement investigated the relation

τῶν λοιπῶν τῶν ἑωρακότων τὸν Κύριον, καὶ ὡς ἀπεμνημόνευε τοὺς λόγους αὐτῶν· καὶ περὶ τοῦ Κυρίου τίνα ἦν ἃ παρ' ἐκείνων ἀκηκόει, καὶ περὶ τῶν δυνάμεων αὐτοῦ, καὶ περὶ τῆς διδασκαλίας, ὡς παρὰ τῶν αὐτοπτῶν τῆς ζωῆς τοῦ Λόγου παρειληφὼς ὁ Πολύκαρπος, ἀπήγγελλε πάντα σύμφωνα ταῖς γραφαῖς. Cf. Eus. Hist. Eccl. v. 20. St. Irenæus succeeded St. Pothinus in the see of Lyons. Pothinus was martyred A.D. 177, and Irenæus died A.D. 202.

[j] Adv. Hær. iii. 1. St. Irenæus was probably born about A.D. 140.

[k] Tertullian was born at Carthage about A.D. 160. Cave places his conversion to Christianity at A.D. 185, and his lapse into the Montanist heresy at A.D. 199. Dr. Pusey (Libr. of Fathers) makes his conversion later, A.D. 195, and his secession from the Church A.D. 201.

[l] Adv. Marc. iv. c. 2: 'Constituimus imprimis evangelicum instrumentum apostolos auctores habere, quibus hoc munus evangelii promulgandi ab Ipso Domino sit impositum. Si et apostolicos, non tamen solos, sed cum apostolis et post apostolos, quoniam prædicatio discipulorum suspecta fieri posset de gloriæ studio, si non adsistat illi auctoritas magistrorum, immo Christi, quæ magistros apostolos fecit. Denique nobis fidem ex apostolis Joannes et Matthæus insinuant, ex apostolicis Lucas et Marcus instaurant.'

[m] Adv. Marc. iv. c. 5: 'Eadem auctoritas ecclesiarum apostolicarum ceteris quoque patrocinabitur Evangeliis, quæ proinde per illas et secundum illas habemus, Joannis dico et Matthæi, licet et Marcus quod edidit Petri affirmetur, cujus interpres Marcus. Nam et Lucæ digestum Paulo adscribere solent. Capit magistrorum videri quæ discipuli promulgarint.'

[n] Adv. Marcion. iv. 5.

of the synoptic Gospels to St. John [o], and he terms the latter the *εὐαγγέλιον πνευματικόν* [p]. It is unnecessary to say that the intellectual atmosphere of that famous Græco-Egyptian school would not have been favourable to any serious countenance of a really suspected document. At Rome St. John's Gospel was certainly received as being the work of that Apostle in the year 170. This is clear from the so-termed Muratorian fragment [q]; and if in receiving it the Roman Church had been under a delusion so fundamental as is implied by the Tübingen hypothesis, St. John's own pupil Polycarp might have been expected to have corrected his Roman brethren when he came to Rome in the year 163 [r]. In the farther East, St. John's Gospel had already been translated as a matter of course into the Peschito Syriac version [s]. It had been translated in Africa into the Latin Versio Itala [t]. At or soon after the middle of the century two works

[o] Westcott, Canon of the New Testament, 5th ed. p. 119. See this writer's remarks on St. Clement's antecedents and position in the Church, ibid. pp. 343, 344. St. Clement lived from about 165 to 220. He flourished as a Christian Father under Severus and Caracalla, 193-220.

[p] Eus. Hist. Eccl. vi. 14, condensing Clement's account, says, *τὸν μέντοι Ἰωάννην ἔσχατον συνιδόντα ὅτι τὰ σωματικὰ ἐν τοῖς εὐαγγελίοις δεδήλωται, προτραπέντα ὑπὸ τῶν γνωρίμων, Πνεύματι θεοφορηθέντα, πνευματικὸν ποιῆσαι εὐαγγέλιον.*

[q] Westcott on the Canon, p. 214. The Muratorian fragment claims to have been written by a contemporary of Pius I., who probably ruled the Roman Church from about A. D. 142 to 157. 'Pastorem vero *nuperrimè temporibus nostris* in urbe Roma Hermas conscripsit, sedente cathedrâ urbis Romæ ecclesiæ Pio episcopo fratre ejus.' Cf. Hilgenfeld, Der Kanon und die Kritik des N. T., p. 39, sqq.

[r] St. Polycarp's martyrdom has been lately fixed in A. D. 155-6. Lightfoot, Cont. Rev. 1875, p. 838. But cf. Wordsworth's Ch. Hist. to Coun. of Nic., p. 161, note. [1881.]

[s] On the difficulty of fixing the exact date of the Peschito version see Westcott, Canon of New Testament, pp. 236-243. Referring (1) to the Syriac tradition of its Apostolic origin at Edessa, repeated by Gregory Bar Hebræus; (2) to the necessary existence of an early Syriac version, implied in the controversial writings of Bardesanes; (3) to the quotations of Hegesippus from the Syriac, related by Eusebius (Hist. Eccl. iv. 22); (4) to the antiquity of the language of the Peschito as compared with that of St. Ephrem, and the high authority in which this version was held by that Father; (5) to the liturgical and general use of it by heretical as well as orthodox Syrians; and (6) to the early translations made from it;—Dr. Westcott concludes that in the absence of more copious critical resources which might serve to determine the date of this version on philological grounds, 'there is no sufficient reason to desert the opinion which has obtained the sanction of the most competent scholars, that its formation is to be fixed *within the first half of the second century*.' (p. 243.) That it was complete then in A. D. 150-160, we may assume without risk of serious error.

[t] This version must have been made before A. D. 170. 'How much more

were published which implied that the four Gospels had long been received as of undoubted authority: I refer to the Harmonies of Theophilus[u], Bishop of Antioch, and of Tatian[v], the heterodox pupil of St. Justin Martyr. St. John is quoted by either writer independently, in the work which was addressed by Theophilus to Autolycus[w], and in the Apology of Tatian[x]. When, about the year 170, Apollinaris of Hierapolis points out the bearings of the different evangelical narratives upon the Quartodeciman controversy, his argument implies a familiarity with St. John. Apollinaris refers to the piercing of our Lord's Side[y], and Polycrates of Ephesus speaks of John as the disciple who lay on the bosom of Jesus[z]. Here we see that the last Gospel must have been read and heard in the Christian Churches with a care which dwells upon its distinctive peculiarities. It is surely inconceivable that a work of such primary claim to speak on the question of highest interest for Christian believers could have been forged, widely circulated, and immediately received by Africans, by Romans, by Gauls, by Syrians, as a work of an Apostle who had passed to his rest some sixty years before. And, if the evidence before us ended here, we might fairly infer that, considering the difficulties of communication between Churches in the sub-apostolic age, and the various elements of moral and intellectual caution, which, as notably in the case of

ancient it really is cannot yet be discovered. Not only is the character of the version itself a proof of its extreme age, but the mutual relation of different parts of it shew that it was made originally by different hands; and if so, it is natural to conjecture that it was coeval with the introduction of Christianity into Africa, and the result of the spontaneous effort of African Christians.' (Westcott on the Canon of the New Testament, p. 258.) Dr. Westcott shews from Tertullian (Adv. Prax. c. 5) that at the end of the century *the Latin translation of St. John's Gospel* had been so generally circulated in Africa, as to have moulded the popular theological dialect. (Ibid. p. 251.)

[u] At latest Theophilus was bishop from A.D. 168 to 180. St. Jerome says: 'Theophilus . . . quatuor evangelistarum in unum opus dicta compingens, ingenii sui nobis monumenta dimisit.' Epist. 121 (al. 151) ad Algas. c. 6.

[v] Eus. Hist. Eccl. iv. 29; Theodoret, Hær. Fab. i. 20; Westcott, Canon, pp. 322, 323, sqq. The recent discovery of the Commentary of St. Ephrem Syrus on Tatian's Diatessaron adds to the evidential importance of that work [1884].

[w] Ad Autol. ii. 31, p. 174, ed. Wolf. Cf. St. John i. 1, 3. Theophilus is the first writer who quotes St. John *by name*.

[x] Orat. contr. Græc. c. 4 (St. John iv. 24); c. 5 (Ibid. i. 1); c. 13 (Ibid. i. 5); c. 19 (Ibid. i. 3).

[y] Chron. Pasch. p. 14; cf. St. John xix. 34; Routh, i. 160, sq.; Westcott, Canon, p. 228 and note 1.

[z] Apud Eus. v. 24. Cf. St. John xiii. 23, xxi. 20.

the Epistle to the Hebrews, were likely to delay the œcumenical reception of a canonical book, St. John's Gospel must have been in existence at the beginning of the second century.

But the evidence does not desert us at this point. Through Tatian we ascend into the earlier portion of the century as represented by St. Justin Martyr. It is remarkable that St. Justin's second Apology, written in 161, contains fewer allusions to the Gospels than the earlier Apology written in 138[a], and than the intermediate composition of this Father, his Dialogue with the Jew Trypho. Now passing by recent theories respecting a Gospel of the Hebrews or a Gospel of Peter, by which an endeavour has been made to weaken St. Justin's witness to the synoptic Evangelists, let us observe that his testimony to St. John is particularly distinct. Justin's emphatic reference of the doctrine of the Logos to our Lord[b], not to mention his quotation of John the Baptist's reply to the messengers of the Jews[c], and of our Saviour's language about the new birth[d], makes his knowledge of St. John's Gospel much more than a probability[e]. Among the great Apostolic fathers, St. Ignatius alludes to St. John in his Letter to the Romans[f], and St. Polycarp quotes the Apostle's first Epistle[g]. In these sub-apostolic writings there are large districts of thought and expression, of a type unmistakeably Johannean[h], which, like

[a] So Gieseler. ii. 3. § 50.

[b] Cf. Tischendorf, Wann wurden unsere Evangelien verfasst? p. 16: 'Die Uebertragung des Logos auf Christus, von der uns keine Spur weder in der Synoptikern noch in den ältesten Parallelschriften derselben vorliegt, an mehreren Stellen Justins von Johannes abzuleiten ist.'

[c] Ibid. Dialog. cum Tryph. 88. Cf. St. John i. 20.

[d] Apolog. i. 61: καὶ γὰρ ὁ Χριστὸς εἶπεν· ''Ἂν μὴ ἀναγεννηθῆτε, οὐ μὴ εἰσέλθητε εἰς τὴν βασιλείαν τῶν οὐρανῶν·' Ὅτι δὲ καὶ ἀδύνατον εἰς τὰς μήτρας τῶν τεκουσῶν τοὺς ἅπαξ γενομένους ἐμβῆναι φανερὸν πᾶσίν ἐστι. Cf. Westcott, Canon of the New Testament, p. 151.

[e] Cf. however Westcott (Canon of the New Testament, p. 145) on the improbability of St. John's being quoted in apologetic writings addressed to Jews and heathen. St. Justin nevertheless does 'exhibit types of language and doctrine which, if not immediately drawn from St. John (why not?), *yet mark the presence of his influence* and the recognition of his authority.' Westcott, Ibid. Besides the passages already alluded to, St. Justin appears to refer to St. John xii. 49 in Dialog. cum Tryph. c. 56; to St. John i. 13 in Dialog. c. 63; to St. John vii. 12 in Dialog. c. 69; to St. John i. 12 in Dialog. c. 123. Cf. Lücke, Comm. Ev. Joh. p. 34, sqq. Comp. Tregelles, Canon Muratorianus, p. 73.

[f] St. Ign. ad Rom. c. 7. Cf. St. John vi. 32, 48, 53, xvi. 11.

[g] Ep. ad Phil. c. 7. Cf. 1 St. John iv. 3.

[h] Cf. St. Barn. Ep. v. vi. xii. (cf. St. John iii. 14); Herm. Past. Simil. ix. 12 (cf. Ibid. x. 7, 9, xiv. 6); St. Ignat. ad Philad. 7 (cf. Ibid. iii. 8);

[LECT.

St. Justin's doctrine of the Logos, witness no less powerfully to the existence of St. John's writings than direct citations. The Tübingen writers lay emphasis upon the fact that in the short fragment of Papias which we possess, nothing is said about St. John's Gospel [i]. But at least we have no evidence that Papias did not speak of it in that larger part of his writings which has been lost; and if his silence is a valid argument against the fourth Gospel, it is equally available against the Gospel of St. Luke, and even against each one of those four Epistles which the Tübingen writers themselves recognise as the work of St. Paul [j].

The testimony of the Catholic Church during this century is supplemented by that of the contemporary heretics. St. Irenæus has pointed out how the system of the celebrated Gnostic,

ad Tral. 8 (cf. Ibid. vi. 51); ad Magnes. 7 (cf. Ibid. xii. 49, x. 30, xiv. 11); ad Rom. 7 (cf. Ibid. vi. 32).

[i] Meyer, Evan. Johann. Einl. p. 14: 'Dass das Fragment des Papias das Evangel. Joh. nicht erwähnt, kann nichts verschlagen, da es überhaupt keine schriftlichen Quellen, aus welchen er seine Nachrichten geschöpft habe, auttührt, vielmehr das Verfahren des Papias dahin bestimmt, dass er bei den Apostelschülern die Aussagen der Apostel erkundet habe, und dessen ausdrücklichen Grundsatz ausspricht: *οὐ γὰρ τὰ ἐκ τῶν βιβλίων τοσοῦτόν με ὠφελεῖν ὑπελάμβανον, ὅσον τὰ παρὰ ζώσης φωνῆς καὶ μενούσης.* Papias wirft hier die damals vorhandenen evangelischen Schriften (*τῶν βιβλίων*) deren eine Menge war (Luk. i. 1) alle ohne Auswahl zusammen, und wie er das Evangel. Matthæi und das des Marcus mit darunter begriffen hat, welche beide er später besonders erwähnt, so kann er auch das Evangel. Joh. mit bei *τῶν βιβλίων* gemeint haben, da Papias einen Begriff von *kanonischen* Evangelien als solchen offenbar noch nicht hat (vergl. Credn. Beitr. i. p. 23), und diese auszuzeichnen nicht veranlasst ist. Wenn aber weiterhin Eusebius noch zwei Aussagen des Papias über die Evangelien des Mark. und Matthäus anführt, so wird damit unser Evangelium nicht ausgeschlossen, welches Papias in *anderen* Theilen seines Buchs erwähnt haben kann, sondern jene beiden Aussagen werden nur deshalb bemerklich gemacht, weil sie über die *Entstehung* jener Evangelien etwas Absonderliches, besonders Merkwürdiges enthalten, wie auch *das* als besonders bemerkenswerth von Eusebius angeführt wird, dass Papias aus zwei *epistolischen* Schriften (1 Joh. u. 1 Petr.) Zeugnisse gebrauche, und eine Erzählung habe, welche sich im Hebräer-Evangel. finde.' Cf. also Westcott, Canon, pp. 76, 77 note 1. Papias is stated by Eusebius (iii. 39) to have quoted St. John's First Epistle. This he could hardly have done, without acknowledging St. John's Gospel.

[j] The newly discovered *διδαχὴ τῶν δώδεκα ἀποστόλων* (ed. Bryennios. Constantinople, 1883) appears to be a product of the Judaising party when almost separating from the Church at the close of the first century. In this document no less than twenty references to St. Matthew's Gospel occur, and six to St. Luke's, but there is not a single quotation from the writings of St. Paul; c. 4 and Eph. vi. 5, 9, and c. 3 and 1 Thess. v. 22 being mere coincidences. That it should contain no reference to St. John is only what its general character would lead us to expect. [1884.]

Valentinus, was mainly based upon a perversion of St. John's Gospel [k]. This assertion is borne out by that remarkable work, the Philosophumena of St. Hippolytus, which, as we in Oxford well remember, was discovered some few years since at Mount Athos [l]. Of the pupils of Valentinus, Ptolemæus quotes from the prologue of St. John's Gospel in his extant letter to Flora [m]. Heracleon, another pupil, wrote a considerable commentary upon St. John [n]. Heracleon lived about 150; Valentinus was a contemporary of Marcion, who was teaching at Rome about 140. Marcion had originally admitted the claims of St. John's Gospel, and only denied them when, for the particular purposes of his heresy, he endeavoured at a later time to demonstrate an opposition between St. Paul and St. John [o]. Basilides taught at Alexandria under Adrian, apparently about the year 120. Basilides is known to have written twenty-four books on the Gospel [p]; but if it cannot be certainly affirmed that any of these books were commentaries on St. John, it is certain from St. Hippolytus that Basilides appealed to texts of St. John

[k] St. Irenæus (Hær. iii. 11. 7) lays down the general position: 'Tanta est circa Evangelia hæc firmitas, ut et ipsi hæretici testimonium reddant eis, et ex ipsis egrediens unusquisque eorum conetur suam confirmare doctrinam.' After illustrating this from the cases of the Ebionites, Marcion, and the Cerinthians, he proceeds, 'Hi autem qui a Valentino sunt, eo [sc. evangelio] quod est secundum Johannem *plenissimè utentes*, ad ostensionem conjugationum suarum; ex ipso detegentur nihil rectè dicentes.' 'Die Valentinianische Gnosis (says Meyer) mit ihren Aeonen, Syzygien u. s. w. verhält sich zum Prolog des Joh. wie das künstlich Gemachte und Ausgesponnene zum Einfachen und Schöpferischen.' (Einl. in Joh. p. 12, note.) For an illustration cf. St. Iren. adv. Hær. i. 8. 5.

[l] Cf. Refut. Hær. vi. 35, init., for Valentinus' use of St. John x. 8.

[m] Apud St. Epiph. adv. Hær. lib. i. tom. i. Hær. 33; Ptol. ad Flor. Cf. St. John i. 3; also Stieren's St. Irenæus, vol. i. p. 924.

[n] Fragments of Heracleon's Commentary on St. John, collected from Origen, are published at the end of the first vol. of Stieren's edition of St. Irenæus, pp. 938-971. St. John iv. is chiefly illustrated by these remains of the great Valentinian commentator. Two points strike one on perusal of them: (1) that before Heracleon's time St. John's Gospel must have acquired, even among heretics, the highest authority; (2) that Heracleon has continually to resort to interpretations so forced (as on St. John i. 3, i. 18, ii. 17; cited by Westcott, Canon, p. 306, note) as 'to prove sufficiently that St. John's Gospel was no Gnostic work.'

[o] Tertullian, adv. Marcion. iv. 3; De Carne Christi, c. 2; quoted by Tischendorf, Wann wurden unsere Evangelien verfasst? pp. 25, 26.

[p] Eusebius, Hist. Eccl. iv. 7. 7: *εἰς μὲν τὸ εὐαγγέλιον τέσσαρα πρὸς τοῖς εἴκοσι σύνταξαι βίβλια.* Was this a Commentary on the Evangelists, or a Life of Christ in the sense of Basilides, or a Dissertation on the Import of Christ's Life? The phrase is indecisive.

in favour of his system [q]. Before Basilides, in the two first decades of the century, we find Ophitic Gnostics, the Naasenians [r], and the Peratæ [s], appealing to passages in St. John's Gospel, which was thus already, we may say in the year 110, a recognised authority among sects external to the Catholic Church.

It may further be observed that the whole doctrine of the Paraclete in the heresy of Montanus is a manifest perversion of the treatise on that subject in St. John's Gospel, the wide reception of which it accordingly presupposes [t]. The Alogi, who were heretical opponents of Montanism, rejected St. John's Gospel for dogmatic reasons, which are really confirmatory of the general tradition in its favour [u]. Nor may we forget Celsus, the keen and satirical opponent of the Christian faith, who wrote, even according to Dr. Hilgenfeld, between 160 and 170, but more probably, as is held by other authorities, as early as 150. Celsus professes very ostentatiously to confine himself to the writings of the disciples of Jesus [x]; but he refers to St. John's Gospel in a manner which would be utterly inconceivable if that book had been in his day a lately completed, or indeed a hardly completed forgery [y].

This evidence might be largely reinforced from other quarters [z],

[q] Refut. Hær. vii. 22, where Basilides uses St. John i. 9, ii. 4. That Basilides, not his disciples, makes the citation, see Sanday, Gospels in Second Century, pp. 298–301.

[r] Refut. Hær. v. 6 sqq., 8 (St. John i. 3, 4); c. 9 (Ibid. iv. 21, and iv. 10): quoted by Tischendorf.

[s] Ibid. v. 12 sqq., 16 (St. John iii. 17, i. 1–4); c. 17 (Ibid. viii. 44).

[t] See however Meyer, Einl. in Joh. p. 13, for the opinion that Montanism originally grew out of belief in the Parousia of our Lord. Baur, Christenthum, p. 213. The Paraclete of Montanus was doubtless very different from the Paraclete of St. John's Gospel. Still St. John's Gospel must have furnished the name; and it is probable that the idea of the Montanistic Paraclete is originally due to the same source, although by a rapid development, contortion, or perversion, the Divine Gift announced by our Lord had been exchanged for Its heretical caricature. The rejection of the promise of the Paraclete alluded to by St. Irenæus (adv. Hær. iii. 11. 9) proceeded not from Montanists, but from opponents to Montanism, who erroneously identified the teaching of St. John's Gospel with that heresy.

[u] St. Epiph. Hær. li. 3. Cf. Pressensé, Jésus-Christ, p. 227.

[x] Origen, contr. Celsum, ii. 74.

[y] Ibid. i. 67; cf. St. John ii. 18. Contr. Celsum, ii. 31, 36, 55; cf. St. John xx. 27.

[z] E. g. the Letter of the Churches of Lyons and Vienne, Eus. v. 1, which quotes St. John xvi. 2 as an utterance of our Lord Himself. Athenagoras, Leg. pro Christianis, 10: cf. St. John i. 1–11, xvii. 21–23. The Clementine Homilies, xix. 22; cf. St. John ix. 2, 3, iii. 52, x. 9, 27. Recognitions, vi. 9; cf. St. John iii. 3–5, ii. 48, v. 23. Ibid. v. 12; cf. St. John viii. 34.

and especially by an examination of that mass of apocryphal literature which belongs to the earlier half of the second century, and the relation of which to St. John's Gospel has lately been very clearly exhibited by an accomplished scholar[a]. But we are already in a position to admit that the facts before us force back the date of St. John's Gospel within the lines of the first century[b]. And when this is done the question of its authenticity is practically decided. It is irrational to suppose that a forgery claiming the name and authority of the beloved disciple could have been written and circulated beneath his very eyes, and while the Church was still illuminated by his oral teaching. Arbitrary theories about the time which is thought necessary to develope an idea cannot rightly be held to counterbalance such a solid block of historical evidence as we have been considering. This evidence shews that, long before the year 160, St. John's Gospel was received throughout orthodox and heretical Christendom, and that its recognition may be traced up to the Apostolic age itself. Ewald shall supply the words with which to close the foregoing considerations. 'Those who since the first discussion of this question have been really conversant with it, never could have had and never have had a moment's doubt. As the attack on St. John has become fiercer and fiercer, the truth during the last ten or twelve years has been more and more solidly established, error has been pursued into its last hiding-places, and at this moment the facts before us are such that no man who does not will knowingly to choose error and to reject truth, can dare to say that the fourth Gospel is not the work of the Apostle John[c].'

[a] Tischendorf, Wann wurden unsere Evangelien verfasst? p. 35, sqq. That the *Acta Pilati* in particular were composed at the beginning of the second century, appears certain from the public appeal to them which St. Justin makes in his Apology to the Roman Emperor. The Acta Pilati 'presuppose not only the synoptists, but particularly and necessarily the Gospel of St. John. It is not that we meet with a passage here and there quoted from that Gospel. If that were the case we might suspect later interpolation. The whole history of the condemnation of Jesus is based essentially upon St. John's narrative; while in the accounts of the Crucifixion and the Resurrection, it is rather certain passages of the synoptists which are particularly suggested.'

[b] Pressensé, Jésus-Christ, p. 232. 'Rien n'est plus vain que de vouloir faire sortir du mouvement des idées au second siècle l'Évangile, qui a précisément donné le branle à ce mouvement, et le domine après l'avoir enfanté.'

[c] Review of Renan's Vie de Jésus, in the Gottingen Scientific Journal, 5 Aug. 1863; quoted by Gratry, Jésus-Christ, p. 119.

Certainly Ewald here expresses himself with vehemence. Some among yourselves may possibly be disposed to complain of him as being too dogmatic. For it may be that you have made impatience of certainty a part of your creed; and you may hold that a certain measure of cautious doubt on all subjects is inseparable from true intellectual culture. You may urge in particular that the weight of external testimony in favour of St. John's Gospel does not silence the difficulties which arise upon an examination of its contents. You point to the use of a mystical and metaphysical terminology, to the repetition of abstract expressions, such as Word, Life, Light, Truth, Paraclete. You remark that St. John's Gospel exhibits the Life of our Lord under an entirely new aspect. Not to dwell immoderately upon points of detail, you insist that the plan of our Lord's life, the main scenes of His ministry, all His exhibitions of miraculous power save two, the form and matter of His discourses, nay, the very attitude and moral physiognomy of His opponents, are so represented in this Gospel as to interfere with your belief in its Apostolical origin.

But are not these peculiarities of the Gospel explained when we consider the purpose with which it was written?

1. St. John's Gospel is in the first place an historical supplement. It was designed to chronicle discourses and events which had been omitted in the narratives of the three preceding Evangelists. Christian antiquity attests this design with remarkable unanimity [d]. It is altogether arbitrary to assert that if St. John had seen the works of earlier Evangelists he would have alluded to them; and that if he had intended to supply the omissions of their narratives he would have formally announced his intention of doing so [e]. It is sufficient to observe that the literary conventionalities of modern Europe were not those of the sacred writers, whether of the Synagogue [f] or of the Church. An inspired writer does his work without the self-consciousness of a modern composer; he is not necessarily careful to define his exact place in literature, his precise obligations to, or his presumed improvements upon, the labours of his

[d] See especially the remarkable passage in Eus. Hist. Eccl. iii. 24, St. Epiph. Hær. ii. 51.

[e] These arguments of Lücke are noticed by Bp. Wordsworth, New Test. part i. p. 206.

[f] 'The later prophets of the Old Testament enlarge upon and complete the prophecies of the earlier. But they do not mention their names, or declare their own purpose to do what they do.' Townson, pp. 134-147; quoted by Bp. Wordsworth, ubi supr.

predecessors. He is the organ of a Higher Intelligence; he owes both what he borrows and what he is believed to originate to the Mind Which inspires him to originate, or Which guides him to select. While the stream of sacred truth is flowing forth from his entranced and burning soul, and is being forthwith crystallized in the moulds of an imperishable language, the eagle-eyed Evangelist does not stoop from heaven to earth for the purpose of guarding or reserving the rights of authorship, by displaying his care to acknowledge its obligations. Certainly St. John does repeat in part the narratives of his predecessors[g]. But this repetition does not interfere with the *supplementary* character of his work as a whole[h]. And yet his Gospel is not only or mainly to be regarded as an historical supplement. It exhibits the precision of method and the orderly development of ideas which are proper to a complete doctrinal essay or treatise. It is indeed rather a treatise illustrated by history, than a history written with a theological purpose. Viewed in its historical relation to the first three Gospels, it is supplemental to them; but this relative character is not by any means an adequate explanation of its motive and function. It might easily have been written if no other Evangelist had written at all; it has a character and purpose which are strictly its own; it is part of a great whole, yet it is also, in itself, organically perfect.

2. St. John's Gospel is a polemical treatise. It is addressed to an intellectual world widely different from that which had been before the minds of the earlier Evangelists. The earliest forms of Gnostic thought are recognisable in the Judaizing theosophists whom St. Paul has in view in his Epistles to the Ephesians and the Colossians. These Epistles were written at the least some thirty years before the fourth Gospel. The fourth Gospel confronts or anticipates a more developed Gnosticism; although we may observe in passing that it certainly

[g] As in chaps. vi. and xii.

[h] M. Renan admits the supplementary character of St. John's Gospel, but attributes to the Evangelist a motive of personal pique in writing it. He was annoyed at the place assigned to himself in earlier narratives! 'On est tenté de croire, que Jean, dans sa vieillesse, ayant lu les récits évangéliques qui circulaient, d'une part, y remarqua diverses inexactitudes, de l'autre, fut froissé de voir qu'on ne lui accordait pas dans l'histoire du Christ une assez grande place; qu'alors il commença à dicter une foule de choses qu'il savait mieux que les autres, *avec l'intention de montrer que, dans beaucoup de cas où on ne parlait que de Pierre, il avait figuré avec et avant lui.*' Vie de Jésus, pp. xxvii. xxviii.

does not contain references to any of the full-grown Gnostic systems which belong to the middle of the second century. The fourth Gospel is in marked opposition to the distinctive positions of Ebionites, of Docetæ, of Cerinthians. But among these the Cerinthian gnosis appears to be more particularly contemplated. In its earlier forms especially, Gnosticism was as much a mischievous intellectual method as a formal heresy. The Gnostic looked upon each revealed truth merely in the light of an addition to the existing stock of materials ready to his hand for speculative discussion. He handled it accordingly with the freedom which was natural to a belief that it was in no sense beyond the range of his intellectual grasp. He commingled it with his cosmical or his psychological theories; he remodelled it; he submitted it to new divisions, to new combinations. Thus his attitude toward Christianity was friendly and yet supercilious. But he threatened the faith with utter destruction, to be achieved by a process of eclectic interpretation. Cerinthus was an early master of this art. Cerinthus as a Chiliastic Judaizer was naturally disposed to Humanitarianism. As an eclectic theorist, who had been trained in the 'teaching of the Egyptians[i],' he maintained that the world had been created by 'some power separate and distinct from Him Who is above all.' Jesus was not born of a virgin; He was the son of Joseph and Mary; He was born naturally like other men. But the Æon Christ had descended upon Jesus after His baptism, in the form of a dove, and had proclaimed the unknown Father, and had perfected the virtues of Jesus. The spiritual impassible Christ had flown back to heaven on the eve of the Passion of Jesus; the altogether human Jesus of Cerinthus had suffered and had risen alone[k]. To this fantastic Christ of the Cerinthian

[i] St. Hippolytus, Refut. Hær. vii. 33.

[k] St. Irenæus, i. 26: 'Et Cerinthus autem quidam in Asiâ non a primo Deo factum esse mundum docuit, sed a virtute quâdam valde separatâ et distante ab eâ principalitate, quæ est super universa, et ignorante eum qui est super omnia, Deum. Jesum autem subjecit, non ex virgine natum (impossibile enim hoc ei visum est); fuisse autem Eum Joseph et Mariæ filium similiter ut reliqui omnes homines, et plus potuisse justitiâ et prudentiâ et sapientiâ ab hominibus. Et post baptismum descendisse in eum ab ea principalitate quæ est super omnia, Christum figurâ columbæ; et tunc annuntiasse incognitum Patrem et virtutes perfecisse; in fine autem revolâsse iterum Christum de Jesu, et Jesum passum esse et resurrexisse; Christum autem impassibilem perseverâsse, existentem spiritalem.' When St. Epiphanius represents Cerinthus as affirming that Jesus would only rise at the general resurrection, he seems to be describing the logical results of the heresy, not the actual doctrine which it embraced. (Hær. xxviii. 6.)

gnosis St. John opposes the counteracting truth of our Lord's Divine and Eternal Nature, as manifested in and through His human life. This Nature was united to the Manhood of Jesus from the moment of the Incarnation. It was not a transient endowment of the Person of Jesus; since it was Itself the seat of His Personality, although clothed with a human form. This Divine Nature was 'glorified' in Christ's Passion, as also in His miracles and His Resurrection. St. John disentangles the Catholic doctrine from the negations and the speculations of Cerinthus; he proclaims the Presence among men of the Divine Word, Himself the Creator of all things, incarnate in Jesus Christ.

3. Thus St. John's Gospel has also a direct, positive, dogmatic purpose. It is not merely a controversial treatise, as it is not merely an historical appendix. Its teaching is far deeper and wider than would have been necessary, in order to refute the errors of Cerinthus. It teaches the highest revealed truth concerning the Person of our Lord. Its substantive and enduring value consists in its displaying the Everlasting Word or Son of God as historically incarnate, and as uniting Himself to His Church.

The peculiarities of St. John's Gospel are explained, when this threefold aspect of it is kept in view. As a supplementary narrative it presents us, for the most part, with particulars concerning our Blessed Lord which are unrecorded elsewhere. It meets the doubts which might naturally have arisen in the later Apostolical age, when the narratives of the earlier Evangelists had been for some time before the Church. If the question was raised, why, if Jesus was so holy and so supernatural a Person, His countrymen and contemporaries did not believe in Him, St. John shews the moral causes which account for their incredulity. He pourtrays the fierce hatred of the Jews against the moral truth which they had rejected; he exhibits this hatred as ever increasing in its intensity as the sanctity of Jesus shines out more and more brightly. If men asked anxiously for more proof that the Death and Resurrection of Jesus were real events, St. John meets that demand by recording his own experience as an eye-witness, and by carefully accumulating the witness of others. If it was objected that Christ's violent Death was inconsistent with His Divine claims, St. John points out that it was strictly voluntary, and even that by it Christ's true glorification was achieved. If the authority of the Apostles and of those who were succeeding them was popularly depreciated on the score of their being rude and illiterate men, St. John shews from the discourse in the supper-room that the claims of Apostles upon the dutiful submission of the Church did not depend upon any natural advantages which they possessed. Jesus had promised a Divine Comforter, Who was to guide them into the whole truth, and to bring to their minds whatever He had said to them[l].

As a polemical writer, St. John selects and marshals his materials with a view to confuting, from historical data, the Humanitarian or Docetic errors of the time. St. John is anxious to bring a particular section of the Life of Jesus to bear upon the intellectual world of Ephesus[m]. He puts forward an aspect of the original truth which was certain to command present and local attention; he is sufficiently in correspondence with the age to which he ministers, and with the speculative temper of the men around him. He had been led to note and to treasure up in his thought certain phases of the teaching and character of Jesus with especial care. He had remembered more accurately those particular discourses, in which Jesus speaks of His eternal relation to the Father, and of the profound mystic communion of life into which He would enter with His followers through the Holy Spirit and the Sacraments. These cherished memories of St. John's earlier years, unshared in their completeness by less privileged Apostles, were well fitted to meet the hard necessities of the Church during the closing years of the beloved disciple. To St. John the gnosis of Cerinthus must have appeared to be in direct contradiction to the sacred certainties which he had heard from the lips of Jesus, and which he treasured in his heart and memory. In order to confute the heresy which separated the man Jesus from the 'Æon' Christ, he had merely to publish what he remembered of the actual words and works of Jesus[n]. His translation of those divine words may be coloured by a phraseology current in the school which he is addressing, sufficiently to make them popularly intelligible. But the peculiarities of his language have been greatly exaggerated by criticism, while they are naturally explained by the polemical and positively doctrinal objects which he had in view. To these objects, the

[l] Cf. Alford, Greek Test. vol. i. Prolegom. p. 60.

[m] St. Irenæus adv. Hær. iii. 1. See Ebrard's discussion of the objections which have been urged against this statement. Gospel History, pt. 2, div. 2, § 127.

[n] Cf. Pressensé, Jésus-Christ, p. 245.

language, the historical arrangement, the selection from conversations and discourses before unpublished, the few deeply significant miracles, the description of opponents by a generic name—the 'Jews'—which ignores the differences of character, class, and sect among them, and notices them only so far as they are in conflict with the central truth manifested in Jesus, —all contribute. But these very peculiarities of the fourth Gospel subserve its positive devotional and didactic aim even more directly than its controversial one [o]. The false gnosis

[o] The internal difficulties urged against St. John's Gospel appear to be overborne by the weight of the external testimony, taken in conjunction with the characteristics and necessities of the later Apostolical age. These difficulties may however be very briefly summarized as follows:—

1. As to time:

(*a*) 'The fourth Gospel implies a long Ministry, with festivals for its landmarks.' But the three (Westcott, Study of Gospels, 267) at least allow of a ministry as long as the fourth can require; while reference to the festivals was natural in a narrative, the main scene of which is laid at Jerusalem.

(*β*) 'The fourth Gospel appears to place the crucifixion on Nisan 14, the three on Nisan 15.' This real difficulty has been explained by various hypotheses, as

e.g. (1) Of an *anticipated* passover, kept by our Lord, on Nisan 13. Westcott, Int. p. 319; Ellicott, Huls. Lect. p. 322, and others. This is perhaps the most satisfactory. The objection drawn from the observance of Nisan 14, by those churches in the second century which inherited St. John's traditions, assumes that such observance was commemorative of the Last Supper, and not, as is probable, of our Lord's Death. Cf. Meyer, Ev. Joh. Einl. p. 18; Mansel, note on St. Matt. xxvi. in Speaker's Commentary.

(2) Of a passover *postponed* by the chief priests. St. Chrys.; Estius; Wordsworth.

(3) Of a difference of computation, as to the true day of the Passover, owing to the variation between the Solar and Lunar reckonings. Petavius, qu. by Neale, Int. East. Ch. ii. 1054.

(4) Of a possible explanation of St. John's language (xviii. 28, &c.), which would make it consistent with the date of Nisan 15, as that of the crucifixion. Dict. of Bible, vol. ii. 720; Edersheim, Life and Times of Jesus, ii. 481, 507; St. Tho. Sum. p. iii. q. 46. a. 9.

If none of these explanations be quite unobjectionable, they may fairly warn us against concluding with our present knowledge that the difficulty is by any means insuperable.

2. As to the scene of Christ's teaching:—'St. John places it chiefly in Judæa; the three in Galilee.' But no Gospel professes to be a complete history of our Lord's actions, and records of a Galilean and of a Judæan ministry respectively leave room for each other. Westcott on the Gospels, p. 265.

3. As to the style of Christ's teaching:—'Si Jésus parlait comme le veut Matthieu, il n'a pu parler comme le veut Jean.' But, the difference of subjects, hearers, and circumstances in the two cases, taken in conjunction

[LECT.

is refuted by an exhibition of the true. The true is set forth for the sake of Christian souls. These things 'are written that ye might believe that Jesus is the Christ, the Son of God; and that believing ye might have life through His Name [p].'

We may perhaps have wondered how a Galilean fisherman could have been the author of a subtle and sublime theosophy, how the son of Zebedee could have appropiated the language of Athens and of Alexandria to the service of the Crucified. The answer is that St. John knew from experience the blessed and tremendous truth that his Lord and Friend was a Divine Person. Apart from the guidance of the Blessed Spirit, St. John's mental strength and refinement may be traced to the force of his keen interest in this single fact. Just as a desperate moral or material struggle brings to light forces and resources unused before, so an intense religious conviction fertilizes intellect, and developes speculative talent, not unfrequently in the most unlearned. Every form of thought which comes even into indirect contact with the truth to which the soul clings adoringly, is scanned by it with deep and anxious interest, whether it be the interest of hope or the interest of apprehension. St. John certainly is a theosophic philosopher, but he is only a philosopher because he is a theologian; he is such a master of abstract thought because he is so devoted to the Incarnate God. The fisherman of Galilee could never have written the prologue of the fourth Gospel, or have guided the religious thought of Ephesus, unless he had clung to this sustaining Truth, which makes him at once so popular and so

with the differing mental peculiarities of the Apostles who report our Lord's words, will account for the difference of style. The phrases assumed to be peculiar to, and really of frequent occurrence in St. John are by no means unknown to the Synoptists. E.g. The antithesis between Light and darkness.

4. As to the matter of Christ's teaching:—Baur begs the whole question by saying that 'the discourses in St. John could not be historical, since they are essentially nothing more than an explanation of the Logos-idea put forth by that writer.' This might be true if the *doctrine* of the Logos had been the product of Gnostic speculations. But if Jesus was really the Divine Son, manifesting Himself as such to men, such language as that reported by St. John is no more than we should expect Him to use at certain times. St. John never represents our Lord as announcing His Divinity in the terms in which it is announced in the Prologue to the Gospel; he would have done so, had he really been creating a fictitious Jesus designed to illustrate a particular theosophic speculation. This is discussed hereafter, p. 272. See Pressensé, Jésus-Christ, p. 244; Luthardt, das Johanneische Evangelium, pp. 26-35.

[p] St. John xx. 31.

profound. For St. John is spiritually as simple, as he is intellectually majestic. In this our day he is understood by the religious insight of the unlettered and the poor, while the learned can sometimes see in him only the weary repetition of metaphysical abstractions. The poor understand this sublime revelation of God, the Creator of the world, as pure Light and Truth. They understand the picture of a moral darkness which commits and excuses sin, and which hates the light. They receive gratefully and believingly the Son of God, made Man, and conquering evil by the laying down His Life. They follow, with the experience of their own temptations, or sins, or hopes, or fears, those heart-searching conversations with Nicodemus, with the Samaritan woman, with the Jews. In truth, St. John's language and, above all, the words of Christ in St. John, are as simple as they are profound. They still speak peace and joy to little children; they are still a stumbling-block to, and a condemnation of, the virtual successors of Cerinthus.

II. If there were nothing else to the purpose in the whole of the New Testament, those first fourteen verses of the fourth Gospel would suffice to persuade a believer in Holy Scripture of the truth that Jesus Christ is absolutely GOD. It is a mistake to regard those fourteen verses as a mere prefatory attack upon the gnosis of Cerinthus, having no necessary connexion with the narrative which follows, and representing nothing essential to the integrity of the Apostle's thought. For, as Baur very truly observes, the doctrine of the prologue is the very fundamental idea which underlies the whole 'Johannean theology[q].' It is not enough to say that between the prologue and the history which follows there exists an intimate organic connexion. The prologue is itself the beginning of the history. 'It is impossible,' says Baur, 'to deny that "the Word made flesh[r]" is one and the same subject with the Man Christ Jesus on the one hand, and with the Word Who "was in the beginning, Who was with God, and Who was God," on the other[s].'

Taking then the prologue of St. John's Gospel in connexion with the verses which immediately succeed it, let us observe that St. John attaches to our Lord's Person two names which together yield a complete revelation of His Divine glory. Our Lord is called the 'Word,' and the 'Only-begotten Son.' It is doubtless true, as Neander observes, that 'the first of these

[q] Vorlesungen, p. 351. [r] St. John i. 14.
[s] Baur, ubi sup., St. John i. 1.

names was' put prominently forward at Ephesus, 'in order to lead those who busied themselves with speculations on the Logos as the centre of all theophanies, from a mere religious idealism to a religious realism, to lead them in short to a recognition of God revealed in Christ[t].' It has already[u] been shewn that the Logos of St. John differs materially from the Logos of Platonizing Jews in Alexandria, while it is linked to great lines of teaching in the Old Testament. No reason can be assigned why St. John had recourse to the word Logos at all, unless he was already in possession of the underlying fact to which this word supplied a philosophical form. If the word did express, in a form familiar to the ears of the men of Ephesus, a great truth which they had buried beneath a heap of errors, that truth, as Bruno Bauer admits, must have been held independently and previously by the Apostle[v]. The direct expression of that truth was St. John's primary motive in using the word; his polemical and corrective action upon the Cerinthian gnosis was a secondary motive.

By the word Logos, then, St. John carries back his history of our Lord to a point at which it has not yet entered into the sphere of sense and time. 'In the four Gospels,' says St. Augustine, 'or rather in the four books of the one Gospel, the Apostle St. John, deservedly compared to an eagle, by reason of his spiritual understanding, has lifted his enunciation of truth to a far higher and sublimer point than the other three, and by this elevation he would fain have our hearts lifted up likewise. For the other three Evangelists walked, so to speak, on earth with our Lord as Man. Of His Godhead they said but a few things. But John, as if he found it oppressive to walk on earth, has opened his treatise as it were with a peal of thunder; he has raised himself not merely above the earth, and the whole compass of the air and heaven, but even above every angel-host, and every order of the invisible powers, and has reached even to Him by Whom all things were made, in that sentence, "In the beginning was the Word[x]."'

Instead of opening his narrative at the Human Birth of our Lord, or at the commencement of His ministry, St. John places himself in thought at the starting-point (as we should conceive

[t] Neander, Kirchengeschichte, p. 549; quoted by Tholuck, Ev. Johan. kap. I.

[u] p. 69.

[v] Kritik der Evangel. Geschichte des Joh. p. 5; quoted by Tholuck, ubi supra.

[x] St. Aug. tr. 36 in Johan.

it) of all time [y]. Nay rather, it would seem that if בראשית at the beginning of Genesis signifies the initial moment of time itself, ἐν ἀρχῇ rises to the absolute conception of that which is anterior to, or rather independent of, time [z]. Then, when time was not, or at a point to which man cannot apply his finite conception of time, there was—the Logos or Word. When as yet nothing had been made, He *was*. What was the *Logos*? Such a term, in a position of such moment, when so much depends on our rightly understanding it, has a moral no less than an intellectual claim upon us, of the highest order. We are bound to try to understand it, just as certainly as we are bound to obey the command to love our enemies. No man who carries his morality into the sphere of religious thought can affect or afford to maintain, that the fundamental idea in the writings of St. John is a scholastic conceit, with which practical Christians need not concern themselves. And indeed St. John's doctrine of the Logos has from the first been scrutinized anxiously by the mind of Christendom. It could not but be felt that the term Logos denotes at the very least something intimately and everlastingly present with God, something as internal to the Being of God as thought is to the soul of man. In truth the Divine Logos is God reflected in His own eternal Thought; in the Logos, God is His own Object. This Infinite Thought, the reflection and counterpart of God, subsisting in God as a Being or Hypostasis, and having a tendency to self-communication,—such is the Logos. The Logos is the Thought of God, not intermittent and precarious like human thought, but subsisting with the intensity of a personal

[y] Meyer in loc., note: 'Völlig unexegetisch ist die Fassung der Socinianer (s. Catech. Racov. p. 135, ed. Oeder): ἐν ἀρχῇ heisse *in initio evangelii*.'

[z] Meyer in loc.: 'Johannes parallelisirt zwar den Anfang seines Evangel. mit dem Anfange der Genesis; aber er steigert den historischen Begriff בְּרֵאשִׁית, welcher (Gen. i. 1) den Anfangsmoment der Zeit selbst bedeutet, zum absoluten Begriffe der *Vorzeitlichkeit*.' This might suffice to refute the assertion of a modern writer that St. John does not teach the Eternity of the Divine Word. 'Une des thèses fondamentales de la spéculation ecclésiastique, c'est idée de l'éternité du Verbe. Depuis que le concile de Nicée en a fait une des pierres angulaires de la théologie Catholique, sa décision est restée l'héritage commun de tous les systèmes orthodoxes. Eh bien! les écrits de Jean n'en parlent pas.' Reuss, Théol. Chrét. ii. 438. The author is mistaken in attributing to ἐν ἀρχῇ a merely relative force, and thence arguing that if the Word is eternal, the world is eternal also (Gen. i. 1). Besides, Θεὸς ἦν ὁ Λόγος. How is the Word other than eternal, if He is thus identified with the ever-existing Being? Cf. Döllinger, Christenthum und Kirche in der Zeit der Grundlegung, p. 169.

[LECT.

form. The very expression seems to court the argument of Athenagoras, that since God could never have been ἄλογος[a], the Logos must have been not created but eternal. It suggests the further inference that since reason is man's noblest faculty, the Uncreated Logos must be at least equal with God. In any case it might have been asked why the term was used at all, if these obvious inferences were not to be deduced from it; but as a matter of fact they are not mere inferences, since they are warranted by the express language of St. John. St. John says that the Word was 'in the beginning.' The question then arises: What was His relation to the Self-existent Being? He was not merely παρὰ τῷ Θεῷ[b], along with God, but πρὸς τὸν Θεόν. This last preposition expresses, beyond the fact of co-existence or immanence, the more significant fact of perpetuated intercommunion. The face of the Everlasting Word, if we may dare so to express ourselves, was ever *directed towards* the face of the Everlasting Father[c]. But was the Logos then an independent being, existing externally to the One God? To conceive of an independent being, anterior to creation, would be an error at issue with the first truth of monotheism; and therefore Θεὸς ἦν ὁ Λόγος[d]. The Word is not merely a Divine Being, but He is in the absolute sense God[e]. Thus from His eternal existence we

[a] Athenag. Suppl. pro Christ. 10 (46 D. ed. Otto): εἶχεν αὐτὸς ἐν ἑαυτῷ τὸν Λόγον, ἀϊδίως λογικὸς ὤν.

[b] St. John xvii. 5.

[c] Meyer in loc.: 'πρός bezeichnet das Befindlichsein des Logos bei Gott im Gesichtspunkte der Richtung der Gemeinschaft.' Bernhardy, Syntax, p. 265.

[d] The omission of the article before Θεός is explained by Meyer in loc.: 'Die Nichtsetzung des Artikels war nothwendig, weil ὁ Θεός nach dem vorherigen πρὸς τὸν Θεόν dem Logos die Identität der *Person* zugesprochen hätte, was aber eben, nachdem πρὸς τὸν Θεόν die *Verschiedenheit* der Person gesetzt hat, ungereimt wäre, dagegen das Nichtartikulirte θεός auf diese persönliche Verschiedenheit der Einheit des Wesens und der Natur folgen lässt.' This is a sufficient reply to Winer, Gr. N. T., iii. § 19. 1.

[e] Here is the essential difference between the Logos of St. John and the Logos of Philo. Meyer, who apparently holds Philo to have definitely considered his Logos as a real hypostasis, states it as follows, in his note on the words καὶ Θεὸς ἦν ὁ Λόγος: 'Wie also Johannes, mit dem nichtartikulirten θεός kein niedrigeres Wesen, als Gott Selbst hat, bezeichnen will; so unterscheidet sich die Johanneische Logos-Idee bestimmt von derjenigen bei Philo, welcher θεός ohne Artikel im Sinne wesentlicher Unterordnung, ja, wie Er Selbst sagt, ἐν καταχρήσει (i. p. 655, ed. Mangey) vom Logos prädicirt;—wie denn auch der Name ὁ δεύτερος θεός, welchen er ihm giebt, nach ii. p. 625. Euseb. præp. Ev. vii. 13, ausdrücklich den Begriff eines Zwischenwesens zwischen Gott und dem Menschen

ascend first to His distinct Personality, and then to the full truth of His substantial Godhead.

Yet the Logos necessarily suggests to our minds the further idea of communicativeness; the Logos is Speech as well as Thought [f]. And of His actual self-communication St. John mentions two phases or stages; the first *creation*, the second *revelation*. The Word unveils Himself to the soul through the mediation of objects of sense in the physical world, and He also unveils Himself immediately. Accordingly St. John says that 'all things were made' by the Word, and that the Word Who creates is also the Revealer: 'the Word was made flesh, and dwelt among us, and we beheld His glory.' He possesses δόξα, that is, in St. John, the totality of the Divine attributes. This 'glory' is not merely something belonging to His Essential Nature; since He allows us to behold It through His veil of Flesh.

What indeed this δόξα or glory was, we may observe by considering that St. John's writings appear to bring God before us, at least more particularly, under a threefold aspect.

1. God is Life (ζωή). The Father is 'living [g];' He 'has life in Himself [h].' God is not merely the living God, that is, the real God, in contrast to the non-existent and feigned deities of the heathen: God is Life, in the sense of Self-existent Being; He is the Focus and the Fountain of universal life. In Him life may be contemplated in its twofold activity, as issuing from its source, and as returning to its object. The Life of God passes forth from Itself; It lavishes Itself throughout the realms of nothingness; It summons into being worlds, systems, intelligences, orders of existences unimagined before. In doing this It obeys no necessary law of self-expansion, but pours Itself forth with that highest generosity that belongs to a perfect freedom. That is to say, that God the Life is God the Creator. On the other hand, God is Being returning into Itself, finding in Itself Its perfect and consummate satisfaction. God is thus

bezeichnen soll, nach dessen Bilde Gott den Menschen geschaffen hat. *Dieser* Subordinatianismus, nach welchem der Logos zwar μεθόριός τις θεοῦ φύσις, aber τοῦ μὲν ἐλάττων, ἀνθρώπου δὲ κρείττων ist (i. p. 683) ist nicht der neu-testamentliche, welcher vielmehr die ewige Wesenseinheit des Vaters und des Sohnes zur Voraussetzung hat (Phil. ii. 6; Kol. i. 15 f.), und die Unterordnung des letztern in dessen Abhängigkeit vom Vater setzt.'

[f] Cf Delitzsch, System der Biblischen Psychologie, p. 138.

[g] St. John vi. 57: ἀπέστειλέ με ὁ ζῶν Πατήρ.

[h] Ibid. v. 26: ὁ Πατὴρ ἔχει ζωὴν ἐν ἑαυτῷ.

the Object of all dependent Life; He is indeed the object of His own Life; all His infinite powers and faculties turn ever inward with uncloyed delight upon Himself as upon their one adequate End or Object. We cannot approach more nearly to a definition of pleasure than by saying that it is the exact correspondence between a faculty and its object. Pleasure is thus a test of vitality; and God, as being Life, is the one Being Who is supremely and perfectly happy.

2. Again, God is Love (ἀγάπη)[i]. Love is the relation which subsists between God and all that lives as He has willed. Love is the bond of the Being of God. Love binds the Father to that Only Son Whom He has begotten from all eternity[j]. Love itself knows no beginning; it proceeds from the Father and the Son from all eternity. God loves created life, whether in nature or in grace; He loves the race of men, the unredeemed world[k]; He loves Christians with a special love[l]. In beings thus external to Himself, God loves the life which He has given them; He loves Himself in them; He is still Himself the ultimate, rightful, necessary Object of His love. Thus love is of His essence; it is the expression of His necessary delight in His own existence.

3. Lastly, God is Light (φῶς). That is to say, He is absolute intellectual and moral Truth; He is Truth in the realms of thought, and Truth in the sphere of action. He is the All-knowing and the perfectly Holy Being. No intellectual ignorance can darken His all-embracing survey of actual and possible fact; no stain can soil His robe of awful Sanctity. Light is not merely the sphere in which He dwells: He is His own sphere of existence; He is Himself Light, and in Him is no darkness at all[m].

[i] 1 St. John iv. 8: *ὁ μὴ ἀγαπῶν, οὐκ ἔγνω τὸν Θεόν· ὅτι ὁ Θεὸς ἀγάπη ἐστίν.* Ibid. ver. 16: *ὁ Θεὸς ἀγάπη ἐστὶ, καὶ ὁ μένων ἐν τῇ ἀγάπῃ, ἐν τῷ Θεῷ μένει, καὶ ὁ Θεὸς ἐν αὐτῷ.*

[j] St. John iii. 35: *ὁ Πατὴρ ἀγαπᾷ τὸν Υἱὸν καὶ πάντα δέδωκεν ἐν τῇ χειρὶ αὐτοῦ.* Ibid. v. 20: *ὁ γὰρ Πατὴρ φιλεῖ τὸν Υἱὸν, καὶ πάντα δείκνυσιν αὐτῷ ἃ αὐτὸς ποιεῖ.* Ibid. x. 17, xv. 9. Ibid. xvii. 24: *ἠγάπησάς με πρὸ καταβολῆς κόσμου.*

[k] St. John iii. 16: *οὕτω γὰρ ἠγάπησεν ὁ Θεὸς τὸν κόσμον, ὥστε τὸν Υἱὸν αὐτοῦ τὸν μονογενῆ ἔδωκεν.* 1 St. John iv. 10: *αὐτὸς ἠγάπησεν ἡμᾶς, καὶ ἀπέστειλε τὸν Υἱὸν αὐτοῦ ἱλασμὸν περὶ τῶν ἁμαρτιῶν ἡμῶν.* Ibid. ver. 19: *ἡμεῖς ἀγαπῶμεν αὐτὸν, ὅτι αὐτὸς πρῶτος ἠγάπησεν ἡμᾶς.*

[l] St. John xiv. 23, xvi. 27.

[m] 1 St. John i. 5: *ὁ Θεὸς φῶς ἐστι, καὶ σκοτία ἐν αὐτῷ οὐκ ἔστιν οὐδεμία.* Ibid. ver. 7: *αὐτός ἐστιν ἐν τῷ φωτί.* Here *ἐν* does not merely point to the sphere in which God dwells. In St. John this preposition is constantly

These three aspects of the Divine Nature, denoted by the terms Life, Love, and Light, are attributed in St. John's writings with abundant explicitness to the Word made flesh.

Thus, the Logos is Light. He is *the* Light, that is, the Light Which is the very essence of God. The Baptist indeed preaches truth; but the Baptist must not be confounded with the Light Which he heralds [n]. The Logos is the true Light [o]. All that has really enlarged the stock of intellectual truth or of moral goodness among men, all that has ever lighted any soul of man, has radiated from Him [p]. He proclaims Himself to be the Light of the world [q], and the Truth [r]; and His Apostle, speaking of the illumination shed by Him upon the Church, reminds Christians that 'the darkness is passing, and the true Light now shineth [s].'

The Logos is Love. He refracts upon the Father the fulness of His love [t]. He loves the Father as the Father loves Himself. The Father's love sends Him into the world, and He obeys out of love [u]. It is love which draws Him together with the Father to make His abode in the souls of the faithful [x].

used to denote the closest possible relationship between two subjects, or, as here, between a subject and its attribute. Cf. Reuss, Théologie Chrétienne, ii. p. 434, for this as well as many of the above observations and references.

[n] St. John i. 7: *οὗτος ἦλθεν εἰς μαρτυρίαν, ἵνα μαρτυρήσῃ περὶ τοῦ φωτός.* Ibid. ver. 8: *οὐκ ἦν ἐκεῖνος τὸ φῶς, ἀλλ' ἵνα μαρτυρήσῃ περὶ τοῦ φωτός.*

[o] Ibid. ver. 9: *ἦν τὸ φῶς τὸ ἀληθινόν.*

[p] Ibid.: *ὃ φωτίζει πάντα ἄνθρωπον ἐρχόμενον εἰς τὸν κόσμον.* 'Das *φωτίζειν πάντα ἄνθρωπον*, als charakteristische Wirksamkeit des wahren Lichts, bleibt wahr, wenngleich empirisch diese Erleuchtung von Vielen nicht empfangen wird. Das empirische Verhältniss kommt darauf zurück: quisquis illuminatur, ab hac luce illuminatur. (Beng.).' Meyer in Joh. i. 9. The Evangelist means more than this: no human being is left without a certain measure of natural light, and this light is given by the Divine Logos in all cases.

[q] St. John viii. 12: *ἐγώ εἰμι τὸ φῶς τοῦ κόσμου· ὁ ἀκολουθῶν ἐμοὶ, οὐ μὴ περιπατήσει ἐν τῇ σκοτίᾳ, ἀλλ' ἕξει τὸ φῶς τῆς ζωῆς.* Ibid. iii. 19: *τὸ φῶς ἐλήλυθεν εἰς τὸν κόσμον*, that is, in the Incarnate Word. Ibid. ix. 5: *ὅταν ἐν τῷ κόσμῳ ὦ, φῶς εἰμι τοῦ κόσμου.* Ibid. xii. 46: *ἐγὼ φῶς εἰς τὸν κόσμον ἐλήλυθα, ἵνα πᾶς ὁ πιστεύων εἰς ἐμὲ, ἐν τῇ σκοτίᾳ μὴ μείνῃ.* Comp. Eph. v. 8.

[r] St. John xiv. 6.

[s] 1 St. John ii. 8: *ἡ σκοτία παράγεται, καὶ τὸ φῶς τὸ ἀληθινὸν ἤδη φαίνει.*

[t] St. John xiv. 31.

[u] 1 St. John iii. 16: *ἐν τούτῳ ἐγνώκαμεν τὴν ἀγάπην* (the absolute charity), *ὅτι ἐκεῖνος ὑπὲρ ἡμῶν τὴν ψυχὴν αὐτοῦ ἔθηκε.* Cf. St. John iii. 16.

[x] St. John xiv. 23: *ἐάν τις ἀγαπᾷ με, τὸν λόγον μου τηρήσει, καὶ ὁ Πατήρ μου ἀγαπήσει αὐτόν, καὶ πρὸς αὐτὸν ἐλευσόμεθα, καὶ μονὴν παρ' αὐτῷ ποιήσομεν.* Ibid. xiii. 1, xv. 9.

The Logos is Life. He is the Life [y], the eternal Life [z], *the* Life Which is the Essence of God. It has been given Him to have life in Himself, as the Father has life in Himself [a]. He can give life [b]; nay, life is so emphatically His prerogative gift, that He is called the Word of Life [c].

Thus the Word reveals the Divine Essence; His Incarnation makes that Life, that Love, that Light, which is eternally resident in God, obvious to souls that steadily contemplate Himself. These terms, Life, Love, Light—so abstract, so simple, so suggestive—meet in God; but they meet also in Jesus Christ. They do not only make Him the centre of a philosophy. They belong to the mystic language of faith more truly than to the abstract terminology of speculative thought. They draw hearts to Jesus; they invest Him with a higher than any intellectual beauty. The Life, the Love, the Light, are the 'glory' of the Word Incarnate which His disciples 'beheld,' pouring its rays through the veil of His human tabernacle [d]. The Light, the Love, the Life, constitute the 'fulness' whereof His disciples received [e]. Herein is comprised that entire body of grace and truth [f], by which the Word Incarnate gives to men the right to become the sons of God [g].

But, as has been already abundantly implied, the Word is also the Son. As applied to our Lord, the title 'Son of God' is protected by epithets which sustain and define its unique significance. In the synoptic Gospels, Christ is termed the 'well-beloved' Son [h]. In St. Paul He is God's 'Own' Son [i]. In St. John He is the Only-begotten Son, or simply the Only-

[y] St. John xi. 25: *ἐγώ εἰμι . . . ἡ ζωή.* Ibid. xiv. 6.

[z] 1 St. John v. 20: *οὗτός ἐστιν . . . ἡ ζωὴ αἰώνιος.* The *οὗτος* is referred to the Father by Lücke and Winer. But see p. 242, note [r].

[a] St. John v. 26: *ἔδωκε καὶ τῷ Υἱῷ ζωὴν ἔχειν ἐν ἑαυτῷ.*

[b] Ibid. i. 3, 4.

[c] 1 St. John i. 1: *ὁ λόγος τῆς ζωῆς.* Reuss, Théol. Chrét. ii. p. 445.

[d] St. John i. 14: *ὁ Λόγος σὰρξ ἐγένετο, καὶ ἐσκήνωσεν ἐν ἡμῖν, καὶ ἐθεασάμεθα τὴν δόξαν αὐτοῦ.*

[e] Ibid. ver. 16: *καὶ ἐκ τοῦ πληρώματος αὐτοῦ ἡμεῖς πάντες ἐλάβομεν.*

[f] Ibid. ver. 14: *πλήρης χάριτος καὶ ἀληθείας.*

[g] Ibid. i. 12: *ὅσοι δὲ ἔλαβον αὐτὸν, ἔδωκεν αὐτοῖς ἐξουσίαν τέκνα Θεοῦ γενέσθαι.*

[h] *ἀγαπητός*, St. Matt. iii. 17, xii. 18, xvii. 5; St. Mark i. 11, ix. 7, xii. 6; St. Luke iii. 22, ix. 35. Cod. Alex. reads *ἐκλελεγμένον*, xx. 13; cf. 2 St. Peter i. 17.

[i] Rom. viii. 32: *τοῦ ἰδίου Υἱοῦ οὐκ ἐφείσατο.* Ibid. ver. 3: *τὸν ἑαυτοῦ Υἱὸν πέμψας.*

begotten[k]. This last epithet surely means, not merely that God has no other such Son, but that His Only-begotten Son is, in virtue of this Sonship, a partaker of that incommunicable and imperishable Essence, Which is sundered from all created life by an impassable chasm. If St. Paul speaks of the Resurrection as manifesting this Sonship to the world[l], the sense of the word *μονογενής* remains in St. John, and it is plainly 'defined by its context to relate to something higher than any event occurring in time, however great or beneficial to the human race[m].' The Only-begotten Son[n] is in the bosom of the Father (*ὁ ὢν εἰς τὸν κόλπον τοῦ Πατρός*) just as the Logos is *πρὸς τὸν Θεόν*, ever contemplating, ever, as it were, moving towards Him in the ceaseless activities of an ineffable communion. The Son is His Father's equal, in that He is partaker of His nature: He is His Subordinate, in that this Equality is eternally derived. But the Father worketh hitherto and the Son works; the Father hath life in Himself, and has given to the Son to have life in Himself; all men are to honour the Son even as they honour the Father[o]. How does the Son of God, as presented to us in Scripture, differ from Him, Whom the Church knows and worships as God the Son?

Each of these expressions, the Word and the Son, if taken alone, might have led to a fatal misconception. In the language of Church history, the Logos, if unbalanced by the idea of Sonship, might have seemed to sanction Sabellianism. The Son, without the Logos, might have been yet more successfully pressed into the service of Arianism. An Eternal Thought or Reason, even although constantly tending to express itself in speech, is of itself

[k] St. John i. 14: *ἐθεασάμεθα τὴν δόξαν αὐτοῦ, δόξαν ὡς μονογενοῦς παρὰ Πατρός.* Ibid. i. 18: *ὁ μονογενὴς Υἱὸς, ὁ ὢν εἰς τὸν κόλπον τοῦ Πατρός.* Ibid. iii. 16: [*ὁ Θεὸς*] *τὸν Υἱὸν αὐτοῦ τὸν μονογενῆ ἔδωκεν.* Ibid. ver. 18: *ὁ δὲ μὴ πιστεύων ἤδη κέκριται, ὅτι μὴ πεπίστευκεν εἰς τὸ ὄνομα τοῦ μονογενοῦς Υἱοῦ τοῦ Θεοῦ.* Cf. 1 St. John iv. 9: *τὸν Υἱὸν αὐτοῦ τὸν μονογενῆ ἀπέσταλκεν ὁ Θεὸς εἰς τὸν κόσμον, ἵνα ζήσωμεν δι' αὐτοῦ.* The word *μονογενής* is used by St. Luke of the son of the widow of Nain (vii. 12), of the daughter of Jairus (viii. 42), and of the lunatic son of the man who met our Lord on His coming down from the mount of the transfiguration (ix. 38). In Heb. xi. 17 it is applied to Isaac. *μονογενής* means in each of these cases 'that which exists once only, that is, singly in its kind.' (Tholuck, Comm. in Joh. i. 14.) God has one Only Son Who by nature and necessity is His Son.

[l] Acts xiii. 32, 33; Rom. i. 4. Compare on the other hand, Heb. v. 8.

[m] Newman's Arians, p. 174.

[n] St. John i. 18, *ὁ μονογενὴς Υἱός*, where the Vat. and Sin. MSS. and Cod. Ephr. read *μονογενὴς ΘΕΟΣ*. Scrivener defends *Υἱός*. Int. N. T. ed. 3. p. 604. For the Patristic evidence, see Alford in loc. [o] St. John v. 17, 23, 26.

too abstract to oblige us to conceive of it as of a personal Subsistence. On the other hand, the filial relationship carries with it the idea of dependence and of comparatively recent origin, even although it should suggest the reproduction in the Son of all the qualities of the Father. Certainly St. John's language in his prologue protects the Personality of the Logos, and unless he believed that God could be divided or could have had a beginning, the Apostle teaches that the Son is co-eternal with the Father. Yet the bare metaphors of 'Word' and 'Son,' taken separately, might lead divergent thinkers to conceive of Him to Whom they are applied, on the one side as an impersonal quality or faculty of God, on the other, as a concrete and personal but inferior and dependent being. But combine them, and each corrects the possible misuse of the other. The Logos, Who is also the Son, cannot be an impersonal and abstract quality; since such an expression as the Son would be utterly misleading, unless it implied at the very least the fact of a personal subsistence distinct from that of the Father. On the other hand, the Son, Who is also the Logos, cannot be of more recent origin than the Father; since the Father cannot be conceived of as subsisting without that Eternal Thought or Reason Which is the Son. Nor may the Son be deemed to be in any respect, save in the order of Divine subsistence, inferior to the Father, since He is identical with the eternal intellectual Life of the Most High. Thus each metaphor reinforces, supplements, and protects the other. Taken together they exhibit Christ before His Incarnation as at once personally distinct from, and yet equal with, the Father; He is That personally subsisting and 'Eternal Life, Which was with the Father, and was manifested unto us[p].'

St. John's Gospel is a narrative of that manifestation. It is a Life of the Eternal Word *tabernacling* in Human Nature among men[q]. The Hebrew schools employed a similar expression to designate the personal presence of the Divinity in this finite world. In St. John's Gospel the Personality of Christ makes Itself felt as Eternal and Divine at wellnigh every step of the narrative[r]. Thus even the Forerunner describes

[p] 1 St. John i. 2. Cf. Newman's Arians, ch. ii. sect. 3.

[q] St. John i. 14: ἐσκήνωσεν ἐν ἡμῖν. The image implies both the reality and the transient character of our Lord's manifestation in the flesh. Olshausen, Meyer, and Lücke see in it an allusion to the 'Shekinah,' in which the Divine glory or radiance (כבוד) dwelt enshrined.

[r] Baur, Dogmengeschichte, i. 602: 'Was das johanneische Evangelium betrifft, so versteht es sich ohnediess von selbst, dass das eigentliche Subject

a Being Who appearing later in time has had an earlier existence[s]; and Who, while coming from above, is yet 'above all[t].' Each discourse, each miracle, nay, each separate word and act, is a fresh ray of glory streaming forth from the Person of the Word through the veil of His assumed Humanity. The miracles of the Word Incarnate are frequently called His works[u]. The Evangelist means to imply that 'the wonderful is only the natural form of working for Him in Whom all the fulness of God dwells.' Christ's Divine Nature must of necessity bring forth works greater than the works of man. The Incarnation is the one great wonder; other miracles follow as a matter of course. The real marvel would be if the Incarnate Being should work no miracles[v]; as it is, they are the natural results of His presence among men, rather than its higher manifestation. His true glory is not perceived except by those who gaze at it with a meditative and reverent intentness[w]. The Word Incarnate is ever conscious of His sublime relationship to the Father. He knows whence He is[x]. He refers not unfrequently to His pre-existent Life[y]. He sees into the deepest purposes of the human hearts around Him[z]. He has a perfect knowledge of all that concerns God[a]. His works are simply the works of God[b]. To believe in the Father

der Persönlichkeit Christi nur der Logos ist, die Menschwerdung besteht daher nur in dem σὰρξ γενέσθαι; dass der Logos Fleisch geworden, im Fleisch erschienen ist, ist seine menschliche Erscheinung.' It will be borne in mind that σάρξ, in its full New Testament meaning, certainly includes ψυχή as well as the animal organism (see Olshausen on Rom. vii. 14), and St. John attributes to the Word Incarnate spiritual experiences which must have had their seat in His human Soul (xi. 33, 38, xiii. 21). But Baur's general position, that in St. John's Gospel the Personality of the Eternal Word is perpetually before us, is unquestionably true.

[s] St. John i. 15: ὁ ὀπίσω μου ἐρχόμενος, ἔμπροσθέν μου γέγονεν, ὅτι πρῶτός μου ἦν.

[t] Ibid. iii. 31: ὁ ἄνωθεν ἐρχόμενος ἐπάνω πάντων ἐστίν.

[u] ἔργα, St. John v. 36, vii. 21, x. 25, 32, 38, xiv. 11, 12, xv. 23. Cf. too St. Matt. xi. 2. The word is applied to the Old Testament miracles in Heb. iii. 9; Ps. xciv. 9, LXX. Cf. Archbishop Trench on the Miracles, p. 7. That, notwithstanding the wider use of ἔργον in St. John xvii. 4, ἔργα in the fourth Gospel *do* mean Christ's miracles, cf. Trench, Mir. p. 8, note †. Cf. Lect. IV. p. 158.

[v] Trench, ubi supra, p. 8.

[w] St. John uses the words θεωρεῖν, θεάσασθαι to describe this.

[x] St. John viii. 14: οἶδα πόθεν ἦλθον.

[y] Ibid. iii. 13, vi. 62, viii. 58, xvi. 28, xvii. 5.

[z] Ibid. ii. 24, iv. 17, v. 14, 42, vi. 15.

[a] Ibid. viii. 55, x. 15.

[b] Ibid. ix. 4, x. 37, sqq., xiv. 10.

is to believe in Him. To have seen Him is to have seen the Father. To reject and hate Him is to reject and hate the Father. He demands at the hands of men the same tribute of affection and submission as that which they owe to the Person of the Father[c].

In St. John's Gospel, the Incarnation is exhibited, not as the measure of the humiliation of the Eternal Word, but as the veil of His enduring and unassailable glory. The angels of God ascend and descend upon Him. Nay, He is still in heaven. Certainly He has taken an earthly form; He has clothed Himself with a human frame. But He has thereby raised humanity rather than abased Himself. In St. John the *status inanitionis*, the intrinsic humiliation of Christ's Incarnate Life, is thrown into the background of the reader's thought. The narrative is throughout illuminated by the never-failing presence of the Word in His glory[d]. Even when Jesus dies, His Death is no mere humilia-

[c] As M. Reuss admits: 'Il résulte (from the prerogatives ascribed to the Word Incarnate in St. John's Gospel) que le Verbe révélateur pouvait demander pour lui-même, de la part des hommes, les mêmes sentiments, et les mêmes dispositions, qu'ils doivent avoir à l'égard de la personne du Père. Ces sentiments sont exprimés par un mot, qui contient la notion d'un respect professé pour un supérieur, la reconnaissance d'une dignité devant laquelle on s'incline. A cet égard, *il y a égalité des deux personnes divines vis-a-vis de l'homme.* On ne croit pas à l'une sans croire à l'autre; qui voit l'une voit l'autre; rejeter, haïr le Fils, c'est rejeter et haïr le Père. (St. Jean iii. 33, 34, xii. 44, xv. 23). Mais dans tout ceci (proceeds M. Reuss) il ne s'agit pas de ce qu'on appele le *culte* dans le langage pratique de l'Église. Le culte appartient à Dieu le Père, et lui sera offert désormais avec d'autant plus d'empressement qu'il est mieux révélé, et que rien ne sépare plus de lui les croyants.' (Reuss, Théol. Chrét. ii. 455.) How inconsequent is this restriction! If the Incarnate Word has a right to demand for Himself the same 'sentiments' and 'dispositions' as those which men cherish towards the Almighty Father, He has a right to the same tribute of an adoration in spirit and in truth as that which is due to the Father. What is worship but a complex act of such 'sentiments' and 'dispositions' as faith, love, self-prostration, self-surrender before the Most Holy? If τιμᾶν (St. John v. 23), within the general meaning of due acknowledgment, includes much else besides adoration, it cannot be applied to the duties of man to God without including adoration. Our Lord's words place Himself and the Father simply on a level; if the Son is not to be adored, neither is the Father; if the Father is to be adored, then must the Son be adored in the same sense and measure. This is certainly not interfered with by St. John iv. 20, sqq.; while the best practical comment upon it is to be found in the confession of St. Thomas, xx. 28; on which see Lect. VII.

[d] This may seem inconsistent with (1) St. John xiv. 28: ὁ Πατήρ μείζων μου ἐστίν. But such a statement would be 'unmeaning' in a mere man. See Lect. IV. pp. 202–204; (2) St. John xvii. 3: αὕτη δέ ἐστιν ἡ αἰώνιος

tion; His Death is the crisis of His exaltation[e], of His glory[f]. Not that He can personally increase in glory. He is already the Son; He is the Word. But He can glorify and exalt that Manhood which is the robe through which His movements are discernible: He can glorify Himself, as God is glorified, by drawing towards His Person the faith and love and reverence of men. It were folly to conceive of Him as enhancing His Divinity; but He can make larger and deeper that measure of homage which ascends towards His throne from human understandings and from human hearts[g].

III. 1. But does St. John's teaching in his earlier writings on the subject of our Lord's Person harmonize with the representations placed before us in the fourth Gospel? The opening words of his first Epistle[h] might go far to answer that question. St. John's position in this Epistle is, that the Eternal immaterial Word of Life resident in God had become historically manifest, and that the Apostles had consciously seen, and heard, and handled Him, and were now publishing their experience to the world[i]. The practical bearing of this announcement lay in the truth that 'he that hath the Son hath the Life, and he that hath not the Son hath not the Life[j].' For 'God hath given to us the Eternal Life, and this, the Life, is in His Son[k].' If then the soul is to hold communion with God in the Life of Light and

ζωὴ, ἵνα γινώσκωσίν σε τὸν μόνον ἀληθινὸν Θεὸν, καὶ ὃν ἀπέστειλας Ἰησοῦν Χριστόν. But here a Socinian sense is excluded, (*a*) by the consideration that 'the knowledge of GOD *and a creature* could not be Eternal Life' (see Alford in loc.); (*b*) by the plain sense of verse 1, which places the Son and the Father on a level: 'What creature could stand before his Creator and say, "Glorify me, that I may glorify Thee?"' Stier apud Alf.; (*c*) by verse 5, which asserts our Lord's pre-existent δόξα. It follows that the restrictive epithets μόνον ἀληθινόν must be held to be exclusive, not of the Son, but of false gods, or creatures external to the Divine Essence. See Estius in loc. Trench, Synonyms of N. T., p. 25, § viii.

[e] St. John iii. 14: ὑψωθῆναι δεῖ τὸν Υἱὸν τοῦ ἀνθρώπου. Ibid. viii. 28, xii. 32.

[f] Ibid. xii. 23: ἐλήλυθεν ἡ ὥρα ἵνα δοξασθῇ ὁ Υἱὸς τοῦ ἀνθρώπου. Ibid. xiii. 31.

[g] Cf. Reuss, Théol. Chrét. ii. 456; although the statements of this writer cannot be adopted without much qualification.

[h] On the authorship of the three Epistles, see Alford, Gk. Test. vol. iv., Prol., chaps. 5, 6, and Westcott, Epistles of St. John, p. liii. ff. See too Appendix, note E.

[i] 1 St. John i. 1–3.

[j] Ibid. v. 12: ὁ ἔχων τὸν Υἱὸν ἔχει τὴν ζωήν· ὁ μὴ ἔχων τὸν Υἱὸν τοῦ Θεοῦ τὴν ζωὴν οὐκ ἔχει.

[k] Ibid. ver. 11: καὶ αὕτη ἐστὶν ἡ μαρτυρία (i.e. the revealed doctrine resting on a Divine authority) ὅτι ζωὴν αἰώνιον ἔδωκεν ἡμῖν ὁ Θεὸς, καὶ αὕτη ἡ ζωὴ ἐν τῷ Υἱῷ αὐτοῦ ἐστιν.

Righteousness and Love, it must be through communion with His Divine Son. Thus all practically depends upon the attitude of the soul towards the Son. Accordingly, 'whosoever denieth the Son, the same hath not the Father[l];' while on the other hand, whosoever sincerely and in practice acknowledges the Son of God in His historical manifestation, enjoys a true communion with the Life of God. 'Whosoever shall confess that Jesus is the Son of God, God dwelleth in him and he in God[m].'

St. John constantly teaches that the Christian's work in this state of probation is to conquer 'the world[n].' It is, in other words, to fight successfully against that view of life which ignores God, against that complex system of attractive moral evil and specious intellectual falsehood, which is marshalled and organized by the great enemy of God, and which permeates and inspires non-Christianized society. The world's force is seen especially in 'the lust of the flesh, in the lust of the eyes, and in the pride of life.' These three forms of concupiscence manifest

[l] 1 St. John ii. 22: οὗτός ἐστιν ὁ ἀντίχριστος, ὁ ἀρνούμενος τὸν Πατέρα καὶ τὸν Υἱόν. A Humanitarian might have urged that it was possible to deny the Son, while confessing the Father. But St. John, on the ground that the Son is the Only and the Adequate Manifestation of the Father, denies this: πᾶς ὁ ἀρνούμενος τὸν Υἱὸν οὐδὲ τὸν Πατέρα ἔχει.

[m] Ibid. iv. 15: ὃς ἂν ὁμολογήσῃ ὅτι Ἰησοῦς ἐστιν ὁ Υἱὸς τοῦ Θεοῦ, ὁ Θεὸς ἐν αὐτῷ μένει, καὶ αὐτὸς ἐν τῷ Θεῷ.

[n] Ibid. ii. 15: ἐάν τις ἀγαπᾷ τὸν κόσμον, οὐκ ἔστιν ἡ ἀγάπη τοῦ Πατρὸς ἐν αὐτῷ. Compare Martensen, Christl. Dogmat. § 96: 'If we consider the effects of the Fall upon the course of historical development, not only in the case of individuals but of the race collectively, the term "world" (κόσμος) bears a special meaning different from that which it would have, were the development of humanity normal. The cosmical principle having been emancipated by the Fall from its due subjection to the Spirit, and invested with a false independence, and the universe of creation having obtained with man a higher importance than really attaches to it, the historical development of the world has become one in which the advance of the kingdom of God is retarded and hindered. The created universe has, in a relative sense, life in itself, *including, as it does, a system of powers, ideas, and aims, which possess a relative value. This relative independence, which ought to be subservient to the kingdom of God, has become a fallen "world-autonomy."* Hence arises the scriptural expression "*this* world" (ὁ κόσμος οὗτος). By this expression the Bible conveys the idea that it regards the world not only ontologically but in its definite and actual state, the state in which it has been since the Fall. "This world" means the world content with itself, in its own independence, its own glory; the world which disowns its dependence on God as its Creator. "This world" regards itself, not as the κτίσις, but only as the κόσμος, as a system of glory and beauty which has life in itself, and can give life. The historical embodiment of "this world" is heathendom, which honoureth not God as God.'

the inner life of the world[o]; if the Christian would resist and beat them back, he must have a strong faith, a faith in a Divine Saviour. 'Who is he that overcometh the world, but he that believeth that Jesus is the Son of God[p]?' This faith, which introduces the soul to communion with God in Light, attained through communion with His Blessed Son, exhibits the world in its true colours. The soul spurns the world as she clings believingly to the Divine Son.

St. John's picture of Christ's work in this first Epistle, and especially his pointed and earnest opposition to the specific heresy of Cerinthus[q], leads us up to the culminating statement that Jesus Himself is the true God and the Eternal Life[r]. Throughout this Epistle the Apostle has been writing to those 'who believe on the Name of the Son of God,' that is to say, on the Divine Nature of Jesus which the verbal symbol guards and

[o] 1 St. John ii. 16: *πᾶν τὸ ἐν τῷ κόσμῳ, ἡ ἐπιθυμία τῆς σαρκὸς, καὶ ἡ ἐπιθυμία τῶν ὀφθαλμῶν, καὶ ἡ ἀλαζονεία τοῦ βίου, οὐκ ἔστιν ἐκ τοῦ Πατρὸς, ἀλλ' ἐκ τοῦ κόσμου ἐστί.*

[p] Ibid. v. 4, 5: *αὕτη ἐστὶν ἡ νίκη ἡ νικήσασα τὸν κόσμον, ἡ πίστις ἡμῶν· τίς ἐστιν ὁ νικῶν τὸν κόσμον, εἰ μὴ ὁ πιστεύων ὅτι Ἰησοῦς ἐστιν ὁ Υἱὸς τοῦ Θεοῦ;*

[q] Specially 1 St. John iv. 2, 3, where the Apostle's words contain a double antithesis to the Cerinthian gnosis, which taught that the Æon Christ entered into the Man Jesus at His baptism, and remained with Him until His Passion. See pp. 223, 224. St. John asserts in opposition (1) that Jesus and the Christ are one and the same Person, (2) that the one Lord Jesus Christ came 'in' not 'into the flesh.' He did not descend into an already existing man, but He appeared clothed in Human Nature. See the exhaustive note of Ebrard, Die Briefe Johannis, in loc.

[r] 1 St. John v. 20: *οὗτός ἐστιν ὁ ἀληθινὸς Θεὸς, καὶ ἡ ζωὴ αἰώνιος.* After having distinguished the *ἀληθινός* from His *Υἱός*, St. John, by a characteristic turn, simply identifies the Son with the *ἀληθινὸς Θεός*. To refer this sentence to the Father, Who has been twice called *ὁ ἀληθινός*, would be unmeaning repetition. Moreover the previous sentence declared, not that we are in God as Father, Son, and Spirit, but that we are in God as being in His Son Jesus Christ. This statement is justified when *οὗτος* is referred to *Υἱῷ*. As to the article before *ἀληθινός*, it has the effect of stating, not merely What, but Who our Lord is; it says not, Christ is Divine, but, Christ is God. This does not really go beyond what the Apostle has already said about the *Λόγος* at the beginning of this Epistle. To object with Düsterdieck that this interpretation obscures the distinction between the Father and the Son, is inaccurate; St. John does not say, This is the Father, but, This is the true God. *Ὁ ἀληθινὸς Θεός* is the Divine Essence, in opposition to all creatures. The Apostle does not enter upon the question of the Son's relation to the Father within the Divine Essence. Our being in the true God depends upon our being in Christ, and St. John clenches this assertion by saying that Christ is the true God Himself. See St. Ath. Or. c. Ar. iii. 19; iv. 26; St. Cyril. Thes. p. 302; Waterland, Wks., ii. 130.

suggests. Throughout this Epistle St. John's object has been to convince believers that by that faith they had the Eternal Life, and to force them to be true to It[s].

In each of St. John's Epistles[t] we encounter that special temper, at once so tender and so peremptory, which is an ethical corollary to belief in an Incarnate God. St. John has been named the Apostle of the Absolute. Those who would concede to Christianity no higher dignity than that of teaching a relative and provisional truth, will fail to find any countenance for their doctrine in the New Testament Scriptures. But nowhere will they meet with a more earnest opposition to it than in the pages of the writer who is pre-eminently the Apostle of charity. St. John preaches the Christian creed as the one absolute certainty. The Christian faith might have been only relatively true, if it had reposed upon the word of a human messenger. But St. John specially insists upon the fact that God has revealed Himself, not merely through, but in, Christ. The Absolute Religion is introduced by a Self-revelation of the Absolute Being Himself. God has appeared, God has spoken; and the Christian faith is the result. St. John then does not treat Christianity as a phase in the history even of true religion, nor as a religion containing elements of truth, even though it were more true than any religion which had preceded it. St. John proclaims that 'we "Christians" are in Him that is True.' Not to admit that Jesus Christ has come in the Flesh, is to be a deceiver and an antichrist. St. John presents Christianity to the soul as a religion which must be its all, if it is not really to be worse than nothing[u]. The opposition between truth and error, between the friends and the foes of Christ, is for St. John as sharp and trenchant a thing as the contrast between light and

[s] 1 St. John v. 13: *ταῦτα ἔγραψα ὑμῖν* [*τοῖς πιστεύουσιν εἰς τὸ ὄνομα τοῦ Υἱοῦ τοῦ Θεοῦ*, Rec.] *ἵνα εἰδῆτε ὅτι ζωὴν ἔχετε αἰώνιον, καὶ ἵνα πιστεύητε* [*οἱ πιστεύοντες*, Tisch.] *εἰς τὸ ὄνομα τοῦ Υἱοῦ τοῦ Θεοῦ.*

[t] In St. John's second Epistle observe (1) the association of Christ with the Father as the source of *χάρις, ἔλεος*, and *εἰρήνη* (ver. 3); (2) the denunciation of the Cerinthian doctrine as anti-Christian (ver. 7); (3) the significant statement that a false progress (*ὁ προάγων*, A.B., not as rec. *ὁ παραβαίνων*) which did not rest in the true Apostolic *διδαχὴ τοῦ Χριστοῦ*, would forfeit all communion with God. We know Him only in Christ His Blessed Son, and to reject Christianity is to reject the only true Theism (vers. 8, 9).

[u] 1 St. John ii. 21: *οὐκ ἔγραψα ὑμῖν ὅτι οὐκ οἴδατε τὴν ἀλήθειαν, ἀλλ' ὅτι οἴδατε αὐτὴν, καὶ ὅτι πᾶν ψεῦδος ἐκ τῆς ἀληθείας οὐκ ἔστι.* Ibid. v. 10: *ὁ μὴ πιστεύων τῷ Θεῷ ψεύστην πεποίηκεν αὐτόν.*

darkness, between life and death [x]. This is the temper of a man who will not enter the public baths along with the heretic who has dishonoured his Lord [y]. This is the spirit of the teacher who warns his flock to beware of eating with a propagator of false doctrine, and of bidding him God speed, lest they should partake of his 'evil deeds [z].' Yet this is also the writer whose pages, beyond any other in the New Testament, beam with the purest, tenderest love of humanity. Side by side with this resolute antagonism to dogmatic error, St. John exhibits and inculcates an enthusiastic affection for humankind as such, which our professed philanthropists could not rival [a]. The man who loves not his brother man, whatever be his spiritual estimate of himself, abideth in death [b]. No divorce is practically possible between the first and the second parts of charity: the man who loves his God must love his brother also [c]. Love is the moral counterpart of intellectual light [d].

It is a modern fashion to represent these two tempers, the dogmatic and the philanthropic, as necessarily opposed. This representation indeed is not even in harmony with modern experience; but in St. John it meets with a most energetic contradiction. St. John is at once earnestly dogmatic and earnestly philanthropic; for the Incarnation has taught him both the preciousness of man and the preciousness of truth. The Eternal Word, incarnate and dying for the truth, inspires St. John to

[x] 1 St. John ii. 15: *ἐάν τις ἀγαπᾷ τὸν κόσμον οὐκ ἔστιν ἡ ἀγάπη τοῦ Πατρὸς ἐν αὐτῷ.* Ibid. ver. 19: *ἐξ ἡμῶν ἐξῆλθον* [scil. *οἱ ἀντίχριστοι*] *ἀλλ' οὐκ ἦσαν ἐξ ἡμῶν· εἰ γὰρ ἦσαν ἐξ ἡμῶν, μεμενήκεισαν ἂν μεθ' ἡμῶν· ἀλλ' ἵνα φανερωθῶσιν ὅτι οὐκ εἰσὶ πάντες ἐξ ἡμῶν.* Ibid. ver. 22: *οὗτός ἐστιν ὁ ἀντίχριστος, ὁ ἀρνούμενος τὸν Πατέρα καὶ τὸν Υἱόν.*

[y] St. Irenæus, adv. Hær. iii. 3, 4: *καὶ εἰσὶν οἱ ἀκηκοότες αὐτοῦ (τοῦ Πολυκάρπου) ὅτι Ἰωάννης ὁ τοῦ Κυρίου μαθητὴς, ἐν τῇ Ἐφέσῳ πορευθεὶς λούσασθαι, καὶ ἰδὼν ἔσω Κήρινθον, ἐξήλατο τοῦ βαλανείου μὴ λουσάμενος ἀλλ' ἐπειπὼν, 'Φύγωμεν, μὴ καὶ τὸ βαλανεῖον συμπέσῃ, ἔνδον ὄντος Κηρίνθου, τοῦ τῆς ἀληθείας ἐχθροῦ.'* Cf. Eus. Hist. Eccl. iii. 28.

[z] 2 St. John 10, 11: *εἴ τις ἔρχεται πρὸς ὑμᾶς, καὶ ταύτην τὴν διδαχὴν οὐ φέρει, μὴ λαμβάνετε αὐτὸν εἰς οἰκίαν, καὶ χαίρειν αὐτῷ μὴ λέγετε· ὁ γὰρ λέγων αὐτῷ χαίρειν, κοινωνεῖ τοῖς ἔργοις αὐτοῦ τοῖς πονηροῖς.*

[a] 1 St. John iii. 11.

[b] Ibid. ver. 14: *ἡμεῖς οἴδαμεν ὅτι μεταβεβήκαμεν ἐκ τοῦ θανάτου εἰς τὴν ζωὴν, ὅτι ἀγαπῶμεν τοὺς ἀδελφούς· ὁ μὴ ἀγαπῶν τὸν ἀδελφὸν μένει ἐν τῷ θανάτῳ.*

[c] Ibid. iv. 20, 21: *ὁ μὴ ἀγαπῶν τὸν ἀδελφὸν αὐτοῦ ὃν ἑώρακε, τὸν Θεὸν ὃν οὐχ ἑώρακε πῶς δύναται ἀγαπᾶν; καὶ ταύτην τὴν ἐντολὴν ἔχομεν ἀπ' αὐτοῦ, ἵνα ὁ ἀγαπῶν τὸν Θεὸν ἀγαπᾷ καὶ τὸν ἀδελφὸν αὐτοῦ.*

[d] Ibid. ii. 9, 10: *ὁ λέγων ἐν τῷ φωτὶ εἶναι, καὶ τὸν ἀδελφὸν αὐτοῦ μισῶν, ἐν τῇ σκοτίᾳ ἐστὶν ἕως ἄρτι. ὁ ἀγαπῶν τὸν ἀδελφὸν αὐτοῦ ἐν τῷ φωτὶ μένει.*

guard it with apostolic chivalry; but also, this revelation of the Heart of God melts him into tenderness towards the race which Jesus has loved so well[e]. To St. John a lack of love for men seems sheer dishonour to the love of Christ. And the heresy which mutilates the Person or denies the work of Christ, does not present itself to St. John as purely speculative misfortune, as clumsy negation of fact, as barren intellectual error. Heresy is with this Apostle a crime against charity; not only because heresy breeds divisions among brethren, but yet more because it kills out from the souls of men that blessed and prolific Truth, which, when sincerely believed, cannot but fill the heart with love to God and to man. St. John writes as one whose eyes had looked upon and whose hands had handled the sensibly present form of Light and Love. That close contact with the Absolute Truth Incarnate had kindled in him a holy impatience of antagonist error; that felt glow of the Infinite Charity of God had shed over his whole character and teaching the beauty and pathos of a tenderness, which, as our hearts tell us while we read his pages, is not of this world.

2. This ethical reflection of the doctrine of God manifest in the flesh is perhaps mainly characteristic of St. John's first Epistle; but it is not wanting in the Apocalypse[f]. The representation of the Person of our Saviour in the Apocalyse is independent of any indistinctness that may attach to the interpretation of the historical imagery of that wonderful book[g]. In the Apocalypse, Christ is the First and the Last; He is the Alpha and the Omega; He is the Eternal; He is the Almighty[h]. He possesses the seven spirits or perfections of

[e] 1 St. John iii. 16: *ἐν τούτῳ ἐγνώκαμεν τὴν ἀγάπην* (i. e. absolute charity), *ὅτι ἐκεῖνος ὑπὲρ ἡμῶν τὴν ψυχὴν αὐτοῦ ἔθηκε· καὶ ἡμεῖς ὀφείλομεν ὑπὲρ τῶν ἀδελφῶν τὰς ψυχὰς τιθέναι.* Ibid. iv. 9: *ἐν τούτῳ ἐφανερώθη ἡ ἀγάπη τοῦ Θεοῦ ἐν ἡμῖν, ὅτι τὸν Υἱὸν αὐτοῦ τὸν μονογενῆ ἀπέσταλκεν ὁ Θεὸς εἰς τὸν κόσμον, ἵνα ζήσωμεν δι' αὐτοῦ.*

[f] On the Johannean authorship of the Apocalypse, see Alford, Gk. Test. vol. iv. pp. 198-229; Wait's remarks in the pref. to Hug's Introduction, pp. 145-177; Schaff, Apost. Church, ii. 89; Leathes, Witness of St. John to Christ, pp. 134, 352.

[g] In the Epistles to the Angels of the Seven Churches, the language used by our Lord is morally inconsistent with any conception of His Person but the highest: Rev. ii. 1-7, 8-11, 12, 13, 14, 16, 19, 20, 21-26, 28, iii. 1-5, 7-13, 14-22. Cf. also the allusion to the *ὀργὴ τοῦ ἀρνίου*, vi. 16, with Ps. vi. 4, vii. 6, xxi. 9; Is. ix. 19, li. 17; Jer. iv. 8, 26, xii. 13; Lam. i. 12; Rom. i. 18, etc.

[h] Rev. i. 8, *ἐγώ εἰμι τὸ Α καὶ τὸ Ω*: Ibid. *ὁ ὢν, καὶ ὁ ἦν, καὶ ὁ ἐρχόμενος, ὁ παντοκράτωρ*: xxi. 6, xxii. 13, *ἀρχὴ καὶ τέλος.*

God[i]. He has a mysterious Name which no man knows save He Himself[j]. His Name is written on the foreheads of the faithful[k]; He is the giver of grace and victory[l]. In the Apocalypse, His Name is called the Word of God[m]; as in the first Epistle He is the Word of Life, and in the Gospel the Word in the beginning. As He rides through heaven on His errand of triumph and of judgment, a Name is written on His vesture and on His thigh; He is 'King of kings, and Lord of lords[n].' St. John had leaned upon His breast at supper in the familiarity of trusted friendship. St. John sees Him but for a moment in His supramundane glory, and forthwith falls at His feet as dead[o]. In the Apocalypse especially we are confronted with the startling truth that the Lord of the unseen world is none other than the Crucified One[p]. The armies of heaven follow Him, clothed as He is in a vesture dipped in blood, at once the symbol of His Passion and of His victory[q]. But of all the teachings of the Apocalypse on this subject, perhaps none is so full of significance as the representation of Christ in His wounded Humanity upon the throne of the Most High. The Lamb, as It had been slain, is in the very centre of the court of heaven[r]; He receives the prostrate adoration of the highest intelligences around the throne[s]; and as the Object of that solemn, uninterrupted, awful worship[t], He is associated with the Father, as being in truth one with the Almighty, Uncreated, Supreme God[u].

[i] Rev. iii. 1: *ὁ ἔχων τὰ ἑπτὰ πνεύματα τοῦ Θεοῦ.*

[j] Ibid. xix. 12: *ἔχων ὄνομα γεγραμμένον ὃ οὐδεὶς οἶδεν εἰ μὴ αὐτός.*

[k] Ibid. iii. 12, where *τὸ ὄνομά μου* is paralleled with *τὸ ὄνομα τοῦ Θεοῦ μου*, although our Lord is speaking as Man. Cf. ii. 17.

[l] Ibid. xxii. 21, iii. 21.

[m] Ibid. xix. 13: *καλεῖται τὸ ὄνομα αὐτοῦ Ὁ Λόγος τοῦ Θεοῦ.*

[n] Ibid. ver. 16: *ἔχει ἐπὶ τὸ ἱμάτιον καὶ ἐπὶ τὸν μηρὸν αὐτοῦ τὸ ὄνομα γεγραμμένον, Βασιλεὺς βασιλέων καὶ Κύριος κυρίων.* Cf. 1 Tim. vi. 15.

[o] Ibid. i. 17: *ὅτε εἶδον αὐτὸν, ἔπεσα πρὸς τοὺς πόδας αὐτοῦ ὡς νεκρός.*

[p] Ibid. xii. 10: *ἡ ἐξουσία τοῦ Χριστοῦ.* Ibid. xiii. 8: *τὸ βίβλιον τῆς ζωῆς τοῦ ἀρνίου τοῦ ἐσφαγμένου.*

[q] Ibid. xix. 13, 14. Cf. Is. lxiii. 1.

[r] Rev. v. 6: *ἐν μέσῳ τοῦ θρόνου . . . Ἀρνίον ἑστηκὸς ὡς ἐσφαγμένον.*

[s] Ibid. v. 8: *τὰ τέσσαρα ζῶα καὶ οἱ εἰκοσιτέσσαρες πρεσβύτεροι ἔπεσον ἐνώπιον τοῦ Ἀρνίου.* Cf. i. 1: *τοῦ ἀγγέλου αὐτοῦ.* The Angel was His property; cf. xxii. 16.

[t] Ibid. ver. 12: *ἄξιόν ἐστι τὸ Ἀρνίον τὸ ἐσφαγμένον λαβεῖν τὴν δύναμιν καὶ πλοῦτον καὶ σοφίαν καὶ ἰσχὺν καὶ τιμὴν καὶ δόξαν καὶ εὐλογίαν.*

[u] Ibid. v. 13: *τῷ καθημένῳ ἐπὶ τοῦ θρόνου καὶ τῷ Ἀρνίῳ ἡ εὐλογία καὶ ἡ τιμὴ καὶ ἡ δόξα καὶ τὸ κράτος εἰς τοὺς αἰῶνας τῶν αἰώνων.* Cf. Ibid. xvii. 14: *τὸ Ἀρνίον νικήσει αὐτοὺς, ὅτι Κύριος κυρίων ἐστὶ καὶ Βασιλεὺς βασιλέων.* See

IV. Whatever, then, may have been the interval between the composition of the Apocalypse and that of the fourth Gospel, we find in the two documents one and the same doctrine, in substance if not in terms, respecting our Lord's Eternal Person; and further, this doctrine accurately corresponds with that of St. John's first Epistle. But it may be asked whether St. John, thus consistent with himself upon a point of such capital importance, is really in harmony with the teaching of the earlier Evangelists? It is granted that between St. John and the three first Gospels there is a broad difference of characteristic phraseology, of the structure, scene, and matter of the several narratives. Does this difference strike deeper still? Is the Christology of the son of Zebedee fundamentally distinct from that of his predecessors? Can we recognise the Christ of the earlier Evangelists in the Christ of St. John?

Now it is obvious to remark that the difference between the three first Evangelists and the fourth, in their respective representations of the Person of our Lord, is in one sense, at any rate, a real difference. There is a real difference in the point of view of the writers, although the truth before them is one and the same. Each from his own stand-point, the first three Evangelists seek and pourtray separate aspects of the Human side of the Life of Jesus. They set forth His perfect Manhood in all Its regal grace and majesty, in all Its Human sympathy and beauty, in all Its healing and redemptive virtue. In one Gospel Christ is the true Fulfiller of the Law, and withal, by a touching contrast, the Man of Sorrows. In another He is the Lord of Nature and the Leader of men; all seek Him; all yield to Him; He moves forward in the independence of majestic strength. In a third He is active and all-embracing Compassion; He is the Shepherd, Who goes forth as for His Life-work, to seek the sheep that was lost; He is the Good Samaritan [v]. Thus the obedience, the force, and the tenderness of His Humanity are successively depicted; but room is left for another aspect of His Life, differing from these and yet in harmony with them. If we may dare so to speak, the synoptists approach their great Subject from without, St. John unfolds it from within. St. John has been guided to pierce the veil of sense; he has penetrated

also the remarkable expression xx. 6, *ἔσονται ἱερεῖς τοῦ Θεοῦ καὶ τοῦ Χριστοῦ*, which clearly associates Christ with the Father in the highest honour which man can render to God, namely, the offering of sacrifice; xxi. 22, 23, xxii. 1, 2.

[v] Cf. Holtzmann, Die Synoptischen Evangelien.

far beyond the Human features, nay even beyond the Human thought and Human will of the Redeemer, into the central depths of His Eternal Personality. He sets forth the Life of our Lord and Saviour on the earth, not in any one of the aspects which belong to It as Human, but as being the consistent and adequate expression of the glory of a Divine Person, manifested to men under a visible form. The miracles described, the discourses selected, the plan of the narrative, are all in harmony with the point of view of the fourth Evangelist, and it at once explains and accounts for them.

Plainly, my brethren, two or more observers may approach the same object from different points of view, and may be even entirely absorbed with distinct aspects of it; and yet it does not follow that any one of these aspects is necessarily at variance with the others. Still less does it follow that one aspect alone represents the truth. Socrates does not lose his identity, because he is so much more to Plato than he is to Xenophon. Each of yourselves may be studied at the same time by the anatomist and by the psychologist. Certainly the aspect of your complex nature which the one study insists upon, is sufficiently remote from the aspect which presents itself to the other. In the eyes of one observer you are purely spirit; you are thought, affection, memory, will, imagination. As he analyses you he is almost indifferent to the material body in which your higher nature is encased, upon which it has left its mark, and through which it expresses itself. But to the other observer this your material body is everything. Its veins and muscles, its pores and nerves, its colour, its proportions, its functions, absorb his whole attention. He is nervously impatient of any speculations about you which cannot be tested by his instruments. Yet is there any real ground for a petty jealousy between the one study of your nature and the other? Is not each student a servant whom true science will own as doing her work? May not each illustrate, supplement, balance, and check the conclusions of the other? Must you necessarily view yourselves as being purely mind, if you will not be persuaded that you are merely matter? Must you needs be materialists, if you will not become the most transcendental of mystics? Or will not a little physiology usefully restrain you from a fanciful supersensualism, while a study of the immaterial side of your being forbids you to listen, even for a moment, to the brutalizing suggestions of consistent materialism?

These questions admit of easy reply; each half of the truth

is practically no less than speculatively necessary to the other. Nor is it otherwise with the general relation of the first three Gospels to the fourth. Yet it should be added that the Synoptists do teach the Divine Nature of Jesus, although in the main His Sacred Manhood is most prominent in their pages. Moreover the fourth Gospel, as has been noticed, abundantly insists upon Christ's true Humanity. Had we not possessed the fourth Gospel, we should have known much less of one side of His Human Character than we actually know. For in it we see Christ engaged in earnest conflict with the worldly and unbelieving spirit of His time, while surrounded by the little company of His disciples, and devoting Himself to them even 'unto the end.' The aspects of our Lord's Humanity which are thus brought into prominence would have remained, comparatively speaking, in the shade, had the last Gospel not been written. But that 'symmetrical conception' of our Lord's Character, which modern critics have remarked upon, as especially distinguishing the fourth Gospel, is to be referred to the manner in which St. John lays bare the Eternal Personality of Jesus. For in It the scattered rays of glory which light up the earlier Evangelists find their point of unity. By laying such persistent stress upon Christ's Godhead, as the true seat of His Personality, the fourth Gospel is doctrinally complemental (how marvellous is the complement!) to the other three; and yet these three are so full of suggestive implications that they practically anticipate the higher teaching of the fourth.

1. For in the synoptic Gospels Christ is called the Son of God in a higher sense than the ethical or than the theocratic. In the Old Testament an anointed king or a saintly prophet is a son of God. Christ is not merely one among many sons. He is the Only, the Well-beloved Son of the Father[1]. His relationship to the Father is unshared by any other, and is absolutely unique. It is indeed probable that of our Lord's contemporaries many applied to Him the title 'Son of God' only as an official designation of the Messiah; while others used it to acknowledge that surpassing and perfect character which proclaimed Jesus of Nazareth to be the One Son, who had appeared on earth,

[1] Compare the voice from heaven at our Lord's baptism, *οὗτός ἐστιν ὁ Υἱός μου ὁ ἀγαπητὸς*, St. Matt. iii. 17, repeated at His transfiguration (Ibid. xvii. 5); the profound sense of His question to the Pharisees, *τίνος υἱός ἐστιν; [sc. ὁ Χριστὸς]* (Ibid. xxii. 41). And that as the *Υἱὸς τοῦ Θεοῦ*, Christ is superhuman, seems to be implied in the questions of the tempter (Ibid. iv. 3, 6; St. Luke iv. 3, 9).

worthily showing forth the moral perfections of our Heavenly Father. But the official and ethical senses of the term are rooted in a deeper sense, which St. Luke connects with it at the beginning of his Gospel. 'The Holy Ghost shall come upon thee,' so ran the angel-message to the Virgin-mother, 'and the power of the Highest shall overshadow thee: therefore also that Holy Thing Which shall be born of thee shall be called the Son of God [y].' This may be contrasted with the prediction respecting St. John the Baptist, that he should be filled with the Holy Ghost even from his mother's womb [z]. St. John then is in existence before his sanctification by the Holy Spirit; but Christ's Humanity Itself is formed by the agency of the Holy Ghost. In like manner St. Matthew's record of the angel's words asserts that our Lord was conceived by the power of the Holy Ghost [a]. But St. Matthew's reference to the prophetic name Emmanuel [b] points to the full truth, that Christ is the Son of God as being of the Divine Essence.

2. Indeed the whole history of the Nativity and its attendant circumstances guards the narratives of St. Matthew and St. Luke [c] against the inroads of Humanitarian interpreters. Our Lord's Birth of a Virgin-mother is as irreconcileable with 'an Ebionitic as it is with a Docetic conception of the entrance of the God-man into connexion with humanity [d].' The worship of the Infant

[y] St. Luke i. 35, where the abstract τὸ γεννώμενον ἅγιον points to a superhuman Being, so far described indefinitely. But His Birth results from the ἐπισκιάζειν of the δύναμις Ὑψίστου, and He is presently announced to be Υἱὸς Θεοῦ.

[z] Ibid. ver. 15: Πνεύματος Ἁγίου πλησθήσεται ἔτι ἐκ κοιλίας μητρὸς αὐτοῦ.

[a] St. Matt. i. 20: τὸ γὰρ ἐν αὐτῇ γεννηθὲν ἐκ Πνεύματός ἐστιν Ἁγίου.

[b] Ibid. ver. 23. This prophecy was fulfilled when our Lord was called Jesus. Cf. Pearson on the Creed (ed. Oxf. 1847), art. ii. p. 89, and note.

[c] For a vindication of these narratives against the mythical theory of Strauss, see Dr. Mill's Christian Advocate's Publications for 1841, 1844, reprinted in his work on the 'Mythical Interpretation.'

[d] Martensen, Christl. Dogm. § 39 (Clark's transl.): 'Christ is born, not of the will of a man, nor of the will of the flesh; but the holy Will of the Creator took the place of the will of man and of the will of the flesh. That is, the Creating Spirit, Who was in the beginning, fulfilled the function of the plastic principle. Christ was born of the Virgin Mary, the chosen woman of the chosen people. It was the task of Israel to provide, not, as has often been said, Christ Himself, but the mother of the Lord; to develope the susceptibility for Christ to a point where it might be able to manifest itself as the profoundest unity of nature and spirit—an unity which found expression in the pure Virgin. In her the pious aspirations of Israel and of mankind, and their faith in the promises, are centred. She is the purest point in history and in nature, and she therefore becomes the appointed

[LECT.

Christ, in St. Matthew by the wise men, in St. Luke by the shepherds of Bethlehem, represents Jesus as the true Lord of humanity, whether Jewish or Gentile, whether educated or unlettered. Especially noteworthy are the greetings addressed to the Mother of our Lord by heavenly as well as earthly visitants. The Lord is with her; she is graced and blessed among women[e]. Her Son will be great; He will be called the Son of the Highest; His kingdom will have no end[f]. Elizabeth echoes the angel's words; Mary is blessed among women, and the Fruit of her womb is Blessed. Elizabeth marvels that such an one as herself should be visited by the Mother of her Lord[g].

The Evangelical canticles, which we owe to the third Gospel, remarkably illustrate the point before us. They surround the cradle of the Infant Saviour with the devotional language of ancient Israel, now consecrated to the direct service of the Incarnate Lord. Mary, the Virgin-mother, already knows that all generations shall call her blessed; for the Mighty One has done great things unto her[h]. And as the moral and social fruits of the Incarnation unfold themselves before her prophetic eye, she proclaims that the promises to the forefathers are at length fulfilled, and that God, 'remembering His mercy, hath holpen His servant Israel[i].' Zacharias rejoices that the Lord God of Israel has in the new-born Saviour redeemed His people[k]. This Saviour is the Lord, whose forerunner has been announced by prophecy[l]; He is the Day-star from on high, bringing a new morning to those who sat in the darkness and death-shadows of

medium for the New Creation. And while we must confess that this Virgin Birth is enveloped in a veil impenetrable to physical reasonings, yet we affirm it to be the only one which fully satisfies the demands of religion and theology. This article of our Creed, 'conceived of the Holy Ghost, born of the Virgin Mary,' is the only sure defence against both the Ebionitic and the Docetic view of the entrance of the God-man into connexion with humanity.'

[e] St. Luke i. 28: *χαῖρε, κεχαριτωμένη· ὁ Κύριος μετὰ σοῦ, εὐλογημένη σὺ ἐν γυναιξίν.*

[f] Ibid. ver. 32: *οὗτος ἔσται μέγας, καὶ υἱὸς ὑψίστου κληθήσεται.* Ver. 33: *τῆς βασιλείας αὐτοῦ οὐκ ἔσται τέλος.*

[g] Ibid. ver. 42: *εὐλογημένη σὺ ἐν γυναιξὶ, καὶ εὐλογημένος ὁ καρπὸς τῆς κοιλίας σοῦ.* Ver. 43: *καὶ πόθεν μοι τοῦτο, ἵνα ἔλθῃ ἡ μήτηρ τοῦ Κυρίου μου πρός με;*

[h] Ibid. ver. 48: *ἀπὸ τοῦ νῦν μακαριοῦσί με πᾶσαι αἱ γενεαί· ὅτι ἐποίησέ μοι μεγαλεῖα ὁ δυνατός.*

[i] Ibid. vers. 51-55.

[k] Ibid. ver. 68.

[l] Ibid. i. 69, Christ is the *κέρας σωτηρίας*. Ibid. ver. 76; to St. John it is said, *προπορεύσῃ γὰρ πρὸ προσώπου Κυρίου, ἑτοιμάσαι ὁδοὺς αὐτοῦ.* Cf. Mal. iii. 1, iv. 5.

the world[m]. Simeon desires to depart in peace, since his eyes have seen his Lord's Salvation. The humble Babe Whom the old man takes in his arms belongs not to the lowly scenes of Bethlehem and Nazareth; He is the destined inheritance of the world. He is the Divine Saviour; all nations are interested in His Birth; He is to shed light upon the heathen; He is to be the pride and glory of the New Israel[n].

The accounts then of our Lord's Birth in two of the synoptic Evangelists, as illustrated by the sacred songs of praise and thanksgiving which St. Luke has preserved, point clearly to the entrance of a superhuman Being into this our human world. Who indeed He was, is stated more explicitly by St. John; but St. John does not deem it necessary to repeat the history of His Advent. The accounts of the Annunciation and of the Miraculous Conception would not by themselves imply the Divinity of Christ. But they do imply that Christ is superhuman; they harmonize with the kind of anticipations respecting Christ's appearance in the world, which might be created by St. John's doctrine of His pre-existent glory. These accounts cannot be forced within the limits, and made to illustrate the laws, of nature. But at least St. John's narrative justifies the mysteries of the synoptic Gospels which would be unintelligible without it; and it is a vivid commentary upon hymns the lofty strains of which might of themselves be thought to savour of exaggeration.

3. If the synoptists are in correspondence with St. John's characteristic doctrine when they describe our Lord's Nativity and its attendant circumstances, that correspondence is even more obvious in their accounts of His teaching and in the pictures which they set before us of His Life and work. They present Him to us mainly, although not exclusively, as the Son of Man. As has already been hinted, that title, besides its direct signification of His true and representative Humanity, is itself the 'product of a self-consciousness, for which the being human is not a matter of course, but something secondary and superinduced[o].' In other words, this title implies an original

[m] St. Luke i. 78: *ἐπεσκέψατο ἡμᾶς ἀνατολὴ ἐξ ὕψους, ἐπιφᾶναι τοῖς ἐν σκότει καὶ σκιᾷ θανάτου καθημένοις· τοῦ κατευθῦναι τοὺς πόδας ἡμῶν εἰς ὁδὸν εἰρήνης.* Isa. ix. 1, xlii. 7, xlix. 9, lx. 2, are thus applied in a strictly spiritual sense.

[n] St. Luke ii. 30-32: *τὸ σωτήριόν σου, ὃ ἡτοίμασας κατὰ πρόσωπον πάντων τῶν λαῶν· φῶς εἰς ἀποκάλυψιν ἐθνῶν, καὶ δόξαν λαοῦ σου Ἰσραήλ.* Cf. Isa. xxv. 7, xliv. 4.

[o] Cf. Dorner, Person Christi, Einl. p. 82: 'Von einem Selbstbewusstseyn

Nature to Which Christ's Humanity was a subsequent accretion, and in Which His true and deepest Consciousness, if we may dare so to speak, was at home. Thus, often in the synoptic Gospels He is called simply the Son [p]. He is the true Son of Man, but He is also the true Son of God. In Him Sonship attains its archetypal form; in Him it is seen in its unsullied perfection. Accordingly He never calls the Father, *our* Father, as if He shared His Sonship with His followers. He always speaks of *My* Father [q]. To this Divine Sonship He received witness from Heaven both at His Baptism and at His Transfiguration. In the parable of the vineyard, the prophets of the old theocracy are contrasted with the Son, not as predecessors or rivals, but as slaves [r]. Thus He lives among men as the One True Son of His Father's home. He is Alone free by birthright among a race of born slaves. Yet instead of guarding His solitary dignity with jealous exclusiveness, He vouchsafes to raise the slaves around Him to an adopted sonship; He will buy them out of bondage by pouring forth His blood; He will lay down His Life, that He may prove the generosity of His measureless love towards them [s].

The synoptic Gospels record parables in which Christ is Himself the central Figure. They record miracles which seem to have no ascertainable object beyond that of exhibiting the superhuman might of the Worker. They tell us of His claim to forgive sins, and that He supported this claim by the exercise of His miraculous powers [t]. Equally with St. John they represent Him as claiming to be not merely the Teacher but the Object of

aus muss diese Bezeichnung ausgeprägt seyn, für welches das Mensch-oder-Menschensohnseyn nicht das Nächstliegende, sich von selbst unmittelbar Verstehende, sondern das Secundäre, Hinzugekommene, war. Ist aber Christi Selbstbewusstseyn so geartet gewesen, dass das Menschseyn ihm als das Secundäre sich darstellte: so muss das Primäre in Seinem Bewusstseyn ein Anderes seyn, dasjenige, was sich, z. B. bei Johannes xvii. 5 ausspricht; und das Ursprüngliche, worin Sein Selbstbewusstseyn sich unmittelbar heimisch weiss (vgl. Luc. ii. 49) muss wenigstens von der Zeit an, wo Er sich selbst ganz hat, wo sein Innerstes Wirklichkeit geworden ist, das Göttliche gewesen seyn.'

[p] St. Matt. xi. 27, xxviii. 20.

[q] Ibid. xviii. 10, 19, 35, xx. 23, xxvi. 53; cf. St. Luke xxiii. 46.

[r] St. Matt. xxi. 34: ἀπέστειλε τοὺς δούλους αὐτοῦ πρὸς τοὺς γεωργούς. Ibid. ver. 36: πάλιν ἀπέστειλεν ἄλλους δούλους. Ibid. ver. 37: ὕστερον δὲ ἀπέστειλε πρὸς αὐτοὺς τὸν υἱὸν αὐτοῦ, λέγων, ''Εντραπήσονται τὸν υἱόν μου.'

[s] Ibid. xx. 28: ἦλθε . . . δοῦναι τὴν ψυχὴν αὐτοῦ λύτρον ἀντὶ πολλῶν. Ibid. xxvi. 28: τὸ αἷμά μου, τὸ τῆς καινῆς διαθήκης, τὸ περὶ πολλῶν ἐκχυνόμενον εἰς ἄφεσιν ἁμαρτιῶν.

[t] St. Matt. ix. 2-6; St. Luke v. 20, 24.

His religion. He insists on faith in His own Person [u]. He institutes the initial Sacrament, and He deliberately inserts His own Name into the sacramental formula; He inserts it between that of the Father and that of the Spirit [x]. Such self-intrusion into the sphere of Divinity would be unintelligible if the synoptists had really represented Jesus as only the teacher and founder of a religious doctrine or character. But if Christ is the Logos in St. John, in these Gospels He is the Sophia [y]. Thus He ascribes to Himself the exclusive knowledge of the Highest. No statement in St. John really goes beyond the terms in which, according to two synoptists, He claims to know and to be known of the Father. 'No man knoweth the Son but the Father, neither knoweth any man the Father save the Son, and he to whomsoever the Son will reveal Him [z].' Here then is a reciprocal relationship of equality: the Son alone has a true knowledge of the Father; the Son is Himself such, that the Father Alone understands Him. In these Gospels, moreover, Christ ascribes to Himself, sanctity; He even places Himself above the holiest thing in ancient Israel [a]. He and His people are greater than the greatest in the old covenant [b]. He scruples not to proclaim His consciousness of having fulfilled His mission. He asserts that all power is committed to Him both on earth and in heaven [c]. All nations are to be made disciples of His religion [d].

When we weigh the language of the first three Evangelists, it will be found that Christ is represented by it as the Absolute Good and the Absolute Truth not less distinctly than in St. John. It is on this account that He is exhibited as in conflict not with subordinate or accidental forms of evil, but with the evil principle itself, with the prince of evil [e]. And, as the

[u] St. Matt. xvi. 16, 17.

[x] Ibid. xxviii. 19. Cf. Waterland's Eighth Sermon at Lady Moyer's Lecture, Works, vol. ii. p. 171.

[y] St. Luke vii. 35: *ἐδικαιώθη ἡ σοφία ἀπὸ τῶν τέκνων αὐτῆς πάντων.* St. Matt. xi. 19, and apparently St. Luke xi. 49, where *ἡ σοφία τοῦ Θεοῦ* corresponds to *ἐγώ* in St. Matt. xxiii. 34.

[z] St. Matt. xi. 27: *οὐδεὶς ἐπιγινώσκει τὸν Υἱὸν εἰ μὴ ὁ Πατήρ· οὐδὲ τὸν Πατέρα τις ἐπιγινώσκει, εἰ μὴ ὁ Υἱὸς, καὶ ᾧ ἐὰν βούληται ὁ Υἱὸς ἀποκαλύψαι.* St. Luke x. 22: *οὐδεὶς γινώσκει τίς ἐστιν ὁ Υἱὸς εἰ μὴ ὁ Πατὴρ, καὶ τίς ἐστιν ὁ Πατὴρ, εἰ μὴ ὁ Υἱὸς, καὶ ᾧ ἐὰν βούληται ὁ Υἱὸς ἀποκαλύψαι.* See Mill on Myth. Interp. p. 59.

[a] St. Matt. xii. 6: *λέγω δὲ ὑμῖν ὅτι τοῦ ἱεροῦ μεῖζόν* [Tisch.] *ἐστιν ὧδε.*

[b] Ibid. xi. 11, xii. 41, 42, xxi. 33, sqq.; St. Luke vii. 28.

[c] St. Matt. xi. 27; St. Luke x. 22; St. Matt. xxviii. 18: *ἐδόθη μοι πᾶσα ἐξουσία ἐν οὐρανῷ καὶ ἐπὶ γῆς.*

[d] St. Matt. xxviii. 19.

[e] St. Luke x. 18: *ἐθεώρουν τὸν Σατανᾶν ὡς ἀστραπὴν ἐκ τοῦ οὐρανοῦ πεσόντα.* St. Matt. iv. 1-11, xii. 27-29, xiii. 38, 39.

Absolute Good, Christ tests the moral worth or worthlessness of men by their acceptance or rejection, not of His doctrine but of His Person. It is St. Matthew who records such sentences as the following: 'Neither be ye called Masters; for One is your Master, even Christ[f];' 'He that loveth father or mother more than Me is not worthy of Me[g];' 'Whosoever shall confess Me before men, him will I confess also before My Father[h];' 'Come unto Me, all ye that labour, and I will give you rest[i];' 'Take My yoke upon you and learn of Me[k].' In St. Matthew then Christ speaks as One Who knows Himself to be a universal and infallible Teacher in spiritual things; Who demands submission of all men, and at whatever cost or sacrifice; Who offers to mankind those deepest consolations which are sought from all others, in vain. Nor is it otherwise with St. Luke and St. Mark. It is indeed remarkable that our Lord's most absolute and peremptory claims[l] to rule over the affections and wills of men are recorded by the first and third, and not by the fourth Evangelist. These royal rights over the human soul can be justified upon no plea of human relationships between teacher and learner, between child and elder, between master and servant, between friend and friend. If the title of Divinity is more explicitly put forward in St. John, the rights which imply it are insisted on in words recorded by the earlier Evangelists. The synoptists represent our Lord, Who is the object of Christian faith no less than the Founder of Christianity, as designing the whole world for the field of His conquests[m], and as claiming the submission of every individual human soul. All are to be brought to discipleship. Only then will the judgment come, when the Gospel has been announced to the whole circle of the nations[n]. Christ, the Good and the Truth Incarnate, must reign throughout all time[o]. He knows, according to the synoptists no less than St. John, that He is a perfect and final Revelation of God. He is the centre-point of the history and of the hopes of man. None shall advance beyond Him: the

[f] St. Matt. xxiii. 10. [g] Ibid. x. 37.
[h] Ibid. ver. 32; St. Luke xii. 8. [i] St. Matt. xi. 28.
[k] Ibid. ver. 29. [l] Ibid. x. 39; St. Luke xiv. 26.
[m] St. Matt. xxviii. 19: *πορευθέντες οὖν μαθητεύσατε πάντα τὰ ἔθνη.* St. Mark xvi. 15; St. Luke xxiv. 47. Cf. St. Matt. xiii. 32, 38, 41, xxiv. 14.
[n] St. Matt. xxiv. 14: *καὶ κηρυχθήσεται τοῦτο τὸ εὐαγγέλιον τῆς βασιλείας ἐν ὅλῃ τῇ οἰκουμένῃ, εἰς μαρτύριον πᾶσι τοῖς ἔθνεσι· καὶ τότε ἥξει τὸ τέλος.*
[o] St. Luke xxii. 69: *ἀπὸ τοῦ νῦν ἔσται ὁ Υἱὸς τοῦ ἀνθρώπου καθήμενος ἐκ δεξιῶν τῆς δυνάμεως τοῦ Θεοῦ.*

pretension to surpass Him is but the symptom of disastrous error and reaction[p].

The Transfiguration is described by all the synoptists; and it represents our Lord in His true relation to the legal and prophetic dispensations, and as visibly invested for the time being with a glory which was rightfully His. The Ascension secures His permanent investiture with that glory; and the Ascension is described by St. Mark and St. Luke. The Resurrection is recorded by the first three Evangelists as accurately as by the fourth; and it was to the Resurrection that He Himself appealed as being the sign by which men were to know His real claim upon their homage. In the first three Gospels, all of Christ's humiliations are consistently linked to the assertion of His power, and to the consummation of His victory. He is buffeted, spat upon, scourged, crucified, only to rise from the dead the third day[q]; His Resurrection is the prelude to His ascent to heaven. He leaves the world, yet He bequeaths the promise of His Presence. He promises to be wherever two or three are gathered in His Name[r]; He institutes the Sacrament of His Body and His Blood[s]; He declares that He will be among His people even to the end of the world[t].

4. But it is more particularly through our Lord's discourses respecting the end of the world and the final judgment, as recorded by the synoptists, that we may discern the matchless dignity of His Person. It is reflected in the position which He claims to fill with respect to the moral and material universe, and in the absolute finality which He attributes to His religion. The Lawgiver Who is above all other legislators, and Who revises all other legislation, will also be the final Judge[u]. At

[p] St. Matt. xxiv. 23–26, &c.

[q] Ibid. xx. 19; St. Mark x. 34; St. Luke xviii. 33.

[r] St. Matt. xviii. 20: *οὗ γάρ εἰσι δύο ἢ τρεῖς συνηγμένοι εἰς τὸ ἐμὸν ὄνομα, ἐκεῖ εἰμὶ ἐν μέσῳ αὐτῶν.*

[s] Ibid. xxvi. 26; St. Mark xiv. 22; St. Luke xxii. 19.

[t] St. Matt. xxviii. 20: *ἐγὼ μεθ' ὑμῶν εἰμι πάσας τὰς ἡμέρας ἕως τῆς συντελείας τοῦ αἰῶνος.*

[u] Ibid. vii. 22: *πολλοὶ ἐροῦσί μοι ἐν ἐκείνῃ τῇ ἡμέρᾳ, 'Κύριε, Κύριε, οὐ τῷ σῷ ὀνόματι προεφητεύσαμεν, καὶ τῷ σῷ ὀνόματι δαιμόνια ἐξεβάλομεν, καὶ τῷ σῷ ὀνόματι δυνάμεις πολλὰς ἐποιήσαμεν;' καὶ τότε ὁμολογήσω αὐτοῖς, ὅτι 'οὐδέποτε ἔγνων ὑμᾶς. ἀποχωρεῖτε ἀπ' ἐμοῦ οἱ ἐργαζόμενοι τὴν ἀνομίαν.'* St. Luke xiii. 25. St. Matt. xiii. 41: *ἀποστελεῖ ὁ Υἱὸς τοῦ ἀνθρώπου τοὺς ἀγγέλους αὐτοῦ, καὶ συλλέξουσιν ἐκ τῆς βασιλείας αὐτοῦ πάντα τὰ σκάνδαλα καὶ τοὺς ποιοῦντας τὴν ἀνομίαν, καὶ βαλοῦσιν αὐτοὺς εἰς τὴν κάμινον τοῦ πυρός.* Ibid. x. 32: St. Mark viii. 38. St. Matt. xxiv. 31: *ἀποστελεῖ τοὺς ἀγγέλους αὐτοῦ μετὰ σάλπιγγος φωνῆς μεγάλης, καὶ ἐπισυνάξουσι τοὺς ἐκλεκτοὺς αὐτοῦ*

that last awful revelation of His personal glory, none shall be able to refuse Him submission. Then will He put an end to the humiliations and the sorrows of His Church; then, out of the fulness of His majesty, He will clothe His despised followers with glory; He will allot the kingdom to those who have believed on Him; and at His heavenly board they shall share for ever the royal feast of life. Certainly the Redeemer and Judge of men, to Whom all spiritual and natural forces, all earthly and heavenly powers must at last submit, is not merely a divinely gifted prophet. His Person 'has a metaphysical and cosmical significance [x].' None could preside so authoritatively over the history and destiny of the world who was not entitled to share the throne of its Creator.

The eschatological discourses in the synoptists do but tally with the prologue of St. John's Gospel. In contemplating the dignity of our Lord's Person, the preceding Evangelists for the most part look forward; St. John looks backward no less than forward. St. John dwells on Christ's Pre-existence; the synoptists, if we may so phrase it, on his Post-existence. In the earlier Evangelists His personal glory is viewed in its relation to the future of the human race and of the universe; in St. John it is viewed in its relation to the origin of created things, and to the solitary and everlasting years of God. In St. John, Christ our Saviour is the First; in the synoptists He is more especially the Last.

In the synoptic Gospels, then, the Person of Christ Divine and Human is the centre-point of the Christian religion. Christ is here the Supreme Lawgiver; He is the Perfect Saint; He is the Judge of all men. He controls both worlds, the physical and the spiritual; He bestows the forgiveness of sins, and the Holy Spirit; He promises everlasting life. His Presence is to be perpetuated on earth, while yet He will reign as Lord of heaven. 'The entire representation,' says Professor Dorner, 'of Christ which is given us by the synoptists, may be placed side by side with that given by St. John, as being altogether identical with it. For a faith moulded in obedience to the synoptic tradition concerning Christ, must have essentially the same features in its resulting conception of Christ as those which belong to the Christ of St. John [y].' In other words, think over the miracles

ἐκ τῶν τεσσάρων ἀνέμων, ἀπ' ἄκρων οὐρανῶν ἕως ἄκρων αὐτῶν. Ibid. xxv. 34-46: St. Luke xii. 35, xvii. 30, 31. See Lect. IV. p. 176.

[x] Martensen, Christl. Dogm. § 128.

[y] Dorner, Person Christi, Einl. p. 89: 'Das synoptische Totalbild von

wrought by Christ and narrated by the synoptists, one by one. Think over the discourses spoken by Christ and recorded by the synoptists, one by one. Look at the whole bearing and scope of His Life, as the three first Evangelists describe It, from His supernatural Birth to His disappearance beyond the clouds of heaven. Mark well how pressing and tender, yet withal how full of stern and majestic Self-assertion, are His words! Consider how merciful and timely, yet also how expressive of immanent and unlimited power, are His miracles! Put the three representations of the Royal, the Human, and the Healing Redeemer together, and deny, if it is possible, that Jesus is Divine. If the Christ of the synoptists is not indeed an unreal phantom, such as Docetism might have constructed, He is far removed above the Ebionitic conception of a purely human Saviour. If Christ's Pre-existence is only obscurely hinted at in the first three Gospels, His relation to the world of spirits is brought out in them even more clearly than in St. John by the discourses which they contain on the subject of the Last Judgment. If St. John could be blotted out from the pages of the New Testament, St. John's central doctrine would still live on in the earlier Evangelists as implicitly contained within a history otherwise inexplicable, if not as the illuminating truth of a heavenly gnosis. There would still remain the picture of a Life Which belongs indeed to human history, but Which the laws that govern human history neither control nor can explain. It would still be certain that One had lived on earth, wielding miraculous powers, and claiming a moral and intellectual place which belongs only to the Most Holy; and if the problem presented to faith might seem for a moment to be more intricate, its final solution could not differ in substance from that which meets us in the pages of the beloved disciple.

V. But what avails it, say you, to shew that St. John is consistent with himself, and that he is not really at variance with the Evangelists who preceded him, if the doctrine which he teaches, and which the Creed re-asserts, is itself incredible? You object to this doctrine that it 'involves an invincible contradiction.' It represents Christ on the one hand as a Personal Being, while on the other it asserts that two mutually self-excluding

Christus dem johanneischen insofern vollkommen an die Seite setzen kann, als der durch Vermittlung der synoptischen Tradition gebildete Glaube wesentlich ganz dieselben Züge in seinem Christusbegriff haben musste, wie sie der johanneische Christus hat.' For the preceding remarks, see Person Christi, Einl. pp. 80-89.

[LECT.

Essences are really united in Him. How can He be personal, you ask, if He be in very truth both God and Man? If He is thus God and Man, is He not, in point of fact, a 'double Being;' and is not unity of being an indispensable condition of personality? Surely, you insist, this condition is forfeited by the very terms of the doctrine. Christ either is not both God and Man, or He is not a single Personality. To say that He is One Person in Two Natures is to affirm the existence of a miracle which is incredible, if for no other reason, simply on the score of its unintelligibility [z].

This is what may be said; but let us consider, first of all, whether to say this does not, however unintentionally, caricature the doctrine of St. John and of the Catholic Creed. Does it not seem as if both St. John and the Creed were at pains to make it clear that the Person of Christ in His pre-existent glory, in His state of humiliation and sorrow, and in the majesty of His mediatorial kingdom, is continuously, unalterably One? Does not the Nicene Creed, for instance, first name the Only-begotten Son of God, and then go on to say how for us men and for our salvation He was Himself made Man, and was crucified for us under Pontius Pilate? Does not St. John plainly refer to One and the Same Agent in such verses as the following? 'All things were made by Him, and without Him was not anything made that was made [a].' 'He riseth from supper, and laid aside

[z] Schenkel, Charakterbild Jesu, p. 2: 'Es gehört vor Allem zum Begriffe einer Person, dass sie im Kerne ihres Wesens eine Einheit bildet; nur unter dieser Voraussetzung lässt sie sich geschichtlich begreifen. Diese Einheit wird durch die herkömmliche Lehre in der Person des Welterlösers aufgehoben. Jesus Christus wird in der kirchlichen Glaubenslehre als ein Doppel-Wesen dargestellt, als die persönliche Vereinigung zweier Wesenheiten, die an sich nichts mit einander gemein haben, sich vielmehr schlechthin widersprechen und nur vermöge eines alle Begriffe übersteigenden Wunders in die engste und unauflöslichste Verbindung mit einander gebracht worden sind. *Er ist demzufolge Mensch und Gott in einer und derselben Person.* Die kirchlichen Theologen haben grosse Anstrengungen gemacht, um die unauflösliche Verbindung von Gott und Mensch in einer Person als begreiflich und möglich darzustellen; sie haben sich aber zuletzt doch immer wieder zu dem Geständniss genöthigt gesehen, dass die Sache unbegreiflich sei, und dass ein undurchdringliches Geheimniss über dem Personleben Jesu Christi schwebe. Allein eine solche Berufung auf Geheimnisse und Wunder ist, wo es auf die Erklärung einer geschichtlichen Thatsache ankommt, für die Wissenschaft ohne allen Werth; sie offenbart uns die Unfähigkeit des theologischen Denkens, das in sich Widersprechende vorstellbar, das geschichtlich Unbegreifliche denkbar zu machen.' Cf. Strauss, Leben Jesu, § 146; Schleiermacher, Glaubenslehre, ii. § 96–98.

[a] St. John i. 3.

His garments; and took a towel, and girded Himself. After that He poureth water into a bason, and began to wash the disciples' feet, and to wipe them with the towel wherewith He was girded [b].' If St. John or the Creed had proceeded to introduce a new subject to whom the circumstances of Christ's earthly Life properly belonged, and who only maintained a mysterious, even although it were an indissoluble connexion with the Eternal Word in heaven, then the charge of making Christ a 'double Being' would be warrantable. Nestorius was fairly liable to that charge. He practically denied that the Man Christ Jesus was One Person with the Eternal Word. In order to heighten the ethical import of the Human Life of Christ, Nestorianism represents our Lord as an individual Man, Who, although He is the temple and organ of the Deity to which He is united, yet has a separate basis of personality in His Human Nature. The individuality of the Son of Mary is thus treated as a distinct thing from that of the Eternal Word; and the Christ of Nestorianism is really a 'double Being,' or rather he is two distinct persons, mysteriously joined in one [c]. But the Church has formally condemned this error, and in so doing she was merely throwing into the form of a doctrinal proposition the plain import of the narrative of St. John's Gospel [d].

[b] St. John xiii. 4, 5.

[c] Ap. Marium Merc. p. 54: 'Non Maria peperit Deum. Non peperit creatura increabilem, sed peperit hominem Deitatis instrumentum. Divido naturas, sed conjungo reverentiam.' Cf. Nestorii Ep. iii. ad Cœlestin. (Mansi, tom. iv. 1197): τὸ προελθεῖν τὸν Θεὸν Λόγον ἐκ τῆς χριστοτόκου παρθένου παρὰ τῆς θείας ἐδιδάχθην γραφῆς· τὸ δὲ γεννηθῆναι Θεὸν ἐξ αὐτῆς, οὐδαμοῦ ἐδιδάχθην. And his 'famous' saying, 'I will never own a child of two months old to be God.' (Labbe, iii. 506.)

[d] St. Leo in Epist. ad Leonem Aug. ed. Ballerino, 165: 'Anathematizetur ergo Nestorius, qui beatam Virginem non Dei, sed hominis tantummodo credidit genitricem, ut aliam personam carnis faceret, aliam Deitatis; nec unum Christum in Verbo Dei et carne sentiret, sed separatum atque sejunctum alterum Filium Dei, alterum hominis prædicaret.' See Confession of the Easterns, accepted by St. Cyril, Labbe, iii. 1107: Ὁμολογοῦμεν τὸν Κύριον ἡμῶν Ἰησοῦν Χριστὸν, τὸν Υἱὸν τοῦ Θεοῦ, Θεὸν τέλειον καὶ ἄνθρωπον τέλειον ἐκ ψυχῆς λογικῆς καὶ σώματος, πρὸ αἰώνων μὲν ἐκ τοῦ Πατρὸς γεννηθέντα κατὰ τὴν Θεότητα, ἐπ' ἐσχάτων δὲ τῶν ἡμερῶν τὸν αὐτὸν ἐκ Μαρίας κατὰ τὴν ἀνθρωπότητα, ὁμοούσιον τῷ Πατρὶ κατὰ τὴν Θεότητα, ὁμοούσιον ἡμῖν κατὰ τὴν ἀνθρωπότητα· δύο γὰρ φύσεων ἕνωσις γέγονε. Κατὰ ταύτην τὴν τῆς ἀσυγχύτου ἑνώσεως ἔννοιαν ὁμολογοῦμεν τὴν ἁγίαν Παρθένον Θεοτόκον, διὰ τὸ τὸν Θεὸν Λόγον σαρκωθῆναι καὶ ἐνανθρωπῆσαι, καὶ ἐξ αὐτῆς τῆς συλλήψεως ἑνῶσαι ἑαυτῷ τὸν ἐξ αὐτῆς ληφθέντα ναόν. Τὰς δὲ εὐαγγελικὰς περὶ τοῦ Κυρίου φωνὰς ἴσμεν τοὺς θεολόγους ἄνδρας τὰς μὲν κοινοποιοῦντας ὡς ἐφ' ἑνὸς προσώπου, τὰς δὲ διαιροῦντας ὡς ἐπὶ δύο φύσεων, καὶ τὰς μὲν θεοπρεπεῖς κατὰ τὴν Θεότητα τοῦ Χριστοῦ, τὰς δὲ ταπεινὰς κατὰ τὴν ἀνθρωπότητα αὐτοῦ παραδιδόντας. The

Undoubtedly, you reply, the Church has not allowed her doctrine to be stated in terms which would dissolve the Redeemer into two distinct agents, and would so altogether forfeit the reality of redemption[e]. But the question is whether the orthodox statement be really successful in avoiding the error which it deprecates. Certainly the Church does say that

definition of Chalcedon is equally emphatic on the subject of the Hypostatic Union. Routh, Scr. Op. ii. 78; Bright, Hist. Ch. p. 4[illegible]. The title Theotokos, assigned to the Blessed Virgin by eminent Fathers before the Nestorian controversy (see Bright, ib. p. 302), and by the whole Church ever since the Council of Ephesus, is essentially a tribute to Christ's personal glory. It is in exact accordance with that well-known Scriptural *usus loquendi*, whereby God is said to have 'purchased the Church with His own Blood' (Acts xx. 28, see Lect. VI.; and compare 1 Cor. ii. 8), as conversely, 'the Son of Man,' while yet on earth, is said to have been 'in heaven' (St. John iii. 13). This 'communicatio idiomatum,' *κοινοποίησις* or *ἀντίδοσις* (St. John Dam. Orth. Fid. iii. 4), as it is technically termed, is only intelligible on the principle that whatever belongs to our Lord in either of His two spheres of Existence belongs to Him as the One Christ, Who is, and is to be spoken of as, both God and Man. In other words, the properties of both His Natures are the properties of His Person. (Hooker, E. P. v. 53; St. Thom. Summ. iii. 16, 4.) In the same sense then as that in which St. Paul could attribute 'crucifixion,' and 'shedding His Blood,' to 'God,' that is to say, to our Divine Saviour in His Manhood, the Church could attribute to Him Birth of a human Mother. The phrase *θεοτόκος* is implicitly sanctioned by the phrase *αἷμα Θεοῦ*. It presupposes the belief that Jesus Christ, the Son of Mary, is our Lord and God; that 'the Son which is the Word of the Father, begotten from everlasting of the Father, very and eternal God, took Man's Nature upon Him in the womb of the Blessed Virgin, of her substance;' art. 2. In sub-apostolic language, *ὁ γὰρ Θεὸς ἡμῶν Ἰησοῦς ὁ Χριστὸς ἐκυοφορήθη ἀπὸ Μαρίας*. Ign. ad Eph. 18. Cf. Bright's observations, Lat. Tr. S. Ath. p. 150 sqq.

[e] Jackson on the Creed, Works, vol. vii. p. 294: 'That proper blood wherewith God is said to have purchased the church, was the blood of the Son of God, the second Person in Trinity, after a more peculiar manner than it was the blood either of God the Father or of God the Holy Ghost. It was the blood of God the Father or of God the Holy Ghost, as all other creatures are, by common right of creation and preservation. It was the blood of God the Son alone by personal union. If this Son of God, and High Priest of our souls, had offered any other sacrifice for us than Himself, or the Manhood thus personally united unto Him, His offering could not have been satisfactory, because in all other things created, the Father and the Holy Ghost had the same right or interest which the Son had, He could not have offered anything to Them which were not as truly Theirs as His. Only the Seed of Abraham, or Fruit of the Virgin's womb Which He assumed into the Godhead, was by the assumption made so His own, as it was not Theirs, His own by incommunicable property of personal union. By reason of this incommunicable property in the woman's seed, the Son of God might truly have said unto His Father, 'Lord, Thou hast purchased the church, yet with My blood:' but so could not the Man Christ Jesus say unto the Son of God, 'Lord, Thou hast paid the ransom for the sins of the world, yet with My blood, not with Thine own.'

'although Christ be God and Man, yet He is not two, but one Christ.' But is this possible? How can Godhead and Manhood thus coalesce without forfeiture of that unity which is a condition of personality?

The answer to this question lies in the fact, upon which St. John insists with such prominence, that our Lord's Godhead is the seat of His Personality. The Son of Mary is not a distinct human person mysteriously linked with the Divine Nature of the Eternal Word[f]. The Person of the Son of Mary is divine and eternal; It is none other than the Person of the Word. When He took upon Him to deliver man, the Eternal Word did not abhor the Virgin's womb. He clothed Himself with man's bodily and man's immaterial nature; He united it to His Own Divinity. He 'took man's Nature upon Him in the womb of the Blessed Virgin, of her substance, so that two whole and perfect Natures, that is to say, the Godhead and Manhood, were joined together in One Person, never to be divided, whereof is One Christ[g].' Thus to speak of Christ as *a* Man, at least without explanation, may lead to a serious misconception; He is *the* Man, or rather He is Man. Christ's Manhood is not of Itself an individual being; It is not a seat and centre of personality; It has no conceivable existence apart from the act whereby the Eternal Word in becoming Incarnate called It into being and made It His Own[h]. It is a vesture which He has folded around His Person; It is an instrument through which He places Himself in contact with men, and whereby He acts upon humanity[i].

[f] St. Ful. de Fide ad Petr. c. 17: 'Deus Verbum non accepit personam hominis, sed naturam; et in æternam personam divinitatis accepit temporalem substantiam carnis.' St. Joh. Damasc. de Fid. Orthod. iii. 11: ὁ Θεὸς Λόγος σαρκωθεὶς οὐ τὴν ἐν τῷ εἴδει θεωρουμένην, οὐ γὰρ πάσας τὰς ὑποστάσεις ἀνέλαβεν· ἀλλὰ τὴν ἐν ἀτόμῳ, ἀπαρχὴν τοῦ ἡμετέρου φυράματος, οὐ καθ' ἑαυτὴν ὑποστᾶσαν καὶ ἄτομον χρηματίσασαν πρότερον, καὶ οὕτως ὑπ' αὐτοῦ προσληφθεῖσαν, ἀλλ' ἐν τῇ αὐτοῦ ὑποστάσει ὑπάρξασαν, αὕτη γὰρ ἡ ὑπόστασις τοῦ Θεοῦ Λόγου ἐγένετο τῇ σαρκὶ ὑπόστασις. He states this in other terms (c. 9) by saying that our Lord's Humanity had no subsistence of itself. It was not ἰδιοσύστατος, nor was it strictly ἀνυπόστατος, but ἐν αὐτῇ τῇ τοῦ Θεοῦ Λόγου ὑποστάσει ὑποστᾶσα, ἐνυπόστατος. He speaks too of Christ's ὑπόστασις σύνθετος. Hooker, E. P. v. 52. 3.

[g] Art. ii.

[h] St. Aug. c. Serm. Arian. c. 6: 'Nec sic assumptus est [homo] ut priùs crearetur, post assumeretur, sed ut in ipsâ assumptione crearetur.' St. Leo, Ep. 25. 3: 'Natura nostra non sic assumpta est ut prius creata, post assumeretur; sed ut ipsâ assumptione crearetur.' Newman's Par. Sermons, ii. 32, vi. 59.

[i] Jackson on the Creed, Works, vol. vii. p. 289: 'The Humanity of Christ is such an instrument of the Divine Nature in His Person, as the hand of man is to the person or party whose hand it is. And it is well

[LECT.

He wears It in heaven, and thus robed in It He represents, He impersonates, He pleads for the race of beings to which It belongs. In saying that Christ 'took our nature upon Him,' we imply that His Person existed before, and that the Manhood which He assumed was Itself impersonal. Therefore He did not make Himself a 'double Being' by becoming incarnate. His Manhood no more impaired the unity of His Person than each human body, with its various organs and capacities, impairs the unity of that personal principle which is the centre and pivot of each separate human existence, and which has its seat within the soul of each one of us.

'As the reasonable soul and flesh is one man, so God and man is one Christ.' As the personality of man resides in the soul, after death has severed soul and body, so the Person of Christ had Its eternal seat in His Godhead before His Incarnation. Intimately as the 'I,' or personal principle within each of us, is associated with every movement of the body, the 'I' itself resides in the soul. The soul is that which is conscious, which remembers, which wills, and which thus realizes personality[j]. Certainly it is true that in our present state of existence we have never as yet realized what personal existence is, apart from the body. But the youngest of us will do this, ere many years have passed. Meanwhile we know that, when divorced from the personal principle which rules and inspires it, the body is but a lump of lifeless clay. The body then does not superadd

observed, whether by Aquinas himself or no I remember not, but by Viguerius, an accurate summist of Aquinas' sums, that albeit the intellectual part of man be a spiritual substance, and separated from the matter or bodily part, yet is the union betwixt the hand and intellectual part of man no less firm, no less proper, than the union between the feet or other organical parts of sensitive creatures, and their sensitive souls or mere physical forms. For the intellectual part of man, whether it be the form of man truly, though not merely physical, or rather his essence, not his form at all, doth use his own hand not as the carpenter doth use his axe, that is, not as an external or separated, but as his proper united instrument: nor is the union between the hand as the instrument and intellective part as the artificer or commander of it an union of matter and form, but an union personal, or at the least such an union as resembles the hypostatical union between the Divine and Human Nature of Christ much better than any material union wherein philosophers or school-divines can make instance.' Cf. Viguerius, Institutiones, c. 20. introd. p. 259, commenting on St. Thom. 3^a. q. 2. a. 1.

[j] Yet when we contrast man's person (ego) and his nature, we understand by nature, not merely the body, but also *soul and spirit*, inasmuch as man's ego is conceived of as distinct from the latter not less than from the former. Delitzsch, Bibl. Psych. iv. § 2.

a second personality to that which is in the soul. It supplies the personal soul with an instrument; it introduces it to a sphere of action; it is the obedient slave, the plastic ductile form of the personal soul which tenants it. The hand is raised, the voice is heard; but these are acts of the selfsame personality as that which, in the invisible voiceless recesses of its immaterial self, goes through intellectual acts of inference, or moral acts of aversion or of love. In short, man is at once animal and spirit, but his personal unity is not thereby impaired: and Jesus Christ is not other than a Single Person, although He has united the Perfect Nature of Man to His Divine and Eternal Being. Therefore, although He says 'I and the Father are One,' He never says 'I and the Son' or 'I and the Word are One.' For He is the Word; He is the Son. And His Human Life is not a distinct self, but a living robe which, as it was created, was forthwith wrapped around His Eternal Personality[k].

But if the illustration of the Creed is thus suggestive of the unity of Christ's Person, is it, you may fairly ask, altogether in harmony with the Scriptural and Catholic doctrine of His Perfect Manhood? If Christ's Humanity stands to His Godhead in the relation of the body of a man to his soul, does not this imply that Christ has no human Soul[l], or at any rate no distinct human Will? You remind me that 'the truth of our Lord's Human Will is essential to the integrity of His Manhood, to the reality of His Incarnation, to the completeness of His redemptive work. It is plainly asserted by Scripture; and the error which denies It has been condemned by the Church. If Nestorius errs on one side, Apollinaris, Eutyches, and finally the Monothelites, warn us how easily we may err on the other. Christ has a Human Will as being Perfect Man, no less than He has a Divine Will as being Perfect God. But this is not suggested by the analogy of the union of body and soul in man. And if there are two Wills in Christ, must there not also be two

[k] On the objection that the illustration in the Athanasian Creed favours Nestorianism, cf. St. Tho. 3^a. 2. 5. It was accepted by St. Cyril himself, but not as complete, Scholia. 8. 28, quo. by Bright, Lat. Tr. of S. Ath. p. 161, note *k*.

[l] This preliminary form of the objection is thus noticed by the Master of the Sentences, Petr. Lomb. l. iii. d. 5 (858): 'Non accepit Verbum Dei *personam* hominis, sed *naturam*. E: A quibusdam opponitur, quod persona assumit personam. Persona enim est substantia rationalis individuæ naturæ, hoc autem est anima. Ergo si animam assumsit, et personam. Quod ideo non sequitur, quia anima non est persona, quando alii rei unita est personaliter, sed quando per se est. Illa autem anima (our Lord's) nunquam fuit, quia esset alii rei conjuncta.'

Persons? and may not the Sufferer Who kneels in Gethsemane be another than the Word by Whom all things were made?'

Certainly, the illustration of the Creed cannot be pressed closely without risk of serious error. An illustration is generally used to indicate correspondence in a single particular; and it will not bear to be erected into an absolute and consistent parallel, supposed to be in all respects analogous to that with which it has a single point of correspondence. But the Creed protects itself elsewhere against any such misuse of this particular illustration. The Creed says that as body and soul meet in a single man, so do Perfect Godhead and Perfect Manhood meet in one Christ. The Perfect Manhood of Christ, not His Body merely but His Soul, and therefore His Human Will, is part of the One Christ. Unless in His condescending love our Eternal Lord has thus taken upon Him our fallen nature in its integrity, that is to say, a Human Soul as well as a Human Body, a Human Will as an integral element of the Human Soul, mankind would not have been really represented on the cross or before the throne. We should not have been truly redeemed or sanctified by a real union with the Most Holy.

Yet in taking upon Him a Human Will, the Eternal Word did not assume a second principle of action which was destructive of the real unity of His Person. Within the precincts of a single human soul may we not observe two principles of volition, this higher and that lower, this animated almost entirely by reason, that as exclusively by passion? St. Paul has described the moral dualism within a single will which is characteristic of the approach to the regenerate life, in a wonderful passage of his Epistle to the Romans[m]. The real self is loyal to God; yet the Christian sees within him a second self, warring against the law of his mind, and bringing him into captivity to that which his central being, in its loyalty to God, energetically rejects[n]. Yet in this great conflict between the old and the new self of the regenerate man, there is, we know, no real schism of

[m] Rom. vii. 14-25. Origen, St. Chrysostom, and Theodoret understand this passage of the state of man before regeneration. St. Augustine was of this mind in his earlier theological life (Confess. vii. 21; Prop. 45 in Ep. ad Rom., quoted by Meyer, Römer. p. 246), but his struggle with the Pelagian heresy led him to understand the passage of the regenerate (Retractat. i. 23, ii. 1; contr. duas Ep. Pelag. i. 10; contr. Faust. xv. 8). This judgment has been accepted by the great divines of the middle ages, St. Anselm and Aquinas, and largely by the moderns. Of late years, the Greek interpretation has been again widely accepted, as doing more perfect justice to the language of the Apostle.

[n] Rom. vii. 17, 22, 23.

an indivisible person, although for the moment antagonist elements within the soul are so engaged as to look like separate hostile agencies. The man's lower nature is not a distinct person, yet it has what is almost a distinct will, and what is thus a shadow of the Created Will which Christ assumed along with His Human Nature. Of course in the Incarnate Christ, the Human Will, although a proper principle of action, was not, could not be, in other than the most absolute harmony with the Will of God [o]. Christ's sinlessness is the historical expression of this harmony. The Human Will of Christ corresponded to the Eternal Will with unvarying accuracy; because in point of fact God, Incarnate in Christ, willed each volition of Christ's Human Will [p]. Christ's Human Will then had a distinct existence, yet Its free volitions were but the earthly echoes of the Will of the All-holy [q]. At the Temptation It was confronted with the personal principle of evil; but the Tempter without was seconded by no pulse of sympathy within. The Human Will of Christ was incapable of willing evil. In Gethsemane It was thrown forward into strong relief as Jesus bent to accept the chalice of suffering from which His Human sensitiveness could not but shrink. But from the first It was controlled by the Divine Will to which It is indissolubly united; just as, if we may use the comparison, in a holy man, passion and impulse are brought entirely under the empire of reason and conscience [r]. As God and Man, our Lord has two Wills; but the Divine Will originates and rules His Action; the Human Will is but the docile servant of that Will of God which has its seat in Christ's Divine and Eternal Person [s]. Here indeed we touch upon the line at

[o] This was the ground taken in the Sixth General Council, A.D. 680, when the language of Chalcedon was adapted to meet the error of the Monothelites. *Δύο φυσικὰς θελήσεις ἤτοι θελήματα ἐν αὐτῷ καὶ δύο φυσικὰς ἐνεργείας ἀδιαιρέτως, ἀτρέπτως, ἀμερίστως, ἀσυγχύτως, κατὰ τὴν τῶν ἁγίων πατέρων διδασκαλίαν κηρύττομεν, καὶ δύο φυσικὰ θελήματα οὐκ ὑπεναντία, μὴ γένοιτο, καθὼς οἱ ἀσεβεῖς ἔφησαν αἱρετικοὶ, ἀλλ' ἑπόμενον τὸ ἀνθρώπινον αὐτοῦ θέλημα, καὶ μὴ ἀντιπίπτον, ἢ ἀντιπαλαῖον μᾶλλον μὲν οὖν καὶ ὑποτασσόμενον τῷ θείῳ αὐτοῦ καὶ πανσθενεῖ θελήματι.* Mansi, tom. xi. p. 637. Routh, Scr. Op. ii. 236; Hooker, E. P. v. 48. 9.

[p] This does not exclude the action upon our Lord's Manhood of the Holy Spirit, Who is One with the Word as with the Father: St. Matt. iv. 1; St. Luke iv. 18; St. John iii. 34; Acts x. 38.

[q] 'In ancient language, a twofold *voluntas* is quite compatible with a single volitio.' Klee, Dogmengesch. ii. 4. 6.

[r] St. Maximus illustrates the two harmonious operations of the Two Wills in Christ, by the physical image of a heated sword which both cuts and burns. Disp. cont. Pyrrh. apud Klee, ubi sup.

[s] St. Ambros. de Fide, v. 6: 'Didicisti, quod omnia sibi Ipsi subjicere

which revealed truth shades off into inaccessible mystery. We may not seek to penetrate the secrets of that marvellous θεανδρικὴ ἐνέργεια: but at least we know that each Nature of Christ is perfect, and that the Person which unites them is One and indissoluble [t].

For the illustration of the Creed might at least remind us that we carry about with us the mystery of a composite nature, which should lead a thoughtful man to pause before pressing such objections as are urged by modern scepticism against the truth of the Incarnation. The Christ Who is revealed in the Gospels and Who is worshipped by the Church, is rejected as being 'an unintelligible wonder!' True, He is, as well in His condescension as in His greatness, utterly beyond the scope of our finite comprehensions. 'Salvâ proprietate utriusque Naturæ, et in unam coeunte personam, suscepta est a majestate humilitas, a virtute infirmitas, ab æternitate mortalitas [u].' We do not profess to solve the mystery of that Union between the Almighty, Omniscient, Omnipresent Being, and a Human Life, with its bounded powers, its limited knowledge, its restricted sphere. We only know that in Christ, the finite and the Infinite are thus united. But we can understand this mysterious union at least as well as we can understand the union of such an organism as the human body to a spiritual immaterial principle like the human soul. How does spirit thus league itself with matter? Where and what is the life-principle of the body? Where is the exact frontier-line between sense and consciousness, between brain and thought, between the act of will and the movement of muscle? Is human nature then so utterly commonplace, and have its secrets been so entirely unravelled by contemporary science, as to entitle us to demand of the Almighty God that when He reveals Himself to us He shall disrobe Himself of

possit secundum operationem utique Deitatis; disce nunc quod secundum carnem omnia subjecta accipiat.'

[t] St. Leo, Ep. xxviii. c. 4: 'Qui verus est Deus, idem verus est Homo; et nullum est in hâc unitate mendacium, dum invicem sunt et humilitas hominis et altitudo deitatis. Agit enim utraque forma cum alterius communione quod proprium est; Verbo scilicet operante quod Verbi est, et carne exsequente quod carnis est. Unum horum coruscat miraculis, alterum succumbit injuriis.' St. Joh. Damasc. iii. 19: Θεοῦ ἐνανθρωπήσαντος, καὶ ἡ ἀνθρωπίνη αὐτοῦ ἐνέργεια θεία ἦν, ἤγουν τεθεωμένη, καὶ οὐκ ἄμοιρος τῆς θείας αὐτοῦ ἐνεργείας· καὶ ἡ θεία αὐτοῦ ἐνέργεια οὐκ ἄμοιρος τῆς ἀνθρωπίνης αὐτοῦ ἐνεργείας· ἀλλ' ἑκατέρα σὺν τῇ ἑτέρᾳ θεωρουμένη. He urges, here and in iii. 15, that Two Natures imply Two Energies co-operating, for no nature is ἀνενέργητος. See St. Tho. 3ª. 19. 1.

[u] St. Leo, Ep. xxviii. c. 3.

mystery? If we reject His Self-revelation in the Person of Jesus Christ on the ground of our inability to understand the difficulties, great and undeniable, although not greater than we might have anticipated, which do in fact surround it; are we also prepared to conclude that, because we cannot explain how a spiritual principle like the soul can be robed in and act through a material body, we will therefore close our eyes to the arguments which certify us that the soul is an immaterial essence, and take refuge from this oppressive sense of mystery in some doctrine of consistent materialism [v]?

Certainly St. John's doctrine of the Divinity of the Word Incarnate cannot be reasonably objected to on the score of its mysteriousness by those who allow themselves to face their real ignorance of the mysteries of our human nature. Nor does that doctrine involve a necessary internal self-contradiction on such a ground as that 'the Word by Whom all things were made, and Who sustains all things, cannot become His Own creature.' Undoubtedly the Word Incarnate does not cease to be the Word; but He can and does assume a Nature which He has created, and in which He dwells, that in it He may manifest Himself. Between the processes of Creation and Incarnation there is no necessary contradiction in Divine revelation, such as is presumed to exist by certain Pantheistic thinkers. He who becomes Incarnate creates the form in which He manifests Himself simultaneously with the act of His Self-manifestation. Doubtless when we say that God creates, we imply that He gives an existence to something other than Himself. On the other hand, it is certain that He does in a real sense Himself exist in each created object, not as being one with it, but as upholding it in being. He is in every such object the constitutive, sustaining, binding force which perpetuates its being. Thus in varying degrees the creatures are temples and organs of the indwelling Presence of the Creator, although in His Essence He is infinitely removed from them. If this is true of the irrational and, in a lower measure, even of the inanimate creatures, much more is it true

[v] The true lesson of such uncomprehended truths has been stated in Dante's imperishable lines:—

'Accender ne dovria più il disio
  Di veder quella essenzia, in che si vede
  Come nostra natura e Dio s'unio.
Li si vedrà ciò che tenem per fede,
  Non dimostrato; ma fia per se noto,
  A guisa del ver primo che l'uom crede.'

PARAD. ii. 40–45.

of the family of man, and of each member of that family. In vast inorganic masses God discovers Himself as the supreme, creative, sustaining Force. In the graduated orders of vital power which range throughout the animal and vegetable worlds, God unveils His activity as the Fountain of all life. In man, a creature exercising conscious reflective thought and free self-determining will, God proclaims Himself a free Intelligent Agent. Man indeed may, if he will, reveal much more than this of the beauty of God. Man may shed abroad, by the free movement of his will, rays of God's moral glory, of love, of mercy, of purity, of justice. Whether a man will thus declare the glory of his Maker depends not upon the necessary constitution of his nature, but upon the free co-operation of his will with the designs of God. God however is obviously able to create a Being who will reveal Him perfectly and of necessity, as expressing His perfect image and likeness before His creatures. All nature points to such a Being as its climax and consummation. And such a Being is the Archetypal Manhood, assumed by the Eternal Word. It is the climax of God's creation; It is the climax also of God's Self-revelation. At this point God's creative activity becomes entirely one with His Self-revealing activity. The Sacred Manhood is a creature, yet It is indissolubly united to the Eternal Word. It differs from every other created being, in that God personally tenants It. So far then are Incarnation and Creation from being antagonistic conceptions of the activity of God, that the absolutely Perfect Creature only exists as a perfect reflection of the Divine glory. In the Incarnation, God creates only to reveal, and He reveals perfectly by That which He creates. 'The Word was made flesh and dwelt among us, and we beheld His glory [w].'

VI. But if belief in our Lord's Divinity, as taught by St. John, cannot be reasonably objected to on such grounds as have been noticed, can it be destroyed by a natural explanation of its upgrowth and formation? Here, undoubtedly, we touch upon a suspicion which underlies much of the current scepticism of the day; and with a few words on this momentous topic we may conclude the present lecture.

Those who reject the doctrine that Christ is God are confronted by the consideration that, after the lapse of eighteen centuries since His appearance on this earth, He is believed in and worshipped as God by a Christendom which embraces the

[w] On this subject, see Martensen, Christl. Dogmat. § 132.

most civilized portion of the human family. The question arises how to account for this fact. There is no difficulty at all in accounting for it if we suppose Him to be, and to have proclaimed Himself to be, a Divine Person. But if we hold that, as a matter of history, He believed Himself to be a mere man, how are we to explain the world-wide upgrowth of so extraordinary a belief about Him, as is this belief in His Divinity? Scepticism may fold its arms and may smile at what it deems the intrinsic absurdity of the dogma believed in; but it cannot ignore the existing prevalence of the belief which accepts the dogma. The belief is a phenomenon which at least challenges attention. How has that belief been spread? How is it that for eighteen hundred years, and at this hour, a conviction of the truth of the Godhead of Jesus dominates over the world of Christian thought? Here, if scepticism would save its intellectual credit, it must cease from the perpetual reiteration of doubts and negations, unrelieved by any frank assertions or admissions of positive truth. It must make a venture; it must commit itself to the responsibilities of a positive position, however inexact and shadowy; it must hazard an hypothesis and be prepared to defend it.

Accordingly the theory which proposes to explain the belief of Christendom in the Godhead of Christ maintains that Christ was 'deified' by the enthusiasm of His first disciples. We are told that 'man instinctively creates a creed that shall meet the wants and aspirations of his understanding and of his heart[x].' The teaching of Christ created in His first followers a passionate devotion to His Person, and a desire for unreserved submission to His dictatorship. Not that Christ's Divinity was decreed Him by any formal act of public honour; it was the spontaneous and irregular tribute of a passionate enthusiasm. Could any expression of reverence seem exaggerated to an admiration and a love which knew no bounds? Could any intellectual price be too high to pay for the advantage of placing the authority of the Greatest of teachers upon that one basis of authority which is beyond assault? Do not love and reverence, centring upon a friend, upon a memory, with eager intensity, turn a somewhat impatient ear to the cautious protestations of the critical reason, when any such voice can make itself heard? Do they not pass by imperceptible degrees into adoration? Does not adoration take for granted the Divinity of the object which it has learned

[x] Feuerbach, Geist. d. Christenth. Einl.

imperceptibly and unreflectingly to adore? The enthusiasm created by Jesus Christ in those around Him, thus comes to be credited with the invention and propagation of the belief in His Divinity. 'So mighty was the enthusiasm, that nothing short of that stupendous belief would satisfy it. The heart of Christendom gave law to its understanding. Christians wished Christ to be God, and they forthwith thought that they had sufficient reasons for believing in His Godhead. The feeling of a society of affectionate friends found its way in process of time into the world of speculation. It fell into the hands of the dialecticians, and into the hands of the metaphysicians; it was analysed, it was defined, it was coloured by contact with foreign speculations; it was enlarged by the accretion of new intellectual material. At length Fathers and Councils had finished their graceless and pedantic task, and that which had at first been the fresh sentiment of simple and loving hearts was duly hardened and rounded off into a solid block of repulsive dogma.'

Now St. John's writings are a standing difficulty in the way of this enterprising hypothesis. We have seen that the fourth Gospel must be recognised as St. John's, unless, to use the words of Ewald, 'we are prepared knowingly to receive falsehood and to reject truth.' But we have also seen that in the fourth Gospel, Jesus Christ is proclaimed to be God by the whole drift of the argument, and in terms as explicit as those of the Nicene Creed. We have not then to deal with any supposed process of deification, whereby the Person of Jesus was 'transfigured' in the apprehension of sub-apostolic or post-apostolic Christendom. It is St. John who proclaims that Jesus is the Word Incarnate, and that the Word is God. How can we account for St. John's conduct in representing Him as God, if He was in truth only man? It will not avail to argue that St. John wrote his Gospel in his old age, and that the memories of his youthful companionship with Jesus had been coloured, heightened, transformed, idealized, by the meditative enthusiasm of more than half a century. It will not avail to say that the reverence of the beloved disciple for his ascended Master was fatal to the accuracy of the portrait which he drew of Him. For what is this but to misapprehend the very fundamental nature of reverence? Truth is the basis, as it is the object of reverence, not less than of every other virtue. Reverence prostrates herself before a greatness the reality of which is obvious to her; but she would cease to be reverence if she could exaggerate the greatness which provokes her homage, not less surely than if she could depreciate or deny it. The sentiment which, in contemplating its object, abandons the guidance of fact for that of imagination, is disloyal to that honesty of purpose which is of the essence of reverence; and it is certain at last to subserve the purposes of the scorner and the spoiler. St. John insists that he teaches the Church only that which he has seen and heard. Even a slight swerving from truth must be painful to genuine reverence; but what shall we say of an exaggeration so gigantic, if an exaggeration it be, as that which transforms a human friend into the Almighty and Everlasting God? If Jesus Christ is not God, how is it that the most intimate of His earthly friends came to believe and to teach that He really is God?

Place yourselves, my brethren, fairly face to face with this difficulty; imagine yourselves, for the moment, in the position of St. John. Think of any whom you have loved and revered, beyond measure, as it has seemed, in past years. He has gone; but you cling to him more earnestly in thought and affection than while he was here. You treasure his words, you revisit his haunts, you delight in the company of his friends, you represent to yourself his wonted turns of thought and phrase, you con over his handwriting, you fondle his likeness. These things are for you precious and sacred. Even now, there are times when the tones of that welcome voice seem to fall with living power upon your strained ear. Even now, the outline of that countenance, upon which the grave has closed, flits, as if capriciously, before your eye of sense. The air around you yields it perchance to your intent gaze, radiant with a higher beauty than it wore of old. Others, you feel, may be forgotten as memory grows weak, and the passing years bring with them the quick succession of new fields and objects of interest, pressing importunately upon the heart and thoughts. But one such memory as I have glanced at, fades not at the bidding of time. It cannot fade; it has become a part of the mind which clings to it. Some who are here may have known those whom they thus remember; a few of us assuredly have known such. But can we conceive it possible that, after any lapse of time, we should ever express our reverence and love for the unearthly goodness, the moral strength, the tenderness of heart, the fearlessness, the justice, the unselfishness of our friend, by saying that he was not an ordinary human being, but a superhuman person? Can we imagine ourselves incorporating our recollections about him with some current theosophic doctrine elevating him to the rank of a Divine hypostasis? While he lies in his silent grave, can

[LECT.

we picture ourselves describing him as the very absolute Light and Life, as the Incarnate Thought of the Most High, as standing in a relationship altogether unique to the Eternal and Self-existent Being, nay, as being literally God? To say that 'St. John lived in a different intellectual atmosphere from our own,' does not meet the difficulty. If Jesus was merely human, St. John's statements about Him are among the most preposterous fictions which have imposed upon the world. They were advanced with a full knowledge of all that they involved. St. John was at least as profoundly convinced as we are of the truth of the unity of the Supreme Being. St. John was at least as alive as we can be to the infinite interval which parts the highest of creatures from the Great Creator. If we are not naturally lured on by some irresistible fascination, by the poetry or by the credulity of our advancing years, to believe in the Godhead of the best man whom we have ever known, neither was St. John. If Jesus had been merely human, St. John would have felt what we feel about a loved and revered friend whom we have lost. In proportion to our belief in our friend's goodness, in proportion to our loving reverence for his character, is the strength of our conviction that we could not now do him a more cruel injury than by entwining a blasphemous fable, such as the ascription of Divinity would be, around the simple story of his merely human life. This 'deification of Jesus by the enthusiasm' of St. John would have been consistent neither with St. John's reverence for God, nor with his real loyalty to a merely human friend and teacher. St. John worshipped the 'jealous' God of Israel; and he has recorded the warning which he himself received against worshipping the angel of the Apocalypse[y]. If Christ had not really been Divine, the real beauty of His Human Character would have been disfigured by any association with such legendary exaggeration, and Christianity would assuredly have perished within the limits of the first century.

The theory that Jesus was deified by enthusiasm assumes the existence of a general disposition in mankind which is unwarranted by experience. Generally speaking men are not eager to believe in the exalted virtue, much less in the superhuman origin or dignity, of their fellow-men. And to do them justice, the writers who maintain that Jesus was invested with Divine honours by popular fervour, illustrate the weakness of their own principle very conspicuously. While they assert that nothing

[y] Rev. xxii. 9.

was more easy and obvious for the disciple of the apostolic age than to believe in the Divinity of his Master, they themselves reject that truth with the greatest possible obstinacy and determination; well-attested though it be, now as then, by historical miracles and by overwhelming moral considerations; but also proclaimed now, as it was not then, by the faith of eighteen centuries, and by the suffrages of all that is purest and truest in our existing civilization.

But, it is suggested that the apostolic narrative itself bears out the doctrine that Jesus was deified through enthusiasm by its account of the functions which are ascribed, especially in St. John's Gospel, to the Comforter. Was not the Comforter sent to testify of Jesus? Is it not said, 'He shall glorify Me'? Does not this language look like the later endeavour of a religious phrenzy, to account for exaggerations of which it is conscious, by a bold claim to supernatural illumination?

Now this suggestion implies that the last Discourse of our Lord is in reality a forgery, which can no more claim to represent His real thought than the political speeches in Thucydides can be seriously supposed to express the minds of the speakers to whom they are severally attributed. Or, at the least, it implies that a purely human feeling is here clothed by language ascribed to our Lord Himself with the attributes of a Divine Person. Of course, if St. John was capable of deliberately attributing to His Master that which He did not say, he was equally capable of attributing to Him actions which He did not do; and we are driven to imagine that the closest friend of Jesus was believed by apostolical Christendom to be writing a history, when in truth he was only composing a biographical novel. But, as Rousseau has observed, in words which have been already quoted, the original inventor of the Gospel history would have been as miraculous a being as its historical Subject. And the moral fascination which the last discourse possesses for every pure and true soul at this hour, combines with the testimony of the Church to assure us that it could have been spoken by no merely human lips, and that it is beyond the inventive scope of even the highest human genius. Those three chapters which M. Renan pronounces to be full of 'the dryness of metaphysics and the darkness of abstract dogmas' have been, as a matter of fact, watered by the tears of all the purest love and deepest sorrow of Christian humanity for eighteen centuries. Never is the New Testament more able to dispense with external evidence than in those matchless words; nowhere more than here is it sensibly divine.

Undoubtedly it is a fact that in these chapters our Lord does promise to His apostles the supernatural aid of the Holy Spirit. It is true that the Spirit was to testify of Christ[z] and to glorify Christ[a], and to guide the disciples into all truth[b]. But how? 'He shall take of Mine and shall shew it unto you[c];' 'He shall teach you all things, and bring all things to your remembrance whatsoever I have said unto you[d].' The Holy Spirit was to bring the words and works and character of Jesus before the illuminated intelligence of the Apostles. The school of the Spirit was to be the school of reflection. But it was not to be the school of legendary invention. Acts, which, at the time of their being witnessed, might have appeared trivial or commonplace, would be seen, under the guidance of the Spirit, to have had a deeper interest. Words, to which a transient or local value had been assigned at first, would now be felt to invite a world-wide and eternal meaning. 'These things understood not His disciples at the first,' is true of much else besides the entry into Jerusalem[e]. Moral, spiritual, physical powers which, though unexplained, could never have passed for the product of purely human activity, would in time be referred by the Invisible Teacher to their true source; they would be regarded with awe as the very rays of Deity.

Thus the work of the Spirit would but complete, systematize, digest the results of previous natural observation. Certainly it was always impossible that any man could 'say that Jesus is the Lord but by the Holy Ghost[f].' The inward teaching of the Holy Ghost alone could make the Godhead of Jesus a certainty of faith as well as a conclusion of the intellect. But the intellectual conditions of belief were at first inseparable from natural contact with the living Human Form of Jesus during the years of His earthly life. Our Lord implies this in saying, 'Ye also shall bear witness, because ye have been with Me from the beginning.' The Apostles lived with One Who combined an exercise of the highest miraculous powers with a faultless human

[z] St. John xv. 26: ἐκεῖνος μαρτυρήσει περὶ ἐμοῦ.
[a] Ibid. xvi. 14: ἐκεῖνος ἐμὲ δοξάσει.
[b] Ibid. ver. 13: ὁδηγήσει ὑμᾶς εἰς πᾶσαν τὴν ἀλήθειαν.
[c] Ibid. vers. 14, 15: ἐκ τοῦ ἐμοῦ λήψεται, καὶ ἀναγγελεῖ ὑμῖν.
[d] Ibid. xiv. 26: ἐκεῖνος ὑμᾶς διδάξει πάντα, καὶ ὑπομνήσει ὑμᾶς πάντα ἃ εἶπον ὑμῖν.
[e] St. John xii. 14–16.
[f] 1 Cor. xii. 3: οὐδεὶς δύναται εἰπεῖν Κύριον Ἰησοῦν, εἰ μὴ ἐν Πνεύματι Ἁγίῳ.

character, and Who asserted Himself, by implication and expressly, to be personally God. The Spirit strengthened and formalized that earlier and more vague belief which was created by His language; but the language which had fallen on the natural ears of the Apostles was His; and it was the germinal principle of their riper faith in His Divinity.

The unbelief of our day is naturally anxious to evade the startling fact that the most intimate of the companions of Jesus is also the most strenuous assertor of His Godhead. There is a proverb to the effect that no man's life should be written by his private servant. That proverb expresses the general conviction of mankind that, as a rule, like some mountain scenery or ruined castles, moral greatness in men is more picturesque when it is viewed from a distance. The proverb bids you not to scrutinize even a good man too narrowly, lest perchance you should discover flaws in his character which will somewhat rudely shake your conviction of his goodness. It is hinted that some unobtrusive weaknesses which escape public observation will be obvious to a man's everyday companion, and will be fatal to the higher estimate which, but for such close scrutiny, might have been formed respecting him. But in the case of Jesus Christ the moral of this cynical proverb is altogether at fault. Jesus Christ chooses one disciple to be the privileged sharer of a nearer intimacy than any other. The son of Zebedee lies upon His bosom at supper; he is 'the disciple whom Jesus loved.' Along with St. Peter and St. James, this disciple is taken to the holy mount, that he may witness the glory of his Transfigured Lord. He enters the empty tomb on the morning of the Resurrection. He is in the upper chamber when the risen Jesus blessed the ten and the eleven. He is on the mount of the Ascension when the Conqueror moves up visibly into heaven. But he also is summoned to the garden where Jesus kneels in agony beneath the olive trees; and alone of the twelve he faces the fierce multitude on the road to Calvary, and stands with Mary beneath the cross, and sees Jesus die. He sees more of the Divine Master than any other, more of His glory, more too of His humiliation. His witness is proportioned to his nearer and closer observation. Whether he is writing Epistles of encouragement and warning, or narrating heavenly visions touching the future of the Church, or recording the experiences of those years when he enjoyed that intimate, unmatched companionship,—St. John, beyond any other of the sacred writers, is the persistent herald and teacher of our Lord's Divinity.

How and by what successive steps it was that the full truth embodied in his Gospel respecting the Person of his Lord made its way into and mastered the soul of the beloved disciple, who indeed shall presume to say? Who of us can determine the exact and varied observations whereby we learn to measure and to revere the component elements even of a great human character? The absorbing interest of such a process is generally fatal to an accurate analysis of its stages. We penetrate deeper and deeper, we mount higher and higher, as we follow the complex system of motives, capacities, dispositions, which, one after another, open upon us. We cannot, on looking back, say when this or that feature became distinctly clear to us. We know not now by what additions and developments the general impression which we have received took its shape and outline. St. John would doubtless have learnt portions of the mighty truth from definite statements and at specified times. The real sense of prophecy[g], the explicit confessions of disciples[h], the assertions by which our Lord replied to the malice or to the ignorance of His opponents[i], were doubtless distinct elements of the Apostle's training in the school of truth. St. John must have learned something of Christ's Divine power when, at His word, the putrid corpse of Lazarus, bound with its grave-clothes, moved forward into air and life. St. John must have learned yet more of his Master's condescension when, girded with a towel, Jesus bent Himself to the earth, that He might wash the feet of the traitor Judas. Each miracle, each discourse supplied a distinct ray of light; but the total impression must have been formed, strengthened, deepened by the incidents of daily intercourse, by the effects of hourly, momentary observation. For every human soul, encased in its earthly prison-house, seeks and finds publicity through countless outlets. The immaterial spirit traces its history with an almost invisible delicacy upon the coarse hard matter which is its servant and its organ. The unconscious, involuntary movements of manner and countenance, the unstudied phrases of daily or of casual conversation, the emphasis of silence not less than the emphasis of speech, help in various ways to complete that self-revelation which every individual character makes to all around, and which is studied by

[g] St. John xii. 41: ταῦτα εἶπεν Ἡσαΐας, ὅτε εἶδε τὴν δόξαν αὐτοῦ, καὶ ἐλάλησε περὶ αὐτοῦ. Isa. vi. 9.

[h] St. John i. 49. After our Lord's words implying His omnipresence, Nathanael says, 'Ῥαββὶ, σὺ εἶ ὁ Υἱὸς τοῦ Θεοῦ.

[i] St. John viii. 58, &c.

all in each. Not otherwise did the Incarnate Word reveal Himself to the purest and keenest love which He found and chose from among the sons of men. One flaw or fault of temper, one symptom of moral impotence or of moral perversion, one hasty word, one ill-considered act, would have shattered the ideal for ever. But, in fact, to St. John the Life of Jesus was as the light of heaven; it was as one constant unfailing outflow of beauty, ever varying its illuminating powers as it falls upon the leaves of the forest oak or upon the countless ripples of the ocean. In the eyes of St. John the Eternal Person of Jesus shone forth through His Humanity with translucent splendour, and wove and folded around Itself, as the days and weeks passed on, a moral history of faultless grandeur. It was not the disciple who idealized the Master; it was the Master Who revealed Himself in His majestic glory to the illumined eye and to the entranced touch of the disciple. No treachery of memory, no ardour of temperament, no sustained reflectiveness of soul, could have compassed the transformation of a human friend into the Almighty and Everlasting Being. Nor was there room for serious error of judgment after a companionship so intimate, so heart-searching, so true, as had been that of Jesus with St. John. And thus to the beloved disciple the Divinity of his Lord was not a scholastic formula, nor a pious conjecture, nor a controversial thesis, nor the adaptation of a popular superstition to meet the demands of a strong enthusiasm, nor a mystic reverie. It was nothing less than a fact of personal experience. 'That Which was from the beginning, Which we have heard, Which we have seen with our eyes, Which we have looked upon and our hands have handled, of the Word of Life; (for the Life was manifested, and we have seen It, and bear witness, and shew unto you that Eternal Life, Which was with the Father, and was manifested unto us;) That Which we have seen and heard declare we unto you.'

LECTURE VI.

OUR LORD'S DIVINITY AS TAUGHT BY ST. JAMES, ST. PETER, AND ST. PAUL.

And when James, Cephas, and John, who seemed to be pillars, perceived the grace that was given unto me, they gave to me and Barnabas the right hands of fellowship; that we should go unto the heathen, and they unto the circumcision.—GAL. ii. 9.

THE meditative temper of thought and phrase, which is so observable in St. John, may be thought to bear in two different manners upon the question before us in these lectures. On the one hand, such a temper, regarded from a point of view entirely naturalistic, must be admitted to be a guarantee against the presumption that St. John, in his enthusiastic devotion to Jesus, committed himself to hasty beliefs and assertions respecting the Person of his Friend and Master. An over-eager and undiscriminating admiration would not naturally express itself in metaphysical terminology of a reflective and mystical character. But on the other hand, it may be asked whether too much stress has not been laid by the argument of the last lecture upon the witness of St. John? Can the conclusions of a mind of high-strung and contemplative temper be held to furnish reasons on which the Church may build a cardinal point of belief in the religion of mankind? May not such a belief be inextricably linked to the moral and intellectual idiosyncrasies of a single man? The belief may indeed be the honest and adequate result of that particular measure and kind of observation and reflection which one saintly mind has achieved; and as such it may be a worthy object of philosophical interest and respect. But is not this respect and interest due to it on the precise ground that it is the true native product of a group of conditions, which co-exist nowhere else save in the particular mind which generated it? Will a faith, of such origin, bear transplantation into the moral and mental soil around? Can it be nourished and handed on by minds of a different calibre, by characters of a distinct cast from that in which it originally grew? Dr. Samuel Johnson, for instance, had private beliefs which were obviously due to the tone and genius of his particular character. These beliefs go far to constitute the charm of the picture with which we are familiar in the pages of Boswell. But our respect for Dr. Johnson does not force us to accept each and all of his quaint convictions. They are peculiar to himself, being such as he was. We admire them as belonging to the attractive and eccentric individuality of the man. We do not suppose that they are capable of being domesticated in the general and diversified mind of England.

Now, if it be hinted that some similar estimate should be formed respecting St. John's doctrine of our Lord's Divinity, the present, for obvious reasons, is not the moment to insist upon a consideration which for us Christians must have paramount weight, namely, that St. John was taught by an infallible Teacher, by none other than God the Holy Ghost. But let us remark, first of all, the fact that St. John did convey to a large circle of minds his own deep conviction that his Friend and Master was a Divine Person; paradoxical as that conviction must at first have seemed to them. If we could have travelled through Asia Minor at the end of the first century of our era, we should have fallen in with a number of persons, in various ranks of society, who so entirely believed in St. John's doctrine, as to be willing to die for it without any kind of hesitation[a]. But it would have been a mistake to suppose that the prevalence of the doctrine was due only to the activity of St. John. While St. John was teaching this doctrine under the form which he had been guided to adopt, a parallel communication of the substance of the doctrine was taking place in several other quarters. St. John was supported, if I may be allowed to use such an expression, by men whose minds were of a totally distinct natural cast, and who expressed their thoughts in a religious phraseology which had little enough in common with that which was current

[a] The Apocalypse was probably written immediately after Domitian's persecution of the Church. Antipas had been martyred at Pergamos. (Rev. ii. 13.) St. John saw the souls of martyrs who had been beheaded with the axe; *εἶδον τὰς ψυχὰς τῶν πεπελεκισμένων διὰ τὴν μαρτυρίαν Ἰησοῦ.* (Rev. xx. 4.) This was the Roman custom at executions. In the persecution under Nero other and more cruel kinds of death had been inflicted. The Bishops of Pergamos (Ibid. ii. 13) and Philadelphia (Ibid. iii. 8) had confessed Christ. St. Clement of Rome alludes to the violence of this persecution. (Ep. ad Cor. 6.) The Apostle himself was banished to Patmos.

in the school of Ephesus. Nevertheless it will be our duty this morning to observe, how radical was their agreement with St. John, in urging upon the acceptance of the human race the doctrine that Jesus Christ is God.

Very ingenious theories concerning a supposed division of the Apostolical Church into schools of thought holding antagonistic beliefs have been advanced of late years. And they have had the effect of directing a large amount of attention to the account which St. Paul gives, in his Epistle to the Galatians, of his interview with the leading Apostles at Jerusalem [b]. The accuracy of that account is not questioned even by the most destructive of the Tübingen divines. According to St. Irenæus and the great majority of authorities, both ancient and modern, the interview took place on the occasion of St. Paul's attendance at the Apostolical Council of Jerusalem. St. Paul says that St. James, St. Peter, and St. John, who were looked upon as 'pillars' of the Church, among the Judaizing Christians as well as among Christians generally, gave the right hands of fellowship to himself and to Barnabas. 'It was agreed,' says St. Paul, 'that we should go unto the heathen, and they unto the circumcision.' Now the historical interest which attaches to this recorded division of labour among the leading Apostles is sufficiently obvious; but the dogmatic interest of the passage, although less direct, is even higher than the historical. This passage warrants us in inferring at least thus much;—that the leading Apostles of our Lord and Saviour Jesus Christ were not hopelessly at issue with each other on a subject of such central and primary importance as the Divine and Eternal Nature of their Master.

It might well seem, at first sight, that to draw such an inference at all within the walls of a Christian church was itself an act for which the faith of Christians would exact an apology. But those who are acquainted with the imaginative licence of recent theories will not deem our inference altogether impertinent and superfluous. Of late years St. James has been represented as more of a Jew than a Christian, and as holding in reality a purely Ebionitic and Humanitarian belief as to the Person of Jesus. St. Paul has been described as the teacher of such a doctrine of the Subordination of the Son as to be practically Arian. St. Peter is then exhibited as occupying a feeble undecided dogmatic position, intermediate to the doctrines of St. Paul and St. James; while all the three are contrasted with

[b] Gal. ii. 1–10.

the distinct and lofty Christology said to be proper to the gnosis of St. John. Now, as has been already remarked, the historical trustworthiness of the passage in the Galatians has not been disputed even by the Tübingen writers. That passage represents St. John as intimately associated, not merely with St. Peter but with St. James. It moreover represents these three apostles as giving pledges of spiritual co-operation and fellowship, from their common basis of belief and action, to the more recent convert St. Paul. Is it to be supposed that St. Paul could have been thus accepted as a fellow-worker on one and the same occasion by the Apostle who is said to be a simple Humanitarian, and by the Apostle whose whole teaching centres in Jesus considered as the historical manifestation of the Eternal Word? Or are we to imagine that the apostles of Christ anticipated that indifference to doctrinal exactness which is characteristic of some modern schools? Did they regard the question of our Lord's Personal Godhead as a kind of speculative curiosity; as a scholastic conceit; as having no necessary connexion with vital, essential, fundamental Christianity? And is St. Paul, in his Epistle to the Galatians, only describing the first great ecclesiastical compromise, in which truths of primary importance were sacrificed for an immediate practical object, more ruthlessly than on any subsequent occasion?

My brethren, the answer to these questions could not be really doubtful to any except the most paradoxical of modern theorists. To say nothing of St. Peter and St. Jude, St. Paul's general language on the subject of heresy[c], and St. John's particular application of such terms as 'the liar' and 'antichrist[d]' to Cerinthus and other heretics, make the supposition of such indifference as is here in question, in the case of the apostles, utterly inadmissible. If the apostles had differed vitally respect-

[c] He speaks of *αἱρέσεις* in the sense of sectarian movements tending to or resulting in separation from the Church, as a form of evil which becomes the unwilling instrument of good (1 Cor. xi. 19). And *αἱρέσεις* are thus classed among the works of the flesh (Gal. v. 20). Using the word in its sense of dogmatic error on vital points, St. Paul bids Titus reject a 'heretic' after two warnings from the communion of the Church: *αἱρετικὸν ἄνθρωπον μετὰ μίαν καὶ δευτέραν νουθεσίαν παραιτοῦ* (Tit. iii. 10). On the inviolate sacredness of the apostolical doctrine, cf. Gal. i. 8: *ἐὰν ἡμεῖς ἢ ἄγγελος ἐξ οὐρανοῦ εὐαγγελίζηται ὑμῖν παρ' ὃ εὐηγγελισάμεθα ὑμῖν, ἀνάθεμα ἔστω.* Cf. 2 Pet. ii. 1.

[d] 1 St. John ii. 22: *τίς ἐστιν ὁ ψεύστης, εἰ μὴ ὁ ἀρνούμενος ὅτι Ἰησοῦς οὐκ ἔστιν ὁ Χριστός; οὗτός ἐστιν ὁ ἀντίχριστος, ὁ ἀρνούμενος τὸν Πατέρα καὶ τὸν Υἱόν. πᾶς ὁ ἀρνούμενος τὸν Υἱὸν, οὐδὲ τὸν Πατέρα ἔχει.* Cf. Ibid. iv. 3; 2 St. John 7.

ing the Person of Christ, they would have shattered the work of Pentecost in its infancy. And the terms in which they speak of each other would be reduced to the level of meaningless or insincere conventionalities [e]. Considering that the Gospel presented itself to the world as an absolute and exclusive draught of Divine truth, contrasted as such with the perpetually-shifting forms of human thought around it; we may deem it antecedently probable, that those critics are mistaken, who profess to have discovered at the very fountain-head of Christianity at least three entirely distinct doctrines, respecting so fundamental a question as the personal rank of Christ in the scale of being.

Undoubtedly it is true that as the Evangelists approach the Person of our Lord from distinct points of view, so do the writers of the apostolic epistles represent different attitudes of the human soul towards the one evangelical truth; and in this way they impersonate types of thought and feeling which have ever since found a welcome and a home in the world-embracing Church of Jesus Christ. St. James insists most earnestly on the moral obligations of Christian believers; and he connects the Old Testament with the New by shewing the place of the law, now elevated and transfigured into a law of liberty, in the new life of Christians. He may indeed for a moment be engaged in refuting a false doctrine of justification by faith [f]. But this is because such a doctrine prevents Christians from duly recognizing those moral and spiritual truths and obligations upon which the Apostle is most eagerly insisting. Throughout his Epistle,

[e] St. Paul associates himself with the other apostles as bearing the stress of a common confessorship for Christ (2 Cor. xii. 12). The apostles are, together with the prophets, the foundations of the Church (Eph. ii. 20). The apostles are first in order (Eph. iv. 11). Although the grace of God in himself had laboured more abundantly than all the apostles, St. Paul terms himself the least of the apostolic college (1 Cor. xv. 9). The equality of the Gentile believers in Christ with the Jewish believers was a truth made known to St. Paul by special revelation, and he called it his Gospel; but it implied no properly doctrinal difference between himself and the apostles of the circumcision. The harmonious action of the apostles as a united spiritual corporation is implied in such passages as 2 Pet. iii. 2, St. Jude 17; and neither of these passages affords ground for Baur's inference respecting the post-apostolic age of the writer. In 2 St. Pet. iii. 15, 16, St. Peter distinguishes between the real mind of 'our beloved brother Paul' as being in perfect agreement with his own, and the abuse which had been made by teachers of error of certain difficult truths put forward in the Pauline Epistles: δυσνόητά τινα, ἃ οἱ ἀμαθεῖς καὶ ἀστήρικτοι στρεβλοῦσιν ὡς καὶ τὰς λοιπὰς γραφὰς, πρὸς τὴν ἰδίαν αὐτῶν ἀπώλειαν.

[f] St. James ii. 14-26.

doctrine is, comparatively speaking, thrown into the background; he is intent upon practical considerations, to the total, or well-nigh total, exclusion of doctrinal topics. St. Paul, on the other hand, abounds in dogmatic statements. Still, in St. Paul, doctrine is, at least, generally brought forward with a view to some immediate practical object. Only in five out of his fourteen Epistles can the doctrinal element be said very decidedly to predominate [g]. St. Paul assumes that his readers have gone through a course of oral instruction in necessary Christian doctrine [h]; he accordingly completes, he expands, he draws out into its consequences what had been already taught by himself or by others. St. Paul's fiery and impetuous style is in keeping with his general relation, throughout his Epistles, to Christian dogma. The calm enunciation of an enchained series of consequences flowing from some central or supreme truth is perpetually interrupted, in St. Paul, by the exclamations, the questions, the parentheses, the anacoloutha, the quotations from hymns, the solemn ascriptions of glory to the Source of all blessings, the outbursts by which argument suddenly melts into stern denunciation, or into versatile expostulation, or into irresistible appeals to sympathy, or into the highest strains of lyrical poetry. Thus it is that in St. Paul primary dogma appears, as it were, rather in flashes of light streaming with rapid coruscations across his pages, than in highly elaborated statements such as might abound throughout a professed doctrinal treatise of some later

[g] And yet in these five Epistles an immediate practical purpose is generally discernible. In the Romans the Apostle is harmonizing the Jewish and Gentile elements within the Catholic Church, by shewing that each section is equally indebted to faith in Jesus Christ for a real justification before God. In the Galatians he is opposing this same doctrinal truth to the destructive and reactionary theory of the Judaizers. In the Ephesians and Colossians he is meeting the mischievous pseudo-philosophy and Cabbalism of the earliest Gnostics, here positively and devotionally, there polemically, by insisting on the dignity of our Lord's Person, and the mystery of His relation to the Church. In the Hebrews, written either by St. Paul himself or by St. Luke under his direction, our Lord's Person and Priesthood are exhibited in their several bearings as a practical reason against apostasy to Judaism (it would seem) of an Alexandrian type.

[h] 1 Thess. iii. 10: *νυκτὸς καὶ ἡμέρας ὑπὲρ ἐκ περισσοῦ δεόμενοι εἰς τὸ ἰδεῖν ὑμῶν τὸ πρόσωπον, καὶ καταρτίσαι τὰ ὑστερήματα τῆς πίστεως ὑμῶν.* The Apostle desires to see the Roman Christians, not that he may teach them any supplementary truths, but to confirm them in their existing belief (*εἰς τὸ στηριχθῆναι ὑμᾶς*, Rom. i. 11) by the interchange of spiritual sympathies with himself. See 1 Cor. xv. 1; Gal. i. 11, 12, iv. 13, 14; 1 Thess. ii. 2; 2 Thess. ii. 15. Compare 1 St. John ii. 21: *οὐκ ἔγραψα ὑμῖν, ὅτι οὐκ οἴδατε τὴν ἀλήθειαν, ἀλλ' ὅτι οἴδατε αὐτήν.*

age; and yet doctrine, although it might seem to be introduced incidentally to some general or special purpose, nevertheless is inextricably bound up with the Apostle's whole drift of practical thought. As for St. John, he is always a contemplative and mystical theologian. The eye of his soul is fixed on God, and on the Word Incarnate. St. John simply describes his intuitions. He does not argue; he asserts. He looks up to heaven, and as he gazes he tells us what he sees. He continually takes an intuition, as it were, to pieces, and recombines it; he resists forms of thought which contradict it; but he does not engage in long arguments, as if he were a dialectician, defending or attacking a theological thesis. Nor is St. John's temper any mere love of speculation divorced from practice. Each truth which the Apostle beholds, however unearthly and sublime, has a directly practical and transforming power; St. John knows nothing of realms of thought which leave the heart and conscience altogether untouched. Thus, speaking generally, the three Apostles respectively represent the moralist, the practical dogmatist, and the saintly mystic; while St. Peter, as becomes the Apostle first in order in the sacred college, seems to blend in himself the three types of Apostolical teachers. His Epistles are not without elements that more especially characterize St. John; while they harmonize in a very striking manner those features of St. Paul and St. James which seem most nearly to approach divergence. It may be added that St. Peter's second Epistle finds its echo in St. Jude.

I. 1. The marked reserve which is observable in St. James' Epistle as to matters of doctrine, combined with his emphatic allusions to the social duties attaching to property and to class distinctions, have been taken to imply that this Epistle represents what is assumed by some theories of development to have been the earliest form of Christianity. The earliest Christians are sometimes referred to, as having been, both in their Christology and in their sociological doctrines, Ebionites. But St. James' Epistle is so far from belonging to the teaching of the earliest apostolical age, that it presupposes nothing less than a very widespread and indirect effect of the distinctive teaching of St. Paul. St. Paul's emphatic teaching respecting faith as the receptive cause of justification must have been promulgated long enough and widely enough to have been perverted into a particular gnosis of an immoral Antinomian type. With that gnosis St. James enters into earnest conflict. Baur indeed maintains that St. James is engaged in a vehement onslaught upon the actual teaching, upon the *ipsissima verba*, of St. Paul himself[i]. Now even if you should adopt that paradox, you would still obviously be debarred from saying that St. James' Epistle is a sample of the earliest Christianity, of the Christianity of the pre-Pauline age of the Church[j]. But in point of fact, as Bishop Bull and others have long since shewn, St. James is attacking an evil which, although it presupposes and is based upon St. Paul's teaching, is as foreign to the mind of St. Paul as to his own. The justification by faith without works which is denounced by St. James is a corruption and a caricature of that sublime truth which is taught us by the author of the Epistles to the Romans and the Galatians. Correspondent to the general temper of mind which, in the later apostolical age, began to regard the truths of faith and morals only as an addition to the intellectual stock of human thinkers, there arose a conception of faith itself which degraded it to the level of mere barren consent on the part of the speculative faculty. This 'faith' had no necessary relations to holiness and moral growth, to sanctification of the affections, and subdual of the will[k]. Thus, for the moment, error had imposed

[i] Baur, Vorlesungen, über N. T. Theologie, p. 277: 'In dem Brief Jacobi dagegen begegnet uns nun eine auf den Mittelpunkt der paulinischen Lehre losgehende Opposition. Dem paulinischen Hauptsatz Röm. iii. 28: *δικαιοῦσθαι πίστει ἀνθρώπον, χωρὶς ἔργων νόμου* wird nun hier der Satz entgegengestellt, Jac. ii. 24: *ὅτι ἐξ ἔργων δικαιοῦται ἄνθρωπος, καὶ οὐκ ἐκ πίστεως μόνον.* Alle Versuche, die man gemacht hat, um der Anerkennung der Thatsache zu entgehen, dass ein directer Widerspruch zwischen diesen beiden Lehrbegriffen stattfinde und der Verfasser des Jacobusbriefs die paulinische Lehre zum unmittelbaren Gegenstand seiner Polemik mache, sind völlig vergeblich.' In his Christenthum (p. 122) Baur speaks in a somewhat less peremptory sense. St. James 'bekämpft eine einseitige, für das praktische Christenthum nachtheilige Auffassung der paulinischen Lehre.'

[j] Baur, Christenthum, p. 122: 'Der Brief des Jacobus, wie unmöglich verkannt werden kann, die paulinische Rechtfertigungslehre voraussetzt, so kann er auch nur eine antipaulinische, wenn auch nicht unmittelbar gegen den Apostel selbst gerichtete Tendenz haben.'

[k] Messmer, Erkl. des Jacobus-briefes, p. 38: 'Der glaube ist bei Jacobus nichts anders als die Annahme, der Besitz oder auch das leere Bekenntniss der christlichen Wahrheiten (sowohl der Glaubens-als-Sitten-wahrheiten,) Resultat des blossen Hörens und eigentlich bloss in der Erkenntniss liegend. . . . . Ein solcher Glaube kann für sich, wie ein unfruchtbarer Keim, völlig wirkungslos für das Leben in Menschen liegen, oder auch in leeren Gefühlen bestehen; er ist nichts als Namen-und-Scheinchristenthum, das keine Heiligkeit hervorbringt. . . . . Das, was diesem Glauben erst die Seele einhaucht, ist die göttliche Liebe, durch welche der Wille und alle Kräfte des Menschen zum Dienste des Glaubens gefangen genommen werden.'

[LECT.

upon the sacred name of faith a sense which emptied it utterly of its religious value, and which St. Paul would have disavowed as vehemently as St. James. St. James denies that this mere consent of the intellect to a speculative position, carrying with it no necessary demands upon the heart and upon the will, can justify a man before God. But when St. Paul speaks of justifying faith, he means an act of the soul, simple indeed at the moment and in the process of its living action, but complex in its real nature, and profound and far-reaching in its moral effect. The eye of the soul is opened upon the Redeemer: it believes. But in this act of living belief, not the intellect alone, but in reality, although imperceptibly, the whole soul, with all its powers of love and resolution, goes forth to meet its Saviour. This is St. Paul's meaning when he insists upon justifying faith as being *πίστις δι' ἀγάπης ἐνεργουμένη*[l]. Faith, according to St. Paul, when once it lives in the soul, is all Christian practice in the germ. The living apprehension of the Crucified One, whereby the soul attains light and liberty, may be separable in idea, but in fact it is inseparable from a Christian life. If the apprehension of revealed truth does not carry within itself the secret will to yield the whole being to God's quickening grace and guidance, it is spiritually worthless, according to St. Paul. St. Paul goes so far as to tell the Corinthians, that even a faith which was gifted with the power of performing stupendous miracles, if it had not charity, would profit nothing[m]. Thus between St. Paul and St. James there is no real opposition. When St. James speaks of a faith that cannot justify, he means a barren intellectual consent to certain religious truths, a philosophizing temper, cold, thin, heartless, soulless, morally impotent, divorced from the spirit as from the fruits of charity. When St. Paul proclaims that we are justified by faith in Jesus Christ, he means a faith which only realizes its life by love, and which, if it did not love, would cease to live. When St. James contends that 'by works a man is justified, and not by faith only,' he implies that faith is the animating motive which gives to works their justifying power, or rather that works only

[l] Gal. v. 6.

[m] 1 Cor. xiii. 2: *ἐὰν ἔχω πᾶσαν τὴν πίστιν, ὥστε ὄρη μεθιστάνειν, ἀγάπην δὲ μὴ ἔχω, οὐδέν εἰμι.* The *γνῶσις* of 1 Cor. viii. 1 seems to be substantially identical with the bare *πίστις* denounced by St. James, although the former was probably of a more purely scientific and intellectual character. The *ἀγάπη* of 1 Cor. viii. 1 is really the *πίστις δι' ἀγάπης ἐνεργουμένη* of Gal. v. 6.

justify as being the expression of a living faith. When St. Paul argues that a man is justified neither by the works of the Jewish law, nor by the works of natural morality, his argument shews that by a 'work' he means a mere material result or product, a soulless act, unenlivened by the presence of that one supernatural motive which, springing from the grace of Christ, can be indeed acceptable to a perfectly holy God. But if on the question of justification St. James' position is in substance identical with that of St. Paul, yet St. James' position, viewed historically, does undoubtedly presuppose not merely a wide reception of St. Paul's teaching, but a perverse development of one particular side of it. In order to do justice to St. James, we have to contemplate first, the fruitless 'faith' of the Antinomian, with which the Apostle is immediately in conflict, and which he is denouncing; next, the living faith of the Christian believer, as insisted upon by St. Paul, and subsequently caricatured by the Antinomian perversion; lastly, the Object of the believer's living faith, Whose Person and work are so prominent in St. Paul's teaching. It is not too much to say that all this is in the mind of St. James. But there was no necessity for his insisting upon what was well understood; he says only so much as is necessary for his immediate purpose. His Epistle is related to the Pauline Epistles in the general scheme of the New Testament, as an explanatory codicil might be to a will. The codicil does not the less represent the mind of the testator because it is not drawn up by the same lawyer as the will itself. The codicil is rendered necessary by some particular liability to misconstruction, which has become patent since the time at which the will was drawn up. Accordingly the codicil defines the real intention of the testator; it guards that intention against the threatened misconstruction. But it does not repeat in detail all the provisions of the will, in order to protect the true sense of a single clause. Still less does it revoke any one of those provisions; it takes for granted the entire document to which it is appended.

The elementary character of parts of the moral teaching of St. James is sometimes too easily assumed to imply that that Apostle must be held to represent the earliest stage of the supposed developments of apostolical Christianity. But is it not possible that in apostolical as well as in later times, 'advanced' Christians may have occasionally incurred the danger of forgetting some important precepts even of natural morality, or of supposing that their devotion to particular truths or forms of thought, or that their experience of particular states of feeling, constituted a religious warrant for such forgetfulness[n]? If this was indeed the case, St. James' Epistle is placed in its true light when we see in it a healthful appeal to that primal morality, which can never be ignored or slighted without the most certain risk to those revealed truths, such as our Lord's plenary Satisfaction for sin, in which the enlightened conscience finds its final relief from the burden and misery of recognized guilt. If the sensitiveness of conscience be dulled or impaired, the doctrines which relieve the anguish of conscience will soon lose their power. St. Paul himself is perpetually insisting upon the nature and claims of Christian virtue, and on the misery and certain consequences of wilful sin. St. James, as the master both of natural and of Christian ethics, is in truth reinforcing St. Paul, the herald and exponent of the doctrines of redemption and justification. Thus St. James' moral teaching generally, not less than his special polemical discussion of the question of justification, appears to presuppose St. Paul. It presupposes St. Paul as we know him now in his glorious Epistles, enjoining the purest and loftiest Christian sanctity along with the most perfect acceptance by faith of the Person and work of the Divine Redeemer. But it also presupposes St. Paul, as Gnostics who preceded Marcion had already misrepresented him, as the idealized sophist of the earliest Antinomian fancies, the sophist who had proclaimed a practical or avowed divorce between the sanctions of morality and the honour of Christ. There is at times a flavour of irony in St. James' language, such as might force a passage for the voice of truth and love through the dense tangle of Antinomian self-delusions. St. James urges that to listen to Christian teaching without reducing it to practice is but the moral counterpart of a momentary listless glance in a polished mirror[o]; and that genuine devotion is to be really tested by such practical results as works of mercy done to the

[n] After making reference to Luther's designation of this Epistle as an 'Epistle of straw,' a modern French Protestant writer proceeds as follows: 'Nous-mêmes, nous ne pouvons considérer la doctrine de Jacques ni comme bien logique, ni comme suffisante; nous y voyons la grande pensée de Jésus rétrécie et appauvrie par le principe légal du mosaïsme. Le christianisme de Jacques n'était qu'à demi émancipé des entraves de la loi; c'était un degré inférieur du Christianisme, et qui ne contenait pas en germe tous les développements futurs de la vérité chrétienne. Il est douteux que cette Épitre ait jamais converti personne.' Premières Transformations du Christianisme, par A. Coquerel fils. Paris, 1866. (p. 65.)

[o] St. James i. 23: *εἴ τις ἀκροατὴς λόγου ἐστὶ καὶ οὐ ποιητὴς, οὗτος ἔοικεν ἀνδρὶ κατανοοῦντι τὸ πρόσωπον τῆς γενέσεως αὐτοῦ ἐν ἐσόπτρῳ· κατενόησε γὰρ ἑαυτὸν, καὶ ἀπελήλυθε, καὶ εὐθέως ἐπελάθετο ὁποῖος ἦν.*

afflicted and the poor, and by conscientious efforts to secure the inward purity of an unworldly life[p].

2. In his earnest opposition to the Antinomian principle St. James insists upon the continuity of the New dispensation with the Old. Those indeed who do not believe the representations of the great Apostles given us in the Acts to have been a romance of the second century, composed with a view to reconciling the imagined dissensions of the sub-apostolical Church, will not fail to note the significance of St. James' attitude at the Council of Jerusalem. After referring to the prophecy of Amos as confirmatory of St. Peter's teaching respecting the call of the Gentiles, St. James advises that no attempt should be made to impose the Jewish law generally upon the Gentile converts[q]. Four points of observance were to be insisted on, for reasons of very various kinds[r]; but the general tenor of the speech proves how radically the Apostle had broken with Judaism as a living system. Yet in his Epistle the real continuity of the Law and the Gospel is undeniably prominent. Considering Christianity as a rule of life based upon a revealed creed, St. James terms it also a Law. But the Christian Law is no mere reproduction of the Sinaitic. The New Law of Christendom is distinguished by epithets which define its essential superiority to the law of the synagogue, and which moreover indirectly suggest the true dignity of its Founder. The Christian law is the law of liberty —*νόμος τῆς ἐλευθερίας*[s]. To be really obeyed it must be obeyed in freedom. A slave cannot obey the Christian law, because it demands not merely the production of certain outward acts, but the living energy of inward motives, whose soul and essence is love. Only a son whom Christ has freed from slavery, and whose heart would rejoice, if so it might be, to anticipate or to go beyond his Father's Will, can offer that free service which is exacted by the law of liberty. That service secures to all his

[p] St. James i. 27: *θρησκεία καθαρὰ καὶ ἀμίαντος παρὰ τῷ Θεῷ καὶ Πατρὶ αὕτη ἐστὶν, ἐπισκέπτεσθαι ὀρφανοὺς καὶ χήρας ἐν τῇ θλίψει αὐτῶν, ἄσπιλον ἑαυτὸν τηρεῖν ἀπὸ τοῦ κόσμου.*

[q] Acts xv. 14-19.

[r] Ibid. ver. 20.

[s] St. James i. 25: *ὁ δὲ παρακύψας εἰς νόμον τέλειον τὸν τῆς ἐλευθερίας, καὶ παραμείνας, οὗτος οὐκ ἀκροατὴς ἐπιλησμονῆς γενόμενος, ἀλλὰ ποιητὴς ἔργου, οὗτος μακάριος ἐν τῇ ποιήσει αὐτοῦ ἔσται.* Ibid. ii. 12: *οὕτω λαλεῖτε καὶ οὕτω ποιεῖτε, ὡς διὰ νόμου ἐλευθερίας μέλλοντες κρίνεσθαι.* Messmer in loc.: 'Gesetz der Freiheit, weil es nicht mehr ein bloss aüsserliches knechtendes Gebot ist, wie das alte Gesetz, sondern mit dem innerlich umgewandelten Willen uebereinstimmt, wir also nicht mehr aus Zwang, sondern mit freier Liebe dasselbe erfüllen.'

faculties their highest play and exercise; the Christian is most conscious of the buoyant sense of freedom when he is most eager to do the Will of his Heavenly Parent. The Christian law, which is the law of love, is further described as the royal law—*νόμος βασιλικός*[t]. Not merely because the law of love is specifically the first of laws, higher than and inclusive of all other laws[u]; but because Christ, the King of Christians, prescribes this law to Christian love. To obey is to own Christ's legislative supremacy. Once more, the Christian law is the perfect law—*νόμος τέλειος*[x]. It is above human criticism. It will not, like the Mosaic law, be completed by another revelation. It can admit of no possible improvement. It exhibits the whole Will of the unerring Legislator respecting man in his earthly state. It guarantees to man absolute correspondence with the true idea of his life, in other words, his perfection; if only he will obey it. In a like spirit St. James speaks of Christian doctrine as the word of truth—*λόγος ἀληθείας*[y]. Christian doctrine is the absolute truth; and it has an effective regenerating force in the spiritual world, which corresponds to that of God's creative word in the region of physical nature. But Christian doctrine is also the engrafted word—*λόγος ἔμφυτος*[z]. It is capable of being

[t] St. James ii. 8: *εἰ μέντοι νόμον τελεῖτε βασιλικὸν, κατὰ τὴν γραφὴν, Ἀγαπήσεις τὸν πλησίον σου ὡς σεαυτὸν, καλῶς ποιεῖτε.* This compendium of the Christian's whole duty towards his neighbour, as enjoined by our Blessed Lord (St. Matt. xxii. 39; St. Mark xii. 31), is not a mere republication of the Mosaic precept (Lev. xix. 18). In the latter the 'neighbour' is apparently 'one of the children of thy people;' in the former it includes any member of the human family, since it embraced even those against whom the Jew had the strongest religious prepossessions. (St. Luke x. 29, sqq.) This injunction of a love of man as man, according to the measure of each man's love of self, is the law of the true King of humanity, Jesus Christ our Lord.

[u] Rom. xiii. 9.

[x] St. James i. 25.

[y] Ibid. ver. 18: *βουληθεὶς ἀπεκύησεν ἡμᾶς λόγῳ ἀληθείας, εἰς τὸ εἶναι ἡμᾶς ἀπαρχήν τινα τῶν αὐτοῦ κτισμάτων.* *ἀποκύειν* is elsewhere used of the female parent. Hence it indicates the tenderness of the Divine love, as shewn in the new birth of souls; just as *βουληθείς* points to the freedom of the grace which regenerates them, and *ἀπαρχήν τινα τῶν κτισμάτων* to the end and purpose of their regeneration. Compare St. John i. 12, 13: *ὅσοι δὲ ἔλαβον αὐτὸν . . ἐκ Θεοῦ ἐγεννήθησαν.*

[z] St. James i. 21: *ἐν πραΰτητι δέξασθε τὸν ἔμφυτον λόγον, τὸν δυνάμενον σῶσαι τὰς ψυχὰς ὑμῶν.* Messmer in loc.: 'Die Offenbarung heisst hier das eingepflanzte, eingewachsene Wort; nämlich bei der Wiedergeburt durch die christliche Lehre eingepflanzt. Wenn nun von einem Aufnehmen der eingepflanzten Lehre die Rede ist, so ist das natürlich nicht die erste Aufnahme, sondern vielmehr das immer innigere Insichhineinnehmen und

taken up into, and livingly united with, the life of human souls. It will thus bud forth into moral foliage and fruits which, without it, human souls are utterly incapable of yielding. This λόγος is clearly not the mere texture of the language in which the faith is taught. It is not the bare thought of the believer moulded into conformity with the ideas suggested by the language. It is the very substance and core of the doctrine; it is He in Whom the doctrine centres; it is the Person of Jesus Christ Himself, Whose Humanity is the Sprout, Shoot, or Branch of Judah, engrafted by His Incarnation upon the old stock of humanity, and sacramentally engrafted upon all living Christian souls. Is not St. James here in fundamental agreement not merely with St. Paul, but with St. John? St. James' picture of the new law of Christendom harmonizes with St. Paul's teaching, that the old law of Judaism without the grace of Christ does but rouse a sense of sin which it cannot satisfy, and that therefore the law of the spirit of life in Christ Jesus has made Christians free from the law of sin and death [a]. St. James' doctrine of the Engrafted Word is a compendium of the first, third, and sixth chapters of St. John's Gospel; the word written or preached does but unveil to the soul the Word Incarnate, the Word Who can give a new life to human nature, because He is Himself the Source of Life.

It is in correspondence with these currents of doctrine that St. James, although our Lord's own first cousin [b], opens his Epistle by representing himself as standing in the same relation to Jesus Christ as to God. He is the slave of God and of our Lord Jesus Christ [c]. In like manner, throughout his Epistle, he appears to apply the word Κύριος to the God of the Old Testament and to Jesus Christ, quite indifferently. Especially

Aneignen derselben und das Sichhineinleben in dieselbe.' See too Dean Alford in loc.: 'The Word whose attribute and ἀρετή it is to be ἔμφυτος, and which is ἔμφυτος, awaiting your reception of it, to spring up and take up your being into it and make you new plants.'

[a] Baur admits that 'dem Verfasser des Briefs auch die paulinische Verinnerlichung des Gesetzes nicht fremd, indem er nicht blos das Gebot der Liebe als königliches Gesetz bezeichnet, sondern auch von einem Gesetze der Freiheit spricht, zu welchem ihm das Gesetz nur dadurch geworden sein kann, dass er, der Aeusserlichkeit des Gesetzes gegenüber sich innerlich ebenso frei von ihm wusste, wie der Apostel Paulus von seinem Standpunkt aus.' Christenthum, p. 122.

[b] Comp. St. Matt. xxvii. 56, St. Mark xv. 40, with St. John xix. 25. See Pearson on Creed, Art. iii.; Mill on Myth. Int. p. 226; Bp. Ellicott, Huls. Lect. pp. 97, 354.

[c] St. James i. 1: Ἰάκωβος Θεοῦ καὶ Κυρίου Ἰησοῦ Χριστοῦ δοῦλος.

[LECT.

noteworthy is his assertion that the Lord Jesus Christ, the Judge of men, is not the delegated representative of an absent Majesty, but is Himself the Legislator enforcing His own laws. The Lawgiver, he says, is One Being with the Judge Who can save and can destroy[d]; the Son of man, coming in the clouds of heaven, has enacted the law which He thus administers. With a reverence which is as practical as his teaching is suggestive, St. James in this one short Epistle reproduces more of the words spoken by Jesus Christ our Lord than are to be found in all the other Epistles of the New Testament taken together[e]. He hints that all social barriers between man and man are as nothing when we place mere human eminence in the light of Christ's majestic Person; and when he names the faith of Jesus Christ, he terms it with solemn emphasis the 'faith of the Lord of Glory,' thus adopting one of the most magnificent of St. Paul's expressions[f], and attributing to our Lord a Majesty altogether above this human world[g]. In short, St. James' recognition of the doctrine of our Lord's Divinity is just what we might expect it to be if we take into account the mainly practical scope of his Epistle. Our Lord's Divinity is never once formally proposed as a doctrine of the faith; but it is largely, although indirectly, implied. It is implied in language which would be exaggerated and overstrained on any other supposition. It is implied in a reserve which may be felt to mean at least as much as the most demonstrative protestations. A few passing expressions of the lowliest reverence disclose the great doctrine of the Church

[d] St. James iv. 12: *εἷς ἐστιν ὁ νομοθέτης καὶ κριτὴς ὁ δυνάμενος σῶσαι καὶ ἀπολέσαι.* (*καὶ κριτὴς* is omitted by text recept., inserted by A. B. א.) So De Wette: 'Einer ist der Gesetzgeber und Richter, der da vermag zu retten und zu verderben.' Cf. Alford in loc., who quotes this.

[e] The following are his references to the Sermon on the Mount. St. James i. 2; St. Matt. v. 10-12. St. James i. 4; St. Matt. v. 48. St. James i. 5; St. Matt. vii. 7. St. James i. 9; St. Matt. v. 3. St. James i. 20; St. Matt. v. 22. St. James ii. 13; St. Matt. vi. 14, 15, v. 7. St. James ii. 14 sqq.; St. Matt. vii. 21 sqq. St. James iii. 17, 18; St. Matt. v. 9. St. James iv. 4; St. Matt. vi. 24. St. James iv. 10; St. Matt. v. 3, 4. St. James iv. 11; St. Matt. vii. 1 sqq. St. James v. 2; St. Matt. vi. 19. St. James v. 10; St. Matt. v. 12. St. James v. 12; St. Matt. v. 33 sqq. And for other discourses of our Lord: St. James i. 14; St. Matt. xv. 19. St. James iv. 12; St. Matt. x. 28. Again, St. James v. 1–6; St. Luke vi. 24 sqq. See reff.; and Alford, vol. iv. p. 107, note.

[f] 1 Cor. ii. 8.

[g] St. James ii. 1: *ἀδελφοί μου, μὴ ἐν προσωποληψίαις ἔχετε τὴν πίστιν τοῦ Κυρίου ἡμῶν Ἰησοῦ Χριστοῦ τῆς δόξης.* Here *τῆς δόξης* is best explained as a second genitive governed by *Κυρίου*. Dean Alford suggests that it may be an epithetal genitive, such as constantly follows the mention of the Divine Name.

respecting the Person of her Lord, throned in the background of the Apostle's thought. And if the immediate interests of his ministry oblige St. James to confine himself to considerations which do not lead him more fully to exhibit the doctrine, we are not allowed, as we read him, to forget the love and awe which veil and treasure it, so tenderly and so reverently, in the inmost sanctuary of his illuminated soul.

II. Of St. Peter's recorded teaching there are two distinct stages in the New Testament. The first is represented by his missionary sermons in the Acts of the Apostles; the second by his general Epistles.

1. Although Jesus Christ is always the central Subject in the sermons of this Apostle, yet the distinctness with which he exhibits our Lord in the glory of His Divine Nature seems to vary with the varying capacity for receiving truth on the part of his audience. Like Jesus Christ Himself, St. Peter teaches as men are able to bear his doctrine; he does not cast pearls before swine. In his missionary sermons he is addressing persons who were believers in the Jewish dispensation, and who were also our Lord's contemporaries. Accordingly, his sermons contain a double appeal; first, to the known facts of our Lord's Life and Death, and above all, of His Resurrection from the dead; and secondly, to the correspondence of these facts with the predictions of the Hebrew Scriptures. Like St. James, St. Peter lays especial stress on the continuity subsisting between Judaism and the Gospel. But while St. James insists upon the moral element of that connexion, St. Peter addresses himself rather to the prophetical. Even before the day of Pentecost, St. Peter points to the Psalter as foreshadowing the fall of Judas[i]. When preaching to the multitude which had just witnessed the Pentecostal gifts, St. Peter observes that these wonders are merely a realization of the prediction of Joel respecting the last days[k]; and he argues elaborately that the language of David in the sixteenth Psalm could not have been fulfilled in the case of the prophet-king himself, still lying among his people in his honoured sepulchre, while it had been literally fulfilled by Jesus Christ[l], Who had notoriously risen from the grave. In his sermon to the multitude after the healing of the lame man in the Porch of Solomon, St. Peter contends that the sufferings of Christ had been 'shewed before' on the part of the God of

[i] Acts i. 16, 20. Cf. Ps. xli. 9, lxix. 25.

[k] Acts ii. 14-21; Joel ii. 28-31.

[l] Acts ii. 24-36.

Israel by the mouth of all His prophets [m], and that in Jesus Christ the prediction of Moses respecting a coming Prophet, to Whom the true Israel would yield an implicit obedience, had received its explanation [n]. When arraigned before the Council [o], the Apostle insists that Jesus is that true 'Corner-stone' of the temple of souls, which had been foretold both by Isaiah [p], and by a later Psalmist [q]; and that although He had been set at nought by the builders of Israel, He was certainly exalted and honoured by God. In the instruction delivered to Cornelius before his baptism, St. Peter states that 'all the prophets give witness' to Jesus, 'that through His Name, whosoever believeth on Him shall receive remission of sins [r].' And we seem to trace the influence of St. Peter, as the first great Christian expositor of prophecy, in the teaching of the deacons St. Stephen and St. Philip. St. Philip's exposition of Christian doctrine to the Ethiopian eunuch was based upon Isaiah's prediction of the Passion [s]. St. Stephen's argument before his judges was cut short by a violent interruption, while it was yet incomplete. But St. Stephen, like St. Peter, appeals to the prediction in Deuteronomy of the Prophet to Whom Israel would hearken [t]. And the drift of the protomartyr's address goes to shew, that the whole course of the history of Israel pointed to the advent of One Who should be greater than either the law or the temple [u], —of One in Whom Israel's wonderful history would reach its natural climax,—of that 'Just One' Who in truth had already come, but Who, like prophets before Him, had been betrayed and murdered by a people, still as of old, 'stiffnecked and uncircumcised in heart and ears [x].'

It is not too much to say that in the teaching of the earliest Church, as represented by the missionary discourses of St. Peter and the deacons, Jesus Christ is the very soul and end of Jewish prophecy. This would of itself suggest an idea of His Person which rises above any merely Humanitarian standard. St. Peter indeed places himself habitually at the point of view which would enable him to appeal to the actual experience of the generation he was addressing. He begins with our Lord's Humiliation, which men had witnessed, and then he proceeds to describe His Exaltation as the honour put by God upon His

[m] Acts iii. 18. [n] Ibid. iii. 22–24; Deut. xviii. 15, 18, 19.
[o] Acts iv. 11. [p] Isa. xxviii. 16.
[q] Ps. cxviii. 22. Our Lord Himself claimed the prophecy, St. Matt. xxi. 42. [r] Acts x. 43. [s] Ibid. viii. 32–35.
[t] Ibid. vii. 37. [u] Ibid. vi. 13. [x] Ibid. vii. 51–53.

Human Nature. He speaks of our Lord's Humanity with fearless plainness[y]. The Man Christ Jesus is exhibited to the world as a miracle-worker; as Man, He is anointed with the Holy Ghost and with power[z]; as the true Servant of God, He is glorified by the God of the patriarchs[a]; He is raised from the dead by Divine Power[b]; He is made by God both Lord and Christ[c]; and He will be sent by the Lord at 'the times of refreshing[d]' as the ordained Judge of quick and dead[e]. But this general representation of the Human Nature by Which Christ had entered into Jewish history, is interspersed with glimpses of His Divine Personality Itself, Which is veiled by His Manhood. Thus we find St. Peter in the porch of Solomon applying to our Lord a magnificent title, which at once carries our thoughts into the very heart of the distinctive Christology of St. John. Christ, although crucified and slain, is yet the Leader or Prince of Life—'Αρχηγὸς τῆς ζωῆς[f]. That He should be held in bondage by the might of death was not possible[g]. The heavens *must* receive Him[h], and He is now the Lord of all things[i]. It is He Who from His heavenly throne has poured out upon the earth the gifts of Pentecost[k]. His Name spoken on earth has a wonder-working power[l]; as unveiling His Nature and office, it is a symbol which faith reverently treasures, and by the might of which the servants of God can relieve even physical suffering[m]. As a refuge for sinners the Name of Jesus stands alone; no other Name has

[y] Acts ii. 22: Ἰησοῦν τὸν Ναζωραῖον, ἄνδρα [not here the generic ἄνθρωπον] ἀπὸ τοῦ Θεοῦ ἀποδεδειγμένον εἰς ὑμᾶς δυνάμεσι καὶ τέρασι καὶ σημείοις, οἷς ἐποίησε δι' αὐτοῦ ὁ Θεὸς ἐν μέσῳ ὑμῶν.

[z] Ibid. x. 38.   [a] Ibid. iii. 13.

[b] Ibid. ii. 24, iii. 15, iv. 10, v. 31, x. 40.   [c] Ibid. ii. 36.

[d] Ibid. iii. 19, 20.   [e] Ibid. x. 42.   [f] Ibid. iii. 15.

[g] Ibid. ii. 24: ὃν ὁ Θεὸς ἀνέστησε, λύσας τὰς ὠδῖνας τοῦ θανάτου, καθότι οὐκ ἦν δυνατὸν κρατεῖσθαι αὐτὸν ὑπ' αὐτοῦ. This 'impossibility' depended not merely on the fact that prophecy had predicted Christ's resurrection, but on the dignity of Christ's Person, implied in the existence of any such prophecy respecting Him.

[h] Ibid. iii. 21: ὃν δεῖ οὐρανὸν μὲν δέξασθαι ἄχρι χρόνων ἀποκαταστάσεως πάντων.

[i] Ibid. x. 36: οὗτός ἐστι πάντων Κύριος.

[k] Ibid. ii. 33: ἐξέχεε τοῦτο ὃ νῦν ὑμεῖς βλέπετε καὶ ἀκούετε.

[l] Ibid. iii. 6: ἐν τῷ ὀνόματι Ἰησοῦ Χριστοῦ τοῦ Ναζωραίου, ἔγειραι καὶ περιπάτει.

[m] Ibid. ver. 16: καὶ ἐπὶ τῇ πίστει τοῦ ὀνόματος αὐτοῦ, τοῦτον ὃν θεωρεῖτε καὶ οἴδατε, ἐστερέωσε τὸ ὄνομα αὐτοῦ. Ibid. iv. 10: γνωστὸν ἔστω πᾶσιν ὑμῖν καὶ παντὶ τῷ λαῷ Ἰσραήλ, ὅτι ἐν τῷ ὀνόματι Ἰησοῦ Χριστοῦ τοῦ Ναζωραίου, ὃν ὑμεῖς ἐσταυρώσατε, ὃν ὁ Θεὸς ἤγειρεν ἐκ νεκρῶν, ἐν τούτῳ οὗτος παρέστηκεν ἐνώπιον ὑμῶν ὑγιής.

been given under heaven whereby the one true salvation can be guaranteed to the sons of men[n]. Here St. Peter clearly implies that the religion of Jesus is the true, the universal, the absolute religion. This implication of itself suggests much beyond as to the true dignity of Christ's Person. Is it conceivable that He Who is Himself the sum and substance of His religion, Whose Name has such power on earth, and Who wields the resources and is invested with the glories of heaven, is notwithstanding in the thought of His first apostles only a glorified man, or only a super-angelic intelligence? Do we not interpret these early discourses most naturally, when we bear in mind the measure of reticence which active missionary work always renders necessary, if truth is to win its way amidst prejudice and opposition? And will not this consideration alone enable us to do justice to those vivid glimpses of Christ's Higher Nature, the fuller exhibition of Which is before us in the Apostle's general Epistles?

2. In St. Peter's general Epistles it is easy to trace the same mind as that which speaks to us in the earliest missionary sermons of the Acts. As addressed to Christian believers[o], these Epistles exhibit Christian doctrine in its fulness, but with an eye to practical objects, and without the methodical completeness of an oral instruction. Christian doctrine is not propounded as a new announcement: the writer takes it for granted as furnishing a series of motives, the force of which would be admitted by those who had already recognized the true majesty and proportions of the faith. St. Peter announces himself as the Apostle of Jesus Christ; he is Christ's slave as well as His Apostle[p]. In his Epistles, St. Peter lays the great stress on prophecy which is so observable in his missionary sermons. Thus, as in his speech before the Council, so in his first Epistle, he specially refers[q] to the prophecy of the Rejected Corner-stone, which our Lord had applied to Himself. But St. Peter's general doctrine of our Lord's relation to Hebrew prophecy should be more particularly noticed. In our day theories have been put forward on this subject which appear to represent the Hebrew prophetical Scrip-

[n] Acts iv. 12: *οὐκ ἔστιν ἐν ἄλλῳ οὐδενὶ ἡ σωτηρία· οὔτε γὰρ ὄνομά ἐστιν ἕτερον ὑπὸ τὸν οὐρανὸν τὸ δεδομένον ἐν ἀνθρώποις, ἐν ᾧ δεῖ σωθῆναι ἡμᾶς.*

[o] 1 St. Pet. i. 1, 2: *ἐκλεκτοῖς παρεπιδήμοις διασπορᾶς, ... κατὰ πρόγνωσιν Θεοῦ Πατρὸς, ἐν ἁγιασμῷ Πνεύματος, εἰς ὑπακοὴν καὶ ῥαντισμὸν αἵματος Ἰησοῦ Χριστοῦ.* 2 St. Pet. i. 1: *τοῖς ἰσότιμον ὑμῖν λαχοῦσι πίστιν.*

[p] 1 St. Pet. i. 1: *ἀπόστολος Ἰησοῦ Χριστοῦ.* 2 St. Pet. i. 1: *δοῦλος καὶ ἀπόστολος Ἰησοῦ Χριστοῦ.*

[q] 1 St. Pet. ii. 6. Cf. Acts iv. 11; Isa. xxviii. 16; Ps. cxviii. 22.

tures as little better than a large dictionary of quotations, to which the writers and preachers of the New Testament are said to have had recourse when they wished to illustrate their subject by some shadowy analogy, or by some vague semblance of a happy anticipation. St. Peter is as widely removed from this position, as it is possible to conceive. According to St. Peter, the prophets of the Old Testament did not only utter literal predictions of the expected Christ, but in doing this they were Christ's own servants, His heralds, His organs. He Who is the subject of the Gospel story, and the living Ruler of the Church, had also, by His Spirit, been Master and Teacher of the prophets. Under His guidance it was that they had foretold His sufferings. It was the Spirit of Christ who was in the prophets, testifying beforehand the sufferings of Christ and the glories that would follow [r]. The prophets did not at first learn the full scope and meaning of the words they uttered [s], but they spoke glorious truths which the Church of Jesus understands and enjoys [t]. Thus the proclamation of Christian doctrine is older than the Incarnation: Christianity strikes its roots far back into the past of ancient Israel. The pre-existent Christ, moulding the utterances of Israel's prophets to proclaim their anticipations of His advent, had indeed reigned in the old theocracy; and yet the privileged terms in which the members of God's elder kingdom upon earth described their prerogatives were really applicable, in a deeper sense, to those who lived within the kingdom of the Divine Incarnation [u]. Indeed, St. Peter's language on the nature and privileges of the Christian life is suggestive of the highest conception of Him Who is

[r] 1 St. Pet. i. 11: *τὸ ἐν αὐτοῖς Πνεῦμα Χριστοῦ, προμαρτυρόμενον τὰ εἰς Χριστὸν παθήματα, καὶ τὰς μετὰ ταῦτα δόξας.* Here *Χριστοῦ* is a genitive of the subject. Olshausen: 'Christus ist dem Petrus vor seiner Erscheinung ein real Existirender, und wirkt selbst durch seinen Geist in den Propheten die Weissagung von sich.' See Huther and Wiesinger in loc.

[s] 1 St. Pet. i. 10, 11: *περὶ ἧς σωτηρίας ἐξεζήτησαν καὶ ἐξηρεύνησαν προφῆται οἱ περὶ τῆς εἰς ὑμᾶς χάριτος προφητεύσαντες, ἐρευνῶντες εἰς τίνα ἢ ποῖον καιρὸν ἐδήλου τὸ ἐν αὐτοῖς Πνεῦμα Χριστοῦ.* Ibid. ver. 12: *οἷς ἀπεκαλύφθη ὅτι οὐχ ἑαυτοῖς, ἡμῖν δὲ διηκόνουν αὐτὰ, ἃ νῦν ἀνηγγέλη ὑμῖν.*

[t] 2 St. Pet. i. 20: *πᾶσα προφητεία γραφῆς ἰδίας ἐπιλύσεως οὐ γίνεται.* The Spirit in the Church understands the Spirit speaking by the prophets.

[u] 1 St. Pet. ii. 9, 10: *ὑμεῖς δὲ γένος ἐκλεκτὸν, βασίλειον ἱεράτευμα, ἔθνος ἅγιον, λαὸς εἰς περιποίησιν, ὅπως τὰς ἀρετὰς ἐξαγγείλητε τοῦ ἐκ σκότους ὑμᾶς καλέσαντος εἰς τὸ θαυμαστὸν αὐτοῦ φῶς· οἱ ποτὲ οὐ λαὸς, νῦν δὲ λαὸς Θεοῦ· οἱ οὐκ ἠλεημένοι, νῦν δὲ ἐλεηθέντες.* Ibid. ver. 5: *ὡς λίθοι ζῶντες οἰκοδομεῖσθε, οἶκος πνευματικὸς, ἱεράτευμα ἅγιον, ἀνενέγκαι πνευματικὰς θυσίας εὐπροσδέκτους τῷ Θεῷ διὰ Ἰησοῦ Χριστοῦ.*

its Author and its Object. St. Peter speaks of conversion from Judaism or heathendom as the 'being called out of darkness into God's marvellous light [x].' It is the happiness of Christians to suffer and to be reviled for the Name of Christ [y]. The Spirit of glory and of God rests upon them. The Spirit is blasphemed by the unbelieving world, but He is visibly honoured by the family of God's children [z]. It is the Person of Jesus in Whom the spiritual life of His Church centres [a]. The Christians whom St. Peter is addressing never saw Him in the days of His flesh; they do not see Him now with the eye of sense. But they love Him, invisible as He is, because they believe in Him. The eye of their faith does see Him. The Lord Christ is present in their hearts; they are to 'sanctify' Him there, as God was 'sanctified' by the worship of Israel [b]. They rejoice in this clear constant inward vision with a joy which language cannot describe, and which is radiant with the glory of the highest spiritual beauty. They are in possession of a spiritual sense [c] whereby the goodness of Jesus may be even tasted; and yet the truths on which their souls are fed are mysteries so profound as to rouse the keen but baffled wonder of the intelligences of heaven [d]. Such language appears to point irresistibly to the existence of a supernatural religion with a superhuman Founder; unless we are to denude it of all spiritual meaning whatever, by saying that it only reflects the habitual exaggeration of Eastern fervour. Why is the intellectual atmosphere of the Church described as 'marvellous light'? Why is suffering for Jesus so much a matter for sincere self-congratulation? Why does the

[x] Ubi supra.

[y] 1 St. Pet. iv. 13: *καθὸ κοινωνεῖτε τοῖς τοῦ Χριστοῦ παθήμασι, χαίρετε, ἵνα καὶ ἐν τῇ ἀποκαλύψει τῆς δόξης αὐτοῦ χαρῆτε ἀγαλλιώμενοι. Εἰ ὀνειδίζεσθε ἐν ὀνόματι Χριστοῦ, μακάριοι.*

[z] Ibid. ver. 14: *ὅτι τὸ τῆς δόξης καὶ τὸ τοῦ Θεοῦ Πνεῦμα ἐφ' ὑμᾶς ἀναπαύεται· κατὰ μὲν αὐτοὺς βλασφημεῖται, κατὰ δὲ ὑμᾶς δοξάζεται.*

[a] Ibid. i. 7, 8: *Ἰησοῦ Χριστοῦ· ὃν οὐκ εἰδότες ἀγαπᾶτε, εἰς ὃν ἄρτι μὴ ὁρῶντες, πιστεύοντες δὲ, ἀγαλλιᾶσθε χαρᾷ ἀνεκλαλήτῳ καὶ δεδοξασμένῃ.*

[b] Ibid. iii. 15: *Κύριον δὲ τὸν Χριστὸν ἁγιάσατε ἐν ταῖς καρδίαις ὑμῶν.* That *Χριστὸν* and not *Θεὸν* is the true reading here, see Scrivener, Introduction to Crit. N. T. p. 456. Cf. Isa. viii. 13. Isaiah is quoted again in 1 St. Pet. ii. 8.

[c] 1 St. Pet. ii. 3: *εἴπερ ἐγεύσασθε ὅτι χρηστὸς ὁ Κύριος.* St. Peter is using the Psalmist's language in reference to Jehovah (Ps. xxxiv. 8), but the context shews him to be speaking of Christ. Cf. Heb. vi. 4: *γευσαμένους τε τῆς δωρεᾶς τῆς ἐπουρανίου.* There is possibly in both passages an indirect reference to sacramental communion.

[d] 1 St. Pet. i. 12: *εἰς ἃ ἐπιθυμοῦσιν ἄγγελοι παρακύψαι.*

Divine Spirit rest so surely upon Christian confessors? Why is the Invisible Jesus the Object of such love, the Source of such inexpressible and glorious joy; if, after all, the religion of Jesus is merely a higher phase of human opinion and feeling, and His Church a human organization, and His Person only human, or at least not literally Divine? The language of St. Peter respecting the Christian life[e] manifestly points to a Divine Christ. And if the Christ of St. Peter had been the Christ, we will not say of a Strauss or of a Renan, but the Christ of a Socinus, nay, the Christ of an Arius, it is not easy to understand what should have moved the angels with that strong desire to bend from their thrones above, that they might gaze with unsuccessful intentness at the humiliations of a created being, their peer or their inferior in the scale of creation. Surely the Angels must be longing to unveil a transcendent mystery, or a series of mysteries, such as are in fact the mystery of the Divine Incarnation and the consequences which depend on it in the kingdom of grace. St. Peter's words are sober and truthful if read by the light of faith in an Incarnate God; divorced from such a faith, they are fanciful, inflated, exaggerated.

St. Peter lays especial stress both on the moral significance and on the atoning power of the Death of Jesus Christ. Here he enters within that circle of truths which are taught most fully in the Epistle to the Hebrews; and his exhibition of the Passion might almost appear to presuppose the particular Christological teaching of that Epistle. St. Peter says that 'Christ has once suffered for sins, the Just for the unjust, that He might bring us to God[f].' This vicarious suffering depended upon the fact that Jesus, when dying, impersonated sinful humanity. 'He bare our sins in His own Body on the tree[g].' Stricken by the anguish of His Passion, the dying Christ is the consummate Model[h] for all Christian sufferers, in His innocence[i], in His silence[j], in His perfect resignation[k]. But also the souls of men,

[e] 1 St. Pet. iii. 16: τὴν ἀγαθὴν ἐν Χριστῷ ἀναστροφήν. Cf. v. 14.

[f] Ibid. ver. 18: Χριστὸς ἅπαξ περὶ ἁμαρτιῶν ἔπαθε, Δίκαιος ὑπὲρ ἀδίκων, ἵνα ἡμᾶς προσαγάγῃ τῷ Θεῷ.

[g] Ibid. ii. 24: ὃς τὰς ἁμαρτίας ἡμῶν αὐτὸς ἀνήνεγκεν ἐν τῷ σώματι αὐτοῦ ἐπὶ τὸ ξύλον.

[h] Ibid. ver. 21: Χριστὸς ἔπαθεν ὑπὲρ ἡμῶν, ἡμῖν ὑπολιμπάνων ὑπογραμμὸν, ἵνα ἐπακολουθήσητε τοῖς ἴχνεσιν αὐτοῦ.

[i] Ibid. ver. 22: ὃς ἁμαρτίαν οὐκ ἐποίησεν, οὐδὲ εὑρέθη δόλος ἐν τῷ στόματι αὐτοῦ. Isa. liii. 9; 2 Cor. v. 21; 1 St. John iii. 5.

[j] 1 St. Pet. ii. 23: ὃς λοιδορούμενος οὐκ ἀντελοιδόρει, πάσχων οὐκ ἠπείλει. In the ἠπείλει there lies the consciousness of power.

[k] Ibid.: παρεδίδου δὲ τῷ κρίνοντι δικαίως.

wounded by the shafts of sin, may be healed by the virtue of that sacred Pain[l]; and a special power to wash out the stains of moral guilt is expressly ascribed to the Redeemer's Blood. The Christian as such is predestined in the Eternal Counsels, not merely to submission to the Christian faith, but also to 'a sprinkling of the Blood of Jesus Christ[m].' The Apostle earnestly insists that it was no mere perishable earthly treasure, no silver or golden wares, whereby Christians had been bought out of their old bondage to the traditional errors and accustomed sins of Judaism or of heathenism. The mighty spell of moral and intellectual darkness had indeed been broken, but by no less a ransom than the Precious Blood of Christ, the Lamb without blemish and Immaculate[n]. Are we to suppose that while using this burning language to extol the Precious Blood of redemption, St. Peter is recklessly following a rhetorical impulse, or that he is obscuring the moral meaning of the Passion, by dwelling upon its details in misleading language, which savours too strongly of the sacrificial ritual of the temple? Is he not even echoing the Baptist[o]? Is he not in correspondence with his brother apostles? Is he not summarizing St. Paul[p]? Is he not anticipating St. John[q]? Certainly this earnest recognition of Christ's true Humanity as the seat of His sufferings is a most essential feature of the Apostle's doctrine[r]; but what is it that gives to Christ's Human acts and sufferings such preterhuman value? Is it not that the truth of Christ's Divine Personality underlies this entire description of

[l] 1 St. Pet. ii. 24: οὗ τῷ μώλωπι αὐτοῦ ἰάθητε.

[m] Ibid. i. 2: εἰς ὑπακοὴν καὶ ῥαντισμὸν αἵματος Ἰησοῦ Χριστοῦ.

[n] Ibid. vers. 18, 19: εἰδότες ὅτι οὐ φθαρτοῖς, ἀργυρίῳ ἢ χρυσίῳ, ἐλυτρώθητε ἐκ τῆς ματαίας ὑμῶν ἀναστροφῆς πατροπαραδότου, ἀλλὰ τιμίῳ αἵματι ὡς ἀμνοῦ ἀμώμου καὶ ἀσπίλου Χριστοῦ. Exod. xii. 5.

[o] St. John i. 29: ἴδε ὁ ἀμνὸς τοῦ Θεοῦ, ὁ αἴρων τὴν ἁμαρτίαν τοῦ κόσμου. It is impossible to doubt that the sacrificial rather than the moral ideas associated with the 'Lamb' are here in question. See Alford in loc.

[p] Acts xx. 28: ποιμαίνειν τὴν ἐκκλησίαν τοῦ Θεοῦ, ἣν περιεποιήσατο διὰ τοῦ ἰδίου αἵματος. 1 Cor. v. 7: τὸ πάσχα ἡμῶν ἐτύθη Χριστός. Heb. ix. 12: διὰ τοῦ ἰδίου αἵματος εἰσῆλθεν ἐφάπαξ εἰς τὰ ἅγια, αἰωνίαν λύτρωσιν εὑράμενος.

[q] 1 St. John i. 7: τὸ αἷμα Ἰησοῦ Χριστοῦ τοῦ Υἱοῦ αὐτοῦ καθαρίζει ἡμᾶς ἀπὸ πάσης ἁμαρτίας. Rev. i. 5: τῷ ἀγαπήσαντι ἡμᾶς καὶ λύσαντι ἡμᾶς ἀπὸ τῶν ἁμαρτιῶν ἡμῶν ἐν τῷ αἵματι αὐτοῦ . . . . αὐτῷ ἡ δόξα καὶ τὸ κράτος εἰς τοὺς αἰῶνας τῶν αἰώνων. ἀμήν. Ibid. v. 9: ἄξιος εἶ λαβεῖν τὸ βιβλίον, καὶ ἀνοῖξαι τὰς σφραγῖδας αὐτοῦ· ὅτι ἐσφάγης καὶ ἠγόρασας τῷ Θεῷ ἡμᾶς ἐν τῷ αἵματί σου.

[r] St. Peter expressly alludes to our Lord's Human Body (1 St. Pet. ii. 24, iii. 18, iv. 1), and to His Human Soul, when descending to preach to the spirits in prison (Ibid. iii. 18), after Its separation from His Body at death.

His redemptive work, rescuing it from the exaggeration and turgidity with which it would be fairly chargeable, if Christ were merely human or less than God? That this is in fact the case is abundantly manifest[s]; and indeed the Person of Christ appears to be hinted at in St. Peter's Epistle, by the same august expression which has been noticed as common to St. James and to St. John. The Logos or Word of God, living and abiding for ever[t], is the Author of the soul's new birth: and Christ Jesus our Lord does not only bring us this Logos from heaven; He is this Logos. And thus in His home of glory, angels and authorities and powers are made subject unto Him[u]; and He is not said to have been taken up into heaven, but to have gone up thither, as though by His own deed and will[v]. And when St. Peter exhorts Christians to act in such a manner that God in all things may be glorified through Jesus Christ, he pauses reverently at this last most precious and sacred Name, to add, 'to Whom is the glory and the power unto ages beyond ages[w].'

St. Peter's second Epistle[x], like his first, begins and ends with Jesus[y]. Its main positive theme is the importance of the higher practical knowledge[z] of our Lord and Saviour Jesus Christ[a]. Jesus is not set before Christians as a revered and departed Teacher whose words are to be gathered up and studied; He is set forth rather as an Invisible and Living Person Who is to be spiritually known by souls. Along with this practical knowledge of Jesus, as with knowledge of God, there will be an increase of grace, and of its resultant inward evidence,

[s] 1 St. Pet. i. 20: φανερωθέντος implies Christ's Pre-existence.

[t] Ibid. ver. 23: ἀναγεγεννημένοι οὐκ ἐκ σπορᾶς φθαρτῆς, ἀλλὰ ἀφθάρτου, διὰ λόγου ζῶντος Θεοῦ καὶ μένοντος εἰς τὸν αἰῶνα. By identifying the λόγος here with the ῥῆμα (ver. 25) that proclaims Him, Baur maintains his paradox, that in St. Peter's Epistles the written word is substituted for, and does the work of, the Person of Christ in St. Paul's writings. Vorlesungen, p. 296.

[u] 1 St. Pet. iii. 22: ὑποταγέντων αὐτῷ ἀγγέλων καὶ ἐξουσιῶν καὶ δυνάμεων.

[v] Ibid.: ὅς ἐστιν ἐν δεξιᾷ τοῦ Θεοῦ πορευθεὶς εἰς οὐρανόν.

[w] Ibid. iv. 11: ἵνα ἐν πᾶσι δοξάζηται ὁ Θεὸς διὰ Ἰησοῦ Χριστοῦ, ᾧ ἐστιν ἡ δόξα καὶ τὸ κράτος εἰς τοὺς αἰῶνας τῶν αἰώνων. ἀμήν. Here ᾧ is naturally referred to Ἰησοῦ Χριστοῦ which immediately precedes it. See, however, Huther, in loc.

[x] For an examination of the arguments which have been urged against the genuineness and authenticity of this Epistle, see Olshausen, Opuscula Theologica, pp. 1-88, and Canon Cook's art. 'Peter,' in Smith's Dict. Bibl.

[y] 2 St. Pet. i. 1, iii. 18.

[z] ἐπίγνωσις.

[a] 2 St. Pet. i. 2, 8, ii. 20, iii. 18.

spiritual peace [b]. For this practical knowledge of Jesus is the crowning point of other Christian attainments [c]. It is the consummate result both of faith and practice, both of the intellectual and of the moral sides of the Christian life. In the long line of graces which this special knowledge implies, are faith and general religious knowledge on the one hand, and on the other, moral strength, self-restraint, patience, piety, brotherly love, and, in its broadest sense, charity [d]. In this higher knowledge of Jesus, all these excellences find their end and their completion. On any other path, the soul is abandoned to spiritual blindness, tending more and more to utter forgetfulness of all past purifications from sin [e]. For this higher practical knowledge of Jesus Christ is the means whereby Christians escape from the polluting impurities of the life of the heathen world [f]. It raises Christian souls towards the Unseen King in His glory; it secures their admission to His everlasting realm [g]. If Christians would not be carried away from their steadfast adherence to the truth and life of Christianity by the errors of those who hate all law, let them endeavour to grow in this blessed knowledge of Jesus [h]. The prominence given to the Person of Christ, in this doctrine of an *ἐπίγνωσις* of which His Person is the Object, leads us up to the truth of His real Divinity. If Jesus, thus known and loved, were not accounted God, then we must say that God is in this Epistle thrown utterly into the background, and that His human messenger has taken His place.

Nor is the negative and polemical side of the Epistle much less significant than its constructive and hortatory side. The special misery of the false teachers of whom the Apostle speaks as likely to afflict the Church, will consist in their 'denying the

[b] 2 St. Pet. i. 2: *χάρις ὑμῖν καὶ εἰρήνη πληθυνθείη ἐν ἐπιγνώσει τοῦ Θεοῦ, καὶ Ἰησοῦ τοῦ Κυρίου ἡμῶν.*

[c] Ibid. ver. 8: *ταῦτα γὰρ* (that is, the eight graces previously enumerated) *ὑμῖν ὑπάρχοντα καὶ πλεονάζοντα, οὐκ ἀργοὺς οὐδὲ ἀκάρπους καθίστησιν εἰς τὴν τοῦ Κυρίου ἡμῶν Ἰησοῦ Χριστοῦ ἐπίγνωσιν.*

[d] Ibid. vers. 5, 6, 7.

[e] Ibid. ver. 9.

[f] Ibid. ii. 20: *ἀποφυγόντες τὰ μιάσματα τοῦ κόσμου ἐν ἐπιγνώσει τοῦ Κυρίου καὶ σωτῆρος Ἰησοῦ Χριστοῦ.* Cf. Ibid. i. 4: *ἀποφυγόντες τῆς ἐν κόσμῳ ἐν ἐπιθυμίᾳ φθορᾶς.*

[g] Ibid. i. 11: *οὕτω γὰρ πλουσίως ἐπιχορηγηθήσεται ὑμῖν ἡ εἴσοδος εἰς τὴν αἰώνιον βασιλείαν τοῦ Κυρίου ἡμῶν καὶ σωτῆρος Ἰησοῦ Χριστοῦ.*

[h] Ibid. iii. 17, 18: *φυλάσσεσθε, ἵνα μὴ τῇ τῶν ἀθέσμων πλάνῃ συναπαχθέντες, ἐκπέσητε τοῦ ἰδίου στηριγμοῦ· αὐξάνετε δὲ ἐν χάριτι καὶ γνώσει τοῦ Κυρίου ἡμῶν καὶ σωτῆρος Ἰησοῦ Χριστοῦ.*

Sovereign that bought them,' and so bringing on themselves swift destruction[i]. Unbelievers might contend that the apostolical teachings respecting the present power and future coming of Jesus were cleverly-invented myths[j]; but St. Peter had himself witnessed the majesty of Jesus in His Transfiguration[k]. The Apostle knows that he himself will quickly die; he has had a special revelation from the Lord Jesus to this effect[l]. Throughout this Epistle the Person of Jesus is constantly before us. As He is the true Object of Christian knowledge, so He is the Lord of the future kingdom of the saints. He is mocked at and denied by the heretics; His Coming it is which the scoffing materialism of the age derides; His judgments are foreshadowed by the great destructive woes of the Old Testament. Again and again, as if with a reverent eagerness which takes pleasure in the sacred words, the Apostle names His Master's Name and titles. He is Jesus our Lord[m]; He is our Lord Jesus Christ[n]; He is the Lord and Saviour[o]; He is our Lord and Saviour Jesus Christ[p]; He is our God and Saviour Jesus Christ[q]. His power is spoken of as Divine[r]; and through the precious things promised by Him to His Church (must we not here especially understand the sacraments?) Christians are made partakers of the Nature of God[s]. To Christ, in His exalted majesty, a tribute of glory is due, both now and unto the day of eternity[t]. Throughout this Epistle Jesus Christ is constantly named where

[i] 2 St. Pet. ii. 1: *παρεισάξουσιν αἱρέσεις ἀπωλείας, καὶ τὸν ἀγοράσαντα αὐτοὺς Δεσπότην ἀρνούμενοι, ἐπάγοντες ἑαυτοῖς ταχινὴν ἀπώλειαν.*

[j] Ibid. i. 16: *οὐ γὰρ σεσοφισμένοις μύθοις ἐξακολουθήσαντες ἐγνωρίσαμεν ὑμῖν τὴν τοῦ Κυρίου ἡμῶν Ἰησοῦ Χριστοῦ δύναμιν καὶ παρουσίαν.*

[k] Ibid.: *ἐπόπται γενηθέντες τῆς ἐκείνου μεγαλειότητος.* Ibid. ver. 18: *ἐν τῷ ὄρει τῷ ἁγίῳ.*

[l] Ibid. ver. 14: *εἰδὼς ὅτι ταχινή ἐστιν ἡ ἀπόθεσις τοῦ σκηνώματός μου, καθὼς καὶ ὁ Κύριος ἡμῶν Ἰησοῦς Χριστὸς ἐδήλωσέ μοι.* Here *ταχινὴ* seems to mean 'soon,' 'not distant,' rather than 'rapid.' Cf. St. John xxi. 18; but some independent revelation, made shortly before these words were written, is probably alluded to. Hegesippus, de Excidio Hierosol. lib. iii. 2; St. Ambros. Serm. contra Auxentium, de Basilicis tradendis, n. 13 in Epist. 21.

[m] 2 St. Pet. i. 2. This occurs elsewhere only at Rom. iv. 24.

[n] 2 St. Pet. i. 14, 16. [o] Ibid. iii. 2. [p] Ibid. i. 11, ii. 20, iii. 18.

[q] Ibid. i. 1. Cf. Bp. Middleton on Gr. Art. p. 433.

[r] 2 St. Pet. i. 3: *τῆς θείας δυνάμεως αὐτοῦ τὰ πρὸς ζωὴν καὶ εὐσέβειαν δεδωρημένης.* *αὐτοῦ* apparently refers to Ἰησοῦ (ver. 2), and is so distinguished from the Eternal Father *τοῦ καλέσαντος ἡμᾶς* (ver. 3).

[s] Ibid. ver. 4: *τίμια ἐπαγγέλματα δεδώρηται, ἵνα διὰ τούτων γένησθε θείας κοινωνοὶ φύσεως.*

[t] Ibid. iii. 18: *αὐτῷ ἡ δόξα καὶ νῦν καὶ εἰς ἡμέραν αἰῶνος.* 'Tota æternitas una dies est.' Estius.

we should expect to find the Name of God. The Apostle does not merely proclaim the Divinity of Jesus in formal terms; he everywhere feels and implies it.

III. Akin to St. Peter's second Epistle in its language and purpose is the short Epistle of St. Jude. Like his brother St. James, St. Jude, although our Lord's first cousin, introduces himself as the slave of Jesus Christ. St. Jude does not also term himself the slave of God[u]. If believing Christians are sanctified in God the Father, they are preserved in a life of faith and holiness by union with Jesus Christ[v]. The religion of Jesus, according to St. Jude, is the final revelation of God, the absolute truth, the true faith. Men should spare no efforts on behalf of the true faith. It is the faith once for all delivered to the saints[w]. The Gnostics alluded to in this Epistle, like those foretold by St. Peter, are said to 'deny our only Sovereign and Lord, Jesus Christ[x].' They are threatened with the punishments awarded by Jesus to Israel in the wilderness[y], and to the rebel angels; they will perish as Sodom and Gomorrha[z]. The Book of Enoch is cited to describe Jesus coming to judgment, surrounded by myriads of saints[a]. The authors of all unholy deeds will then be convicted of their crimes; the hard things spoken against the Judge by impious sinners will be duly punished. Christians, however, are to build themselves up upon their most holy faith[b]: their life is fashioned in devotion to the Blessed Trinity. It is a life of prayer: their souls live in the Holy Spirit as in an atmosphere[c]. It is a life of persevering love, whereof the Almighty Father is the Object[d]. It is a life of expectation: they look forward to the indulgent mercy which

[u] St. Jude ver. 1: Ἰησοῦ Χριστοῦ δοῦλος, ἀδελφὸς δὲ Ἰακώβου.

[v] Ibid.: τοῖς ἐν Θεῷ πατρὶ ἡγιασμένοις καὶ Ἰησοῦ Χριστῷ τετηρημένοις κλητοῖς.

[w] Ibid. ver. 3: παρακαλῶν ἐπαγωνίζεσθαι τῇ ἅπαξ παραδοθείσῃ τοῖς ἁγίοις πίστει.

[x] Ibid. ver. 4: τὸν μόνον Δεσπότην καὶ Κύριον ἡμῶν Ἰησοῦν Χριστὸν ἀρνούμενοι.

[y] Ibid. ver. 5, where Ἰησοῦς is found in A, B, 13, Vulg., Copt., Æth., St. Jer., Cyr. Ὁ Θεός, Κύριος, and ὁ Κύριος are less fully attested.

[z] Ibid. vers. 5-7.

[a] Ibid. ver. 14: ἦλθε Κύριος ἐν μυριάσιν ἁγίαις αὐτοῦ, ποιῆσαι κρίσιν κατὰ πάντων. On 'Enoch' see Pusey, Daniel the Prophet, p. 393, note 3.

[b] Ibid. ver. 20: ὑμεῖς δέ, ἀγαπητοί, τῇ ἁγιωτάτῃ ὑμῶν πίστει ἐποικοδομοῦντες ἑαυτούς.

[c] Ibid.: ἐν Πνεύματι Ἁγίῳ προσευχόμενοι.

[d] Ibid. ver. 21: ἑαυτοὺς ἐν ἀγάπῃ Θεοῦ τηρήσατε.

our Lord Jesus Christ will shew them at His coming[e]. Christ is the Being to whom they look for mercy; and the issue of His compassion is everlasting life. Could any merely human Christ have had this place in the heart and faith of Christians, or on the judgment-seat of God?

IV. But it is time that we should proceed to consider, however briefly, the witness of that great Apostle, whose Epistles form so much larger a contribution to the sacred volume of the New Testament than is supplied by any other among the inspired servants of Christ.

1. In comparing St. Paul with St. John, a modern author has remarked that at first sight two objects stand out prominently in the theological teaching of the beloved disciple, while three immediately challenge observation in the writings of the Apostle of the Gentiles. At first sight, St. John's doctrine appears to place us face to face only with God and the human world. Christ as the Eternal Logos is in St. John plainly identical with God; although when we contemplate the life of the Godhead He is discerned to be personally distinct from the Father. But we cannot really understand St. John, and withal establish in our thought an essential separation between God and the Word Incarnate. Although Jesus is a manifestation of God's glory in the world of sense, He is ever internal to that Divine Essence Whose glory He manifests; He is with God, and He is God. In St. Paul, on the other hand, we are confronted more distinctly with three objects. These are, God, the human world, and between the two, Jesus Christ, Divine and human, the One Mediator between God and man. Of course the *primâ facie* impression produced on the mind by the sacred writers is all that is here in question, and this impression is not to be confounded with their real relations to each other. The Christ of St. John is as truly Human as the Christ of St. Paul is literally Divine; St. John exhibits the Mediator not less truly than St. Paul, St. Paul the Divine Son of the Father not less truly than St. John. But the observation referred to enables us to do justice to the form of St. Paul's Christology; and we may well observe in his writings the prominence which is given to two truths which supply the foil, on this side and on that, to the doctrine of our Lord's essential Godhead.

(*a*) St. Paul insists with particular earnestness upon the truth

[e] St. Jude ver. 21: *προσδεχόμενοι τὸ ἔλεος τοῦ Κυρίου ἡμῶν Ἰησοῦ Χριστοῦ, εἰς ζωὴν αἰώνιον.*

of our Lord's real Humanity. This truth is not impaired by such expressions as the 'form of a servant [f],' the 'fashion of a man [g],' the 'likeness of sinful flesh [h],' which are employed either to describe Christ's Humanity as a mode of being, or to hint at Its veiling a Higher Nature undiscerned by the senses of man, or to mark the point at which, by Its glorious inaccessibility to sin, It is in contrast with the nature of that frail and erring race to which It truly belongs. Nor is our Lord's Humanity conceived of as a phantom, when the Apostle has reached a point of spiritual growth at which the outward circumstances of Christ's Life are wellnigh forgotten in an overmastering perception of His spiritual and Divine glory [i]. St. Paul speaks plainly of our Lord as being manifest in the flesh [k]; as possessing a Body of material flesh [l]; as being 'made of a woman [m];' as being 'born of the seed of David according to the flesh [n];' as having drawn the substance of His Flesh from the race of Israel [o]. As a Jew, Jesus Christ was born under the yoke of the Law [p]. His Human Life was not merely one of self-denial [q] and obedience; it was pre-eminently a life of sharp suffering [r]. The Apostle uses energetic expressions to describe our Lord's real share in our physical human weakness [s], as well as in those various forms of pain, mental and bodily, which He willed to undergo, and which reached their climax in the supreme agonies of the Passion [t]. If however Christ became obedient unto death, even the death of the cross [u], this, as is implied, was of His own free condescension; and St. Paul dwells with rapture upon the glory of Christ's risen Body, to which our bodies of humiliation will

[f] Phil. ii. 7: μορφὴν δούλου.
[g] Ibid. ver. 8: σχήματι εὑρεθεὶς ὡς ἄνθρωπος.
[h] Rom. viii. 3: ἐν ὁμοιώματι σαρκὸς ἁμαρτίας.
[i] 2 Cor. v. 16: εἰ δὲ καὶ ἐγνώκαμεν κατὰ σάρκα Χριστὸν, ἀλλὰ νῦν οὐκ ἔτι γινώσκομεν.
[k] 1 Tim. iii. 16: ἐφανερώθη ἐν σαρκί.
[l] Col. i. 22: ἐν τῷ σώματι τῆς σαρκὸς αὐτοῦ.
[m] Gal. iv. 4: γενόμενον ἐκ γυναικός.
[n] Rom. i. 3: τοῦ γενομένου ἐκ σπέρματος Δαβὶδ κατὰ σάρκα.
[o] Ibid. ix. 5: ἐξ ὧν ὁ Χριστὸς τὸ κατὰ σάρκα.
[p] Gal. iv. 4: γενόμενον ὑπὸ νόμον.
[q] Rom. xv. 3: καὶ γὰρ ὁ Χριστὸς οὐκ ἑαυτῷ ἤρεσεν.
[r] Heb. v. 8: καίπερ ὢν υἱὸς, ἔμαθεν ἀφ' ὧν ἔπαθε τὴν ὑπακοήν.
[s] 2 Cor. xiii. 4: ἐσταυρώθη ἐξ ἀσθενείας.
[t] Ibid. i. 5: τὰ παθήματα τοῦ Χριστοῦ. Phil. iii. 10: τὴν κοινωνίαν τῶν παθημάτων αὐτοῦ. Col. i. 24: τὰ ὑστερήματα τῶν θλίψεων τοῦ Χριστοῦ.
[u] Phil. ii. 8: ἐταπείνωσεν ἑαυτὸν, γενόμενος ὑπήκοος μέχρι θανάτου, θανάτου δὲ σταυροῦ.

hereafter in their degrees, by His Almighty Power, be assimilated[v]. Upon two features of our Lord's Sacred Humanity does St. Paul lay especial stress. First, Christ's Manhood was clearly void of sin, both in Soul and Body; and in this respect It was unlike any one member of the race to which It belonged[x]. This sinlessness, however, did but restore humanity 'in Christ' to its original type of perfection. Thus, secondly, Christ's Manhood is representative of the human race; it realizes the archetypal idea of humanity in the Divine Mind. Christ, the Second Adam, according to St. Paul, stands in a relation to the regenerate family of men analogous to that ancestral relationship in which the first Adam stands to all his natural descendants. But this correspondence is balanced by a contrast. In two great passages St. Paul exhibits the contrast which exists between the Second Adam and the first[y]. This contrast is physical, psychological, moral, and historical. The body of the first Adam is corruptible and earthly; the Body of the Second Adam is glorious and incorruptible[z]. The first Adam enjoys natural life; he is made a living soul. The Second Adam is a supernatural Being, capable of communicating His Higher Life to others; He is a quickening Spirit[a]. The first Adam is a sinner, and his sin compromises the entire race which springs from him. The Second Adam sins not; His Life is one mighty act of righteousness[b]; and they who are in living communion with Him share in this His righteousness[c]. The historical consequence of the action of the first Adam is death, the death of the body and of the soul. This consequence is transmitted to his

[v] Phil. iii. 21: *ὃς μετασχηματίσει τὸ σῶμα τῆς ταπεινώσεως ἡμῶν, ... σύμμορφον τῷ σώματι τῆς δόξης αὐτοῦ, κατὰ τὴν ἐνέργειαν τοῦ δύνασθαι αὐτὸν καὶ ὑποτάξαι ἑαυτῷ τὰ πάντα.* 1 Cor. xv. 44: *σῶμα πνευματικόν.*

[x] 2 Cor. v. 21: *τὸν γὰρ μὴ γνόντα ἁμαρτιαν, ὑπὲρ ἡμῶν ἁμαρτίαν ἐποίησεν.* Gal. ii. 17: *ἆρα Χριστὸς ἁμαρτίας διάκονος; μὴ γένοιτο.* Rom. viii. 3; cf. Art. xv.

[y] Rom. v. 12-21; 1 Cor. xv. 45-49.

[z] 1 Cor. xv. 47: *ὁ πρῶτος ἄνθρωπος ἐκ γῆς, χοϊκός· ὁ δεύτερος ἄνθρωπος [ὁ Κύριος], ἐξ οὐρανοῦ. Οἷος ὁ χοϊκὸς, τοιοῦτοι καὶ οἱ χοϊκοί· καὶ οἷος ὁ ἐπουράνιος, τοιοῦτοι καὶ οἱ ἐπουράνιοι.*

[a] Ibid. ver. 45: *ἐγένετο ὁ πρῶτος ἄνθρωπος Ἀδὰμ εἰς ψυχὴν ζῶσαν· ὁ ἔσχατος Ἀδὰμ εἰς πνεῦμα ζωοποιοῦν.* Cf. vers. 21, 22.

[b] *δικαίωμα*, Rom. v. 18.

[c] Rom. v. 18, 19: *ἄρα οὖν ὡς δι' ἑνὸς παραπτώματος, εἰς πάντας ἀνθρώπους, εἰς κατάκριμα· οὕτω καὶ δι' ἑνὸς δικαιώματος, εἰς πάντας ἀνθρώπους, εἰς δικαίωσιν ζωῆς. ὥσπερ γὰρ διὰ τῆς παρακοῆς τοῦ ἑνὸς ἀνθρώπου ἁμαρτωλοὶ κατεστάθησαν οἱ πολλοὶ, οὕτω καὶ διὰ τῆς ὑπακοῆς τοῦ ἑνὸς δίκαιοι κατασταθήσονται οἱ πολλοί.*

descendants along with his other legacy of transmitted sin. The historical consequence of the action and suffering of the Second Adam is life; and communion with His living righteousness is the gauge and assurance to His faithful disciples of a real exemption from the law of sin and death [d]. Such a contrast, you observe, might well suggest that the Second Adam, Representative of man's race, its true Archetype, its Restorer and its Saviour, is Himself more than man. Certainly; but nevertheless it is as Man that Christ is contrasted with our first parent; and it is in virtue of His Manhood that He is our Mediator, our Redeemer [e], our Saviour from Satan's power, our Intercessor with the Father [f]. Great stress indeed does St. Paul lay upon the Manhood of Christ as the instrument of His mediation between earth and heaven, as the channel through which intellectual truth and moral strength descend from God into the souls of men, as the Exemplar wherein alone human nature has recovered its ideal beauty, as entering a sphere wherein the Sinless One could offer the perfect, world-representing sacrifice of a truly obedient Will. So earnestly and constantly does St. Paul's thought dwell on our Lord's mediating Humanity, that to unreflecting persons his language might at times appear to imply that Jesus Christ is personally an inferior being, external to the Unity of the Divine Essence [g]. Thus he tells the Corinthians that Christians have one Lord Jesus Christ as well as one God [h]. Thus he reminds St. Timothy that there is One

[d] Rom. v. 12: *δι' ἑνὸς ἀνθρώπου ἡ ἁμαρτία εἰς τὸν κόσμον εἰσῆλθε, καὶ διὰ τῆς ἁμαρτίας ὁ θάνατος.* Ibid. ver. 17: *εἰ γὰρ ἐν ἑνὶ* [*τῷ τοῦ ἑνὸς*, text. rec.] *παραπτώματι ὁ θάνατος ἐβασίλευσε διὰ τοῦ ἑνὸς, πολλῷ μᾶλλον οἱ τὴν περισσείαν τῆς χάριτος καὶ τῆς δωρεᾶς τῆς δικαιοσύνης λαμβάνοντες, ἐν ζωῇ βασιλεύσουσι διὰ τοῦ ἑνὸς Ἰησοῦ Χριστοῦ.* Cf. Ibid. ver. 21.

[e] 1 Tim. ii. 5, 6: *ἄνθρωπος Χριστὸς Ἰησοῦς, ὁ δοὺς ἑαυτὸν ἀντίλυτρον ὑπὲρ πάντων.*

[f] Heb. ii. 14: *ἐπεὶ οὖν τὰ παιδία κεκοινώνηκε σαρκὸς καὶ αἵματος, καὶ αὐτὸς παραπλησίως μετέσχε τῶν αὐτῶν, ἵνα διὰ τοῦ θανάτου καταργήσῃ τὸν τὸ κράτος ἔχοντα τοῦ θανάτου, τουτέστι, τὸν διάβολον.* Ibid. v. 1.

[g] As in 1 Cor. iii. 23, xi. 3. Compare Eph. ii. 18-20.

[h] 1 Cor. viii. 6: *εἷς Κύριος Ἰησοῦς Χριστός.* Here however (1) *Κύριος*, as contrasted with *Θεὸς*, implies no necessary inferiority; else we must say that the Father is not *Κύριος*; cf. St. Chrys. de Incompr. Dei Nat. v. 2; in 1 Cor. x. 20, 21, *Κύριος* is used of Christ in contrast with the demon-gods of heathendom: while (2) the clause *δι' οὗ τὰ πάντα, καὶ ἡμεῖς δι' αὐτοῦ*, (which could not be restricted to our Lord's redemptive work without great arbitrariness, since it plainly refers to His creation of the universe,) places Jesus Christ on a level with the Father. Compare the position of *διὰ* between *ἐξ* and *εἰς*, Rom. xi. 36; cf. Col. i. 16. Our Lord is here distinguished from the 'One God,' as being Human as well as Divine; cf. the

God and One Mediator between God and man, the Man Christ Jesus, Who gave Himself a ransom for all [i]. Thus he looks forward to a day when the need for Christ's mediatorial Royalty having ceased, His Manhood, shall be subject to Him That put all things under Him, that God may be all in all [j]. It is at least certain that no modern Humanitarian could recognise the literal reality of our Lord's Humanity with more explicitness than did the Apostle who had never seen Him on earth, and to whom He had been manifested in visions which a Docetic enthusiast might have taken as sufficient warrant for denying His actual participation in our flesh and blood [k].

(β) On the other hand, St. Paul is as strict a monotheist as any unconverted pupil of Gamaliel; he does not merely retain

relation of μεσίτης to Θεὸς in 1 Tim. ii. 5. But the real antithesis lies not between εἷς Θεὸς and εἷς Κύριος, but between the εἷς Θεὸς ὁ Πατὴρ and the θεοὶ πολλοί of heathendom, and the εἷς Κύριος and the heathen κύριοι πολλοί: cf. ver. 5. Baur's remarks on 1 Cor. viii. 6 (Vorlesungen, p. 193), which proceed upon the assumption that only four Epistles of St. Paul are extant, and therefore that Col. i. 16, 17 is nothing to the purpose, and which moreover endeavour to impose the plain redemptive reference of 2 Cor. v. 17, 18 upon this passage, are so capricious as to shew very remarkably the strength and truth of the Catholic interpretation. Cf. Waterland, Works, ii. 54.

[i] 1 Tim. ii. 5, 6: εἷς γὰρ Θεὸς, εἷς καὶ μεσίτης Θεοῦ καὶ ἀνθρώπων, ἄνθρωπος Χριστὸς Ἰησοῦς. Cf. Wilberforce, Doctr. Inc. pp. 212–214, ed. 3.

[j] 1 Cor. xv. 28: ὅταν δὲ ὑποταγῇ αὐτῷ τὰ πάντα, τότε καὶ αὐτὸς ὁ Υἱὸς ὑποταγήσεται τῷ ὑποτάξαντι αὐτῷ τὰ πάντα, ἵνα ᾖ ὁ Θεὸς τὰ πάντα ἐν πᾶσιν. That our Lord's Humanity is the subject of ὑποταγήσεται is the opinion of St. Augustine (de Trin. i. c. 8), St. Jerome (adv. Pelag. i. 6), Theodoret (in loc.). If αὐτὸς ὁ Υἱὸς means the Divine Son most naturally, the predicate ὑποταγήσεται is an instance of communicatio idiomatum (cf. Acts xx. 28; 1 Cor. ii. 8; Rom. viii. 32, ix. 5; Heb. vi. 6; St. John iii. 13); since it *can* only apply to a created nature. A writer who believed our Lord to be literally God (Rom. ix. 5) could not have supposed that, at the end of His mediatorial reign as Man, a new relation would be introduced between the Persons of the Godhead. The subordination (κατὰ τάξιν) of the Son is an eternal fact in the inner Being of God. See Lect. IV. p. 202. But the *visible* subjection of His Humanity (with Which His Church is so organically united as to be called 'Christ' 1 Cor. xii. 12) to the supremacy of God will be realized at the close of the present dispensation. Against the attempt to infer from this passage an ἀποκατάστασις of men and devils, cf. Meyer in loc.; and against Pantheistic inferences from τὰ πάντα ἐν πᾶσιν, cf. Julius Müller, Lehre von d. Sünde, i. p. 157, quoted ibid.

[k] There seems, however, to be a distinction between such visions and trances as those of 2 Cor. xii. 1–4; Acts xviii. 9; xxii. 17, and the appearance of Jesus Christ at midday, at St. Paul's conversion, Acts ix. 17. Of this last St. Paul appears to speak more especially in 1 Cor. ix. 1, and xv. 8. Cf. Macpherson on the Resurrection, p. 330.

his hold upon the primal truth of God's inviolate Unity; he is especially devoted to it.

God is parted from the very highest forms of created life by a measureless interval, and yet the universe is a real reflection of His Nature[l]. The relation of the creatures to God is threefold. Nothing exists which has not proceeded originally from God's creative Hand. Nothing exists which is not upheld in being and perfected by God's sustaining and working energy. Nothing exists which shall not at the last, whether mechanically or consciously, whether willingly or by a terrible constraint, subserve God's high and resistless purpose. For as He is the Creator and Sustainer, so He is the One last End of all created existences. Of Him, and through Him, and unto Him, are all things[m]. So absolute an idea of God excludes all that is local, transient, particular, finite. God's supreme Unity is the truth which determines the universality of the Gospel; since the Gospel unveils and proclaims the One supreme, world-controlling God[n]. Hence the Apostle infers the deep misery of Paganism. The Pagan representation of Deity was 'a lie' by which this essential truth of God's Being[o] was denied. The Pagans had forfeited that partial apprehension of the glory of the incorruptible God which the physical universe and the light of natural conscience placed within their reach. They had yielded to those instincts of creature-worship[p] which mere naturalism is ever prone to indulge. The Incarnation alone subdues these instincts by consecrating them to the service of God Incarnate; while beyond

[l] Rom. i. 20: τὰ γὰρ ἀόρατα αὐτοῦ ἀπὸ κτίσεως κόσμου τοῖς ποιήμασι νοούμενα καθορᾶται.

[m] Ibid. xi. 36: ὅτι ἐξ αὐτοῦ καὶ δι' αὐτοῦ καὶ εἰς αὐτὸν τὰ πάντα. 'Alles ist *aus Gott* (*Urgrund*), in sofern Alles aus Gottes Schöpferkrafte hervorgegangen ist; *durch Gott* (*Vermittelungsgrund*), in sofern nichts ohne Gottes Vermittelung (continuirliche Einwirkung) existirt; *für Gott* (*teleologische Bestimmung*), in sofern Alles den Zwecken Gottes dient.' Meyer in loc.

[n] Baur, Vorlesungen, p. 205: 'Auf dieser Auffassung der Idee Gottes beruht der Universalismus des Apostels, wie er diess in dem Satz ausspricht, dass Gott sowohl der Heiden als der Juden Gott sei. Rom. ii. 11, iii. 29, x. 12. Das Christenthum ist selbst nichts anderes (it *is* this, but it is a great deal more) als die Aufhebung alles Particularistischen, damit die reine absolute Gottes-Idee in der Menschheit sich verwirkliche, oder in ihr zum Bewusstsein komme.' The Pantheistic touch of the last phrase does not destroy the general truth of the observation.

[o] Rom. i. 25: μετήλλαξαν τὴν ἀλήθειαν τοῦ Θεοῦ ἐν τῷ ψεύδει.

[p] Ibid. vers. 18-25; especially 23: ἤλλαξαν τὴν δόξαν τοῦ ἀφθάρτου Θεοῦ ἐν ὁμοιώματι εἰκόνος φθαρτοῦ ἀνθρώπου καὶ πετεινῶν καὶ τετραπόδων καὶ ἑρπετῶν, κ.τ.λ.

the Church they perpetually threaten naturalistic systems witl an utter and disastrous subjection to the empire of sense. When man then had fairly lost sight of the Unity and Spirituality of God, Paganism speedily allowed him to sink beneath a flood of nameless sensualities; he had abandoned the Creator to become, in the most debased sense, the creature's slave[q].

At another time the Apostle's thought rests for an instant upon the elegant but impure idolatries to which the imagination and the wealth of Greece had consecrated those beautiful temples which adorned the restored city of Corinth. 'To us Christians,' he fervently exclaims, 'there is but one God, the Father; all things owe their existence to Him, and we live for His purposes and His glory[r].' In after years, St. Paul is writing to a fellow-labourer for Christ, and he has in view some of those Gnostic imaginations which already proposed to link earth with heaven by a graduated hierarchy of Æons, thus threatening the re-introduction either of virtual polytheism or of conscious creature-worship. Against this mischievous speculation the Apostle utters his protest; but it issues from his adoring soul upwards to the footstool of the One Supreme and Almighty Being in the richest and most glorious of the doxologies which occur in his Epistles. God is the King of the ages of the world; He is the imperishable, invisible, only wise Being[s]. God is the Blessed and Only Potentate, the King of kings and Lord of lords; He only has from Himself, and originally, immortality; He dwells in the light which is inaccessible to creatures; no man has seen Him; no man can see Him; let honour and power be for ever ascribed to Him[t].

[q] Rom. i. 24: *παρέδωκεν αὐτοὺς ὁ Θεὸς ἐν ταῖς ἐπιθυμίαις τῶν καρδιῶν αὐτῶν εἰς ἀκαθαρσίαν.* Ibid. ver. 26: *εἰς πάθη ἀτιμίας.* Ibid. ver. 28: *εἰς ἀδόκιμον νοῦν.* See the whole context.

[r] 1 Cor. viii. 5, 6: *καὶ γὰρ εἴπερ εἰσὶ λεγόμενοι θεοὶ, εἴτε ἐν οὐρανῷ, εἴτε ἐπὶ γῆς* (the two spheres of polytheistic invention) *ὥσπερ εἰσὶ θεοὶ πολλοὶ, καὶ κύριοι πολλοί· ἀλλ' ἡμῖν εἷς Θεὸς ὁ Πατὴρ, ἐξ οὗ τὰ πάντα, καὶ ἡμεῖς εἰς αὐτόν.*

[s] 1 Tim. i. 17: *τῷ δὲ βασιλεῖ τῶν αἰώνων, ἀφθάρτῳ, ἀοράτῳ μόνῳ σοφῷ Θεῷ, τιμὴ καὶ δόξα εἰς τοὺς αἰῶνας τῶν αἰώνων.* Here *μόνῳ σοφῷ Θεῷ* excludes current Gnostic claims on behalf of Æons; in Rom. xvi. 27 (with which compare St. Jude 25) it contrasts the Divine Wisdom manifested in the plan of Redemption through Jesus Christ with human schemes and theories, whether Jewish or Gentile.

[t] 1 Tim. vi. 15, 16: *ὁ μακάριος καὶ μόνος δυνάστης, ὁ βασιλεὺς τῶν βασιλευόντων, καὶ Κύριος τῶν κυριευόντων, ὁ μόνος ἔχων ἀθανασίαν, φῶς οἰκῶν ἀπρόσιτον, ὃν εἶδεν οὐδεὶς ἀνθρώπων, οὐδὲ ἰδεῖν δύναται, ᾧ τιμὴ καὶ κράτος αἰώνιον, ἀμήν.*

St. Paul is, beyond all question, an earnest monotheist; his faith is sensitively jealous on behalf of the supremacy and the rights of God. What then is the position which he assigns to Jesus Christ in the scale of being? That he believed Jesus Christ to be merely a man is a paradox which could be maintained by no careful reader of his Epistles. But if, according to St. Paul, Christ is more than man, what is He? Is He still only an Arian Christ? or is He a Divine Person? In St. Paul's thought this question could not have been an open one. His earnest, sharply-defined faith in the One Most High God must force him to say either that Christ is a created Being, or that He is internal to the Essence of God. Nor is the subject of such a nature as to admit of accommodation or compromise in its treatment. In practical matters, and where the law of God permits, St. Paul may become all things to all men that he may by all means save some [u]. But he cannot, as if he were a pagan politician of old, or a modern man of the world, compliment away his deepest faith [x]. He cannot ascribe Divinity to a fellow-creature by way of panegyrical hyperbole; his belief in God is too powerful, too exacting, too keen, too real. St. Paul may teach the Athenians that we live and move and have our being in the all-present, all-encompassing Life of God [y]; he may bid the Corinthians expect a time when God shall be known and felt by every member of His great family to be all in all [z]. But St. Paul cannot merge the Maker and Ruler of the universe, so gloriously free in His creative and providential action [a], in any conception which identifies Him with the work of His hands, or which reduces Him to the level of an impersonal quality or force. The Apostle may contemplate the vast hierarchy of the blessed angels, ranging in their various degrees of glory between the throne of God and the children of men [b]. But no heavenly intelligence, however exalted, is seen in his pages to trench for one moment upon the incommunicable prerogatives of God. St. Paul may describe the regenerate life of Christians in such terms as to warrant us in saying that Christ's true members become divine by spiritual communion with God in His Blessed Son [c]. But the saintliest of men, the most exalted and majestic of seraphs, are alike removed by an infinite interval from the One Uncreated, Self-existent, Incor-

[u] 1 Cor. ix. 22. [x] 2 Cor. i. 18, ii. 17. [y] Acts xvii. 28.
[z] 1 Cor. xv. 28. [a] Rom. ix. 21.
[b] Col. i. 16. These hierarchical distinctions appear to have been preserved among the fallen angels (Eph. vi. 12).
[c] 1 Cor. iii. 16, 17; vi. 19, 20.

ruptible Essence[d]. There is no room in St. Paul's thought for an imaginary being like the Arian Christ, hovering indistinctly between created and Uncreated life; since, where God is believed to be so utterly remote from the highest creatures beneath His throne, Christ must either be conceived of as purely and simply a creature with no other than a creature's nature and rights, or He must be adored as One Who is for ever and necessarily internal to the Uncreated Life of the Most High.

2. It has been well observed by the author of 'Ecce Homo' that 'the trait in Christ which filled St. Paul's whole mind was His condescension;' and that 'the charm of that condescension lay in its being voluntary[e].' Certainly. But condescension is the act of bending from a higher station to a lower one; and the question is, from what did Christ condescend? If Christ was merely human, what was the human eminence from which St. Paul believed Him to be stooping? Was it a social eminence? But as the favourite of the synagogue, and withal as protected by the majesty of the Roman franchise[f], St. Paul occupied a social position not less widely removed from that of a Galilean peasant leading a life of vagrancy, than are your circumstances, my brethren, who belong to the middle and upper classes of this country, removed from the lot of the homeless multitudes who day by day seek relief in our workhouses. Was it an intellectual eminence? But the Apostle who had sat at the feet of Gamaliel, and had drawn largely from the fountains of Greek thought and culture, had at least enjoyed educational advantages which were utterly denied to the Prophet of Nazareth. Was it then a moral eminence? But, if Jesus was merely Man, was He, I do not say morally perfect, but morally eminent at all? Was not His self-assertion such as to be inconsistent with any truthful recognition whatever of the real conditions of a created existence? But was the eminence from which Christ condescended angelical as distinct from human? St. Paul has drawn the sharpest distinction between Christ and the angels; Christ is related to the angels, in the belief of the Apostle, simply as the Author of their being[g]; while the appointed duties of the angels are to worship His Person and to serve His servants[h].

What then was the position from which Christ condescended? Two stages of condescension are indeed noted, one within and

[d] Rom. xi. 34-36.

[e] Ecce Homo, p. 49.
[f] Acts xxii. 29.
[g] Col. i. 16.
[h] Heb. i. 6, 14.

[LECT.

one beyond the limits of our Lord's Human Life. Being found in fashion as a Man, He voluntarily humbled Himself and became obedient unto death[i]. But the earlier and the greater act of condescension was that whereby He had become Man out of a state of pre-existent glory[k]. St. Paul constantly refers to the pre-existent Life of Jesus Christ. The Second Adam differs from the first in that He is 'from heaven[l].' When ancient Israel was wandering in the desert, Christ had been Himself invisibly present as Guardian and Sustainer of the Lord's people[m]. St. Paul is pleading on behalf of the poor Jewish Churches with their wealthier Corinthian brethren; and he points to the grace of our Lord Jesus Christ, Who, when He was rich, for our sakes became poor, that we through His poverty might be rich[n]. Here Christ's eternal wealth is in contrast with His temporal impoverishment. For His poverty began with the manger of Bethlehem; He became poor by the act of His Incarnation; being rich according to the unbegun, unending Life of His Higher Nature, He became poor in time[o]. When St. Paul says that our Lord was 'manifested in the flesh[p],'

[i] Phil. ii. 8: *σχήματι εὑρεθεὶς ὡς ἄνθρωπος, ἐταπείνωσεν ἑαυτὸν, γενόμενος ὑπήκοος μέχρι θανάτου, θανάτου δὲ σταυροῦ.*

[k] Ibid. vers. 6, 7: *ἐν μορφῇ Θεοῦ ὑπάρχων, . . ἑαυτὸν ἐκένωσε, μορφὴν δούλου λαβών.*

[l] 1 Cor. xv. 47: *ὁ δεύτερος ἄνθρωπος [ὁ Κύριος] ἐξ οὐρανοῦ.* Cf. Tert. adv. Marc. v. 10.

[m] 1 Cor. x. 4: *ἡ δὲ πέτρα* [the *πέτρα ἀκολουθοῦσα* commemorated by Jewish traditions] *ἦν ὁ Χριστός.* Ibid. ver. 9: *μηδὲ ἐκπειράζωμεν τὸν Χριστὸν, καθὼς καί τινες αὐτῶν ἐπείρασαν.*

[n] 2 Cor. viii. 9: *γινώσκετε γὰρ τὴν χάριν τοῦ Κυρίου ἡμῶν Ἰησοῦ Χριστοῦ, ὅτι δι' ὑμᾶς ἐπτώχευσε πλούσιος ὤν, ἵνα ὑμεῖς τῇ ἐκείνου πτωχείᾳ πλουτήσητε.*

[o] Baur suggests that *ἐπτώχευσε* need mean no more than that Christ was poor. (Vorlesungen, p. 193.) But 'der *Aorist* bezeichnet das einst geschehene *Eintreten* des Armseins (denn *πτωχεύειν* heisst nicht arm *werden*, sondern arm *sein*), nicht das von Christo geführte *ganze Leben* in Armuth und Niedrigkeit, wobei er gleichwohl reich an Gnade gewesen sei.' (Meyer in 2 Cor. viii. 9.)

[p] 1 Tim. iii. 16: *ἐφανερώθη ἐν σαρκί.* Cf. Bishop Ellicott in loc. The bishop pronounces *ὃς* to be the reading of the Codex A, 'after minute personal inspection,' and has adopted it in his text. Mr. Scrivener however has examined the Codex more recently, and with a different result. 'On holding the leaf,' he says, 'up to the light one singularly bright hour, February 7, 1861, and gazing at it with and without a lens, with eyes which have something of the power and too many of the defects of a microscope, I saw clearly the tongue of the ϵ through the attenuated vellum, crossing the circle about two thirds up, (much above the thick modern line), the knob at its extremity falling without the circle. On laying

he at least implies that Christ existed before this manifestation; when St. Paul definitely ascribes to our Lord the function of a Creator who creates not for a Higher Power but for Himself, we rise from the idea of pre-existence to the idea of a relationship towards the universe, which can belong to One Being alone. This will presently be considered.

Certainly St. Paul used the terms 'form of God,' 'image of God,' when speaking of the Divinity of Jesus Christ[q]. But these terms do not imply that Christ's Divinity only resembles or is analogous to the Divinity of the Father. They do not mean that, as Man, He represents the Divine Perfections in an inferior and partial manner to our finite intelligence which is incapable of raising itself sufficiently to contemplate the transcendent reality. They are necessary in order to define the personal distinction which exists between the Divine Son and the Eternal Father. Certainly it is no mere human being or seraph Whom St. Paul describes as being 'over all, God blessed for ever[r].' You remind me that these words are referred by some modern scholars to the Eternal Father. Certainly they are: but on what grounds? Of scholarship? What then is St. Paul's general purpose when he uses these words? He has just been enumerating those eight privileges of the race of Israel, the thought of which kindled in his true Jewish heart the generous and passionate desire to be made even anathema for his rejected countrymen. To these privileges he subjoins a climax. The Israelites were they, *ἐξ ὧν ὁ Χριστὸς τὸ κατὰ σάρκα, ὁ ὢν ἐπὶ πάντων Θεὸς εὐλογητὸς εἰς τοὺς αἰῶνας.* It was from the blood of Israel that the true Christ had sprung, so far as His Human Nature was concerned; but Christ's Israelitic descent is, in the Apostle's eyes, so consummate a glory for Israel, because Christ is much more than one of the sons of men; because

down the leaf I saw immediately after (but not at the same moment) the slight shadow of the real ancient diameter, only just above the recent one.' Still, on a review of the whole mass of external proof, particularly of the verdict of Codex ℵ, and of the versions and Fathers, Mr. Scrivener decides for ὃς as the probable reading although 'he dares not pronounce θεὸς a corruption.' See the very full statement in his 'Introduction to the Criticism of the N. T., 3rd ed.,' pp. 637–642. If then it be admitted that the reading ΘΣ is too doubtful to be absolutely relied on; in any case our Lord's Pre-existence lies in the *ἐφανερώθη* (1 St. John i. 2), which cannot without violence be watered down into the sense of Christ's manifestation in the teaching and belief of the Church, as distinct from His manifestation in history.

[q] Phil. ii. 6; Col. i. 15.

[r] Rom. ix. 5.

by reason of His Higher Pre-existent Nature He is 'over all, God blessed for ever.' This is the natural [s] sense of the passage. If the passage occurred in a profane author and its sense and structure alone had to be considered, few critics would think of overlooking the antithesis between Χριστὸς τὸ κατὰ σάρκα and Θεὸς εὐλογητός [t]. Still less possible would it be to destroy this antithesis outright, and to impoverish the climax of the whole passage, by cutting off the doxology from the clause which precedes it, and so erecting it into an independent ascription of praise to God the Father [u]. If we should admit that the

[s] Reuss, Théol. Chrét. ii. 76, note. M. Reuss says that the Catholic interpretation of Rom ix. 5 is 'l'explication la plus simple et la plus naturelle.' 'Man hat hier verschiedene Auswege gesucht, der Nothwendigkeit zu entgehen, [ὁ] ὢν ἐπὶ πάντων Θεός auf Christum zu beziehen; aber bei jedem bieten sie solche Schwierigkeiten dar, die immer wieder auf die einfachste und von der Grammatik gebotene Auslegung zurückführen.' (Usteri, Entwickelung des Paulinischen Lehrbegriffes, p. 309.) That the text was understood in the early Church to apply to Jesus Christ will appear from St. Iren. iii. 16. 3; Tert. adv. Prax. 13, 15; St. Hipp. c. Noet. 6; Origen in Rom. vii. 13; Conc. Ant. A.D. 269, ap. Routh, Reliq. Sacr. iii. 292; St. Athan. Orat. c. Ar. i. 10, iv. 1, sub init.; Theodoret, Hær. Fab. v. 14; St. Chrys. de Incompr. Dei Nat. v. 2; in Joan. hom. xxxiii. 1; in 1 Cor. hom. xx. 3; St. Cyr. Alex. Contr. Julianum, x. 328. It seems probable that any non-employment of so striking a passage by the Catholics during their earlier controversial struggles with the Arians is to be attributed to their fear of being charged with construing it in a Sabellian sense. (Cf. Olsh. in loc.; Reiche, Comm. ii. 268, note.) The language of the next age was unhesitating: εἶπεν αὐτὸν 'ἐπὶ πάντων' . . . 'Θεὸν' . . . 'εὐλογητὸν' . . . ἔχοντες οὖν τὸν Χριστὸν καὶ ὄντα Θεὸν καὶ εὐλογητὸν, αὐτῷ προσκυνήσωμεν. St. Procl. ad Arm. (Labbe, iii. 1231.) Wetstein erroneously assumed that those early fathers who refused to apply ὁ ἐπὶ πάντων Θεὸς to Christ would have objected to the predicate actually employed by the Apostle, ἐπὶ πάντων Θεός. (Cf. Fritzsche, Comm. in Rom. i. p. 262 sqq.) And indeed Socinus himself (see Tholuck in loc.) had no doubt of the reference of this passage to Christ; although he explained it of a conferred, not of a 'natural' Divinity. (Cat. Rac. 159 sqq.) See too Dr. Vaughan, Comm. in loc., against the 'harsh, evasive and most needless interpretation,' which applies it to the Father.

[t] Observe Rom. i. 3, where ἐκ σπέρματος Δαβὶδ κατὰ σάρκα is in contrast with Υἱοῦ Θεοῦ . . . κατὰ Πνεῦμα Ἁγιωσύνης. Here as σάρξ designates the lower human Nature in Christ, Πνεῦμα Ἁγιωσύνης must mean His Higher Divine Nature, conceived of generally, according to which He is the Son of God. The Holy Spirit is nowhere called πνεῦμα ἁγιωσύνης in the New Testament, while πνεῦμα is used of the Divine Nature in St. John iv. 24; 2 Cor. iii. 17; Heb. ix. 14. See Philippi in loc.; Lect. VI. p. 344, note.

[u] As to the punctuation of this passage the early MSS. themselves of course determine nothing; but the citations and versions to which Lachmann generally appeals for the formation of his text are decisively in favour of referring ὁ ὢν to Χριστός. The Sabellian use of the text to prove that

doctrine of Christ's Godhead is not stated in this precise form elsewhere in St. Paul's writings [x], that admission cannot be held

the Father became Man, and the orthodox replies shewing that this was not the sense of the passage, equally assume that the doxological clause refers to Christ. Nothing can with safety be inferred as to the received reading in the Church from the general and of course prejudiced statement of the Emperor Julian, that τὸν γοῦν Ἰησοῦν οὔτε Παῦλος ἐτόλμησεν εἰπεῖν Θεόν. St. Cyril. cont. Jul. x. init., Op. tom. vi. p. 327. Besides CL (Tisch. ed. 8), two cursive MSS. of the twelfth century (5 and 47) interpose a punctuation after σάρκα, and so raise the following clause into an independent doxology addressed to God the Father. But the construction which is thus rendered necessary (1) makes the participle ὢν altogether superfluous. In 2 Cor. xi. 31, ὁ ὢν εὐλογητὸς εἰς τοὺς αἰῶνας is an exactly parallel construction to that of Rom. ix. 5. (Cf. also Rom. i. 25.) It is instructive to observe the facility with which the natural force of the passage is at once recognised in the former and denied in the latter case (see Prof. Jowett in loc., and Baur, Vorlesungen, p. 194, who begs the question,—'Christus ist noch wesentlich Mensch, nicht Gott'). There is no authority for transposing ὁ ὢν into ὢν ὁ (with Schlichting, Whiston, and Whitby), in order to evade the natural force of the participle. (2) The construction which the isolation of the clause renders necessary violates the invariable usage of Biblical Greek. 'If the Apostle had wished to express "God, Who is over all, be blessed for ever," he must, according to the unvarying usage of the New Testament and the LXX. (which follows the use of ברוך), have placed εὐλογητός first, and written εὐλογητὸς ὁ ὢν κ.τ.λ. There are about forty places in the Old Testament and five in the New in which this formula of doxology occurs, and in every case the arrangement is the same, "Blessed be the God Who is over all, for ever."' (Christ. Rem. April 1856, p. 469.) In the only apparent exception, Ps. lxviii. 19, LXX. (cited by Winer, N. T. Gr. Eng. Tr. p. 573), Κύριος ὁ Θεὸς εὐλογητὸς, εὐλογητὸς Κύριος, the first εὐλογητός has no corresponding word in the Hebrew text, and if not interpolated is a paraphrastic clause, intended to concentrate rhetorical emphasis on the doxology of the usual form, which follows. Dean Alford observes that 1 Kings x. 6; 2 Chron. ix. 8; Job i. 21; Ps. cxii. 2, are not exceptions; 'since in all of them the verb εἴη or γένοιτο is expressed, requiring the substantive to follow it closely.' We may be very certain that, if ἐπὶ πάντων Θεός could be proved to be an unwarranted reading, no scholar would hesitate to say that ὁ ὢν εὐλογητὸς κ.τ.λ. should be referred to the proper name which precedes it.

[x] Our Lord is not, we are reminded, called εὐλογητός elsewhere in the New Testament. But εὐλογημένος is certainly applied to Him, St. Matt. xxi. 9; St. Luke xix. 28; and as regards εὐλογητός, the limited number of the doxologies addressed to Him might account for the omission. The predicate could only be refused to Him on the ground of His being, in the belief of St. Paul, merely a creature; whereas St. Paul calls Him Θεός, Eph. v. 5. See Lect. VI. p. 340, note; Harless and Rückert in loc.; Col. ii. 2, τοῦ Θεοῦ Χριστοῦ; Tisch. 8th ed., where the comma before Χριστοῦ is unwarranted; and Tit. ii. 13, μέγας Θεός (cf. note y, p. 319). It is arbitrary to maintain that no word can possibly be applied to a given subject because there is not a second instance of such application within a limited series of books. Even if the application of ὁ ὢν ἐπὶ πάντων Θεὸς εὐλογητός to

to justify us in violently breaking up the passage, in order to escape from its natural meaning, unless we are prepared to deny that St. Paul could possibly have employed an ἅπαξ λεγόμενον. Nor in point of fact does St. Paul say more in this famous text than when in writing to Titus he describes Christians as 'looking for the blessed hope and appearing of the glory of our great God and Saviour Jesus Christ, Who gave Himself for us[y].' Here the grammar apparently, and the context certainly, oblige us to recognise the identity of 'our Saviour Jesus Christ' and 'our Great God.' As a matter of fact, Christians are not waiting for any manifestation of the Father. And He Who

Christ were an ἅπ. λεγ., it would be justified by the consideration that a writer who habitually thinks of Christ as God (Col. i. 15, 16, 17; Eph. i. 23; Rom. i. 7; 1 Cor. i. 3; Rom. x. 13; Phil. ii. 10, 11) would naturally call Him God in a passage designed to express in the most vivid terms the crowning privilege of Israel. Against ἐπὶ πάντων Θεός, besides the foregoing objection, it is further urged that it *cannot* be applied to our Lord, Who, although consubstantial with, is subordinate to, the Eternal Father, and withal personally distinct from Him; cf. Eph. iv. 5; 1 Cor. viii. 6, where, however, see p. 309, note h. But St. Paul does not call our Lord ὁ ἐπὶ πάντων Θεὸς; the article would lay the expression open to a Sabellian construction; St. Paul says that Christ is ἐπὶ πάντων Θεός, where the Father of course is not included among τὰ πάντα, 1 Cor. xv. 27; and the sense corresponds substantially with Acts x. 36, Rom. x. 12. It asserts that Christ is internal to the Divine Essence, without denying His personal distinctness from, or His filial relation to, the Father. Cf. Alford in loc.; Usteri, Entwickelung des Paulinischen Lehrbegriffes, p. 309 sqq.; Olshausen, Comm. in loc.

[y] Tit. ii. 13: προσδεχόμενοι τὴν μακαρίαν ἐλπίδα καὶ ἐπιφάνειαν τῆς δόξης τοῦ μεγάλου Θεοῦ καὶ Σωτῆρος ἡμῶν Ἰησοῦ Χριστοῦ, ὃς ἔδωκεν ἑαυτὸν ὑπὲρ ἡμῶν. 'Nicht Gott und Christus, sondern bloss Christus gemeint ist; denn es ist von der herrlichen Wiederkunft Christi die Rede, und eine Erscheinung Gottes (of the Father) anzunehmen, wäre ausser aller Analogie; auch bedürfte Gott der Vater nicht erst des erhebenden und preisenden Epithets μέγας, vielmehr deutet auch dieses auf Christum.' (Usteri, Lehrbegriff, p. 310.) For St. Paul's habitual association of ἐπιφανεία τῆς δόξης with Christ, cf. 2 Thess. ii. 8; 1 Tim. vi. 14: 2 Tim. i. 10; 2 Tim. iv. 1, 8. To these arguments Bishop Ellicott adds that the subsequent allusion to our Lord's profound Self-humiliation accounts for St. Paul's ascribing to Him, by way of reparation, 'a title, otherwise unusual, that specially and antithetically marks His glory,' and that two ante-Nicene writers, Clemens Alexandr. (Protrep. 7) and St. Hippolytus, together with the great bulk of post-Nicene fathers, although not all, concur in this interpretation. The bishop holds that grammatically there is a presumption in favour of this interpretation, but, on account of the defining genitive ἡμῶν, nothing more. Nevertheless, taking the great strength of the exegetical evidence into account, he sees in this text a 'direct, definite, and even *studied* declaration of the Divinity of the Eternal Son.' See his note; Wordsworth in loc.; Middleton, Greek Article, ed. Rose, p. 393; Pfleiderer Paulinismus, Kap. xi. p. 474.

gave Himself for us can be none other than our Lord Jesus Christ.

Reference has already been made to that most solemn passage in the Epistle to the Philippians, which is read by the Church in the Communion Service on Palm Sunday [z], in order, as it would seem, to remind Christians of the real dignity of their suffering Lord. Our Lord's Divine Nature is here represented as the seat of His Eternal Personality; His Human Nature is a clothing which He assumed in time. Ἐν μορφῇ Θεοῦ ὑπάρχων, . . . ἑαυτὸν ἐκένωσε, μορφὴν δούλου λαβών [a]. It is impossible not to be struck by the mysterious statement that Christ, being in the form of God, did not look upon equality with God (τὸ εἶναι ἴσα Θεῷ) as a prize to be seized and kept hold on [b] (οὐκ ἁρπαγμὸν ἡγήσατο). It has been maintained that St. Paul is here contrasting the apostolic belief in our Lord's condescending love with an early Gnostic speculation respecting an Æon. This Æon desired by an immediate and violent assault to lay hold on the invisible and incomprehensible God; whereas God could only be really known to and contemplated by the Monogenes. The ambition of the fabled Æon is thus said to be in contrast with the 'self-emptying' of the Eternal Christ. Such a contrast, if it had been in the Apostle's mind, would have implied the Absolute Pre-existent Divinity of Christ. Christ voluntarily lays aside the glory which was His; the fabled Æon would violently grasp a glory

[z] See Epistle for Sunday next before Easter.

[a] Phil. ii. 6, 7. 'Die Gnostiker sprachen von einem Aeon, welcher das absolute Wesen Gottes auf unmittelbare Weise erfassen wollte, und weil er so das an sich Unmögliche erstrebte aus dem πλήρωμα in das κένωμα herabfiel. Dieser Aeon begieng so gleichsam einen Raub, weil er, der in der Qualität eines göttlichen Wesens an sich die Fähigkeit hatte, sich mit dem Absoluten zu vereinigen, diese Identität, welche erst durch den ganzen Weltprocess realisirt werden konnte, gleichsam sprungweise, mit Einem Male, durch einen gewaltsamen Act, oder wie durch einen Raub an sich reissen wollte. So erhält erst die bildliche Vorstellung eines ἁρπαγμός ihre eigentliche Bedeutung.' (Baur, Vorlesungen, p. 266.) Compare, however, Meyer, Philipperbrief, p. 68, Anmerkung. Baur has spun a large web out of St. Irenæus, Adv. Hær. I. 2. 1. 2. The notion that the Æon sought to attain an identity with God,—and this assumption is necessary in order to construct a real parallel with St. Paul's words,—has no foundation in the text of St. Irenæus.

[b] Cf. Bp. Ellicott in loc.; and in Aids to Faith, p. 436; Döllinger, First Age of the Church, p. 163. (E. T.) renders ἁρπαγμὸν as 'a spoil which was not His by right, and of which He might be deprived.' ἁρπ. is clearly a thing or state, not an action. Thus the description of the glory from which our Lord stooped ends at ὑπάρχων; the description of His condescension begins with οὐχ ἁρπαγμὸν, and ἀλλ' has its full force.

[LECT.

which could not rightfully belong to him. But if this explanation of the energetic negative phrase of the Apostle should not be accepted, it is in any case clear that the force of St. Paul's moral lesson in the whole passage must depend upon the real Divinity of the Incarnate and Self-immolating Christ. The point of our Lord's example lies in His emptying Himself of the glory or 'form' of His Eternal Godhead. Worthless indeed would have been the force of His example, had He been in reality a created Being, who only abstained from grasping tenaciously at Divine prerogatives which a creature could not have arrogated to himself without impious folly [c]. Christians are to have in themselves the Mind of Christ Jesus; but what that mind is they can only understand, by considering what His Apostle believed Christ Jesus to have been, before He took on Him the form of a servant and became obedient unto death.

Perhaps the most exhaustive assertion of our Lord's Godhead which is to be found in the writings of St. Paul, is that which occurs in the Epistle to the Colossians [d]. This magnificent dogmatic passage is introduced, after the Apostle's manner, with a strictly practical object. The Colossian Church was exposed to the intellectual attacks of a theosophic doctrine, which degraded Jesus Christ to the rank of one of a long series of inferior beings, supposed to range between mankind and the supreme God. Against this position St. Paul asserts that Christ is the *εἰκὼν τοῦ Θεοῦ τοῦ ἀοράτου*—the Image of the Invisible God [e]. The expression *εἰκὼν τοῦ Θεοῦ* supplements the title of 'the Son.' As 'the Son' Christ is derived eternally from the Father, and He is of One Substance with the Father. As 'the Image,' Christ is, in that One Substance, the exact likeness of the Father, in all things except being the Father. The Son is the Image of the Father, not as the Father, but as God: the Son is 'the Image

[c] The Arian gloss upon this text was this: *ὅτι θεὸς ὢν ἐλάττων οὐχ ἥρπασε τὸ εἶναι ἴσα τῷ Θεῷ τῷ μεγάλῳ καὶ μείζονι.* St. Chrysostom comments thus: *Καὶ μικρὸς καὶ μέγας Θεὸς ἔνι; καὶ τὰ Ἑλληνικὰ τοῖς τῆς ἐκκλησίας δόγμασιν ἐπεισάγετε; . . . Εἰ γὰρ μικρὸς, πῶς καὶ Θεός;* (Hom. vi. in loc.) *Μορφὴ* is the 'manner of existence;' and only God could have the 'manner of existence' of God. Trench. Syn. N. T. p. 248. Cp. *δόξα*, St. John xvii. 5. Of this *μορφὴ* (as distinct from Deity Itself) our Lord *ἐκένωσεν ἑαυτόν.* The word *ὑπάρχων* points to our Lord's 'original subsistence' in the splendour of the Godhead. The expression *ἐν μορφῇ Θεοῦ ὑπάρχων* is virtually equivalent to *τὸ εἶναι ἴσα Θεῷ.* See Dean Alford's exhaustive note upon this passage.

[d] Col. i. 15-17.

[e] Cf. 2 Cor. iv. 4: *ὅς ἐστιν εἰκὼν τοῦ Θεοῦ.*

of God.' The εἰκὼν is indeed originally God's unbegun, unending reflection of Himself in Himself; but the εἰκὼν is also the Organ whereby God, in His Essence invisible, reveals Himself to His creatures. Thus the εἰκὼν is, so to speak, naturally the Creator, since creation is the first revelation which God has made of Himself. Man is the highest point in the visible universe; in man, God's attributes are most luminously exhibited; man is the image and glory of God [f]. But Christ is the Adequate Image of God, God's Self-reflection in His Own thought, eternally present with Himself. As the εἰκὼν, Christ is the πρωτότοκος πάσης κτίσεως: that is to say, *not* the First in rank among created beings, *but* born before any created beings [g]. That this is a true sense of the expression is etymologically certain [h]; but it is also the only sense which is in real harmony with the relation in which, according to the context, Christ is said to stand to the

[f] 1 Cor. xi. 7: εἰκὼν καὶ δόξα Θεοῦ.

[g] πρωτότοκος was apparently preferred by St. Paul to πρωτόγονος, the favourite Alexandrian word, because it suggested that Christ was the true Messiah as well as the true Logos. Lightfoot, Colossians, p. 212.

[h] As εἰκὼν here defines our Lord's relation to God the Father, so πρωτότοκος defines His relation to the creatures. *βούλεται δεῖξαι ὅτι πρὸ πάσης τῆς κτίσεώς ἐστιν ὁ Υἱός· πῶς ὤν; διὰ γεννήσεως· οὐκοῦν καὶ τῶν ἀγγέλων πρότερος, καὶ οὕτως, ὥστε καὶ αὐτὸς ἔκτισεν αὐτούς.* (Theophyl. in loc.) Christ is not the first of created spirits; He exists before them, and as One 'begotten not made.' 'Der *genit.* πάσης κτίσεως ist nicht Genit. *partitiv.* (obwohl diess noch *de Wette* für unzweifelhaft hält), weil πᾶσα κτίσις nicht *die ganze Schöpfung* heisst, mithin nicht die *Kategorie* oder *Gesammtheit* aussagen kann, zu welcher Christus als ihr erstgebornes Individuum gehöre: es heisst, *jedwedes Geschöpf;* vrgl. z. πᾶσα οἰκοδομή, Eph. ii. 21), sondern es ist der Genit. *comparat.: der Erstgeborne in Vergleich mit jedem Geschöpfe* (s. Bernhardy, p. 139), d. h. *eher* geboren *als* jedes Geschöpf. Vrgl. Bähr z. St. u. Ernesti Ursprung d. Sünde, p. 241. Anders ist das Verhältniss Apoc. i. 5: πρωτότοκος τῶν νεκρῶν, wo τῶν νεκρῶν die Kategorie anzeigt, vrgl. πρωτότοκος ἐν πολλοῖς ἀδελφοῖς (Rom. viii. 29). Unser Genit. ist ganz zu fassen wie der vergleichende Genit. bei πρῶτος Joh. i. 15, 30; *Winer*, p. 218; *Fritzsche* ad Rom. ii. p. 421. Das Vergleichungs-Moment ist das Verhältniss der *Zeit*, und zwar in Betreff des *Ursprungs:* da aber letzterer bei jeder κτίσις *anders* ist als bei Christo, so ist nicht πρωτόκτιστος oder πρωτόπλαστος gesagt, welches von Christo eine gleiche Art der Entstehung wie von der Creatur anzeigen würde, sondern πρωτότοκος gewählt, welches in der Zeitvergleichung des Ursprungs die absonderliche *Art* der Entstehung in Betreff *Christi* anzeigt, dass er nämlich von Gott nicht *geschaffen* sei, wie die anderen Wesen, bei denen diess in der Benennung κτίσις liegt, sondern *geboren*, aus dem Wesen Gottes gleichartig hervorgegangen. Richtig *Theodoret:* οὐχ ὡς ἀδελφὴν ἔχων τὴν κτίσιν, ἀλλ' ὡς πρὸ πάσης κτίσεως γεννηθείς. Wortwidrig ist daher die *Arianische* Erklärung, dass Christus als das *erste Geschöpf Gottes* bezeichnet werde.' Meyer, Kolosserbrief, p. 184. See Lightfoot, Colossians. p. 212.

created universe[i]. That relation, according to St. Paul, is threefold. Of all things in earth and heaven, of things seen and unseen, of the various orders of the angelic hierarchy, of thrones, of dominions, of principalities, of powers—it is said that they were created in Christ, by Christ, and for Christ. Ἐν αὐτῷ, ἐκτίσθη . . . . δι' αὐτοῦ, καὶ εἰς αὐτὸν ἔκτισται[j]. *In Him.* There was no creative process external to and independent of Him; since the archetypal forms after which the creatures are modelled, and the sources of their strength and consistency of being, eternally reside in Him[k]. *By Him.* The force which has summoned the worlds out of nothingness into being, and which upholds them in being, is His; He wields it; He is the One Producer and Sustainer of all created existence. *For Him.* He is not, as Arianism afterwards pretended, merely an inferior workman, creating for the glory of a higher Master, for a God superior to Himself. He creates for Himself; He is the End of created things as well as their immediate Source; and in living for Him every creature finds at once the explanation and the law of its being. For 'He is before all things, and by Him all things consist[l].' After such a statement it follows naturally

[i] Schleiermacher's desire to apply to the new creation, what is here said of the natural, illustrates his tendency 'to expound the Bible by the verdict of his consciousness, instead of permitting his consciousness to be regulated by the Bible.' Auberlen on the Divine Revelation, pt. 2. iv. 2. a.

[j] Compare Rom. xi. 36: ἐξ αὐτοῦ καὶ δι' αὐτοῦ καὶ εἰς αὐτὸν τὰ πάντα. As in this passage the Apostle is speaking of God, without hinting at any distinction of Persons within the Godhead, he writes ἐξ αὐτοῦ, not ἐν αὐτῷ. The Eternal Father is the ultimate Source of all life, both *intra* and extra Deum; while the production of created beings depends immediately upon the Son. The other two prepositions—the last being theologically of most import—correspond in the two passages.

[k] ἐκτίσθη describes the *act* of creation; ἔκτισται points to creation as a completed and enduring fact. In ἐν αὐτῷ, the preposition signifies that 'in Christo beruhete (ursächlich) der Act der Schöpfung, so dass die Vollziehung derselben *in Seinen Person begründet war,* und ohne ihn nicht geschehen wäre.' Cf. St. John i. 3: χωρὶς αὐτοῦ ἐγένετο οὐδὲ ἕν, ὃ γέγονεν. But although the preposition immediately expresses the dependence of created life upon Christ as its cause, it hints at the reason of this dependence, namely, that our Divine Lord is the *causa exemplaris* of creation, the κόσμος νοητὸς, the Archetype of all created things, 'die Dinge ihrer Idee nach, Selbst, er trägt ihre Wesenheit in sich.' (Olshausen in loc.)

[l] Col. i. 17: καὶ αὐτός ἐστι πρὸ πάντων, καὶ τὰ πάντα ἐν αὐτῷ συνέστηκε. Meyer in loc. 'Und Er (Er eben), durch welchen und für welchen τὰ πάντα ἔκτισται, hat eine frühere Existenz als Alles, und das Sämmtliche besteht in ihm. . . . . πρὸ πάντων wie πρωτότοκος von der *Zeit,* nicht vom Range; *wiederholt und nachdrücklich* betont wird von P. die Präexistenz Christi. Statt ἔστι hatte er ἦν sagen können (Joh. i. 1); jenes aber ist

that the πλήρωμα, that is to say, the entire cycle of the Divine attributes, considered as a series of powers or forces, dwells in Jesus Christ; and this, not in any merely ideal or transcendental manner, but with that actual reality which men attach to the presence of material bodies which they can feel and measure through the organs of sense. Ἐν αὐτῷ κατοικεῖ πᾶν τὸ πλήρωμα τῆς θεότητος σωματικῶς [m]. Although throughout this Epistle the word λόγος is never introduced, it is plain that the εἰκὼν of St. Paul is equivalent in His rank and functions to the λόγος of St. John. Each exists prior to creation; each is the one Agent in creation; each is a Divine Person; each is equal with God and shares His essential Life; each is really none other than God.

Indeed with this passage in the Colossians only two others in the entire compass of the New Testament can, on the whole, be compared. Allusion has already been made to the prologue of St. John's Gospel; and it is no less obvious to refer to the opening chapter of the Epistle to the Hebrews. Most of those writers who earnestly reject the Pauline authorship of that Epistle admit that it is of primary canonical authority, and assign to its author the highest place of honour in 'the school of St. Paul.' There are reasons for believing that, at the utmost, it is not more distantly related to his mind than is the Gospel of St. Luke; if indeed it does not furnish a crowning instance of the spiritual versatility of the great Apostle, addressing himself to a set of circumstances unlike any other of which the records of his ministry have given us information [n]. Throughout the

gesagt, weil Er die *Permanenz* des Seins Christi im Auge hat und darstellt, nicht aber historisch über ihn berichten will, was nur in den Hülfssätzen mit ὅτι vers. 16. u. 19. geschieht.' Cf. St. John viii. 58.

[m] Col. ii. 9: πᾶν τὸ πλήρωμα. Meyer in loc.: 'Wird durch τῆς θεότητος näher bestimmt, welches angiebt, *was* seiner ganzen Fülle nach, d. i. nicht etwa blos theilweise, sondern in seiner Gesammtheit, in Christo wohne. . . . ἡ θεότης *die Gottheit* (Lucian, Icarom. 9; Plut. Mor. p. 415, C.) das Abstractum von ὁ Θεός, ist zu unterscheiden von ἡ θειότης dem Abstractum von θεῖος (Rom. i. 20; Sap. xviii. 9; Lucian de Calumn., 17). Jenes ist *Deitas, das Gottsein*, d. i. die göttliche *Wesenheit, Gottheit;* dieses aber die *Divinitas*, d. i. die göttliche *Qualität, Göttlichkeit*.' So Bengel: 'Non modò divinæ virtutes, sed ipsa divina natura.' See too Abp. Trench, Syn. N. T. i. p. 8. Thus in this passage the πλήρωμα must be understood in the metaphysical sense of the Divine Essence, even if in Col. i. 19 it is referred to the fulness of Divine grace. Contrast too the permanent fact involved in the present κατοικεῖ of the one passage with the historical aorist εὐδόκησε of the other.

[n] The Pauline authorship of the Epistle has been maintained with great

Epistle to the Hebrews a comparison is instituted between Christianity and Judaism; and this comparison turns partly on the spiritual advantages which belong to the two systems respectively, and partly on the relative dignity of the persons who represent the two dispensations, and who mediate accordingly, in whatever senses, between God and humanity. Thus our Incarnate Lord as the one great High-priest is contrasted with Aaron [o] and his successors. Thus too as the one perfect Revealer of God, He is compared with Moses [p] and the Jewish prophets. As the antitype of Melchisedec, Christ is a higher Priest than Aaron [q]; as a Son reigning over the house of God, Christ is a greater Ruler than the legislator whose praise it was that he had been a faithful servant [r]. As Author of a final, complete, and unique revelation, Christ stands altogether above the prophets by whom God had revealed His Mind in many modes and in many fragments, in revelations very various as to their forms, and, at certain epochs, almost incessant in their occurrence [s]. But if the superiority of Christianity to Judaism was to be completely established, a further comparison was necessary. The later Jewish theologians had laid much stress upon the delivery of the Sinaitic Law through the agency of angels acting as delegates for the Most High God [t]. The Author of Christianity might be superior to Moses and the prophets, but could He challenge comparison with those pure and mighty spirits compared with whom the greatest of the sons of Israel, as beings of flesh and blood, were insignificant and sinful? The answer is, that if Christ is not the peer of the

ability by Biesenthal, 'Das Trostschreiben des Ap. Paulus an die Hebräer,' Leipzig, 1878, cf. pp. 19-43 [1881].

[o] Heb. v. 4; x. 11.

[p] Ibid. iii. 1-6.

[q] Ibid. vii. 1-22.

[r] Ibid. iii. 5, 6: *καὶ Μωσῆς μὲν πιστὸς ἐν ὅλῳ τῷ οἴκῳ αὐτοῦ, ὡς θεράπων, ... Χριστὸς δὲ, ὡς υἱὸς ἐπὶ τὸν οἶκον αὐτοῦ, οὗ οἶκός ἐσμεν ἡμεῖς.* The preceding words are yet more noteworthy: Moses and the house of Israel stand to Jesus Christ in the relation of creature to the Creator. *πλείονος γὰρ δόξης οὗτος παρὰ Μωσῆν ἠξίωται, καθ' ὅσον πλείονα τιμὴν ἔχει τοῦ οἴκου ὁ κατασκευάσας αὐτόν. πᾶς γὰρ οἶκος κατασκευάζεται ὑπό τινος· ὁ δὲ τὰ πάντα κατασκευάσας* (sc. Jesus Christ), *Θεός.* So too the *ἀπὸ Θεοῦ ζῶντος* of ver. 12 refers most naturally to our Lord, not to the Father.

[s] Ibid. i. 1: *πολυμερῶς καὶ πολυτρόπως πάλαι ὁ Θεὸς λαλήσας τοῖς πατράσιν ἐν τοῖς προφήταις.*

[t] Ibid. ii. 2: *ὁ δι' ἀγγέλων λαληθεὶς λόγος.* Acts vii. 38: *μετὰ τοῦ ἀγγέλου τοῦ λαλοῦντος αὐτῷ ἐν τῷ ὄρει Σινᾶ.* Ibid. ver. 53: *οἵτινες ἐλάβετε τὸν νόμον εἰς διαταγὰς ἀγγέλων.* Gal. iii. 19: *ὁ νόμος . . . προσετέθη . . . διαταγεὶς δι' ἀγγέλων.*

angels, this is because He is their Lord and Master [u]. The angels are ministers of the Divine Will; they are engaged in stated services enjoined on them towards creatures lower than themselves, yet redeemed by Christ [v]. But He, in His glory above the heavens, is invested with attributes to which the highest angel could never pretend. In His crucified but now enthroned Humanity, He is seated at the right hand of the Majesty on high [w]; He is seated there, as being Heir of all things [x]; the angels are themselves but a portion of His vast inheritance. The dignity of His titles is indicative of His essential rank [y]. Indeed He is expressly addressed as God [z]; and when He is termed the Son of God, or the Son, the full sense of that term is drawn out in language adopted, as it seems, from the Book of Wisdom [a], and not less explicit than that which we have been considering in the Epistle to the Colossians, although of a distinct type. That He is One with God as having streamed forth eternally from the Father's Essence, like a ray of light from the parent fire with which it is unbrokenly joined, is implied in the expression *ἀπαύγασμα τῆς δόξης* [b]. That He is both personally distinct from, and yet literally equal to, Him of Whose Essence He is the adequate imprint, is taught us in the phrase *χαρακτὴρ τῆς ὑποστάσεως* [c]. By Him,

[u] Heb. ii. 3: *σωτηρίας . . . ἀρχὴν λαβοῦσα λαλεῖσθαι διὰ τοῦ Κυρίου.*

[v] Ibid. i. 14: *λειτουργικὰ πνεύματα, εἰς διακονίαν ἀποστελλόμενα διὰ τοὺς μέλλοντας κληρονομεῖν σωτηρίαν.*

[w] Ibid. ver. 3: *ἐκάθισεν ἐν δεξιᾷ τῆς μεγαλωσύνης ἐν ὑψηλοῖς.* The superiority of Christ to the Angels is already implied in the climax at Gal. iv. 14, while the elevation of Christ's Manhood above all orders of Angelic life is taught in Eph. i. 20, 21.

[x] Heb. i. 2: *κληρονόμον πάντων.*

[y] Ibid. ver. 4: *τοσούτῳ κρείττων γενόμενος τῶν ἀγγέλων, ὅσῳ διαφορώτερον παρ' αὐτοὺς κεκληρονόμηκεν ὄνομα.* As to *γενόμενος*, it will be borne in mind that the subject of the whole passage is the Word now truly Incarnate, and not, as is sometimes assumed, the pre-existent Logos alone. The *γενόμενος* would therefore refer to the exaltation of our Lord's Humanity. (See Ebrard, Comm. in loc.) St. Cyril observes that it does not imply that in Christ's superior nature He could be *made* superior to angels. Thes. p. 199.

[z] Heb. i. 8: *πρὸς δὲ τὸν Υἱὸν, 'ὁ θρόνος σου, ὁ Θεὸς, εἰς τὸν αἰῶνα τοῦ αἰῶνος.'* Ps. xlv. 6.

[a] Wisd. vii. 26; cf. Lect. II. p. 63.

[b] Heb. i. 3.

[c] Ibid. A. V. has 'Express image of His Person.' 'So Beza, who dreaded Arianism, and accordingly used 'Person' instead of 'Substance,' from an apprehension that the latter rendering would here imply something inconsistent with the Homoousion.

therefore, the universe was made[d]; and at this moment all things are preserved and upheld in being by the fiat of His almighty word[e]. What created angel can possibly compare with Him? In the Name which He bears and which unveils His Nature[f]; in the honours which the heavenly intelligences themselves may not refuse to pay Him, even when He is entering upon His profound Self-humiliation[g]; in the contrast between their ministerial duties and His Divine and unchanging Royalty[h]; in His relationship of Creator both to earth and heaven[i]; and in the majestic certainty of His trumph over all who shall oppose the advance of His kingdom[k],—we recognise a Being, for Whose Person, although It be clothed in a finite Human Nature[l], there is no real place between humanity and God. While the Epistle to the Hebrews lays even a stronger emphasis than any other book of the New Testament upon Christ's true Humanity[m], it is nevertheless certain that no other book more explicitly asserts the reality of His Divine prerogatives[n].

3. Enough will have been said, to shew that the Apostle Paul believed in the Divinity of Jesus Christ, not in the moral sense of Socinianism, nor in the ditheistic sense, so to speak, of Arianism, but in the literal, metaphysical, and absolute sense of the Catholic Church. Those passages in his writings which may appear to interfere with this conclusion are certainly to be referred either to his anxiety to insist upon the reality of our Lord's Manhood, or to his recognition of the truth that Christ's Eternal Sonship is Itself derived from the Person of the Father. From the Father Christ eternally receives an equality of life and power, and therefore, as being a recipient, He is so far subordinate to the Father. We have indeed

[d] Heb. i. 2: *δι' οὗ καὶ τοὺς αἰῶνας ἐποίησεν.* See Delitzsch and Biesenthal, in loc.

[e] Ibid. ver. 3: *φέρων τε τὰ πάντα τῷ ῥήματι τῆς δυνάμεως αὐτοῦ.*

[f] Ibid. ver. 5: *Υἱός μου εἶ σύ.* See Biesenthal, in loc.

[g] Ibid. ver. 6: *προσκυνησάτωσαν αὐτῷ πάντες ἄγγελοι Θεοῦ.* Psalm xcvii. 7.

[h] Heb. i. 7–9, 14.

[i] Ibid. ver. 10: *σὺ κατ' ἀρχὰς, Κύριε, τὴν γῆν ἐθεμελίωσας, καὶ ἔργα τῶν χειρῶν σου εἰσὶν οἱ οὐρανοί.*

[k] Ibid. ver. 13: *πρὸς τίνα δὲ τῶν ἀγγέλων εἴρηκέ ποτε, 'Κάθου ἐκ δεξιῶν μου, ἕως ἂν θῶ τοὺς ἐχθρούς σου ὑποπόδιον τῶν ποδῶν σου;'*

[l] Ibid. iii. 2: *πιστὸν ὄντα τῷ ποιήσαντι αὐτόν.*

[m] Ibid. ii. 14, 18, iv. 15, v. 7. So xiii. 20.

[n] Cf. especially Heb. xiii. 8, than which no stronger language could be employed to describe the Alone Unchangeable.

already seen that Christ's eternal derivation from the Father is set forth nowhere more fully than in the Gospel of St. John, and by the mouth of our Lord Himself. But the doctrine before us, as it lies in the writings of St. Paul, is not to be measured only by an analysis of those particular texts which proclaim it in terms. The evidence for this great doctrine is not really in suspense until such time as the critics may have finally decided by their microscopical and chemical apparatus, whether the bar of the Θ in a famous passage of St. Paul's first Epistle to Timothy is or is not really discernible in the Alexandrian manuscript. The doctrine lies too deep in the thought of the Apostle, to be affected by such contingencies[o]. You cannot make St. Paul a preacher of Humanitarianism, without warping, mutilating, degrading his whole recorded mind. Particular texts, when duly isolated from the Apostle's general teaching, may be pressed with plausible effect into the service of Arian or Humanitarian theories; but take St. Paul's doctrine as a whole, and it must be admitted to centre in One Who is at once and truly God as well as Man.

St. Paul never speaks of Jesus Christ as a pupil of less originality and genius might speak of a master in moral truth, whose ideas he was recommending, expanding, defining, defending, popularizing, among the men of a later generation. St. Paul never professes to be working on the common level of human power and knowledge with a master from whom he differed, as an inferior teacher might differ, only in the degree of his capacity and authority. St. Paul always writes and speaks as becomes the slave of Jesus. He is indeed a most willing and enthusiastic slave, reverently gathering up and passionately enforcing all that touches the work and glory of that Divine Master to Whom he has freely consecrated his liberty and his life.

In St. Paul's earliest sermons, we do not find the moral precepts of Jesus a more prominent element than the glories of His Person and of His redemptive work. That the reverse

[o] This is indirectly recognised by those writers who would, for instance, deny the Pauline authorship of such Epistles as those to the Ephesians and Colossians, for this reason among others, that our Lord's profound relations to the Church, as set forth in these Epistles, involve a doctrine of His Person, which they reject; cf. Baur, Vorlesungen über N. T. Theologie, 272, sqq. Pfleiderer regards the Epistle to the Colossians as due to the later influence of Alexandrianism upon St. Paul's doctrine; while that to the Ephesians, he says, belongs to the transition stage from 'Paulinism' to 'Catholicism.' 'Paulinismus,' 1873. pp. 366, 431 [1881].

is the case is at once apparent from a study of the great discourse which was pronounced in the synagogue of the Pisidian Antioch. The past history of Israel is first summarized from a point of view which regards it as purely preparatory to the manifestation of the anticipated Saviour [p]; and then the true Messiahship of Jesus is enforced by an appeal to the testimony of John the Baptist [q], to the correspondence of the circumstances of Christ's Death with the prophetic announcements [r], and to the historical fact of His resurrection from the grave [s], which had been witnessed by the apostles as distinctly [t] as it had been foretold by the prophets [u]. Thus the Apostle reaches his practical conclusion. To believe in Jesus Christ is the one condition of receiving remission of sins and (how strangely must such words have sounded in Jewish ears!) justification from all things from which men could not be justified by the divinely-given law of Moses [v]. To deny Jesus Christ is to incur those penalties which the Hebrew Scriptures denounced against scornful indifference to the voice of God and to the present tokens of His Love and Power [w].

At first sight, St. Paul's sermon from the steps of the Areopagus might seem to be rather Theistic than Christian. St. Paul had to gain the ear of a 'philosophical' audience which imagined that 'Jesus and the Resurrection' were two 'strange demons [x],' who might presently be added to the stock of deities already venerated by the Athenian populace. St. Paul is therefore eager to set forth the lofty spirituality of the God of Christendom; but, although he insists chiefly on those Divine attributes which are observable in Nature and Providence, his sermon ends with Jesus. After shewing what God is in Himself [y], and what are the natural relations which subsist between God and mankind [z], St. Paul touches the conscience of his Athenian audience by a sharp denunciation of the vulgar idolatry which it despised [a], and he calls men to repent by a reference to the coming judgment,

[p] Acts xiii. 17-23. [q] Ibid. vers. 24, 25. [r] Ibid. vers. 26-30.

[s] Ibid. ver. 30. [t] Ibid. ver. 31. [u] Ibid. vers. 32-37.

[v] Ibid. vers. 38, 39: διὰ τούτου ὑμῖν ἄφεσις ἁμαρτιῶν καταγγέλλεται· καὶ ἀπὸ πάντων ὧν οὐκ ἠδυνήθητε ἐν τῷ νόμῳ Μωσέως δικαιωθῆναι, ἐν τούτῳ πᾶς ὁ πιστεύων δικαιοῦται.

[w] Ibid. ver. 40: βλέπετε οὖν μὴ ἐπέλθῃ ἐφ' ὑμᾶς τὸ εἰρημένον ἐν τοῖς προφήταις· ''Ἴδετε, οἱ καταφρονηταὶ, καὶ θαυμάσατε καὶ ἀφανίσθητε· ὅτι ἔργον ἐγὼ ἐργάζομαι ἐν ταῖς ἡμέραις ὑμῶν.' Hab. i. 5.

[x] Acts xvii. 18: ξένων δαιμονίων δοκεῖ καταγγελεὺς εἶναι.

[y] Ibid. vers. 24, 25. [z] Ibid. vers. 26 28.

[a] Ibid. vers. 29, 30.

which conscience itself foreshadowed. But the certainty of that judgment has been attested by the historical fact of the resurrection of Jesus; the risen Jesus is the future Judge [b].

Or, listen to St. Paul as with fatherly authority and tenderness he is taking his leave of his fellow-labourers in Christ, the presbyters of Ephesus, on the strand of Miletus. Here the Apostle's address moves incessantly round the Person of Jesus. He protests that to lead men to repentance towards God and faith towards the Lord Jesus Christ [c], had been the single object of his public and private ministrations at Ephesus. He counts not his life dear to himself, if only he can complete the mission which is so precious to him because he has received it from the Lord Jesus [d]. The presbyters are bidden to 'shepherd the Church of God which He has purchased with His Own Blood [e];' and the Apostle concludes by quoting a saying of the Lord Jesus which has not been recorded in the Gospels, but which was then reverently treasured in the Church, to the effect that 'it is more blessed to give than to receive [f].'

In the two apologetic discourses delivered, the one from the stairs of the tower of Antonia before the angry multitude, and the other in the council-chamber at Cæsarea before King Agrippa II. of Chalcis, St. Paul justifies his missionary activity by dwelling upon the circumstances which accompanied and immediately followed his conversion. Everything had turned upon a fact which the Apostle abundantly insists upon;—he had received a revelation of Jesus Christ in His heavenly glory. It was Jesus Who had spoken to St. Paul from heaven [g]; it was Jesus Who had revealed Himself as persecuted in His suffering Church [h]; it was to Jesus that St. Paul had surrendered his moral liberty [i]; it was from Jesus that he had received specific

[b] Acts xvii. 31; 1 Thess. ii. 19.

[c] Acts xx. 21: *διαμαρτυρόμενος . . . . τὴν εἰς τὸν Θεὸν μετάνοιαν, καὶ πίστιν τὴν εἰς τὸν Κύριον ἡμῶν Ἰησοῦν Χριστόν.*

[d] Ibid. ver. 24.

[e] Ibid. ver. 28: *ποιμαίνειν τὴν ἐκκλησίαν τοῦ Θεοῦ* [Κυρίου, Tisch. al.] *ἣν περιεποιήσατο διὰ τοῦ αἵματος τοῦ ἰδίου.* See Dr. Wordsworth's note in loc. In the third edition of his Greek Testament, Dean Alford restored the reading τοῦ Θεοῦ, which he had abandoned for Κυρίου in the two former editions. See especially the note in his fifth edition. For Κυρίου are A, C, D, E; for Θεοῦ, B, ℵ, Syr., Vulg. Compare Scrivener, Introduction to Criticism of the N. T., ed. 3, p. 620 sqq.

[f] Acts xx. 35: *μνημονεύειν τε τῶν λόγων τοῦ Κυρίου Ἰησοῦ, ὅτι αὐτὸς εἶπε· 'Μακάριόν ἐστι μᾶλλον διδόναι ἢ λαμβάνειν.'*

[g] Ibid. xxii. 7; xxvi. 14. [h] Ibid. xxii. 8; xxvi. 15. [i] Ibid. xxii. 10.

[LECT.

orders to go into Damascus[k]; Jesus had commissioned him to be a minister and witness both of what he had seen, and of the truths which were yet to be disclosed to him[l]; it was by Jesus that he was sent both to Jews and Gentiles, 'to open their eyes, and to turn them from darkness to light, and from the power of Satan unto God, that,' continued the Heavenly Speaker, 'they may receive forgiveness of sins, and inheritance among them which are sanctified by faith that is in Me[m].' It was Jesus Who had appeared to St. Paul when he was in an ecstasy in the Temple, had bidden him leave Jerusalem suddenly, and had sent him to the Gentiles[n]. The revelation of Jesus had been emphatically the turning-point of the Apostle's life; it had first determined the direction and had then quickened the intensity of his action. He could plead with truth before Agrippa that he had not been disobedient unto the heavenly vision[o]. But who can fail to see that the Lord who in His glorified Manhood thus speaks to His servant from the skies, and Who is withal revealed to him in the very centre of his soul[p], is no created being, is neither saint nor seraph, but in very truth the Master of consciences, the Monarch Who penetrates, inhabits, and rules the secret life of spirits, the King Who claims the fealty and Who orders the ways of men?

St. Paul's popular teaching then is emphatically a 'preaching of Jesus Christ[q].' Our Lord is always the Apostle's theme; but the degree in which His Divine glory is unveiled varies with the capacities of the Jewish or heathen listeners for bearing the great discovery. The doctrine is distributed, if we may so speak, in a like varying manner over the whole text of St. Paul's Epistles. It lies in those greetings[r] by which the Apostle

[k] Acts xxii. 10. [l] Ibid. xxvi. 16. [m] Ibid. vers. 17, 18.

[n] Ibid. xxii. 17: *ἐγένετο . . . . προσευχομένου μου ἐν τῷ ἱερῷ, γενέσθαι με ἐν ἐκστάσει, καὶ ἰδεῖν αὐτὸν λέγοντά μοι, Σπεῦσον καὶ ἔξελθε ἐν τάχει ἐξ Ἱερουσαλήμ.* Ibid. ver. 21: *εἰς ἔθνη μακρὰν ἐξαποστελῶ σε.*

[o] Ibid. xxvi. 19: *οὐκ ἐγενόμην ἀπειθὴς τῇ οὐρανίῳ ὀπτασίᾳ.*

[p] Gal. i. 15, 16: *εὐδόκησεν ὁ Θεὸς . . . . ἀποκαλύψαι τὸν Υἱὸν αὐτοῦ ἐν ἐμοί.*

[q] Acts ix. 20, xvii. 3, 18, xxviii. 31: *διδάσκων τὰ περὶ τοῦ Κυρίου Ἰησοῦ.* Cf. Ibid. v. 42; 1 Cor. i. 23; 2 Cor. iv. 5; Phil. i. 15, 17, 18. Hence Rom. xvi. 25: *τὸ κήρυγμα Ἰησοῦ Χριστοῦ.*

[r] Rom. i. 7: *χάρις ὑμῖν καὶ εἰρήνη ἀπὸ Θεοῦ Πατρὸς ἡμῶν καὶ Κυρίου Ἰησοῦ Χριστοῦ.* 1 Cor. i. 3; 2 Cor. i. 2; Gal. i. 3; Eph. i. 2; Phil. i. 2; Col. i. 2; 1 Thess. i. 1; 2 Thess. i. 2; Philemon 3. In 1 Tim. i. 2; 2 Tim. i. 2; *ἔλεος* is inserted between *χάρις* and *εἰρήνη*, probably because Timothy, on account of his ministerial responsibilities, needed the pitying mercy of God more than unordained Christians.

associates Jesus Christ with God the Father, as being the source no less than the channel of the highest spiritual blessings. It is pointedly asserted when the Galatians are warned that St. Paul is 'an Apostle not from men nor by man, *but* by Jesus Christ and God the Father [s].' It is implied in commands and benedictions [t] which are pronounced in the Name of Christ without naming the Name of God [u]. It underlies those early apostolical hymns, sung, as it would seem, in the Redeemer's honour [v]; it

[s] Gal. i. 1: *οὐκ ἀπ' ἀνθρώπων οὐδὲ δι' ἀνθρώπου, ἀλλὰ διὰ Ἰησοῦ Χριστοῦ καὶ Θεοῦ Πατρός.* Compare vers. 11, 12.

[t] 2 Thess. iii. 6, 12.

[u] Rom. xvi. 20: *ἡ χάρις τοῦ Κυρίου ἡμῶν Ἰησοῦ Χριστοῦ μεθ' ὑμῶν.* 1 Cor. xvi. 23; 2 Cor. xiii. 13. In Gal. vi. 18, *μετὰ τοῦ πνεύματος ὑμῶν.* Phil. iv. 23; 1 Thess. v. 28. 2 Thess. ii. 16: *αὐτὸς δὲ ὁ Κύριος ἡμῶν Ἰησοῦς Χριστὸς, καὶ ὁ Θεὸς καὶ Πατὴρ ἡμῶν, ὁ ἀγαπήσας ἡμᾶς καὶ δοὺς παράκλησιν αἰωνίαν καὶ ἐλπίδα ἀγαθὴν ἐν χάριτι, παρακαλέσαι ὑμῶν τὰς καρδίας, καὶ στηρίξαι ὑμᾶς ἐν παντὶ λόγῳ καὶ ἔργῳ ἀγαθῷ.* 2 Thess. iii. 18.

[v] Such are 1 Tim. i. 15, from a hymn on redemption:—

Χριστὸς Ἰησοῦς
ἦλθεν εἰς τὸν κόσμον
ἁμαρτωλοὺς σῶσαι.

And Ibid. iii. 16, from a hymn on our Lord's Incarnation and triumph:—

ἐφανερώθη ἐν σαρκὶ,
ἐδικαιώθη ἐν πνεύματι,
ὤφθη ἀγγέλοις,
ἐκηρύχθη ἐν ἔθνεσιν,
ἐπιστεύθη ἐν κόσμῳ,
ἀνελήφθη ἐν δόξῃ.

And 2 Tim. ii. 11–13, from a hymn on the glories of martyrdom:—

εἰ συναπεθάνομεν, καὶ συζήσομεν·
εἰ ὑπομένομεν, καὶ συμβασιλεύσομεν·
εἰ ἀρνούμεθα, κἀκεῖνος ἀρνήσεται ἡμᾶς·
εἰ ἀπιστοῦμεν, ἐκεῖνος πιστὸς μένει·
ἀρνήσασθαι ἑαυτὸν οὐ δύναται.

And Tit. iii. 4–7, from a hymn on the way of salvation; cf. Keble's Sermons Acad. and Occ., p. 182:—

ὅτε δὲ ἡ χρηστότης καὶ ἡ φιλανθρωπία ἐπεφάνη τοῦ Σωτῆρος ἡμῶν ΘΕΟΥ,
οὐκ ἐξ ἔργων τῶν ἐν δικαιοσύνῃ ὧν ἐποιήσαμεν ἡμεῖς,
ἀλλὰ κατὰ τὸν αὐτοῦ ἔλεον, ἔσωσεν ἡμᾶς,
διὰ λουτροῦ παλιγγενεσίας, καὶ ἀνακαινώσεως ΠΝΕΥΜΑΤΟΣ ἉΓΙΟΥ,
οὗ ἐξέχεεν ἐφ' ἡμᾶς πλουσίως, διὰ ἸΗΣΟΥ ΧΡΙΣΤΟΥ τοῦ Σωτῆρος ἡμῶν,
ἵνα δικαιωθέντες τῇ ἐκείνου χάριτι,
κληρονόμοι γενώμεθα κατ' ἐλπίδα ζωῆς αἰωνίου.

Although in Tit. iii. 4 *Σωτῆρος Θεοῦ* refers to the Father, it is Jesus Christ our Saviour through Whom He has given the Spirit and the sacraments, the grace of justification, and an inheritance of eternal life. Jesus is the more prominent Subject of the hymn. Compare the fragment of a hymn, whether for a baptism or on penitence, based on Isa. lx. 1, and quoted in Eph. v. 14:—

justifies the thanksgivings and doxologies which set forth His praise[w]. It alone can explain the application of passages, which are used in the Old Testament of the Lord Jehovah, to the Person of Jesus Christ[x]; such an application would have been impossible unless St. Paul had renounced his belief in the authority and sacred character of the Hebrew Scriptures, or had explicitly recognised the truth that Jesus Christ was Jehovah Himself visiting and redeeming His people.

Mark too how the truth before us mingles with the current topics of St. Paul's Epistles; how it is often presupposed even where it is not asserted in terms. Does that picture of the future Judge Whose Second Coming is again and again brought before us in the Epistles to the Thessalonians befit one who is not Divine[y]? Is the Justifier of humanity in the Epistles to the Romans and the Galatians, to Whom the whole of the Old Testament points as its fulfilment, only a human martyr after all[z]? Why then is the effect of His Death so distinct in kind from any which has followed upon the martyrdom of His servants[a]? How comes it that by dying He has achieved that restoration of the rightful relations of man's being towards God and moral truth[b], which the law of nature and the Law of Sinai had alike failed to secure? Does not the whole representation of the Second Adam in the Epistle to the Romans and in the first Epistle to the Corinthians point to a dignity more than human? Can He, Who is not merely a living soul, but a quickening Spirit; from Whom life radiates throughout renewed humanity[c]; from Whom there flows a stream of grace more abundant than the inheritance of sin which was bequeathed

ἔγειραι ὁ καθεύδων
καὶ ἀνάστα ἐκ τῶν νεκρῶν,
καὶ ἐπιφαύσει σοι ὁ Χριστός.

Cf. Münter, über die älteste Christliche Poesie, p. 29.

[w] Rom. ix. 5; and perhaps xvi. 27, see Ols. in loc.; 1 Tim. i. 12: χάριν ἔχω τῷ ἐνδυναμώσαντί με Χριστῷ Ἰησοῦ τῷ Κυρίῳ ἡμῶν κ.τ.λ. Cf. Heb. xiii. 20.

[x] e.g. certainly Joel ii. 32 in Rom. x. 13; and very probably Jer. ix. 23, 24 in 1 Cor. i. 31, etc.

[y] 1 Thess. ii. 19, iii. 13, iv. 2, 6, 16, 17, v. 23; 2 Thess. i. 7, 8, 9, 10, ii. 8. Compare Rom. xiv. 10, 11, 12.

[z] Rom. x. 4; Gal. iii. 24.

[a] Rom. iii. 25, 26; Gal. ii. 16, etc. St. Paul's argument in Gal. iii. 20 implies our Lord's Divinity; since, if Christ is merely human, He would be a mediator in the same sense in which Moses was a mediator. Of the two parties, God and Israel, the μεσίτης of the Law could properly represent Israel alone. The μεσίτης of 1 Tim. ii. 5 is altogether higher.

[b] δικαιοσύνη. Comp. Rom. v. 1, 2, 11.

[c] Rom. v. 18, 19; xv. 18.

by our fallen parent [d],—can He be, in His Apostle's mind, merely one of the race which He thus blesses and saves [e]? And if Jesus Christ be more than man, is it possible to suggest any intermediate position between humanity and the throne of God, which St. Paul, with his earnest belief in the God of Israel, could have believed Him to occupy?

In the Epistles to the Corinthians St. Paul is not especially maintaining any one great truth of revelation; he is entering with practical versatility into the varied active life and pressing wants of a local Church. Yet these Epistles might alone suffice to shew the high and unrivalled honour paid to Jesus Christ in the Apostle's heart and thought. Is the Apostle contrasting his preaching with the philosophy of the Greek and the hopes of the Jewish world around him? Jesus crucified [f] is his central subject; Jesus crucified is his whole philosophy [g]. Is he prescribing the law of apostolic labours in building up souls or Churches? 'Other foundation can no man lay' than 'Jesus Christ [h].' Is he unfolding the nature of the Church? It is not a self-organized multitude of religionists who agree in certain tenets, but 'the Body of Christ [i].' Is he arguing against sins of impurity? Christians have only to remember that they are members of Christ [j]. Is he deepening a sense of the glory and of the responsibility of being a Christian? Christians are reminded that Jesus Christ is in them except they be reprobates [k]. Is he excommunicating or reconciling a flagrant offender against natural law? He delivers to Satan in the Name of Christ; he

[d] Rom. v. 15; xv. 29.

[e] St. Paul styles himself in Rom. i. 1, δοῦλος Χριστοῦ Ἰησοῦ: and his value for this designation appears from Gal. i. 10, εἰ ἔτι ἀνθρώποις ἤρεσκον, Χριστοῦ δοῦλος οὐχ ἂν ἤμην, where observe the antithesis between Χριστοῦ and ἀνθρώποις: cf. Eph. vi. 6. With these compare his earnest precept, 1 Cor. vii. 23, μὴ γίνεσθε δοῦλοι ἀνθρώπων. How much is implied too in the stern description, Rom. xvi. 18, τῷ Κυρίῳ ἡμῶν Χριστῷ οὐ δουλεύουσιν, ἀλλὰ τῇ ἑαυτῶν κοιλίᾳ. Cf. Phil. iii. 19.

[f] 1 Cor. i. 23, 24: ἡμεῖς δὲ κηρύσσομεν Χριστὸν ἐσταυρωμένον .... Θεοῦ δύναμιν καὶ Θεοῦ σοφίαν.

[g] Ibid. ii. 2: οὐ γὰρ ἔκρινα τοῦ εἰδέναι τι ἐν ὑμῖν, εἰ μὴ Ἰησοῦν Χριστὸν, καὶ τοῦτον ἐσταυρωμένον.

[h] Ibid. iii. 11: θεμέλιον γὰρ ἄλλον οὐδεὶς δύναται θεῖναι παρὰ τὸν κείμενον, ὅς ἐστιν Ἰησοῦς ὁ Χριστός. Isa. xxviii. 16; Eph. ii. 20.

[i] 1 Cor. xii. 27: ὑμεῖς δέ ἐστε σῶμα Χριστοῦ καὶ μέλη ἐκ μέρους. Thus he even identifies the Church with Christ. Ibid. ver. 12: καθάπερ γὰρ τὸ σῶμα ἕν ἐστι, καὶ μέλη ἔχει πολλὰ .... οὕτω καὶ ὁ Χριστός.

[j] Ibid. vi. 15: οὐκ οἴδατε ὅτι τὰ σώματα ὑμῶν μέλη Χριστοῦ ἐστιν;

[k] 2 Cor. xiii. 5: ἢ οὐκ ἐπιγινώσκετε ἑαυτοὺς, ὅτι Ἰησοῦς Χριστὸς ἐν ὑμῖν ἐστιν; εἰ μή τι ἀδόκιμοί ἐστε.

absolves in the Person of Christ [l]. Is he rebuking irreverence towards the Holy Eucharist? The broken bread and the cup of blessing are not picturesque symbols of an absent Teacher, but veils of a gracious yet awful Presence; the irreverent receiver is guilty of the Body and Blood of the Lord Which he does not 'discern [m].' Is he pointing to the source of the soul's birth and growth in the life of light? It is the 'illumination of the Gospel of the Glory of Christ, Who is the Image of God;' it is the 'illumination of the knowledge of the glory of God in the Person of Jesus Christ [n].' Is he describing the spirit of the Christian life? It is perpetual self-mortification for the love of Jesus, that the moral life of Jesus may be manifested to the world in our frail human nature [o]. Is he sketching out the intellectual aim of his ministry? Every thought is to be brought as a captive into submission to Christ [p]. Is he unveiling the motive which sustained him in his manifold sufferings? All was undergone for Christ [q]. Is he suffering from a severe bodily or spiritual affliction? Thrice he prays to Jesus Christ for relief. And when he is told that the trial will not be removed, since in possessing Christ's grace he has all that he needs, he rejoices in the infirmity against which he had prayed, 'that the power of Christ may tabernacle upon him [r].' Would he summarize the relations of the Christian to Christ? To Christ

[l] 1 Cor. v. 4, 5: *ἐν τῷ ὀνόματι τοῦ Κυρίου ἡμῶν Ἰησοῦ, ... σὺν τῇ δυνάμει τοῦ Κυρίου ἡμῶν Ἰησοῦ Χριστοῦ παραδοῦναι τὸν τοιοῦτον τῷ Σατανᾷ.* 2 Cor. ii. 10: *καὶ γὰρ ἐγὼ εἴ τι κεχάρισμαι, ᾧ κεχάρισμαι, δι' ὑμᾶς, ἐν προσώπῳ Χριστοῦ, ἵνα μὴ πλεονεκτηθῶμεν ὑπὸ τοῦ Σατανᾶ.*

[m] Ibid. x. 16: *τὸ ποτήριον τῆς εὐλογίας ὃ εὐλογοῦμεν, οὐχὶ κοινωνία τοῦ αἵματος τοῦ Χριστοῦ ἐστι; τὸν ἄρτον ὃν κλῶμεν, οὐχὶ κοινωνία τοῦ σώματος τοῦ Χριστοῦ ἐστι;* Ibid. xi. 27: *ὃς ἂν ἐσθίῃ τὸν ἄρτον τοῦτον ἢ πίνῃ τὸ ποτήριον τοῦ Κυρίου ἀναξίως, ἔνοχος ἔσται τοῦ σώματος καὶ αἵματος τοῦ Κυρίου.* Ibid. ver. 29: *ὁ γὰρ ἐσθίων καὶ πίνων [ἀναξίως], κρίμα ἑαυτῷ ἐσθίει καὶ πίνει, μὴ διακρίνων τὸ σῶμα τοῦ Κυρίου.*

[n] 2 Cor. iv. 4. The god of this world has blinded the thoughts of the unbelievers, *εἰς τὸ μὴ αὐγάσαι αὐτοῖς τὸν φωτισμὸν τοῦ εὐαγγελίου τῆς δόξης τοῦ Χριστοῦ, ὅς ἐστιν εἰκὼν τοῦ Θεοῦ.* On the other hand, God, Who bade light shine out of darkness, has shined in the hearts of believing Christians, *πρὸς φωτισμὸν τῆς γνώσεως τῆς δόξης τοῦ Θεοῦ ἐν προσώπῳ Ἰησοῦ Χριστοῦ* (ver. 6).

[o] Ibid. ver. 10: *ἵνα καὶ ἡ ζωὴ τοῦ Ἰησοῦ ἐν τῷ σώματι ἡμῶν φανερωθῇ.*

[p] Ibid. x. 5: *αἰχμαλωτίζοντες πᾶν νόημα εἰς τὴν ὑπακοὴν τοῦ Χριστοῦ.*

[q] Ibid. xii. 10: *εὐδοκῶ ἐν ἀσθενείαις, ἐν ὕβρεσιν, ἐν ἀνάγκαις, ἐν διωγμοῖς, ἐν στενοχωρίαις ὑπὲρ Χριστοῦ.*

[r] Ibid. vers. 7-9: *ἐδόθη μοι σκόλοψ τῇ σαρκὶ . . . . ὑπὲρ τούτου τρὶς τὸν Κύριον παρεκάλεσα, ἵνα ἀποστῇ ἀπ' ἐμοῦ· καὶ εἴρηκέ μοι, "Ἀρκεῖ σοι ἡ χάρις μου· ἡ γὰρ δύναμίς μου ἐν ἀσθενείᾳ τελειοῦται." ἥδιστα οὖν μᾶλλον καυχήσομαι ἐν ταῖς ἀσθενείαις μου, ἵνα ἐπισκηνώσῃ ἐπ' ἐμὲ ἡ δύναμις τοῦ Χριστοῦ.*

he owes his mental philosophy, his justification before God, his progressive growth in holiness, his redemption from sin and death [s]. Would he mark the happiness of instruction in that 'hidden philosophy' which was taught in the Church among the perfect, and which was unknown to the rulers of the non-Christian world? It might have saved them from crucifying the Lord of Glory [t]. Would he lay down an absolute criterion of moral ruin? 'If any man love not the Lord Jesus Christ, let him be Anathema Maran-atha [u].' Would he impart an apostolical benediction? In one Epistle he blesses his readers in the Name of Christ alone [v]; in the other he names the Three Blessed Persons: while 'the grace of our Lord Jesus Christ' is mentioned, not only before 'the fellowship of the Holy Ghost,' but before 'the love of God [w].'

Here are texts, selected almost at random from those two among the longer Epistles of St. Paul which are most entirely without the form and method of a doctrinal treatise, dealing as they do with the varied contemporary interests and controversies of a particular Church [x]. Certainly some of these texts, taken alone, do not assert the Divinity of Jesus Christ. But put them together; add, as you might add, to their number; and consider whether the whole body of language before you, however you interpret it, does not imply that Christ held a place in the thought, affections, and teaching of St. Paul, higher than that which a sincere Theist would assign to any creature, and, if Christ be only a creature, obviously inconsistent

[s] 1 Cor. i. 30: ὃς ἐγενήθη ἡμῖν σοφία ἀπὸ Θεοῦ, δικαιοσύνη τε καὶ ἁγιασμὸς καὶ ἀπολύτρωσις.

[t] Ibid. ii. 8: εἰ γὰρ ἔγνωσαν, οὐκ ἂν τὸν Κύριον τῆς δόξης ἐσταύρωσαν.

[u] Ibid. xvi. 22: εἴ τις οὐ φιλεῖ τὸν Κύριον Ἰησοῦν Χριστὸν, ἤτω ἀνάθεμα, μαρὰν ἀθά.

[v] Ibid. ver. 23.

[w] 2 Cor. xiii. 13; cf. 1 Cor. i. 8: ὃς καὶ βεβαιώσει ὑμᾶς ἕως τέλους.

[x] Thus to the passages already quoted from 2 Cor. may be added, those on our Lord's unchangeableness, i. 19, 20, comp. Numb. xxiii. 19, Mal. iii. 6, St. James i. 17, and Heb. xiii. 8; His being the Divine Πνεῦμα, iii. 17, comp. note, p. 317; the φόβος τοῦ Κυρίου, with reference to His coming to judgment, v. 11; the explanation of ὑπὲρ Χριστοῦ πρεσβεύομεν by ὡς τοῦ Θεοῦ παρακαλοῦντος δι' ἡμῶν, v. 20, cf. ver. 19; Christ's condescension, viii. 9, cf. p. 314; the implied force of viii. 19, 23; Christ's bestowal of ἐξουσία, x. 8, xiii. 10; His being the 'boast' of Christians, x. 17-18, comp. vers. 7, 14, and 1 Cor. i. 31, although this reference to our Lord admits of being disputed; His being Bridegroom of the Church, xi. 2, cf. Rev. xix. 7, as Jehovah is of Israel in Ezek. xvi. 8-14, Is. lxii. 5, etc.; the adjurations, xi. 10, xii. 19, cf. Is. lxv. 16; Christ's speaking in His servants, xiii. 3, through the Holy Spirit, St. Matt. x. 20.

with the supreme and exacting rights of God. In these Epistles, it is not the teaching, but the Person and Work of Jesus Christ, upon which St. Paul's eye appears to rest. Christ Himself is, in St. Paul's mind, the Gospel of Christ; and if Christ be not God, St. Paul cannot be acquitted of assigning to Him generally a prominence which is inconsistent with serious loyalty to monotheistic truth.

Still more remarkably do the Epistles of the First Imprisonment present us with a picture of our Lord's Work and Person which absolutely presupposes, even where it does not in terms assert, the doctrine of His Divinity. The Epistles to the Ephesians and the Colossians are even more intimately related to each other than are those to the Romans and the Galatians. They deal with the same lines of truth; they differ only in method of treatment. That to the Ephesians is devotional and expository; that to the Colossians is polemical. In the Colossians the dignity of Christ's Person is put forward most explicitly as against the speculations of a Judaizing theosophy which degraded Christ to the rank of an archangel [z], and which recommended, as a substitute for Christ's redemptive work, ascetic observances, grounded on a trust in the cleansing and hallowing properties and powers of nature [a]. In the Epistle to the Ephesians our Lord's Personal dignity is asserted more indirectly. It is implied in His reconciliation of Jews and heathens to each other and to God, and still more in His relationship to the predestination of the saints [b]. In both Epistles we encounter two

[z] Baur, Vorlesungen, p. 274: 'Die im Colosserbrief gemeinten Engelsverehrer setzten ohne Zweifel Christus selbst in die Classe der Engel, als ἕνα τῶν ἀρχαγγέλων, wie diess Epiphanius als einen Lehrsatz der Ebioniten angibt, wogegen der Colosserbrief mit allem Nachdruck auf ein solches κρατεῖν τὴν κεφαλὴν dringt, dass *alles, was nicht das Haupt selbst ist, nur in einem absoluten Abhängigkeits-verhältniss zu Ihm stehend gedacht wird*, ii. 19.'

[a] Ibid. 'Eine Lehre, welche den Menschen in religiöser Hinsicht von seinem natürlichen bürgerlichen Sein, von der materiellen Natur abhängig machte, und sein religiöses Heil durch die reinigende und heiligende Kraft, die man den Elementen und Substanzen der Welt zuschrieb, den Einfluss der Himmels-cörper, das natürlich Reine im Unterschied von dem für unrein Gehaltenen vermittelt werden liess, setzte die στοιχεῖα τοῦ κόσμου an dieselbe Stelle, welche nur Christus als Erlöser haben sollte. In diesem Sinne werden V. 8 die στοιχεῖα τοῦ κόσμου und Christus einander gegenübergestellt. Das ist die Philosophie in dem Sinne in welchem das Wesen der Philosophie als Weltweisheit bezeichnet wird, als die Wissenschaft, die es mit den στοιχεῖα τοῦ κόσμου zu thun hat. Als solche ist sie auch nur eine κενὴ ἀπάτη, eine blosse παράδοσις τῶν ἀνθρώπων.'

[b] Ibid. p. 270: 'Der transcendenten Christologie dieser Briefe und ihrer

prominent lines of thought, each, in a high degree, pointing to Christ's Divine dignity. The first, the absolute character of the Christian faith as contrasted with the relative character of heathenism and Judaism [c]; the second, the re-creative power of the grace of Christ [d]. In both Epistles the Church is considered as a vast spiritual society [e] which, besides embracing as its heritage all races of the world, pierces the veil of the unseen, and includes the families of heaven [f] in its majestic compass. Of this society Christ is the Head [g], and it is 'His Body, the fulness of Him That filleth all in all.' Christ is the predestined point of unity in which earth and heaven, Jew and Gentile, meet and are one [h]. Christ's Death is the triumph of peace in the spiritual world. Peace with God is secured through the taking away of the law of condemnation by the dying Christ, Who nails it to His Cross and openly triumphs over the powers of darkness [i]. Peace among men is secured, because the Cross is the centre of the regenerated world, as of the moral universe [j].

darauf beruhenden Anschauung von dem alles umfassenden und über alles übergreifenden Charakter des Christenthums ist es ganz gemäss, dass sie in der Lehre von der Beseligung der Menschen auf eine überzeitliche Vorherbestimmung zurückgehen, Eph. i. 4, f.'

[c] Baur, Vorlesungen, p. 273: 'So ist . . . auch die absolute Erhabenheit des Christenthums über Judenthum und Heidenthum ausgesprochen. Beide verhalten sich gleich negativ (but by no means in the same degree) zum Christenthum, das ihnen gegenüber *ὁ λόγος τῆς ἀληθείας* ist Eph. i. 13, oder *φῶς* im Gegensatz von *σκότος* (v. 8). Die Juden und die Heiden waren wegen der allgemeinen Sündhäftigkeit dem göttlichen Zorn verfallen, Eph. ii. 3. Der religiöse Charakter des Heidenthums wird noch besonders dadurch bezeichnet, dass die Heiden *ἄθεοι ἐν τῷ κόσμῳ* sind (ii. 12), *ἐσκοτωμένοι τῇ διανοίᾳ ὄντες* (iv. 18), *ἀπηλλοτριωμένοι τῆς ζωῆς τοῦ Θεοῦ διὰ τὴν ἄγνοιαν τὴν οὖσαν ἐν αὐτοῖς* (iv. 18), *περιπατοῦντες κατὰ τὸν αἰῶνα τοῦ κόσμου τούτου κατὰ τὸν ἄρχοντα τῆς ἐξουσίας τοῦ ἀέρος* (ii. 2). Beiden Religionen gegenüber ist das Christenthum die absolute Religion. *Der absolute Charakter des Christenthums selbst aber ist bedingt durch die Person Christi.*'

[d] Col. iii. 9; Eph. iv. 21 sqq.; cf. Ibid. ii. 8-10. Baur, Vorlesungen, p. 270: 'Die Gnade ist das den Menschen durch den Glauben an Christus neu schaffende Princip. Etwas Neues muss nämlich der Mensch durch das Christenthum werden.'

[e] Col. i. 5, 6: *τοῦ εὐαγγελίου, τοῦ παρόντος εἰς ὑμᾶς, καθὼς καὶ ἐν παντὶ τῷ κόσμῳ, καὶ ἔστι καρποφορούμενον.* Eph. i. 13.

[f] Eph. iii. 15.

[g] Eph. i. 22, 23: *αὐτὸν ἔδωκε κεφαλὴν ὑπὲρ πάντα τῇ ἐκκλησίᾳ, ἥτις ἐστὶ τὸ σῶμα αὐτοῦ, τὸ πλήρωμα τοῦ πάντα ἐν πᾶσι πληρουμένου.* v. 23, 30.

[h] Ibid. ver. 10: *ἀνακεφαλαιώσασθαι τὰ πάντα ἐν τῷ Χριστῷ, τά τε ἐν τοῖς οὐρανοῖς καὶ τὰ ἐπὶ τῆς γῆς· ἐν αὐτῷ, ἐν ᾧ καὶ ἐκληρώθημεν.*

[i] Col. ii. 14, 15.

[j] Col. i. 20, 21: *δι' αὐτοῦ ἀποκαταλλάξαι τὰ πάντα εἰς αὐτὸν, εἰρηνοποιήσας*

Divided races, religions, nationalities, classes, meet beneath the Cross; they embrace as brethren; they are fused into one vast society which is held together by an Indwelling Presence, reflected in the general sense of boundless indebtedness to a transcendent Love [k]. Hence in these Epistles such marked emphasis is laid upon the unity of the Body of Christ [l]; since the reunion of moral beings shews forth Christ's Personal Glory. Christ is the Unifier. As Christ in His Passion is the Combiner and Reconciler of all things in earth and heaven; so He ascends to heaven, He descends to hell on His errand of reconciliation and combination [m]. He institutes the hierarchy of the Church [n]; He is the Root from which her life springs, the Foundation on

διὰ τοῦ αἵματος τοῦ σταυροῦ αὐτοῦ, δι' αὐτοῦ, εἴτε τὰ ἐπὶ τῆς γῆς, εἴτε τὰ ἐν τοῖς οὐρανοῖς.

[k] Col. iii. 11: *οὐκ ἔνι Ἕλλην καὶ Ἰουδαῖος, περιτομὴ καὶ ἀκροβυστία, βάρβαρος, Σκύθης, δοῦλος, ἐλεύθερος· ἀλλὰ τὰ πάντα καὶ ἐν πᾶσι Χριστός.* Observe the moral inferences in vers. 12–14, the measure of charity being *καθὼς καὶ ὁ Χριστὸς ἐχαρίσατο ὑμῖν.* Especially Jews and Gentiles are reconciled beneath the Cross, because the Cross cancelled the obligatoriness of the ceremonial law. Eph. ii. 14–17: *αὐτὸς γάρ ἐστιν ἡ εἰρήνη ἡμῶν, ὁ ποιήσας τὰ ἀμφότερα ἕν, καὶ τὸ μεσότοιχον τοῦ φραγμοῦ λύσας, τὴν ἔχθραν ἐν τῇ σαρκὶ αὐτοῦ, τὸν νόμον τῶν ἐντολῶν ἐν δόγμασι, καταργήσας· ἵνα τοὺς δύο κτίσῃ ἐν ἑαυτῷ εἰς ἕνα καινὸν ἄνθρωπον, ποιῶν εἰρήνην, καὶ ἀποκαταλλάξῃ τοὺς ἀμφοτέρους ἐν ἑνὶ σώματι τῷ Θεῷ διὰ τοῦ σταυροῦ, ἀποκτείνας τὴν ἔχθραν ἐν αὐτῷ.* Col. iii. 15.

[l] Baur, Christenthum, p. 119: 'Die Einheit ist das eigentliche Wesen der Kirche, diese Einheit ist mit allen zu ihr gehörenden Momenten durch das Christenthum gegeben, es ist Ein Leib, Ein Geist, Ein Herr, Ein Glaube, Eine Taufe u. s. w. Eph. iv. 4, f. . . . . Von diesem Punkte aus steigt die Anschauung höher hinauf, bis dahin, wo der Grund aller Einheit liegt. Die einigende, eine allgemeine Gemeinschaft stiftende Kraft des Todes Christi lässt sich nur daraus begreifen, *dass Christus überhaupt der alles tragende und zusammenhaltende Centralpunkte des ganzen Universums ist.* . . . . Die Christologie der beiden Briefe hängt aufs Innigste zusammen mit dem in der unmittelbaren Gegenwart gegebenen Bedürfniss der Einigung in der Idee der Einen, alle Unterschiede und Gegensätze in sich aufhebenden Kirche. Es ist, wenn wir uns in die Anschauungsweise dieser Briefe hineinversetzen, schon ein ächt katholisches Bewusstsein das sich in ihnen ausspricht.' This may be fully admitted without accepting Baur's conclusions as to the date and authorship of the two Epistles.

[m] Eph. iv. 10: *ὁ καταβὰς, αὐτός ἐστι καὶ ὁ ἀναβὰς ὑπεράνω πάντων τῶν οὐρανῶν, ἵνα πληρώσῃ τὰ πάντα.* St. Aug. Ep. 187, ad Dardanum: 'Christum Dominum . . . ubique totum præsentem esse, non dubites, *tanquam Deum.*'

[n] Eph. iv. 11–13: *καὶ αὐτὸς ἔδωκε τοὺς μὲν ἀποστόλους, τοὺς δὲ προφήτας, τοὺς δὲ εὐαγγελιστὰς, τοὺς δὲ ποιμένας καὶ διδασκάλους, πρὸς τὸν καταρτισμὸν τῶν ἁγίων, εἰς ἔργον διακονίας, εἰς οἰκοδομὴν τοῦ σώματος τοῦ Χριστοῦ· μέχρι καταντήσωμεν οἱ πάντες εἰς τὴν ἑνότητα τῆς πίστεως καὶ τῆς ἐπιγνώσεως τοῦ Υἱοῦ τοῦ Θεοῦ, εἰς ἄνδρα τέλειον, εἰς μέτρον ἡλικίας τοῦ πληρώματος τοῦ Χριστοῦ.* Compare 1 Cor. xii. 28: *ἔθετο ὁ Θεός.*

which her superstructure rests [o]; He is the quickening, organizing, Catholicizing Principle within her [p]. The closest of natural ties is the chosen symbol of His relation to her; she is His bride. For her, in His love, He gave Himself to death, that He might sanctify her by the cleansing virtue of His baptism, and might so present her to Himself, her Lord,—blameless, immaculate, glorious [q]. And thus He is the Standard of perfection with which she must struggle to correspond. Her members must grow up unto Him in all things. Accordingly, not to mention the great passage, already referred to, in the Epistle to the Colossians, Jesus Christ is said in that Epistle to possess the intellectual as well as the other attributes of Deity [r]. In the allusions to the Three Most Holy Persons, which so remarkably underlie the structure and surface-thought of the Epistle to the Ephesians, Jesus Christ is associated most significantly with the Father and the Spirit [s]. He is the Invisible King, Whose slaves Christians are [t]. Nay, His Realm is termed explicitly 'the kingdom of Him Who is Christ and God [u];' the Church is subject to Him [v]. He is the object of Christian study, and of Christian hope [x]. In the Epistle to the Philippians it is expressly said that all created beings in heaven, on earth, and in hell, when His triumph is complete, shall acknowledge the

[o] Col. ii. 7: *ἐρριζωμένοι καὶ ἐποικοδομούμενοι ἐν αὐτῷ.*

[p] Eph. iv. 15, 16: *ὁ Χριστὸς, ἐξ οὗ πᾶν τὸ σῶμα συναρμολογούμενον καὶ συμβιβαζόμενον διὰ πάσης ἀφῆς τῆς ἐπιχορηγίας, κατ' ἐνέργειαν ἐν μέτρῳ ἑνὸς ἑκάστου μέρους, τὴν αὔξησιν τοῦ σώματος ποιεῖται εἰς οἰκοδομὴν ἑαυτοῦ ἐν ἀγάπῃ.* Col. ii. 19.

[q] Eph. v. 25–27: *ὁ Χριστὸς ἠγάπησε τὴν ἐκκλησίαν, καὶ ἑαυτὸν παρέδωκεν ὑπὲρ αὐτῆς· ἵνα αὐτὴν ἁγιάσῃ, καθαρίσας τῷ λουτρῷ τοῦ ὕδατος ἐν ῥήματι, ἵνα παραστήσῃ αὐτὴν ἑαυτῷ ἔνδοξον, τὴν ἐκκλητίαν, μὴ ἔχουσαν σπίλον ἢ ῥυτίδα ἤ τι τῶν τοιούτων, ἀλλ' ἵνα ᾖ ἁγία καὶ ἄμωμος.*

[r] Col. ii. 2, 3: *ἐν ᾧ εἰσὶ πάντες οἱ θησαυροὶ τῆς σοφίας καὶ τῆς γνώσεως ἀπόκρυφοι.* Scrivener, Introd. Crit. N. T., p. 451. Col. i. 19, ii. 9.

[s] Eph. i. 3: *Πατὴρ τοῦ Κυρίου.* Ibid. ver. 6: *ἐν τῷ ἠγαπημένῳ.* Ibid. ver. 13: *ἐσφραγίσθητε τῷ Πνεύματι.* Ibid. ii. 18: *δι' αὐτοῦ ἔχομεν τὴν προσαγωγὴν οἱ ἀμφότεροι ἐν ἑνὶ Πνεύματι πρὸς τὸν Πάτερα.* Ibid. iii. 6: *συγκληρόνομα, καὶ σύσσωμα, καὶ συμμέτοχα,* where the Father Whose heirs we are, the Son of Whose Body we are members, the Spirit of Whose gifts we partake, seem to be glanced at by the adjectives denoting our relationship to the *ἐπαγγελία.* Cf. Ibid. iii. 14–17.

[t] Ibid. vi. 6: *μὴ κατ' ὀφθαλμοδουλείαν ὡς ἀνθρωπάρεσκοι, ἀλλ' ὡς δοῦλοι τοῦ Χριστοῦ.* Cf. ver. 5: *ὡς τῷ Χριστῷ.* Cf. p. 334, note.

[u] Ibid. v. 5: *ἐν τῇ βασιλείᾳ τοῦ Χριστοῦ καὶ Θεοῦ,* where, 'in the absence of the article before *Θεοῦ,* Christ and God are presented as a single conception.' See Harless in loc. Col. i. 13.

[v] Eph. v. 24: *ἡ ἐκκλησία ὑποτάσσεται τῷ Χριστῷ.*

[x] Ibid. iv. 20; i. 12; vi. 6–9.

majesty even of His Human Nature [y]. The preaching of the Gospel is described as the preaching Christ [z]. Death is a blessing for the Christian, since by death he gains the eternal presence of Christ [a]. The Philippians are specially privileged in being permitted, not merely to believe on Christ, but to suffer for Him [b]. The Apostle trusts in Jesus as in Providence to be able to send Timothy to Philippi [c]. He contrasts the selfishness of ordinary Christians with a disinterestedness that seeks the things (it is not said of God, but) of Christ [d]. The Christian 'boast' centres in Christ, as did the Jewish in the Law [e]; the Apostle had counted all his Jewish privileges as dung that he might win Christ [f]; Christ has taken possession of him [g]; Christ strengthens him [h]; Christ will one day change this body of our humiliation, that it may become of like form with the Body of His glory, according to the energy of His ability even to subdue all things unto Himself [i]. In this Epistle, as in those to the Corinthians, the Apostle is far from pursuing any one line of doctrinal statement: moral exhortations, interspersed with allusions to persons and matters of interest to himself and to the Philippians, constitute the staple of his letter. And yet how constant are the references to Jesus Christ, and how inconsistent are they, taken as a whole, with any conception of His Person which denies His Divinity [j]!

[y] Phil. ii. 10: ἵνα ἐν τῷ ὀνόματι Ἰησοῦ πᾶν γόνυ κάμψῃ ἐπουρανίων καὶ ἐπιγείων καὶ καταχθονίων. Cf. St. Cyril Alex. Thes. p. 128.

[z] Phil. i. 16: τὸν Χριστὸν καταγγέλλουσιν. Ibid. ver. 18: Χριστὸς καταγγέλλεται.

[a] Ibid. ver. 23: ἐπιθυμίαν ἔχων εἰς τὸ ἀναλῦσαι, καὶ σὺν Χριστῷ εἶναι. Cf. 2 Cor. v. 8; 1 Thess. iv. 17.

[b] Phil. i. 29: ὑμῖν ἐχαρίσθη τὸ ὑπὲρ Χριστοῦ, οὐ μόνον τὸ εἰς αὐτὸν πιστεύειν, ἀλλὰ καὶ τὸ ὑπὲρ αὐτοῦ πάσχειν. Cf. i. 20: μεγαλυνθήσεται Χριστὸς ἐν τῷ σώματί μου.

[c] Ibid. ii. 19: ἐλπίζω δὲ ἐν Κυρίῳ Ἰησοῦ, Τιμόθεον ταχέως πέμψαι ὑμῖν.

[d] Ibid. ver. 21: οἱ πάντες γὰρ τὰ ἑαυτῶν ζητοῦσιν, οὐ τὰ τοῦ Χριστοῦ Ἰησοῦ.

[e] Ibid. iii. 3: καυχώμενοι ἐν Χριστῷ Ἰησοῦ.

[f] Ibid. ver. 8: δι' ὃν τὰ πάντα ἐζημιώθην· καὶ ἡγοῦμαι σκύβαλα εἶναι, ἵνα Χριστὸν κερδήσω, καὶ εὑρεθῶ ἐν αὐτῷ. Cf. St. Matt. x. 37, 39, xiii. 44, 46; St. Luke xiv. 33.

[g] Ibid. iii. 12: κατελήφθην ὑπὸ Χριστοῦ Ἰησοῦ.

[h] Ibid. iv. 13: πάντα ἰσχύω ἐν τῷ ἐνδυναμοῦντί με [Χριστῷ]. Cf. i. 19: ἐπιχορηγία τοῦ Πνεύματος Ἰησοῦ Χριστοῦ.

[i] Ibid. iii. 20, 21: ὃς μετασχηματίσει τὸ σῶμα τῆς ταπεινώσεως ἡμῶν, εἰς τὸ γενέσθαι αὐτὸ σύμμορφον τῷ σώματι τῆς δόξης αὐτοῦ, κατὰ τὴν ἐνέργειαν τοῦ δύνασθαι αὐτὸν καὶ ὑποτάξαι ἑαυτῷ τὰ πάντα. Cf. iv. 4: ὁ Κύριος ἐγγύς.

[j] It should be added that in the Epistle to Philemon our Lord is associated with the Father as the source of grace and peace, ver. 3, while He

The Pastoral Epistles are distinguished, not merely by the specific directions which they contain respecting the Christian hierarchy and religious societies in the apostolical Church [k], but also and especially by the stress which they lay upon the vital distinction between heresy and orthodoxy [l]. Each of these lines of teaching radiates from a most exalted conception of Christ's Person, whether He is the Source of ministerial power [m], or the Sun and Centre-point of orthodox truth [n]. In stating the doctrine of redemption these Epistles insist strongly upon its universality [o]. The whole world was redeemed in the inten-

is represented as the object of Christian faith and activity, vers. 5, 6; and the pregnant phrases ἐν Χριστῷ, ἐν Κυρίῳ, occur four times in this short Epistle.

[k] 1 Tim. iii. iv. v.; Tit. i. 5-9; ii. 1-10, etc.

[l] St. Paul's language implies that the true faith is to the soul what the most necessary conditions of health are to the body. ὑγιαίνουσα διδασκαλία (1 Tim. i. 10; Tit. i. 9, ii. 1); so λόγος ὑγιὴς (Tit. ii. 8), λόγοι ὑγιαίνοντες (2 Tim. i. 13). Thus the orthodox teaching is styled ἡ καλὴ διδασκαλία (1 Tim. iv. 6), or simply ἡ διδασκαλία (Ibid. vi. 1), as though no other deserved the name. Any deviation (ἑτεροδιδασκαλεῖν, Ibid. i. 3; vi. 3) is self-condemned as being such. The heretic prefers his own self-chosen private way to the universally-received doctrine; he is to be cut off, after two admonitions, from the communion of the Church (Tit. iii. 10) on the ground that ἐξέστραπται ὁ τοιοῦτος, καὶ ἁμαρτάνει, ὢν αὐτοκατάκριτος (Ibid.). Heresy is spoken of by turns as a crime and a misfortune, περὶ τὴν πίστιν ἐναυάγησαν (1 Tim. i. 19); ἀπεπλανήθησαν ἀπὸ τῆς πίστεως (Ibid. vi. 10); περὶ τὴν ἀλήθειαν ἠστόχησαν (2 Tim. ii. 18). Deeper error is characterized in severer terms, ἀποστήσονταί τινες τῆς πίστεως, προσέχοντες πνεύμασι πλάνοις καὶ διδασκαλίαις δαιμονίων .... κεκαυτηριασμένων τὴν ἰδίαν συνείδησιν κ.τ.λ. (1 Tim. iv. 1, 2); οὗτοι ἀνθίστανται τῇ ἀληθείᾳ, ἄνθρωποι κατεφθαρμένοι τὸν νοῦν, ἀδόκιμοι περὶ τὴν πίστιν (2 Tim. iii. 8); ἀπὸ τῆς ἀληθείας τὴν ἀκοὴν ἀποστρέψουσιν, ἐπὶ δὲ τοὺς μύθους ἐκτραπήσονται (Ibid. iv. 4). Heresy eats its way into the spiritual body like a gangrene, ὁ λόγος αὐτῶν ὡς γάγγραινα νομὴν ἕξει (Ibid. ii. 17). It is observable that throughout these Epistles πίστις is not the subjective apprehension, but the objective body of truth; not *fides quâ creditur*, but *the* Faith. And the Church is στύλος καὶ ἑδραίωμα τῆς ἀληθείας (1 Tim. iii. 15). This truth, which the Church supports, is already embodied in a ὑποτύπωσις ὑγιαινόντων λόγων (2 Tim. i. 13).

[m] 1 Tim. i. 12: θέμενος εἰς διακονίαν. 2 Tim. ii. 3: στρατιώτης Ἰησοῦ Χριστοῦ. So when the young widows who have entered into the Order of widows wish to marry again, this is represented as an offence against Christ, with Whom they have entered into a personal engagement, ὅταν γὰρ καταστρηνιάσωσι τοῦ Χριστοῦ, γαμεῖν θέλουσιν, ἔχουσαι κρίμα, ὅτι τὴν πρώτην πίστιν ἠθέτησαν (1 Tim. v. 11, 12).

[n] 1 Tim. vi. 3, where moral and social truth is specially in question.

[o] Ibid. ii. 3. Intercession is to be offered for all. τοῦτο γὰρ καλὸν καὶ ἀπόδεκτον ἐνώπιον τοῦ Σωτῆρος ἡμῶν Θεοῦ, ὃς πάντας ἀνθρώπους θέλει σωθῆναι καὶ εἰς ἐπίγνωσιν ἀληθείας ἐλθεῖν. εἷς γὰρ Θεὸς, εἷς καὶ μεσίτης Θεοῦ καὶ

[LECT.

tion of Christ, however that intention might be limited in effect by the will of man. As the theories, Judaizing and Gnostic, which confined the benefits of Christ's redemptive work to races or classes, were more or less Humanitarian in their estimate of His Person; so along with the recognition of a world-embracing redemption was found the belief in a Divine Redeemer. Accordingly in the Pastoral Epistles the Divinity of our Lord is taught both in express terms [p] and by tacit implication [q]. His functions as the Awarder of indulgence and mercy [r], His invisible Presence among angelic attendants [s], His active providence over His servants, and His ready aid in trouble [t], are introduced naturally as familiar topics. And if the Manhood of the One Mediator is prominently alluded to as being the instrument of His Mediation [u], His Pre-existence in a Higher Nature is as clearly intimated [v].

After what has already been said on the prominence of the doctrine of Christ's Divinity in the Epistle to the Hebrews, it may suffice here to remark that the power [w] of His Priestly

ἀνθρώπων, ἄνθρωπος Χριστὸς Ἰησοῦς, ὁ δοὺς ἑαυτὸν ἀντίλυτρον ὑπὲρ πάντων. Cf. Ibid. iv. 10; Tit. ii. 11.

[p] Tit. ii. 13: τοῦ μεγάλου Θεοῦ καὶ Σωτῆρος ἡμῶν Ἰησοῦ Χριστοῦ. Cf. p. 319, note y.

[q] e.g. 2 Tim. i. 1, ii. 1. Cf. St. John i. 14, 16; 2 Tim. i. 9, 10. Cf. Tit. ii. 11, iii. 4, etc.

[r] 1 Tim. i. 16: διὰ τοῦτο ἠλεήθην, ἵνα ἐν ἐμοὶ πρώτῳ ἐνδείξηται Ἰησοῦς Χριστὸς τὴν πᾶσαν μακροθυμίαν. Cf. ver. 13. Compare the intercession for the (apparently) deceased Onesiphorus: δῴη αὐτῷ ὁ Κύριος εὑρεῖν ἔλεος παρὰ Κυρίου ἐν ἐκείνῃ τῇ ἡμέρᾳ (2 Tim. i. 18); where the second Κύριος also is Jesus Christ (Gen. xix. 24; St. Luke xi. 17; St. Matt. xii. 26) the Judge, at Whose Hands St. Paul himself expects to receive the crown of righteousness (Ibid. iv. 8, 14).

[s] Observe the adjurations, διαμαρτύρομαι ἐνώπιον τοῦ Θεοῦ καὶ Κυρίου Ἰησοῦ Χριστοῦ καὶ τῶν ἐκλεκτῶν ἀγγέλων (1 Tim. v. 21); παραγγέλλω σοι ἐνώπιον τοῦ Θεοῦ τοῦ ζωοποιοῦντος τὰ πάντα, καὶ Χριστοῦ Ἰησοῦ τοῦ μαρτυρήσαντος ἐπὶ Ποντίου Πιλάτου τὴν καλὴν ὁμολογίαν (Ibid. vi. 13). Cf. 2 Tim. iv. 1.

[t] 2 Tim. iii. 11: ἐκ πάντων [sc. διωγμῶν] με ἐῤῥύσατο ὁ Κύριος. Ibid. iv. 17: ὁ δὲ Κύριός μοι παρέστη, καὶ ἐνεδυνάμωσέ με. Ibid. ver. 18: ῥύσεταί με ὁ Κύριος ἀπὸ παντὸς ἔργου πονηροῦ. Cf., yet more, Ibid. ii. 10: σωτηρίας τῆς ἐν Χριστῷ Ἰησοῦ, μετὰ δόξης αἰωνίου. Cf. St. John x. 28, xvii. 22.

[u] 1 Tim. ii. 5.

[v] Ibid. iii. 16. Baur, Vorlesungen, p. 351: 'Mensch wird zwar Christus ausdrücklich genannt (1 Tim. ii. 5) aber von einem menschlichen Subject kann doch eigentlich nicht gesagt werden ἐφανερώθη ἐν σαρκί. Es passt diess nur für ein höheres übermenschliches Wesen.'

[w] Heb. vii. 25: σώζειν εἰς τὸ παντελὲς δύναται. Ibid. ix. 12: αἰωνίαν λύτρωσιν.

Mediation as there insisted on, although exhibited in His glorified Humanity, does of itself imply a superhuman Personality [x]. This indeed is more than hinted at in the terms of the comparison which is instituted between Melchisedec and His Divine Antitype. History records nothing of the parents, of the descent, of the birth, or of the death of Melchisedec; he appears in the sacred narrative as if he had no beginning of days or end of life. In this he is 'made like unto the Son of God,' with His eternal Pre-existence and His endless days [y]. This Eternal Christ can save to the uttermost, because He has a Priesthood that is unchangeable, since it is based on His Own Everlasting Being [z].

In short, if we bear in mind that, as the Mediator, Christ is God and Man, St. Paul's language about Him is explained by its twofold drift. On the one hand, the true force of the distinction between 'One God' and 'One Lord' or 'One Mediator' becomes apparent in those passages, where Christ in His assumed Manhood is for the moment in contrast with the Unincarnate Deity of the Father [a]. On the other hand, it is only possible to read the great Christological passages of the Apostle without doing violence to the plain force of his language, when we believe that Christ is God. Doubtless the Christ of St. Paul is shrouded in mystery; but could any real intercourse between God and man have been re-established which should be wholly unmysterious? Strip Christ of His Godhead that you may denude Him of mystery, and what becomes, I do not say of particular texts, but of all the most characteristic teaching of St. Paul? Substitute, if you can, throughout any one Epistle the name of the first of the saints or of the highest among the angels, for the Name of the Divine Redeemer, and see how it reads. Accept the Apostle's implied challenge. Imagine for a moment that Paul was crucified for you; that

[x] That it was our Lord's Divine Nature which gave its supreme value to His sacrifice on the Cross seems to be taught in Heb. ix. 14, where πνεῦμα is the nature of God, Who is Spirit; see Rom. i. 4, 1 Tim. iii. 16, and St. John iv. 24. Cf. Bisping in loc.

[y] Heb. vii. 3: *ἀπάτωρ, ἀμήτωρ, ἀγενεαλόγητος· μήτε ἀρχὴν ἡμερῶν, μήτε ζωῆς τέλος ἔχων· ἀφωμοιωμένος δὲ τῷ Υἱῷ τοῦ Θεοῦ.* Bengel: 'Non dicitur Filius Dei assimilatus Melchisedeko, sed contra. Nam Filius Dei est antiquior, et archetypus.'

[z] Heb. vii. 24, 25: *ὁ δὲ, διὰ τὸ μένειν αὐτὸν εἰς τὸν αἰῶνα, ἀπαράβατον ἔχει τὴν ἱερωσύνην· ὅθεν καὶ σώζειν εἰς τὸ παντελὲς δύναται.*

[a] 1 Cor. viii. 6; Eph. iv. 5; 1 Tim. ii. 5.

you were baptized in the name of Paul[a]; that wisdom, holiness, redemption, come from the Apostle; that the Church is not Christ's, but Paul's[b]. Conceive, if you can, that the Apostle ascends his Master's throne; that he says anathema to any who loves not the Apostle Paul; that he is bent upon bringing every thought captive to the obedience of Paul; that he announces that in Paul are hid all the treasures of wisdom and knowledge; that instead of protesting 'We preach not ourselves, but Christ Jesus the Lord, and ourselves your servants for Jesus' sake[c],' he could say, Paul is 'the end of the law to every one that believeth[d],' or 'I beseech you for Paul's sake and for the love of the Spirit[e].' What is it in the Name of Christ which renders this language, when applied to Him, other than intolerable? Why is it that when coupled with any other name, however revered and saintly, the words of Paul respecting Jesus Christ must seem not merely strained, but exaggerated and blasphemous? Is it not that truth answers to truth, that all through these Epistles, and not merely in particular assertions, there is an underlying idea of Christ's Divinity which is taken for granted, as being the very soul and marrow of the entire series of doctrines? that when this is lost sight of, all is misshapen and dislocated? that when this is recognised, all falls into its place as the exhibition of infinite Power and Mercy, clothed in a vesture of humiliation and sacrifice, and devoted to the succour and enlightenment of man?

4. It is with the prominent features of St. Paul's characteristic teaching as with the general drift of his great Epistles; they irresistibly imply a Christ Who is Divine.

(*a*) Every reader of the New Testament associates St. Paul with the special advocacy of the necessity of faith as the indispensable condition of man's justification before God. What is this 'faith' of St. Paul? It is in experience the most simple of the movements of the soul; and yet, if analysed, it turns out

[a] 1 Cor. i. 13: *μὴ Παῦλος ἐσταυρώθη ὑπὲρ ὑμῶν; ἢ εἰς τὸ ὄνομα Παύλου ἐβαπτίσθητε;*

[b] Rom. xvi. 16: *αἱ ἐκκλησίαι πᾶσαι τοῦ Χριστοῦ.* Gal. i. 22. Comp. St. Matt. xvi. 18: *μου τὴν ἐκκλησίαν.* The more usual expression, it is significant to note, is *ἐκκλησία τοῦ Θεοῦ.* 1 Cor. i. 2, x. 32, xi. 16, 22, xv. 9; 2 Cor. i. 1; Gal. i. 13; 1 Tim. iii. 5, 15.

[c] 2 Cor. iv. 5.

[d] Rom. x. 4.

[e] Rom. xv. 30: *παρακαλῶ δὲ ὑμᾶς, ἀδελφοί, διὰ τοῦ Κυρίου ἡμῶν Ἰησοῦ Χριστοῦ, καὶ διὰ τῆς ἀγάπης τοῦ Πνεύματος.*

to be one of the most complex among the religious ideas in the New Testament. The word πίστις implies, first of all, both faithfulness and confidence[f]; but religious confidence is closely allied to belief, that is to say, to a persuasion that some unseen fact is true[g]. And this belief, having for its object the unseen, is opposed by St. Paul to 'sight[h].' It is fed by, or rather it is in itself, a higher intuition than any of which nature is capable[i]; it is the continuous exercise of a new sense of spiritual truth with which man has been endowed by grace. It is indeed a spiritual second-sight; and yet reason has ancillary duties towards it. Reason may prepare the way of faith in the soul by removing intellectual obstacles to its claims; or she may arrange, digest, explain, systematize, and so express the intuitions of faith in accordance with the needs of a particular locality or time. This active intellectual appreciation of the object-matter of faith, which analyses, discusses, combines, infers, is by no means necessary to the life of the Christian soul. It is a special grace or accomplishment, which belongs only to a small fraction of the whole body of the faithful. Their faith is supplemented by what St. Paul terms, in this peculiar sense, 'knowledge[j].' Faith itself, by which the soul lives, is mainly passive, at least in respect of its intellectual ingredients: the believing soul may or may not apprehend with scientific accuracy that which its faith receives. The 'word of knowledge,' that is, the power of analysis and statement which is wielded by theological science, is thus a distinct gift, of great value to the Church, although cer-

[f] Rom. iii. 3. πίστις Θεοῦ is the faithfulness of God in accomplishing His promises. Cf. πιστὸς ὁ Θεός, 1 Cor. i. 9; 1 Thess. v. 24. πίστις is confidence in God, Rom. iv. 19, 20; as πεπίστευμαι, 'I have been entrusted with' (Gal. ii. 7; 1 Tim. i. 11).

[g] The transition is observable in Rom. vi. 8: εἰ δὲ ἀπεθάνομεν σὺν Χριστῷ, πιστεύομεν ὅτι καὶ συζήσομεν αὐτῷ. For belief in the truth of an unseen fact upon human testimony, cf. 1 Cor. xi. 18: ἀκούω σχίσματα ἐν ὑμῖν ὑπάρχειν, καὶ μέρος τι πιστεύω.

[h] 2 Cor. v. 7: διὰ πίστεως γὰρ περιπατοῦμεν, οὐ διὰ εἴδους.

[i] 1 Cor. xii. 3: οὐδεὶς δύναται εἰπεῖν· Κύριος Ἰησοῦς, εἰ μὴ ἐν Πνεύματι Ἁγίῳ.

[j] 1 Cor. xii. 8: ἄλλῳ δὲ [δίδοται] λόγος γνώσεως, κατὰ τὸ αὐτὸ Πνεῦμα. 2 Cor. viii. 7: ἐν παντὶ περισσεύετε, πίστει, καὶ λόγῳ, καὶ γνώσει. So in 1 Cor. xiii. 2 πᾶσα ἡ γνῶσις evidently means intellectual appreciation of the highest revealed truths, of which it is said in ver. 8 that καταργηθήσεται. Of course this γνῶσις was from the first capable of being abused; only, when it is so abused, to the hindrance of Divine truth, the Apostle maintains that it does not deserve the name (ἀντιθέσεις τῆς ψευδωνύμου γνώσεως. 1 Tim. vi. 20).

tainly not of absolute necessity for all Christians. But 'without faith' itself 'it is impossible to please God;' and in its simplest forms, faith pre-supposes a proclamation of its object by the agency of preaching[k]. Sometimes indeed the word preached does not profit, 'not being mixed with faith in them that hear it[l].' But when the soul in very truth responds to the message of God, the complete responsive act of faith is threefold. This act proceeds simultaneously from the intelligence, from the heart, and from the will of the believer. His intelligence recognises the unseen object as a fact[m]. His heart embraces the object thus present to his understanding; his heart opens instinctively and unhesitatingly to receive a ray of heavenly light[n]. And his will too resigns itself to the truth before it; it places the soul at the disposal of the object which thus rivets its eye and conquers its affections[o]. The believer accordingly merges his personal existence in that of the object of his faith; he lives, yet not he, but Another lives in him[p]. He gazes on truth, he loves it, he yields himself to it, he loses himself in it. So true is it, that in its essence, and not merely in its consequences, faith has a profoundly moral character. Faith is not merely a perception of the understanding; it is a kindling of the heart, and a resolve of the will; it is, in short, an act of the whole soul, which, by one simultaneous complex movement, sees, feels, and obeys the truth presented to it.

Now, according to St. Paul, it is Jesus Christ Who is eminently the Object of Christian faith. The intelligence, the heart, the will of the Christian unite to embrace Him. How

[k] Rom. x. 14-17: ἡ πίστις ἐξ ἀκοῆς. Cf. λόγος ἀκοῆς, 1 Thess. ii. 13.

[l] Heb. iv. 2.

[m] 1 Thess. iv. 14, πιστεύειν is used of recognising two past historical facts; Rom. vi. 8, of recognising a future fact; 2 Thess. ii. 11, of believing that to be a fact which is a falsehood.

[n] Rom. x. 9, 10: ἐὰν ὁμολογήσῃς ἐν τῷ στόματί σου Κύριον Ἰησοῦν, καὶ πιστεύσῃς ἐν τῇ καρδίᾳ σου ὅτι ὁ Θεὸς αὐτὸν ἤγειρεν ἐκ νεκρῶν, σωθήσῃ· καρδίᾳ γὰρ πιστεύεται εἰς δικαιοσύνην. Thus coincidently with the act of faith, ἡ ἀγάπη τοῦ Θεοῦ ἐκκέχυται ἐν ταῖς καρδίαις ἡμῶν (Rom. v. 5). The love of God is infused into the heart at the moment when His truth enters the understanding; and it is in this co-operation of the moral nature that the essential power of faith resides: hence faith is necessarily δι' ἀγάπης ἐνεργουμένη.

[o] Rom. vii. 4: εἰς τὸ γενέσθαι ὑμᾶς ἑτέρῳ, τῷ ἐκ νεκρῶν ἐγερθέντι. Ibid. xiv. 8, 9; 2 Cor. v. 15; Col. iii. 17.

[p] Gal. ii. 20: ζῶ δὲ οὐκ ἔτι ἐγώ, ζῇ δὲ ἐν ἐμοὶ Χριστός. Phil. i. 21: ἐμοὶ γὰρ τὸ ζῆν, Χριστός.

versatile and many-sided a process this believing apprehension of Christ is, might appear from the constantly varied phrase of the Apostle when describing it. Yet of faith in all its aspects Christ is the legitimate and constant Object. Does St. Paul speak as if faith were a movement of the soul towards an end? That end is Christ[q]. Does he hint that faith is a repose of the soul resting upon a support which guarantees its safety? That support is Christ[r]. Does he seem to imply that by faith the Christian has entered into an atmosphere which encircles and protects, and fosters the growth of his spiritual life? That atmosphere is Christ[s]. Thus the expression 'the faith of Christ' denotes the closest possible union between Christ and the faith which apprehends Him[t]. And this union, affected on man's side by faith, on God's by the instrumentality of the sacraments[u], secures man's real justification. The believer is justified by this identification with Christ, Whose perfect obedience and expiatory sufferings are thus transferred to him. St. Paul speaks of belief in Christ as involving belief in the Christian creed[v]; Christ has warranted the ventures which faith makes, by assuring the believer that He has guaranteed the truth of the whole object-matter of faith[w]. Faith then is the starting-point and the strength of the new life; and this faith must be pre-eminently faith in Christ[x]. The precious

[q] This seems to be the force of *εἰς* with *πιστεύειν*. Col. ii. 5: *τὸ στερέωμα τῆς εἰς Χριστὸν πίστεως ὑμῶν*. Phil. i. 29; Rom. x. 14. The preposition *πρὸς* indicates the direction of the soul's gaze, without necessarily implying the idea of movement in that direction. In Philem. 5: *τὴν πίστιν, ἣν ἔχεις πρὸς* [*εἰς* A. C. D.] *τὸν Κύριον Ἰησοῦν*. Cf. 1 Thess. i. 8.

[r] 1 Tim. i. 16: *πιστεύειν ἐπ' αὐτῷ* (sc. Jesus Christ) *εἰς ζωὴν αἰώνιον*. *Πιστεύειν ἐπὶ* is used with the acc. of trust in the Eternal Father. Cf. Rom. iv. 5, 24.

[s] Gal. iii. 26: *πάντες γὰρ υἱοὶ Θεοῦ ἐστε διὰ τῆς πίστεως ἐν Χριστῷ Ἰησοῦ*. Eph. i. 15: *ἀκούσας τὴν καθ' ὑμᾶς πίστιν ἐν τῷ Κυρίῳ Ἰησοῦ*. 2 Tim. iii. 15. The Old Testament can make wise unto salvation, *διὰ πίστεως τῆς ἐν Χριστῷ Ἰησοῦ*. 1 Tim. iii. 13: *παρρησίαν ἐν πίστει τῇ ἐν Χριστῷ Ἰησοῦ*.

[t] Rom. iii. 22: *διὰ πίστεως Ἰησοῦ Χριστοῦ*. Gal. ii. 16. This genitive seems to have the force of the *construct state* in Hebrew.

[u] Tit. iii. 5; 1 Cor. x. 16.

[v] 1 Tim. iii. 16: *ἐπιστεύθη ἐν κόσμῳ*. Christ's Person is here said to have been believed in as being the Centre of the New Dispensation.

[w] 2 Tim. i. 12: *οἶδα γὰρ ᾧ πεπίστευκα, καὶ πέπεισμαι ὅτι δυνατός ἐστι τὴν παραθήκην μου φυλάξαι εἰς ἐκείνην τὴν ἡμέραν*. Rom. i. 16.

[x] Gal. ii. 16: *ἡμεῖς εἰς Χριστὸν Ἰησοῦν ἐπιστεύσαμεν, ἵνα δικαιωθῶμεν ἐκ πίστεως Χριστοῦ*. So Rom. i. 17: *δικαιοσύνη γὰρ Θεοῦ ἐν αὐτῷ* (Christ's Gospel) *ἀποκαλύπτεται ἐκ πίστεως εἰς πίστιν*. In like manner the Christian is termed *ὁ ἐκ πίστεως Ἰησοῦ*: his spiritual life dates from, and depends

Blood of Christ, not only as representing the obedience of His Will, but as inseparably joined to His Majestic Person, is itself an object in which faith finds life and nutriment; the baptized Christian is bathed in it, and his soul dwells on its pardoning and cleansing power. It is Christ's Blood; and Christ is the great Object of Christian faith [y]. For not Christ's teaching alone, not even His redemptive work alone, but emphatically and beyond all else the Person of the Divine Redeemer is set forth by St. Paul before the eyes of Christians, as being That upon Which their souls are more especially to gaze in an ecstasy of chastened and obedient love [z].

Now if our Lord had been, in the belief of His Apostle, only a created being, is it conceivable that He should have been thus put forward as having a right well-nigh to engross the vision, the love, the energy of the human soul? For St. Paul does expressly, as well as by implication, assert that the hope [a] and the love [b] of the soul, no less than its belief, are to centre in Christ. He never tells us that a bare intellectual realization of Christ's existence or of Christ's work will avail to justify the sinner before God. By faith the soul is to be moving ever towards Christ, resting ever upon Christ, living ever in Christ. Christ is to be the end, the support, the very atmosphere of its life [c]. But how is such a relation possible, if Christ be not God? Undoubtedly faith does perceive and apprehend the existence of invisible creatures as well as of the Invisible God. Certainly the angels are discerned by faith; the Evil One himself is an object of faith. That is to say, the supernatural sense of the soul perceives these inhabitants of the unseen world in their different spheres of wretchedness and bliss. But angels and devils are

upon his faith. Rom. iii. 26. So, οἱ ἐκ πίστεως (Gal. iii. 7); and, with an allusion to the Church as the true home of faith, οἰκείους τῆς πίστεως (Gal. vi. 10.)

[y] Rom. iii. 25: διὰ τῆς πίστεως ἐν τῷ αὐτοῦ αἵματι. We might have expected ἐπί; and St. Paul would doubtless have used it, if he had meant to express no more than confidence in the efficacy of Christ's Blood.

[z] Thus it is that our Lord is, in the fullest sense, τῆς πίστεως ἀρχηγὸς καὶ τελειωτής, Heb. xii. 2, where ἀρχηγός means not 'leader' but 'author,' as Acts iii. 15, ἀρχηγὸς τῆς ζωῆς, Heb. ii. 10, ἀρχηγὸς τῆς σωτηρίας. He is ἀρχηγὸς τῆς πίστεως, as 'docens quæ credenda sunt et donans ut credamus,' and He is Himself the object-matter of the grace which is His gift, and which He will reward hereafter with the vision of Himself.

[a] 1 Tim. i. 1; 1 Cor. xv. 19; Col. i. 27; 1 Thess. i. 3.

[b] 1 Cor. xvi. 22.

[c] 2 Tim. iii. 12. The phrase εὐσεβῶς ζῆν ἐν Χριστῷ Ἰησοῦ could be used of no created being, 'extra Christum nulla pietas.'

not objects of the faith which saves humanity from sin and death. The blessed spirits command not that loyalty of heart and will which welcomes Christ to the Christian soul. The soul loves them as His ministers, not as its end. No creature can be the legitimate satisfaction of a spiritual activity so complex in its elements, and so soul-absorbing in its range, as is the faith which justifies. No created form can thus be gazed at, loved, obeyed in that inmost sanctuary of a soul, which is consecrated to the exclusive glory of the great Creator. If Christ were a creature, we may dare to affirm that St. Paul's account of faith in Christ ought to have been very different from that which we have been considering. If, in the belief of St. Paul, Christ is only a creature, then it must be said that St. Paul, by his doctrine of faith in Christ, does lead men to live for the creature rather than for the Creator. In the spiritual teaching of St. Paul, Christ eclipses God if He is not God; since it is emphatically Christ's Person, as warranting the preciousness of His work, Which is the Object of justifying faith. Nor can it be shewn that the intellect and heart and will of man could conspire to give to God a larger tribute of spiritual homage than they are required by the Apostle to give to Christ.

(β) Again, how much is implied as to the Person of Christ by the idea of Regeneration, as it is brought before us in the writings of St. Paul! St. Paul uses the word itself only once [d]. But the idea recurs continually throughout his writings; it is not less prominent in them than is the idea of faith. This idea of regeneration is sometimes expressed by the image of a change of vesture [e]. The regenerate nature has put off the old man, with his deeds of untruthfulness and lust, and has put on the new or ideal man, the Perfect Moral Being, the Christ. Sometimes the idea of regeneration is expressed more closely by the image of a change of form [f]. The regenerate man has been metamorphosed. He is made to correspond to the Form of

[d] *παλιγγενεσία*, Tit. iii. 5. In St. Matt. xix. 28 the word has a much wider and a very distinct sense.

[e] Col. iii. 9, 10: *ἀπεκδυσάμενοι τὸν παλαιὸν ἄνθρωπον . . . . . . καὶ ἐνδυσάμενοι τὸν νέον.* Eph. iv. 22–24: *ἀποθέσθαι . . . . . . τὸν παλαιὸν ἄνθρωπον τὸν φθειρόμενον κατὰ τὰς ἐπιθυμίας τῆς ἀπάτης· ἀνανεοῦσθαι δὲ τῷ πνεύματι τοῦ νοὸς ὑμῶν, καὶ ἐνδύσασθαι τὸν καινὸν ἄνθρωπον τὸν κατὰ Θεὸν κτισθέντα ἐν δικαιοσύνῃ καὶ ὁσιότητι τῆς ἀληθείας.* Gal. iii. 27: *Χριστὸν ἐνεδύσασθε.* Rom. xiii. 14.

[f] Rom. xii. 2: *μεταμορφοῦσθε τῇ ἀνακαινώσει τοῦ νοὸς ὑμῶν.* Ibid. viii. 29: *οὓς προέγνω, καὶ προώρισε συμμόρφους τῆς εἰκόνος τοῦ Υἱοῦ αὐτοῦ.* Cf. Col. iii. 10: *κατ' εἰκόνα τοῦ κτίσαντος αὐτόν.*

Christ; he is renewed in the Image of Christ; his moral being is reconstructed. Sometimes, however, and most emphatically, regeneration is paralleled with natural birth. Regeneration is a second birth. The regenerate man is a new creature [g]; he is a work of God [h]; he has been created according to a Divine standard [i]. But—and this is of capital importance—he is also said to be created in Christ Jesus [j]; Christ is the sphere of the new creation [k]. The instrument of regeneration on Christ's part, according to St. Paul, is the sacrament of baptism [l], to which the Holy Spirit gives its efficacy, and which, in the case of an adult recipient, must be welcomed to the soul by repentance and faith. Regeneration thus implies a double process, one destructive, the other constructive; by it the old life is killed, and the new life forthwith bursts into existence. This double process is effected by the sacramental incorporation of the baptized, first with Christ crucified and dead [m], and then with Christ rising from the dead to life; although the language of the Apostle distinctly intimates that a continued share in the resurrection-life depends upon the co-operation of the will of the Christian [n]. But the moral realities of the Christian life, to which the grace of baptism originally introduces the Christian, correspond with, and are effects of, Christ's Death and Resurrection. Regarded historically, these events belong to the irrevocable past. But for us Christians the Crucifixion and the Resurrection are not merely past events of history; they are energizing facts from which no lapse of centuries can sever us; they are perpetuated to the end of time within the kingdom of the Redemption [o]. The Christian is, to the end of time,

[g] Gal. vi. 15: *καινὴ κτίσις.*

[h] Eph. ii. 10: *αὐτοῦ γάρ* [sc. *Θεοῦ*] *ἐσμεν ποίημα.*

[i] Ibid. iv. 24: *τὸν κατὰ Θεὸν κτισθέντα.*

[j] Ibid. ii. 10: *κτισθέντες ἐν Χριστῷ Ἰησοῦ ἐπὶ ἔργοις ἀγαθοῖς.*

[k] 2 Cor. v. 17; and perhaps 1 Cor. viii. 6, where *ἡμεῖς* means 'we regenerate Christians.'

[l] Tit. iii. 5: *ἔσωσεν ἡμᾶς, διὰ λουτροῦ παλιγγενεσίας καὶ ἀνακαινώσεως Πνεύματος Ἁγίου.* Gal. iii. 27: *ὅσοι γὰρ εἰς Χριστὸν ἐβαπτίσθητε, Χριστὸν ἐνεδύσασθε.* 1 Cor. xii. 13.

[m] Rom. vi. 3, 4: *ἢ ἀγνοεῖτε ὅτι ὅσοι ἐβαπτίσθημεν εἰς Χριστὸν Ἰησοῦν, εἰς τὸν θάνατον αὐτοῦ ἐβαπτίσθημεν; συνετάφημεν οὖν αὐτῷ διὰ τοῦ βαπτίσματος εἰς τὸν θάνατον.*

[n] Ibid. vers. 4, 5: *ἵνα ὥσπερ ἠγέρθη Χριστὸς ἐκ νεκρῶν διὰ τῆς δόξης τοῦ Πατρὸς, οὕτω καὶ ἡμεῖς ἐν καινότητι ζωῆς περιπατήσωμεν. Εἰ γὰρ σύμφυτοι γεγόναμεν τῷ ὁμοιώματι τοῦ θανάτου αὐτοῦ, ἀλλὰ καὶ τῆς ἀναστάσεως ἐσόμεθα.*

[o] Reuss, Théol. Chrét. ii. 140: 'La régénération en tant qu'elle comprend ces deux éléments d'une mort et d'une renaissance, est tout naturellement

crucified with Christ [p]; he dies with Christ [q]; he is buried with Christ [r]; he is quickened together with Christ [s]; he rises with Christ [t]; he lives with Christ [u]. He is not merely made to sit together in heavenly places as being in Christ Jesus [v], he is a member of His Body, as out of His Flesh and out of His Bones [w]. And of this profound incorporation baptism is the original instrument. The very form of the sacrament of regeneration, as it was administered to the adult multitudes who in the early days of the Church pressed for admittance into her communion, harmonizes with the spiritual results which it effects. As the

mise en rapport direct avec la mort et la résurrection de Jésus-Christ. Ce rapport a été compris par quelques théologiens comme si le fait historique était un symbole du fait psychologique, pour lequel il aurait fourni la terminologie figurée. Mais assurément la pensée de l'apôtre *va au delà d'un simple rapprochement idéal et nous propose le fait d'une relation objective et réelle.* Nous nous trouvons encore une fois sur le terrain du mysticisme évangélique; il est question très-positivement *d'une identification avec la mort et la vie du Sauveur, et il n'y a ici de figurée que l'expression,* puisqu'au fond il ne s'agit pas de l'existence physique du Chrétien. Oui, d'après Paul, le croyant meurt avec Christ, pour ressusciter avec lui; et cette phrase ne s'explique pas par ce que nous pourrions appeler un jeu de mots spirituel, ou un rapprochement ingénieux; *elle est l'application du grand principe de l'union personnelle, d'après lequel l'existence propre de l'homme cesse réellement, pour se confondre avec celle du Christ,* qui répète, pour ainsi dire, la sienne, avec ses deux faits capitaux, dans chaque individualité se donnant à lui.' O si sic omnia!

[p] Rom. vi. 6: ὁ παλαιὸς ἡμῶν ἄνθρωπος συνεσταυρώθη. Gal. ii. 20: Χριστῷ συνεσταύρωμαι.

[q] 2 Tim. ii. 11: συναπεθάνομεν. Rom. vi. 8: ἀπεθάνομεν σὺν Χριστῷ.

[r] Rom. vi. 4: συνετάφημεν οὖν αὐτῷ διὰ τοῦ βαπτίσματος. Col. ii. 12: συνταφέντες αὐτῷ ἐν τῷ βαπτίσματι.

[s] Eph. ii. 5: συνεζωοποίησε τῷ Χριστῷ. Col. ii. 13: συνεζωοποίησε σὺν αὐτῷ. The Aorists point to a definite event in the past.

[t] Eph. ii. 6: συνήγειρε [τῷ Χριστῷ]. There is no sufficient reason for understanding Eph. ii. 5, 6 of the future resurrection alone; although in that passage the idea of the future resurrection (cf. ver. 7) is probably combined with that of the spiritual resurrection of souls in the kingdom of grace. We have been raised with Christ here, that we may live with Him hereafter. Col. ii. 12: ἐν ᾧ καὶ [sc. ἐν Χριστῷ] συνηγέρθητε διὰ τῆς πίστεως τῆς ἐνεργείας τοῦ Θεοῦ. Ibid. iii. 1.

[u] Rom. vi. 8: συζήσομεν αὐτῷ. 2 Tim. ii. 11: εἰ γὰρ συναπεθάνομεν, καὶ συζήσομεν. 1 Thess. v. 10.

[v] Eph. ii. 6: συνεκάθισεν ἐν τοῖς ἐπουρανίοις ἐν Χριστῷ Ἰησοῦ.

[w] Ibid. v. 30: μέλη ἐσμὲν τοῦ σώματος αὐτοῦ, ἐκ τῆς σαρκὸς αὐτοῦ, καὶ ἐκ τῶν ὀστέων αὐτοῦ. Although omitted by ℵ. A. B., this passage is retained by ℵ^c. D. E. F. G. L. P. and verss. except Copt. Cf. Meyer, App. Crit. in loc. Cf. Hooker, Eccl. Pol. v. 56, 7: 'We are of Him and in Him, even as though our very flesh and bones should be made continuate with His.'

neophyte is plunged beneath the waters, so the old nature is slain and buried with Christ. As Christ, crucified and entombed, rises with resistless might from the grave which can no longer hold Him, so, to the eye of faith, the Christian is raised from the bath of regeneration radiant with a new and supernatural life. His gaze is to be fixed henceforth on Christ, Who, being raised from the dead, dieth no more. The Christian indeed may fail to persevere; he may fall from this high grace in which he stands. But he need not do so; and meanwhile he is bound to account himself as 'dead indeed unto sin, but alive unto God through Jesus Christ our Lord [x].'

This regenerate or Christian life is further described by two most remarkable expressions. The Apostle speaks sometimes of Christians being in Christ [y]; sometimes of Christ being in Christians [z]. The most recent criticism refuses to sanction the efforts which in former years have been made to empty these expressions of their literal and natural force. Hooker has observed that it is 'too cold an interpretation whereby some men expound being in Christ to import nothing else but only that the selfsame nature which maketh us to be men is in Him, and maketh Him man as we are. For what man in the world is there which hath not so far forth communion with Jesus Christ [a]?' Nor will it suffice to say that in such phrases as are here in question, 'Christ' means only the moral teaching of Christ, and that a Christian is 'in Christ' by the force of a mere intellectual loyalty to the Sermon on the Mount. The expression is too energetic to admit of this treatment; it resists any but a literal explanation. By a vigorous metaphor an enthusiastic Platonist might perhaps speak of his 'living in' Plato, meaning thereby that his whole intellectual activity is absorbed by and occupied with the recorded thought of that philosopher. But he would scarcely say that he is 'in' Plato; since such a phrase would imply not merely an intellectual communion with Plato's mind, but an objective inherence in his nature or being. Still less

[x] Rom. vi. 10, 11: ὃ γὰρ ἀπέθανε [sc. ὁ Χριστὸς], τῇ ἁμαρτίᾳ ἀπέθανεν ἐφάπαξ· ὃ δὲ ζῇ, ζῇ τῷ Θεῷ. οὕτω καὶ ὑμεῖς λογίζεσθε ἑαυτοὺς νεκροὺς μὲν εἶναι τῇ ἁμαρτίᾳ, ζῶντας δὲ τῷ Θεῷ ἐν Χριστῷ Ἰησοῦ τῷ Κυρίῳ ἡμῶν. Col. iii. 3, 4.

[y] Rom. viii. 1; xii. 5; xvi. 7, 11; 1 Cor. i. 2, 30; xv. 22; 2 Cor. ii. 17; v. 17; xii. 19; Gal. i. 22; iii. 26, 28; Eph. i. 1, 3, 10; ii. 10; iii. 6; Phil. i. 1; 1 Thess. ii. 14; iv. 16. Comp. St. John xv. 4, 5.

[z] Rom. viii. 10; Gal. ii. 20; Eph. iii. 17; 2 Cor. xiii. 5; Col. i. 27.

[a] Hooker, Eccl. Pol. v. 56, 7.

possible would it be to adopt the alternative phrase, and say that Plato is 'in' the student of Plato. When St. Paul uses these expressions to denote a Christian's relation to Christ, he plainly is not recording any subjective impression of the human mind; he is pointing to an objective and independent fact, strictly peculiar to the kingdom of the Incarnation. The regenerate Christian is as really 'in' Christ, as every member of the human family is 'in' our first parent Adam [b]. Christ is indeed much more to the Christian than is Adam to his descendants; Christ is the sphere in which the Christian moves and breathes; but Christ is also the Parent of that new nature in which he shares; Christ is the Head of a Body, whereof he is really a member; nay, the Body of which he is a member is itself Christ [c]. From Christ, risen, ascended, glorified, as from an exhaustless storehouse, there flow powers of unspeakable virtue [d]; and in this life-stream the believing and baptized Christian is bathed and lives. And conversely, Christ lives in the Christian; the soul and body of the Christian are the temple of Christ; the Christian is well assured that Jesus Christ is in him, except he be reprobate [e].

My brethren, what becomes of this language if Jesus Christ be not truly God? No conceivable relationship to a human teacher or to a created being will sustain its weight. If it be not a mass of crude, vapid, worthless, misleading metaphor, it indicates relationship with One Who is altogether higher than the sons of men, altogether higher than the highest archangel. It is true that we are in Him, by being joined to His Human Nature; but what is it which thus makes His Human Nature a re-creative and world-embracing power? Why is it that if any man be in Christ, there is a new creation [f] of his moral being? And how can Christ really be in us, if He is not one with the Searcher of hearts? Surely He only Who made the soul can thus sound its depths, and dwell within it, and renew its powers, and enlarge its capacities. If Christ be not God, must not this renewal of man's nature rest only on an empty fiction, must not this regeneration of man's soul be but the ecstasy of an enthusiastic dreamer?

(γ) It would, then, be a considerable error to recognize the doctrine of our Lord's Divinity only in those passages of St. Paul's writings which distinctly assert it. The indirect evidence of the

[b] See Olshausen on the Epistle to the Romans, § 9, 'Parallel between Adam and Christ,' chap. v. 12–21, Introductory Remarks.

[c] 1 Cor. xii. 12.

[d] Eph. iv. 7: ἐδόθη ἡ χάρις κατὰ τὸ μέτρον τῆς δωρεᾶς τοῦ Χριστοῦ.

[e] 2 Cor. xiii. 5.

[f] Ibid. v. 17: εἴ τις ἐν Χριστῷ, καινὴ κτίσις.

[LECT.

Apostle's hold upon the doctrine is much wider and deeper than to admit of being exhibited in a given number of isolated texts; since the doctrine colours, underlies, interpenetrates the most characteristic features of his thought and teaching. The proof of this might be extended almost indefinitely; but let it suffice to observe that the doctrine of our Lord's Divinity is the key to the greatest polemical struggle of the Apostle's whole life. Of themselves, neither the importation of Jewish ceremonial, nor even the disposition to sacrifice the Catholicity of the Church to a petty nationalism, would fully account for the Apostle's attitude of earnest hostility to those Judaizing teachers whom he encountered at Corinth, in Galatia, and, in a somewhat altered guise, at Colossæ and at Ephesus. For, in point of fact, the Judaizers implied more than they expressly asserted. They implied that Christ's religion was not of so perfect and absolute a character as to make additions to it an irreverent impertinence. They implied that they did its Founder no capital wrong, when, instead of recognizing Him as the Saviour of the whole human family, they practically purposed to limit the applicability of His work to a narrow section of it. They implied that there was nothing in His majestic Person which should have forbidden them to range those dead rites of the old law, which He had fulfilled and abolished, side by side with the Cross and Sacraments of Redemption. The keen instinct of the Apostle detected the wound thus indirectly but surely aimed at his Master's honour; and St. Paul's love for Christ was the exact measure of his determined opposition to the influence and action of the Judaizers. If the Judaizers had believed in the true Divinity of Jesus, they could not have returned to the 'weak and beggarly elements' of systems which had paled and died away before the glories of His Advent. If they had fully and clearly believed Jesus to be God, that faith must have opposed an insurmountable barrier to these reactionary yearnings for 'the things which had been destroyed.' Their attempt to re-introduce circumcision into the Galatian Churches was a reflection upon the glory of Christ's finished work, and so, ultimately, upon the transcendent dignity of His Person. They knew not, or heeded not, that they were members of a kingdom in which circumcision and uncircumcision were insignificant accidents, and in which the new creation of the soul by the atoning and sacramental grace of the Incarnate Saviour was the one matter of vital import[g].

[g] Gal. vi. 15: *ἐν γὰρ Χριστῷ Ἰησοῦ οὔτε περιτομή τι ἰσχύει οὔτε ἀκροβυστία, ἀλλὰ καινὴ κτίσις.* Here regeneration is viewed from without, on the side

Although they had not denied Christ in terms, yet He had become of no effect to them; and the Apostle sorrowfully proclaimed that as many of them as were justified by the law had fallen from grace[h]. They had practically rejected the plenary efficacy of Christ's saving and re-creating power; they had implicitly denied that He was a greater than Moses. Their work did not at once perish from among men. For the Judaizing movement bequeathed to the Churches of the Lesser Asia many of those theological influences which were felt by later ages in the traditional temper of the School of Antioch; while outside the Church it was echoed in the long series of Humanitarian mutterings which culminated in the blasphemies of Paulus of Samosata. It must thus be admitted to figure conspicuously in the intellectual ancestry of the Arian heresy; and St. Paul, not less than St. John, is an apostolical representative of the cause and work of Athanasius.

Although the foregoing observations may have taxed your indulgent patience somewhat severely, they furnish at best only a sample of the evidence which might be brought to illustrate the point before us. But enough will have been urged to dispose of the suspicion, that St. John's belief and teaching respecting the Divinity of Jesus Christ was only an intellectual or spiritual peculiarity of that Apostle. If the form and clothing of St. John's doctrine was peculiar to him, its substance was common to all the Apostles of Jesus Christ. Just as the titles and position assigned to Jesus Christ in the narrative of the fourth Gospel are really in harmony with the powers which He wields and with the rights which He claims in the first three Evangelists, so St. John's doctrine of the Eternal Word is substantially one with St. Paul's doctrine of the 'Image of the Father,' and with his whole description of the redemptive work of Christ, and of the attitude of the Christian soul towards Him. St. John's fuller statements do but supply the key to the fervid doxologies of St. Peter, and to the profound and significant reverence of St. James. Indeed from these Apostles he might seem to differ in point of intellectual temper and method, even less than he differs from St. Paul. Between St. Paul and St. John how great

of the Divine Energy Which causes it; in Gal. v. 6, where it is equally contrasted with legal circumcision, it is viewed from within the soul, as consisting essentially in *πίστις δι' ἀγάπης ἐνεργουμένη*. Cf. Lect. VI. p. 287.

[h] Gal. v. 4: *κατηργήθητε ἀπὸ τοῦ Χριστοῦ, οἵτινες ἐν νόμῳ δικαιοῦσθε, τῆς χάριτος ἐξεπέσατε.* Cf. Ibid. v. 2: *ἐὰν περιτέμνησθε, Χριστὸς ὑμᾶς οὐδὲν ὠφελήσει.*

is the contrast! In St. Paul we are struck mainly by the wealth of sacred thought; in St. John by its simplicity. St. Paul is versatile and discursive; St. John seems to be fixed in the entranced bliss of a perpetual intuition. St. Paul is a dialectician who teaches us by reasoning; he refutes, he infers, he makes quotations, he deduces corollaries, he draws out his demonstrations more or less at length, he presses impetuously forward, reverently bending before the great dogmas which he proclaims, yet moving in an atmosphere of perpetual conflict. St. John speaks as if the highest life of his soul was the wondering study of one vast Apocalypse: he teaches, not by demonstrating truths, but by exhibiting his contemplations; he states what he sees; he repeats the statement, he inverts it, he repeats it once more; he teaches, as it seems, by the exquisite tact of scarcely disguised but uninterrupted repetition, which is justified because there is no higher attainable truth than the truth which he repeats. St. Paul begins with anthropology, St. John with theology; St. Paul often appeals to theology that he may enforce truths of morals; St. John finds the highest moral truth in his most abstract theological contemplations. St. Paul usually describes the redemptive gift of Christ as Righteousness, as the restoration of man to the true law of his being; St. John more naturally contemplates it as Life, as the outflow of the Self-existent Being of God into His creatures through the quickening Humanity of the Incarnate Word. In St. Paul the ethical element predominates, in St. John the mystical. St. John is more especially the spiritual ancestor of such fathers as was St. Gregory Nazianzen; St. Paul of such as St. Augustine. It may be said, with some reservations, that St. Paul is the typical Apostle of Western, as St. John is of Eastern Christendom; that the contemplative side of the Christian life finds its pattern in St. John, the active in St. Paul. Yet striking as are such differences of spiritual method and temper, they are found in these great apostles side by side with an entire unity of teaching as to the Person of our Lord. 'Certainly,' says Neander, with deep truth, 'it could be nothing merely accidental which induced men so differently constituted and trained as Paul and John to connect such an idea [as that of Divinity] with the doctrine of the Person of Christ. This must have been the result of a higher necessity, which is founded in the nature of Christianity, in the power of the impression which the life of Christ had made on the lives of men, in the reciprocal relation between the appearance of Christ and the archetype that presents itself as an inward revelation of God in the depths of the higher self-consciousness. And all this has found its point of connection and its verification in the manner in which Christ, the Unerring Witness, expressed His consciousness of the indwelling of the Divine Essence with Him[i].'

This is indeed the only reasonable explanation of the remarkable fact before us, namely, that the persecutor who was converted on the road to Damascus, and the disciple who had laid on Christ's breast at supper, were absolutely agreed as to the Divine prerogatives of their Master. And if we, my brethren, have ever been tempted to think that a creed like that of St. John befits only a contemplative or mystic life, alien to the habits of our age and to the necessities of our position, let us turn our eyes towards the great Apostle of the Gentiles. It would be difficult, even in this busy day, to rival St. Paul's activity; and human weakness might well shrink from sharing his burden of pain and care. It is given to few to live 'in journeyings often, in perils of waters, in perils of robbers, in perils from a man's own countrymen, in perils by the heathen, in perils in the city, in perils in the wilderness, in perils in the sea, in perils among false brethren[k],' for a purely unselfish object. Few rise to the heroic scope of a life passed 'in weariness and painfulness, in watchings often, in hunger and thirst, in fastings often, in cold and nakedness[l].' But this is certain,—that at many lower levels of moral existence, there is much to be done, and much, sooner or later, to be endured, which we can only do manfully and bear meekly in the strength of the Apostle's great conviction. If St. Paul can suffer the loss of all things that at

[i] Planting and Training, i. 505, Bohn's edit. Neander adds: 'Had the doctrine of Christ's Eternal Sonship, when it was first promulgated by Paul, been altogether new and peculiar to himself, it must have excited much opposition as contradicting the common monotheistic belief of the Jews, even among the apostles, to whom, from their previous habits, such a speculative theosophic element must have remained unknown, unless it had found a point of connexion in the lessons received from Christ, and in their Christian knowledge.' Of such opposition, direct and avowed, there is no trace. Cf. Meyer. Ev. Joh. p. 49. 'Die Materie der Lehre war bei Johannes, ehe er in jener gnostischen Form die entsprechende Darstellung fand, das Fundament seines Glaubens und der Inhalt seiner Erkenntniss, wie sie bei Paulus und bei allen anderen Aposteln es war, welche nicht, (ausser dem Verf. des Hebräerbriefs) von der Logos-Speculation berührt wurden; diese Materie der Lehre ist schlechthin auf Christum selbst zurückzuführen, dessen Eröffnungen an seine Jünger und dessen unmittelbarer Eindruck auf diese (Joh. i. 14) ihnen den Stoff gab, welcher sich später die verschiedenen Formen der Darstellung dienstbar machte.'

[k] 2 Cor. xi. 25, 26. [l] Ibid. ver. 27. Cf. Ibid. vi. 4–10, and xi. 5 sqq.

[LECT.

the last he may win Christ, if he can do all things through One That strengtheneth him, it is because he is consciously reaching towards or leaning on the arm of a Saviour Who is God as well as Man. And if we, looking onward to the unknown changes and chances of this mortal life, and beyond them, to death, would fain live and die like Christians, we too must see to it that we fold to our inmost souls that central truth of the Christian creed which was the strength and joy of the first servants of Christ. We too must believe and confess, that that Human Friend Whose words enlighten us, Whose Blood cleanses us, Whose Sacraments have renewed and even now sustain us, is in the truth of His Higher Nature none other and no less than the Unerring, the All-merciful, the Almighty God.

LECTURE VII.

THE HOMOOUSION.

Holding fast the faithful word as he hath been taught, that he may be able by sound doctrine both to exhort and to convince the gainsayers.
TIT. i. 9.

A GREAT doctrine which claims to rule the thought of men and to leave its mark upon their conduct must of necessity encounter some rude and probing tests of its vitality as it floats along the stream of time. The common speech of mankind, embodying the verdict of man's experience, lays more emphasis upon the 'ravages' than upon the conservative or constructive effects of time:—

'Tempus edax rerum, tuque invidiosa vetustas,
Omnia destruitis, vitiataque dentibus ævi
Paulatim lenta consumitis omnia morte [a].'

The destructive force of time is no less observable in the sphere of human ideas and doctrines than in that of material and social facts. Time exposes every doctrine or speculation to the action of causes which, if more disguised and subtle, are not less certainly at work than those which threaten political systems or works of art with decay and dissolution.

A doctrine is liable to suffer with the lapse of time from without and from within. From within it is exposed to the risk of decomposition by analysis. When once it has been launched into the ocean of our public intellectual life, it is forthwith subjected, as a condition of its acceptance, to the play and scrutiny of many and variously constituted minds. The several ingredients which constitute it, the primary truths to which it appeals

[a] Ovid, Met. xv. 234.

[LECT.

and upon which it ultimately reposes, are separately and constantly examined. It may be that certain elements of the doctrine, essential to its perfect representation, are rejected altogether. It may be that all its constitutive elements are retained, while the proportions in which they are blended are radically altered. It may be that an impulse is given to some active intellectual solvent, hitherto dormant, but from the first latent in the constitution of the doctrine, and likely, according to any ordinary human estimate, to break it up. Or some point of attraction between the doctrine and a threatening philosophy outside it is discovered and insisted on; and the philosophy, in a patronizing spirit, proposes to meet the doctrine half way, and to ratify one half of it if the other may be abandoned. Or some subtle intellectual poison is injected into the doctrine; and while men imagine that they are only adapting it to the temper of an age, or to the demands of a line of thought, its glow and beauty are forfeited, or its very life and heart are eaten out. Then for awhile its shell or its skeleton lies neglected by the side of the great highway of thought; until at length some one of those adventurers who in every age devote themselves to the manufacture of eclectic systems assigns to the intellectual fossil a place of honour in his private museum, side by side with the remains of other extinct theories, to which in its lifetime it was fundamentally opposed

But even if a doctrine be sufficiently compact and strong to resist internal decomposition, it must in any case be prepared to encounter the shock of opposition from without. To no doctrine is it given to be absolutely inoffensive; and therefore sooner or later every doctrine is opposed. Every doctrine, however frail and insignificant it may be, provokes attacks by the mere fact of its existence. It challenges a certain measure of attention which is coveted by some other doctrines. It takes up a certain amount of mental room which other doctrines would fain appropriate, if indeed it does not jostle inconveniently against them, or contradict them outright. Thus it rouses against itself resentment, or, at any rate, opposition; and this opposition is reinforced by an appetite which is shared in by those who hold the opposed doctrine no less than by those who oppose it. The craving for novelty is by no means peculiar to quickwitted races like the Athenians of the apostolical age or the French of our own day. It is profoundly and universally human; and it enters into our appreciation of subject-matters the most various. Novelty confers a charm upon high efforts of thought and enquiry as well as upon works of art or of imagination, or even upon fashions in amusement or in dress. To treat this yearning for novelty as though it were only a vicious frivolity is to overlook its profound significance. For, even in its lowest and unloveliest forms, it is a living and perpetual witness to the original nobility of the soul of man. It is the restlessness of a desire which One Being alone can satisfy; it reminds us that the Infinite One has made us for Himself, and that no object, person, or doctrine, that is merely finite and earthly, can take His place in our heart and thought, and bid us finally be still. And therefore as man passes through life on his short and rapid pilgrimage, unless his eye be fixed on that treasure in heaven which 'neither moth nor rust doth corrupt,' he is of necessity the very slave of novelty. Each candidate for his admiration wins from him, it may be, a passing glance of approval; but, unsatisfied at heart, he is ever seeking for some new stimulant to his evanescent sympathies. He casts to the winds the faded flower which he had but lately stooped to gather with such eager enthusiasm; he buries beneath the waves the useless pebble which, when his eye first detected it sparkling on the shore, had yielded him a moment of such bright enjoyment. Nothing human can insure its life against the attractions of something more recent than itself in point of origin; no doctrine of earthly mould can hope to escape the sentence of superannuation when it is fairly confronted with the intellectual creations of an age later than its own. A human doctrine may live for a few years, or it may live for centuries. Its duration will depend partly upon the amount of absolute truth which it embodies, and partly upon the strength of the rivals with which it is brought into competition. But it cannot always satisfy the appetite for novelty; its day of extinction can only be deferred.

οὐκ ἔχω προσεικάσαι
πάντ' ἐπισταθμώμενος,
πλὴν Διὸς, εἰ τὸ μάταν ἀπὸ φροντίδος ἄχθος
χρὴ βαλεῖν ἐτητύμως.
οὐδ' ὅστις πάροιθεν ἦν μέγας,
παμμάχῳ θράσει βρύων,
οὐδὲν ἂν λέξαι πρὶν ὤν,
ὃς δ' ἔπειτ' ἔφυ, τρια-
κτῆρος οἴχεται τυχών[b].

So it must ever fare with a religious dogma of purely human authorship. In obedience to the lapse of time it must

[b] Æsch. Ag. 163-171.

of necessity be modified, corrupted, revolutionized, and then yield to some stronger successor.

> 'Our little systems have their day,
> They have their day and cease to be.'

This is the true voice of human speculation on Divine things, conscious that it is human, conscious of its weakness, and mindful of its past and ever-accumulating experience. He only, 'with Whom is no variableness neither shadow of turning,' can be the Author of a really unchanging doctrine; and, as a matter of historical fact, 'His truth endureth from generation to generation.'

When the doctrine of our Lord's Divinity entered into the world of human thought, it was not screened from the operation of the antagonistic and dissolvent influences which have just been noticed. It was confronted with the passion for novelty beneath the eyes of the Apostles themselves. The passion for novelty at Colossæ appears to have combined a licentious fertility of the religious imagination with a taste for such cosmical speculations as were current in that age; while in the Galatian Churches it took the form of a return to the discarded ceremonial of the Jewish law. In both cases the novel theory was opposed to the apostolical account of our Lord's personal dignity; and in another generation the wild imaginings of a Basilides or of a Valentinus illustrated the attractive force of a new fashion in Christological speculation still more powerfully. Somewhat later the dialectical habits of the Alexandrian writers subjected the doctrine to a searching analysis, while the neo-Platonic philosophy brought a powerful intellectual sympathy to bear upon it, which, as an absorbing or distorting influence, might well have been fatal to a human dogma. Lastly, the doctrine was directly opposed by a long line of Humanitarian teachers, reaching, with but few intermissions, from the Ebionitic period to the Arian.

In the history of the doctrine of Christ's Divinity the Arian heresy was the climax of difficulty and of triumph; it tested the doctrine at one and the same time in each of the three modes which have been noticed. Arianism was ostentatiously anxious to appear to be an original speculation, and accordingly it taunted the Nicene fathers with their intellectual poverty; it branded them as ἀφελεῖς καὶ ἰδιῶται because they adhered to the ground of handing on simply what they had received. Its method of conducting discussion is traceable to the schools of the Sophists at Antioch; and by this method, as well as by the assumption that certain philosophical *placita* were granted, Arianism endeavoured to kill the doctrine from within by a destructive analysis. And it need scarcely be added that Arianism inherited and intensified the direct opposition which had been offered to the doctrine by earlier heresies; Arianism is immortalized, however ingloriously, in those sufferings, in those struggles, in those victories of the great Athanasius, of which its own bitter hostility to our Lord's Essential Godhead was the immediate cause.

That such a doctrine as our Lord's Divinity should be thus opposed was not unnatural. It is in itself so startling, so awful; it endows the man who honestly and intelligently believes it with a conception of the worth and drift of Christianity, so altogether unique; it is so utterly intolerable if you admit a suspicion of its being false; it is so necessarily exacting when once you have recognised it as true; it makes such large and immediate demands, not merely upon the reason and the imagination, but also upon the affections and the will; that a specific opposition to it, as distinct from a professed general opposition to the religion of which it is the very heart and soul, is only what might have been expected. Certainly, such a doctrine could not at first bring peace on earth; rather it could not but bring division. It could not but divide families, cities, nations, continents; it could not but arm against itself the edge and point of every weapon that might be forged or whetted by the ingenuity of a passionate animosity. It could not but have collapsed utterly and vanished away when confronted with the heat of opposition which it provoked, had it not descended from the Source of Truth, had it not reposed upon an absolute and indestructible basis. The Arian controversy broke upon it as an intellectual storm, the violence of which must have shattered any human theory. But when the storm had spent itself, the doctrine emerged from the conciliar decisions of the fourth century as luminous and perfect as it had been when it was proclaimed by St. Paul and St. John. Resistance does but strengthen truth which it cannot overthrow: and when the doctrine had defied the craving for novelty, the disintegrating force of hostile analysis, and the vehement onslaught of passionate denunciation, it was seen to be vitally unlike those philosophical speculations which might have been confused with it by a superficial observer. The doctrine was unaltered; it still involved and excluded precisely what it had excluded and involved from the first. But henceforth it was to be held with a clearer recognition of its real frontier, and with a stronger sense of the necessity for insisting upon that recognition. In the Homoousion, after such hesitation as found expression at Antioch, the Church felt that she had lighted upon a symbol practically adapted to tell forth the truth that never had been absent from her heart and mind, and withal, capable of resisting the intellectual solvents which had seemed to threaten that truth with extinction. The Homoousion did not change, it protected the doctrine. It clothed the doctrine in a vesture of language which rendered it intelligible to a new world of thought while preserving its strict unchanging identity. It translated the apostolical symbols of the Image and the Word of God into a Platonic equivalent; and it remains with us to this hour, in the very heart of our Creed, as the complete assertion of Christ's absolute oneness with the Essence of Deity, as the monument which records the greatest effort and the greatest defeat of its antagonist error, as the guarantee that the victorious truth maintains and will maintain an unshaken empire over the thought of Christendom.

We are all sufficiently familiar with the line of criticism to which such a formula as the Homoousion is exposed in our day and generation. A contrast is depicted and insisted upon with more vehemence than accuracy, between the unfixed popular faith of Christians in the first age of the Church and the keen theological temper of the fourth century. It is said that the Church's earliest faith was unformed, simple, vague, too full of childlike wonder to analyse itself, too indeterminate to satisfy the requirements of a formalized theology. It is asserted that at Alexandria the Church learned how to fix her creed in precise, rigid, exclusive moulds; that she there gradually crystallized what had once been fluid, and cramped and fettered what had before been free. And it is insinuated that in this process, whereby the fresh faith of the infant Church 'was hardened into the creed of the Church of the Councils,' there was some risk, or more than risk, of an alteration or enlargement of the original faith. 'How do you know,' men ask, 'that the formulary which asserts Christ's Consubstantiality with the Father is really expressive of the simple faith in which the first Christians lived and died? Do not probabilities point the other way? Is it not likely that when this effort was made to fix the expression of the faith in an unchanging symbol, there was a simultaneous growth, however unsuspected and unrecognised, in the subject-matter of the faith expressed? May not the hopes and feelings of a passionate devotion, as well as the inferential arguments of an impetuous logic, have contributed something to fill up the outline and to enhance the significance of the original and revealed germ of truth? May not the Creed of Nicæa be thus in reality a creed distinct from, if not indeed more extensive than, the creed of the apostolic age?' Such is the substance of many a whispered question, or of many a confident assertion, which we hear around us; and it is necessary to enquire, whether the admitted difference of form between the apostolic and Nicene statements does really, or only in appearance, involve a deeper difference—a difference in the object of faith.

I. Let it then be considered that a belief may be professed either by stating it in terms, or by acting in a manner which necessarily implies that you hold it. A man may profess a creed with which his life is at variance; but he may also live a creed, if I may so speak, which he has not the desire or the skill to put into exact words. There is no moral difference between the sincere expression of a conviction in language, and its consistent reflection in action. There is, for example, no difference between my saying that a given person is not to be relied upon when dealing with money matters, and my pointedly declining to act with him on this particular trust, when I am asked to do so. It is not necessary that I should express my complete opinion of his character, until I am obliged to express it. I content myself with acting in the only manner which is prudent under the circumstances. Meanwhile my line of action speaks for itself; its meaning is evident to all who are practically interested in the subject. Until I am challenged for an explanation; until the assumption upon which I act is denied; there is no necessity for my putting into words an opinion which has already been stated in the language of action and with such unmistakeable decision.

Did then the ante-Nicene Church as a whole—did its congregations of worshippers as well as its councils of divines—did its poor, its young, its unlettered multitudes, as well as its saints and doctors, so act and speak as to imply a belief that Jesus Christ is actually God?

A question such as this may at first sight seem to be difficult to answer, by reason of the one-sidedness and caprice of history. History for the most part concerns herself with the actions and opinions of the great and the distinguished, that is to say, of the few. Incidentally, or on particular occasions, she may glance at what passes beyond the region of courts and battle-fields; but it is not her wont to enable us readily to ascertain the real

[LECT.

currents of thought and feeling which have swayed the minds of multitudes in a distant age.

Such at any rate is the rule with secular history; but the genius of the Church of Christ is of a nature to limit the force of the observation. In her eyes, the interests of the many, the customs, the deeds, the sufferings of the illiterate and of the poor, are, to say the least, not less precious and noteworthy than those of kings and prelates. For the standard of aristocracy within her borders is not an intellectual or a social, but a moral standard; and her Founder has put the highest honour not upon those who rule and are of reputation, but upon those who serve and are unknown. The history of the Christian Church does therefore serve to illustrate the point before us; and it proves the belief of Christian people in the Godhead of Jesus by its witness to the early and universal practice of adoring Him.

The early Christian Church did not content herself with 'admiring' Jesus Christ. She adored Him. She approached His glorious Person with that very tribute of prayer, of self-prostration, of self-surrender, by which all serious Theists, whether Christian or non-Christian, are accustomed to express their felt relationship as creatures to the Almighty Creator. For as yet it was not supposed that a higher and truer knowledge of the Infinite God would lead man to abandon the sense and the expression of complete dependence upon Him and of unmeasured indebtedness to Him, which befits a reasonable creature whom God has made, and whom God owns and can dispose of, when such a creature is dealing with God. As yet it was not imagined that this bearing would or could be exchanged for the more easy demeanour of an equal, or of one deeming himself scarcely less than an equal, who is intelligently appreciating the existence of a remarkably wise and powerful Being, entitled by His activities to a very large share of speculative attention[c]. The Church simply adored God; and she

[c] Cf. Lecky, History of Rationalism, i. 309. Contrasting the Christian belief in a God Who can work miracles with the 'scientific' belief in a god who is the slave of 'law,' Mr. Lecky remarks, that the former 'predisposes us most to prayer,' the latter to 'reverence and admiration.' Here the antithesis between 'reverence' and 'prayer' seems to imply that the latter word is used in the narrow sense of petition for specific blessings, instead of in the wider sense which embraces the whole compass of the soul's devotional activity, and among other things, adoration. Still, if Mr. Lecky had meant to include under 'reverence' anything higher than we yield to the highest forms of human greatness, he would scarcely have coupled it with 'admiration.'

adored Jesus Christ, as believing Him to be God. Nor did she destroy the significance of this act by conceiving that admiration differs from adoration only in degree; that a sincere admiration is practically equivalent to adoration; that adoration after all is only admiration raised to the height of an enthusiasm.

You will not deem it altogether unnecessary, under our present intellectual circumstances, to consider for a moment whether this representation of the relationship between admiration and adoration be strictly accurate. So far indeed is this from being the case, that adoration and admiration are at one and the same moment and with reference to a single object mutually exclusive of each other. Certainly, in the strained and exaggerated language of poetry or of passion, you may speak of adoring that on which you lavish an unlimited admiration. But the common sense and judgment of men refuses to regard admiration as an embryo form of adoration, or as other than a fundamentally distinct species of spiritual activity. Adoration may be an intensified reverence, but it certainly is not an intensified admiration. The difference between admiration and adoration is observable in the difference of their respective objects; and that difference is immeasurable. For, speaking strictly, we admire the finite; we adore the Infinite. Why is this? It is because admiration requires a certain assumption of equality with the object admired, an assumption of ideal, if not of literal equality[d]. Admiration such as is here in question is not a vague unregulated wonder; it involves a judgment; it is a form of criticism. And since it is a criticism, it consists in our internally referring the object which we admire to a criterion. That criterion is an ideal of our own, and the act by which we compare the admired object with the ideal is our own act. We may have borrowed the ideal from another; and we do not for a moment suppose that we ourselves could give it perfect expression, or even could produce a rival to the object which commands our critical admiration. Yet, after all, the ideal is before us; it is, by right of possession, our own. We take credit to ourselves for possessing it, and for

[d] It is on this account that the apotheosis of men involves the capital sin of pride in those who decree or sanction not less than in those who accept it. The worshipper is himself the 'fountain of honour;' and in 'deifying' a fellow-creature, he deifies human nature, and so by implication himself. Wisd. xiv. 20; Acts xii. 22, 23; xiv. 11–15; xxviii. 6; Rom. i. 23.

comparing the object before us with it; nay, we identify ourselves more or less with this ideal when we compare it with the object before us. When you, my brethren, express your admiration of a good painting, you do not mean to assert that you yourselves could have painted it. But you do imply that you have before your mind an ideal of what a good painting should be, and that you are able to form an opinion as to the correspondence of a particular work of art with that ideal. Thus it is that, whether justifiably or not, your admiration of the painting has the double character of self-appreciation and of patronage. Indeed it may be questioned whether as art-critics, intent upon the beauty of your ideal, you are not much more disposed secretly to claim for yourselves a share of merit than would have been the case if you had been the artist himself whose success you consent to admire; since the artist, we may be sure, is at least conscious of some measure of failure, and is humbled, if not depressed, by a sense of the difficulty of translating his ideal into reality, by the anxieties and struggles which always accompany the process of production.

Now this element of self-esteem, or at any rate of approving reflection upon self, which enters so penetratingly into admiration, is utterly incompatible with the existence of genuine adoration. For adoration is no mere prostration of the body; it is a prostration of the soul. It is reverence carried to the highest point of possible exaggeration. It is mental self-annihilation before a Greatness Which utterly transcends all human and finite standards. In That Presence self knows that it has neither plea nor right to any consideration; it is overwhelmed by the sense of its utter insignificance. The adoring soul bends thought and heart and will before the footstool of the One Self-existing, All-creating, All-upholding Being; the soul wills to be as nothing before Him, or to exist only that it may recognise His Glory as altogether surpassing its words and thoughts. If any one element of adoration be its most prominent characteristic, it is this heartfelt uncompromising renunciation of the claims of self.

Certainly admiration may lead up to adoration; but then real admiration dies away when its object is seen to be entitled to something higher than and distinct from it. Admiration ceases when it has perceived that its Object altogether transcends any standard of excellence or beauty with which man can compare Him. Admiration may be the ladder by which we mount to adoration; but it is useless, or rather it is an impertinence, when adoration has been reached. Every man of intelligence and modesty meets in life with many objects which call for his free and sincere admiration, and he himself gains both morally and intellectually by answering to such a call. But while the objects of human admiration are as various as the minds and tastes of men,

'Denique non omnes eadem mirantur amantque,'

One Only Being can be rightfully adored. To 'admire' God would involve an irreverence only equal to the impiety of adoring a fellow-creature. It would be as reasonable to pay Divine worship to our every-day associates, as to substitute for that incommunicable honour which is due to the Most High some one of the tranquil and self-satisfied forms of a favourable notice with which we greet accomplishments or excellence in our fellow-men. 'When I saw Him,' says St. John, speaking of Jesus in His glory, 'I fell at His feet as dead[e].' That was something more than admiration, even the most enthusiastic; it was an act, in which self had no part; it was an act of adoration.

If Jesus Christ had been only a morally perfect Man, He would have been entitled to the highest human admiration; although it may be questioned, as we have seen, whether He can be deemed morally perfect if He is in reality only human. But the historical fact before us is, that from the earliest age of Christianity, Jesus Christ has been adored as God. This adoration was not yielded to Him in consequence of the persuasions of theologians who had pronounced Him to be a Divine Person. It had nothing in common with the fulsome and servile insincerities which ever and anon rose like incense around the throne of some pagan Cæsar who had received the equivocal honour of an apotheosis. It was not the product of a spiritual fascination, too subtle or too strong to be analyzed by those who felt its power, but easy of explanation to a later age. You cannot trace the stages of its progressive development[f]. You cannot

[e] Rev. i. 17: ὅτε εἶδον αὐτὸν, ἔπεσα πρὸς τοὺς πόδας αὐτοῦ ὡς νεκρός.

[f] The expressions Κυριακὸν δεῖπνόν, 1 Cor. xi. 20, for the Holy Eucharist, and Κυριακὴ ἡμέρα, Rev. i. 10, are, in this connection, significant. In both cases the adjective undoubtedly refers to Jesus Christ; while the Eucharist corresponds to 'the Lord's Passover,' Exod. xii. 11, and the Lord's Day to the 'Sabbath of the Lord thy God,' Exod. xx. 10. The Gospel Rites are to the Jewish as the substance to the shadow; but their very names suggest that Jesus already has a claim upon the devotion of His people corresponding to that of Jehovah.

name the time at which it was regarded only as a pious custom or luxury, and then mark this off from a later period when it had become, in the judgment of Christians, an imperious Christian duty. Never was the adoration of Jesus protested against in the Church as a novelty, derogatory to the honour and claims of God. Never was there an age when Jesus was only 'invoked' as if He had been an interceding saint, by those who had not yet learned to prostrate themselves before His throne as the throne of the Omnipotent and the Eternal. In vain will you endeavour to establish a parallel between the adoration of Jesus and some modern 'devotion,' unknown to the early days of Christendom, but now popularized largely in portions of the Christian Church; since the adoration of Jesus is as ancient as Christianity. Jesus has been ever adored on the score of His Divine Personality, of Which this tribute of adoration is not merely a legitimate but a necessary acknowledgment.

1. During the days of His earthly life our Lord was surrounded by a varied homage, extending, as it might seem, so far as the intentions of those who offered it were concerned, from the wonted forms of Eastern courtesy up to the most direct and conscious acts of Divine worship. As an Infant, He was 'worshipped' by the Eastern sages[g]; and during His ministry He constantly received and welcomed acts and words expressive of an intense devotion to His Sacred Person on the part of those who sought or who had received from Him some supernatural aid or blessing. The leper worshipped Him, crying out, 'Lord, if Thou wilt, Thou canst make me clean[h].' Jairus worshipped Him, saying, 'My daughter is even now dead: but come and lay Thy hand upon her, and she shall live[i].' The mother of Zebedee's children came near to Him, worshipping Him, and asking Him to bestow upon her sons the first places of honour in His kingdom[j]. The woman of Canaan, whose daughter was 'grievously vexed with a devil,' 'came and worshipped Him, saying, Lord, help me[k].' The father of the poor lunatic, who met Jesus as He descended from the Mount of Transfiguration, 'came, kneeling down to Him, and saying,

[g] St. Matt. ii. 11: πεσόντες προσεκύνησαν αὐτῷ.

[h] Ibid. viii. 2: Κύριε, ἐὰν θέλῃς, δύνασαί με καθαρίσαι.

[i] Ibid. ix. 18: προσεκύνει αὐτῷ, λέγων, '"Οτι ἡ θυγάτηρ μου ἄρτι ἐτελεύτησεν· ἀλλὰ ἐλθὼν ἐπίθες τὴν χεῖρά σου ἐπ' αὐτὴν, καὶ ζήσεται.'

[j] Ibid. xx. 20: προσῆλθεν αὐτῷ ἡ μήτηρ τῶν υἱῶν Ζεβεδαίου μετὰ τῶν υἱῶν αὐτῆς, προσκυνοῦσα καὶ αἰτοῦσά τι παρ' αὐτοῦ.

[k] Ibid. xv. 25: ἡ δὲ ἐλθοῦσα προσεκύνει αὐτῷ, λέγουσα, 'Κύριε βοήθει μοι.'

'Lord, have mercy on my son[l].' These are instances of worship accompanying prayers for special mercies. And did not the dying thief offer at least a true inward worship to the Crucified Ruler of the unseen world, while he uttered the words, 'Remember me when Thou comest into Thy kingdom[m]'?

At other times such visible 'worship' of our Saviour was an act of acknowledgment or of thanksgiving for mercies received. Thus it was with the grateful Samaritan leper, who, 'when he saw that he was healed, turned back, and with a loud voice glorified God, and fell down on his face at His feet, giving Him thanks[n].' Thus it was when Jesus had appeared walking on the sea and had quieted the storm, and 'they that were in the ship came and worshipped Him, saying, Of a truth Thou art the Son of God.' Thus too was it after the miraculous draught of fishes, that St. Peter, astonished at the greatness of the miracle, 'fell down at Jesus' knees, saying, Depart from me; for I am a sinful man, O Lord[o].' Thus the penitent, 'when she knew that Jesus sat at meat in the Pharisee's house, brought an alabaster box of ointment, and stood at His feet behind Him weeping, and began to wash His feet with tears, and did wipe them with the hairs of her head, and kissed His feet, and anointed them with the ointment[p].' Thus again when the man born blind confesses his faith in 'the Son of God,' he accompanies the confession by an act of adoration. 'And he said, Lord, I believe. And he worshipped Him[q].' Thus the holy women,

[l] St. Matt. xvii. 14, 15: *προσῆλθεν αὐτῷ ἄνθρωπος γονυπετῶν αὐτῷ, καὶ λέγων, 'Κύριε, ἐλέησόν μου τὸν υἱόν.'*

[m] St. Luke xxiii. 42: *ἔλεγε τῷ 'Ιησοῦ, 'Μνήσθητί μου, Κύριε* [*'Ιησοῦ*, Tisch. ed. 8, Tregell.] *ὅταν ἔλθῃς ἐν τῇ βασιλείᾳ σου.'*

[n] St. Luke xvii. 15, 16: *εἷς δὲ ἐξ αὐτῶν, ἰδὼν ὅτι ἰάθη, ὑπέστρεψε, μετὰ φωνῆς μεγάλης δοξάζων τὸν Θεόν· καὶ ἔπεσεν ἐπὶ πρόσωπον παρὰ τοὺς πόδας αὐτοῦ, εὐχαριστῶν αὐτῷ.* That *εὐχαριστεῖν* is not used in the Apostolic Epistles with reference to Christ may possibly be explained as an early anticipation of the devotional instinct referred to in Lect. vii. 397.

[o] St. Matt. xiv. 32, 33: *ἐκόπασεν ὁ ἄνεμος· οἱ δὲ ἐν τῷ πλοίῳ ἐλθόντες προσεκύνησαν αὐτῷ, λέγοντες, ''Αληθῶς Θεοῦ Υἱὸς εἶ.'* St. Luke v. 8: *ἰδὼν δὲ Σίμων Πέτρος προσέπεσε τοῖς γόνασι τοῦ 'Ιησοῦ, λέγων, ''Εξελθε ἀπ' ἐμοῦ, ὅτι ἀνὴρ ἁμαρτωλός εἰμι, Κύριε.'*

[p] St. Luke vii. 37, 38: *κομίσασα ἀλάβαστρον μύρου, καὶ στᾶσα παρὰ τοὺς πόδας αὐτοῦ ὀπίσω κλαίουσα, ἤρξατο βρέχειν τοὺς πόδας αὐτοῦ τοῖς δάκρυσι, καὶ ταῖς θριξὶ τῆς κεφαλῆς αὐτῆς ἐξέμασσε, καὶ κατεφίλει τοὺς πόδας αὐτοῦ, καὶ ἤλειφε τῷ μύρῳ.* These actions were expressive of a passionate devotion; they had no object beyond expressing it.

[q] St. John ix. 35-38: *ἤκουσεν ὁ 'Ιησοῦς ὅτι ἐξέβαλον αὐτὸν ἔξω· καὶ εὑρὼν αὐτὸν, εἶπεν αὐτῷ, 'Σὺ πιστεύεις εἰς τὸν Υἱὸν τοῦ Θεοῦ;' 'Απεκρίθη ἐκεῖνος καὶ*

[LECT.

when the Risen 'Jesus met them, saying, "All hail," came . . . and held Him by the feet, and worshipped Him[r].' Thus apparently Mary of Magdala, in her deep devotion, had motioned to embrace His feet in the garden, when Jesus bade her 'Touch Me not[s].' Thus the eleven disciples met our Lord by appointment on a mountain in Galilee, and 'when they saw Him,' as it would seem, in their joy and fear, 'they worshipped Him[t].' Thus, pre-eminently, St. Thomas uses the language of adoration, although it is not said to have been accompanied by any corresponding outward act. When, in reproof for his scepticism, he had been bidden to probe the Wounds of Jesus, he burst forth into the adoring confession, 'My Lord and my God[u].' Thus, when the Ascending Jesus was being borne upwards into heaven, the disciples, as if thanking Him for His great glory, worshipped Him; and then 'returned to Jerusalem with great joy[x].'

It may be that in some of these instances the 'worship' paid to Jesus did not express more than a profound reverence. Sometimes He was 'worshipped' as a Superhuman Person, wielding superhuman powers; sometimes He was worshipped by those who instinctively felt His moral majesty, which forced them, they knew not how, upon their knees. But if He had been only a 'good man,' He must have checked such worship[y].

εἶπε, 'Τίς ἐστι, Κύριε, ἵνα πιστεύσω εἰς αὐτόν;' Εἶπε δὲ αὐτῷ ὁ 'Ιησοῦς, 'Καὶ ἑώρακας αὐτὸν, καὶ ὁ λαλῶν μετὰ σοῦ, ἐκεῖνός ἐστιν.' 'Ο δὲ ἔφη, 'Πιστεύω, Κύριε·' καὶ προσεκύνησεν αὐτῷ.

[r] St. Matt. xxviii. 9: *ὁ 'Ιησοῦς ἀπήντησεν αὐταῖς, λέγων, 'Χαίρετε.' Αἱ δὲ προσελθοῦσαι ἐκράτησαν αὐτοῦ τοὺς πόδας, καὶ προσεκύνησαν αὐτῷ.*

[s] St. John xx. 17.

[t] St. Matt. xxviii. 17: *καὶ ἰδόντες αὐτὸν, προσεκύνησαν αὐτῷ· οἱ δὲ ἐδίστασαν.* If some doubted, the worship offered by the rest may be presumed to have been a very deliberate act. For the use of *προσκυνεῖν* in the strict sense of adoring the Deity, cf. St. Matt. iv. 9, 10; St. John iv. 23, 24; Rev. xix. 10.

[u] St. John xx. 28: *καὶ ἀπεκρίθη ὁ Θωμᾶς, καὶ εἶπεν αὐτῷ, ''Ο Κύριός μου καὶ ὁ Θεός μου.'* Against the attempt of Theodore of Mopsuestia and others to resolve this into an ejaculation addressed to the Father, see Alford in loc.; Pye Smith on Messiah, ii. 53. The *αὐτῷ* is of itself decisive.

[x] St. Luke xxiv. 51, 52: *καὶ ἀνεφέρετο εἰς τὸν οὐρανόν. καὶ αὐτοὶ προσκυνήσαντες αὐτὸν, ὑπέστρεψαν εἰς 'Ιερουσαλὴμ μετὰ χαρᾶς μεγάλης.*

[y] This consideration is remarkably overlooked by Channing, who might have been expected to feel its force. Channing is 'sure' that 'the worship paid to Christ during His public ministry was rendered to Him only as a Divine Messenger.' But prophets and Apostles were messengers from God. Why were they not worshipped? Channing insists further that such titles as 'Son of David,' shew that those who used them had no thought of Christ's being 'the Self-existent Infinite Divinity.' It may be true that the full

He had Himself re-affirmed the foundation-law of the religion of Israel: 'Thou shalt worship the Lord thy God, and Him only shalt thou serve[z].' Yet He never hints that danger lurked in this prostration of hearts and wills before Himself; He welcomes, by a tacit approval, this profound homage of which He is the Object. His rebuke to the rich young man implies, not that He Himself had no real claim to be called 'Good Master,' but that such a title, in the mouth of the person before Him, was an unmeaning compliment[a]. He seems to invite prayer to Himself, even for the highest spiritual blessings, in such words as those which He addressed to the woman of Samaria: 'If thou knewest the gift of God, and Who it is that saith unto thee, Give Me to drink; thou wouldest have asked of Him, and He would have given thee living water[b].' He predicts indeed a time when the spiritual curiosity of His disciples would be satisfied in the joy of perfectly possessing Him; but He nowhere hints that He would Himself cease to receive their prayers[c]. He claims all the varied homage which the sons of men, in their want and fulness, in their joy and sorrow, may rightfully and profitably pay to the Eternal Father; all men are to 'honour the Son even as they honour the Father.'

2. Certain it is that no sooner had Christ been lifted up from the earth, in death and in glory, than He forthwith began to draw all men unto Him[d]. This attraction expressed itself,

truth of His Divine Nature was not known to these first worshippers; but it does not hold good that a particular title employed in prayer exhausts the idea which the petitioner has formed of the Person whom he addresses. Above all Channing urges the indifference of the Jews 'to the frequent prostrations of men before Jesus.' He thinks this indifference unintelligible on the supposition of their believing such prostrations to involve the payment of divine honours. That many of these prostrations were not designed to involve anything so definite is freely conceded. That the Jews suspected the intention to honour Christ's Divinity in none of them would not prove that none of them were designed to honour It. The Jews were not present at the confession of St. Thomas after the Resurrection; but there is no reasonable room for questioning either the devotional purpose or the theological force of the Apostle's exclamation, 'My Lord and my God.' But see Channing, Works, ii. 194.

[z] St. Matt. iv. 10.

[a] See Lect. iv. 196.

[b] St. John iv. 10: εἰ ᾔδεις τὴν δωρεὰν τοῦ Θεοῦ, καὶ τίς ἐστιν ὁ λέγων σοι, 'Δός μοι πιεῖν,' σὺ ἂν ᾔτησας αὐτὸν, καὶ ἔδωκεν ἄν σοι ὕδωρ ζῶν.

[c] Ibid. xvi. 22: πάλιν δὲ ὄψομαι ὑμᾶς, καὶ χαρήσεται ὑμῶν ἡ καρδία, καὶ τὴν χαρὰν ὑμῶν οὐδεὶς αἴρει ἀφ' ὑμῶν· καὶ ἐν ἐκείνῃ τῇ ἡμέρᾳ ἐμὲ οὐκ ἐρωτήσετε οὐδέν. Here ἐρωτήσετε clearly means 'question.'

[d] Ibid. xii. 32.

not merely in an assent to His teaching, but in the worship of His Person. No sooner had He ascended to His throne than there burst upwards from the heart of His Church a tide of adoration which has only become wider and deeper with the lapse of time. In the first days of the Church, Christians were known as 'those who called upon the name of Jesus Christ[e].' Prayer to Jesus Christ, so far from being a devotional eccentricity, was the universal practice of Christians; it was the act of devotion which specially characterized a Christian. It would seem more than probable that the prayer offered by the assembled apostles at the election of St. Matthias, was addressed to Jesus glorified[f]. A few months later the

[e] Thus Ananias pleads to our Lord that Saul 'hath authority from the chief priests to bind *πάντας τοὺς ἐπικαλουμένους τὸ ὄνομά σου*.' (Acts ix. 14.) On St. Paul's first preaching in Jerusalem, 'All that heard him were amazed, and said, Is not this he that destroyed in Jerusalem *τοὺς ἐπικαλουμένους τὸ ὄνομα τοῦτο*;' (Ibid. ver. 21.) Thus the title was applied to Christians both by themselves and by Jews outside the Church. In after years St. Paul inserts it at the beginning of his first Epistle to the Corinthians, which is addressed to the Church of God at Corinth *σὺν πᾶσι τοῖς ἐπικαλουμένοις τὸ ὄνομα τοῦ Κυρίου ἡμῶν Ἰησοῦ Χριστοῦ*. (1 Cor. i. 2.) The expression is illustrated by the dying prayer of St. Stephen, whom his murderers stoned *ἐπικαλούμενον καὶ λέγοντα, 'Κύριε Ἰησοῦ, δέξαι τὸ πνεῦμά μου.'* (Acts vii. 59.) It cannot be doubted that in Acts xxii. 16, 2 Tim. ii. 22, the Person Who is addressed is our Lord Jesus Christ. *Ἐπικαλεῖσθαι* is not followed by an accusative except in the sense of appealing to God or man. Its meaning is clear when it is used of prayer to the Eternal Father, 1 St. Pet. i. 17; Acts ii. 21 (but cf. Rom. x. 13); or of appeal to Him, 2 Cor. i. 23; or of appeal to a human judge, Acts xxv. 11, 12, 21, 25; xxvi. 32, xxviii. 19. Its passive use occurs in texts of a different construction: Acts iv. 36; x. 18; xii. 12; xv. 17; Heb. xi. 16; St. James ii. 7.

[f] Acts i. 24: *καὶ προσευξάμενοι εἶπον, 'Σὺ Κύριε καρδιογνῶστα πάντων, ἀνάδειξον ἐκ τούτων τῶν δύο ἕνα ὃν ἐξελέξω' κ.τ.λ.* The selection of the twelve apostles is always ascribed to Jesus Christ. Acts i. 2: *οὓς ἐξελέξατο*. St. Luke vi. 13: *προσεφώνησε τοὺς μαθητὰς αὐτοῦ· καὶ ἐκλεξάμενος ἀπ' αὐτῶν δώδεκα, οὓς καὶ ἀποστόλους ὠνόμασε*. St. John vi. 70: *οὐκ ἐγὼ ὑμᾶς τοὺς δώδεκα ἐξελεξάμην*; Ibid. xiii. 18: *ἐγὼ οἶδα οὓς ἐξελεξάμην*. Ibid. xv. 16: *οὐχ ὑμεῖς με ἐξελέξασθε, ἀλλ' ἐγὼ ἐξελεξάμην ὑμᾶς*. Ibid. ver. 19: *ἐγὼ ἐξελεξάμην ὑμᾶς ἐκ τοῦ κόσμου*. Meyer quotes Acts xv. 7: *ὁ Θεὸς ἐξελέξατο διὰ τοῦ στόματός μου ἀκοῦσαι τὰ ἔθνη τὸν λόγον τοῦ εὐαγγελίου*, in order to shew that the Eternal Father must have been addressed. But this assumes that *Θεός* can have no reference to our Lord. Moreover St. Peter is clearly referring, not to his original call to the apostolate, but to his being directed to evangelize the Gentiles. St. Paul was indeed accustomed to trace up his apostleship to the Eternal Father as the ultimate Source of all authority (Gal. i. 15; 2 Cor. i. 1; Eph. i. 1; 2 Tim. i. 1); but this is not inconsistent with the fact that Jesus Christ chose and sent all the apostles, and in particular himself: 1 Tim. i. 12, *θέμενος εἰς διακονίαν*: Rom. i. 5, *δι' οὗ ἐλάβομεν χάριν καὶ ἀποστολήν*. The epithet *καρδιογνώστης*, and still more the word

dying martyr St. Stephen passed to his crown. His last cry was a prayer to our Lord, moulded upon two of the seven sayings which our Lord Himself had uttered on the Cross. Jesus had prayed the Father to forgive His executioners. Jesus had commended His Spirit into the Father's hands[g]. The words which are addressed by Jesus to the Father, are by St. Stephen addressed to Jesus. To Jesus Stephen turns in that moment of supreme agony; to Jesus he prays for pardon on his murderers; to Jesus, as to the King of the world of spirits, he commends his parting soul. It is suggested that St. Stephen's words were 'only an ejaculation forced from him in the extremity of his anguish,' and that as such they are 'highly unfitted to be made the premiss of a theological inference.' But the question is, whether the earliest apostolical Church did or did not pray to Jesus Christ. And St. Stephen's dying prayer is strictly to the point. An 'ejaculation' may shew more clearly than any set formal prayer the ordinary currents of devotional thought and feeling; an ejaculation is more instinctive, more spontaneous, and therefore a truer index of a man's real mind, than a prayer which has been used for years. And how could the martyr's cry to Jesus have been the product of a 'thoughtless impulse'? Dying men do not cling to devotional fancies or to precarious opinions; the soul in its last agony instinctively falls back upon its deepest certainties. Nor can the unpremeditated ejaculation of a person dying in shame and torture be credited with that element of dramatic artifice which may in rare cases have coloured parting words and actions when, alas! on the brink of eternity, men have thought more of a 'place in history' than of the awful Presence into which they were hastening. Is it hinted that St. Stephen was a recent convert, not yet entirely instructed in the complete faith and mind of the apostles, and not unlikely to exaggerate particular features of their teaching? But St. Stephen is expressly described as a man 'full of faith and of the Holy Ghost[h].'

Κύριος, are equally applicable to the Father and to Jesus Christ. For the former, see St. John i. 49, ii. 25, vi. 64, xvi. 30, xxi. 17; Rev. ii. 23. It was natural that the apostles should thus apply to Jesus Christ to fill up the vacant chair, unless they had believed Him to be out of the reach of prayer or incapable of helping them. See Alford and Ols. in loc.; Baumgarten's Apost. Hist. in loc.; Waterland, Works, ii. 555.

[g] Acts vii. 59, 60: ἐλιθοβόλουν τὸν Στέφανον, ἐπικαλούμενον καὶ λέγοντα, 'Κύριε Ἰησοῦ, δέξαι τὸ πνεῦμά μου.' Θεὶς δὲ τὰ γόνατα, ἔκραξε φωνῇ μεγάλῃ, 'Κύριε, μὴ στήσῃς αὐτοῖς τὴν ἁμαρτίαν ταύτην.'

[h] Acts vi. 5: ἄνδρα πλήρη πίστεως καὶ Πνεύματος Ἁγίου.

As such he had recently been chosen to fill an important office in the Church; and as a prominent missionary and apologist of the Gospel he might seem almost to have taken rank with the apostles themselves. Is it urged that St. Stephen's prayer was offered under the exceptional circumstances of a vision of Christ vouchsafed in mercy to His dying servant[i]? But it does not enter into the definition of prayer or worship that it must of necessity be addressed to an invisible Person. And the vision of Jesus standing at the right hand of God may have differed in the degree of sensible clearness, but in its general nature it did not differ, from that sight upon which the eye of every dying Christian has rested from the beginning. St. Stephen would not have prayed to Jesus Christ *then*, if he had never prayed to Him before; the vision of Jesus would not have tempted him to innovate upon the devotional law of his life; the sight of Jesus would have only carried him in thought upwards to the Father, if the Father alone had been the Object of the Church's earliest adoration. St. Stephen would never have prayed to Jesus, if he had been taught that such prayer was hostile to the supreme prerogatives of God; and the apostles, as monotheists, must have taught him thus, unless they had believed that Jesus is God, Who with the Father is worshipped and glorified.

Indeed St. Stephen's prayer may be illustrated, so far as this point is concerned, by that of Ananias at Damascus. To Ananias Jesus appeared in a vision, and desired him to go to the newly-converted Saul of Tarsus 'in the street that is called Straight.' The reply of Ananias is an instance of that species of prayer in which the soul trustfully converses with God even to the verge of argument and remonstrance[j], while yet it is controlled by the deepest sense of God's awful greatness: 'Lord, I have heard by many of this man, how much evil he hath done to Thy saints at Jerusalem: and here he hath authority from the chief priests to bind all that call on Thy Name[k].' Our Lord overrules the

[i] So apparently Meyer in loc.: 'Das Stephanus Jesum anrief, war höchst natürlich, da er eben Jesum für ihn bereit stehend gesehen hatte.'

[j] For similar colloquies with God in prayers, see Gen. xviii. 23-33; Exod. iv. 10-13; 1 Kings xx. 14; Jer. i. 6-9; Jonah iv. 9, 10; Acts x. 13-15. Compare Ps. lxxiv. 1-11; Ps. xliv. passim, and Imitat. Christi, Lib. iii. 17, etc.

[k] Acts ix. 13, 14: Κύριε, ἀκήκοα ἀπὸ πολλῶν περὶ τοῦ ἀνδρὸς τούτου, ὅσα κακὰ ἐποίησε τοῖς ἁγίοις σου ἐν Ἱερουσαλήμ· καὶ ὧδε ἔχει ἐξουσίαν παρὰ τῶν ἀρχιερέων, δῆσαι πάντας τοὺς ἐπικαλουμένους τὸ ὄνομά σου.

objections of His servant. But what man has not at times prayed for exemption, when God has made it plain that He wills him to undertake some difficult duty, or to embrace some sharp and heavy cross? Who has not pleaded with God the claims of His interests and His honour against what appears to be His Will, so long as it has been possible to doubt whether His Will is really what it seems to be? Ananias' 'remonstrance' is a prayer; it is a spiritual colloquy; it is a form of prayer which implies daily, hourly familiarity with its Object; it is the language of a soul habituated to constant communion with Jesus. It shews very remarkably how completely Jesus occupies the whole field of vision in the soul of His servant. The 'saints' whom Saul of Tarsus has persecuted at Jerusalem, are the 'saints,' it is not said of God, but of Jesus; the Name which is called upon by those whom Saul has authority to bind at Damascus, is the Name of Jesus. Ananias does not glance at One higher than Jesus, as if Jesus were lower than God; Jesus is to Ananias his God, the Recipient of his worship, and yet the Friend before Whom he can plead the secret thoughts of his heart with earnestness and freedom.

But he to whom, at the crisis of a far greater destiny, Ananias brought consolation and relief from Jesus, was himself conspicuous for his devotion to the adorable Person of our Lord[l]. Even at the very moment of his conversion, Saul of Tarsus sought guidance from Jesus Christ in prayer, as from the lawful Lord of his being. 'Lord,' he cried, 'what shall I do[m]?' And when afterwards in the temple our Lord bade St. Paul, 'Make haste and get thee quickly out of Jerusalem,' we find the Apostle, like Ananias, unfolding to Jesus his secret thoughts, his fears, his regrets, his confessions; laying them out before Him, and waiting for an answer from Jesus in the secret chambers of his soul[n]. Indeed St. Paul constantly uses language which shews that he habitually thought of Jesus as of Divine Providence in a Human Form, watching over, befriending, consoling, guiding, providing for him and his, with Infinite fore-

[l] That Acts ix. 11, ἰδοὺ. γὰρ προσεύχεται, refers to prayers addressed to Christ is rendered at least probable by the prayers of St. Paul at his conversion and in the temple. Acts xxii. 10, 19, 20. For the use of προσεύχεσθαι, of prayer to Christ, see Acts i. 24.

[m] Acts xxii. 10, τί ποιήσω, Κύριε;

[n] Ibid. vers. 19, 20: Κύριε, αὐτοὶ ἐπίστανται, ὅτι ἐγὼ ἤμην φυλακίζων καὶ δέρων κατὰ τὰς συναγωγὰς τοὺς πιστεύοντας ἐπὶ σέ· καὶ ὅτε ἐξεχεῖτο τὸ αἷμα Στεφάνου τοῦ μάρτυρός σου, καὶ αὐτὸς ἤμην ἐφεστὼς καὶ συνευδοκῶν τῇ ἀναιρέσει αὐτοῦ, καὶ φυλάσσων τὰ ἱμάτια τῶν ἀναιρούντων αὐτόν.

sight and power, but also with the tenderness of a human sympathy. In this sense Jesus is placed on a level with the Father in St. Paul's two earliest Epistles. 'Now God Himself and our Father, and our Lord Jesus Christ, direct our way unto you [o];' 'Now our Lord Jesus Christ Himself, and God, even our Father, Which hath loved us, and hath given us everlasting consolation and good hope through grace, comfort your hearts, and stablish you in every good word and work [p].' Thus Jesus is associated with the Father, in one instance as directing the outward movements of the Apostle's life, in another as building up the inward life of the recent converts to Christianity. In other devotional expressions the Name of Jesus stands alone. 'I trust in the Lord Jesus,' so the Apostle writes to the Philippians, 'to send Timotheus shortly unto you [q].' 'I thank Christ Jesus our Lord,' so he assures St. Timothy, 'Who hath given me power, for that He counted me faithful, putting me into the ministry [r].' Is not this the natural language of a soul which is constantly engaged in communion with Jesus, whether it be the communion of praise or the communion of prayer? Jesus is to St. Paul, not a deceased teacher or philanthropist, who has simply done his great work and then has left it as a legacy to the world; He is God, ever living and ever present, the Giver of temporal and of spiritual blessings, the Guide and Friend of man both in man's outward and in his inward life. If we had no explicit records of prayers offered by St. Paul to Jesus, we might be sure that such prayers were offered, since otherwise the language which he employs could not have been used. But, in point of fact, the Apostle has not left us in doubt as to his faith or his practice in this respect. 'If,' he asserts, 'thou shalt confess with thy mouth the Lord Jesus, and shalt believe in thine heart that God hath raised Him from the dead, thou shalt be saved. For with the heart man believeth unto righteousness; and with

[o] 1 Thess. iii. 11: Αὐτὸς δὲ ὁ Θεὸς καὶ Πατὴρ ἡμῶν, καὶ ὁ Κύριος ἡμῶν Ἰησοῦς Χριστὸς, κατευθύναι τὴν ὁδὸν ἡμῶν πρὸς ὑμᾶς.

[p] 2 Thess. ii. 16, 17: αὐτὸς δὲ ὁ Κύριος ἡμῶν Ἰησοῦς Χριστὸς, καὶ ὁ Θεὸς καὶ Πατὴρ ἡμῶν, ὁ ἀγαπήσας ἡμᾶς καὶ δοὺς παράκλησιν αἰωνίαν καὶ ἐλπίδα ἀγαθὴν ἐν χάριτι, παρακαλέσαι ὑμῶν τὰς καρδίας, καὶ στηρίξαι ὑμᾶς ἐν παντὶ λόγῳ καὶ ἔργῳ ἀγαθῷ.

[q] Phil. ii. 19: ἐλπίζω δὲ ἐν Κυρίῳ Ἰησοῦ, Τιμόθεον ταχέως πέμψαι. 'This hope was ἐν Κυρίῳ Ἰησοῦ: it rested and centred in Him; it arose from no *extraneous* feelings or expectations, and so would doubtless be fulfilled.' Bp. Ellicott in loc. Compare, too, Bp. Lightfoot in loc.

[r] 1 Tim. i. 12: καὶ χάριν ἔχω τῷ ἐνδυναμώσαντί με Χριστῷ Ἰησοῦ τῷ Κυρίῳ ἡμῶν, ὅτι πιστόν με ἡγήσατο, θέμενος εἰς διακονίαν.

VII]

the mouth confession is made to salvation. For the Scripture saith, Whosoever believeth on Him shall not be ashamed. For there is no difference between the Jew and the Greek: for the Same is Lord over all, rich unto all that call upon Him. For whosoever shall call upon the Name of the Lord shall be saved[s].' The prophet Joel had used these last words of prayer to the Lord Jehovah. St. Paul, as the whole context shews beyond reasonable doubt, understands them of prayer to Jesus[t]. And what are the Apostle's benedictions in the name of Christ but indirect prayers offered to Christ that His blessing might be vouchsafed to the Churches which the Apostle is addressing? 'Grace be to you from God our Father, and from the Lord Jesus Christ[u].' 'The grace of our Lord Jesus Christ be with you all[v].' Or what shall we say of St. Paul's entreaties that he might be freed from the mysterious and humiliating infirmity which he terms his 'thorn in the flesh'? He tells us that three times he besought the Lord Jesus Christ that it might depart from him, and that in mercy his prayer was refused[w]. Are we to imagine that that prayer to Jesus was an isolated act in St. Paul's spiritual life? Does any such religious act stand alone in the spiritual history of an earnest and moderately consistent man? Apostles believed that

[s] Rom. x. 9-13: ἐὰν ὁμολογήσῃς ἐν τῷ στόματί σου Κύριον Ἰησοῦν, καὶ πιστεύσῃς ἐν τῇ καρδίᾳ σου ὅτι ὁ Θεὸς αὐτὸν ἤγειρεν ἐκ νεκρῶν, σωθήσῃ· καρδίᾳ γὰρ πιστεύεται εἰς δικαιοσύνην, στόματι δὲ ὁμολογεῖται εἰς σωτηρίαν. Λέγει γὰρ ἡ γραφή, 'Πᾶς ὁ πιστεύων ἐπ' αὐτῷ οὐ καταισχυνθήσεται.' Οὐ γάρ ἐστι διαστολὴ Ἰουδαίου τε καὶ Ἕλληνος· ὁ γὰρ αὐτὸς Κύριος πάντων, πλουτῶν εἰς πάντας τοὺς ἐπικαλουμένους αὐτόν. 'Πᾶς γὰρ ὃς ἂν ἐπικαλέσηται τὸ ὄνομα Κυρίου, σωθήσεται. Cf. Isa. xxviii. 16; Joel ii. 32. Here St. Paul applies to Jesus the language which prophets had used of the Lord Jehovah. Cf. Acts ii. 21.

[t] Cf. Meyer in Rom. x. 12: ὁ γὰρ αὐτὸς Κύριος πάντων. 'Dieser Κύριος ist Christus, der αὐτός ver. 11 und der mit diesem αὐτός nothwendig identische Κύριος ver. 13. Wäre *Gott* (i.e. the Father) gemeint, so müsste man grade den *christlichen* Charakter der Beweisführung erst hinzutragen (wie *Olsh.*: 'Gott in Christo'), was aber willkürlich wäre.' For Κύριος πάντων, see Phil. ii. 11. Cf. St. Chrys. in loc.

[u] 1 Cor. i. 3.

[v] Rom. xvi. 20; cf. Rom. i. 7.

[w] 2 Cor. xii. 8, 9: ὑπὲρ τούτου τρὶς τὸν Κύριον παρεκάλεσα, ἵνα ἀποστῇ ἀπ' ἐμοῦ· καὶ εἴρηκέ μοι, 'Ἀρκεῖ σοι ἡ χάρις μου· ἡ γὰρ δύναμίς μου ἐν ἀσθενείᾳ τελειοῦται.' ἥδιστα οὖν μᾶλλον καυχήσομαι ἐν ταῖς ἀσθενείαις μου, ἵνα ἐπισκηνώσῃ ἐπ' ἐμὲ ἡ δύναμις τοῦ Χριστοῦ. Meyer in loc.: 'τὸν Κύριον, nicht *Gott* (the Father), sondern *Christum* (s. v. 9, ἡ δύναμις τοῦ Χριστοῦ), der ja der mächtige Bezwinger des Satan's ist. . . . . *Wie* Paulus die Antwort, den χρηματισμός (Matt. ii. 12: Luk. ii. 6: Act. x. 22) von Christo empfangen habe, ist uns völlig unbekannt.'

when the First-begotten was brought into the inhabited world, the angels of heaven were bidden to worship Him [x]. They declared Him [y], when His day of humiliation and suffering had ended, to have been so highly exalted that the Name which He had borne on earth, and which is the symbol of His Humanity, was now the very atmosphere and nutriment of all the upward

[x] Heb. i. 6: *ὅταν δὲ πάλιν εἰσαγάγῃ τὸν πρωτότοκον εἰς τὴν οἰκουμένην, λέγει, 'Καὶ προσκυνησάτωσαν αὐτῷ πάντες ἄγγελοι Θεοῦ.'* On this passage see the exhaustive note of Delitzsch, Comm. zum. Br. an die Hebräer, pp. 24–29. 'Die LXX. übers. hier ganz richtig *προσκυνήσατε*, denn הִשְׁתַּחֲווּ ist ja kein *praet. consec.*, und Augustin macht die den rechten Sinn treffende schöne Bemerkung: "adorate Eum;" cessat igitur adoratio angelorum, qui non adorantur, sed adorant; mali angeli volunt adorari, boni adorant nec se adorari permittunt, ut vel saltem eorum exemplo idolatriæ cessent.' Es fragt sich nun aber: mit welchem Rechte oder auch nur auf welchem Grunde bezieht der Verf. eine Stelle, die von Jehova handelt, auf Christum?' After discussing some unsatisfactory replies, he proceeds: 'Der Grundsatz, von welchem der Verf. ausgeht, ist . . . . dieser: Ueberall wo im A. T. von einer endzeitigen letztentscheidenden Zukunft (Parusie), Erscheinung und Erweisung Jehova's in seiner zugleich richterlichen und heilwärtigen Macht und Herrlichkeit die Rede ist, von einer gegenbildlich zur mosaischen Zeit sich verhaltenden Offenbarung Jehova's, von einer Selbstdarstellung Jehova's als Königs seines *Reiches:* da ist Jehova = Jesus Christus; denn dieser ist Jehova, geoffenbaret im Fleisch; Jehova, eingetreten in die Menscheit und ihre Geschichte; Jehova, aufgegangen als Sonne des Heils über seinem Volke. Dieser Grundsatz ist auch unumstösslich wahr; auf ihm ruht der heilsgeschichtliche Zusammenhang, die tiefinnerste Einheit beider Testamente. Alle neutest. Schriftsteller sind dieses Bewusstseins voll, welches sich gleich auf der Schwelle der evangelischen Geschichte ausspricht; denn dem יום ה' soll Elia vorausgehn Mal. iii. 23 f. und *πρὸ προσώπου Κυρίου* Johannes Lc. i. 76, vgl. 17. Darum sind auch alle Psalmen in welchen die Verwirklichung des weltüberwindenden Königthums Jehova's besungen wird, messianisch und werden von unserem Verf. als solche betrachtet, denn die schliessliche Glorie der Theokratie ist nach heilsgeschichtlichem Plane keine andere als die der Christokratie, das Reich Jehova's und das Reich Christi ist Eines.'

[y] Phil. ii. 9, 10: *ὁ Θεὸς αὐτὸν ὑπερύψωσε, καὶ ἐχαρίσατο αὐτῷ ὄνομα τὸ ὑπὲρ πᾶν ὄνομα· ἵνα ἐν τῷ ὀνόματι Ἰησοῦ πᾶν γόνυ κάμψῃ ἐπουρανίων καὶ ἐπιγείων καὶ καταχθονίων· καὶ πᾶσα γλῶσσα ἐξομολογήσηται ὅτι Κύριος Ἰησοῦς Χριστὸς εἰς δόξαν Θεοῦ Πατρός.* See Alford in loc.: 'The general aim of the passage is . . . . the *exaltation of Jesus.* The *εἰς δόξαν Θεοῦ Πατρός* below is no deduction from this, but rather an additional reason why we should carry on the exaltation of Jesus *until this new particular is introduced.* This would lead us to infer that the universal prayer is to be *to* Jesus. And this view is confirmed by the next clause, where every tongue is to confess that Jesus Christ is *Κύριος*, when we remember the common expression, *ἐπικαλεῖσθαι τὸ ὄνομα Κυρίου*, for prayer. Rom x. 12; 1 Cor. i. 2; 2 Tim. ii. 22.' For *ἐν τῷ ὀνόματι*, comp. 1 Kings viii. 44, LXX; Ps. xliv. 10. Bp. Lightfoot in loc.: 'It seems clear from the context that the Name of Jesus is not only the medium, but the object of adoration.'

torrents of prayer which rise from the moral world beneath His throne; that as the God-Man He was worshipped by angels, by men, and by the spirits of the dead. The practice of the Apostles did but illustrate their faith; and the prayers offered to Jesus by His servants on earth were believed to be but a reflection of that worship which is offered to Him by the Church of heaven.

If this belief is less clearly traceable in the brief Epistles of St. Peter [z], it is especially observable in St. John. St. John is speaking of the Son of God, when he exclaims, 'This is the confidence that we have in Him, that, if we ask anything according to His Will, He heareth us: and if we know that He hear us, ... we know that we have the petitions that we desired of Him [a].' These petitions of the earthly Church correspond to the adoration above, where the wounded Humanity of our Lord is throned in the highest heavens. 'I beheld, and lo, in the midst of the throne .... stood a Lamb as It had been slain [b].' Around Him are three concentric circles of adoration. The inmost proceeds from the four mysterious creatures and the four and twenty elders who 'have harps, and golden vials full of odours, which are the prayers of the saints [c].' These are the courtiers who are placed on the very steps of the throne; they represent more distant worshippers. But they too fall down before the throne, and sing the new song which is addressed to the Lamb slain and glorified [d]: 'Thou wast slain, and hast redeemed us to God by Thy Blood out of every kindred, and tongue, and people, and nation; and hast made us unto our God kings and priests, and we shall reign on the earth [e].' Around these, at a greater

[z] Yet 1 St. Pet. iv. 11 is a doxology 'framed, as it might seem, for common use on earth and in heaven.' See also 2 St. Pet. iii. 18.

[a] 1 St. John v. 13–15: *ἵνα πιστεύητε εἰς τὸ ὄνομα τοῦ Υἱοῦ τοῦ Θεοῦ. Καὶ αὕτη ἐστὶν ἡ παῤῥησία ἣν ἔχομεν πρὸς αὐτὸν, ὅτι ἐάν τι αἰτώμεθα κατὰ τὸ θέλημα αὐτοῦ, ἀκούει ἡμῶν· καὶ ἐὰν οἴδαμεν ὅτι ἀκούει ἡμῶν, ὃ ἂν αἰτώμεθα, οἴδαμεν ὅτι ἔχομεν τὰ αἰτήματα ἃ ᾐτήκαμεν παρ' αὐτοῦ.* The *natural* construction of this passage seems to oblige us to refer *αὐτοῦ* and *τὸ θέλημα* to the Son of God (ver. 13). The passage 1 St. John iii. 21, 22 does not forbid this; it only shews how fully, in St. John's mind, the honour and prerogatives of the Son are those of the Father.

[b] Rev. v. 6: *καὶ εἶδον, καὶ ἰδοὺ ἐν μέσῳ τοῦ θρόνου καὶ τῶν τεσσάρων ζώων καὶ ἐν μέσῳ τῶν πρεσβυτέρων, ἀρνίον ἑστηκὸς ὡς ἐσφαγμένον.*

[c] Ibid. ver. 8: *ἔχοντες ἕκαστος κιθάρας, καὶ φιάλας χρυσᾶς γεμούσας θυμιαμάτων, αἵ εἰσιν αἱ προσευχαὶ τῶν ἁγίων.*

[d] Ibid.: *ἔπεσον ἐνώπιον τοῦ ἀρνίου .... καὶ ᾄδουσιν ᾠδὴν καινήν.*

[e] Ibid. ver. 9: *ἐσφάγης, καὶ ἠγόρασας τῷ Θεῷ ἡμᾶς ἐν τῷ αἵματί σου, ἐκ πάσης φυλῆς καὶ γλώσσης καὶ λαοῦ καὶ ἔθνους, καὶ ἐποίησας ἡμᾶς τῷ Θεῷ ἡμῶν βασιλεῖς καὶ ἱερεῖς· καὶ βασιλεύσομεν ἐπὶ τῆς γῆς.*

distance from the Most Holy, there is a countless company of worshippers: 'I heard the voice of many angels round about the throne and the creatures and the elders: and the number of them was ten thousand times ten thousand, and thousands of thousands; saying with a loud voice, Worthy is the Lamb That was slain to receive power, and riches, and wisdom, and strength, and honour, and glory, and blessing [f].' Beyond these again, the entranced Apostle discerns a third sphere in which a perpetual worship is maintained. Lying outside the two inner circles of conscious adoration offered by the heavenly intelligences, there is in St. John's vision an assemblage of all created life, which, whether it wills or not, lives for Christ's as for the Father's glory: 'And every creature which is in heaven, and on the earth, and under the earth, and such as are in the sea, and all that are in them, heard I saying, Blessing, and honour, and glory, and power, be unto Him that sitteth upon the throne, and unto the Lamb for ever and ever [g].' This is the hymn of the whole visible creation, and to it a response comes from the inmost circle of adoring beings, ratifying and harmonizing this sublime movement of universal life: 'And the four creatures said, Amen [h].' And how does the redeemed Church on earth bear her part in the universal chorus of praise? 'Unto Him That loved us, and washed us from our sins in His Own Blood, and hath made us kings and priests unto God and His Father; to Him be glory and dominion for ever and ever. Amen [i].' It is surely impossible to mistake the force and meaning of this representation of the adoration of the Lamb in the Apocalypse. This representation cannot be compared with the Apocalyptic pictures of the future fortunes of the Church, where the imagery employed frequently leaves room for allusions so diverse, that no interpretation can be positively assigned to a particular symbol without a certain intellectual and spiritual immodesty in the

[f] Rev. v. 11, 12: καὶ εἶδον, καὶ ἤκουσα φωνὴν ἀγγέλων πολλῶν κυκλόθεν τοῦ θρόνου καὶ τῶν ζώων καὶ τῶν πρεσβυτέρων. . . . . καὶ χιλιάδες χιλιάδων, λέγοντες φωνῇ μεγάλῃ, 'Ἄξιόν ἐστι τὸ ἀρνίον τὸ ἐσφαγμένον λαβεῖν τὴν δύναμιν καὶ πλοῦτον καὶ σοφίαν καὶ ἰσχὺν καὶ τιμὴν καὶ δόξαν καὶ εὐλογίαν.'

[g] Ibid. ver. 13: καὶ πᾶν κτίσμα ὅ ἐστιν ἐν τῷ οὐρανῷ, καὶ ἐν τῇ γῇ, καὶ ὑποκάτω τῆς γῆς, καὶ ἐπὶ τῆς θαλάσσης ἅ ἐστι, καὶ τὰ ἐν αὐτοῖς πάντα, ἤκουσα λέγοντας, 'Τῷ καθημένῳ ἐπὶ τοῦ θρόνου καὶ τῷ ἀρνίῳ ἡ εὐλογία καὶ ἡ τιμὴ καὶ ἡ δόξα καὶ τὸ κράτος εἰς τοὺς αἰῶνας τῶν αἰώνων. Cf. vii. 9, 10.

[h] Ibid. ver. 14: καὶ τὰ τέσσαρα ζῶα ἔλεγον, Ἀμήν.

[i] Ibid. i. 5, 6: τῷ ἀγαπήσαντι ἡμᾶς καὶ λούσαντι ἡμᾶς ἀπὸ τῶν ἁμαρτιῶν ἡμῶν ἐν τῷ αἵματι αὐτοῦ· καὶ ἐποίησεν ἡμᾶς βασιλεῖς καὶ ἱερεῖς τῷ Θεῷ καὶ Πατρὶ αὐτοῦ· αὐτῷ ἡ δόξα καὶ τὸ κράτος εἰς τοὺς αἰῶνας τῶν αἰώνων. ἀμήν.

interpreter who essays to do so. You may in vain endeavour satisfactorily to solve the questions which encompass such points as the number of the beast or the era of the millennium; but you cannot doubt for one moment Who is meant by 'the Lamb,' or what is the character of the worship that is so solemnly offered to Him.

But upon this worship of Jesus Christ as we meet with it in the apostolical age, let us here make three observations.

a. First, then, it cannot be accounted for, and so set aside, as being part of an undiscriminating cultus of heavenly or superhuman beings in general. Such a cultus finds no place in the New Testament, except when it, or something very much resembling it, is expressly discountenanced. By the mouth of our Lord Jesus Christ the New Testament reaffirms the Sinaitic law which restricts worship to the Lord God Himself[k]. St. Peter will not sanction the self-prostrations of the grateful Cornelius, lest Cornelius should think of him as more than human[l]. When, at Lystra, the excited populace, with their priest, desired to offer sacrifice to St. Paul and St. Barnabas, as to 'deities who had come down to them in the likeness of men,' the Apostles in their unfeigned distress protested that they were but men of like feelings with those whom they were addressing, and claimed for the living God that service which was His exclusive right[m]. When St. John fell at the feet of the angel of the Apocalypse, in profound acknowledgment of the marvellous privileges of sight and sound to which he had been admitted, he was peremptorily checked on the ground that the angel too was only his fellow-slave, and that God was the one true Object of worship[n]. One of the most salient features of the Gnostico-Jewish theosophy which threatened the faith of the Church of Colossæ was the worshipping of angels; and St. Paul censures

[k] St. Matt. iv. 10; Deut. vi. 13; x. 20. See Lect. I. 27; II. 95.

[l] Acts x. 25: συναντήσας αὐτῷ ὁ Κορνήλιος, πεσὼν ἐπὶ τοὺς πόδας προσεκύνησεν. ὁ δὲ Πέτρος αὐτὸν ἤγειρε λέγων, ''Ανάστηθι· κἀγὼ αὐτὸς ἄνθρωπός εἰμι.'

[m] Ibid. xiv. 14, 15: διαῤῥήξαντες τὰ ἱμάτια αὐτῶν εἰσεπήδησαν εἰς τὸν ὄχλον, κράζοντες καὶ λέγοντες, ''Ανδρες, τι ταῦτα ποιεῖτε; καὶ ἡμεῖς ὁμοιοπαθεῖς ἐσμεν ὑμῖν ἄνθρωποι, εὐαγγελιζόμενοι ὑμᾶς ἀπὸ τούτων τῶν ματαίων ἐπιστρέφειν ἐπὶ τὸν Θεὸν τὸν ζῶντα.'

[n] Rev. xxii. 8, 9: καὶ ἐγὼ 'Ιωάννης ὁ βλέπων ταῦτα καὶ ἀκούων· καὶ ὅτε ἤκουσα καὶ ἔβλεψα, ἔπεσα προσκυνῆσαι ἔμπροσθεν τῶν ποδῶν τοῦ ἀγγέλου τοῦ δεικνύοντός μοι ταῦτα. καὶ λέγει μοι, ''Ορα μή· σύνδουλός σου γάρ εἰμι καὶ τῶν ἀδελφῶν σου τῶν προφητῶν, καὶ τῶν τηρούντων τοὺς λόγους τοῦ βιβλίου τούτου· τῷ Θεῷ προσκύνησον.'

it because it tended to loosen men's hold upon the incommunicable prerogatives of the great Head of the Church [o]. Certainly the New Testament does teach that we Christians have close communion with the blessed angels and with the sainted dead, such as would be natural to members of one great and really undivided family. The invisible world is not merely above, it is around us; we have come into it; and Christ's kingdom on earth and in heaven [p] forms one supernatural whole. But the worship claimed for, accepted by, and paid to Jesus, stands out in the New Testament in the sharpest relief. This relief is not softened or shaded off by any instances of an inferior homage paid, whether legitimately or not, to created beings. We do not meet with any clear distinction between a primary and a secondary worship, by which the force of the argument might have been more or less seriously weakened. Worship is claimed for, and is given to, God alone; and if Jesus is worshipped, this is simply because Jesus is God [q].

β. The worship paid to Jesus in the apostolic age was certainly in many cases that adoration which is due to the Most High God, and to Him alone, from all His intelligent creatures. God Himself must needs have been, then as ever, the One Object of real worship. But the Eternal Son, when He became

[o] Col. ii. 18: *μηδεὶς ὑμᾶς καταβραβευέτω θέλων ἐν ταπεινοφροσύνῃ καὶ θρησκείᾳ τῶν ἀγγέλων.* The Apostle condemns this (1) on the *moral* ground that the Gnostic teacher here alluded to claimed to be in possession of truths respecting the unseen world of which he really was ignorant, ἃ [μὴ C. K. L.] *ἑώρακεν ἐμβατεύων, εἰκῇ φυσιούμενος ὑπὸ τοῦ νοὸς τῆς σαρκὸς αὐτοῦ*: (2) On the *dogmatic* ground of a resulting interference with due recognition of the Headship of Jesus Christ, the One Source of the supernatural life of the Church, *καὶ οὐ κρατῶν τὴν κεφαλὴν, ἐξ οὗ πᾶν τὸ σῶμα διὰ τῶν ἁφῶν καὶ συνδέσμων ἐπιχορηγούμενον καὶ συμβιβαζόμενον, αὔξει τὴν αὔξησιν τοῦ Θεοῦ.*

[p] Heb. xii. 22: *προσεληλύθατε Σιὼν ὄρει, καὶ πόλει Θεοῦ ζῶντος, Ἱερουσαλὴμ ἐπουρανίῳ, καὶ μυριάσιν ἀγγέλων, πανηγύρει καὶ ἐκκλησίᾳ πρωτοτόκων ἐν οὐρανοῖς ἀπογεγραμμένων, καὶ κριτῇ Θεῷ πάντων, καὶ πνεύμασι δικαίων τετελειωμένων, καὶ διαθήκης νέας μεσίτῃ Ἰησοῦ.*

[q] The 'worship' of Buddha has sometimes been compared to that of our Divine Lord, as if Buddha were regarded as a real divinity by his followers. But 'le Bouddha reste homme, et ne cherche jamais à dépasser les limites de l'humanité, au delà de laquelle il ne conçoit rien. L'enthousiasme de ses disciples a été aussi réservé que lui-même: dans le culte innocent qu'ils lui rendaient, *leur ferveur s'adressait à un souvenir consolateur et fortifiant; jamais leur superstition intéressée ne s'adressait à sa puissance* .... Ni l'orgueil de Çâkyamouni, ni le fanatisme des croyants, n'a conçu un sacrilège; le Bouddha, tout grand qu'il se croit, n'a point risqué l'apothéose; .... jamais personne n'a songé à en faire un dieu.' Saint-Hilaire, Le Bouddha, p. 168.

Man, ceased not to be God. As God, He received from those who believed in Him the only worship which their faith could render[r]. This is clear from the representations of heavenly worship in the Apocalypse, which we have been considering, even if we take no other passages into account. The Apocalyptic worship of our glorified Lord is not any mere honorary acknowledgment that His redemptive work is complete. Even at the moment[s] of His Incarnation worship is addressed to Christ's Divine and Eternal Person. Doubtless the language of devotion to Him which we find in the Gospels represents many postures of the human soul, ranging between that utter self-prostration which we owe to the Most High, and that trustful familiarity with which we pour our joys and sorrows, our hopes and fears into the ear of a human friend. Such 'lower forms' of worship lead up to, and are explained by, the higher. They illustrate the condescension and purpose of the Incarnation. But the familiar confidence which the Incarnation invites cannot be pleaded against the rights of the Incarnate God. A free, trustful, open-hearted converse with Christ is compatible with the lowliest worship of His Person; Christian confidence even 'leans upon His breast at supper,' while Christian faith discerns His Glory, and 'falls at His feet as dead.'

γ. The apostolic worship of Jesus Christ embraced His Manhood no less than it embraced His Godhead[t]. According to

[r] Meyer's remarks are very far from satisfactory. 'Das *Anrufen Christi* ist nicht *das Anbeten schlechthin*, wie es nur in Betreff des Vaters, als *des einigen absoluten Gottes* (!) geschieht, wohl aber die Anbetung nach der durch das Verhältniss Christi *zum Vater* (dessen wesensgleicher Sohn, Ebenbild, Throngenosse, Vermittler, und Fürsprecher für die Menschen u. s. w. er ist) bedingten Relativität im betenden Bewusstsein . . . . Der Christum Anrufende ist sich bewusst, er rufe ihn nicht *als den schlechthinigen Gott*, sondern als den gottmenschlichen Vertreter und Mittler Gottes an.' In Rom. x. 12 our Lord is represented as being equal with the Father (p. 380, note), and equally with Him entitled to adoration. Adoration is strictly due to the Uncreated Substance of God, and to Jesus Christ as being personally of It. The mediatorial functions of His Manhood cannot affect the bearings of this truth. See Waterland's profound remarks on 'Scripture's seeming in some places to found Christ's title to worship not so much upon what He is in Himself, as upon what He has done for us.' Works, vol. i. p. 435.

[s] Cat. Rac. p. 164.

[t] Cf. Pearson, Minor Theological Works, vol. i. p. 307: 'Christus sive Homo Ille Qui est Mediator, adoratus est. Heb. i. 6; Apoc. v. 11, 12. Hæc est plenissima descriptio adorationis. Et hic Agnus occisus erat Homo ille, Qui est Mediator; Ergo Homo Ille, Qui est Mediator est adorandus. St. Greg. Nazianzen. Epist. ci.: Εἴτις μὴ προσκυνεῖ τὸν ἐσταυρωμένον, ἀνάθεμα

St. Paul His Human Name of Jesus, that is, His Human Nature, is worshipped on earth, in heaven, and among the dead. It is not the Unincarnate Logos, but the wounded Humanity of Jesus, Which is enthroned and adored in the vision of the Apocalypse. To adore Christ's Deity while carefully refusing to adore His Manhood would be to forget that His Manhood is for ever joined to His Divine and Eternal Person, Which is the real Object of our adoration. Since He has taken the Manhood into God, It is an inseparable attribute of His Personal Godhead; every knee must bend before It; henceforth the angels themselves around the throne must adore, not as of yore the Unincarnate Son, but 'the Lamb as It had been slain.'

3. Thus rooted in the doctrine and practice of the apostles, the worship of Jesus Christ was handed down to succeeding ages as an integral and recognised element of the spiritual life of the Church. The early Fathers refer to the worship of our Lord as to a matter beyond dispute. The apostolic age had scarcely passed, when St. Ignatius bids the Roman Christians 'put up supplications to Christ' on his behalf, that he might attain the distinction of martyrdom [u]. St. Polycarp's Epistle to the Philippians opens with a benediction which is in fact a prayer to Jesus Christ, as being, together with the Almighty Father, the Giver of peace and mercy [x]. Polycarp prays that 'the God and Father of our Lord Jesus Christ, and the Eternal Priest Himself, Jesus Christ, the Son of God, would build up his readers in faith and truth and in all meekness, . . . and would give them a part and lot among the saints [y].' And at a later

ἔστω, καὶ τετάχθω μετὰ τῶν θεοκτόνων.' Cf. also Ibid. p. 308: 'Christus, quâ est Mediator, est unicâ adoratione colendus. Concil. Gen. V. Collat. viii. can. 9. Si quis adorari in duabus naturis dicit Christum, ex quo duas adorationes introducat, semotim Deo Verbo, et semotim Homini: aut si quis . . . . . adorat Christum, sed non *unâ adoratione* Deum Verbum Incarnatum cum Ejus Carne adorat, extra quod sanctæ Dei ecclesiæ ab initio traditum est; talis anathema sit.' See the whole of this and the preceding 'Determination.' And compare St. Cyril's 8th Anathema; Damasc., iv. 3; Hooker, E. P. v. 54, 9.

[u] St. Ign. ad Rom. 4: *λιτανεύσατε τὸν Χριστὸν* [*τὸν Κύριον* ed. Dressel, which, however, must here mean our Lord] *ὑπὲρ ἐμοῦ, ἵνα διὰ τῶν ὀργάνων τούτων* [*Θεῷ* ed. Dressel] *θυσία εὑρεθῶ.* Cf. ad Magn. 7.

[x] St. Polyc. ad Phil. 1: *ἔλεος ὑμῖν καὶ εἰρήνη παρὰ Θεοῦ παντοκράτορος καὶ Κυρίου Ἰησοῦ Χριστοῦ τοῦ Σωτῆρος ἡμῶν πληθυνθείη.*

[y] Ibid. 12: 'Deus autem et Pater Domini nostri Jesu Christi, et ipse Sempiternus Pontifex, Dei Filius Jesus Christus, ædificet vos in fide et veritate et in omni mansuetudine, ... et det vobis sortem et partem inter sanctos suos.'

day, standing bound at the pyre of martyrdom, he cries, 'For all things, O God, do I praise and bless and glorify Thee, together with the Eternal and Heavenly Jesus Christ, Thy well-beloved Son, with Whom, to Thee and the Holy Ghost, be glory, both now and for ever. Amen [z].' After his death, Nicetas begged the proconsul not to deliver up his body for burial, 'lest the Christians should desert the Crucified One, and should begin to worship this new martyr [a].' The Jews, it appears, employed an argument which may have been the language of sarcasm or of a real anxiety. 'They know not,' continues the encyclical letter of the Church of Smyrna, 'that neither shall we ever be able to desert Christ Who suffered for the salvation of all who are saved in the whole world, nor yet to worship any other. For Him indeed, as being the Son of God, we do adore; but the martyrs, as disciples and imitators of the Lord, we worthily love by reason of their unsurpassed devotion to Him their own King and Teacher. God grant that we too may be fellow-partakers and fellow-disciples with them [b].' The writers of this remarkable passage were not wanting in love and honour to the martyr of Christ. 'Afterward,' say they, 'we, having taken up his bones, which were more precious than costly stones, and of more account than gold, placed them where it was fitting [c].' But they draw the sharpest line between such a tribute of affection and the worship of the Redeemer; Jesus was worshipped as 'being the Son of God.' The Apologists point to the adoration of Jesus Christ, as well as to that of the Father, when replying to the heathen charge of atheism. St. Justin protests to the emperors that the Christians worship God alone [d]. Yet he also asserts that the Son and the Spirit share in the reverence and worship which is offered to the Father [e]; and

[z] Mart. St. Polyc. c. 14, apud Hefele, Patr. Ap. p. 131.

[a] Ibid. c. 17: *μή, φησίν, ἀφέντες τὸν ἐσταυρωμένον, τοῦτον ἄρξωνται σέβεσθαι.*

[b] Ibid.: *ἀγνοοῦντες, ὅτι οὔτε τὸν Χριστόν ποτε καταλιπεῖν δυνησόμεθα τὸν ὑπὲρ τῆς τοῦ παντὸς κόσμου τῶν σωζομένων σωτηρίας παθόντα, οὔτε ἕτερόν τινα σέβεσθαι. τοῦτον μὲν γὰρ Υἱὸν ὄντα τοῦ Θεοῦ προσκυνοῦμεν· τοὺς δὲ μάρτυρας, ὡς μαθητὰς καὶ μιμητὰς τοῦ Κυρίου, ἀγαπῶμεν ἀξίως, ἕνεκα εὐνοίας ἀνυπερβλήτου τῆς εἰς τὸν ἴδιον βασιλέα καὶ διδάσκαλον· ὧν γένοιτο καὶ ἡμᾶς συγκοινωνούς τε καὶ συμμαθητὰς γενέσθαι.*

[c] Ibid. c. 18.

[d] Apol. i. § 17, p. 44, ed. Otto. After quoting St. Luke xx. 22–25 he proceeds: *ὅθεν Θεὸν μὲν μόνον προσκυνοῦμεν, ὑμῖν δὲ πρὸς τὰ ἄλλα χαίροντες ὑπηρετοῦμεν.*

[e] Ibid. i. § 6, p. 14, ed. Otto: *Καὶ ὁμολογοῦμεν τῶν τοιούτων νομιζομένων θεῶν ἄθεοι εἶναι, ἀλλ' οὐχὶ τοῦ ἀληθεστάτου καὶ πατρὸς δικαιοσύνης καὶ σωφρο-*

in controversy with Trypho he especially urges that prophecy foretold the adoration of Messiah[f]. St. Irenæus insists that the miracles which were in his day of common occurrence in the Church were not to be ascribed to any invocation of angels, nor yet to magical incantations, nor to any form of evil curiosity. They were simply due to the fact that Christians constantly prayed to God the Maker of all things, and called upon the Name of His Son Jesus Christ[g]. Clement of Alexandria has left us three treatises, designed to form a missionary trilogy. In one he is occupied with converting the heathen from idolatry to the faith of Christ; in a second he instructs the new convert in the earlier lessons and duties of the Christian faith; while in his most considerable work he labours to impart the higher knowledge to which the Christian is entitled, and so to render him 'the perfect Gnostic.' In each of these treatises, widely different as they are in point of practical aim, Clement bears witness to the Church's worship of our Lord. In the first, his Hortatory Address to the Greeks, he winds up a long

σύνης καὶ τῶν ἄλλων ἀρετῶν, ἀνεπιμίκτου τε κακίας θεοῦ· ἀλλ' ἐκεῖνόν τε, καὶ τὸν παρ' αὐτοῦ Υἱὸν ἐλθόντα καὶ διδάξαντα ἡμᾶς ταῦτα καὶ τὸν τῶν ἄλλων, ἑπομένων καὶ ἐξομοιουμένων ἀγαθῶν ἀγγέλων στρατὸν, Πνεῦμά τε τὸ προφητικὸν σεβόμεθα καὶ προσκυνοῦμεν λόγῳ καὶ ἀληθείᾳ τιμῶντες. With regard to the clause of this passage which has been the subject of so much controversy (καὶ τὸν τῶν ἄλλων . . . . ἀγγέλων στρατὸν), (1) it is impossible to make στρατὸν depend upon σεβόμεθα καὶ προσκυνοῦμεν without involving St. Justin in self-contradiction (cf. the passage quoted above), and Bellarmine's argument based on this construction (de Beatitud. Sanctor. lib. i. c. 13) proves, if anything, too much for his purpose, viz. that *the same* worship was paid to the angels as to the Persons of the Blessed Trinity. Several moderns (quoted by Otto in loc.) who adopt this construction use it for a very different object. (2) It is difficult to accept Bingham's rendering (Ant. bk. 13, c. 2, § 2) which joins ἀγγέλων στρατὸν and ἡμᾶς with διδάξαντα, and makes Christ the Teacher not of men only but of the angel host. This idea, however, seems to have no natural place in the passage, and we should have expected ταῦτα ἡμᾶς not ἡμᾶς ταῦτα. (3) It seems better, therefore, with Bull, Chevallier (Transl. p. 152), Möhler (Tübing. Theol. Quartalsch. 1833, Fasc. i. p. 53 sqq., quoted by Otto) to make ἀγγέλων στρατὸν and ταῦτα together dependent upon διδάξαντα: 'the Son of God taught us not merely about these (viz. evil spirits, cf. § 5) but also concerning the good angels,' &c.; τὸν ἀγγέλων στρατὸν being elliptically put for τὰ περὶ τοῦ . . . ἀγγέλων στρατοῦ.

[f] Dial. cum Tryph. c. 68: γραφὰς, αἳ διαῤῥήδην τὸν Χριστὸν καὶ παθητὸν καὶ προσκυνητὸν καὶ Θεὸν ἀποδεικνύουσιν. Ibid. c. 76: Καὶ Δαυὶδ . . . . Θεὸν ἰσχυρὸν καὶ προσκυνητὸν, Χριστὸν ὄντα, ἐδήλωσε.

[g] Hær. ii. § 32: 'Ecclesia . . . . . nomen Domini nostri Jesu Christi invocans, virtutes ad utilitates hominum, sed non ad seductionem, perficit.' Observe too the argument which follows.

argumentative invective against idolatry with a burst of fervid entreaty: 'Believe, O man,' he exclaims, 'in Him Who is both Man and God; believe, O man, in the living God, Who suffered and Who is adored [h].' The Pædagogus concludes with a prayer of singular beauty ending in a doxology [i], and in these the Son is worshipped and praised as the Equal of the Father. In the Stromata, as might be expected, prayer to Jesus Christ is rather taken for granted; the Christian life is to be a continuous worship of the Word, and through Him of the Father [k]. Tertullian in his Apology grapples with the taunt that the Christians worshipped a Man Who had been condemned by the Jewish tribunals [l]. Tertullian does not deny or palliate the charge; he justifies the Christian practice. Whatever Christ might be in the opinion of the pagan world, Christians knew Him to be of one substance with the Father [m]. The adoration of Christ, then, was not a devotional eccentricity; it was an absolute duty. In one passage Tertullian argues against mixed marriages with the heathen, because in these cases there could be no joint worship of the Redeemer [n]; elsewhere he implies that the worship of Jesus was co-extensive with faith in Christianity [o].

Origen's erratic intellect may have at times betrayed him, on this as on other subjects, into language [p], more or less incon-

[h] Protrept. c. x. p. 84, ed. Potter: *πίστευσον, ἄνθρωπε, ἀνθρώπῳ καὶ Θεῷ· πίστευσον, ἄνθρωπε, τῷ παθόντι καὶ προσκυνουμένῳ Θεῷ ζῶντι· πιστεύσατε οἱ δοῦλοι τῷ νεκρῷ· πάντες ἄνθρωποι, πιστεύσατε μόνῳ τῷ πάντων ἀνθρώπων Θεῷ· πιστεύσατε καὶ μισθὸν λάβετε σωτηρίαν κ.τ.λ.*

[i] Pædagog. lib. iii. c. 7, p. 311, ed. Potter: *ὅπερ οὖν λοιπὸν ἐπὶ τοιαύτῃ πανηγύρει τοῦ Λόγου, τῷ Λόγῳ προσευξώμεθα· Ἵλαθι τοῖς σοῖς, παιδαγωγὲ, παιδίοις, Πατὴρ, ἡνίοχε Ἰσραὴλ, Υἱὲ καὶ Πατὴρ, Ἓν ἄμφω Κύριε. δὸς δὲ ἡμῖν τοῖς σοῖς ἑπομένοις παραγγέλμασι τὸ ὁμοίωμα πληρῶσαι . . . . . αἰνοῦντας εὐχαριστεῖν, [εὐχαριστοῦντας] αἰνεῖν, τῷ μόνῳ Πατρὶ καὶ Υἱῷ, Υἱῷ καὶ Πατρὶ, παιδαγωγῷ καὶ διδασκάλῳ Υἱῷ, σὺν καὶ τῷ ἁγίῳ Πνεύματι, πάντα τῷ Ἑνὶ, ἐν ᾧ τὰ πάντα, δι' ὃν τὰ πάντα ἕν, . . . ᾧ ἡ δόξα καὶ νῦν καὶ εἰς αἰῶνας.*

[k] See the fine passage, Stromat. lib. vii. c. 7, ad init. p. 851, ed. Potter.

[l] Apolog. c. 21: 'Sed et vulgus jam scit Christum ut hominum aliquem, qualem Judæi judicaverunt, quo facilius quis nos hominis cultores existimaverit. Verum neque de Christo erubescimus, cum sub nomine ejus deputari et damnari juvat.'

[m] Ibid.: 'Hunc ex Deo prolatum didicimus, et prolatione generatum, et idcirco Filium Dei *et Deum dictum, ex unitate Substantiæ*.'

[n] Ad Uxor. lib. ii. c. 6: 'Audiat . . . de ganeâ. Quæ Dei mentio? quæ Christi invocatio?'

[o] Adv. Jud. c. 7: 'Ubique creditur, ab omnibus gentibus suprà enumeratis colitur, ubique regnat, ubique adoratur.'

[p] Particularly in the treatise, De Oratione, c. 15, vol. i. ed. Ben. p. 223: *πῶς δὲ οὐκ ἔστι κατὰ τὸν εἰπόντα· 'Τί με λέγεις ἀγαθόν; οὐδεὶς ἀγαθὸς εἰ μὴ*

sistent with his own general line of teaching, by which it must in fairness be interpreted. Origen often insists upon the worship of Jesus Christ as being a Christian duty[q]; he illustrates this duty, especially in his Homilies, by his personal example[r]; he bases it upon the great truth which justifies and demands such a practical acknowledgment[s]. It is in keeping with this that

εἷς ὁ Θεὸς, ὁ Πατήρ·' εἰπεῖν ἄν· Τί ἐμοὶ προσεύχῃ; Μόνῳ τῷ Πατρὶ προσεύχεσθαι χρὴ, ᾧ κἀγὼ προσεύχομαι· ὅπερ διὰ τῶν ἁγίων γραφῶν μανθάνετε· Ἀρχιερεῖ γὰρ τῷ ὑπὲρ ἡμῶν κατασταθέντι ὑπὸ τοῦ Πατρὸς, καὶ παρακλήτῳ ὑπὸ τοῦ Πατρὸς εἶναι λαβόντι, εὔχεσθαι ἡμᾶς οὐ δεῖ, ἀλλὰ δι' ἀρχιερέως καὶ παρακλήτου κ.τ.λ. This indefensible language was a result of the line taken by Origen in opposing the Monarchians. 'As the latter, together with the distinction of substance in the Father and the Son, denied also that of the Person, so it was with Origen a matter of practical moment, on account of the systematic connexion of ideas in his philosophical system of Christianity, to maintain in opposition to them the personal independence of the Logos. Sometimes in this controversy he distinguishes between *unity of substance* and personal unity or unity of subject, so that it only concerned him to controvert the latter. And this certainly was the point of greatest practical moment to him; and he must have been well aware that many of the Fathers who contended for a *personal distinction* held firmly at the same time to a *unity of substance*. But according to the internal connexion of his own system (Neander means his Platonic doctrine of the τὸ ὄν) both fell together; wherever he spoke, therefore, from the position of that system, he affirmed at one and the same time the ἑτερότης τῆς οὐσίας and the ἑτερότης τῆς ὑποστάσεως or τοῦ ὑποκειμένου.' Neander, Ch. Hist. ii. 311, 312. From this philosophical premiss Origen deduces his practical inference above noticed: εἰ γὰρ ἕτερος, ὡς ἐν ἄλλοις δείκνυται, κατ' οὐσίαν καὶ ὑποκείμενός ἐστιν ὁ Υἱὸς τοῦ Πατρὸς, ἤτοι προσκυνητέον τῷ Υἱῷ καὶ οὐ τῷ Πατρὶ, ἢ ἀμφοτέροις, ἢ τῷ Πατρὶ μόνῳ. De Orat. c. 15, sub init. p. 222. Although, then, Origen expresses his conclusion in Scriptural terminology, it is a conclusion which is traceable to his philosophy as distinct from his strict religious belief, and it is entirely contradicted by a large nmber of other passages in his writings.

[q] Contr. Cels. v. 12, sub fin. vol. i. p. 587. Also Ibid. viii. 12, p. 750 (in juxta-position with some inconsistent language): ἕνα οὖν Θεὸν, ὡς ἀποδεδώκαμεν, τὸν Πατέρα καὶ τὸν Υἱὸν θεραπεύομεν· καὶ μένει ἡμῖν ὁ πρὸς τοὺς ἄλλους ἀτενὴς λόγος· καὶ οὐ τὸν ἔναγχός γε φανέντα, ὡς πρότερον οὐκ ὄντα, ὑπερθρησκεύομεν. Ibid. viii. 26: μόνῳ γὰρ προσευκτέον τῷ ἐπὶ πᾶσι Θεῷ, καὶ προσευκτέον γε τῷ Μονογενεῖ, καὶ Πρωτοτόκῳ πάσης κτίσεως, Λόγῳ Θεοῦ.

[r] See his prayer on the furniture of the tabernacle, as spiritually explained, Hom. 13 in Exod. xxxv. p. 176: 'Domine Jesu, præsta mihi, ut aliquid monumenti habere merear in tabernaculo Tuo. Ego optarem (si fieri posset), esse aliquid meum in illo auro, ex quo propitiatorium fabricatur, vel ex quo arca contegitur, vel ex quo candelabrum fit luminis et lucernæ. Aut si aurum non habeo, argentum saltem aliquid inveniar offerre, quod proficiat in columnas, vel in bases earum. Aut certe vel æris aliquid . . . . Tantum ne in omnibus jejunus et infecundus inveniar.' Cf. too Hom. i. in Lev., Hom. v. in Lev., quoted by Bingham, Ant. xiii. 2, § 3.

[s] Comm. in Rom. x. lib. viii. vol. 4, p. 624, ed. Ben., quoted by Bingham, ubi supra: '[Apostolus] in principio Epistolæ quam ad Corinthios scribit,

Origen explains the frankincense offered by the wise men to our Infant Saviour as an acknowledgment of His Godhead; since such an action obviously involved that adoration which is due only to God [t]. This explanation could not have been put forward by any but a devout worshipper of Jesus. In the work on the Trinity [u], ascribed to Novatian, in the treatises and letters [x] of St. Cyprian, in the apologetic works of Arnobius [y] and Lac-

ubi dicit, "Cum omnibus qui invocant nomen Domini nostri Jesu Christi, in omni loco ipsorum et nostro" eum cujus nomen invocatur, Dominum Jesum Christum esse pronuntiat. Si ergo et Enos, et Moyses, et Aaron, et Samuel, "invocabant Dominum et ipse exaudiebat eos," sine dubio Christum Jesum Dominum invocabant; et si invocare nomen Domini et orare Dominum unum atque idem est; sicut invocatur Deus, invocandus est Christus; et sicut oratur Deus, ita et orandus est Christus; et sicut offerimus Deo Patri primo omnium orationes, ita et Domino Jesu Christo; et sicut offerimus postulationes Patri, ita offerimus postulationes et Filio; et sicut offerimus gratiarum actiones Deo, ita et gratias offerimus Salvatori. Unum namque utrique honorem deferendum, id est Patri et Filio, divinus edocet sermo, cum dicit: "Ut omnes honorificent Filium, sicut honorificant Patrem."'

[t] Contr. Cels. i. 60, p. 375: *φέροντες μὲν δῶρα, ἃ (ἵν' οὕτως ὀνομάσω) συνθέτῳ τινὶ ἐκ Θεοῦ καὶ ἀνθρώπου θνητοῦ προσήνεγκαν, σύμβολα μὲν, ὡς βασιλεῖ τὸν χρυσὸν, ὡς δὲ τεθνηξομένῳ τὴν σμύρναν, ὡς δὲ Θεῷ τὸν λιβανωτόν· προσήνεγκαν δὲ, μαθόντες τὸν τόπον τῆς γενέσεως αὐτοῦ. Ἀλλ' ἐπεὶ Θεὸς ἦν, ὁ ὑπὲρ τοὺς βοηθοῦντας ἀνθρώποις ἀγγέλους ἐνυπάρχων Σωτὴρ τοῦ γένους τῶν ἀνθρώπων, ἄγγελος ἠμείψατο τὴν τῶν μάγων ἐπὶ προσκυνῆσαι τὸν Ἰησοῦν εὐσέβειαν, χρηματίσας αὐτοῖς 'μὴ ἥκειν πρὸς τὸν Ἡρώδην, ἀλλ' ἐπανελθεῖν ἄλλῃ ὁδῷ εἰς τὰ οἰκεῖα.'* Cf. St. Iren. adv. Hær. iii. 9. 2.

[u] Novat. de Trin. c. 14, quoted by Bingham: 'Si homo tantummodo Christus, quomodo adest ubique invocatus, quum hæc hominis natura non sit, sed Dei, ut adesse omni loco possit?'

[x] St. Cyprian. de Bono Patientiæ, p. 220, ed. Fell.: 'Pater Deus præcepit Filium suum adorari: et Apostolus Paulus, divini præcepti memor, ponit et dicit: "Deus exaltavit illum et donavit illi nomen quod est super omne nomen; ut in nomine Jesu omne genu flectatur, cœlestium, terrestrium, et infernorum:" et in Apocalypsi angelus Joanni volenti adorari se resistit et dicit: "Vide ne feceris, quia conservus tuus sum et fratrum tuorum; Jesum Dominum adora." Qualis Dominus Jesus, et quanta patientia ejus, ut qui in cœlis adoratur, necdum vindicetur in terris?' In Rev. xx. 9, St. Cyprian probably read *τῷ Κυρίῳ* instead of *τῷ Θεῷ*. See his language to Lucius, Bishop of Rome, who had recently been a confessor in a sudden persecution of Gallus, A.D. 252 (Ep. 61, p. 145, ed. Fell.): 'Has ad vos literas mittimus, frater carissime, et repræsentantes vobis per epistolam gaudium nostrum, fida obsequia caritatis expromimus; hic quoque in sacrificiis atque in orationibus nostris non cessantes Deo Patri, et Christo Filio Ejus Domino nostro gratias agere, et orare pariter ac petere, ut qui perfectus est atque perficiens, custodiat et perficiat in vobis confessionis vestræ gloriosam coronam.'

[y] Arnobius adv. Gentes, i. 36: 'Quotidianis supplicationibus adoratis.' And Ibid. i. 39: 'Neque [Christus] omni illo qui vel maximus potest excogitari divinitatis afficiatur cultu?' [ed. Oehler].

tantius[z], references to the subject are numerous and decisive. But our limits forbid any serious attempt to deal with the materials which crowd upon us as we advance into the central and later decades of the third century; and at this point it may be well to glance at the forms with which the primitive Church actually approached the throne of the Redeemer.

It is clear that Christian hymnody has ever been prized and hated for its services in popularising the worship of Jesus Christ. Hymnody actively educates, while it partially satisfies, the instinct of worship; it is a less formal and sustained act of worship than prayer, yet it may really involve transient acts of the deepest adoration. But, because it is less formal; because in using it the soul can pass, as it were, unobserved and at will from mere sympathetic states of feeling to adoration, and from adoration back to passive although reverent sympathy;—hymnody has always been a popular instrument for the expression of religious feeling. And from the first years of Christianity it seems to have been especially consecrated to the honour of the Redeemer. We have already noted traces of such apostolical hymns in the Pauline Epistles; but some early Humanitarian teachers did unintentional service, by bringing into prominence the value of hymns as witnesses to Christian doctrine, and as efficient means of popular dogmatic teaching. When the followers of Artemon maintained that the doctrine of Christ's Godhead was only brought into the Church during the episcopate of Zephyrinus, a Catholic writer, quoted by Eusebius, observed, by way of reply, that 'the psalms and hymns of the brethren, which, from the earliest days of Christianity, had been written by the faithful, all celebrate Christ, the Word of God, proclaiming His Divinity[a].' Origen pointed out that hymns were addressed only to God and to His Only-begotten Word, Who is also God[b]. And the practical value of these hymns as teaching the doctrine of Christ's Deity was illustrated by the conduct of Paulus of Samosata. He banished from his own and neighbouring churches the psalms which were sung to our Lord Jesus Christ; he spoke of them contemptuously as being merely modern compositions. This was very natural in a prelate who 'did not wish to confess with the Church that the

[z] Lactantius, Div. Inst. iv. 16.

[a] Eus. Hist. Eccl. v. 28: ψαλμοὶ δὲ ὅσοι καὶ ᾠδαὶ ἀδελφῶν ἀπ' ἀρχῆς ὑπὸ πιστῶν γραφεῖσαι, τὸν Λόγον τοῦ Θεοῦ τὸν Χριστὸν ὑμνοῦσι θεολογοῦντες.

[b] Contr. Cels. viii. 67: ὕμνους γὰρ εἰς μόνον τὸν ἐπὶ πᾶσι λέγομεν Θεὸν, καὶ τὸν μονογενῆ αὐτοῦ Λόγον καὶ Θεόν· καὶ ὑμνοῦμέν γε Θεὸν καὶ τὸν Μονογενῆ αὐτοῦ.

Son of God had descended from heaven[c];' but it shews how the hymnody of the primitive Church protected and proclaimed the truths which she taught and cherished.

Of the early hymns of the Church of Christ some remain to this day among us as witnesses and expressions of her faith in Christ's Divinity. Such are the Tersanctus and the Gloria in Excelsis. Both belong to the second century; both were introduced, it is difficult to say how early, into the Eucharistic Office; both pay Divine honours to our Blessed Lord. As each morning dawned, the Christian of primitive days repeated in private the Gloria in Excelsis; it was his hymn of supplication and praise to Christ. How wonderfully does it blend the appeal to our Lord's human sympathies with the confession of His Divine prerogatives! 'O Lord God, Lamb of God, Son of the Father, That takest away the sins of the world, have mercy upon us.' How thrilling is that burst of praise, which at last drowns the plaintive notes of entreaty that have preceded it, and hails Jesus Christ glorified on His throne in the heights of heaven! 'For Thou only art holy; Thou only art the Lord; Thou only, O Christ, with the Holy Ghost, art most high in the glory of God the Father.' Each evening too, in those early times, the Christian offered another hymn, less known among ourselves, but scarcely less beautiful. It too was addressed to Jesus in His majesty:—

'Hail! gladdening Light, of His pure glory poured,
Who is th' Immortal Father, heavenly, blest,
Holiest of Holies—Jesus Christ our Lord!
Now we are come to the sun's hour of rest,
The lights of evening round us shine,
We hymn the Father, Son, and Holy Spirit Divine!
Worthiest art Thou at all times to be sung
With undefiled tongue,
Son of our God, Giver of life, Alone!
Therefore in all the world, Thy glories, Lord, they own[d].'

[c] Eus. Hist. Eccl. vii. 30: ψαλμοὺς δὲ τοὺς μὲν εἰς τὸν Κύριον ἡμῶν Ἰησοῦν Χριστὸν παύσας, ὡς δὴ νεωτέρους καὶ νεωτέρων ἀνδρῶν συγγράμματα. The account continues: εἰς ἑαυτὸν δὲ ἐν μέσῃ τῇ ἐκκλησίᾳ, τῇ μεγάλῃ τοῦ πάσχα ἡμέρᾳ ψαλμῳδεῖν γυναῖκας παρασκευάζων, ὧν καὶ ἀκούσας ἄν τις φρίξειεν. They seem to have sung in this prelate's own presence, and with his approbation, odes which greeted him as 'an angel who had descended from heaven,' although Paulus denied our Lord's pre-existence. Vanity and unbelief are naturally and generally found together. The historian adds expressly: τὸν μὲν γὰρ Υἱὸν τοῦ Θεοῦ οὐ βούλεται συνομολογεῖν ἐξ οὐρανοῦ κατεληλυθέναι.

[d] Cf. Lyra Apostolica, No. 63. The original is given in Routh's Reliquiæ Sacr. iii. p. 515:—

A yet earlier illustration is afforded by the ode with which the Alexandrian Clement concludes his Pædagogus. Although its phraseology was strictly adapted to the 'perfect Gnostic' at Alexandria in the second century, yet it seems to have been intended for congregational use. It celebrates our Lord, as 'the Dispenser of wisdom,' 'the Support of the suffering,' the 'Lord of immortality,' 'the Saviour of mortals,' 'the Mighty Son,' 'the God of peace.' It thrice insists on the 'sincerity' of the praise thus offered Him. It concludes:—

'Sing we sincerely
The Mighty Son;
We, the peaceful choir,
We, the Christ-begotten ones,
We, the people of sober life,
Sing we together the God of peace[e].'

Nor may we forget a hymn which, in God's good providence, has been endeared to all of us from childhood. In its present form, the Te Deum is clearly Western, whether it belongs to the age of St. Augustine, with whose baptism it is connected by the popular tradition, or, as is probable, to a later period. But we can scarcely doubt that portions of it are of Eastern origin, and that they carry us up wellnigh to the sub-apostolic period. The Te Deum is at once a song of praise, a creed, and a supplication. In each capacity it is addressed to our Lord. In the Te Deum how profound is the adoration offered to Jesus, whether as One

Φῶς ἱλαρὸν ἁγίας δόξης ἀθανάτου Πατρὸς
οὐρανίου, ἁγίου, μάκαρος,
Ἰησοῦ Χριστὲ,
ἐλθόντες ἐπὶ τοῦ ἡλίου δύσιν,
ἰδόντες φῶς ἑσπερινὸν,
ὑμνοῦμεν Πατέρα, καὶ Υἱὸν, καὶ Ἅγιον Πνεῦμα Θεοῦ.
ἄξιος εἶ ἐν πᾶσι καιροῖς ὑμνεῖσθαι φωναῖς ὁσίαις,
Υἱὲ Θεοῦ, ζωὴν ὁ διδούς·
διὸ ὁ κόσμος σε δοξάζει.

St. Basil quotes it in part, De Spir. Sanct. 73. It is still the Vesper Hymn of the Greek Church.

[e] Clem. Alex. Pæd. iii. 12, fin. p. 313; Daniel, Thesaurus Hymnologicus, tom. iii. p. 3. 'Der Ton des Liedes ist . . . . gnostisch versinnlichend.' (Fortläge Gesänge Christlicher Vorzeit, p. 357, qu. by Daniel):—

μέλπωμεν ἁπλῶς
παῖδα κρατερόν,
χορὸς εἰρήνης
οἱ χριστόγονοι,
λαὸς σώφρων,
ψάλλωμεν ὁμοῦ Θεὸν εἰρήνης.

of the Most Holy Three, or more specially in His Personal distinctness as the King of Glory, the Father's Everlasting Son! How touching are the supplications which remind Him that when He became incarnate 'He did not abhor the Virgin's womb,' that when His Death-agony was passed He 'opened the kingdom of heaven to all believers!' How passionate are the pleadings that He would 'help His servants whom He has redeemed with His most precious Blood,' that He would 'make them to be numbered with His saints in glory everlasting!' Much of this language is of the highest antiquity; all of it is redolent with the fragrance of the earliest Church; and, as we English Christians use it still in our daily services, we may rejoice to feel that it unites us altogether in spirit, and to a great extent in the letter, with the Church of the first three centuries [f].

The Apostolical Constitutions contain ancient doxologies which associate Jesus Christ with the Father as 'inhabiting the praises of Israel,' after the manner of the Gloria Patri [g]. And the Kyrie Eleison, that germinal type of supplication, of which the countless litanies of the modern Church are only the varied expansions, is undoubtedly sub-apostolic. Together with the Tersanctus and the Gloria in Excelsis it shews very remarkably, by its presence in the Eucharistic Office, how ancient and deeply rooted was the Christian practice of prayer to Jesus Christ. For the Eucharist has a double aspect: it is a gift from heaven to earth, but it is also an offering from earth to heaven. In the Eucharist the Christian Church offers to the Eternal Father the 'merits and Death of His Son Jesus Christ;' since Christ

[f] On this subject, see Daniel, Thesaur. Hymnolog. tom. ii. pp. 279–299.

[g] Constitutiones, viii. 12 (vol. i. p. 482, ed. Labbe), quoted by Bingham: *παρακαλοῦμέν σε . . . . ὅπως ἅπαντας ἡμᾶς διατηρήσας ἐν τῇ εὐσεβείᾳ, ἐπισυναγάγῃς ἐν τῇ βασιλείᾳ τοῦ Χριστοῦ σου τοῦ Θεοῦ πάσης αἰσθητῆς καὶ νοητῆς φύσεως, τοῦ βασιλέως ἡμῶν, ἀτρέπτους, ἀμέμπτους, ἀνεγκλήτους· ὅτι σοι πᾶσα δόξα, σέβας καὶ εὐχαριστία, τιμὴ καὶ προσκύνησις τῷ Πατρὶ, καὶ τῷ Υἱῷ, καὶ τῷ Ἁγίῳ Πνεύματι καὶ νῦν καὶ ἀεὶ καὶ εἰς τοὺς ἀνελλειπεῖς καὶ ἀτελευτήτους αἰῶνας τῶν αἰώνων.* Ibid. 13 (p. 483): *διὰ τοῦ Χριστοῦ σου· μεθ' οὗ σοι δόξα, τιμὴ, αἶνος, δοξολογία, εὐχαριστία, καὶ τῷ Ἁγίῳ Πνεύματι, εἰς τοὺς αἰῶνας, ἀμήν.* Ibid.: *εὐλογημένος ὁ ἐρχόμενος ἐν ὀνόματι Κυρίου Θεὸς, Κύριος, καὶ ἐπέφανεν ἡμῖν· Ὡσαννὰ ἐν τοῖς ὑψίστοις.* Ibid. 14 (p. 486): *ἑαυτοὺς τῷ Θεῷ τῷ μόνῳ ἀγεννήτῳ Θεῷ, καὶ τῷ Χριστῷ αὐτοῦ παραθώμεθα.* Ibid. 15 (p. 486): *πάντας ἡμᾶς ἐπισυνάγαγε εἰς τὴν τῶν οὐρανῶν βασιλείαν, ἐν Χριστῷ Ἰησοῦ τῷ Κυρίῳ ἡμῶν· μεθ' οὗ σοι δόξα, τιμὴ καὶ σέβας καὶ τῷ Ἁγίῳ Πνεύματι εἰς τοὺς αἰῶνας, ἀμήν.* Ibid. (p. 487): *ὅτι σοι δόξα, αἶνος, μεγαλοπρέπεια, σέβας, προσκύνησις, καὶ τῷ σῷ παιδὶ Ἰησοῦ τῷ Χριστῷ σου τῷ Κυρίῳ ἡμῶν καὶ Θεῷ καὶ βασιλεῖ, καὶ τῷ Ἁγίῳ Πνεύματι, νῦν καὶ ἀεὶ καὶ εἰς τοὺς αἰῶνας τῶν αἰώνων, ἀμήν.*

Himself has said, 'Do this in remembrance of Me.' The canon of Carthage accordingly expresses the more ancient law and instinct of the Church: 'Cum altari adsistitur, semper ad Patrem dirigatur oratio [h].' Yet so strong was the impulse to offer prayer to Christ, that this canon is strictly observed by no single liturgy, while some rites violate it with the utmost consistency. The Mozarabic rite is a case in point: its collects witness to the Church's long struggle with, and final victory over, the tenacious Arianism of Spain [i]. It might even appear

[h] Conc. Carth. iii. c. 23, Labbe, vol. ii. p. 1170.

[i] Taking a small part of the Mozarabic Missal, from Advent Sunday to Epiphany inclusive, we find sixty cases in which prayer is offered, during the altar service, to our Lord. These cases include (1) three 'Illations' or Prefaces, for the third Sunday in Advent, Circumcision, and Epiphany (and part at least of this Mass for the Epiphany is considered by Dr. Neale in his Essays on Liturgiology, p. 138, to be at least not later 'than the middle of the fourth century'); also (2) several prayers in which our Lord's agency in sanctifying the Eucharistic sacrifice, or even in receiving it, is implied—e.g. 'Jesu, bone Pontifex . . . . . sanctifica hanc oblationem;' or, in a 'Post Pridie' for fifth Sunday in Advent: 'Hæc oblata Tibi . . . . . benedicenda assume libamina (. . . . tui Adventûs gloriam, &c.).' (Miss. Moz. p. 17.) So again, on Mid-Lent Sunday: 'Ecce, Jesu . . . deferimus Tibi hoc sacrificium nostræ redemptionis . . . . . accipe hoc sacrificium;' on which Leslie quotes St. Fulgentius, de Fide, c. 19: 'Cui (i.e. to the Incarnate Son) cum Patre et Spiritu Sancto . . . . sacrificium panis et vini . . . . Ecclesia . . . . offerre non cessat.' Again, in the Mass for Easter Friday, in an 'Alia Oratio:' 'Ecce, Jesu Mediator . . . . hanc Tibi afferimus victimam sacrificii singularis.' From Palm Sunday to Easter Day inclusive, the prayers offered to Christ, according to this Missal, are twenty-nine. The zeal of the Spanish Church for the Divinity of the Holy Spirit is remarkably shewn in a 'Post Pridie' for Whitsunday: 'Suscipe . . . . . Spiritus Sancte, omnipotens Deus, sacrificia;' on which Leslie's note says, 'Ariani negabant sacrificium debere Dei Filio offerri, aut Spiritui Sancto . . . . contra quos Catholici Gotho-Hispani Filio et Spiritui Sancto sacrificium Eucharisticum distinctè offerunt;' and he proceeds to quote another passage from Fulgentius that worship and sacrifice were offered alike to all the Three Persons, 'hoc est, Sanctæ Trinitati.' The Gallican Liturgies, though in a less degree, exhibit the same feature of Eucharistic prayer to our Lord. In the very old series of fragmentary Masses, discovered by Mone, and edited by the Rev. G. H. Forbes and Dr. Neale (in Ancient Liturgies of the Gallican Church, part i.), as the 'Missale Richenovense' (from the abbey of Reichenau, where they were found), there are four cases of prayer to Christ; one of them, in the ninth Mass, being in a 'Contestatio' or Preface. In the 'Gothic' (or southern-Gallic) Missal, prayer is made to Him about seventy-six times. Some of these cases are very striking. Thus on Christmas Day, 'Suscipe, ... Domine Jesu, omnipotens Deus, sacrificium laudis oblatum.' (Muratori, Lit. Rom. ii. 521; Forbes and Neale, p. 35.) The 'Immolatio' (another term for the Contestatio) of Palm Sunday is addressed to Christ. The 'Old Gallican' Missal, belonging to central Gaul, has sixteen cases of prayer to Him, including the 'Immolatio' of Easter

to substitute for the rule laid down at Carthage, the distinct but (considering the indivisible relation of the Three Holy Persons to each other) perfectly consistent principle that the Eucharist is offered to the Holy Trinity. This too would seem to be the mind of the Eastern Church[k]. It is unnecessary to observe that at this day, both in the Eucharistic Service and elsewhere, prayer to Jesus Christ is as integral a feature of the devotional system of the Church of England, as it was of the ancient, or as it is of the contemporary Use of Western Christendom[l].

Nor was the worship of Jesus Christ by the early Christians an esoteric element of their religious activity, obvious only to those who were within the Church, who cherished her creed, and who took part in her services. It was not an abstract doctrine,

Saturday. The 'Gallican Sacramentary' (called also the Sacramentarium Bobiense, and by Mr. Forbes, the Missal of Besançon) has twenty-eight such cases, including three Contestations. The Canon of the Ambrosian Rite has prayers to Christ.

[k] The principle affirmed in the old Spanish rite, that the Eucharist was to be offered to the whole Trinity, and therefore to the Son, is also affirmed in the daily Liturgy of the Eastern Church. The prayer of the Cherubic Hymn, which indeed was not originally a part of St. Chrysostom's Liturgy, having been inserted in it not earlier than Justinian's reign, has this conclusion: *Σὺ γὰρ εἶ ὁ προσφέρων καὶ προσφερόμενος, καὶ προσδεχόμενος, καὶ διαδιδόμενος, Χριστὲ ὁ Θεὸς ἡμῶν, καὶ σοὶ τὴν δόξαν ἀναπέμπομεν κ.τ.λ.* About 1155 a dispute arose as to *προσδεχόμενος*, and Soterichus Panteugenus, patriarch-elect of Antioch, who taught that the sacrifice was not offered to the Son, but only to the Father and the Holy Spirit, was condemned in a council at Constantinople, 1156. 'This,' says Neale (Introd. to East. Church, i. 434), 'was the end of the controversy that for more than seven hundred years had vexed the Church on the subject of the Incarnation.' Between this event and the condemnation of Monothelitism, Neale reckons the condemnation of Adoptionism, in 794. Compare also, in the present Liturgy of St. James, a prayer just before the 'Sancta Sanctis,' addressed to our Lord, in which the phrase occurs, '*Thy* holy and bloodless sacrifices.' The same Liturgy has other prayers addressed to Him. In St. Mark's Liturgy, among other prayers to Christ, one runs thus, 'Shew Thy face on this bread and these cups.' After the Lord's Prayer, the Deacon says, 'Bow your heads to Jesus,' and the response is, 'To Thee, O Lord.' In fact, the East seems never to have accepted the maxim that Eucharistic prayer was always addressed to the Father. Our 'Prayer of St. Chrysostom,' addressed to the Son, is the 'prayer of the third Antiphon' in Lit. St. Chrys.; and the same rite, and the Armenian, have the remarkable prayer, 'Attend, O Lord Jesus Christ our God . . . . . and come to sanctify us,' &c. In the Coptic Liturgy of St. Basil, our Lord is besought to send down the Spirit on the elements. The present Roman rite has three prayers to Christ between the 'Agnus Dei' and the 'Panem cœlestem.'

[l] See Note F in Appendix.

but a living and notorious practice, daily observed by, and recommended to, Christians. As such it challenged the observation of the heathen from a very early date. It is probable indeed that the Jews, as notably on the occasion of St. Polycarp's martyrdom [m], drew the attention of pagan magistrates to the worship of Jesus, in order to stir up contempt and hatred against the Christians. But such a worship was of itself calculated to strike the administrative instincts of Roman magistrates as an unauthorized addition to the registered religions of the empire, even before they had discovered it to be irreconcileable with public observance of the established state ceremonies, and specially with any acknowledgment of the divinity of the reigning emperor. The younger Pliny is drawing up a report for the eye of his imperial master Trajan; and he writes with the cold impartiality of a pagan statesman who is permitting himself to take a distant philosophical interest in the superstitions of the lower orders. Some apostates from the Church had been brought before his tribunal, and he had questioned them as to the practices of the Christians in Asia Minor. It appeared that on a stated day the Christians met before daybreak, and sang among themselves, responsively, a hymn to Christ as God [n]. Here it should be noted that Pliny is not recording a vague report, but a definite statement, elicited from several persons in cross-examination, moreover touching a point which, in dealing with a Roman magistrate, they might naturally have desired to keep in the background [o]. Again, the emperor Adrian, when writing to Servian, describes the population of Alexandria as divided between the worship of Christ and the worship of Serapis [p]. That One Who had been adjudged by the law to

[m] Martyr. St. Polyc. c. 17.

[n] Plin. Ep. lib. x. ep. 97: 'Alii ab indice nominati esse se Christianos dixerunt, et mox negaverunt; fuisse quidem sed desiisse; quidam ante triennium, quidam ante plures annos, non nemo etiam ante viginti quoque. Omnes et imaginem tuam, deorumque simulacra venerati sunt, ii et Christo maledixerunt. Adfirmabant autem, hanc fuisse summam vel culpæ suæ vel erroris, quod essent soliti stato die ante lucem convenire, carmenque Christo, quasi Deo, dicere secum invicem, seque sacramento non in scelus aliquod obstringere, sed ne furta, ne latrocinia, ne adulteria committerent.'

[o] That the 'carmen' was an incantation, or that Christ was saluted as a hero, not as a Divine Person, are glosses upon the sense of this passage, rather than its natural meaning. See Augusti, Denkwürdigkeiten, tom. v. p. 33.

[p] Apud Lamprid. in vitâ Alex. Severi: 'ab aliis Serapidem, ab aliis adorari Christum.'

death as a criminal should receive Divine honours, must have been sufficiently perplexing to the Roman official mind; but it was much less irritating to the statesmen than to the philosophers. In his life of the fanatical cynic and apostate Christian, Peregrinus Proteus, whose voluntary self-immolation he himself witnessed at Olympia in A.D. 165, Lucian gives vent to the contemptuous sarcasm which was roused in him, and in men like him, by the devotions of the Church. 'The Christians,' he says, 'are still worshipping that great man who was gibbeted in Palestine[q].' He complains that the Christians are taught that they stand to each other in the relation of brethren, as soon as they have broken loose from the prevailing customs, and have denied the gods of Greece, and have taken to the adoration of that impaled Sophist of theirs[r]. The Celsus with whom we meet in the treatise of Origen may or may not have been the friend of Lucian[s]. Celsus, it has been remarked, represents a class of intellects which is constantly found among the opponents of Christianity; Celsus has wit and acuteness without moral earnestness or depth of research; he looks at things only on the surface, and takes delight in constructing and putting forward difficulties and contradictions[t]. The worship of our Lord was certain to engage the perverted ingenuity of a mind of this description; and Celsus attacks the practice upon a variety of grounds which are discussed by Origen. The general position taken up by Celsus is that the Christians had no right to denounce the polytheism of the pagan world, since their own worship of Christ was essentially polytheistic. It was absurd in the Christians, he contends, to point at the heathen gods as idols, whilst they worshipped one who was in a much more wretched condition than the idols, and indeed was not even an idol at all, since he was a mere corpse[u]. The Christians, he

[q] De Morte Peregrini, c. 11: τὸν μέγαν οὖν ἐκεῖνον ἔτι σέβουσιν ἄνθρωπον, τὸν ἐν Παλαιστίνῃ ἀνασκολοπισθέντα.

[r] Ibid. c. 13: ἐπειδὰν ἅπαξ παραβάντες, θεοὺς μὲν Ἑλληνικοὺς ἀπαρνήσωνται, τὸν δ' ἀνεσκολοπισμένον ἐκεῖνον σοφιστὴν αὐτῶν προσκυνῶσι.

[s] Neander decides in the negative (Ch. Hist. i. 225 sqq.), (1) on the ground of the vehemence of the opponent of Origen, as contrasted with the moderation of the friend of Lucian; (2) because the friend of Lucian was an Epicurean, the antagonist of Origen a neo-Platonist.

[t] See the remarks of Neander, Ch. Hist. vol. i. p. 227, ed. Bohn.

[u] Contr. Cels. vii. 40, p. 722: ἵνα μὴ παντάπασιν ἦτε καταγέλαστοι τοὺς μὲν ἄλλους, τοὺς δεικνυμένους θεοὺς, ὡς εἴδωλα βλασφημοῦντες· τὸν δὲ καὶ αὐτῶν ὡς ἀληθῶς εἰδώλων ἀθλιώτερον, καὶ μηδὲ εἴδωλον ἔτι, ἀλλ' ὄντως νεκρὸν, σέβοντες, καὶ Πατέρα ὅμοιον αὐτῷ ζητοῦντες.

urges, worshipped no God, no, not even a demon, but only a dead man [x]. If the Christians were bent upon religious innovations; if Hercules, and Æsculapius, and the gods who had been of old held in honour, were not to their taste; why could they not have addressed themselves to such distinguished mortals as Orpheus, or Anaxarchus, or Epictetus, or the Sibyl? Nay, would it not have been better to have paid their devotions to some of their own prophets, to Jonah under the gourd, or to Daniel in the lions' den, than to a man who had lived an infamous life, and had died a miserable death [y]? In thus honouring a Jew who had been apprehended and put to death, the Christians were no better than the Getæ who worshipped Zamolxis, than the Cilicians who adored Mopsus, than the Acarnanians who prayed to Amphilochus, than the Thebans with their cultus of Amphiaraus, than the Lebadians who were so devoted to Trophonius [z]. Was it not absurd in the Christians to ridicule the heathen for the devotion which they paid to Jupiter on the score of the exhibition of his sepulchre in Crete, while they themselves adored one who was himself only a tenant of the tomb [a]? Above all, was not the worship of Christ fatal to the Christian doctrine of the Unity of God? If the Christians really worshipped no God but One, then their reasoning against the heathen might have had force in it. But while they offer an excessive adoration to this person who has but lately appeared in the world, how can they think that they commit no offence against God, by giving such Divine honours to His servant [b]?

In his replies Origen entirely admits the fact upon which

[x] Contr. Cels. vii. 68, p. 742: *διελέγχονται σαφῶς οὐ Θεὸν, ἀλλ' οὐδὲ δαίμονα ἀλλὰ νεκρὸν σέβοντες.*

[y] Ibid. vii. 53, p. 732: *πόσῳ δ' ἦν ὑμῖν ἄμεινον, ἐπειδή γε καινοτομῆσαί τι ἐπεθυμήσατε, περὶ ἄλλον τινὰ τῶν γενναίως ἀποθανόντων, καὶ θεῖον μῦθον δέξασθαι δυναμένων, σπουδάσαι; Φέρε, εἰ μὴ ἤρεσκεν Ἡρακλῆς, καὶ Ἀσκληπιὸς, καὶ οἱ πάλαι δεδοξασμένοι, Ὀρφέα εἴχετε κ.τ.λ.* Cf. 57.

[z] Ibid. iii. 34, p. 469: *μετὰ ταῦτα 'παραπλήσιον ἡμᾶς' οἴεται 'πεποιηκέναι,' τὸν (ὥς φησιν ὁ Κέλσος) ἁλόντα καὶ ἀποθανόντα θρησκεύοντας,' τοῖς Γέταις σέβουσι τὸν Ζάμολξιν, καὶ Κίλιξι τὸν Μόψον, καὶ Ἀκαρνᾶσι τὸν Ἀμφίλοχον, καὶ Θηβαίοις τὸν Ἀμφιάρεων, καὶ Λεβαδίοις τὸν Τροφώνιον.'*

[a] Ibid. iii. 43, p. 475: *μετὰ ταῦτα λέγει περὶ ἡμῶν 'ὅτι καταγελῶμεν τῶν προσκυνούντων τὸν Δία, ἐπεὶ τάφος αὐτοῦ ἐν Κρήτῃ δείκνυται· καὶ οὐδὲν ἧττον σέβομεν τὸν ἀπὸ τοῦ τάφου' κ.τ.λ.*

[b] Ibid. viii. 12, p. 750: *δόξαι δ' ἄν τις ἑξῆς τούτοις πιθανόν τι καθ' ἡμῶν λέγειν ἐν τῷ, 'Εἰ μὲν δὴ μηδένα ἄλλον ἐθεράπευον οὗτοι πλὴν ἕνα Θεὸν, ἦν ἄν τις αὐτοῖς ἴσως πρὸς τοὺς ἄλλους ἀτενὴς λόγος· νυνὶ δὲ τὸν ἔναγχος φανέντα τοῦτον ὑπερθρησκεύουσι, καὶ ὅμως οὐδὲν πλημμελεῖν νομίζουσι περὶ τὸν Θεὸν, εἰ καὶ ὑπηρέτης αὐτοῦ θεραπευθήσεται.'*

Celsus comments in this lively spirit of raillery. He does not merely admit that prayer to Christ was the universal practice of the Church; he energetically justifies it. When confronting the heathen opponent of his Master's honour, Origen writes as the Christian believer, rather than as the philosophizing Alexandrian [c]. He deals with the language of Celsus patiently and in detail. The objects of heathen worship were unworthy of worship; the Jewish prophets had no claim to it; Christ was worshipped as the Son of God, as God Himself. 'If Celsus,' he says, 'had understood the meaning of this, "I and the Father are One," or what the Son of God says in His prayer, "As I and Thou are One," he would never have imagined that we worship any but the God Who is over all; for Christ says, "The Father is in Me and I in Him [d]."' Origen then proceeds, although by a questionable analogy, to guard this language against a Sabellian construction: the worship addressed to Jesus was addressed to Him as personally distinct from the Father. Origen indeed, in vindicating this worship of our Lord, describes it elsewhere as prayer in an improper sense [e], on the ground that true prayer is offered to the Father only. This has been explained to relate only to the mediatorial aspect of His Manhood as our High Priest [f]; and Bishop Bull further understands him to argue that the Father, as the Source of Deity, is ultimately the Object of all adoration [g]. But Origen entirely admits the broad fact that Jesus received Divine honours; and he defends such worship of Jesus as being an integral element of the Church's life [h].

The stress of heathen criticism, however, still continued to be directed against the adoration of our Lord. 'Our gods,' so ran the heathen language of a later day, 'are not displeased

[c] See however Contr. Cels. v. 11, sub fin. p. 586, where, nevertheless, the conclusion of the passage shews his real mind in De Orat. c. 15, quoted above.

[d] Contr. Cels. viii. 12, p. 750: *εἴπερ νενοήκει ὁ Κέλσος τό· ''Ἐγὼ καὶ ὁ Πατὴρ ἕν ἐσμεν·' καὶ τὸ ἐν εὐχῇ εἰρημένον ὑπὸ τοῦ Υἱοῦ τοῦ Θεοῦ ἐν τῷ· ''Ὡς ἐγὼ καὶ σὺ ἕν ἐσμεν,' οὐκ ἂν ᾤετο ἡμᾶς καὶ ἄλλον θεραπεύειν, παρὰ τὸν ἐπὶ πᾶσι Θεόν. ''Ὁ γὰρ Πατὴρ,' φησὶν, 'ἐν ἐμοὶ, κἀγὼ ἐν τῷ Πατρί.'*

[e] Ibid. v. 4: *τῆς περὶ προσευχῆς κυριολεξίας καὶ καταχρήσεως.*

[f] Ibid. viii. 13, 16. 'Loquitur de Christo,' says Bishop Bull, 'ut Summo Sacerdote.' Def. Fid. Nic. ii. 9, 15.

[g] Bull, Def. Fid. Nic. sect. ii. c. 9, n. 15: '*Sin Filium intueamur relatè, quâ Filius est*, et ex Deo Patre trahit originem, tum rursus certum est, cultum et venerationem omnem, quem ipsi deferimus, ad Patrem redundare, in ipsumque, ut *πηγὴν θεότητος* ultimo referri.'

[h] See Reading's note on Orig. de Orat. § 15.

[LECT.

with you Christians for worshipping the Almighty God. But you maintain the Deity of One Who was born as a man, and Who was put to death by the punishment of the cross (a mark of infamy reserved for criminals of the worst kind); you believe Him to be still alive, and you adore Him with daily supplications [i].' 'The heathen,' observes Lactantius, 'throw in our teeth the Passion of Christ; they say that we worship a man, and a man too who was put to death by men under circumstances of ignominy and torture [k].' Lactantius and Arnobius reply to the charge in precisely the same manner. They admit the truth of Christ's Humanity, and the shame of His Passion; but they earnestly assert His literal and absolute Godhead. However the heathen might scorn, the Godhead of Christ was the great certainty upon which the eye of His Church was persistently fixed; it was the truth by which her practice of adoring Him was necessarily determined [l].

If the Gospel had only enjoined the intellectual acceptance of some philosophical theistic theory, its popular impotence would have earned the toleration which is easily secured by cold, abstract, passionless religions. In that case it would never have provoked the earnest scorn of a Lucian or of a Celsus. They would have condoned or passed it by, even if they had not cared to patronize it. But the continuous adoration of Jesus by His Church made the neutrality of such men as these morally impossible. They knew what it meant, this worship of

[i] Arnob. adv. Gentes, i. 36: 'Sed non idcirco Dii vobis infesti sunt, quod omnipotentem colatis Deum: sed quod hominem natum, et (quod personis infame est vilibus) crucis supplicio interemptum, et Deum fuisse contenditis, et superesse adhuc creditis, et quotidianis supplicationibus adoratis.'

[k] Lact. Div. Inst. iv. 16: 'Venio nunc ad ipsam Passionem, quæ velut opprobrium nobis objectari solet, quod et hominem, et ab hominibus insigni supplicio adfectum et excruciatum colamus: ut doceam eam ipsam Passionem ab Eo cum magnâ et divinâ ratione susceptam, et in eâ solâ et virtutem, et veritatem, et sapientiam contineri.'

[l] Arnob. adv. Gentes, i. 42: 'Natum hominem colimus. Etiamsi esset id verum, locis ut in superioribus dictum est, tamen pro multis et tam liberalibus donis, quæ ab eo profecta in nobis sunt, Deus dici appellarique deberet. Cum vero Deus sit re certâ, et sine ullius rei dubitationis ambiguo, inficiaturos arbitramini nos esse, quam maxime illum a nobis coli, et præsidem nostri corporis nuncupari? Ergone, inquiet aliquis furens, iratus, et percitus, Deus ille est Christus? Deus, respondebimus, et interiorum potentiarum Deus; et quod magis infidos acerbissimis doloribus torqueat, rei maximæ causâ a summo Rege ad nos missus.' Lact. Div. Inst. iv. 29: 'Quum dicimus Deum Patrem et Deum Filium, non diversum dicimus, nec utrumque secernimus: siquidem nec Pater sine Filio nuncupari, nec Filius potest sine Patre generari.'

the Crucified; it was too intelligible, too soul-enthralling, to be ignored or to be tolerated. And the lowest orders of the populace were for many long years, just as intelligently hostile to it as were the philosophers. Witness that remarkable caricature of the adoration of our crucified Lord, which was discovered not long since beneath the ruins of the Palatine palace[m]. It is a rough sketch, traced, in all probability, by the hand of some pagan slave in one of the earliest years of the third century of our era[n]. A human figure with an ass's head is represented as

[m] See 'Deux Monuments des Premiers Siècles de l'Église expliqués, par le P. Raphaël Garrucci,' Rome, 1862. He describes the discovery and appearance of this 'Graffito Blasfemo' as follows:—'Comme tant d'autres ruines, le palais des Césars récélait aussi de nombreuses inscriptions dictées par le caprice. Après avoir recueilli celles qui couvraient les parois de toute une salle, nous arrivâmes à trouver quelques paroles grecques, inscrites au sommet d'un mur enseveli sous les décombres. Ce fut là un précieux indice qui nous fit poursuivre nos recherches. Bientôt apparut le contour d'une tête d'animal sur un corps humain, dont les bras étaient étendus comme ceux des *orantes* dans les Catacombes. La découverte paraissait avoir un haut intérêt: aussi Mgr. Milesi, Ministre des travaux publics, nous autorisa-t-il, avec sa bienveillance accoutumée, à faire enlever la terre et les débris qui encombraient cette chambre, le 11 Novembre, 1857. Nous ne tardâmes point à contempler une image que ces ruines avaient conservée intacte à travers les siècles, et dont nous pûmes relever un calque fidèle.

'Elle répésente une croix, dont la forme est celle du *Tau* grec, surmonté d'une cheville qui porte une tablette. Un homme est attaché à cette croix, mais la tête de cette figure n'est point humaine, c'est celle du cheval ou plutôt de l'onagre. Le crucifié est revêtu de la tunique de dessous, que les anciens désignaient sous le nom d'*interula*, et d'une autre tunique sans ceinture; des bandes appelées *crurales* enveloppent la partie inférieure des jambes. À la gauche du spectateur, on voit un autre personnage, qui sous le même vêtement, semble converser avec la monstrueuse image, et élève vers elle sa main gauche, dont les doigts sont separés. À droite, au dessus de la croix, se lit la lettre Υ; et au dessous, l'inscription suivante:

ΑΛΕΞΑΜΕΝΟΣ ΣΕΒΕΤΕ (pour ΣΕΒΕΤΑΙ)
ΘΕΟΝ
Alexamenos adore son Dieu.'

For the reference to this interesting paper I am indebted to the kindness of Professor Westwood. See Wordsworth's Tour in Italy, ii. p. 143; and for engravings of the Graffito, Tyrwhitt's Art Teaching of the Primitive Church, p. 7; Northcote and Brownlow, Roma Sotterranea, p. ii, p. 346. Champfleury, Histoire de la Caricature Antique, c. xxiv. p. 287, sqq.

[n] P. Garucci fixes this date on the following grounds: (1) Inscriptions on tiles and other fragments of this part of the Palatine palace shew that it was constructed during the reign of the Emperor Adrian. The dates 123 and 126 are distinctly ascertained. (Deux Monuments, &c., p. 10.) The inscription therefore is not earlier than this date. (2) The calumny of the worship of the ass's head by the Christians is not mentioned by any of the Apologists who precede Tertullian, nor by any who succeed Minucius

fixed to a cross; while another figure in a tunic stands on one side. This figure is addressing himself to the crucified monster, and is making a gesture which was the customary pagan expression of adoration. Underneath there runs a rude inscription: *Alexamenos adores his God.* Here we are face to face with a touching episode of the life of the Roman Church in the days of Severus or of Caracalla. As under Nero, so, a century and a half later, there were worshippers of Christ in the household of the Cæsar. But the paganism of the later date was more intelligently and bitterly hostile to the Church than the paganism which had shed the blood of the Apostles. The Gnostic invective which attributed to the Jews the worship of an ass, was applied by the pagans with facile indifference both to Jews and Christians. Tacitus attributes the custom to a legend respecting services rendered by wild asses to the Israelites in the desert [o]; 'and so, I suppose,' observes Tertullian, 'it was thence presumed that we, as bordering on the Jewish religion, were taught to worship such a figure [p].' A story of this kind once current, was

Felix; which may be taken to prove that this misrepresentation of Christian worship was only in vogue among pagan critics in Rome and Africa at the close of the second and at the beginning of the third century. (3) It is certain from Tertullian that there were Christians in the imperial palace during the reign of the Emperor Severus: 'Even Severus himself, the father of Antoninus, was mindful of the Christians; for he sought out Proculus a Christian, who was surnamed Torpacion, the steward of Euodia, who had once cured him by means of oil, and kept him in his own palace, even to his death: whom also Antoninus very well knew, nursed as he was upon Christian milk.' Ad Scapulam, c. 4. Caracalla's playmate was a Christian boy; see Dr. Pusey's note on Tertull. p. 148, Oxf. Tr. Libr. Fath. (4) 'Rien dans le monument du Palatin ne contredit cette opinion, ni la paléographie, qui trahit la même époque, tant à cause de l'usage simultané de l'E carré et de l'E semicirculaire dans la même inscription, que par la forme générale des lettres; ni moins encore l'ortographe, car on sait que le changement de l'AI en E a plus d'un exemple à Rome, même sur les monuments grecs du règne d'Auguste. Enfin les autres inscriptions grecques de cette chambre, qui sans préjudice pour notre thèse, pourraient être d'une autre temps, ne font naître aucune difficulté sérieuse, étant parfaitement semblables à celle dont nous nous occupons.' Garucci, Ibid. p. 13.

[o] Tac. Hist. v. c. 4. He had it probably from Apion: see Josephus, c. Ap. ii. 10. It is repeated by Plutarch, Symp. iv. 5: *τὸν ὄνον ἀναφήναντα αὐτοῖς πηγὴν ὕδατος τιμῶσι.* And by Democritus: *Χρυσῆν ὄνου κεφαλὴν προσεκύνουν.* Apud Suidas, voc. Ἰουδάς.

[p] Apolog. 16. Tertullian refutes Tacitus by referring to his own account of the examination of the Jewish temple by Cn. Pompeius after his capture of Jerusalem; Pompey 'found no image' in the temple. For proof that the early Christians were constantly identified with the Jews by the pagan world, see Dr. Pusey's note on Tert. ubi supra, in the Oxf. Tr. Libr. Fath.

easily adapted to the purposes of a pagan caricaturist. Whether from ignorance of the forms of Christian worship, or in order to make his parody of it more generally intelligible to the pagan public, the draughtsman has ascribed to Alexamenos the gestures of a heathen devotee [q]. But the real object of this coarse caricature is too plain to be mistaken. Jesus Christ, we may be sure, had other confessors and worshippers in the imperial palace who knelt side by side with Alexamenos. The moral pressure of the advancing Church was making itself felt throughout all ranks of pagan society; ridicule was invoked to do the work of argument; and the social persecution which crowned all true Christian devotion was often only the prelude to a sterner test of that loyalty to a crucified Lord, which could meet heathen scorn with the strength of patient faith, and heathen cruelty with the courage of heroic endurance.

The death-cry of the martyrs must have familiarized the heathen mind with the honour paid to the Redeemer by Christians. Of the worship offered in the Catacombs, of the stern yet tender discipline whereby the early Church stimulated, guided, moulded the heavenward aspirations of her children, paganism knew, could know, nothing. But the bearing and the exclamations of heroic servants of Christ when arraigned before the tribunals of the empire, or when exposed to a death of torture and shame in the amphitheatres, were matters of public notoriety. The dying prayers of St. Stephen expressed the instinct, if they did not provoke the imitation, of many a martyr of later days. What matters it to Blandina of Lyons that her pagan persecutors have first entangled her limbs in the meshes of a large net, and then have exposed her to the fury of a wild bull? She is insensible to pain; she is entranced in a profound communion with Christ [r]. What matters it to that servant-boy in Palestine, Porphyry, that his mangled body is 'committed to a slow fire?' He does but call more earnestly in his death-struggle upon Jesus [s]. Felix, an African bishop, after a long series of persecutions, has been condemned to be beheaded at Venusium for refusing to give up the sacred books

[q] Job xxxi. 27. St. Hieronym. in Oseam, c. 13: 'Qui adorant solent deosculari manum suam.' Comp. Minuc. Fel. Oct. c. 2.

[r] Eus. Hist. Ecc. v. 1: εἰς γύργαθον βληθεῖσα, ταύρῳ παρεβλήθη· καὶ ἱκανῶς ἀναβληθεῖσα πρὸς τοῦ ζώου, μηδὲ αἴσθησιν ἔτι τῶν συμβαινόντων ἔχουσα διὰ τὴν ἐλπίδα καὶ ἐποχὴν τῶν πεπιστευμένων καὶ ὁμιλίαν πρὸς Χριστόν.

[s] Ibid. Mart. Pal. 11: καθαψαμένης αὐτοῦ τῆς φλογὸς ἀπέῤῥηξε φωνὴν, τὸν Υἱὸν τοῦ Θεοῦ Ἰησοῦν βοηθὸν ἐπιβοώμενος.

to the proconsul. 'Raising his eyes to heaven, he said with a clear voice . . . "O Lord God of heaven and earth, Jesu Christ, to Thee do I bend my neck by way of sacrifice, O Thou Who abidest for ever, to Whom belong glory and majesty, world without end. Amen[t]."' Theodotus of Ancyra has been betrayed by the apostate Polychronius, and is joining in a last prayer with the sorrowing Church. 'Lord Jesu Christ,' he cries, 'Thou Hope of the hopeless, grant that I may finish the course of my conflict, and offer the shedding of my blood as a libation and sacrifice, to the relief of all those who suffer for Thee. Do Thou lighten their burden; and still this tempest of persecution, that all who believe in Thee may enjoy rest and quietness[u].' And afterwards, in the extremity of his torture, he prays thus: 'Lord Jesu Christ, Thou Hope of the hopeless, hear my prayer, and assuage this agony, seeing that for Thy Name's sake I suffer thus[x].' And when the pain had failed to bend his resolution, and the last sentence had been pronounced by the angry judge, 'O Lord Jesu Christ,' the martyr exclaims, 'Thou Maker of heaven and earth, Who forsakest not them that put their hope in Thee, I give Thee thanks for that Thou hast made me meet to be a citizen of Thy heavenly city, and to have a share in Thy kingdom. I give Thee thanks, that Thou hast given me strength to conquer the dragon, and to bruise his head. Give rest unto Thy servants, and stay the fierceness of the enemies in my

[t] Ruinart, Acta Martyrum Sincera, ed. Veronæ, 1731, p. 314. Acta S. Felicis Episcopi, anno 303: 'Felix Episcopus, elevans oculos in cœlum, clarâ voce dixit, *Deus, gratias Tibi. Quinquaginta et sex annos habeo in hoc sæculo. Virginitatem custodivi, Evangelia servavi, fidem et veritatem prædicavi. Domine Deus cœli et terræ, Jesu Christe, Tibi cervicem meam ad victimam flecto, Qui permanes in æternum; Cui est claritas et magnificentia in sæcula sæculorum. Amen.*'

[u] Ibid. p. 303, Passio S. Theodoti Ancyrani, et septem virginum: 'Theodotus, valedicens fratribus, jubensque ne ab oratione cessarent, sed Deum orarent ut corona ipsi obtingeret, præparavit se ad verbera sustinenda. Simul igitur perstiterunt in oratione cum martyre, qui prolixe precatus, tandem ait: *Domine Jesu Christe, spes desperatorum, da mihi certaminis cursum perficere, et sanguinis effusionem pro sacrificio et libatione offerre, omnium eorum causâ qui propter Te affliguntur. Alleva onus eorum; et compesce tempestatem, ut requie et profundâ tranquillitate potiantur omnes qui in Te credunt.*'

[x] Ibid. p. 307: 'Videns ergo Præses se frustra laborare, et fatigatos tortores deficere, depositum de ligno jussit super ignitas testulas collocari. Quibus etiam interiora corporis penetrantibus gravissimum dolorem sentiens Theodotus, oravit dicens, *Domine Jesu Christe, spes desperatorum, exaudi orationem meam, et cruciatum hunc mitiga; quia propter Nomen Sanctum Tuum ista patior.*'

person. Give peace unto Thy Church, and set her free from the tyranny of the devil [y].'

Thus it was that the martyrs prayed and died. Their voices reach us across the chasm of intervening centuries; but time cannot impair the moral majesty, or weaken the accents of their strong and simple conviction. One after another their piercing words, in which the sharpest human agony is so entwined with a superhuman faith, fall upon our ears. 'O Christ, Thou Son of God, deliver Thy servants [z].' 'O Lord Jesu Christ, we are Christians; Thee do we serve; Thou art our Hope; Thou art the Hope of Christians; O God Most Holy, O God Most High, O God Almighty [a].' 'O Christ,' cries a martyr again and again amidst his agonies, 'O Christ, let me not be confounded [b].' 'Help, I pray Thee, O Christ, have pity. Preserve my soul, guard my spirit, that I be not ashamed. I pray Thee, O Christ, grant me power of endurance [c].' 'I pray Thee,

[y] Ruinart, Acta, p. 307: 'Cumque ad locum pervenissent, orare cœpit Martyr in hæc verba: *Domine Jesu Christe, cœli terræque conditor, qui non derelinquis sperantes in Te, gratias Tibi ago, quia fecisti me dignum cœlestis Tuæ Urbis civem, Tuique regni consortem. Gratias Tibi ago, quia donasti mihi draconem vincere, et caput ejus conterere. Da requiem servis Tuis, atque in me siste violentiam inimicorum. Da Ecclesiæ Tuæ pacem, eruens eam a tyrannide diaboli.*'

[z] Ibid. p. 340; Acta SS. Saturnini, Dativi, et aliorum plurimorum martyrum in Africâ, a. 304: 'Thelica martyr, mediâ de ipsâ carnificum rabie hujusmodi preces Domino cum gratiarum actione effundebat: Deo gratias. *In Nomine Tuo, Christe Dei Fili, libera servos Tuos.*'

[a] Ibid.: 'Cum ictibus ungularum concussa fortius latera sulcarentur, profluensque sanguinis unda violentis tractibus emanaret, Proconsulem sibi dicentem audivit: Incipies sentire quæ vos pati oporteat. Et adjecit: *Ad gloriam. Gratias ago Deo regnorum. Apparet regnum æternum, regnum incorruptum. Domine Jesu Christe, Christiani sumus; Tibi servimus; Tu es spes nostra; Tu es spes Christianorum; Deus sanctissime; Deus altissime; Deus omnipotens.*'

[b] Ibid. p. 341: 'Advolabant truces manus jussis velocibus leviores, secretaque pectoris, disruptis cutibus, visceribusque divulsis, nefandis adspectibus profanorum adnexâ crudelitate pandebant. Inter hæc Martyris mens immobilis perstat: et licet membra rumpantur, divellantur viscera, latera dissipentur, animus tamen martyris integer, inconcussusque perdurat. Denique dignitatis suæ memor Dativus, qui et Senator, tali voce preces Domino sub carnifice rabiente fundebat: *O Christe Domine, non confundar.*' Ibid. p. 342: 'At martyr, inter vulnerum cruciatus sævissimos pristinam suam repetens orationem: *Rogo*, ait, *Christe, non confundar.*'

[c] Ibid. p. 342: 'Spectabat interea Dativus lanienam corporis sui potius quam dolebat: et cujus ad Dominum mens animusque pendebat, nihil dolorem corporis æstimabat, sed tantum ad Dominum precabatur, dicens; *Subveni, rogo, Christe, habe pietatem. Serva animam meam; custodi spiritum meum ut non confundar. Rogo, Christe, da sufferentiam.*'

[LECT.

Christ, hear me. I thank Thee, my God; command that I be beheaded. I pray Thee, Christ, have mercy; help me, Thou Son of God[d].' 'I pray Thee, O Christ: all praise to Thee. Deliver me, O Christ; I suffer in Thy Name. I suffer for a short while; I suffer with a willing mind, O Christ my Lord: let me not be confounded[e].'

Or listen to such an extract from an early document as the following:—'Calvisianus, interrupting Euplius, said, "Let Euplius, who hath not in compliance with the edict of the emperors given up the sacred writings, but readeth them to the people, be put to the torture." And while he was being racked, Euplius said, "I thank Thee, O Christ. Guard Thou me, who for Thee am suffering thus." Calvisianus the consular said, "Cease, Euplius, from this folly. Adore the gods, and thou shalt be set at liberty." Euplius said, "I adore Christ; I utterly hate the demons. Do what thou wilt: I am a Christian. Long have I desired what now I suffer. Do what thou wilt. Add yet other tortures: I am a Christian." After he had been tortured a long while, the executioners were bidden hold their hands. And Calvisianus said, "Unhappy man, adore the gods. Pay worship to Mars, Apollo, and Æsculapius." Euplius said, "I worship the Father and the Son and the Holy Ghost. I adore the Holy Trinity, beside Whom there is no God. Perish the gods who did not make heaven and earth, and all that is in them. I am a Christian." Calvisianus the præfect said, "Offer sacrifice, if thou wouldest be set at liberty." Euplius said, "I sacrifice myself only to Christ my God: more than this I cannot do. Thy efforts are to no purpose; I am a Christian." Calvisianus gave orders that he should be tortured again more severely. And while he was being tortured, Euplius said, "Thanks to Thee, O Christ. Help me, O Christ. For Thee do I suffer thus, O Christ." And he said this repeatedly. And as his strength gradually failed him, he went on repeating these or other exclamations, with his lips only—his voice was gone[f].'

[d] Acta, p. 342: 'Ne inter moras torquentium exclusa anima corpus supplicio pendente desereret, tali voce Dominum presbyter precabatur: *Rogo Christe, exaudi me. Gratias Tibi ago, Deus: jube me decollari. Rogo Christe, miserere. Dei Fili, subveni.*'

[e] Ibid. p. 343: 'Emeritus martyr ait: . . . . . *Rogo, Christe, Tibi laudes: libera me, Christe, patior in Nomine Tuo. Breviter patior, libenter patior, Christe Domine; non confundar.*'

[f] Ruinart, p. 362; Acta S. Euplii Diaconi et Martyris, a. 304: 'Calvisianus interlocutus dixit: *Euplius qui secundum Edictum Principum non tradidit Scripturas, sed legit populo, torqueatur.* Cumque torqueretur,

You cannot, as I have already urged [g], dismiss from your consideration such prayers as these, on the ground of their being 'mere ejaculations.' Do serious men, who know they are dying, 'ejaculate' at random? Is it at the hour of death that a man would naturally innovate upon the devotional habits of a life-time? Is it at such an hour that he would make hitherto unattempted enterprises into the unseen world, and address himself to beings with whom he had not before deemed it lawful or possible to hold spiritual communion? Is not the reverse of this supposition notoriously the case? Surely, those of us who have witnessed the last hours of the servants of Christ cannot hesitate as to the answer. As the soul draws nigh to the gate of death, the solemnities of the eternal future are wont to cast their shadows upon the thought and heart; and whatever is deepest, truest, most assured and precious, thenceforth engrosses every power. At that dread yet blessed hour, the soul clings with a new intensity and deliberation to the most certain truths, to the most prized and familiar words. The mental creations of an intellectual over-subtlety, or of a thoughtless enthusiasm, or of an unbridled imagination, or of a hidden perversity of will, or of an unsuspected unreality of character, fade away or are discarded. To gaze upon the naked truth is the one necessity; to plant the feet upon the Rock Itself, the supreme desire, in that awful, searching, sifting moment. Often, too, at a man's last hour, will habit strangely assert its mysterious power of recovering, as if from the grave, thoughts and memories which seemed to have been lost for ever. Truths which have been half forgotten or quite forgotten since childhood, and prayers

dixit Euplius: *Gratias Tibi, Christe. Me custodi qui propter Te hæc patior.* Dixit Calvisianus Consularis: *Desiste, Eupli, ab insaniâ hâc. Deos adora et liberaberis.* Euplius dixit: *Adoro Christum, detestor dæmonia. Fac quod vis, Christianus sum. Hæc diu optavi. Fac quod vis. Adde alia, Christianus sum.* Postquam diu tortus esset, jussi sunt cessare carnifices. Et dixit Calvisianus: *Miser, adora deos: Martem cole, Apollinem et Æsculapium.* Dixit Euplius: *Patrem et Filium et Spiritum Sanctum adoro: Sanctam Trinitatem adoro, præter quam non est Deus. Pereant dii qui non fecerunt cœlum et terram, et quæ in eis sunt. Christianus sum.* Calvisianus præfectus dixit: *Sacrifica, si vis liberari.* Euplius dixit: *Sacrifico modo CHRISTO DEO me ipsum: quid ultra faciam, non habeo. Frustra conaris: Christianus sum.* Calvisianus præcepit iterum torqueri acriùs. Cumque torqueretur, dixit Euplius: *Gratias Tibi, Christe. Succurre, Christe. Propter Te hæc patior, Christe.* Et dixit sæpius. Et deficientibus viribus, dicebat labiis tantum, absque voce hæc vel alia.'

[g] Lect. VII. p. 376.

which were learned at a mother's knee, return upon the soul with resistless persuasiveness and force, while the accumulations of later years disappear and are lost sight of. Depend upon it, the martyrs prayed to Jesus in their agony because they had prayed to Him long before, many of them from infancy; because they knew from experience that such prayers were blessed and answered. They had been taught to pray to Him; they had joined in prayers to Him; they had been taunted and ridiculed for praying to Him; they had persevered in praying to Him; and when at last their hour of trial and of glory came, they had recourse to the prayers which they knew full well to be the secret of their strength, and those prayers carried them on through their agony, to the crown beyond it.

And, further, you will have remarked that the worship of Jesus by the martyrs was full of the deepest elements of worship. It was made up of trust, of resignation, of self-surrender, of self-oblation. Nothing short of a belief in the absolute Godhead of Jesus could justify such worship. The Homoousion was its adequate justification. Certainly the Arians worshipped our Lord, although they rejected the Homoousion. So clear were the statements of Scripture, so strong and so universal was the tradition of Christendom, that Arianism could not resist the claims of a practice which was nevertheless at variance with its true drift and principle. For, as St. Athanasius pointed out, the Arians did in reality worship one whom they believed to be a being distinct from the Supreme God. The Arians were creature-worshippers not less than the heathen[h]. Some later Arians appear to have attempted to retort the charge of creature-worship by pointing to the adoration of our Lord's Humanity in the Catholic Church. But, as St. Athanasius explains, our Lord's Manhood was adored, not as a distinct and individual Being, but only as inseparably joined to the adorable Person of the Everlasting Word[i]. A refusal to adore Christ's Manhood must imply that after the Incarnation men could truly conceive of It as separate from Christ's Eternal

[h] St. Athanas. Epist. ad Adelphium, § 3: *οὐ κτίσμα προσκυνοῦμεν, μὴ γένοιτο, ἐθνικῶν γὰρ καὶ Ἀρειανῶν ἡ τοιαύτη πλάνη· ἀλλὰ τὸν Κύριον τῆς κτίσεως σαρκωθέντα τὸν τοῦ Θεοῦ Λόγον προσκυνοῦμεν.*

[i] Ibid.: *εἰ γὰρ καὶ ἡ σὰρξ αὐτὴ καθ' ἑαυτὴν μέρος ἐστὶ τῶν κτισμάτων, ἀλλὰ Θεοῦ γέγονε σῶμα. καὶ οὔτε τὸ τοιοῦτον σῶμα καθ' ἑαυτὸ διαιροῦντες ἀπὸ τοῦ Λόγου προσκυνοῦμεν, οὔτε τὸν Λόγον προσκυνῆσαι θέλοντες μακρύνομεν αὐτὸν ἀπὸ τῆς σαρκός· ἀλλ' εἰδότες, καθὰ προείπομεν, τὸ 'ὁ Λόγος σὰρξ ἐγένετο,' τοῦτον καὶ ἐν σαρκὶ γενόμενον ἐπιγινώσκομεν Θεόν.*

Person[j]. There was no real analogy between this worship and the Arian worship of a being who was in no wise associated with the Essence of God; and Arianism was either virtually ditheistic or consciously idolatrous. It was idolatrous, if Christ was a created being; it was ditheistic, if He was conceived of as really Divine, yet distinct in essence from the Essence of the Father[k].

The same phenomenon of the vital principle of a heresy being overridden for a while by the strength of the tradition of universal Christendom was reproduced, twelve centuries later, in the case of Socinianism. The earliest Socinians taught that the Son of God was a mere man, who was conceived of the Holy Ghost, and was therefore called the Son of God. But they also maintained that on account of His obedience, He was, after finishing His work of redemption, exalted to Divine dignity and honour[l]. Christians were to treat Him as if He were God: they were to trust Him implicitly; they were to adore Him[m]. Faustus Socinus[n] zealously insisted upon the duty of adoring Jesus Christ; and the Racovian Catechism expressly asserts that those who do not call upon or adore Christ are not to be

[j] St. Athanas. Epist. ad Adelphium, § 3: *τίς τοιγαροῦν οὕτως ἄφρων ἐστὶν ὡς λέγειν τῷ Κυρίῳ, ἀπόστα ἀπὸ τοῦ σώματος ἵνα σε προσκυνήσω; κ.τ.λ.* Compare Ibid. § 5: *ἵνα καὶ τολμῶσι λέγειν* (sc. Ariani), *οὐ προσκυνοῦμεν ἡμεῖς τὸν Κύριον μετὰ τῆς σαρκὸς, ἀλλὰ διαιροῦμεν τὸ σῶμα καὶ μόνῳ τούτῳ λατρεύομεν.*

[k] St. Athanas. contr. Arian. Orat. ii. § 14, sub fin. p. 482. Orat. iii. § 16, p. 565, *εἰ γὰρ μὴ οὕτως ἔχει, ἀλλ' ἐξ οὐκ ὄντων ἐστὶ κτίσμα καὶ ποίημα ὁ Λόγος, ἢ οὐκ ἔστι Θεὸς ἀληθινὸς, διὰ τὸ εἶναι αὐτὸν ἕνα τῶν κτισμάτων, ἢ εἰ Θεὸν αὐτὸν ὀνομάζουσιν ἐντρεπόμενοι παρὰ τῶν γραφῶν, ἀνάγκη λέγειν αὐτοὺς δύο θεοὺς, ἕνα μὲν κτίστην, τὸν δὲ ἕτερον κτιστὸν, καὶ δύο κυρίοις λατρεύειν, ἑνὶ μὲν ἀγενήτῳ, τῷ δὲ ἑτέρῳ γενητῷ καὶ κτίσματι . . . . . οὕτω δὲ φρονοῦντες πάντως καὶ πλείονας συνάψουσι θεούς· τοῦτο γὰρ τῶν ἐκπεσόντων ἀπὸ τοῦ ἑνὸς Θεοῦ τὸ ἐπιχείρημα. διατί οὖν οἱ 'Αρειανοὶ τοιαῦτα λογιζόμενοι καὶ νοοῦντες οὐ συναριθμοῦσιν ἑαυτοὺς μετὰ τῶν 'Ελλήνων;*

[l] Socin. de Justif. Bibl. Fr. Pol. tom. i. fol. 601, col. 1.

[m] Cat. Racov.: 'Qu. 236. *Quid præterea Dominus Jesus huic præcepto addidit?* Resp. *Id quod etiam Dominum Jesum pro Deo agnoscere tenemur, id est, pro eo, qui in nos potestatem habet divinam, et cui nos divinum exhibere honorem obstricti sumus.* Qu. 237. *In quo is honor divinus Christo debitus consistit?* Resp. *In eo, quod quemadmodum adoratione divinâ eum prosequi tenemur, ita in omnibus necessitatibus nostris ejus opem implorare possumus. Adoramus verò eum propter ipsius sublimem et divinam ejus potestatem.*' Cf. Möhler, Symbolik. Mainz. 1864, p. 609.

[n] The tenacity of the Christian practice may be still more remarkably illustrated from the death-cry of Servetus, as given in a MS. account of his execution, cited by Roscoe, Life of Leo X, c. 19. 'Ipse horrendâ voce clamans; *Jesu, Fili Dei æterni, miserere mei.*'

accounted Christians[o]. But this was only the archæology, or at most the better feeling of Socinianism. Any such mere feeling was destined to yield surely and speedily to the logic of a strong destructive principle. In vain did Blandrata appeal to Faustus Socinus himself[p], when endeavouring to persuade the Socinians of Transylvania to adore Jesus Christ: the Transylvanians would not be persuaded to yield an act of adoration to any creature[q]. In vain did the Socinian Catechism draw a distinction between a higher and a lower worship, of which the former was reserved for the Father, while the latter was paid to Christ[r]. Practically this led on to a violation of the one positive fundamental principle of Socinianism; it obscured the incommunicable prerogatives of the Supreme Being. Accordingly, in spite of the texts of Scripture upon which their worship of Christ was rested by the Socinian theologians, such worship was soon abandoned; and the later practice of Socinians[s] has illustrated the true doctrinal force and meaning of

[o] Cat. Racov.: 'Qu. 246. *Quid verò sentis de iis hominibus, qui Christum non invocant, nec adorandum censent?* Resp. *Prorsùs non esse Christianos sentio, cum Christum non habeant.* Et licet verbis id negare non audeant, reipsâ negant tamen.' In his sermon on 'Satan Transformed,' South quotes Socinus as saying that 'Præstat Trinitarium esse, quam asserere Christum non esse adorandum.'

[p] See Socinus' tractates, Bibl. Frat. Pol. ii. p. 709, sqq.

[q] Cf. Möhler, Symbolik, p. 609; Bp. Pearson, Minor Works, vol. i. p. 300, and note. Coleridge's Table Talk, 2nd ed. p. 304: 'Faustus Socinus worshipped Jesus Christ, and said that God had given Him the power of being omnipresent. Davidi, with a little more acuteness, urged that mere audition or creaturely presence could not possibly justify worship from men;—that a man, how glorified soever, was no nearer God than the most vulgar of the race. Prayer therefore was inapplicable.' On the responsibility of Socinus for Davidi's subsequent persecution for this negation, see Priestley, Corr. of Christ., Part i. § 11. For himself Coleridge says (Ibid. p. 50), 'In no proper sense of the term can I call Unitarians and Socinians believers in Christ; at least not in the only Christ of Whom I have read or know anything.'

[r] Cat. Rac.: 'Qu. 245. *Ergo is honor et cultus ad eum modum tribuitur, ut nullum sit inter Christum et Deum hoc in genere discrimen?* Resp. *Imo, permagnum est. Nam adoramus et colimus Deum, tanquam causam primam salutis nostræ; Christum tanquam causam secundam; aut ut cum Paulo loquamur, Deum tanquam Eum ex quo omnia, Christum ut eum per quem omnia.*' Cf. Bibl. Frat. Pol. tom. ii. fol. 466, qu. by Möhler, Symbolik, p. 609. Möhler observes that 'man sieht dass an Christus eine Art von Invocation gerichtet wird, die mit der Katholischen Anrufung der Heiligen einige Aehnlichkeit hat.'

[s] Cf. Priestley, Corr. of Christ., Part i. § 11: 'It is something *extraordinary* that the Socinians in Poland thought it their duty, as Christians, and indeed essential to Christianity, to pray to Jesus Christ, notwithstanding

that adoration which Socinianism refuses, but which the Church unceasingly offers to Jesus, the Son of God made Man. Of this worship the only real justification is that full belief in Christ's Essential Unity with the Father which is expressed by the Homoousion.

II. But the Homoousion did not merely justify and explain the devotional attitude of the Church towards Jesus Christ: it was, in reality, in keeping with the general drift and sense of her traditional language.

Reference has already been made to the prayers of the primitive martyrs; but the martyrs professed in terms their belief in Christ's divinity, as frequently as they implied that belief by their adorations of Christ. This is the more observable because it is at variance with the suggestions by which those who do not share the faith of the martyrs, sometimes attempt to account for the moral spectacle which martyrdom presents. It has been said that the martyrs did not bear witness to any definite truth or dogma; that the martyr-temper, so to term it, was composed of two elements, a kind of military enthusiasm for an unseen Leader, and a strange unnatural desire to brave physical suffering; that the prayers uttered by the martyrs were the product of this compound feeling, but that such prayers did not imply any defined conceptions respecting the rank and powers of Him to Whom they were addressed. Now, without denying that the martyrs were sustained by a strictly supernatural contempt for pain, or that their devotion to our Lord was of the nature of an intense personal attachment which could not brook the least semblance of slight or disloyalty, or that they had not analysed their intellectual apprehension of the truth before them in the manner of the divines of the Nicene age, I nevertheless affirm that the martyrs did suffer on behalf of a doctrine which was dearer to them than life. The Christ with Whom they held such close and passionate communion, and for Whose honour they shed their blood, was not to them a vague floating idea, or a being of whose rank and powers they imagined themselves to be ignorant. If there be one doctrine of the faith which they especially confessed at death, it is the doctrine of our Lord's Divinity. This truth was not only confessed by bishops and presbyters. Philosophers,

that they believed Him to be a mere man, whose presence with them, and whose knowledge of their situation, they could not therefore be assured of.' This work appeared in 1782.

like Justin[t]; soldiers, such as Maurice[u], and Tarachus[v], and Theodorus[x]; young men of personal beauty like Peter of Lampsacus[y], or literary friends of high mental cultivation as were Epipodius and Alexander[z]; widows, such as Symphorosa[a]; and

[t] Ruinart, Acta, p. 49: '*Ego quidem ut homo imbecillis sum, et longè minor quam ut de infinitâ illius Deitate aliquid magnum dicere possim: Prophetarum munus hoc esse fateor.*'

[u] Ibid. p. 243: '*Milites sumus, Imperator, tui: sed tamen servi, quod liberè confitemur, Dei . . . . . . Habes hic nos confitentes Deum Patrem auctorem omnium; et Filium Ejus Jesum Christum DEUM credimus.*'

[v] Ibid. p. 377: Τάραχος εἶπεν· 'Νῦν ἀληθῶς φρονιμώτερόν με ἐποίησας, ταῖς πληγαῖς ἐνδυναμώσας με, ἔτι μᾶλλον πεποιθέναι με ἐν τῷ ὀνόματι τοῦ Θεοῦ καὶ τοῦ Χριστοῦ αὐτοῦ.' Μάξιμος ἡγεμὼν εἶπεν· ''Ανοσιώτατε καὶ τρισκατάρατε, πῶς δυσὶ θεοῖς λατρεύεις, καὶ αὐτὸς ὁμολογῶν, τοὺς θεοὺς ἀρνῇ;' Τάραχος εἶπεν· ''Εγὼ Θεὸν ὁμολογῶ τὸν ὄντως ὄντα.' Μάξιμος ἡγεμὼν εἶπεν· 'Καὶ μὴν καὶ Χριστόν τινα ἔφης εἶναι Θεόν.' Τάραχος εἶπεν· 'Οὕτως ἔχει· αὐτὸς γάρ ἐστιν ὁ Χριστὸς ὁ Υἱὸς τοῦ Θεοῦ τοῦ ζῶντος, ἡ ἐλπὶς τῶν Χριστιανῶν, δι' ὃν καὶ πάσχοντες σωζόμεθα.'

[x] Ibid. p. 425: '*Vos autem erratis qui dæmonas fallaces et impostores Dei appellatione honoratis; mihi vero Deus est Christus, Dei Unigenitus Filius. Pro pietate igitur atque confessione Istius, et qui vulnerat incidat; et qui verberat laceret; et qui cremat flammam admoveat; et qui his vocibus meis offenditur, linguam eximat.*'

[y] Ibid. p. 135: 'Comprehensus est quidam, Petrus nomine, valdè quidem fortis in fide; pulcher animo et speciosus corpore. Proconsul dixit: *Habes ante oculos decreta invictissimorum principum. Sacrifica ergo magnæ deæ Veneri.* Petrus respondit: *Miror, si persuades mihi, optime Proconsul, sacrificare impudicæ mulieri et sordidæ, quæ talia opera egit ut confusio sit enarrare . . . . Oportet ergo me magis* DEO *vivo et vero, Regi sæculorum omnium Christo sacrificium offerre orationis deprecationis, compunctionis et laudis.* Audiens hæc Proconsul jussit eum adhuc ætate adolescentulum tendi in rotâ, et inter ligna in circuitu posita, vinculis ferreis totum corpus ejus fecit constringi: ut contortus et confractus [?] minutatim ossa ejus comminuerentur. Quanto autem plus torquebatur famulus Dei, tanto magis fortior apparebat. Constans vero aspectu, et ridens de ejus stultitiâ, conspiciens in cœlum ait: *Tibi ago gratias, Domine Jesu Christe, qui mihi hanc tolerantiam dare dignatus es ad vincendum nequissimum tyrannum.* Tunc Proconsul videns tantam ejus perseverantiam, et nec his quidem defecisse tormentis, jussit eum gladio percuti.'

[z] Acta, p. 65, circ. a. 178: 'Ita literis eruditissimi, concordiâ crescente, adeo provecti sunt: . . . . . ad hæc beatus Epipodius. . . . . . *Sempiternum vero Dominum nostrum Jesum Christum quem crucifixum memoras, resurrexisse non nosti, qui ineffabili mysterio homo pariter et Deus, famulis suis tramitem immortalitatis instituit, ... Christum cum Patre ac Spiritu Sancto Deum esse confiteor, dignumque est ut illi animam meam refundam, qui mihi et Creator est et Redemptor.*'

[a] Ibid. p. 21, a. 120: '*Si pro nomine Christi Dei mei incensa fuero, illos dæmones tuos magis exuro.*'

poor women like Domnina [b]; and slaves such as Vitalis [c]; and young boys such as Martialis [d];—the learned and the illiterate, the young and the old, the noble and the lowly, the slave and his master, united in this confession. Sometimes it is wrung from the martyr reluctantly by cross-examination; sometimes it is proclaimed as a truth with which the Christian heart is full to bursting, and which, out of the heart's abundance, the Christian mouth cannot but speak. Sometimes Christ's Divinity is professed as belonging to the great Christian contradiction of the polytheism of the heathen world around; sometimes it is explained as involving Christ's Unity with the Father, against the pagan imputation of ditheism [e]; sometimes it is proclaimed as justifying the worship which, as the heathens knew, Christians paid to Christ. The martyrs look paganism in the face, and maintain that, although Christ was crucified, yet nevertheless Christ is God; that even while His very Name is cast out as

[b] Ruinart, Acta, p. 235: '*Ne in ignem æternam incidam, et tormenta perpetua, Deum colo et Christum ejus, qui fecit cœlum et terram.*'

[c] Ibid. p. 410 (cf. St. Ambr. de Exh. Virgin. c. 1), circ. a. 304: 'Martyri nomen Agricola est, cui Vitalis servus fuit ante, nunc consors et collega martyrii. Præcessit servus, ut provideret locum; secutus est dominus . . . cumque sanctus Vitalis cogeretur a persequentibus ut Christum negaret, et ille ampliùs profiteretur Dominum nostrum Jesum Christum, omnia tormentorum genera in eum exercentes, ut non esset in corpore ejus sine vulnere locus, orationem fudit ad Dominum dicens; *Domine Jesu Christe, Salvator meus, et Deus meus; jube suscipi spiritum meum; quia jam desidero ut accipiam coronam, quam angelus tuus sanctus mihi ostendit.* Et completâ oratione emisit spiritum.'

[d] Ibid., Passio S. Felicitatis et Septem Filiorum Ejus, p. 23: 'Hoc quoque amoto, jussit septimum Martialem ingredi, eique dixit: Crudelitatis vestræ factores effecti, Augustorum instituta contemnitis, et in vestrâ pernicie permanetis. Respondit Martialis: *O si nosses quæ pœnæ idolorum cultoribus paratæ sunt! Sed adhuc differt Deus iram suam in vos et idola vestra demonstrare. Omnes enim qui non confitentur* CHRISTUM VERUM *esse* DEUM *in ignem æternum mittentur.*'

[e] Ibid. p. 122: 'Post hæc cum adstante haud procul Asclepiade, quis diceretur inquireret [Polemon scilicet] respondit Asclepiades, *Christianus.* Polemon: Cujus ecclesiæ? Asclepiades: *Catholicæ.* Polemon: Quem Deum colis? Respondit: *Christum.* Polemon: Quid ergo? iste alter est? Respondit: *Non, sed ipse quem et ipsi paullo ante confessi sunt.*'

Cf. Prudentius, Peristeph. Hymn. 10. 671:—

'Arrisit infans, nec moratus retulit:
Est quidquid illud, quod ferunt homines Deum
Unum esse oportet, et quod uni est unicum.
Cum Christus hoc sit, Christus est verus Deus.
Genera deorum multa nec pueri putant.'

[LECT.

evil, Christ is really Master of the fortunes of Rome and Disposer of the events of history; that the pagan empire itself did but unwittingly subserve His purposes and prepare His triumph[f]; that He Who is the Creator of heaven and earth, can afford to wait, and is certain of the future. This was the faith which made any compromise with paganism impossible[g].

[f] Prudentius has given a poetical amplification of the last prayer of St. Laurence, which, whatever its historic value, at any rate may be taken to represent the primitive Christian sentiment respecting the relation of Jesus Christ to the pagan empire. It should be noticed that neither St. Ambrose nor St. Augustine, in their accounts of the martyrdom, report anything of this kind; Prudentius *may* have followed a distinct and trustworthy tradition. The martyr is interceding for Rome:—

'O Christe, numen unicum,
O splendor, O virtus Patris,
O factor orbis et poli,
Atque auctor horum mœnium!

Qui sceptra Romæ in vertice
Rerum locasti, sanciens
Mundum Quirinali togæ
Servire, et armis cedere

Ut discrepantum gentium
Mores, et observantiam,
Linguasque et ingenia et sacra
Unis domares legibus.

En omne sub regnum Remi
Mortale concessit genus:
Idem loquuntur dissoni
Ritus, id ipsum sanciunt.

Hoc destinatum quo magis
Jus Christiani nominis,
Quodcumque terrarum jacet
Uno illigaret vinculo.

Da, Christe, Romanis tuis
Sit Christiana ut civitas:
Per quem dedisti, ut cæteris
Mens una sacrorum foret.'

Peristeph. 2, 413.

[g] Prud. Peristeph. Hymn. 5. 57; qu. by Ruinart, Acta, p. 330. De S. Vincentii martyrio:—

'Vox nostra quæ sit accipe.
Est Christus et Pater Deus:
Servi hujus ac testes sumus;
Extorque si potes fidem.

Tormenta, carcer, ungulæ
Stridensque flammis lamina
Atque ipsa pœnarum ultima;
Mors Christianis ludus est.'

'What God dost thou worship?' enquired the judges of the Christian Pionius. 'I worship,' replied Pionius, 'Him Who made the heavens, and Who beautified them with stars, and Who has enriched the earth with flowers and trees.' 'Dost thou mean,' asked the magistrates, 'Him Who was crucified?' 'Certainly,' replied Pionius; 'Him Whom the Father sent for the salvation of the world[h].'

The point before us notoriously admits of the most copious illustration[i]: and it is impossible to mistake its significance. If the dying words of this or that martyr are misreported, or exaggerated, or coloured by the phraseology of a later age, the general phenomenon cannot but be admitted, as a fact beyond dispute. The martyrs of the primitive Church died, in a great number of cases, expressly for the dogma of Christ's Divinity. The confessions of the martyrs explain and justify the prayers of the martyrs; the Homoousion combines, summarizes, fixes the sense of their confessions. The martyrs did not pray to or confess a creature external to the Essence of God, however dignified, however powerful, however august. They prayed to Christ as God, they confessed that Christ is God, they died for Christ as God. They prayed to Him and they spoke of Him as of a distinct Person, Who yet was one with God. Does not this simple faith of the Christian people cover the same area as the more clearly defined faith of the Nicene fathers? Or could it be more fairly or more accurately summarized by any other symbol than it is by the Homoousion?

But you admit that the Nicene decision did very fairly embody and fix in a symbolical form the popular creed of earlier centuries. 'This,' you say, 'is the very pith of our objection; it was the popular creed to which the Council gave the sanction of its authority.' You suggest that although a dying martyr may be an interesting ethical study, yet that the moral force which carries him through his sufferings is itself apt to be a form of fanaticism hostile to any severely intellectual conception of the worth and bearings of his creed. You admit that the martyr

[h] Ruinart, p. 125: 'Judices interim dixerunt: *Quem Deum colitis?* Pionius respondit: *Hunc qui cœlum fecit, et sideribus ornavit, qui terram statuit, et floribus arboribusque decoravit; qui ordinavit circumflua terræ et maria, et statuta terminorum vel litorum lege signavit.* Tum illi: *Illum dicis qui crucifixus est?* Et Pionius: *Illum dico quem pro salute orbis Pater misit.*'

[i] Ibid., Acta Sincera, p. 210, for the confession of Sapricius, who afterwards fell; p. 235; p. 256 for that of Victor at Marseilles; pp. 274, 314, 341, 435, 438, 439, 467, 470, 479, 483, 506, 513, 514, 521.

represents the popular creed; but then you draw a distinction between a popular creed, as such, and the 'ideas' of the 'thinkers.' 'What is any and every creed of the people,' say you, 'but the child of the wants and yearnings of humanity, fed at the breast of mere heated feeling, and nursed in the lap of an ignorance more or less profound?' A popular creed, you admit, may have a restricted interest, as affording an insight into the intellectual condition of the people which holds it; but you deem it worthless as a guide to absolute truth. The question, you maintain, is not, What was believed by the primitive Christians at large? The question is, What was taught by the well-instructed teachers of the early Church? Did the creed of the people, with all its impulsiveness and rhetoric, keep within the lines of the grave, reserved, measured, hesitating, cautious language of the higher minds of primitive Christendom?

Now here, my brethren, I might fairly take exception to your distinction between a popular and an educated creed, as in fact inapplicable to the genius and circumstances of early Christianity. Are not your criteria really derived from your conceptions of modern societies, political and religious? It was once said of an ancient state, that each of its citizens was so identified with the corporate spirit and political action of his country, as to be in fact a statesman. And in the primitive Church, it was at least approximately true that every Christian, through the intensity and intelligence of the popular faith, was a sound divine. Men did not then die for rhetorical phrases, any more than they would do so now; and if the martyrs were, as a rule, men of the people, it is also notorious that not a few among them were bishops and theologians of repute. But that we may do justice to the objection, let us enquire briefly what the great Church teachers of the first three centuries have taught respecting the Higher and Eternal Nature of Jesus Christ.

And here let us remark, first of all, that a chain of representative writers, reaching from the sub-apostolic to the Nicene age, does assert, in strong and explicit language, the belief of the Church that Jesus Christ is God.

Thus St. Ignatius of Antioch dwells upon our Lord's Divine Nature as a possession of the Church, and of individual Christians; he calls Jesus Christ 'my God,' 'our God.' 'Jesus Christ our God,' he says, 'was carried in the womb of Mary[k].' The

[k] Ad Eph. 18: *ὁ γὰρ Θεὸς ἡμῶν Ἰησοῦς ὁ Χριστὸς ἐκυοφορήθη ὑπὸ Μαρίας.* Cf. Ibid. 7: *ἐν σαρκὶ γενόμενος Θεός.*

Blood of Jesus is the Blood of God [l]. Ignatius desires to imitate the sufferings of his God [m]. The sub-apostolic author of the Letter to Diognetus teaches that 'the Father hath sent to men, not one of His servants, whether man or angel, but the very Architect and Author of all things, by Whom all has been ordered and settled, and on Whom all depends.... He has sent Him as being God [n].' And because He is God, His Advent is a real revelation of God; He has shewn Himself to men, and by faith men have seen and known their God [o]. St. Polycarp appeals to Him as to the Everlasting Son of God [p]; all things on earth and in heaven, all spirits obey Him [q]; He is the Author of our justification; He is the Object of our hope [r]. Justin Martyr maintains that the Word is the First-born of God, and so God [s]; that He appeared in the Old Testament as the God of Abraham, Isaac, and Jacob [t]; that He is sometimes called the Glory of the Lord, sometimes the Son, sometimes the Wisdom, sometimes the Angel, sometimes God [u]. St. Justin argues against Tryphon that if the Jews had attentively considered what the prophets have written, they would not have denied that Christ is God, and the Only Son of the Unbegotten God [x]. He maintains that the Word is Himself the witness to His own

[l] Eph. 1: *ἀναζωπυρήσαντες ἐν αἵματι τοῦ Θεοῦ.*

[m] Rom. 6: *ἐπιτρέψατέ μοι μιμητὴν εἶναι τοῦ πάθους τοῦ Θεοῦ μου.*

[n] Ep. ad Diogn. 7: *αὐτὸς ὁ παντοκράτωρ καὶ παντοκτίστης καὶ ἀόρατος Θεὸς . . . . . οὐ καθάπερ ἄν τις εἰκάσειεν, ἀνθρώποις ὑπηρέτην τινὰ πέμψας ἢ ἄγγελον, ἢ ἄρχοντα, ἤ τινὰ τῶν διεπόντων τὰ ἐπίγεια, ἤ τινὰ τῶν πεπιστευμένων τὰς ἐν οὐρανοῖς διοικήσεις, ἀλλ' αὐτὸν τὸν τεχνίτην καὶ δημιουργὸν τῶν ὅλων . . . . ὡς Θεὸν ἔπεμψεν, ὡς πρὸς ἀνθρώπους ἔπεμψεν, ὡς σώζων ἔπεμψεν.*

[o] Ep. ad Diogn. c. 8: *τίς γὰρ ὅλως ἀνθρώπων ἠπίστατο τί ποτ' ἐστὶ Θεὸς, πρὶν αὐτὸν ἐλθεῖν . . . . ἀνθρώπων δὲ οὐδεὶς οὔτε εἶδεν οὔτε ἐγνώρισεν, αὐτὸς δὲ ἑαυτὸν ἐπέδειξεν, ἐπέδειξε δὲ διὰ πίστεως, ᾗ μόνῃ Θεὸν ἰδεῖν συγκεχώρηται.*

[p] Epist. Eccl. Smyrn. de Mart. S. Polyc. n. 14.

[q] Ad Phil. 2: *Ὧι ὑπετάγη τὰ πάντα ἐπουράνια καὶ ἐπίγεια· ᾧ πᾶσα πνοὴ λατρεύει.* In Phil. 6: *τοῦ Κυρίου καὶ Θεοῦ* apparently refers to Christ.

[r] Ibid. 8: *ἀδιαλείπτως οὖν προσκαρτερῶμεν τῇ ἐλπίδι ἡμῶν καὶ τῷ ἀῤῥαβῶνι τῆς δικαιοσύνης ἡμῶν, ὅς ἐστι Χριστὸς Ἰησοῦς.*

[s] Apol. i. n. 63: *ὃς Λόγος καὶ πρωτότοκος ὢν τοῦ Θεοῦ, καὶ Θεὸς ὑπάρχει.*

[t] Ibid.

[u] See the argument of the whole passage, Contr. Tryph. 57–61: *ἀρχὴν πρὸ πάντων τῶν κτισμάτων ὁ Θεὸς γεγέννηκε δύναμίν τινα ἐξ ἑαυτοῦ λογικὴν, ἥτις καὶ δόξα Κυρίου ὑπὸ τοῦ Πνεύματος τοῦ Ἁγίου καλεῖται, ποτὲ δὲ Υἱὸς, ποτὲ δὲ Σοφία, ποτὲ δὲ Ἄγγελος, ποτὲ δὲ Θεός.*

[x] Ibid. 126: *εἰ νενοήκατε τὰ εἰρημένα ὑπὸ τῶν προφητῶν, οὐκ ἂν ἐξηρνεῖσθε αὐτὸν εἶναι Θεὸν τοῦ μόνου καὶ ἀγεννήτου Θεοῦ Υἱόν.* Cf. Ibid. 63: *προσκυνητός—καὶ Θεός.* Justin expresses the truth of our Lord's distinct Personality by the phrase *Θεὸς ἕτερος ἀριθμῷ ἀλλ' οὐ γνώμῃ* (Ibid. 56).

Divine Generation of the Father[y]; and that the reality of His Sonship is itself a sufficient evidence of His True Divinity[z]. Tatian is aware that the Greeks deem the faith of the Church utter folly; but he nevertheless will assert that God has appeared on earth in a human form[a]. Athenagoras proclaims with special emphasis the oneness of the Word with the Father, as Creator and Ruler of the universe[b]. Melito of Sardis speaks of Jesus as being both God and Man[c]: 'Christians,' he says, 'do not worship senseless stones, as do the heathen, but God and His Christ, Who is God the Word[d].' St. Irenæus perhaps represents the purest and deepest stream of apostolic doctrine which flowed from St. John through Polycarp into the Western Church. St. Irenæus speaks of Christ as sharing the Name of the only true God. He maintains against the Valentinians that the Divine Name in its strictest sense was not given to any angel; and that when in Scripture the Name of God is given to any other than God Himself there is always some explanatory epithet or clause in order to shew that the full sense of the word is not intended[e]. None is directly called God save God the Father of all things and His Son Jesus Christ[f]. In both Testaments Christ is preached as God and Lord, as the King Eternal, as the Only-begotten, as the Word Incarnate[g]. If Christ is

[y] Contr. Tryph. 61: μαρτυρήσει δέ μοι ὁ Λόγος τῆς σοφίας αὐτὸς ὢν οὗτος ὁ Θεὸς ἀπὸ τοῦ Πατρὸς τῶν ὅλων γεννηθείς.

[z] Ibid. 126; Apolog. i. 63.

[a] Adv. Græc. c. 21: οὐ γὰρ μωραίνομεν, ἄνδρες Ἕλληνες, οὐδὲ λήρους ἀπαγγέλλομεν, Θεὸν ἐν ἀνθρώπου μορφῇ γεγονέναι. Cf. Ibid. n. 13: τοῦ πεπόνθοτος Θεοῦ.

[b] Legat. n. 10: πρὸς αὐτοῦ γὰρ καὶ δι' αὐτοῦ πάντα ἐγένετο, ἑνὸς ὄντος τοῦ Πατρὸς καὶ τοῦ Υἱοῦ.

[c] See Eus. Hist. Eccl. v. 28. Compare the magnificent passage from St. Melito's treatise on Faith, given in Cureton's Spicilegium Syriacum, pp. 53, 54, and quoted by Westcott on the Canon, p. 196.

[d] Apol. apud Auct. Chron. Pasch. (Gall. tom. i. p. 678): οὐκ ἐσμὲν λίθων οὐδεμίαν αἴσθησιν ἐχόντων θεραπευταί, ἀλλὰ μόνου Θεοῦ τοῦ πρὸ πάντων καὶ ἐπὶ πάντων, καὶ ἔτι τοῦ Χριστοῦ αὐτοῦ ὄντος Θεοῦ Λόγου πρὸ αἰώνων ἐσμὲν θρησκευταί. Routh, Rel. Sacr. i. 118, 133.

[e] Adv. Hær. iii. 6, n. 3.

[f] Ibid. iii. 6, n. 2: 'Nemo igitur alius Deus nominatur, aut Dominus appellatur nisi qui est omnium Deus et Dominus, qui et Moysi dixit, Ego sum Qui sum, ... et Hujus Filius Jesus Christus.' Cf. iii. 8, n. 3: 'Deus Solus.'

[g] Ibid. iii. 19, n. 2: 'Quoniam autem Ipse propriè præter omnes qui fuerunt tunc homines, Deus, et Dominus, et Rex Æternus et Unigenitus, et Verbum Incarnatum prædicatur, et a prophetis omnibus et apostolis, et ab ipso Spiritu, adest videre omnibus qui vel modicum veritatis attigerint.'

worshipped[h], if Christ forgives sins[i], if Christ is Mediator between God and man[k], this is because He is really a Divine Person.

And if from Gaul we pass to Africa, and from the second to the third century, the force and number of primitive testimonies to the Divinity of our Lord increase upon us so rapidly as to render it impossible that we should do more than glance at a few of the more prominent. At Alexandria we find Clement speaking of That Living God Who suffered and Who is adored[l]; of the Word, Who is both God and man, and the Author of all blessings[m]; of God the Saviour[n], Who saves us, as being the Author and Archetype of all existing beings. Clement alludes to our Lord's Divinity as explaining His equality with the Father[o], His prescience during His Human Life[p], His revelation of the Father to men[q]. Origen maintains Christ's true Divinity against the contemptuous criticisms of Celsus[r]. Origen more than once uses the expression 'the God Jesus[s].' He teaches that the Word, the Image of God, is God[t]; that the Son is as truly Almighty as the Father[u]; that Christ is the Very Word, the Absolute Wisdom, the Absolute Truth, the Absolute Righteousness Itself[x]. Christ, according to Origen, possesses all the attributes of Deity[y]; God is contemplated in

[h] Adv. Hær. iii. 9, 2. 'Thus [obtulerunt magi] quoniam Deus.'

[i] Ibid. v. 17, n. 3.

[k] Ibid. iii. 18, 7.

[l] Protrept. 10, § 106: *πίστευσον, ἄνθρωπε, ἀνθρώπῳ καὶ Θεῷ, τῷ παθόντι καὶ προσκυνουμένῳ Θεῷ ζῶντι.*

[m] Ibid. 1, § 7: *αὐτὸς οὗτος ὁ Λόγος, ὁ μόνος ἄμφω, Θεός τε καὶ ἄνθρωπος, ἁπάντων ἡμῖν αἴτιος ἀγαθῶν.*

[n] Strom. ii. 9, § 45: *Θεῷ τῷ Σωτῆρι*; Ibid. v. 6, § 38: *ὁ Θεὸς Σωτὴρ κεκλημένος, ἡ τῶν ὅλων ἀρχὴ, ἥτις ἀπεικόνισται μὲν ἐκ τοῦ Θεοῦ τοῦ ἀοράτου πρώτη καὶ πρὸ αἰώνων, τετύπωκεν δὲ τὰ μέθ' ἑαυτὴν ἅπαντα γενόμενα.*

[o] Protrept. 10, § 110: *ὁ φανερώτατος ὄντως Θεὸς, ὁ τῷ Δεσπότῃ τῶν ὅλων ἐξισωθείς.*

[p] Quis Div. Salv. 6: *προεῖδε ὡς Θεὸς, ἃ μέλλει διερωτηθήσεσθαι.*

[q] Pæd. i. 8. We know God from our knowledge of Jesus—*ἐκ τρυτάνης ἰσοσθενοῦς.*

[r] Contr. Cels. ii. 9, 16 sqq.; vii. 53, etc. But iii. 28 is less satisfactory.

[s] *Θεὸν Ἰησοῦν*, Ibid. v. 51; vi. 66.

[t] Select. in Gen. In Gen. ix. 6.

[u] Princ. 1. ii. n. 10: 'Ut autem unam eandemque Omnipotentiam Patris et Filii esse cognoscas, sicut unus atque idem est cum Patre Deus et Dominus, audi hoc modo Johannem in Apocalypsi dicentem: Hæc dixit Dominus Deus, qui est et qui erat, et qui venturus est, Omnipotens; qui enim venturus est, quis est alius nisi Christus.'

[x] Contr. Cels. iii. 41: *αὐτόλογος, αὐτοσοφία, αὐτοαλήθεια.* Ibid. v. 39: *αὐτοδικαιοσύνης.*

[y] In Jerem. Hom. viii. n. 2: *πάντα γὰρ ὅσα τοῦ Θεοῦ, τοιαῦτα ἐν αὐτῷ*

[LECT.

the contemplation of Christ[z]. Christ's Incarnation is like the economical language of parables which describe Almighty God as if He were a human being. So real is Christ's Deity, that His assumption of our Nature, like the speech of a parable, is to be looked upon as only a condescension to finite intelligences[a]. There is no Highest Good in existence which is superior to Christ[b]; as Very God, Christ is present in all the world; He is present with every man[c]. Origen continually closes his Homilies with a doxology to our Lord; and he can only account for refusal to believe in His Divinity by the hypothesis of some kind of mental obliquity[d]. Tertullian's language is full of Punic fire, but in speaking of Christ's Divinity he is dealing with opponents who would force him to be accurate, even if there were not a higher motive for accuracy. Tertullian anticipates the Homoousion in terms: Christ, he says, is called God, by reason of His oneness of substance with God[e]. Christ alone is begotten of God[f]; He is God and Lord over all men[g]. Tertullian argues at length that an Incarnation of God is possible[h]; he dwells upon its consequences in language which must appear paradoxical to unbelief or half-belief, but which is natural to a sincere and intelligent faith in its reality. Tertullian speaks of

ἔστι, ὁ Χριστός ἐστι σοφία τοῦ Θεοῦ . . . . αὐτὸς ἀπολύτρωσις, αὐτὸς φρόνησίς ἐστι Θεοῦ.

[z] In Joan. t. xxxii. n. 18: θεωρεῖται γὰρ ἐν τῷ Λόγῳ, ὄντι Θεῷ καὶ εἰκόνι τοῦ Θεοῦ ἀοράτου.

[a] In Matt. t. xvii. n. 20: ὥσπερ ὁ Θεὸς ἀνθρώπους οἰκονομῶν ὡς ἐν παραβολαῖς ἄνθρωπος λέγεται, τάχα δέ πως καὶ γίνεται· οὕτως καὶ ὁ Σωτὴρ προηγουμένως Υἱὸς ὢν τοῦ Θεοῦ καὶ Θεός ἐστιν, καὶ Υἱὸς τῆς ἀγάπης αὐτοῦ, καὶ εἰκὼν τοῦ Θεοῦ τοῦ ἀοράτου· οὐ μένει δὲ ἐν ᾧ ἐστι προηγουμένως, ἀλλὰ γίνεται κατ' οἰκονομίαν τοῦ ἐν παραβολαῖς λεγομένου ἀνθρώπου ὄντως δὲ Θεοῦ, Υἱὸς ἀνθρώπου κατὰ τὸ μιμεῖσθαι, ὅταν ἀνθρώπους οἰκονομῇ, τὸν Θεὸν λεγόμενον ἐν παραβολαῖς καὶ γινόμενον ἄνθρωπον.

[b] In Joan. t. i. n. 11: οὐ σιωπητέον . . . τὸν μετὰ τὸν Πατέρα τῶν ὅλων Θεὸν Λόγον, οὐδενὸς γὰρ ἔλαττον ἀγαθοῦ καὶ τοῦτο τὸ ἀγαθόν.

[c] Ibid. t. vi. n. 15: δοξολογίαν περὶ τῆς προηγουμένης οὐσίας Χριστοῦ διηγεῖται, ὅτι δύναμιν τοσαύτην ἔχει, ὡς καὶ ἀόρατος εἶναι τῇ θειότητι αὐτοῦ, παρὼν παντὶ ἀνθρώπῳ, παντὶ δὲ καὶ τῷ ὅλῳ κόσμῳ συμπαρεκτεινόμενος.

[d] Contr. Cels. iii. 29.

[e] Apol. c. 21: 'Hunc ex Deo prolatum didicimus, et prolatione generatum, et idcirco Filium Dei, et Deum dictum ex *unitate substantiæ*.' See Lect. VII. p. 390. Ibid.: 'Quod de Deo profectum est, Deus est, et Dei Filius, et Unus ambo.' Adv. Prax. 4: 'Filium non aliunde deduco, sed de substantiâ Patris.' Ibid. 3: 'Consortibus [Filio et Spiritu Sancto] substantiæ Patris.'

[f] Adv. Prax. 7: 'Solus ex Deo genitus.'

[g] Adv. Jud. 7: 'Christus omnibus Deus et Dominus est.' Cf. c. 12.

[h] Cf. De Carne Christi, c. 3, 4.

a Crucified God[i]; of the Blood of God, as the price of our redemption[k]. Christians, he says, believe in a God Who was dead, and Who nevertheless reigns for ever[l]. St. Cyprian argues that those who believe in Christ's power to make a temple of the human soul must needs believe in His Divinity; nothing but utter blindness or wickedness can account for a refusal to admit this truth[m]. St. Hippolytus had urged it against Jews and Sabellians[n]; Arnobius determines to indent it upon the pagan mind by dint of constant repetition[o]. Theonas of Alexandria instructs a candidate for the imperial librarianship how he may gradually teach it to his pagan master[p]. Dionysius of Alexandria vehemently repudiates as a cruel scandal the report of his having denied it[q]. St. Peter of Alexandria would prove it from an examination of Christ's miracles[r]. For the rest, St. Methodius of Tyre may represent the faith of western

[i] Adv. Marc. ii. 27: 'Deum crucifixum.'

[k] Ad Uxor. ii. 3: 'Non sumus nostri, sed pretio empti, et quali pretio? Sanguine Dei.'

[l] Adv. Marc. ii. 16: 'Christianorum est etiam Deum mortuum credere, et tamen viventem in ævo ævorum.'

[m] Ep. 73, ad Jubaianum, 12: 'Si peccatorum remissam consecutus est . . . et templum Dei factum est, quæro cujus Dei? Si Creatoris, non potuit in eum qui non credidit. Si Christi, nec ejus fieri potest templum qui negat Deum Christum.' Cf. Ep. 74, c. 6: 'Quæ verò est animæ cæcitas, quæ pravitas, fidei unitatem de Deo Patre, et de Jesu Christi Domini et Dei nostri traditione venientem nolle agnoscere,' &c.

[n] Adv. Jud. c. 6: Θεὸς ὢν ἀληθινῶς. Contr. Noet. c. 6: *οὗτος ὁ ὢν ἐπὶ πάντων Θεός ἐστιν· λέγει γὰρ οὕτω μετὰ παῤῥησίας· Πάντα μοι παραδέδοται ὑπὸ τοῦ Πατρός. 'ὁ ὢν ἐπὶ πάντων Θεὸς εὐλογητὸς,' γεγένηται, καὶ ἄνθρωπος γενόμενος, Θεός ἐστιν εἰς τοὺς αἰῶνας.* Apud Routh, Opusc. i. p. 59. And c. 17: *Θεὸς Λόγος ἀπ' οὐρανῶν κατῆλθεν εἰς τὴν ἁγίαν παρθένον.* Adv. Beron. et Helic. n. 2: *ὁ τῶν ὅλων Θεός* is later: cf. Döll. Hipp. and Call. E. T. p. 295. In Eus. v. 28, He is called our *εὔσπλαγχνος Θεός.*

[o] Adv. Gent. ii. 60: 'Ideo Christus, licet vobis invitis, Deus; Deus inquam Christus—hoc enim sæpe dicendum est, ut infidelium dissiliat et disrumpatur auditus—Dei principis jussione loquens sub hominis formâ.' Ibid. i. 53: 'Deus ille sublimis fuit; Deus radice ab intimâ, Deus ab incognitis regnis, et ab omnium principe Deus sospitator est missus.'

[p] Apud Routh, Rel. Sacr. iii. p. 443; Ep. ad Lucian. Cubicul. Præpos. c. 7: 'Interdum et divinas scripturas laudare conabitur . . . . laudabitur et interim Evangelium Apostolusque pro divinis oraculis: insurgere poterit Christi mentio, explicabitur paullatim ejus sola Divinitas.'

[q] Ep. ad Dionys. Rom. apud S. Athan. Op. tom. i. p. 255: *καὶ δι' ἄλλης ἐπιστολῆς ἔγραψα, ἐν οἷς ἤλεγξα καὶ ὃ προφέρουσιν ἔγκλημα κατ' ἐμοῦ, ψεῦδος ὄν, ὡς οὐ λέγοντος τὸν Χριστὸν ὁμοούσιον εἶναι τῷ Θεῷ.*

[r] Apud Routh, Rel. Sac. iv. 48: *τὰ δὲ σημεῖα πάντα ἃ ἐποίησε καὶ αἱ δυνάμεις δεικνῦσιν αὐτὸν Θεὸν εἶναι ἐνανθρωπήσαντα. τὰ συναμφότερα τοίνυν δείκνυται· ὅτι Θεὸς ἦν φύσει, καὶ γέγονεν ἄνθρωπος φύσει.*

[LECT.

Asia[s]; the martyred Felix that of the Roman chair[t]; and, to omit other illustrations[u], the letter of the Council to Paulus of Samosata summarizes the belief both of eastern and western Christendom during the latter half of the third century[x].

This language of the preceding centuries does in effect and substance anticipate the Nicene decision. When once the question of Christ's Divinity had been raised in the metaphysical form which the Homoousion presupposes, no other answer was possible, unless the Nicene fathers had been prepared to renounce the most characteristic teaching of their predecessors. Certainly it did not occur to them that the Catholic language of earlier writers had been 'mere rhetoric,' and could, as such, be disregarded. What is the real meaning of this charge of 'rhetoric' which is brought so freely against the early Christian fathers? It really amounts to saying that a succession of men who were at least intelligent and earnest, were nevertheless, when writing upon the subject which lay nearest to their hearts, wholly unable to command that amount of jealous self-control, and cautious accuracy in the use of language, which might save them from misrepresenting their most fundamental convictions. Let us ask ourselves whether this judgment be morally probable? Doubtless the fathers felt strongly, and, being sincere men, they wrote as they felt. But they were not always exhorting or declaiming or perorating: they wrote, at times, in the temper of cold unimpassioned reasoners, who had to dispute their ground inch by inch with pagan or heretical opponents. Tertullian is not always 'fervid'; St. Chrysostom is not always eloquent; Origen does not allegorize under all circumstances; St. Ambrose can interpret Scripture literally and morally as well as mystically. The fathers were not a uniform series of poets or transcendentalists. Many of them were eminently practical, or, if you will,

[s] De Symeon. et Annâ, n. 6: *Σὺ Θεὸς πρῶτος, ἔμπροσθέν σου οὐκ ἐγεννήθη θεὸς ἄλλος ἐκ Θεοῦ Πατρὸς, καὶ μετὰ σοῦ οὐκ ἔσται ἄλλος Υἱὸς τῷ Πατρὶ ὁμοούσιος καὶ ὁμότιμος.* n. 8: *διὰ τοῦ μονογενοῦς καὶ ἀπαραλλάκτου καὶ ὁμοουσίου Παιδός σου τὴν λύτρωσιν ἡμῖν ποιησάμενος.* n. 14: *φῶς ἀληθινὸν ἐκ φωτὸς ἀληθινοῦ, Θεὸς ἀληθινὸς ἐκ Θεοῦ ἀληθινοῦ.* Quoted by Klee.

[t] Ep. ad Maximin. Epp. et Cler. Alex.: 'De Verbi autem Incarnatione et fide credimus in Dominum nostrum Jesum Christum, ex Virgine Mariâ natum, quod Ipse est sempiternus Dei Filius et Verbum, non autem homo a Deo assumptus, ut alius sit ab Illo; neque enim hominem assumpsit Dei Filius, ut alius ab ipso exsistat. Sed cum perfectus Deus esset, factus est simul Homo Perfectus ex Virgine Incarnatus.' Labbe et Coss. Conc. iii. 511.

[u] Cf. more especially St. Greg. Thaumaturgus, Orat. Panegyr. in Origenem, n. 4; Lact. Div. Inst. iv. 22, 29.

[x] Labbe et Coss. i. 845–850.

prosaic; and they continually wrote in view of hostile criticism, as well as in obedience to strong personal convictions. To men like Justin, Origen, and Cyprian the question of the Divinity of our Lord was one of an interest quite as pressing and practical as any that moves the leaders of political or commercial or scientific opinion in the England of to-day. And when men write with their lives in their hands, and moreover believe that the endless happiness of their fellow-creatures depends in no slight degree upon the conscientious accuracy with which they express themselves, they are not likely to yield to the temptation of writing for the miserable object of mere rhythmical effect;—they may say what others deem strong and startling things without being, in the depreciatory sense of the term, 'rhetorical.'

But,—to be just,—those who insist most eagerly upon the 'rhetorical' shortcomings of the fathers, are not accustomed to deny to them under all circumstances the credit of writing with intelligence and upon principle. If, for example, a father uses expressions, however inadvertently or provisionally, which appear to contradict the general current of Church teaching, he is at once welcomed as a serious writer who is entitled to marked and respectful attention. Critics who lay most stress upon the charge of unprincipled rhetoric as brought against the fathers are often anxious to take advantage of the argument which screens the fathers and which they themselves reject. 'Give that argument,' they say, 'its full and honest scope. If the Nicene fathers were not mere rhetoricians, neither were the ante-Nicene. If Athanasius, Basil, and the Gregories are to be taken at their word, so are Justin Martyr, Clement, Origen, and their contemporaries. If the orthodox language of one period is not rhetoric, then the doubtful or unorthodox language of another period is not rhetoric. If for the moment we admit the principle upon which you are insisting, we claim that it shall be applied impartially,—to the second century as to the fourth, to the language which is said to favour Arius, no less than to the language which is insisted upon by the friends of Athanasius.'

'Is it not notorious,' men ask, 'that some ante-Nicene writers at times use language which falls short of, if it does not contradict, the doctrine of the Nicene Council? Does not St. Justin Martyr, for instance, speak of the Son as subserving the Father's Will [y]? nay, as being begotten of Him at His Will [z]? Does not

[y] Tryph. 126: ὑπηρετῶν τῇ βουλῇ αὐτοῦ. Cf. Athan. Treat. i. 118, note *n*.

[z] Ibid. 128. But cf. Athan. Treat. ii. p. 486, note *g*.

Justin even speak of Christ as "another God under the Creator[a]?" Do not Athenagoras, Tatian, Theophilus, and St. Hippolytus apply the language of Scripture respecting the generation of the Word to His manifestation at the creation of the world, as a distinct being from God? Do they not so distinguish between the λόγος ἐνδιάθετος and the λόγος προφορικὸς as to imply that the Word was hypostatized only at the creation[b]? Does not Clement of Alexandria implicitly style the Word the Second Principle of things[c]? Does he not permit himself to say that the Nature of the Son is *most close* to the Sole Almighty One[d]? Although Origen first spoke of the Saviour as being "ever-begotten[e]," has he not, amidst much else that is questionable, contrasted the Son, as the immediate Creator of the world, with the Father as the original Creator[f]? Did not Dionysius of Alexandria use language which he was obliged to account for, and which is repudiated by St. Basil[g]? Was not Lucian of Antioch excommunicated, and, martyr though he was, regarded as the founder of an heterodox sect[h]? Is not Tertullian said to be open to the charge that he combated Praxeas with arguments which did the work of Arius[i]? Has he not, in his anxiety to avoid the Monarchianist confusion of Persons, spoken of the Son as a "derivation from, and portion of, the whole Substance of the Father[k]," or even as if He once was not[l]? Does any Catholic writer undertake to apologise for the expressions of Lactantius. Has not recent criticism tended somewhat to enhance the

[a] Dial. contr. Tryph. c. 56: Θεὸς ἕτερος ὑπὸ τὸν ποιητήν.

[b] Petav. 3. 6; Newman's Arians, p. 106. But see Athan. Treat. i. 113, note z; and Bull, Def. Fid. Nic. iii. 5. 6. 7, 8.

[c] Strom. lib. vii. 3, p. 509, apud Pet.: δεύτερον αἴτιον.

[d] Ibid. 2, p. 504: ἡ Υἱοῦ φύσις, ἡ τῷ μόνῳ Παντοκράτορι προσεχεστάτη. Bull, Def. Fid. Nic. ii. 6, 6.

[e] ὁ Σωτὴρ ἀεὶ γεννᾶται. Apud Routh, Rel. Sacr. iv. 354.

[f] Orig. contr. Cels. vi. 60, apud Petav. de Trin. i. 4, 5: τὸν μὲν προσεχῶς δημιουργὸν εἶναι τὸν Υἱὸν τοῦ Θεοῦ Λόγον καὶ ὡσπερεὶ αὐτουργὸν τοῦ κόσμου· τὸν δὲ Πάτερα . . . εἶναι πρώτως δημιουργόν.

[g] Cf. Pet. de Trin. i. 4, 10; St. Bas. Ep. 9. But cf. Athan. Sent. Dion.

[h] Alexander ap. Theodoret. Hist. lib. i. c. 4; Pet. de Trin. i. 4, 13.

[i] Petavius attacks him especially on the score of this treatise. De Trin. i. 5, 2: 'Opinionem explicat suam,' says Petavius, 'quæ etiam Arianorum hæresim impietate et absurditate superat.' For a fairer estimate, see Klee, Dogmengeschichte, ii. c. 2.

[k] Adv. Prax. c. 9: 'Pater enim tota Substantia est, Filius verò derivatio totius et portio.' See the remarks of Baur, Dogmengeschichte, i. 444, to which, however, a study of the context will yield a sufficient answer; e. g. c. 8: 'Sermo in Patre semper . . . . nunquam separatus a Patre.'

[l] Adv. Hermog. c. 3. See Bull, Def. iii. 10. Comp. Ibid. ii. 7.

reputation of Petavius at the expense of Bishop Bull[m]? Nay, is not Bull's great work itself an illustration of what is at least the *primâ facie* state of the case? Does it not presuppose a considerable apparent discrepancy between some ante-Nicene and the post-Nicene writers? Is it not throughout explanatory and apologetic? Can we deny that out of the long list of writers whom Bull reviews, he has, for one cause or another, to explain the language of nearly one-half?'

This line of argument in an earlier guise has been discussed so fully by a distinguished predecessor[n] in the present Lecture, that it may suffice to notice very summarily the considerations which must be taken into account, if justice is to be done, both to its real force and to the limits which ought to be, but which are not always, assigned to it.

(*a*) Undoubtedly, it should be frankly granted that some of the ante-Nicene writers do at times employ terms which, judged by a Nicene standard, must be pronounced unsatisfactory. You might add to the illustrations which have already been quoted; and you might urge that, if they admit of a Catholic interpretation, they do not always invite one. For in truth these ante-Nicene fathers were feeling their way, not towards the substance of the faith, which they possessed in its fulness, but towards that intellectual mastery both of its relationship to outer forms of thought, and of its own internal harmonies and system, which is obviously a perfectly distinct gift from the simple possession of the faith itself. As Christians they possessed the faith itself. The faith, delivered once for all, had been given to the Church in its completeness by the apostles. But the finished intellectual survey and treatment of the faith is a superadded acquirement; it is the result of conflict with a hostile criticism, and of devout reflections matured under the guidance of the Spirit of Truth. Knowledge of the drift and scope of particular lines of speculation, knowledge of the real force and value of a new terminology, comes, whether to a man or to a society, in the way of education and after the discipline of partial and temporary failure. Heresy indirectly contributed to form the Church's mind: it gave point and sharpness to current conceptions of truth by its mutilations and denials; it illustrated the fatal tendencies of novel lines of speculation, or even of misleading terms; it unwittingly forced

[m] The writer himself would on no account be understood to assent to this opinion. Even in criticizing Bull, Dr. Newman admits that he does his work 'triumphantly.' Developm. p. 159.

[n] Dr. Burton.

[LECT.

on an elucidation of the doctrines of the Church by its subtle and varied opposition. But before heresy had thus accomplished its providential work, individual Church teachers might in perfect good faith attempt to explain difficulties, or to win opponents, by enterprising speculations, in this or that direction, which were not yet shewn to be perilous to truth. Not indeed that the Universal Church, in her collective capacity, was ever committed to any of those less perfect statements of doctrine which belong to the ante-Nicene period. Particular fathers or schools of thought within her might use terms and illustrations which she afterwards disavowed; but then, they had no Divine guarantee of inerrancy, such as had been vouchsafed to the entire body of the faithful. They were in difficult and untried circumstances; they were making experiments in unknown regions of thought; their language was tentative and provisional. Compared with the great fathers of the fourth and fifth centuries, who spoke when collective Christendom had expressed or was expressing its mind in the Œcumenical Councils, and who therefore more nearly represented it, and were in a certain sense its accepted organs, such ante-Nicene writers occupy a position inferior, if not in love and honour, yet certainly in weight of authority. If without lack of reverence to such glorious names the illustration is permissible, the Alexandrian teachers of the second and third centuries were, relatively to their successors of the age of the Councils, in the position of young or half-educated persons, who know at bottom what they mean, who know yet more distinctly what they do not mean, but who as yet have not so measured and sounded their thoughts, or so tested the instrument by which thought finds expression, as to avoid misrepresenting their meaning more or less considerably, before they succeed in conveying it with accuracy. When, for example, St. Justin, and after him Tertullian, contrast the visibility of the Son with the invisibility of the Father, all that their language is probably intended to convey is that the Son had from everlasting designed to assume a nature which would render Him visible. When again St. Justin speaks of the Son as a *Minister of God*, this expression connects Him without explanation with the ministering Angel of the Old Testament. Yet it need involve nothing beyond a reference to His humiliation in the days of His Flesh. A like interpretation may fairly be put upon the ultra-subordinationist terms used by Origen and Tertullian in dealing with two forms of heretical Monarchianism; and upon the misconstrued phrases of the saintly Dionysius which expressed his resistance to a full-blown Sabellianism [o]. Language was employed which obviously admitted of being misunderstood. It would not have been used at a later period. 'It may be,' says St. Jerome, with reference to some of the ante-Nicene fathers, 'that they simply fell into errors, or that they wrote in a sense distinct from that which lies on the surface of their writings, or that the copyists have gradually corrupted their writings. Or at any rate before that Arius, like "the sickness that destroyeth in the noonday," was born in Alexandria, these writers spoke, in terms which meant no harm, and which were less cautious than such as would be used now, and which accordingly are open to the unfriendly construction which ill-disposed persons put upon them [p].'

Indeed it is observable that the tentative and perplexing Christological language which was used by earlier fathers, at a time when the quicksands of religious thought had not yet been explored by the shipwrecks of heresy, does not by any means point, as is sometimes assumed, in an Arian direction exclusively. If, for instance, a few phrases in St. Justin may be cited by Arianism with a certain plausibility, a similar appeal to him is open from the opposite direction of Sabellianism. In his anxiety to discountenance Emanatist conceptions of the relation of the Logos to the Father, Justin hastily refers the beginning of the Personal Subsistence of the Word to revelation or to the creation, and he accordingly speaks of the Word as being caused by the Will of God. But Justin did not place the Son on the footing of a creature; he did not hold a strict subordinationism [q]; since he teaches distinctly that the Logos is of the Essence of God, that He is a Power eternally begotten of God Himself [r]. Thus St. Justin's language at first sight seems to embrace two opposite and not yet refuted heresies: both can appeal to him with equal justice, or rather with equal want of it [s].

[o] Petav. de Trin. i. 4, 10.

[p] Apolog. adv. Ruffin. ii. Oper. tom. iv. p. ii. p. 409, apud Petav. de Trin. i. 1: 'Fieri potest, ut vel simpliciter erraverint, vel alio sensu scripserint, vel a librariis imperitis eorum paullatim scripta corrupta sint. Vel certè, antequam in Alexandriâ, quasi dæmonium meridianum, Arius nasceretur, innocenter quædam et minus cautè locuti sunt, et quæ non possint perversorum hominum calumniam declinare.' Cf. St. Athan. contr. Ar. iii. 59.

[q] Dorner, Person Christi, Erster Theil, p. 426, n. 22.

[r] Contr. Tryph. c. 61: πρὸ πάντων τῶν κτισμάτων ὁ Θεὸς γεγέννηκε δύναμίν τινα ἐξ ἑαυτοῦ λογικήν.

[s] Dorner, Person Christi, Erster Theil, p. 426. See the whole passage, in which this is very ably argued against Semisch.

(β) Reflect further that a doctrine may be held in its integrity, and yet be presented to men of two different periods, under aspects in many ways different. So it was with the doctrine of Christ's Divinity, in the ante-Nicene as compared with the post-Nicene age of its promulgation. When the Gospel was still struggling with paganism throughout the empire, the Church undoubtedly laid the utmost possible stress upon the Unity of the Supreme Being. For this was the primal truth which she had to assert most emphatically in the face of polytheism. In order to do this it was necessary to insist with particular emphasis upon those relations which secure and explain the Unity of the Divine Persons in the Blessed Trinity. That, in the ineffable mystery of the Divine Life, the Father is the Fount or Source of Godhead, from Whom by eternal Generation and Procession respectively, the Son and the Spirit derive their Personal Being, was the clear meaning of the theological statements of the New Testament. When, then, Origen speaks of the Father as the 'first God[t],' he means what the Apostle meant by the expression, 'One God and Father of all, Who is above all.' He implicitly means that, independently of all time and inferiority, the Son's Life was derived from, and, *in that sense*, subordinate to the Life of the Father. Now it is obvious that to speak with perfect accuracy upon such a subject, so as to express the ideas of derivation and subordinateness, while avoiding the cognate but false and disturbing ideas of posteriority in time and inferiority of nature, was difficult. For as yet the dogmatic language of the Church was comparatively unfixed, and a large discretion was left to individual teachers. They used material images to express what was in their thoughts. These images, drawn from created things, were of course not adequate to the Uncreated Object Which they were designed to illustrate. Yet they served to introduce an imperfect conception of It[u].

[t] Contr. Cels. vi. 47: ὁ πρῶτος καὶ ἐπὶ πᾶσι Θεός.

[u] 'In some instances [of ante-Nicene language] which are urged, it is quite obvious on the surface that the writer is really wishing to express the idea of the Son's generation being absolutely coeval with the Eternal Being of the Father, and is using the examples from the natural world, where the derivation is most immediately consequent upon the existence of the thing derived from, in order broadly to impress that idea of coeval upon the reader's mind. "The Son," says St. Clement of Alexandria, "issues from the Father quicker than light from the sun." Here, however, the very aim of the illustration to express simultaneousness is turned against it, and special attention is called to the word "*quicker*," as if the writer had only degrees of quickness in his mind, and only made the Son's

The fathers who employed them, having certain Emanatist theories in view, repeatedly urged that the Son is derived from the Father *in accordance with* the Divine attributes of Will and Power. Looking to our human experience, we conceive of will as prior to that which it calls into being; but in God the Eternal Will and the Eternal Act are coincident; and the phrase of St. Justin which refers the existence of the Logos to the Divine Will is only misunderstood because it is construed in an anthropomorphic sense. In like manner the Alexandrian distinction between the λόγος ἐνδιάθετος and the λόγος προφορικὸς fell in naturally with the subordinationist teaching in the ante-Nicene Church. It could, in a sense, be said that the Son left the Bosom of the Father when He went forth to create, and the act of creation was thus described as a kind of second generation of the Son. But the expression did not imply, as it has been understood to imply, a denial of His eternal Generation, and of His unbegotten, unending Subsistence in God. This indeed is plain from the very writers who use it [x]. Generally speaking, the early fathers are bent on insisting on the subordination (κατὰ τάξιν) of the Son, as protecting and explaining the doctrine of the Divine Unity. If some of these expressed themselves too incautiously or boldly, the general truth itself was never discredited in the Church. Subordinationism was indeed allowed to fall somewhat into the shade, when the decline of paganism made it possible, and the activities of Arianism made it necessary, to contemplate Jesus Christ in the absoluteness of His Personal Godhead rather than in that relation of a subordinate, in the sense of an eternally derived subsistence, in which He also stands to the Eternal Father. But Bishop Bull has shewn how earnestly such a doctrine of subordination was also taught in the Nicene period; and at this day we confess it in the Nicene Creed itself. And the stress which was laid upon it in the second and third centuries, and which goes far to explain much of the language which is sometimes held to be of doubtful orthodoxy, is in reality perfectly consistent with the broad fact that from the first the general current of Church language proclaims the truth that Jesus Christ is God.

(γ) For that truth was beyond doubt the very central feature of the teaching of the ante-Nicene Church, even when Church

generation from His source "*quicker*" than that of light from its source, and not absolutely coeval.' Mozley on the Theory of Development, p. 183.

[x] See the examination of passages in Newman's Arians, pp. 215-218.

[LECT.

teachers had not yet recognised all that it necessarily involved, and had not yet elaborated the accurate statement of its relationship to other truths around it. The writers whose less-considered expressions are brought forward in favour of an opposite conclusion do not sustain it. If, as we have seen, Justin may be quoted by those who push the Divinity of Christ to the denial of His Personal distinction from the Father [y], no less than by Arianizers; so also, as Petavius himself admits [z], do both Origen and Tertullian anticipate the very language of the Nicene Creed. Nor, when their expressions are fairly examined, can it be denied that the writers who imported the philosophical category of the λόγος ἐνδιάθετος and προφορικὸς into Christian theology did really believe with all their hearts in the eternal Generation of the Word. For it should especially be remarked that when the question of our Lord's Divinity was broadly proposed to the mind of the ante-Nicene Church, the answer was not a doubtful or hesitating one. Any recognised assault upon it stirred the heart of the Church to energetic protest. When Victor of Rome excommunicated the Quarto-decimans, his censures were answered either by open remonstrance or by tacit disregard, throughout Gaul and the East [a]. When he cut off Theodotus from the communion of the Church, the act commanded universal acquiescence; the Christian heart thrilled with indignation at 'the God-denying apostasy' of the tanner of Byzantium [b]. When Dionysius of Alexandria, writing with incautious zeal against the Sabellians, was charged with heterodoxy on the subject of our Lord's Divine Nature, he at once addressed to Dionysius of Rome an explanation which is in fact an anticipation of the language of Athanasius [c]. When Paulus of Samosata appeared in one of the first sees of Christendom, the universal excitement, the emphatic protests, the final, measured, and solemn condemnation which he provoked, proved how deeply the Divinity of Jesus Christ was rooted in the heart of the Church of the third century. Moreover, unless Christ's absolute Godhead had been thus a matter of Catholic belief, the rise of such a heresy as that of Sabellianism would have been impossible. Sabellianism overstates that which Arianism denies. Sabellianism presupposes the truth of Christ's Godhead, which, if we may so speak, it exaggerates even to the point of rejecting

[y] Petav. de Trin. i. 6, 6. [z] Ibid. i. 4, 6; 5, 3.
[a] Eus. Hist. Eccl. v. 24.
[b] Eus. Hist. Eccl. v. 28: τῆς ἀρνησιθέου ἀποστασίας. Epiphan. Hær. 54.
[c] See St. Athan. de Sent Dionysii, c. 4, sqq.

His Personal distinctness from the Father. If the belief of the ante-Nicene Church had been really Arianizing, Noetus could not have appealed to it as he did, while perverting it to a denial of hypostatic distinctions in the Godhead [d]; and Arius himself might have only passed for a representative of the subordinationism of Origen, and of the literalism of Antioch, instead of being condemned as a sophistical dialectician who had broken altogether with the historical tradition of the Church, by daring to oppose a central truth of her unchanging faith.

The idea that our Lord's Divinity was introduced into the belief and language of the Church at a period subsequent to the death of the apostles, was indeed somewhat adventurously put forward by some early Humanitarians. Reference has already been made in another connection to an important passage, which is quoted by Eusebius from an anonymous writer who appears to have flourished in the early part of the third century [e]. This passage enables us to observe the temper and method of treatment encountered by any such theory in ante-Nicene times.

The Humanitarian Artemon seems to have been an accomplished philosopher and mathematician; and he maintained that the Divinity of Christ was imported into the Church during the episcopate of Zephyrinus, who succeeded Victor in the Roman chair. Now if this story could have been substantiated, it would have been necessary to suppose, either that the Church was the organ of a continuous and not yet completed revelation, or else that the doctrine was a human speculation unwarrantably added to the simpler creed of an earlier age. But the writer to whom I have referred meets the allegation of Artemon by denying it point-blank. 'Perchance,' he archly observes, 'what they [the Artemonites] say might be credible, were it not that the Holy Scriptures contradict them; and then also there are works of certain brethren, older than the days of Victor, works written in defence of the truth, and against the heresies then prevailing. I speak of Justin and Miltiades, and Tatian and Clement, and many others, by all of whom the Divinity of Christ is asserted. For who,' he continues, 'knows not the works of Irenæus and Melito, and the rest, in which Christ is announced as God and Man [f]?' This was the argument upon

[d] St. Hippol. contr. Hær. Noeti, c. 1: *ὁ δὲ ἀντίστατο λέγων, 'Τί οὖν κακὸν ποιῶ δοξάζων τὸν Χριστόν;'* See also Epiphanius, Hær. 57.

[e] Cf. Lect. VII. p. 393, note.

[f] Eus. Hist. Eccl. v. 28. It is probable that St. Hippolytus wrote 'The Little Labyrinth.'

which the Church of those ages instinctively fell back when she was accused of adding to her creed. Particular writers might have understated truth; or they might have ventured upon expressions requiring explanation; or they might have written economically as in view of particular lines of thought, and have been construed by others without the qualifications which were present to their own minds. But there could be no mistake about the continuous drift and meaning of the belief around which they moved, and which was always in the background of their ideas and language. There could be no room for the charge that they had invented a new dogma, when it could be shewn that the Church from the beginning, and the New Testament itself, had taught what they were said to have invented.

III. Of the objections to which the Homoousion is exposed in the present day, there are two which more particularly demand our attention.

(*a*) 'Is not the Homoousion,' it is said, 'a development? Was it not rejected at the Council of Antioch sixty years before it was received at Nicæa? Is not this fact indicative of a forward movement in the mind of the Church? Does it not shew that the tide of dogmatic belief was rising, and that it covered ground in the Nicene age which it had deliberately left untouched in the age preceding? And, if this be so, if we admit the principle of a perpetual growth in the Church's creed, why should we not accept the latest results of such a principle as unequivocally as we close with its earlier results? If we believe that the Nicene decision is an assertion of the truth of God, why should we hesitate to adopt a similar belief respecting that proclamation of the sinless conception of the Blessed Virgin which startled Christendom twelve years ago, and which has since that date been added to the official creed of the largest section of the Christian Church?'

Here, the first point to be considered turns on a question of words. What do we mean by a doctrinal development? Do we mean an explanation of an already existing idea or belief, presumably giving to that belief greater precision and exactness in our own or other minds, but adding nothing whatever to its real area [g]? Or do we mean the positive substantial growth of

[g] In this sense a Development of Doctrine must necessarily be admitted. When the life of the individual soul is vigorous and healthy, there must be a continuously increasing knowledge of Divine Truth. St. Aug. in Joan. Ev. Tract. xiv. c. 3. n. 5: 'Crescat ergo Deus qui semper perfectus est, crescat in te. Quantò enim magis intelligis Deum, et quantò magis capis, videtur in

the belief itself, whether through an enlargement from within, just as the acorn developes into the oak, or through an accretion from without of new intellectual matter gathered around it, like the aggrandisements whereby the infant colony developes into the powerful empire?

Now if it be asked, which is the natural sense of the word 'development,' I reply that we ordinarily mean by it an actual enlargement of that which is said to be developed. And in that sense I proceed to deny that the Homoousion was a development. It was not related to the teaching of the apostles as an oak is related to an acorn. Its real relation to their teaching was that of an exact and equivalent translation of the language of one intellectual period into the language of another. The New Testament had taught that Jesus Christ is the Lord of nature [h] and of men [i], of heaven, and of the spiritual world [j];

te crescere Deus; in se autem non crescit, sed semper perfectus est. Intelligebas heri modicum; intelligis hodiè ampliùs, intelliges cras multò ampliùs: lumen ipsum Dei crescit in te; ita velut Deus crescit, qui semper perfectus manet. Quemadmodum si curarentur alicujus oculi ex pristinâ cæcitate, et inciperet videre paululum lucis, et aliâ die plus videret, et tertiâ die ampliùs, *videretur* illi lux crescere: lux tamen perfecta est, sive ipse videat, sive non videat. Sic est et interior homo: proficit quidem in Deo, et Deus in illo *videtur* crescere; ipse tamen minuitur, ut à gloriâ suâ decidat, et in gloriam Dei surgat.' A somewhat analogous progress in the knowledge of Truth, received from Christ and His Apostles, is found in the collective Christian Society. Vincent. Lirinens. Commonit. c. 28: 'Nullusne ergò in Ecclesiâ Dei profectus? Habeatur planè et maximus: nam quis ille est tam invidus hominibus, tam exosus Deo, qui illud prohibere conetur? Crescat igitur oportet, et multum vehementerque proficiat tam singulorum quam omnium, tam unius hominis quam totius ecclesiæ ætatum ac sæculorum gradibus, intelligentiâ, scientiâ, sapientiâ.' Not that this increasing apprehension of the true force and bearings of the truth revealed in its fulness once for all involves any addition to or subtraction from that one unchanging body of truth. Commonit. c. 30: 'Fas est enim ut prisca illa cœlestis philosophiæ dogmata processu temporis excurentur, limentur, poliantur; sed nefas est ut commutentur, nefas ut detruncentur, nefas ut mutilentur. Accipiant licet evidentiam, lucem, distinctionem; sed retineant necesse est plenitudinem, integritatem, proprietatem.' There is then no real increase in the body of truth committed to the Church, but only a clearer perception on the part of the Church of the force and bearings of that truth which she had possessed in its completeness from the first. With some few drawbacks, this is fairly stated by Staudenmaier. Wetzer and Welte's Diction. Encycl.; art. Dogma.

[h] St. John v. 17; St. Matt. viii. 3, 13; ix. 6, 22, 25, 29; St. John iv. 50; v. 8. This power over nature He delegated to others: St. Matt. x. 1, 8; St. Mark xvi. 17; St. Luke x. 17; St. John xiv. 12; Acts iii. 6, 12, 16; ix. 34; xvi. 18. [i] St. Matt. xxviii. 18-20; St. John v. 21, 22; xvii. 2.

[j] St. Matt. vii. 21, 23; xviii. 18; xxvi. 64; St. John i. 51; xx. 12, etc.

that He is the world's Legislator, its King and its Judge [k]; that He is the Searcher of hearts [l], the Pardoner of sins [m], the Well-spring of life [n]; that He is Giver of true blessedness and salvation [o], and the Raiser of the dead [p]; it distinctly attributed to Him omnipresence [q], omnipotence [r], omniscience [s]; eternity [t], absolute likeness to the Father [u], absolute oneness with the Father [x], an equal share in the honour due to the Father [y], a like claim upon the trust [z], the faith [a], and the love [b] of humanity. The New Testament had spoken of Him as the Creator [c] and Preserver of the world [d], as the Lord of all things, as the King of kings [e], the Distributor of all graces [f], the Brightness of the Father's Glory and the Impress of His Being [g]; as being in the form of God [h], as containing in Himself all the fulness of the Godhead [i], as being God [k]. This and much more to the same purpose had been said in the New Testament. When therefore the question was raised whether Jesus Christ was or was not 'of one substance with' the Father, it became clear that of two courses one must be adopted. Either an affirmative answer must be given, or the teaching of the apostles themselves must

[k] St. Matt. v.–vii.; xi. 29, 30; xv. 18; xviii. 19; xxv. 34, 40; St. John viii. 36; xiv. 21; xv. 12; xx. 23, etc.

[l] St. John i. 47–50; ii. 24, 25; iv. 17, 18; vi. 15, 70; xvi. 19, 32; Rev. ii. 23.

[m] St. Matt. ix. 2, 6; St. Luke v. 20, 24; vii. 48; xxiv. 47; and St. John xx. 23, where He delegates the absolving power to others.

[n] St. John iv. 13, 14; v. 21, 26, 40; vi. 47, 51–58; x. 28.

[o] St. Matt. vii. 21 sq.; St. John vi. 39, 40; x. 28; Acts iv. 12; Heb. ii. 10, 14.

[p] St. John v. 21, 25; xi. 25. Christ raises Himself from death: St. John ii. 19; x. 18.

[q] Ibid. iii. 13; St. Matt. xviii. 20.

[r] St. Matt. xxviii. 18; Phil. iii. 21; Heb. i. 3.

[s] St. Matt. xi. 27; St. John iii. 11–13; vi. 46; x. 15; Col. ii. 3.

[t] St. John viii. 58; xvii. 5; Rev. i. 8; ii. 8; xxii. 12, 13.

[u] St. John v. 17, 19, 21, 26; x. 28, 29; xiv. 7.

[x] Ibid. x. 28, 30; xiv. 10.

[y] Ibid. v. 23.

[z] Ibid. xiv. 1; xvi. 33; Col. i. 27; St. Matt. xii. 21.

[a] St. John vi. 27; 1 St. John iii. 23; Acts xvi. 31; xx. 21.

[b] 1 Cor. xvi. 22; St. John xiv. 23.

[c] St. John i. 3; Col. i. 16; Heb. i. 2, 10.

[d] Col. i. 17; Heb. i. 3.

[e] Acts x. 36; Jude 4; Rev. xvii. 14; xix. 16.

[f] St. John i. 12, 14, 16, 17; 2 Thess. ii. 16.

[g] Heb. i. 3; Col. i. 15; 2 Cor. iv. 4.

[h] Phil. ii. 6.

[i] Col. ii. 9; St. John i. 14, 16.

[k] St. John i. 1; Acts xx. 28; Rom. ix. 5; Titus ii. 13; 1 St. John v. 20. Compare Rom. viii. 9–11 with Rom. xiv. 10–12.

be explained away[l]. As a matter of fact the Nicene fathers only affirmed, in the philosophical language of the fourth century, what our Lord and the apostles had taught in the popular dialects of the first. If then the Nicene Council developed, it was a development by explanation. It was a development which placed the intrinsically unchangeable dogma, committed to the guardianship of the Church, in its true relation to the new intellectual world that had grown up around Christians in the fourth century. Whatever vacillations of thought might have been experienced here or there, whatever doubtful expressions might have escaped from theologians of the intervening period, no real doubt could be raised as to the meaning of the original teachers of Christianity, or as to the true drift and main current of the continuous traditional belief of the Church. The Nicene divines interpreted in a new language the belief of their first fathers in the faith. They did not enlarge it; they vehemently protested that they were simply preserving and handing on what they had received. The very pith of their objection to Arianism was its novelty: it was false because it was of recent origin[m]. They themselves were forced to say what they meant by their creed, and they said it. Their explanation added to the sum of authoritative ecclesiastical language, but it did not add to the number of articles in the Christian faith: the area of the creed was not enlarged. The Nicene Council did not vote a new honour to Jesus Christ which He had not before possessed: it defined more clearly the original and unalterable bases of that supreme place which from the days of the apostles He had held in the thought and heart, in the speculative and active life of Christendom.

The history of the symbol Homoousion during the third century might, at first sight, seem to favour the position, that its adoption at Nicæa was of the nature of an accretive development. Already, indeed, Dionysius and others (perhaps Origen) had employed it to express the faith of the Church; but it had been, so to speak, disparaged and discoloured by the patronage of the Valentinians and the Manichæans. In the Catholic theo-

[l] Möhler, Symbolik, p. 610: 'Wären sie (the Socinians) schärfere Denker gewesen, so mussten sie zur Einsicht gelangen, dass, wenn das Evangelium den Sohn als ein persönliches Wesen, und zugleich als Gott darstellt, wie die Socinianer nicht laügneten (Christ. Relig. institut. bibl. frat. Pol. tom. i. p. 655. Es wird Joh. i. 1; xx. 21 citirt.), kein anderes Verhältniss zwischen ihm und dem Vater *denkbar* sei, als jenes, welches die katholische Kirche von Anfang an geglaubt hatte.'

[m] Socr. Hist. Eccl. i. 6.

logy the word denoted full participation in the absolute self-existing Individuality of God [n]. Besides this, the word suggested the distinct personality of its immediate Subject; unless it had suggested this, it would have been tautologous. In ordinary language it was applied to things which are only similar to each other, and are considered as one by an abstraction of our minds. No such abstraction was possible in the contemplation of God. His οὐσία is Himself, peculiar to Himself, and One; and therefore to be ὁμοούσιος with Him is to be internal to that Uncreated Nature Which is utterly and necessarily separate from all created beings. But the Valentinians used the word to denote the relation of their Æons to the Divine Pleroma; and the Manichæans said that the soul of man was ὁμοούσιον τῷ Θεῷ, in a materialistic sense. When then it was taken into the service of these Emanatist doctrines, the Homoousion implied nothing higher than a generic or specific bond of unity [o]. These uses of the word implied that οὐσία itself was something beyond God, and moreover, as was suggested by its Manichæan associations, something material. Paulus of Samosata availed himself of this depreciation of the word to attack its Catholic use as being really materialistic. Paulus argued that 'if the Father and the Son were ὁμοούσιοι, there was some common οὐσία in which they partook,' higher than, and 'distinct from, the Divine Persons themselves [p].' Firmilian and Gregory were bent, not upon the philological object of restoring the word ὁμοούσιος to its real sense, but upon the religious duty of asserting the true relation of the Son to the Father, in language the meaning of which would be plain to their contemporaries. The Nicene Fathers, on the other hand, were able, under altered circumstances, to vindicate for the word its Catholic meaning, unaffected by any

[n] St. Cyril of Alexandria defines οὐσία as πρᾶγμα αὐθύπαρκτον, μὴ δεόμενον ἑτέρου πρὸς τὴν ἑαυτοῦ σύστασιν. Apud Suicer. in voc. οὐσία. As οὐσία meant sometimes individuality or personality, ὁμοούσιον had for some minds even a Sabellian import.

[o] Ὁμοούσιος properly means of the same nature—i.e. under the same general nature or species. It is applied to things which are but similar to each other, and are considered as one by an abstraction of our minds. Thus Aristotle speaks of the stars being 'ὁμοούσια with each other.' Newman, Arians, p. 203. 'Valentinianism,' he says (p. 206), 'applied the word to the Creator and His creatures in this its original philosophical sense. The Manichees followed . . . . they too were Emanatists,' &c. But such a usage offends against 'the great revealed principle' of 'the incommunicable . . . . Individuality of the Divine Essence:' according to which principle ὁμοούσιος, as used of the Son, defined Him as 'necessarily included in That Individuality.' See Dr. Newman's valuable note on St. Athanasius' Treatises, i. 152, note *a* (Libr. Fath.); Ibid. 35, note *t*; and Soc. i. 8.

[p] Newman, Arians, p. 209. See the whole passage.

Emanatist gloss; and accordingly, in their hands it protected the very truth which at Antioch, sixty years earlier, it would have obscured. St. Athanasius tells us that 'the fathers who deposed the Samosatene took the word Homoousion in a corporeal sense. For Paulus sophisticated by saying that if.... Christ was consubstantial with the Father, there must necessarily be three substances, one which was prior and two others springing from it. Therefore, with reason, to avoid that sophism of Paulus, the fathers said that Christ was not consubstantial, that is, that He was not in that relation to the Father which Paulus had in his mind. On the other hand,' continues St. Athanasius, 'those who condemned the Arian heresy saw through the cunning of Paulus, and considered that in things incorporeal, especially in God, "consubstantial" did not mean what he had supposed; so they, knowing the Son to be begotten of the Substance,..... with reason called Him consubstantial[q].' Paulus, as a subtle and hardheaded dialectician, had endeavoured to connect with the term a sense, which either made the Son an inferior being or else destroyed the Unity of God. He used the word, so St. Hilary says, as mischievously as the Arians rejected the use of it[r]; while the fathers at Antioch set it aside from a motive as loyal to Catholic truth as was that which led to its adoption at Nicæa[s]. Language is worth, after all, just what it means to those who employ it. Origen had rejected and Tertullian had defended the προβολή from an identical theological motive; and the opposite lines of action, adopted by the Councils of Antioch and Nicæa respectively, are so far from proving two distinct beliefs respecting the higher Nature of Jesus Christ, that when closely examined, they exhibit an absolute identity of creed and purpose brought

[q] St. Athan. De Synodis, § 45; cf. Cave, Hist. Lit. i. 134. 'Non aliud dicit Athanasius quam Paulum ex detorto Catholicorum vocabulo sophisticum argumentum contra Christi Divinitatem excogitasse; nempe, nisi confiteremur Christum ex homine Deum factum esse, sequeretur ipsum Patri esse ὁμοούσιον, ac proinde tres esse substantias, unam quidem primariam, duas ex illâ derivatas: σωματικῶς enim et crasso sensu vocabulum accepit, quasi in essentiâ divinâ, perinde ac in rebus corporeis usu venit, ut ab unâ substantiâ altera, eaque diversa, derivetur. Quocirca, ne hac voce hæretici ulteriùs abuterentur, silentio supprimendam censuerunt patres Antiocheni: non quod Catholicum vocis sensum damnarent, sed ut omnem sophisticè cavillandi occasionem hæreticis præriperent, ut ex Athanasio, Basilio, aliisque, abunde liquet.'

[r] St. Hil. de Syn. 86: 'Malè Homoousion Samosatenus confessus est, sed nunquam meliùs Ariani negaverunt.'

[s] Routh, Rel. Sacr. iii. 360, ed. 1846. See too Dr. Newman's note 2, in St. Athanasius' Select Treatises, i. p. 166. (Oxf. Libr. Fath.).

[LECT.

face to face with two distinct sets of intellectual circumstances. The faith and aim of the Church was one and unchanging. But the question, whether a particular symbol would represent her mind with practical accuracy, received an answer at Antioch which would have been an error at Nicæa. The Church looked hard at the Homoousion at Antioch, when heresy had perverted its popular sense; and she set it aside. She examined it yet more penetratingly at Nicæa; and from then until now it has been the chosen symbol of her unalterable faith in the literal Godhead of her Divine Head.

Therefore between the imposition of the Homoousion and the recent definition of the Immaculate Conception, there is no real correspondence. It is not merely that the latter is accepted only by a section of the Christian Church, and was promulgated by an authority whose modern claims the fathers of Nicæa would have regarded with sincere astonishment. The difference between the two cases is still more fundamental; it lies in the substance of the two definitions respectively. The Nicene fathers did but assert a truth which had been held to be of primary, vital import from the first; they asserted it in terms which brought it vividly home to the intelligence of their day. They were explaining old truth; they were not setting forth as truth that which had before been matter of opinion. But the recent definition asserts that an hypothesis, unheard of for centuries after the first promulgation of the Gospel, and then vehemently maintained and as vehemently controverted[t] by theologians of at least equal claims to orthodoxy, is a fact of Divine revelation, to be received by all who would receive the true faith of the Redeemer. In the one case an old truth is vindicated by an explanatory reassertion; in the other the assertion of a new fact is added to the Creed. The Nicene fathers only maintained in the language of their day the original truth that Jesus Christ is God: but the question whether the Conception of Mary was or was not sinless is a distinct question of fact, standing by itself, with no necessary bearing upon her office in the economy of the Incarnation, and not related in the way of an explanatory vindication of any originally revealed truth beyond it. It is one thing to reassert the revealed Godhead of Jesus; it is, in principle, a fundamentally distinct thing to 'decree a new honour' to Mary. The Nicene

[t] Cf. especially the treatise of the Dominican, John de Torquemada, Cardinal de Turrecremata, entitled, Tractatus de Veritate Conceptionis B. Virginis. Romæ, 1547, 4to; Oxon. 1869. ed. Pusey. Note G in App.

decision is the act of a Church believing itself commissioned to guard a body of truth which had been delivered from heaven in its integrity, once for all. The recent definition appears to presuppose a Church which can do more than guard the ancient faith, which is empowered to make actual additions to the number of revealed certainties, which is the organ no less than the recipient of a continuous revelation [u]. It is one thing to say that language has changed its value, and that a particular term which was once considered misleading will now serve to vindicate an acknowledged truth; it is another thing to claim the power of transfiguring a precarious and contradicted opinion, resting on no direct scriptural or primitive testimony, and impugned in terms by writers of the date and authority of Aquinas [x], into a certainty, claiming submission from the faith of Christendom on nothing less than a Divine authority. There is then no real reason for the statement that those who now reject the Immaculate

[u] I have been reminded that Roman Catholics do not admit this (see the 'Month,' Nov. 1867), and, at the instance of my reviewer, I quote with pleasure the following language of the Bull *Ineffabilis*, which is substantially that of Vincent of Lerins, and which will command the assent of English Churchmen. The Church of Christ, says the Bull, 'sedula depositorum apud se dogmatum custos, et vindex, nihil in his unquam permutat, nihil minuit, *nihil addit*, sed omni industriâ vetera fideliter sapienterque tractando si quà antiquitùs informata sunt, et Patrum fides sevit, ita limare expolire studet, ut prisca illa cœlestis doctrinæ dogmata accipiant evidentiam, lucem, distinctionem, sed retineant plenitudinem, integritatem, proprietatem, ac in suo tantum genere crescant, in eodem scilicet dogmate, eodem sensu, eâdemque sententiâ,' p. 11. But the question is whether, if the principle thus stated had been really adhered to, the Immaculate Conception of the Blessed Virgin Mary could have been defined to be an article of necessary faith. It is one thing to propose a new and necessary definition or explanation of a truth which has been confessed from the first; it is another thing to say that a fact, the truth of which has been controverted by a series of writers of the highest authority, is now so certain that it must be received as matter of faith. Should not the 'nihil addit' of the Bull alone have sufficed to render the definition impossible? See Observations d'un Théologien sur la Bulle de Pie IX, relative à la Conception de la Sainte Vierge, Paris, 1855, pp. 28–38; La Croyance à l'Immaculée Conception de la Sainte Vierge ne peut devenir dogme de foi, par M. l'Abbé Laborde, Paris, 1854, pp. 77–83. Can the assertion that the Immaculate Conception of the Blessed Virgin is a certainty of faith, be really rested upon any other ground, than an assumption in the modern Church of some power to discern and proclaim truths which were altogether unknown to the Church of the Apostles?

[x] Sum. Th. iii. a. 27, q. 2: 'B. Virgo contraxit quidem originale peccatum, sed ab eo fuit mundata antequam ex utero nasceretur.' Cf. St. Bernard. Ep. 174; Durandus, Rationale Divinorum Officiorum, vii. 7. 4; St. Bonaventur. Sent. iii. Dist. 3, pars i. art. i. quæst. 2.

Conception would of old have rejected the Homoousion. There is nothing to shew that those who bow with implicit faith before the Nicene decision are bound, as a matter of consistency, to yield the same deference of heart and thought to the most modern development of doctrine within the Latin portion of Catholic Christendom.

(β) But it may be rejoined: 'Why was a fresh definition deemed needful at Nicæa at all? Why could not the Church of the Nicene age have contented herself with saying that Jesus Christ is God, after the manner of the Church of earlier days? Why was the thought of Christendom to be saddled with a metaphysical symbol which at least transcends, if it does not destroy, the simplicity of the Church's first faith in our Lord's Divinity?'

(1) Now the answer is simply as follows. In the Arian age it was not enough to say that Jesus Christ is God, because the Arians had contrived to impoverish and degrade the idea conveyed by the Name of God so completely as to apply that sacred word to a creature [y]. Of course, if it had been deemed a matter of sheer indifference whether Jesus Christ is or is not God, it would have been a practical error to have insisted on the truth of His real Divinity, and an equivocal expression might have been allowed to stand. If the Church of Christ had been, not the school of revealed truth, in which the soul was to make knowledge the food and stimulant of love, but a world-wide debating club, 'ever seeking and never coming to the knowledge of the truth,' it would then have been desirable to keep this and all other fundamental questions open [z]. Perhaps in that case the Nicene decision might with truth have been described as the 'greatest misfortune that has happened to Christendom.' But the Church believed herself to possess a revelation from God, essential to the eternal well-being of the soul of man. She further believed that the true Godhead of Jesus Christ was a clearly-revealed truth of such fundamental and capital import,

[y] In the same way modern Socinians 'believe in the Divinity of Christ.' Channing, Objections to Unitarian Christianity Considered, Works, vol. ii. p. 361. Yet they also believe that Christ 'is a Being distinct from the one God.' Ibid. p. 510. Such a confession of Christ's 'Divinity' implies of course no more than might be said of St. John, and shews how completely language may be emptied of its original value. Cf. Lect. I. p. 26.

[z] See the letter addressed in Constantine's name to St. Alexander and to Arius (Soc. i. 7), in which the writer—probably Eusebius of Nicomedia—insists 'that the points at issue are minute and trivial.' Bright's Hist. Ch. p. 20. Neale, Hist. Alex. i. 134.

that, divorced from it, the creed of Christendom must perish outright. Plainly therefore it was the Church's duty to assert this truth in such language as might be unmistakably expressive of it. Now this result was secured by the Homoousion. It was at the time of its first imposition, and it has been ever since, a working criterion of real belief in the Godhead of our Lord. It excluded the Arian sense of the word God, and on this account it was adopted by the orthodox. How much it meant was proved by the resistance which it then encountered, and by the subsequent efforts which have been made to destroy or to evade it. The sneer of Gibbon about the iota which separates the semi-Arian from the Catholic symbol[a] (Homoiousion from Homoousion) is naturally repeated by those who believe that nothing was really at stake beyond the emptiest of abstractions, and who can speak of the fourth century as an age of meaningless logomachies. But to men who are concerned, not with words, but with the truths which they enshrine, not with the mere historic setting of a great struggle, but with the vital question at issue in it, the full importance of the Nicene symbol will be sufficiently obvious. The difference between Homoiousion and Homoousion convulsed the world for the simple reason, that in that difference lay the whole question of the real truth or falsehood of our Lord's actual Divinity. If in His Essence He was only like God, He was still a distinct Being from God, and therefore either created, or (*per impossibile*) a second God. In a great engagement, when man after man is laid low in defence of the colours of his regiment, it might seem to a bystander, unacquainted with the forms of war, a prodigious absurdity that so great a sacrifice of life should be incurred for a piece of silk or cotton of a particular hue; and he might make many caustic epigrams at the expense of the struggling and suffering combatants. But a soldier would tell him that the flag is a symbol of the honour and prowess of his country; and that he is not dying for a few yards of coloured material, but for the moral and patriotic idea which the material represents. If ever there was a man who was not the slave of language, who had his eye upon ideas, truths, facts, and who made language submissively do their work, that man was the great St. Athanasius. He advocated the Homoousion at Nicæa, because he was convinced that it was the sufficient and necessary symbol and safeguard of the treasure

[a] An equally reasonable sneer might be levelled, on Pantheistic grounds, at the number of letters which distinguishes 'Creature' from 'Creator.'

of truth committed to the Church: but years afterwards, he would not press it upon semi-Arians whom he knew to be at heart loyal to the truth which it protected[b]. He was sure that, if he gave them time, they would end by accepting it. And during fifteen centuries experience has not shewn that any large number of real believers in our Saviour's Godhead have objected to the Nicene statement; while its efficacy in guarding against a lapse into Arian error has amply confirmed the far-sighted wisdom, which, full of jealousy for the rightful honour of Jesus[c], and of charity for the souls of men, has incorporated it for ever with the most authoritative profession of faith in the Divinity of Christ which is possessed by Christendom.

(2) It may indeed be urged that freedom from creeds is ideally and in the abstract the highest state of Christian communion. It may be pleaded that a public confession of faith will produce in half-earnest and superficial souls a formal and mechanical devotion; that the exposure of the most sacred truth in a few condensed expressions to the scepticism and irreverence of those who are strangers to its essence will lead to inevitable ribaldry and scandal. But it is sufficient to reply that these liabilities do not outweigh the necessity for a clear 'form of sound words,' since formalists will be formal, and sceptics will be irreverent, with or without it. And those who depreciate creeds among us now, do not really mean to recommend that truth should be kept hidden, as in the first centuries, in the secret mind of the Church: they have far other purposes in view. Rousseau might draw pictures of the superiority of simple primitive savage life to the enervated civilization of Paris; but it would not have been prudent in the Parisians at the end of the last century to have attempted a return to the barbaric life of their ancestors, who had roamed as happy savages in the great forests of Europe. The Latitudinarians who suggest that the Church might dispense with the Catholic

[b] De Synod. 41: *Πρὸς δὲ τοὺς ἀποδεχομένους τὰ μὲν ἄλλα πάντα τῶν ἐν Νικαίᾳ γραφέντων, περὶ δὲ μόνον τὸ Ὁμοούσιον ἀμφιβάλλοντας, χρὴ μὴ ὡς πρὸς ἐχθροὺς διακεῖσθαι . . . . ἀλλ' ὡς ἀδελφοὶ πρὸς ἀδελφοὺς διαλεγόμεθα, τὴν αὐτὴν μὲν ἡμῖν διάνοιαν ἔχοντας, περὶ δὲ τὸ ὄνομα μόνον διστάζοντας. . . . . Οὐ μακρὰν εἰσιν ἀποδέξασθαι καὶ τὴν τοῦ Ὁμοουσίου λέξιν.* He repeatedly declares that the Homoousion in its Nicene sense is intended to guard the reality of the Divine Sonship as being uncreated. Ibid. 39, 45, 48, 54.

[c] St. Athanasius' 'zeal for the Consubstantiality had its root in his loyalty to the CONSUBSTANTIAL. He felt that in the Nicene dogma were involved the worship of Christ and the life of Christianity.' Bright's Hist. Ch. p. 149.

creeds, advise us to revert to the defencelessness of ecclesiastical childhood. But, alas! they cannot guarantee to us its innocence, or its immunities. We could not, if we would, reverse the thought of centuries, and ignore the questions which heresy has opened, and which have been œcumenically decided. We might not thus do despite to the kindly providence of Him, Who, with the temptations to faith that came with the predestined course of history, has in the creeds opened to us such 'a way to escape that we may be able to bear them.'

Certainly if toil and suffering confer a value on the object which they earn or preserve; if a country prizes the liberties which were baptized in the blood of her citizens; if a man rejoices in the honour which he has kept unstained at the risk of life; then we, who are the heirs of the ages of Christendom, should cling with a peculiar loyalty and love to the great Nicene confession of our Lord's Divinity. For the Nicene definition was wrung from the heart of the agonized Church by a denial of the truth on which was fed, then as now, her inmost life. In the Arian heresy the old enemies of the Gospel converged as for a final and desperate effort to achieve its destruction. The carnal, gross, external, Judaizing spirit, embodied in the frigid literalism of the school of Antioch; the Alexandrian dialectics, substituting philosophical *placita* for truths of faith; nay, Paganism itself, vanquished in the open field, but anxious to take the life of its conqueror by private assassination;—these were the forces which reappeared in Arianism [d]. It was no mere exasperation of rhetoric which saw Porphyry in Arius, and which compared Constantius to Diocletian. The life of Athanasius after the Nicene Council might well have been lived before the Edict of Milan. Arianism was a political force; it ruled at court. Arianism was a philosophical disputant, and was at home in the schools. Arianism was, moreover, a proselytizer; it had verses and epigrammatic arguments for the masses of the people; and St. Gregory of Nyssa, in a passage [e] which is

[d] St. Greg. Nyssa, contr. Eunom. xii. p. 728. Arianism is ἡ τῆς Ἰουδαϊκῆς ἀπάτης συνήγορος, ἔχουσά τι καὶ τῆς Ἑλληνικῆς ἀθεΐας. So St. Gregory Nazianz. (Orat. i. vol. i. p. 16) describes the Arian conception of the Divine Nature as marked by an Ἰουδαϊκὴ πενία, meaning the hard abstract monotheism of the later Jewish creed. Quoted by Baur, Lehre von der Dreieinigkeit. i. pp. 352, 353, note.

[e] See Dr. Newman's translation of it in Athan. Treatises, i. 213, note *a*: 'Men of yesterday and the day before, mere mechanics, off-hand dogmatists in theology, servants too, and slaves that have been flogged . . . . are solemn with us and philosophical about things incomprehensible. . . . Ask

[LECT.

classical, has described its extraordinary success among the lower orders. Never was a heresy stronger, more versatile, more endowed with all the apparatus of controversy, more sure, as it might have seemed, of the future of the world. It was a long, desperate struggle, by which the original faith of Christ conquered this fierce and hardy antagonist. At this day the Creed of Nicæa is the living proof of the Church's victory[f]; and as we confess it we should, methinks, feel somewhat of the fire of our spiritual ancestors, some measure of that fresh glow of thankfulness, which is due to God after a great deliverance, although wrought out in a distant age. To unbelief this creed may be only an ecclesiastical 'test,' only an additional 'incubus,' weighing down 'honest religious thought.' But to the children of faith, the Nicene confession must ever furnish the welcome expression of their most cherished conviction. Let us henceforth repeat it, at those most solemn moments when the Church puts it into our mouths, with a renewed and deepened sense of gratitude and joy. Not as if it were the mere trophy of a controversial victory, or the dry embodiment of an abstract truth in the language of speculation, should we welcome this glorious creed to our hearts and lips. Rather let us greet it, as the intellectual sentinel which guards the shrine of faith in our inmost souls from the profanation of error; as the good angel who warns us that since the Incarnation we move in the very ante-chamber of a Divine Presence; as a mother's voice reminding us of that tribute of heartfelt love and adoration, which is due from all serious Christians to the Lord Jesus Christ our Saviour and our God.

about pence, and he will discuss the Generate and Ingenerate; inquire the price of bread, he answers, "Greater is the Father, and the Son is subject;" say that a bath would suit you, and he defines that the Son is out of nothing.' See also St. Athan. Orat. Ari. i. 22, on the profane questions put to boys and women in the Agora; and Ibid. 4 sqq. on the 'Thalia' of Arius. Cf. also St. Greg. Nyssen, De Deitate Filii et Sp. Sancti. Opp. iii. 466.

[f] The stress here laid upon the Nicene Creed will not be supposed to imply forgetfulness of the great claims, in its due place, of the symbol *Quicunque.* Coleridge, indeed, has said that the Athanasian Creed is, in his judgment, 'heretical in the omission or implicit denial of the Filial subordination in the Godhead, which is the doctrine of the Nicene Creed.' (Table-Talk, p. 41.) But when the Athanasian Creed asserts that the Son is 'of the Father,' it virtually affirms the Subordination; and when the Nicene Creed calls the Son 'Very God' and 'Consubstantial,' it emphatically confesses the Coequality. Coleridge's judgment can only be sustained by supposing that the Nicene Creed teaches a doctrine of Subordination in which the Nicene Council would assuredly have detected Arianism. See Bright, Sermons of St. Leo, note 99.

LECTURE VIII.

SOME CONSEQUENCES OF THE DOCTRINE OF OUR LORD'S DIVINITY.

He That spared not His Own Son, but delivered Him up for us all, how shall He not with Him also freely give us all things?—ROM. viii. 32.

OF late years we have been familiarized with cautions and protests against what has been termed by way of disparagement 'Inferential Theology.' And no one would deny that in all ages of the Church, the field of theology has been the scene of hasty, unwarrantable, and misleading inferences. False conclusions have been drawn from true premisses; and very doubtful or false premisses have been occasionally assumed if not asserted to be true. Moreover, some earnest believers have seemed to forget that in a subject-matter such as the creed of Christendom, they are confessedly below truth and not above it. They have forgotten that it is given us here to see a part only, and not the whole. In reality we can but note the outskirts of a vast economy, whose body and substance stretch far away from our gaze into infinitude. Many an intercepting truth, not the less true because unseen and unsuspected, ought to arrest the hardy and confident logic, which insists upon this or that particular conclusion as following necessarily upon these or those premises of which it is already in possession. But this caution has not always been kept in view. And when once pious affection or devout imagination have seized the reins of religious thought, it is easy for individuals or schools to wander far from the beaten paths of a clear yet sober faith, into some theological wonderland, the airiest creation of the liveliest fancy, where, to the confusion and unsettlement of souls, the wildest fiction and the highest truth may be inextricably intertwined in an entanglement of hopeless and bewildering disorder.

[LECT.

But if this should be admitted, it would not follow that theology is in no sense 'inferential.' Within certain limits, and under due guidance, 'inference' is the movement, it is the life of theology. The primal records of revelation itself, as we find them in Scripture, are continually inferential; and it is at least the business of theology to observe and marshal these revealed inferences, to draw them out, and to make the most of them. The illuminated reason of the collective Church has for ages been engaged in studying the original materials of the Christian revelation. It thus has shaped, rather than created, the science of theology. What is theology, but a continuous series of observed and systematized inferences, respecting God in His Nature and His dealings with mankind, drawn from premises which rest upon God's authority? Do you say that no 'inference' is under any circumstances legitimate; that no one truth in theology necessarily implies another; that the Christian mind ought to preserve in a jealous and sterile isolation each proposition that can be extracted from Scripture? Do you suppose that the several truths of the Christian creed are so many separate, unsuggestive, unfruitful dogmas, having no traceable relations towards each other? Do you take it for granted that each revealed truth involves nothing that is not seen plainly to lie on the very surface of the terms which express it? In short, are the doctrines of the Church to be regarded now as only so many barren abstractions, which a merely human speculation on divine things has from age to age drawn out into form and system? If so, of course it is natural enough to deprecate any earnest scrutiny of the worth and consequences of these abstractions; you deprecate it as interfering with moral and practical interests; you deem an inferential theology alike illusory and mischievous. If I here touch the secret of your thought, at least, my brethren, I admit its consistency; but then your governing premise is of a character to put you out of all relations with the Christian Church, except those of fundamental opposition. The Christian Church believes that God has really spoken; and she assumes that no subject can have a higher practical interest for man than a consideration of the worth and drift of what He has said. Of course no one would waste his time upon systematizing what he believed to be only a series of abstract phantoms. And if a man holds a doctrine with so slight and doubtful a grasp that it illuminates nothing within him, that it moves nothing, that it leads on to nothing beyond itself, he is in a fair way to forfeit it altogether.

We scan anxiously and cross-question keenly only that which we really possess and cherish as solid truth: a living faith is pretty certain to draw inferences. The seed which has not shrivelled up into an empty husk cannot but sprout, if you place it beneath the sod; the living belief, which has really been implanted in the soil of thought and feeling, cannot but bear its proper flower and fruit in the moral and intellectual life of a thoughtful and earnest man. If you would arrest the growth of the seed, you must cut it off from contact with the soil, and so in time you must kill it: you may, for awhile, isolate a religious conviction by some violent moral or intellectual process; but be sure that the conviction which cannot germinate in your heart and mind is already condemned to death[a].

If theology is inferential, she infers under guidance and within restricted limits. If the eccentric reasonings of individual minds are to be received with distrust, the consent of many minds, of many ages, of many schools and orders of thought, may command at least a respectful attention. If we reject conclusions drawn professedly from the substance of revelation, but really enlarging instead of explaining it, it does not follow that we should reject inferences which are simply explanatory, or which exhibit the bearing of one revealed truth upon another. This indeed is the most fruitful and legitimate province of inference in theological enquiry. Such 'inference' brings out the meaning of the details of revelation. It raises this feature to prominence; it throws that into the shade. It places language to which a too servile literalism might have attributed the highest force, in the lower rank of metaphor and symbol; it elicits pregnant and momentous truths from incidents which, in the absence of sufficient guidance or reflection, may have been thought to possess only a secondary degree of significance.

To-day we reach the term of those narrow limits within which some aspects of a subject in itself exhaustless have been so briefly and imperfectly discussed. And it is natural for any earnest man to ask himself—'If I believe in Christ's Divinity, what does this belief involve? Is it possible that such a faith can be for me a dead abstraction, having no real influence upon my daily life of thought and action? If this great doctrine be true, is there not, when I am satisfied of its truth, still something to be done besides proving it? Can it be other than a

[a] See, on this point, University Sermons, by Rev. R. Scott, D.D., Master of Balliol College, pp. 174-176. The rejection of 'inferential theology' was a characteristic feature of Sadduceeism.

practical folly, to have ascertained the truth that Jesus is God, and then to consign so momentous a conclusion to a respectful oblivion in some obscure corner of my mind, as if it were a well-bound but disused book that could only ornament the shelves of a library? Must I not rather enshrine it in the very centre of my soul's life? Must I not contemplate it, nay, if it may be, penetrate it, feed on it by repeated contemplation, that it may illuminate, sustain, transfigure my whole inward being? Must I not be reasonably anxious till this great conviction shall have moulded all that it can bear on, or that can bear on it—all that I hold in any degree for religious truth? Must not such a faith at last radiate through my every thought? Must it not invigorate with a new and deeper motive my every action? If Jesus, Who lived and died and rose for me, be indeed God, can my duties to Him end with a bare confession of His Divinity? Will not the greatness of His Life and of His Death, will not the binding force of His commands, will not the nature and reality of His promises and gifts, be felt to have a new and deeper meaning, when I survey them in the light of this glorious truth? Must not all which the Divine Christ blesses and sanctions have in some sense about it, the glory and virtue of His Divinity?'

Undoubtedly, brethren, the doctrine of Christ's Godhead is, both in the sphere of belief and in that of morals, as fruitful and as imperious as you anticipate. St. Paul's question in the text is in substantial harmony with the spirit of your own. St. Paul makes the doctrine of a Divine Christ, given for the sins of men to a Life of humiliation and to a Death of anguish, the premise of the largest consequences, the warrant of the most unbounded expectations. 'He That spared not His Own Son, but gave Him up for us all, how shall He not with Him also freely give us all things?' Let us then hasten to trace this somewhat in detail; and let us remark, in passing, that on the present occasion we shall not be leaving altogether the track of former lectures. For in studying the results of a given belief, we may add to the number of practical evidences in its favour; we may approach the belief itself under conditions which are more favourable for doing justice to it than those which a direct argument supplies. To contemplate such a truth as the Godhead of our Lord *in itself*, is like gazing with open eyelids at the torturing splendour of the noon-day sun. We can best admire the sun of the natural heavens when we take note of the beauty which he sheds over the face of the world, when we mark the floods of light which stream from him, and the deep shadows which he casts, and the colours and forms which he lights up and displays before us. In like manner, perchance, we may most truly enter into the meaning of the Divinity of the Sun of Righteousness, by observing the truths which depend more or less directly on that glorious doctrine,—truths on which it sheds a significance so profound, so unspeakably awful, so unspeakably consoling.

There are three distinct bearings of the doctrine of our Lord's Divinity which it is more especially of importance to consider. This doctrine protects truths prior to itself, and belonging both to natural and to revealed theology. It also illuminates the meaning, it asserts the force of truths which depend upon itself, which are, to speak humanly, below it, and which can only be duly appreciated when they are referred to it as justifying and explaining them. Lastly, it fertilizes the Christian's moral and spiritual life, by supplying a motive to the virtues which are most characteristically Christian, and without which Christian ethics sink down to the level of Pagan morality.

I. Observe, first, the conservative force of the doctrine. It protects the truths which it presupposes. Placed at the centre of the faith of Christendom, it looks backward as well as forward; it guards in Christian thought the due apprehension of those fundamental verities without which no religion whatever is possible, since they are the postulates of all religious thought and activity.

1. What, let us ask, is the practical relation of the doctrine before us to the primal truth that a Personal God really exists?

(*a*) Both in the last century and in our own day, it has been the constant aim of a philosophical deism to convince the world that the existence of a Supreme Being would be more vividly, constantly, practically realized, if the dogma of His existence were detached from the creed of Christendom. The pure Theistic idea, we are told, if it were only freed from the earthly and material accessories of an Incarnation, if it were not embarrassed by the 'metaphysical conception' of distinct personal Subsistencies within the Godhead, if it could be left to its native force, to its spirituality of essence, to its simplicity of form,—would exert a prodigious influence on human thought, if not on human conduct. This influence is said to be practically impossible, so long as Theistic truth is overlaid by the 'thick integument' of Christian doctrine. Accordingly a real belief in God is to be deepened and extended, and atheism is to be expelled from the minds of men, by the destruction of dogmatic Christianity. But has any such anticipation as yet been realized by deism? Is it in the way to be realized at this hour? Need I remind you, that throughout Europe, the most earnest assaults of infidelity upon the Christian creed within the last ten years have been directed against its *Theistic*, as distinct from its peculiarly Christian elements? When the possibility of miracle is derided; when a Providence is scouted as the fond dream of man's exaggerated self-love; when belief in the power of prayer is treated as a crude superstition, illustrative of man's ignorance of the scientific conception of law; when the hypothesis of absolutely invariable law, and the cognate conception of nature as a self-evolved system of self-existent forces and self-existent matter, are advancing with giant strides in large departments of the literature of the day;—it is not Christianity as such, it is Theism, which is really jeopardized and insulted. Among the forces arrayed against Christianity at this hour, the most formidable, because the most consistent and the most sanguine, is that pure materialism, which has been intellectually organized in the somewhat pedantic form of Positivism. To the Positivist the most etherealized of deistic theories is just as much an object of pitying scorn as the creed of a St. John and a St. Athanasius. Both are relegated to 'the theological period' of human development. And if we may judge from the present aspect of the controversy between non-Christian spiritualists and the apostles of Positivism, it must be sorrowfully acknowledged that the latter appear to gain steadily and surely on their opponents. This fact is more evident on the continent of Europe than in our own country. It cannot be explained by supposing that the spiritualistic writers are intellectually inferior to the advocates of materialism. Still less is an explanation to be sought in the intrinsic indefensibility of the truth which the spiritualists defend; it is really furnished by the conditions under which they undertake to defend it. A living, energetic, robust faith, a faith, as it has been termed, not of ether, but of flesh and blood, is surely needed, in order to stand the reiterated attacks, the subtle and penetrating misgivings, the manifold wear and tear of a protracted controversy with so brutal an antagonist. Can deism inspire this faith? The pretension of deists to refine, to spiritualize, to etherealize the idea of God almost indefinitely, is fatal to the living energy of their one conviction. Where an abstract deism is not killed out by the violence of atheistic materialism, it is apt, although left to itself, to die by an unperceived process of evaporation. For a living faith in a Supreme Being, the human mind requires motives, corollaries, consequences, supports. These are not supplied by the few abstract considerations which are entertained by the philosophical deists. Whatever may be the intellectual strength of their position against atheism, the practical weakness of that position is a matter of notoriety; and if this weakness is apparent in the case of the philosophers themselves, how much more patent is it when deism attempts to make itself a home in the heart of the people! That abstract and inaccessible being who is placed at the summit of deistic systems is too subtle for the thought and too cold for the heart of the multitudes of the human family. When God is regarded less as the personal Object of affection and worship than as the necessary term of an intellectual equation, the sentiment of piety is not really satisfied; it hungers, it languishes, it dies. And this purely intellectual manner of apprehending God, which kills piety, is so predominant in every genuine deistic system as to bring about, in no long lapse of time, its impotence and extinction as a popular religious force. The Supreme Agent, without whom the deist cannot construct an adequate or satisfactory theory of being, is gradually divested of all personal characteristics, and is resolved into a formula expressing only supreme agency. His moral perfections fall into the background of thought, while he is conceived of, more and more exclusively, as the Universal Mind. And his intellectual attributes are in turn discarded, when for the Supreme Mind is substituted the conception of the Mightiest Force. Long before this point is reached, deistic philosophy is nervously alarmed, lest its God should still be supposed to penetrate as a living Providence down into this human world of suffering and sin. Accordingly, professing much anxiety for his true dignity and repose, deism weaves around his liberty a network of imaginary law; and if he has not been previously destroyed by the materialistic controversialists, he is at length conducted by the cold respect of deistic thinkers to the utmost frontier of the conceivable universe, where, having been enthroned in a majestic inaction, he is as respectfully abandoned. As suggesting a problem which may rouse a faint spasmodic intellectual instinct, his name may still be mentioned from time to time in the world of letters. But the interest which he creates is at the best on a level with that of the question whether the planets are or are not inhabited. As an energetic, life-controlling, life-absorbing power, the God of deism is extinct.

[LECT.

Now the doctrine that Jesus of Nazareth is the Incarnate God protects this primal theistic truth which non-Christian deism is so incapable of popularizing, and even of retaining. The Incarnation bridges over the abyss which opens in our thought between earth and heaven; it brings the Almighty, Allwise, Illimitable Being down to the mind and heart of His reasonable creatures. The Word made Flesh is God condescending to our finite capacities; and this condescension has issued in a clear, strong sense of the Being and Attributes of God, such as is not found beyond the bounds of Christendom. The last prayer of Jesus, that His redeemed might know the only true God, has been answered in history. How profound, how varied, how fertile is the idea of God, of His Nature and of His attributes, in St. John, in St. Paul, in St. Gregory Nazianzen, in St. Augustine! How energetic is this idea, how totally is it removed from the character of an impotent speculation! How does this keen, strong sense of God's present and majestic Life leave its mark upon manners, literatures, codes of law, national institutions, national characters! How utterly does its range of energy transcend any mere employment of the intellect; how does it, again and again, bend wills, and soften hearts, and change the current and drift of lives, and transfigure the souls of men! And why is this? It is because the Incarnation rivets the apprehension of God on the thought and heart of the Church, so that within the Church theistic truth bids defiance to those influences which tend perpetually to sap or to volatilize it elsewhere. Instead of presenting us with some fugitive abstraction, inaccessible to the intellect and disappointing to the heart, the Incarnation points to Jesus. Jesus is the Almighty, restraining His illimitable powers; Jesus is the Incomprehensible, voluntarily submitting to bonds; Jesus is Providence, clothed in our own flesh and blood; Jesus is the Infinite Charity, tending us with the kindly looks and tender handling of a human love; Jesus is the Eternal Wisdom, speaking out of the depths of infinite thought in a human language. Jesus is God making Himself, if I may dare so to speak, our tangible possession; He is God brought 'very nigh to us, in our mouth and in our heart;' we behold Him, we touch Him, we cling to Him, and lo! we are θείας κοινωνοὶ φύσεως[b], partakers of the Nature of Deity through our actual membership in His Body[c]; we dwell, if we will, evermore in Him, and He in us.

[b] 2 St. Pet. i. 4.

[c] 1 Cor. xii. 27.

This then is the result of the Divine Incarnation: it brings God close to the inmost being of man, yet without forfeiting, nay, rather while guarding most carefully, in man's thought, the spirituality of the Divine Essence. Nowhere is the popular idea of God more refined, more spiritual, than where faith in the Divinity of Jesus is clearest and strongest. No writers have explained and asserted the immateriality, the simplicity, the indivisibility of the Essence of God more earnestly, than those who have most earnestly asserted and explained the doctrines of the Holy Trinity and of the Divine Incarnation. For if we know our happiness in Christ, we Christians are united to God, we possess God, we consciously live, and move, and have our being in God. Our intelligence and our heart alike apprehend God in His majestic and beautiful Life so truly and constantly, because He has taken possession of our whole nature, intellectual, moral, and corporeal, and has warmed and illuminated and blessed it by the quickening Manhood of Jesus. We cannot reflect upon and rejoice in our union with Jesus, without finding ourselves face to face with the Being and Attributes of Him with Whom in Jesus we are made one. Holy Scripture has traced the failure and misery of all attempts on the part of a philosophical deism to create or to maintain in the soul of man a real communion with our heavenly Parent. 'Whosoever denieth the Son, the same hath not the Father [d].' And the Christian's practical security against those speculative difficulties to which his faith in a living God may be exposed, lies in that constant contemplation of and communion with Jesus, which is of the essence of the Christian life. 'God, who commanded the light to shine out of darkness, hath shined in our hearts, to give the light of the knowledge of the glory of God in the Face of Jesus Christ [e].'

(β) But if belief in our Saviour's Godhead protects Christian thought against the intellectual dangers which await an arid Deism, does it afford an equally effective safeguard against Pantheism? In conceiving of God, the choice before a pantheist lies between alternatives from which no genius has as yet devised a real escape. God, the pantheist must assert, is literally everything; God is the whole material and spiritual universe; He is humanity in all its manifestations; He is by inclusion every moral and immoral agent; and every form and exaggeration of moral evil, no less than every variety of moral

[d] 1 St. John ii. 23.

[e] 2 Cor. iv. 6.

excellence and beauty, is part of the all-pervading, all-comprehending movement of His Universal Life. If this revolting blasphemy be declined, then the God of pantheism must be the barest abstraction of abstract being; He must, as with the Alexandrian thinkers, be so exaggerated an abstraction as to transcend existence itself; He must be conceived of as utterly unreal, lifeless, non-existent; while the only real beings are these finite and determinate forms of existence whereof 'nature' is composed [f]. This dilemma haunts all the historical transformations of pantheism, in Europe as in the East, to-day as two thousand years ago. Pantheism must either assert that its God is the one only existing being whose existence absorbs and is identified with the universe and humanity; or else it must admit that he is the rarest and most unreal of conceivable abstractions; in plain terms, that he is no being at all. And the question before us is, Does the Incarnation of God, as taught by the Christian doctrine, expose Christian thought to this dilemma? Is God 'brought very nigh to us' Christians in such sort, as to bury the Eternal in the temporary, the Infinite in the finite, the Absolute and Self-existent in the transient and the relative, the All-holy in the very sink of moral evil, unless, in order to save His honour in our thought, we are prepared to attenuate our idea of Him into nonentity?

Now, not merely is there no ground for this apprehension, but the Christian doctrine of an Incarnate God is our most solid protection against the inroads of pantheistic error.

The strength of pantheistic systems lies in that craving both of the intellect and of the heart for union with the Absolute Being, which is the most legitimate and the noblest instinct of our nature. This craving is satisfied by the Christian's union with the Incarnate One. But while satisfying it, the Incarnation raises an effective barrier against its abuse after the fashion of pantheism. Against the dogma of an Incarnate God, rooted in the faith of a Christian people, the waves of pantheistic thought may surge and lash themselves and break in vain. For the Incarnation presupposes that master-truth which pantheism most passionately denies. It presupposes the truth that between the finite and the Infinite, between the Creator and the Cosmos, between God and man, there is of necessity a measureless abyss. On this point its opposition to pantheism is as earnest as that of the most jealous deism; but the

[f] Saisset, Philosophie Religieuse, i. 181; ii. 368.

Christian creed escapes from the deistic conception of an omnipotent moral being, surveying intelligently the vast accumulation of sin and misery which we see on this earth, yet withal remaining unmoved, inactive, indifferent. The Christian creed spans this gulf which yawns between earth and heaven, by proclaiming that the Everlasting Son has taken our nature upon Him. In His Person a Created Nature is joined to the Uncreated, by a union which is for ever indissoluble. But what is that truth which underlies this transcendent mystery? What sustains it, what even enhances it, what forbids it to melt away in our thought into a chaotic confusion out of which neither the Divine nor the Human could struggle forth into the light for distinct recognition? It is, I reply, the truth that the Natures thus united in the Person of Jesus are radically, by their essence, and for ever, distinct. It is by reason of this ineffaceable distinctness that the union of the Godhead and Manhood in Jesus is such an object of wondering and thankful contemplation to Christians. Accordingly, at the very heart of the creed of Christendom, we have a guarantee against the cardinal error of pantheism; while yet by our living fellowship as Christians with the Divine and Incarnate Son, we realize the aspiration which pantheism both fosters and perverts. Christian intellect, so long as it is Christian, can never be betrayed into the admission that God is the universe; Christian faith can never be reduced to the extremity of choosing between a denial of moral distinctions and an assertion that God is the parent of all immoral action, or to the desperate endeavour to escape this alternative by volatilizing God into non-existence. And yet Christian love, while it is really Christian, cannot for one moment doubt that it enfolds and possesses and is united to its Divine Object. But this intellectual safeguard and this moral satisfaction alike vanish, if the real Deity of Jesus be denied or obscured: since it is the Deity of our truly human Lord which satisfies the Christian heart, while it protects the Christian intellect against fatal aberrations. Certainly a deism which would satisfy the heart, inevitably becomes pantheistic in its awkward attempts to become devotional; and although pantheism should everywhere breathe the tenderness which almost blinds a reader of Spinosa's ethics to a perception of their real character, still pantheism is at bottom and in its results not other than a graceful atheism. But to partake of the Divine Nature incarnate in Christ is not to bury God in the filth of moral pollution, nor is it to transcendentalize Him into

[LECT.

an abstraction, which mocks us, when we attempt to grasp it, as an unsubstantial phantom [g].

2. One more sample shall be given of this protective efficacy of the doctrine before us. If it guards in our thought the honour, the majesty, the Life of God, it also protects the true dignity and the rights of man. The unsettled spirit of our time, when it has broken with the claims of faith, oscillates, whether from caprice or in bewilderment, between the most inconsistent errors. If at one while its audacity would drive the Great God from His throne in heaven to make way for the lawless intellect and will of His creature, at another it seems possessed by an infatuated passion for the degradation of mankind. It either ignores such features of the higher side of our complex being as are the powers of reflection and of inference, or it arbitrarily assumes that they are only the products of civilization. It fixes its attention exclusively upon the graduated variety of form perceptible in a long series of crania which it has arranged in its museum, and then it proclaims with enthusiasm that a Newton or a Herschel is after all only the cultivated descendant of a grotesque and irrational ape. It even denies to man the possession of any spiritual nature whatever; thought is asserted to be inherent in the substance of the brain; belief in the existence of an immaterial essence is treated as an unscientific and superstitious prejudice; virtuous and vicious actions are alluded to as alike results of purely physical agencies [h]; man is to all intents and purposes a soulless brute. My brethren, you will not suppose that I am desiring to derogate, however indirectly, from the claims of that noble science which patiently investigates the physiology of our animal nature; I am only protesting against a rash and insulting hypothesis, for which science, if her sons could speak with one voice, would be loath to make herself responsible, since by it her true utterances

[g] M. Renan's frequent mention of 'God' in his 'Vie de Jésus' does not imply that he believes in a Supreme Being. 'God' means with M. Renan only 'the category of the ideal,' and not any existing personal being whatever. Questions contemporaines, p. 224: 'Les sciences historiques ne diffèrent en rien par la méthode des sciences physiques et mathématiques: elles supposent qu'aucun agent surnaturel ne vient troubler la marche de l'humanité; que cette marche est la résultante immédiate de la liberté qui est dans l'homme et de la fatalité qui est dans la nature; qu'il n'y a pas d'être libre supérieur à l'homme auquel on puisse attribuer une part appréciable dans la conduite morale, non plus que dans la conduite matérielle de l'univers.'

[h] Cf. M. Taine, Histoire de la Littérature Anglaise, Introduction, p. xv: 'Le vice et la vertu sont des produits comme le sucre et le vitriol.'

are piteously caricatured. It cannot be said that such a theory is a harmless eccentricity of over-eager speculation; for it destroys that high and legitimate estimate of God's natural gifts to man which is an important element of earnest and healthy morality in the individual, and which is still more essential to the onward march of our social progress.

But so long as the Christian Church believes in the true Divinity of our Incarnate Lord, it is not probable that theories which deny the higher aspects of human nature will meet with large acceptance. We Christians can bear to be told that the skull of this or that section of the human family bears this or that degree of resemblance to the skull of a gorilla. We know, indeed, that as receivers of the gift of life we are simply on a level with the lowest of the lower creatures; we owe all that we are and have to God. Do we not thank Him for our creation, preservation, and all the blessings of this life? Might He not have given us less than we have? Might He not have given us nothing? What have we, what are we, that we have not received? The question of man's place in the universe touches not any self-achieved dignity of our own, but the extent and the nature of the Divine bounty. But while we believe the creed of Christendom, we cannot view such a question as open, or listen with any other feelings than those of sorrow and repugnance to the arguments of the apostles of human degradation. We cannot consent to suppose ourselves to be mere animal organisms, without any immaterial soul or future destiny, parted by no distinctive attribute from the perishing beasts around us. For the true nobility of our nature has received the seal of a recognition, which forbids our intellectual complicity with the physics or the 'psychology' of materialism. Do not we Christians call to mind, often, every day of our lives, that God has put such high and distinctive honour upon our common humanity as to clothe Himself in it, and to bear it to heaven in its glorious and unsullied perfection, that for all eternity it may be the partner of His throne?

Tremunt videntes angeli
Versam vicem mortalium;
Peccat caro, mundat Caro,
Regnat Deus Dei Caro.

But this exaltation of our human nature would be the wildest dream, unless Jesus were truly God as well as Man. His Divinity is the warrant that in Him our race is 'crowned with glory and honour,' and that in taking upon Him 'not the nature of angels, but the seed of Abraham,' He was vindicating our individual capacity for the highest greatness. Apart from the phenomena of reflection and reason, the hopes which are raised by the Incarnation utterly forbid speculations that would degrade man to the level of a brute incapable of any real morality. If we are told that such hopes are not direct replies to the arguments of physiology, we answer that physiology can and does often correct by her scientific demonstrations, the eccentricities of those who would force her to take part against man's best hopes and instincts. But, as a practical matter of fact, Christendom maintains its faith in the dignity of man amidst the creatures of God by its faith in the Incarnation of the Divine Son. 'Beloved, now are we the sons of God, and it doth not yet appear what we shall be: but we know that, when He shall appear, we shall be like Him; for we shall see Him as He is[1].'

II. These are but a few out of many illustrations of the protection afforded by the doctrine of Christ's Divinity to sundry imperilled truths of natural religion. Let us proceed to consider the illuminative or explanatory relation in which the doctrine stands to truths which are internal to the Christian revelation, and which themselves presuppose some definite belief respecting the Person of Christ.

Now our Lord's whole Mediatorial work, while it is discharged through His assumed Humanity, is efficacious and complete, simply because the Mediator is not merely Man but God. As a Prophet, His utterances are infallible. As a Priest, He offers a prevailing sacrifice. As a King, He wields an authority which has absolute claims upon the conscience, and a power which will ultimately be proved to be resistless.

(*a*) A sincere and intelligent belief in the Divinity of Jesus Christ obliges us to believe that Jesus Christ, as a Teacher, is infallible. His infallibility is not a gift, it is an original and necessary endowment of His higher Nature. If indeed Christ had been merely man, He might still have been endowed with an infallibility such as was that of His own apostles. As it is, to charge Him with error is to deny that He is God. Unless God's wisdom can be foolishness, or His veracity can be sullied by the suspicion of deceit; unless God can Himself succumb to error, or can consent to deceive His reasonable creatures; a sincere believer in the true Divinity of Jesus Christ will bow before His words in all their possible range of significance,

[1] 1 St. John iii. 2.

as before the words of a literally infallible Master. So obvious an inference would only be disputed under circumstances of an essentially transitional character, such as are those which have perplexed the Church of England during the last few years. Deny that Jesus Christ is God, and you may or may not proceed to deny that He is infallible. But confess His Godhead, and the common sense of men of the world will concur with the judgment of divines, in bidding you avoid the irrational as well as blasphemous conception of a fallible Deity. To maintain, on the one hand, that Jesus Christ is God, and, on the other, that He is a teacher and propagator, not of trivial and unimportant, but of far-reaching and substantial errors;—this would have appeared to ancient Christendom a paradox so singular as to be absolutely incredible. But we have lived to hear men proclaim the legendary and immoral character of considerable portions of those Old Testament Scriptures, upon which our Lord has set the seal of His infallible authority [k]. And yet, side by side with this rejection of Scriptures so deliberately sanctioned by Christ, there is an unwillingness which, illogical as it is, we must sincerely welcome, to profess any explicit rejection of the Church's belief in Christ's Divinity. Hence arises the endeavour to intercept a conclusion, which might otherwise have seemed so plain as to make arguments in its favour an intellectual impertinence. Hence a series of singular refinements, by which Christ is presented to the modern world as really Divine, yet as subject to fatal error; as Founder of the true religion, yet as the credulous patron of a volume replete with worthless legends; as the highest Teacher and Leader of humanity, yet withal as the ignorant victim of the prejudices and follies of an unenlightened age.

It will be urged by those who impugn the trustworthiness of the Pentateuch without denying in terms the Divinity of Christ, that such a representation as the foregoing does them a certain measure of injustice. They do not wish to deny that

[k] Colenso on the Pentateuch, vol. iii. p. 623: '[In Matt. iv. 4, 7, 10] we have quotations from Deut. viii. 3; vi. 16; vi. 13; x. 20. And it is well known that there are many other passages in the Gospels and Epistles, in which this book is referred to, and in some of which Moses is expressly mentioned as the writer of the words in question, *e.g.* Acts iii. 22; Rom. x. 19. And, though it is true that, in the texts above quoted, the words are not, indeed, ascribed to Moses, but are merely introduced with the phrase 'It is written,' yet in Matt. xix. 7 the Pharisees refer to a passage in Deut. xxiv. 1 as a law of Moses; and our Lord in His reply, ver. 8, repeats their language, and practically adopts it as correct, and makes it His own.

Christ, as the Eternal Son of God, is infallible. But the Christ Who speaks in the Gospels is, they contend, '*a* Son of man,' and as such He is subject to the human infirmities of ignorance and error[1]. 'Does He not profess Himself,' they ask, 'in the plainest words, ignorant of the day of the last judgment? Does not His Evangelist assure us that He increased in "wisdom" as well as in stature? This being so, was not His human knowledge limited; and was not error possible, if not inevitable, when He passed beyond the limits of such knowledge as He possessed? Why should He be supposed to speak of the Pentateuch with a degree of critical acumen, to which the foremost learning of His day and country had not yet attained? Take care,' so they warn us, 'lest in your anxiety to repudiate Arius and Nestorius, you deny the reality of Christ's Human Soul, and become the unconscious associate of Apollinaris or of Eutyches. Take care, lest you make Christianity answer with its life for the truth of a "theory" about the historical trustworthiness of the Old Testament, which, although it certainly was sanctioned and put forward by Jesus Christ, yet has been as decidedly condemned by the "higher criticism" of the present day.'

Let us remark in this position, first of all, the indirect admission that Christ, as the Eternal Son of God, is strictly infallible. Obvious as such a truth should be to Christians, Arianism, be it remembered, did not confess it. Arianism held that the Word Himself was ignorant of the day of judgment. Such a tenet was perfectly consistent with the denial that the

[1] Colenso on the Pentateuch, vol. i. p. xxxi: 'It is perfectly consistent with the most entire and sincere belief in our Lord's Divinity to hold, as many do, that, when He vouchsafed to become a "Son of Man," He took our nature fully, and voluntarily entered into all the conditions of humanity, and, among others, into that which makes our growth in all ordinary knowledge *gradual* and *limited*. We are expressly told, in Luke ii. 52, that "Jesus increased in *wisdom*," as well as in "stature." It is not supposed that, in His human nature, He was acquainted, more than any educated Jew of the age, with the mysteries of all modern sciences; nor, with St. Luke's expressions before us, can it be seriously maintained that, as an *infant* or *young child*, He possessed a knowledge surpassing that of the most pious and learned adults of His nation, upon the subject of the authorship and age of the different portions of the Pentateuch. At what period, then, of His life upon earth, is it to be supposed that He had granted to Him, as the Son of Man, *supernaturally*, full and accurate information on these points, so that He should be expected to speak about the Pentateuch in other terms than any other devout Jew of that day would have employed? Why should it be thought that he would speak with certain *Divine* knowledge on this matter, more than upon other matters of ordinary science or history?'

Word was consubstantial with the Omniscient God; but it was utterly at variance with any pretension honestly to believe in His Divinity[m]. Yet it must be recorded with sorrow, that some writers who would desire nothing less than to uphold the name and errors of the opponent of Athanasius, do nevertheless at times seem to speak as if it were seriously possible that the Infallible could have erred, or that the boundless knowledge of the Eternal Mind could be really limited. Let us then note and welcome the admission that the Eternal Son of God is literally infallible, even though it be made in quarters where His authority, as the Incarnate Christ, teaching unerringly substantial truth, is directly impugned and repudiated.

It is of course urged that our Lord's Human Soul is the seat of that 'fallibility' which is insisted upon as being so fatal to His authority as a Teacher. Let us then enquire what the statements of Scripture on this mysterious subject would really appear to affirm.

1. When St. Luke tells us that our Lord increased in wisdom and stature[n], we can scarcely doubt that an intellectual development of some kind in Christ's human Soul is indicated. This development, it is implied, corresponded to the growth of His bodily frame. The progress in wisdom was real and not merely apparent, just as the growth of Christ's Human Body was a real growth. If only an increasing manifestation of knowledge had been meant, it might have been meant also that Christ only manifested increase of stature, while His Human Body did not really grow. But on the other hand, St. Luke had previously spoken of the Child

[m] St. Athanasius comments as follows upon St. Mark xiii. 32, *οὐδὲ ὁ Υἱός*. Contr. Arian. Or. iii. c. 44: διὰ τοῦτο καὶ περὶ ἀγγέλων λέγων οὐκ εἴρηκεν ἐπαναβαίνων, ὅτι οὐδὲ τὸ Πνεῦμα τὸ ἅγιον, ἀλλ' ἐσιώπησε, δεικνὺς κατὰ δύο ταῦτα, ὅτι εἰ τὸ Πνεῦμα οἶδεν, πολλῷ μᾶλλον ὁ Λόγος ᾗ Λόγος ἐστὶν οἶδε, παρ' οὗ καὶ τὸ Πνεῦμα λαμβάνει, καὶ ὅτι περὶ τοῦ Πνεύματος σιωπήσας φανερὸν πεποίηκεν, ὅτι περὶ τῆς ἀνθρωπίνης αὐτοῦ λειτουργίας ἔλεγεν· οὐδὲ ὁ Υἱός· καὶ τούτου τεκμήριον, ὅτι ἀνθρωπίνως εἰρηκὼς, οὐδε ὁ Υἱὸς οἶδε, δείκνυσιν ὅμως θεϊκῶς ἑαυτὸν τὰ πάντα εἰδότα. ὃν γὰρ λέγει Υἱὸν τὴν ἡμέραν μὴ εἰδέναι, τοῦτον εἰδέναι λέγει τὸν Πατέρα· οὐδεὶς γὰρ, φησὶ, γινώσκει τὸν Πατέρα εἰ μὴ ὁ Υἱός. πᾶς δὲ πλὴν τῶν Ἀρειανῶν συνομολογήσειεν, ὡς ὁ τὸν Πατέρα γινώσκων πολλῷ μᾶλλον οἶδεν τῆς κτίσεως τὸ ὅλον, ἐν δὲ τῷ ὅλῳ καὶ τὸ τέλος ἐστὶ ταύτης.

Olshausen observes, in Ev. Matt. xxiv. 36, Comm. i. p. 909: 'Ist aber vom Sohne Gottes hier die Rede, so kann das von ihm prädicirte Nichtwissen der ἡμέρα und ὥρα kein absolutes seyn, indem die *Wesenseinheit des Vaters und des Sohnes* das Wissen des Sohnes und des Vaters nicht specifisch zu trennen gestattet; es muss vielmehr nur von dem Zustande der κένωσις des Herrn in Stande seiner Niedrigkeit verstanden werden.'

[n] St. Luke ii. 52: Ἰησοῦς προέκοπτε σοφίᾳ καὶ ἡλικίᾳ.

Jesus as 'being filled with wisdom [o],' and St. John teaches that as the Word Incarnate, Jesus was actually 'full of truth.' St. John means not only that our Lord was veracious, but that He was fully in possession of objective truth [p]. It is clearly implied that, according to St. John, this fulness of truth was an element of that glory which the first disciples beheld or contemplated [q]. This statement appears to be incompatible with the supposition that the Human Soul of Jesus, through spiritual contact with Which the disciples 'beheld' the glory of the Eternal Word, was Itself not 'full of truth.' St. John's narrative does not admit of our confining this 'fulness of truth' to the later days of Christ's ministry, or to the period which followed His Resurrection. There are then two representations before us, one suggesting a limitation of knowledge, the other a fulness of knowledge in the human soul of Christ. In order to harmonize these statements, we need not fall back upon the vulgar rationalistic expedient of supposing that between St. John's representation of our Lord's Person, and that which is given in the three first Gospels, there is an intrinsic and radical discrepancy. If we take St. John's account together with that of St. Luke, might it not seem that we have here a special instance of that tender condescension, by which our Lord willed to place Himself in a relation of real sympathy with the various experiences of our finite existence? If by an infused knowledge He was, even as a Child, 'full of truth,' yet that He might enter with the sympathy of experience into the various conditions of our intellectual life, He would seem to have acquired, by the slow labour of observation and inference, a new mastery over truths which He already, in another sense, possessed. Such a co-existence of growth in knowledge with a possession of all its ultimate results would not be without a parallel in ordinary human life. In moral matters, a living example may teach with a new power some law of conduct, the truth of which we have before recognised intuitively. In another field of knowledge, the telescope or the theodolite may verify a result of which we have been previously informed by a mathematical calculation [r]. We can then conceive that the reality of our

[o] St. Luke ii. 40: πληρούμενον σοφίας.

[p] St. John i. 14: πλήρης χάριτος καὶ ἀληθείας.

[q] Ibid.: ἐθεασάμεθα τὴν δόξαν αὐτοῦ.

[r] In the same way, every man's stock of opinions is of a twofold character; it is partly traditional and partly acquired by personal investigation and thought. The traditionally received element in the mind, may be held, as such, with the utmost tenacity; and yet there is a real 'increase in

Lord's intellectual development would not necessarily be inconsistent with the simultaneous perfection of His knowledge. As Man, He might have received an infused knowledge of all truth, and yet have taken possession through experience and in detail of that which was latent in His mind, in order to correspond with the intellectual conditions of ordinary human life. But, let us suppose that this explanation be rejected[s], that St. John's statement be left out of sight, and that St. Luke's words be understood to imply simply that our Lord's Human Soul acquired knowledge which It did not in any sense possess before. Does even any such 'increase in wisdom' as this during Christ's early years, warrant our saying that, in the days of His ministry, our Lord was still ignorant of the real claims and worth of the Jewish Scriptures? Does it enable us to go further, and to maintain that, when He made definite statements on the subject, He was both the victim and the propagator of serious error? Surely such inferences are not less unwarranted by the statements of Scripture than they are destructive of Christ's character and authority as a teacher of truth!

2. But it may be pleaded that our Lord, in declaring His ignorance of the day of the last judgment, does positively assign a specified limit to the knowledge actually possessed by His Human Soul during His ministry. 'Of that day,' He says, 'and that hour knoweth no man, no, not the angels which are in heaven, neither the Son, but the Father[t].' 'If these words,' you

wisdom,' when this element is, so to speak, taken possession of a second time by means of personal inquiry and reflection. This is, of course, a very remote analogy to the Sacred Subject discussed in the text, but it may serve to suggest how the facts of an infused knowledge and a real προέκοπτε σοφίᾳ in our Lord's Human Soul may have been compatible.

[s] The following remarks of Dr. Klee will be read with interest. Dogmatik, p. 511: 'Der Menschheit Christi kann keine absolute Vollendung und Imperfectibilität der Erkenntniss von Anfang an zugelegt werden, weil dann Christus im Eingange in seine Glorie in Bezug auf sie unverherrlicht geblieben wäre, was nicht wohl angenommen werden kann; weil ferner dann in Christo eine wahrhafte Allwissenheit angenommen werden müsste, was mit der menschlichen Natur und dem menschlichen Willen nicht wohl zu vereinbaren ist; und wenn Einige sich damit helfen zu können glaubten, dass diese Allwissenheit immer nur eine aus Gnade mitgetheilte wäre, so ist dagegen zu bemerken, dass die Menschheit dann aus Gnade auch die andern göttlichen Attribute, z. B. Allmacht haben könnte, und wenn man dieses mit der Entgegnung aus dem Felde zu schlagen glaubt, dass die Allmacht die Gottheit selbst, mithin absolut incommunicabel ist, so muss erwidert werden, dass die Allwissenheit ebenso Gottes Wesen selbst, somit unmittheilbar ist.'

[t] St. Mark xiii. 32: περὶ δὲ τῆς ἡμέρας ἐκείνης καὶ τῆς ὥρας, οὐδεὶς οἶδεν, οὐδὲ οἱ ἄγγελοι οἱ ἐν οὐρανῷ, οὐδὲ ὁ Υἱὸς, εἰ μὴ ὁ Πατήρ.

[LECT.

urge, 'do not refer to His ignorance as God, they must refer to His ignorance in the only other possible sense, that is to say, to His ignorance as Man.'

Of what nature then is the 'ignorance' to which our Lord alludes in this much-controverted text? Is it a real matter-of-fact ignorance, or is it an ignorance which is only ideal and hypothetical? Is it an ignorance to which man, as man, is naturally subject, but to which the Soul of Christ, the Perfect Man, was not subject, since His human intelligence was always illuminated by an infused omniscience [u]? or is it an economical as distinct from a real ignorance? Is it the ignorance of the Teacher, who withholds from His disciples a knowledge which He actually possesses, but which it is not for their advantage to acquire [x]? or is it the ignorance which is compatible with implicit knowledge? Does Christ implicitly know the date of the day of judgment, yet, that He may rebuke the forwardness of His disciples, does He refrain from contemplating that which is potentially within the range of His mental vision? Is He deliberately turning away His gaze from the secrets which are open to it, and which a coarse, earthly curiosity would have greedily and quickly investigated [y]?

With our eye upon the literal meaning of our Lord's words, must we not hesitate to accept any of these explanations? It is indeed true that to many very thoughtful and saintly minds, the words, 'neither the Son,' have not appeared to imply any 'ignorance' in the Son, even as Man. But antiquity does not furnish any decisive consent in favour of this belief; and it might seem, however involuntarily, to put a certain force upon the direct sense of the passage. There is no sufficient ground for questioning the correctness of the text [z]; and here, as always, 'if a literal explanation will stand, the furthest from the letter is commonly the worst.' If elsewhere, in the course of these lectures, we have appealed to the literal force of the great texts in

[u] St. Greg. Magn. Epist. lib. x. 39. ad Eulog.: '*In* naturâ quidem humanitatis novit diem et horam judicii, sed tamen hunc non *ex* naturâ humanitatis novit.'

[x] St. Aug. de Trin. i. 12: 'Hoc enim nescit, quod nescientes facit, id est, quod non ita sciebat ut tunc discipulis indicaret.' St. Ambros. de Fide, v. § 222: 'Nostrum assumpsit affectum, ut nostrâ ignoratione nescire se diceret, non quia aliquid ipse nesciret.' St. Hil. de Trin. ix. 62. See the passages accumulated by Dr. Newman, Select Treatises of St. Athanasius, p. 464, note *f*, Lib. Fath.

[y] So Lange, Leben Jesu, ii. 3, p. 1280.

[z] St. Ambr. de Fid. v. § 193: 'Primum veteres non habent codices Græci, quia nec Filius scit.'

St. John and St. Paul, as yielding a witness to the Catholic doctrine, can we substitute for the literal sense of the passage before us, a sense which, to say the least, is not that suggested by the letter? If then we should understand that our Lord in His Human Soul was, at the time of His speaking, actually ignorant of the day of the last judgment, we shall find ourselves sheltered by Fathers of unquestioned orthodoxy[a]. St. Irenæus discovers in our Lord's Human ignorance a moral argument against the intellectual self-assertion of his own Gnostic contemporaries[b]; while he attributes Omniscience to the Divine Nature of Christ in the clearest terms. St. Athanasius insists that the explanation which he gives, restricting our Lord's ignorance to His Human Soul, is a matter in which the faithful are well instructed[c]. He is careful to assert again and again our Lord's omniscience as God the Word; he attributes Christ's 'ignorance' as Man to the condescending love by which He willed to be like unto us in all things[d], and compares it, accordingly, to His hunger

[a] Klee says: 'It was impossible, in virtue of the Hypostatic Union, to ascribe to the Human Soul of Christ an absolute science and a perfect knowledge. On this subject, however, there is a very marked difference between the Fathers.' Dogmengeschichte, ii. 4. 7. Of the Fathers cited by Klee the majority assert a limitation of knowledge in our Lord's Human Soul.

[b] St. Iren. adv. Hær. ii. 28, 6: 'Irrationabiliter autem inflati, audaciter inenarrabilia Dei mysteria scire vos dicitis; quandoquidem et Dominus, ipse Filius Dei, ipsum judicii diem et horam concessit scire solum Patrem, manifestè dicens, "De die autem illâ et horâ nemo scit, neque Filius, sed Pater solus." (Marc. xiii. 32.) Si igitur scientiam diei illius Filius non erubuit referre ad Patrem, sed dixit quod verum est; neque nos erubescamus, quæ sunt in quæstionibus majora secundum nos, reservare Deo. Nemo enim super Magistrum est.' That St. Irenæus is here referring to our Lord's humanity is clear from the appeal to His example. Of His Divinity he says (ii. 28, 7): 'Spiritus Salvatoris, qui in eo est, scrutatur omnia, et altitudines Dei.' Cf. Bull, Def. Fid. Nic. ii. 5, 8.

[c] St. Athan. contr. Arian. Orat. iii. c. 45: *οἱ δὲ φιλόχριστοι καὶ χριστοφόροι γινώσκωμεν, ὡς οὐκ ἀγνοῶν ὁ Λόγος ᾗ Λόγος ἐστὶν ἔλεγεν, 'οὐκ οἶδα,' οἶδε γὰρ, ἀλλὰ τὸ ἀνθρώπινον δεικνὺς, ὅτι τῶν ἀνθρώπων ἴδιόν ἐστι τὸ ἀγνοεῖν, καὶ ὅτι σάρκα ἀγνοοῦσαν ἐνεδύσατο, ἐν ᾗ ὢν σαρκικῶς ἔλεγεν.* Dr. Mill resents the suggestion 'that when even an Athanasius could speak (with the Scriptures) of the limitation of human knowledge in the Incarnate Son, the improved theology of later times is entitled to censure the sentiment, as though impeaching His Divine Personality.' On the Nature of Christianity, p. 18.

[d] Ibid. c. 43: *ἀμέλει λέγων ἐν τῷ εὐαγγελίῳ περὶ τοῦ κατὰ τὸ ἀνθρώπινον αὐτοῦ· Πάτερ, ἐλήλυθεν ἡ ὥρα· δόξασόν σου τὸν Υἱόν· δῆλός ἐστιν ὅτι καὶ τὴν περὶ τοῦ πάντων τέλους ὥραν ὡς μὲν Λόγος γινώσκει, ὡς δὲ ἄνθρωπος ἀγνοεῖ· ἀνθρώπου γὰρ ἴδιον τὸ ἀγνοεῖν, καὶ μάλιστα ταῦτα. ἀλλὰ καὶ τοῦτο τῆς φιλανθρωπίας ἴδιον τοῦ Σωτῆρος. ἐπειδὴ γὰρ γέγονεν ἄνθρωπος, οὐκ ἐπαισχύνεται διὰ τὴν σάρκα τὴν ἀγνοοῦσαν εἰπεῖν, οὐκ οἶδα, ἵνα δείξῃ ὅτι εἰδὼς ὡς Θεὸς ἀγνοεῖ*

[LECT.

and thirst[e]. 'To whom,' exclaims St. Gregory Nazianzen, 'can it be a matter of doubt that Christ has a knowledge of that hour as God, but says that He is ignorant of it as Man[f]?' St. Cyril of Alexandria argues that our Lord's 'ignorance' as Man is in keeping with the whole economy of the Incarnation. As God, Christ did know the day of judgment; but it was consistent with the law of self-humiliation prescribed by His infinite love that He should assume all the conditions of real humanity, and therefore, with the rest, a limitation of knowledge. There would be no reasonable ground for offence at that which was only a consequence of the Divine Incarnation[g]. You will remark, my brethren, the significance of such a judgment when advanced by this great father, the uncompromising opponent of Nestorian error, the strenuous assertor of the Hypostatic Union, the chief

σαρκικῶς. οὐκ εἴρηκε γοῦν, οὐδὲ ὁ Υἱὸς τοῦ Θεοῦ οἶδεν, ἵνα μὴ ἡ θεότης ἀγνοοῦσα φαίνηται· ἀλλ' ἁπλῶς, 'οὐδὲ ὁ Υἱός,' ἵνα τοῦ ἐξ ἀνθρώπων γενομένου Υἱοῦ ἡ ἄγνοια ᾖ.

[e] St. Athan. contr. Arian. Orat. iii. c. 46: *ὥσπερ γὰρ ἄνθρωπος γενόμενος μετὰ ἀνθρώπων πεινᾷ καὶ διψᾷ καὶ πάσχει, οὕτως μετὰ μὲν τῶν ἀνθρώπων ὡς ἄνθρωπος οὐκ οἶδε, θεϊκῶς δὲ ἐν τῷ Πατρὶ ὢν Λόγος καὶ Σοφία οἶδε, καὶ οὐδέν ἐστιν ὃ ἀγνοεῖ.* Cf. ad Serap. ii. 9.

[f] St. Greg. Naz. Orat. xxx. 15: *καίτοι πῶς ἀγνοεῖ τι τῶν ὄντων ἡ Σοφία ὁ ποιητὴς τῶν αἰώνων, ὁ συντελεστὴς καὶ μεταποιητὴς, τὸ πέρας τῶν γενομένων; . . . ἢ πᾶσιν εὔδηλον, ὅτι γινώσκει μὲν, ὡς Θεὸς, ἀγνοεῖν δέ φησιν, ὡς ἄνθρωπος, ἄν τις τὸ φαινόμενον χωρίσῃ τοῦ νοουμένου; . . . . ὥστε τὴν ἄγνοιαν ὑπολαμβάνειν ἐπὶ τὸ εὐσεβέστερον, τῷ ἀνθρωπίνῳ, μὴ τῷ Θείῳ ταύτην λογιζομένους.*

[g] St. Cyril. Alex. Thesaurus, Op. tom. v. p. 221: *ὥσπερ οὖν συγκεχώρηκεν ἑαυτὸν ὡς ἄνθρωπον γενόμενον μετὰ ἀνθρώπων καὶ πεινᾷν καὶ διψῆν καὶ τὰ ἄλλα πάσχειν ἅπερ εἴρηται περὶ αὐτοῦ, τὸν αὐτὸν δὴ τρόπον ἀκόλουθον μὴ σκανδαλίζεσθαι κἂν ὡς ἄνθρωπος λέγῃ μετὰ ἀνθρώπων ἀγνοεῖν, ὅτι τὴν αὐτὴν ἡμῖν ἐφόρεσε σάρκα· οἶδε μὲν γὰρ ὡς Σοφία καὶ Λόγος ὢν ἐν Πατρί· μὴ εἰδέναι δέ φησι δι' ἡμᾶς καὶ μεθ' ἡμῶν ὡς ἄνθρωπος.* But see the whole discussion of the bearing of St. Mark xiii. 32 upon the Homoousion (Thesaurus, pp. 217–224). Certainly St. Cyril refers to the *οἰκονομία*, and he speaks of Christ's 'saying that He did not know, on our account,' and of His professing not to know 'humanly.' But this language does not amount to saying that Christ really did know, as Man, while for reasons of His own, which were connected with His love and *φιλανθρωπία*, He said He knew not. St. Cyril's mind appears to be, that our Lord did know as God, but in His love He assumed all that belongs to real manhood, and, therefore, actual limitation of knowledge. The word *οἰκονομία* does not seem to mean here simply a gracious or wise arrangement, but the Incarnation, considered as involving Christ's submission to human limitations. The Latin translator renders it 'administrationi sive Incarnationi.' St. Cyr. Op. v. p. 218. St. Cyril does not say that Christ really did know *as Man*; he must have said so, considering the bearing of his argument, had he believed it. He thus states the principle which he kept in view: *οὕτω γὰρ ἕκαστον τῶν λεγομένων ἐν τῇ οἰκείᾳ τάξει κείσεται· οὔτε τῶν ὅσα πρέπει γυμνῷ τῷ Λόγῳ καταφερομένων εἰς τὸ ἀνθρώπινον, οὔτε μὴν τῶν ἀνθρωπίνων ἀναβαινόντων εἰς τὸν τῆς θεότητος λόγον.* Thes. p. 253.

inheritor of all that is most characteristic in the theological mind of St. Athanasius. It is of course true that a different belief was already widely received within the Church: it is enough to point to the 'retractation' of Leporius, to which St. Augustine was one of the subscribing bishops[h]. But although a contrary judgment subsequently predominated in the West, it is certain that the leading opponents of Arianism did not shrink from recognising a limitation of knowledge in Christ's Human Soul, and that they appealed to His own words as a warrant for doing so[i].

'But have we not here,' you ask, 'albeit disguised under and recommended by the sanction of great names, the old heresy of the Agnoetæ?' No. The Agnoetæ attributed ignorance not merely to our Lord's Human Soul, but to the Eternal Word. They seem to have imagined a confusion of Natures in Christ, after the Eutychian pattern, and then to have attributed ignorance to that Divine Nature into which His Human Nature, as they held, was absorbed[k]. They were thus, on this point, in agreement with the Arians: while Eulogius of Alexandria, who wrote against them, admitted that Catholic fathers before him had taught that, as Man, Christ had been subject to a certain limitation of knowledge[l].

[h] Quoted by Petavius, De Incarn. xi.; c. 1, § 14. Leporius appears to have answered the Arian objections by restricting the ignorance to our Lord's Human Soul, after the manner of St. Athanasius. He retracts as follows: 'Ut autem et hinc nihil cuiquam in suspicione derelinquam, tunc dixi, immò ad objecta respondi, Dominum nostrum Jesum Christum secundum hominem ignorare: sed nunc non solum dicere non præsumo, verum etiam priorem anathematizo prolatam in hâc parte sententiam.' Leporius, however, seems really to have anticipated Nestorius in teaching a complete separation of our Lord's Two Natures. Klee, Dogmengesch. ii. 4. 4.

[i] Compare Bishop Forbes on Nic. Creed, p. 146, 2nd ed. And see St. Hil. in Matt. Comm. c. 26, n. 4; Theodoret in Ps. xv. § 7, quoted by Klee.

[k] See Suicer in voc. 'Αγνοηταὶ, i. p. 65: 'Hi docebant divinam Christi naturam (hanc enim solam post Unionem agnoscebant, tanquam absorpta esset planè humana), quædam ignorâsse, ut horam extremi judicii.' Eulogius of Alexandria, who wrote against them, denied any actual limitation of knowledge in Christ's Manhood, but admitted that earlier Fathers had taught this, *πρὸς τὴν τῶν 'Αρειανῶν μανίαν ἀντιφερόμενοι*; but, as he thinks, because *οἰκονομικώτερον ἐδοκίμασαν ἐπὶ τῆς ἀνθρωπότητος ταῦτα φέρειν ἢ παραχωρεῖν ἐκείνους μεθέλκειν ταῦτα κατὰ τῆς θεότητος.* Apud Photium, Cod. 230, ed. Bekker. p. 284, 6, sub fin. Klee distinguishes between the teaching of those Fathers who denied that the Human Soul of Christ possessed unlimited knowledge, and that of the Agnoetæ, who 'speaking of the Person of Christ without any limitations,' maintained that He did not know the day of judgment. Dogmengeschichte, ii. 4. § 7.

[l] It is remarkable that 'die Ansicht dass Christi Menschheit gleich nach der Vereinigung mit dem Logos Alles wusste, als Irrthum des Arnold von

'At any rate,' you rejoin, 'if our Lord's words are to be taken literally, if they are held to mean that the knowledge of His Human Soul is in any degree limited, are we not in danger of Nestorian error? Does not this conjunction of "knowledge" and "ignorance" in one Person, and with respect to a single subject, dissolve the unity of the God-man [m]? Is not this intellectual dualism inconsistent with any conception we can form of a single personality? Cannot we understand the indisposition of later theologians to accept the language of St. Athanasius and others without an explanation, even although a sense which it does not of itself suggest is thereby forced upon it?'

The question to be considered, my brethren, is whether such an objection has not a wider scope than you intend. Is it not equally valid against other and undisputed contrasts between the Divine and Human Natures of the Incarnate Son? For example, as God, Christ is omnipresent; as Man, He is present at a particular point in space [n]. Do you say that this, however mysterious, is more conceivable than the co-existence of ignorance and knowledge, with respect to a single subject in a single personality? Let me then ask whether this co-existence of ignorance and knowledge is more mysterious than a co-existence of absolute blessedness and intense suffering? If the Scriptural words which describe the sufferings of Jesus are understood literally, without establishing Nestorianism; why are we in danger of Nestorianism if we understand Him to be speaking of His Manhood, when He asserts that the Son is ignorant of the day of judgment? If Jesus, as Man, did not enjoy the Divine attribute of perfect blessedness, yet without prejudice to His full possession of it, as God; why could He not, in like manner, as Man, be without the Divine attribute of perfect knowledge? If as He knelt in Gethsemane, He was in one sphere of existence All-blessed, and in another 'sore amazed, very heavy, sorrowful even unto death;' might He not with equal truth be in the

Villanova 1309 förmlich verurtheilt worden.' Klee, Dogmatik, p. 511. Arnold attempted to maintain that his opinion was a necessary consequence of the Hypostatic Union. 'Quantum citò anima Christi fuit unita Divinitati, statim ipsa anima scivit omnia, quæ Deus scit; quia alias, ut dicebat, non fuisset cum eâ una persona, præcipuè quia scire est circumstantia pertinens ad suppositum individuale, et non ad naturam.' Eimeric. Direct. inquis. ii. qu. 11. qu. by Klee, Dogmengesch. ii. 4, 8.

[m] Stier, Reden Jesu in Matt. xxiv. 36.

[n] Scotus Erigena first taught the ubiquity of our Lord's Manhood; in more recent times it was prominently put forward by Luther, as an explanation of his teaching on the Eucharist. See Hooker, E. P. v. 55. 2-7.

one Omniscient, and in the other subject to limitations of knowledge? The difficulty [o] is common to all the contrasts of the Divine Incarnation; but these contrasts, while they enhance our sense of our Lord's love and condescension, do not destroy our apprehension of the Personal Unity of the Incarnate Christ [p]. His Single Personality has two spheres of existence; in the one It is all-blessed, undying, and omniscient; in the other It meets with pain of mind and body, with actual death, and with a correspondent liability to a limitation of knowledge. No such limitation, we may be sure, can interfere with the completeness of His redemptive office. It cannot be supposed to involve any ignorance of that which the Teacher and Saviour of mankind should know; while yet it suffices to place Him as Man in a perfect sympathy with the actual conditions of the mental life of His brethren [q].

If then this limitation of our Lord's human knowledge be admitted, to what does the admission lead? It leads, properly speaking, to nothing beyond itself. It amounts to this: that at the particular time of His speaking, the Human Soul of Christ was restricted as to Its range of knowledge in one particular direction.

For it is certain from Scripture that our Lord was constantly giving proofs, during His earthly life, of an altogether superhuman range of knowledge. There was not merely in Him the quick and penetrating discernment of a very holy soul,—not merely 'that unction from the Holy One' whereby Christians instinctively 'know all things' that concern their salvation. It

[o] Bishop Ellicott, in Aids to Faith, p. 445: 'Is there really any greater difficulty in such a passage [as St. Mark xiii. 32] than in John xi. 33, 35, where we are told that those holy cheeks were still wet with human tears, while the loud Voice was crying, "Lazarus, come forth!"'

[p] See Leibnitz's reply to Wissowatius, quoted by Lessing, Sammtl. Schrift. ix. 277: 'Potest quis ex nostrâ hypothesi simul esse ille qui nescit diem judicii, nempe homo, et ille qui est Deus Altissimus. Quæ hypothesis nostra, quod idem simul possit esse Deus et homo, quamdiu non evertitur, tamdiu contrarium argumentum petit principium.'

[q] See Klee, Dogmatik, p. 511: 'Auch das kann nicht gesagt werden, dass die menschliche Natur, wenn sie nicht absolut vollkommen und imperfectibel ist, dann mit Unwissenheit behaftet ist; denn nicht-allwissend ist nicht unwissend, sonst war Adam vor seinem Falle schon, und sind die Engel und Heiligen in ihrer Glorie immerfort in der Unwissenheit. Unwissenheit ist Negation des nothwendigen und ziemenden Wissens, und solche ist in der Menschheit Christi nicht, in welche die ihr verbundene Gottheit alles zu ihrem Berufe gehörige und durch sie alles zum Heile der Menschheit gehörige überströmte. Darum war auch die Steigerung der Wissenschaft der Menschheit keine Erlösung derselben, und fällt der Einwand, dass, wenn die Menschheit etwas nicht gewusst hätte, sie eine erlösungsbedürftige gewesen wäre, was doch nicht angenommen werden könne, weg.'

was emphatically a knowledge of hard matters of fact, not revealed to Him by the senses, and beyond the reach of sense. Thus He knows the exact coin which will be found in the mouth of the first fish which His apostle will presently take[r]. He bases His discourse on the greatest in the kingdom of heaven, on an accurate knowledge of the secret communings in which His conscience-stricken disciples had indulged on the road to Capernaum[s]. He gives particular instructions to the two disciples as to the finding of the ass on which He will make His entry into Jerusalem[t]. He is perfectly cognizant of the secret plottings of the traitor, although no human informant had disclosed them[u]. Nor is this knowledge supernaturally communicated at the moment; it is the result of an actual supra-sensuous sight of that which He describes. 'Before that Philip called thee,' He says to Nathanael, 'when thou wast under the fig-tree, I saw thee[x].' Do you compare this to the knowledge of secrets ascribed to Elisha[y], to Daniel[z], to St. Peter[a]? In these instances, as eminently in that of Daniel, the secret was revealed to the soul of the prophet or apostle. In the case of Christ we hear of no such revelation; He speaks of the things of heaven with a calm familiarity, which is natural to One Who knows them as beholding them 'in Himself[b].'

Indeed, our Lord's knowledge embraced two districts, each of which really lies open only to the Eye of the Most High. We will not dwell on His knowledge of the unsuspected future, a knowledge inherent in Him, as it was imparted to those prophets in whom His Spirit had dwelt. We will not insist on His knowledge of a strictly contingent futurity, such as is involved in His positive assertion that Tyre and Sidon would have repented of their sins, *if* they had enjoyed the opportunities of Chorazin and Bethsaida[c]; although such knowledge as this, considering the vast survey of motives and circumstances which it implies, *must* be strictly proper to God alone. But He knew the secret heart of man, and He knew the hidden thought and purpose of the Most High God. Such a 'discerner' was He 'of the thoughts and intents' of human hearts[d], so truly did His

[r] St. Matt. xvii. 27.
[s] St. Luke ix. 47: *ἰδὼν τὸν διαλογισμὸν τῆς καρδίας αὐτῶν.*
[t] St. Matt. xxi. 2; St. Mark xi. 2; St. Luke xix. 30.
[u] St. John xiii. 11. [x] Ibid. i. 49. [y] 2 Kings vi. 9, 32.
[z] Dan. ii. 19. [a] Acts v. 3. [b] St. John vi. 61: *ἐν ἑαυτῷ.*
[c] St. Matt. xi. 21.
[d] Heb. iv. 12: *κριτικὸς ἐνθυμήσεων καὶ ἐννοιῶν καρδίας.*

Apocalyptic title, the 'Searcher of the reins and hearts [e],' belong to Him in the days of His historical manifestation, that 'He needed not that any should testify to Him of men, for He knew what was in man [f].' This was not a result of His taking careful note of peculiarities of action and character manifested to the eye by those around Him, but of His 'perceiving in His Spirit' and 'knowing in Himself [g]' the unuttered reasonings and volitions which were taking shape, moment by moment, within the secret souls of men, just as clearly as He saw physical facts not ordinarily appreciated except by sensuous perception. This was the conviction of His apostles. 'We are sure,' they said, 'that Thou knowest all things [h].' 'Lord, Thou knowest all things,' cries St. Peter, 'Thou knowest that I love Thee [i].' Yet more, in the Eternal Father Jesus encounters no impenetrable mysteries; for Jesus no clouds and darkness are round about Him, nor is His way in the sea, nor His path in the deep waters, nor His footsteps unknown. On the contrary, our Lord reciprocates the Father's knowledge of Himself by an equivalent knowledge of the Father. 'As the Father knoweth Me, even so know I the Father [k].' 'No Man knoweth Who the Son is, but the Father; and Who the Father is, but the Son, and he to whom the Son will reveal Him [l].' Even if our Lord should be speaking, in this passage, primarily at least, of His Divine omniscience, He is also plainly speaking of a knowledge infused into and possessed by His Human Soul, and thus His words supply the true foil to His statement respecting the day of judgment. If that statement be construed literally, it manifestly describes, not the normal condition of His Human Intelligence, but an exceptional restriction. For the Gospel history implies that the knowledge infused into the Human Soul of Jesus was ordinarily and practically equivalent to omniscience. 'We may conjecture,' says Hooker, 'how the powers of that Soul are illuminated, Which, being so inward unto God, cannot choose but be privy unto all things which God worketh, and must therefore of necessity be endued with knowledge so far forth universal, though not with infinite knowledge peculiar to Deity Itself [m].'

[e] Rev. ii. 23. The message from Jesus to each of the angels of the seven Churches begins with the word οἶδα, as if in order to remind these bishops of His soul-penetrating omniscience.

[f] St. John ii. 25: οὐ χρείαν εἶχεν ἵνα τὶς μαρτυρήσῃ περὶ τοῦ ἀνθρώπου· αὐτὸς γὰρ ἐγίνωσκε τί ἦν ἐν τῷ ἀνθρώπῳ. [g] St. Mark ii. 8; v. 30.

[h] St. John xvi. 30: νῦν οἴδαμεν ὅτι οἶδας πάντα.

[i] Ibid. xxi. 17: Κύριε, σὺ πάντα οἶδας· σὺ γινώσκεις ὅτι φιλῶ σε.

[k] Ibid. x. 15. [l] St. Luke x. 22. [m] Eccl. Pol. v. 54. 7.

[LECT.

St. Paul's assertion that 'in Christ are hidden all the treasures of wisdom and knowledge [n],' may practically be understood of Christ's earthly life, no less than of His life of glory. If then His Human Intellect, flooded as it was by the infusion of boundless light streaming from His Deity, was denied, at a particular time, knowledge of the date of a particular future event, this may well be compared with that deprivation of the consolations of Deity, to which His Human affections and will were exposed when He hung dying on the Cross. If 'the Divine Wisdom,' as Bishop Bull has said, 'impressed its effects upon the Human Soul of Christ *pro temporum ratione*, in the degree required by particular occasions or emergencies [o],' this would be only one application of the principle recognised by St. Irenæus and Theodoret, and rendered familiar to many of us in the language of Hooker. 'As the parts, degrees, and offices of that mystical administration did require, which He voluntarily undertook, the beams of Deity did in operation always accordingly restrain or enlarge themselves [p].' We may not attempt rashly to specify the exact motive which may have determined our Lord to deny to His Human Soul at one particular date the point of knowledge here in question; although we may presume generally that it was a part of that condescending love which led Him to become 'in all things like unto His brethren.' That He was ever completely ignorant of aught else, or that He was ignorant on this point at any other time, are inferences for which we have no warrant, and which we make at our peril.

But it is not on this account alone that our Lord's Human ignorance of the day of judgment, if admitted, cannot be made the premiss of an argument intended to destroy His authority, when He sanctions the Mosaic authorship and historical trustworthiness of the Pentateuch. That argument involves a confusion between limitation of knowledge and liability to error; whereas, plainly enough, a limitation of knowledge is one thing,

[n] Col. ii. 3: *ἐν ᾧ εἰσι πάντες οἱ θησαυροὶ τῆς σοφίας καὶ τῆς γνώσεως ἀπόκρυφοι.*

[o] Bull, Def. Fid. Nic. ii. 5, 8: 'Quippe divinam Sapientiam menti humanæ Christi effectus suos impressisse *pro temporum ratione*, Christumque, quâ Homo fuit, *προκόψαι σοφίᾳ*, profecisse sapientiâ (Luc. ii. 52) adeoque pro tempore suæ ἀποστολῆς, quo istâ scientiâ opus non habebat (this seems to hint at more than anything which the text of the New Testament warrants) diem judicii universalis ignorare potuisse, nemini sano absurdum videbitur.'

[p] Hooker, Eccl. Pol. v. 54. 6. See Mr. Keble's references from Theodoret (Dial. iii. t. 4, pars. i. 232) and St. Iren. Hær. iii. c. 19. 3.

and fallibility is another. St. Paul says that 'we know in part[q],' and that 'we see through a glass darkly[r].' Yet St. Paul is so certain of the truth of that which he teaches, as to exclaim, 'If we or an angel from heaven preach any other Gospel to you than that which we have preached unto you, let him be accursed[s].' St. Paul clearly believed in his own infallibility as a teacher of religious truth; and the Church of Christ has ever since regarded his Epistles as part of an infallible literature. But it is equally clear that St. Paul believed his knowledge of religious truth to be limited. Infallibility does not imply omniscience, any more than limited knowledge implies error. Infallibility may be conferred on a human teacher with very limited knowledge, by a special endowment preserving him from error. When we say that a teacher is infallible, we do not mean that his knowledge is encyclopædic, but merely that, when he does teach, he is incapable of propounding as truth that which, in point of fact, is not true[t].

Now the argument in question assumes that Christ our Lord, when teaching religious truth, was not merely fallible, but actually in serious error. If indeed our Lord had believed Himself to be ignorant of the authorship or true character of the Book of Deuteronomy, we may presume that He would not have fallen below the natural level of ordinary heathen honesty, by speaking with authority upon a subject with which He was consciously unacquainted. It is admitted that He spoke as believing Himself to be teaching truth. But was He, in point of fact, *not* teaching truth? Was that which He believed to be knowledge nothing better than a servile echo of contemporary ignorance? Was His knowledge really limited on a subject-matter, where He was Himself unsuspicious of the existence of a limitation? Was He then not merely deficient in information,

[q] 1 Cor. xiii. 9: *ἐκ μέρους γὰρ γινώσκομεν.*

[r] Ibid. ver. 12: *βλέπομεν γὰρ ἄρτι δι' ἐσόπτρου ἐν αἰνίγματι.*

[s] Gal. i. 8, 9.

[t] Cf. Bishop H. Browne, Pentateuch and Elohistic Psalms, p. 13: 'Ignorance does not of necessity involve error. Of course in *our* present state of being, and with our propensity to lean on our wisdom, ignorance is extremely likely to lead to error. But ignorance is not error: and there is not one word in the Bible which could lead us to suppose that our blessed Lord was liable to error in any sense of the word or in any department of knowledge. I do not say that we have any distinct statements to the contrary, but there is nothing like a hint that there was such a liability: whereas His other human infirmities, weakness, weariness, sorrow, fear, suffering, temptation, ignorance, all these are put forward prominently, and many of them frequently.'

but fallible; not merely fallible, but actually in error? and has it been reserved for the criticism of the nineteenth century to set Him right? It must be acknowledged that our Lord's statement respecting the day of judgment will not avail to sustain a deduction which supposes, not an admitted limitation of knowledge, but an unsuspected self-deception of a character and extent which, in the case of a purely human teacher, would be altogether destructive of any serious claim to teach substantial truth [u].

Nor is this all. The denial of our Lord's infallibility, in the form in which it has come before us of late years, involves an unfavourable judgment, not merely of His intellectual claims, but of the penetration and delicacy of His moral sense. This is the more observable because it is fatal to a distinction which has been projected, between our Lord's authority as a teacher of spiritual or moral truth, and His authority when dealing with those questions which enter into the province of historical criticism. If in the latter sphere He is said to have been liable and subject to error, in the former, we are sometimes told, His instinct was invariably unerring. But is this the case, if our Lord was really deceived in His estimate of the Book of Deuteronomy, and if further the account of the origin and composition of that book which is put forward by His censors be accepted as satisfactory? Our Lord quotes Deuteronomy as a work of the highest authority on the subject of man's relations and duties to God [x]. Yet we are assured that in point of fact this book was nothing better than a pious forgery of the age of Jeremiah, if indeed it was not a work of that prophet, in which he employed the name and authority of Moses as a restraint upon the increasing polytheism of the later years of king Josiah [y]. That

[u] If a human teacher were to decline to speak on a given subject, by saying that he did not know enough about it, this would not be a reason for disbelieving him when he proceeded to speak confidently on a totally distinct subject, thereby at least implying that he did know enough to warrant his speaking. On the contrary, his silence in the one case would be a reason for trusting his statements in the other. The argument which is under consideration in the text would have been really sound, if our Saviour had fixed the date of the day of judgment, and the event had shewn Him to have been mistaken.

[x] St. Matt. iv. 4, Deut. viii. 3; St. Matt. iv. 7, Deut. vi. 16; St. Matt. iv. 10, Deut. vi. 13, and x. 20.

[y] Colenso on the Pentateuch, vol. ii. p. 427: 'Supposing (to fix our ideas) that Jeremiah really wrote the book, we must not forget that he was a prophet, and, as such, habitually disposed to regard all the special impulses

hypothesis has been discussed elsewhere and by others on its own critical merits. Here it may suffice to observe, that if it could have been seriously entertained it would involve our Lord in something more than intellectual fallibility. If Deuteronomy is indeed a forgery, Jesus Christ was not merely ignorant of a fact of literary history. His moral perceptions were at fault. They were not sufficiently fine to miss the consistency, the ring of truth, in a document which professed to have come from the great Lawgiver with a Divine authority; while, according to modern writers, it was only the 'pious' fiction of a later age, and its falsehood had only not been admitted by its author, lest its 'effect' should be counteracted [z].

When, in the middle of the ninth century, the pseudo-

of his mind to religious activity as direct inspirations from the Divine Source of Truth. To us, with our inductive training and scientific habits of mind, the correct statement of *facts* appears of the first necessity; and consciously to misstate them, or to state as fact what we do not know or believe from *external* testimony to be fact, is a crime against truth. But to a man who believed himself to be in *immediate* communication with the Source of all Truth, this condition must have been reversed. The *inner* voice, which he believed to be the voice of the Divine Teacher, would become all-powerful—would silence at once all doubts and questionings. What it ordered him to do, he would do without hesitation, as by direct command of God, and all considerations as to morality or immorality would either not be entertained at all, or would only take the form of misgivings as to whether, possibly, in any particular case, the command itself was really Divine.

'Let us imagine, then, that Jeremiah, or any other contemporary seer, meditating upon the condition of his country, and the means of weaning his people from idolatry, *became possessed* with the idea of writing to them an address, as in the name of Moses, of the kind which we have just been considering, in which the laws ascribed to him, and handed down from an earlier age, which were now in many respects unsuitable, should be adapted to the present circumstances of the times, and re-enforced with solemn prophetical utterances. This thought, we may believe, would take in the prophet's mind the form of a Divine command. All question of *deception* or *fraus pia* would vanish.'

[z] Colenso on the Pentateuch, vol. ii. p. 429: 'Perhaps, at first, it was felt to be difficult or undesirable to say or do anything which might act as a check upon the zeal and energy which the king himself exhibited, and in which, as it seems, he was generally supported by the people, in putting down by force the gross idolatries which abounded in his kingdom. That impulsive effort, which followed immediately the reading of the "Book," might have been arrested, if he had been told at once the true origin of those awful words which had made so strong an impression on him. They were not less awful, indeed, or less true, because uttered in the name of Moses by such a prophet as Jeremiah. But still it is obvious that *their effect was likely to be greatly intensified under the idea that they were the last utterances of Moses himself.*'

Isidorian decretals were first brought from beyond the Alps to Rome, they were almost immediately cited by Nicholas I. in reply to an appeal of Hincmar of Rheims, in order to justify and extend the then advancing claims of the Roman Chair[a]. We must then either suppose that this Pope was really incapable of detecting a forgery, which no Roman Catholic writer would now think of defending[b], or else we must imagine that, in order to advance an immediate ecclesiastical object, he could condescend to quote a document which he knew to have been recently forged, as if it had been of ancient and undoubted authority. The former supposition is undoubtedly most welcome to the common sense of Christian charity; but it is of course fatal to any belief in the personal infallibility of Pope Nicholas I. A like dilemma awaits us in the Gospel history, if those unhappy theories respecting the Pentateuch to which I have alluded are seriously adopted. Before us is no mere question as to whether Christ's knowledge was or was not limited; the question is, whether as a matter of fact He taught or implied the truth of that which is not true, and which a finer moral sense than His might have seen to be false. The question is plainly, whether He was a trustworthy teacher of religious no less than of historical truth. The attempted distinction between a critical judgment of historical or philological facts, and a moral judgment of strictly spiritual and moral truths, is inapplicable to a case in which the moral judgment is no less involved than the intellectual; and we have really to choose between the infallibility, moral no less than intellectual, of Jesus Christ our Lord on the one hand, and the conjectural speculations of critics, of whatever degree of critical eminence, on the other.

Indeed, as bearing upon this vaunted distinction between spiritual truth, in which our Lord is still, it seems, to be an authority, and historical truth, in which His authority is to be set aside, we have words of His own which prove how truly He made the acceptance of the lower portions of His teaching a preliminary to belief in the higher. 'If I have told you earthly things, and ye believe not, how shall ye believe if I tell you of heavenly things[c]?' How indeed? If, when He sets the seal of His authority upon the writings of Moses as a whole, and upon the most miraculous incidents which they relate in detail, He

[a] Dean Milman, History of Latin Christianity, vol. ii. p. 379.
[b] Compare Walter, Lehrbuch des Kirchenrechts, pp. 206 210.
[c] St. John iii. 12.

is really only the uneducated Jew who ignorantly repeats and reflects the prejudice of a barbarous age; how shall we be sure that when He reveals the Character of God, or the precepts of the new life, or the reality and nature of the endless world, He is really trustworthy—trustworthy as an Authority to whom we are prepared to cling in life and in death? You say that here your conscience ratifies His teaching,—that the 'enthusiasm of humanity' which is in you sets its seal upon this higher teaching of the Redeemer of men. Is then your conscience in very truth the ultimate and only teacher? Have you anticipated, and might you dispense with, the teaching of Christ? And what if your conscience, as is surely not impossible, has itself been warped or misled? What if, in surveying even the moral matter of His teaching, you still assume to exercise a 'verifying faculty,' and object to this precept as ascetic, and to that command as exacting, and to yonder most merciful revelation of an endless woe as 'Tartarology!' Alas! brethren, experience proves it, the descent into the Avernus of unbelief is only too easy. There are broad highways in the life of faith, just as in the life of morality, which a man cannot leave without certain risk of losing his way in a trackless wilderness. To deny our Lord's infallibility, on the precarious ground of a single known limitation of knowledge in His human intellect, is not merely an inconsequence, it is inconsistent with any serious belief in His real Divinity. The common sense of faith assures us that if Christ is really Divine, His infallibility follows as a thing of course. The man who sincerely believes that Jesus Christ is God will not doubt that His every word standeth sure, and that whatever has been sealed and sanctioned by His supreme authority is independent of, and unassailable by, the fallible judgment of His creatures respecting it.

(β) If the doctrine of Christ's Divinity implies that as a teacher of truth He is infallible, it also illuminates His suffering death upon the Cross with an extraordinary significance.

The degrees of importance which are attributed to the several events and stages of our Lord's life on earth, will naturally vary with the variations of belief respecting His Person. With the Humanitarian, for instance, the dominant, almost the exclusive, interest will be found to centre in Christ's Ministry, as affording the largest illustrations of His Human Character and of His moral teaching. The mysteries which surround His entrance into and His departure from our human world, will have been thrown into the background as belonging to questions of a very inferior degree of importance, or possibly, as at best serving to illustrate the legendary creativeness of a subsequent age. Perhaps a certain historical and chronological value will still be allowed to attach to Christ's Birth. Perhaps, if His Resurrection be admitted to have been a matter of historical occurrence, a high evidential significance will continue to be assigned to it, such as was recognised by Priestley and by all Socinians of the last generation. And to a Humanitarian, the interest of Christ's Death will be of a yet higher kind. For Christ's Death enters into His moral Self-manifestation; it is the heroic climax of His devotion to truth; it is the surest seal which a teacher can set upon his doctrine. Thus a Humanitarian will admit that the dying Christ saves the world by enriching its stock of moral life, by setting before the eyes of men, for all future time, the example of a transcendent sacrifice of self. But in the bare fact that Jesus died, Humanitarianism sees no mystery beyond that which attaches to the death of any ordinary man. The Crucifixion is simply regarded as a practical appendix to the Sermon on the Mount. And thus to the Socinian pilgrim, the mountain of the beatitudes and the shores of the Sea of Galilee will always and naturally appear more worthy of reverence and attention, than the spot on which Mary brought her Son into the world, or than the hill on which Jesus died.

Far otherwise must it ever be with a sincere believer in our Saviour's Godhead. Not that he can be insensible to the commanding moral interest which the Life and teaching of the Perfect Man ever rouses in the heart of Christians. That Life and that teaching have indeed for him a meaning into which the Humanitarian cannot enter; since the believer knows that it is God Who lives and speaks in Jesus. But contemplating Jesus as the Incarnate God, he is necessarily attracted by those points in our Lord's earthly Life, at which the contrast is most vividly marked between His Divine and Eternal Nature and His state of humiliation as Man.

This attraction is reflected in the believer's religious thought, in his devotions, in the instinctive attitude of his interest towards the Life of Jesus. The creed expresses the thought of the whole company of the faithful. After stating that the Only-begotten Son, consubstantial with the Father, for us men and for our salvation came down from heaven and was made Man, the creed proceeds to speak of His Crucifixion, Sufferings, Burial, Resurrection, and Ascension. The creed makes no allusion to His example, or to the nature and contents of His doctrine. In an analogous sense the Litany gives utterance to the devotion of the collective Church. In the Litany, Jesus, our 'Good Lord,' is entreated to deliver us 'by' the successive mysteries of His earthly Self-manifestation. Dependent on the mystery of His holy Incarnation are His 'holy Nativity and Circumcision,' His 'Baptism, Fasting, and Temptation,' His 'Agony and Bloody Sweat,' His 'Cross and Passion,' His 'precious Death and Burial,' His 'glorious Resurrection and Ascension.' Here again there is no reference to His sinless example, or to His words of power. Why is this? Is it not because the thought of the Church centres most persistently upon the Person of Jesus? His teaching and His example, although they presuppose His Divinity, yet in many ways appeal to us independently of it. But the significance of His birth into the world, of His varied sufferings[d], of His death, of His rising from the tomb, and of His ascent to heaven, resides chiefly, if not altogether, in the fact that His Person is Divine. That truth illuminates these features of His earthly Self-manifestation, which else might be thrown into the shade by the moral beauty of His example or of His doctrine. The birth and death of a mere man, and even the resurrection and glorification of a mere man, would only be the accessories of a higher interest centring in the range and influence of his ideas, in the force and consistency of his conduct, in the whole bearing of his moral and intellectual action upon the men of his time. But when He Who is born, Who suffers, Who dies, Who rises and ascends, is known to be personally and literally God, it is inevitable that the interest of thought and devotion should take a direction in which the 'mystery of godliness' is most directly and urgently felt. Christian devotion necessarily hovers around those critical turning-points in the Self-manifestation of the Infinite and Almighty Being, at which His gracious and immeasurable Self-humiliation most powerfully illustrates His boundless love, by the contrast which it yields to the majesty of His Divine and Eternal Person. No one would care for the birthplace or grave of the philosopher, when he could visit the scene of his intellectual victories; but the Christian pilgrim, in all ages of the Church, is less riveted by the lake-side and mountains of Galilee, than by those sacred sites, where his God and Saviour

[d] Cf. in this connection Heb. x. 29, where an apostate from the Faith is described as *ὁ τὸν Υἱὸν τοῦ Θεοῦ καταπατήσας*, and 1 Cor. ii. 8, *τὸν Κύριον τῆς δόξης ἐσταύρωσαν*.

first drew human breath and where He poured forth His Blood upon the Cross of shame.

Let us imagine, if we can, that our Lord's life had been written, not by the blessed Evangelists, but by some modern Socinian or Humanitarian author. Would not the relative proportions assigned to the several parts of His life have been very different from those which we find in the New Testament? We should have been presented with an analytical exposition of the moral greatness of Christ, in its several bearings upon the individual and social life of man; and His teaching would have been insisted upon as altogether eclipsing in importance any questions which might be raised as to His 'origin' or His 'place in the world of spirits.' As for His Death, it would of course have been introduced as the natural result of His generous conflict with the great evils and corruptions of His day. But this closing episode would have been treated hurriedly and with reserve. The modern writer would have led us to the foot of Calvary. There he would have left us to our imagination, and all that followed would have been summarized in a couple of sentences. The modern writer would have avoided any appearance of giving prominence to the 'physical aspects' of the tragedy, to the successive insults, cruelties, cries, which indicated so many distinct phases of mental or bodily agony in the sufferer. He would have argued that to dwell intently on these things was unnecessarily harrowing to the feelings, and moreover, that it might distract attention from the general moral interest to which the Death of Jesus was, in his judgment, only subsidiary. Clearly he would not have followed in the track of the Evangelists. For the four Evangelists, while the plan and materials of their several narratives present many points of difference, yet concur in assigning an extraordinary importance, not merely to the general narrative of the Passion, but to its minute details. This is more in harmony with the genius of St. Mark and St. Luke than with that of St. Matthew; but considering the scope and drift of the fourth Gospel, it is at first sight most remarkable in St. John. For instead of veiling the humiliations of the Word Incarnate, St. John regards them as so many illustrations of His 'glory;' and, indeed, each of the four evangelical narratives, however condensed may be its earlier portions, expands into the minute particularity of a diary, as it approaches the foot of the Cross.

Now this concurrent disposition of the four Evangelists is eminently suggestive. It implies that there is a momentous interest attaching, not merely to the Death of Christ as a whole, but to each stage and feature of the great agony in detail. It implies that this interest is not merely moral and human, but of a higher and distinct kind. The moral requirements of the history would have been satisfied, had we been compendiously informed that Christ died at last in attestation of the moral truth which He taught; but this detailed enumeration of the successive stages and shades of suffering, both physical and mental, leads the devout Christian insensibly to look beneath the varying phases of protracted agony, at the unruffled, august, eternal Person of the insulted Sufferer; and thus Christian thought rests with more and more of anxious intensity upon the possible or probable results of an event so stupendous as the Death of Christ.

Upon such a problem, human reason, left to itself, could shed no light whatever. It could only be sure of this:—that much more must be involved in the Death of Christ than in the death of the best of men. Had Christ been merely human, greater love among men, greater enthusiasm for truth as truth, greater devotion to the sublimest of moral teachings and to the Will of the Universal Father, greater contempt for pleasure when pleasure is in conflict with duty, and for pain when pain is recommended by conscience, would certainly have followed upon His Death. These effects follow in varying degrees upon every sincere and costly act of human self-renouncement; and the moral kingdom of God is a vast treasure-house of saintly and living memories, in which the highest place of honour is for ever assigned to those who exhibit the most perfect sacrifice of self. Nor, most assuredly, is any the least and lowest act of sacrifice destined to perish: it thrills on in its undying force through the ages; it kindles, first in one and then in another unit of the vast company of moral beings, a new devotion to truth, to duty, to man, to God. But when we know that Jesus Christ is God, we are prepared to hear that something much more stupendous than any moral impulse, however strong and enduring, must have resulted from His Death—something (as yet we know not what) reaching far beyond the sphere and laws of history, beyond the world of sense and of time, of natural moral sequence, and of those ascertainable or hidden influences which pass on from man to man and from age to age.

Nowhere is the illuminative force of Christ's Divinity more felt than here. The tremendous premiss, that He Who died upon the Cross is truly God, when seriously and firmly believed, avails to carry the believer forward to any representation of the efficacy of His Death which rests upon an adequate authority.

'No person,' says Hooker [e], 'was born of the Virgin but the Son of God, no person but the Son of God baptized, the Son of God condemned, the Son of God and no other person crucified; which one only point of Christian belief, *the infinite worth of the Son of God*, is the very ground of all things believed concerning life and salvation by that which Christ either did or suffered as man in our behalf.' 'That,' says Bishop Andrewes, 'which setteth the high price upon this Sacrifice is this, that He which offereth it to God, is God [f].' 'Marvel not,' says St. Cyril of Jerusalem, 'if the whole world has been redeemed, for He Who has died for us is no mere man, but the Only-begotten Son of God [g].' 'Christ,' says St. Cyril of Alexandria, 'would not have been equivalent [as a sacrifice] for the whole creation, nor would He have sufficed to redeem the world, nor have laid down His life by way of a price for it, and poured forth for us His precious Blood, if He be not really the Son, and God of God, but a creature [h].'

This, as has been already noticed, is St. Peter's meaning when he says that we were not redeemed with corruptible things, as silver and gold, but with the precious Blood of Christ, as of a Lamb without blemish and immaculate [i]. This underlies St. Paul's contrast between the blood of bulls and goats and the

[e] Eccl. Pol. v. 52. 3.

[f] Second Sermon on the Passion. For other references, see Rev. W. Bright's Sermons of St. Leo, p. 89.

[g] Catech. 13. 2: μὴ θαυμάζῃς εἰ κόσμος ὅλος ἐλυτρώθη, οὐ γὰρ ἦν ἄνθρωπος ψιλὸς, ἀλλ' Υἱὸς Θεοῦ μονογενὴς ὁ ὑπεραποθνήσκων. St. Proclus, Hom. in Incarn. c. 5: ἔδει τοίνυν δυοῖν θάτερον, ἢ πᾶσιν ἐπαχθῆναι τὸν ἐκ τῆς καταδίκης θάνατον, ἐπειδὴ καὶ πάντες ἥμαρτον· ἢ τοιοῦτον δοθῆναι πρὸς ἀντίδοσιν τίμημα, ᾧ πᾶν ὑπῆρχε δικαίωμα πρὸς παραίτησιν. Ἄνθρωπος μὲν οὖν σῶσαι οὐκ ἠδύνατο, ὑπέκειτο γὰρ τῷ χρέει τῆς ἁμαρτίας. Ἄγγελος ἐξαγοράσασθαι τὴν ἀνθρωπότητα οὐκ ἴσχυεν, ἠπόρει γὰρ τοιούτου λύτρου. Λοιπὸν οὖν ὁ ἀναμάρτητος Θεὸς ὑπὲρ τῶν ἡμαρτηκότων ἀποθανεῖν ὤφειλεν· αὕτη γὰρ ἐλείπετο μόνη τοῦ κακοῦ ἡ λύσις. c. 6: ὢ τῶν μεγάλων πραγμάτων! ἄλλοις ἐπραγματεύσατο τὸ ἀθάνατον, αὐτὸς γὰρ ὑπῆρχεν ἀθάνατος. τοιοῦτος γὰρ ἄλλος κατ' οἰκονομίαν οὔτε γέγονεν, οὔτε ἦν, οὔτε ἔσται ποτὲ, ἢ μόνος ἐκ τῆς παρθένου τεχθεὶς Θεὸς καὶ ἄνθρωπος· οὐκ ἀντιταλαντεύουσαν μόνον ἔχων τὴν ἀξίαν τῷ πλήθει τῶν ὑποδίκων, ἀλλὰ καὶ πάσαις ψήφοις ὑπερέχουσαν. c. 9: ἄνθρωπος ψιλὸς σῶσαι οὐκ ἴσχυε, Θεὸς γυμνὸς παθεῖν οὐκ ἠδύνατο. τί οὖν; αὐτὸς ὢν Θεὸς ὁ Ἐμμανουὴλ, γέγονεν ἄνθρωπος. (Labbe, iii. 13 sq.)

[h] St. Cyril. Alex. de Sanctâ Trinitate, dial. 4, tom. v. pp. 508, 509. See too Ad Reginas, i. c. 7; Labbe, iii. 112.

[i] 1 St. Pet. i. 19.

Blood of Christ offering Himself without spot to God[j]. This is the substance of St. John's announcement that the Blood of Jesus Christ the Son of God cleanseth us from all sin[k]. Apart from this illuminating doctrine of the Godhead of Jesus Christ crucified, how overstrained and exaggerated are the New Testament representations of the effects of His Death! He has redeemed man from a moral and spiritual slavery[l]; He has made a propitiation for our sins[m]; He has really reconciled God and His creatures[n]. But how is such a redemption possible, unless the price be infinitely costly? How could such a propitiation be offered, save by One Whose intrinsic worth might tender some worthy offering from a boundless Love to a perfect Justice? How was a real reconciliation between God and His creatures to be effected, unless the Reconciler had some natural capacity for mediating, unless He could represent God to man no less truly than man to God? How could He 'exchange' Divine glory for human misery, or raise man in his misery to companionship with God, unless He were Himself Divine? Alas! brethren, if Jesus Christ be not God, the promises of redemption to which penitent and dying sinners cling with such thankful tenacity, forthwith dissolve into the evanescent forms of Jewish modes of thought, and unsubstantial misleading metaphors. If Jesus be not God, we stand face to face in the New Testament, not with the unsearchable riches, the boundless mercy of a Divine Saviour, able 'to save to the uttermost those that come unto God by Him,' but only with the crude and clinging prejudices of His uneducated or semi-educated followers. But if it be certain that 'in this was manifested the love of God towards us, because that God sent His Only-begotten Son into the world, that we might live through

[j] Heb. ix. 13, 15. See Lect. VI, p. 344, note x.

[k] 1 St. John i. 7.

[l] Ἀπολύτρωσις presupposes the slavery of humanity, from which Christ our Lord redeems us by the λύτρον of His precious Blood. St. Matt. xx. 28; 1 Cor. i. 30; Eph. i. 7, 14; iv. 30. The idea of purchase out of bondage is vividly expressed by the verb ἐξαγοράζειν, Gal. iii. 13; iv. 5.

[m] ἱλασμός presupposes the unexpiated sin of humanity, for which Christ makes a propitiation. 1 St. John ii. 2; iv. 10; Heb. ii. 17. Our Lord Himself is the θυσία, the προσφορά (Eph. v. 2; Heb. x. 12); He is the πάσχα (1 Cor. v. 7); He is the sacrificial ἀμνός (St. John i. 29, 36; 1 St. Peter i. 19); He is the slain ἀρνίον (Rev. v. 6, 8, 12, 13; vi. 1).

[n] καταλλαγή presupposes the existence of an enmity between God and man, which is done away by Christ's 'exchanging' His glory for our misery and pain, while He gives us His glory. Rom. v. 10; 2 Cor. v. 18, 19.

[LECT.

Him [o],' then the disclosures of revelation respecting the efficacy of His Death do not appear to be excessive. Vast as is the conclusion of a world of sinners redeemed, atoned for, reconciled, the premiss that Jesus Crucified is truly God more than warrants it. And the accompaniments of the Passion are such as might have been anticipated by the faith of the Church. Why those darkened heavens? Why that rent veil in the temple? Why those shattered rocks? Why do those 'bodies of the saints which slept' return from the realms of death to the city of the living? Nature, could she speak, would answer that her Lord is crucified. But her convulsive homage before the Cross of Christ is as nothing when compared to a moral miracle of which the only sensible symptoms are an entreaty and a promise, uttered alike in human words. 'Not when Christ raised the dead, not when He rebuked the sea and the winds, not when He expelled the devils,—but when He was crucified, pierced with the nails, insulted, spit upon, reproached, reviled,—had He strength to change the evil disposition of the robber, to draw to Himself that soul, harder though it were than the rocks around, and to honour it with the promise, 'To-day shalt thou be with Me in Paradise [p].' That promise was a revelation of the depth and height of His redemptive power; it was a flash of His Godhead, illuminating the true meaning of His humiliations as Man. If then we believe Him to be God, we bow our heads before His Cross, as in the presence of fathomless mystery, while we listen to His apostles as they unfold the results of His Death. If we are perplexed with some difficulties in contemplating these results, we may remember that we are but hovering on the outskirts of a vast economy of mercy reaching far away beyond our furthest sight, and that the seen will one day be explained by the unseen. But at least no magnitude of redemptive mercies can possibly surprise us, when the Redeemer is known to be Divine; we say to ourselves with St. Paul, 'If God spared not His Own Son, but freely gave Him up for us all, how shall He not with Him also freely give us all things?'

(γ) As our Lord's Divinity is the truth which illuminates and sustains the world-redeeming virtue of His death, so in like manner it explains and justifies the power of the Christian Sacraments, as actual channels of supernatural grace.

To those who deny that Jesus Christ is God, the Sacraments are naturally nothing more than 'badges or tokens' of social co-

[o] 1 St. John iv. 9. Compare Eph. iv. 32: *ὁ Θεὸς ἐν Χριστῷ ἐχαρίσατυ ὑμῖν.* Tit. ii. 11; iii. 4.

[p] St. Chrysost. De Cruce et Latrone, Hom. i. § 2. tom. ii. 404.

operation[q]. The one Sacrament is only 'a sign of profession and mark of difference, whereby Christian men are discerned from others that be not christened[r].' The other is at best 'only a sign of the love that Christians ought to have one towards another[s].' Thus sacraments are viewed as altogether human acts; God gives nothing in them; He has no special relation to them[t]. They are regarded as purely external ceremonies, which may possibly suggest certain moral ideas by recalling the memory of a Teacher who died many centuries ago[u]. They help to save His name from dying out among men. Thus they discharge the functions of a public monument, or of a ribbon or medal implying membership in an association, or of an anniversary festival instituted to celebrate the name of some departed historical worthy. It cannot be said that in point of effective moral power they rise to the level of a good statue or portrait; since a merely outward ceremonial cannot recall character and suggest moral sympathy as effectively as an accurate rendering of the human countenance in stone, or colour, or the lines of an engraving. Rites, with a function so purely historical, are not likely to survive any serious changes in human feelings and associations. Men gradually determine to commemorate the object of their regard in some other way, which may perhaps be more in harmony with their personal tastes; they do not admit that this particular form of commemoration, although enjoined by the Author of Christianity, binds their consciences with the force of any moral obligation; they end by deciding that it is just as well to neglect such commemorations altogether.

If the Socinian and Zwinglian estimate of the Sacraments had been that of the Church of Christ, the Sacraments would long ago have been abandoned as useless ceremonies. But the Church has always seen in them not mere outward signs addressed to the taste or to the imagination, nor even signs (as Calvinism asserts) which are tokens of grace received inde-

[q] Art. XXV. condemns this Zwinglian account of Sacraments generally.

[r] Art. XXVII. condemns this Zwinglian account of Baptism.

[s] Art. XXVIII. condemns this Zwinglian account of the Holy Communion.

[t] Cat. Rac. Qu. 202: 'Quomodo confirmare potest nos in fide id, *quod nos ipsi facimus*, quodque, licet a Domino institutum, *opus tamen nostrum est, nihil prorsus miri in se continens*?'

[u] Ibid. Qu. 334: 'Christi institutum ut fideles ipsius panem frangant et comedant, et è calice bibant, mortis ipsius annuntiandæ causâ.' Ibid. 337: 'Nonne alia causa, ob quam cœnam instituit Dominus, superest? Nulla prorsus. Etsi homines multas excogitarint.'

pendently of them [x], but signs which, through the power of the promise and words of Christ, effect what they signify. They are '*effectual* signs of grace and God's good-will towards us, by the which He doth work invisibly in us [y].' Thus in baptism the Christian child is made 'a member of Christ, a child of God, and an inheritor of the Kingdom of Heaven [z].' And 'the Body and Blood of Christ are verily and indeed taken and received by the faithful in the Lord's Supper [a].'

This lofty estimate of the effective power of the Christian Sacraments is intimately connected with belief in the Divinity of the Incarnate Christ. The importance attached to the words in which Christ institutes and explains the Sacraments, varies concomitantly with belief in the Divinity of the Speaker. If the Speaker be held to be only man, then, in order to avoid imputing to him the language of inflated and thoughtless folly, it becomes necessary to empty the words of their natural and literal force by violent exegetical processes which, if applied generally, would equally destroy the witness of the New Testament to the Atonement or to the Divinity of Christ. But if Christ be in very truth believed to be the Eternal Son of God, then the words in which He provides for the communication of His life-giving Humanity in His Church to the end of time may well be allowed to stand in all the force and simplicity of their natural meaning. Baptism will then be the laver of a real regeneration [b]; the Eucharist will be a real 'communion of the

[x] See Cartwright, quoted by Hooker, Eccl. Pol. v. 60. 3, note.

[y] Art. XXV. Cf. P. Lombard, lib. iv. d. 1. 2: 'Sacramentum est invisibilis gratiæ visibilis forma. . . . Ita signum est gratiæ Dei, et invisibilis gratiæ forma, ut ipsius imaginem gerat et causa existat.' Church Catechism: 'An outward and visible sign of an inward and spiritual grace given unto us, ordained by Christ Himself, as a *means whereby* we receive the same, and a pledge to assure us thereof.' See Martensen, Christ. Dogm. p. 418, Clark's Transl.: 'The essential difference' [between Prayer and Sacraments] 'consists in this: the sacred tokens of the New Covenant contain also an *actual communication of the Being and Life* of the risen Christ, Who is the Redeemer and Perfecter, not only of man's spiritual, but of man's corporeal nature. In Prayer there is only a *unio mystica*, a real, yet only spiritual, psychological union: but in the Sacraments the deepest mystery rests in the truth that in them Christ communicates Himself, not only spiritually, but in His glorified corporeity.'

[z] Church Catechism.

[a] Ibid. Mr. Fisher observes that 'out of twenty-five questions of which the Catechism now consists, no less than seventeen relate exclusively to the nature and efficacy of the Sacraments.' Liturgical Purity, p. 293, 1st ed.

[b] Tit. iii. 5: διὰ λουτροῦ παλιγγενεσίας. Common Prayer-book, Office of Private Baptism: 'This child, who being born in original sin and in the

Body and Blood' of the Incarnate Jesus[c]. If, with our eye upon Christ's actual Godhead, we carefully weigh the momentous sentences in which He ordained[d], and the still more explicit terms in which He explained[e], His institutions; if we ponder well His earnestly enforced doctrine, that they who would have part in the Eternal Life must be branches of that Living Vine[f] whose trunk is Himself; if we listen to His

wrath of God, is now by the laver of regeneration in Baptism received into the number of the children of God.' For the connection between Baptismal grace and our Lord's Divinity, see St. Cyril Alex. de Rectâ Fide, c. 37: *Τί δρᾷς, ὦ οὗτος, κατακομίζων ἡμῶν εἰς γῆν τὴν ἐλπίδα; βεβαπτίσμεθα γὰρ οὐκ εἰς ἄνθρωπον ἁπλῶς, ἀλλ' εἰς Θεὸν ἐνηνθρωπηκότα, καὶ ἀνιέντα ποινῆς καὶ τῶν ἀρχαίων αἰτιαμάτων τοὺς τὴν εἰς αὐτὸν πίστιν ἐκδεδεγμένους . . . . ἀπολύων γὰρ ἁμαρτίας τὸν αὐτῷ προσκείμενον, τῷ ἰδίῳ λοιπὸν καταχρίει πνεύματι· ὅπερ ἐνίησι μὲν αὐτὸς, ὡς ἐκ Θεοῦ Πατρὸς Λόγος, καὶ ἐξ ἰδίας ἡμῖν ἀναπηγάζει φύσεως.* He quotes Rom. viii. 9, 10.

[c] 1 Cor. x. 16: *κοινωνία τοῦ αἵματος τοῦ Χριστοῦ . . . κοινωνία τοῦ σώματος τοῦ Χριστοῦ.* St. Just. Mart. Apol. i. 66: *Οὐ γὰρ ὡς κοινὸν ἄρτον οὐδὲ κοινὸν πόμα ταῦτα λαμβάνομεν· ἀλλ' ὃν τρόπον διὰ Λόγου Θεοῦ σαρκοποιηθεὶς Ἰησοῦς Χριστὸς ὁ Σωτὴρ ἡμῶν καὶ σάρκα καὶ αἷμα ὑπὲρ σωτηρίας ἡμῶν ἔσχεν, οὕτως καὶ τὴν δι' εὐχῆς λόγου τοῦ παρ' αὐτοῦ εὐχαριστηθεῖσαν τροφὴν, ἐξ ἧς αἷμα καὶ σάρκες κατὰ μεταβολὴν τρέφονται ἡμῶν, ἐκείνου τοῦ σαρκοποιηθέντος Ἰησοῦ καὶ σάρκα καὶ αἷμα ἐδιδάχθημεν εἶναι.* Cf. Dorner, Person Christi, Erster Theil, p. 435, note 47: 'Justin denkt sich den ganzen Christus in Verbindung mit dem Abendmahl. Auch so kann er sich diese unter dem Bilde der Incarnation denken, indem Christus die Elemente zum sichbaren Organ seiner Wirksamkeit und Selbstmittheilung macht, und das durch seine Erhöhung verlorne Moment der Sichtbarkeit seiner objectiven Erscheinung sich in jedem Abendmahl durch Assumtion der sichtbaren Elemente wieder herstellt.' For the connection between the Holy Eucharist and our Lord's Divinity, see St. Cyril Alex. Epist. Synod. ad Nestorium, c. 7: *Τὴν ἀναίμακτον ἐν ταῖς ἐκκλησίαις τελοῦμεν θυσίαν, πρόσιμέν τε οὕτω ταῖς μυστικαῖς εὐλογίαις καὶ ἁγιαζόμεθα, μέτοχοι γενόμενοι τῆς τε ἁγίας σαρκὸς, καὶ τοῦ τιμίου αἵματος τοῦ πάντων ἡμῶν Σωτῆρος Χριστοῦ· καὶ οὐχ ὡς σάρκα κοινὴν δεχόμενοι (μὴ γένοιτο) οὔτε μὴν ὡς ἀνδρὸς ἡγιασμένου καὶ συναφθέντος τῷ Λόγῳ κατὰ τὴν ἑνότητα τῆς ἀξίας, ἤγουν ὡς θείαν ἐνοίκησιν ἐσχηκότος, ἀλλ' ὡς ζωοποιὸν ἀληθῶς καὶ ἰδίαν αὐτοῦ τοῦ Λόγου. Ζωὴ γὰρ ὢν κατὰ φύσιν ὡς Θεὸς, ἐπειδὴ γέγονεν ἓν πρὸς τὴν ἑαυτοῦ σάρκα, ζωοποιὸν ἀπέφηνεν αὐτήν.* This epistle, given in Routh, Scr. Opusc. ii. 17, ed. 3, was written Nov. 430, and read with tacit approval, as it seems, at the General Council of Ephesus in 431. (See Bright's Hist. Ch. pp. 326, 333.) A similar passage is in St. Cyril's Explanatio xii. Capitum (tom. vi. p. 156), to the effect that the Body and Blood in the Holy Eucharist are *οὐχ ἑνὸς τῶν καθ' ἡμᾶς καὶ ἀνθρώπου κοινοῦ*, but *ἴδιον σῶμα καὶ αἷμα τοῦ τὰ πάντα ζωογονοῦντος Λόγου· κοινὴ γὰρ σὰρξ ζωοποιεῖν οὐ δύναται, καὶ τούτου μάρτυς αὐτὸς ὁ Σωτὴρ, λέγων, "Ἡ σὰρξ οὐκ ὠφελεῖ οὐδὲν, τὸ πνεῦμά ἐστι τὸ ζωοποιοῦν.'* So in his Comm. in Joan. lib. iv. (tom. iv. p. 361) he says that as Christ's Flesh, by union with the Word, Who is essentially Life, *ζωοποιὸς γέγονε*, therefore, *ὅταν αὐτῆς ἀπογευσόμεθα, τότε τὴν ζωὴν ἔχομεν ἐν ἑαυτοῖς.*

[d] St. Matt. xxviii. 19; xxvi. 26.

[e] St. John iii. 5; vi. 53 sqq.

[f] St. John xv. 1 sqq.

[LECT.

Apostle proclaiming that we are members of His Body, from His Flesh and from His Bones[g]; then in a sphere, so inaccessible to the measurements of natural reason, so absolutely controlled by the great axioms of faith, it will not seem incredible that 'as many as have been baptized into Christ' should really 'have put on Christ[h],' or that 'the Body of Jesus Christ which was given for us' should now, when received sacramentally, 'preserve our bodies and souls unto everlasting life[i].' In view of our Lord's Divinity, we cannot treat as so much profitless and vapid metaphor the weighty sentences which Apostles have traced around the Font and the Altar, any more than we can deal thus lightly with the precious hopes and promises that are graven by the Divine Spirit upon the Cross. The Divinity of Christ warrants the realities of sacramental grace as truly as it warrants the cleansing virtue of the Atoning Blood. If it forbids our seeing in the Great Sacrifice for sin, nothing higher than a moral exemplar, it also forbids our degrading the august institutions of the Divine Redeemer to the level of the dead ceremonies of the ancient law. And conversely, belief in the reality of sacramental grace protects belief in a Christ Who is really Divine. Sacraments, if fully believed in, furnish outworks in the religious thought and in the daily habits of the Christian, which necessarily and jealously guard the prerogatives and honour of his adorable Lord.

That depreciation of the Sacraments has often been followed by depreciation of our Lord's Eternal Person is a simple matter of history[j]. True, there have been and are earnest believers in our Lord's Divinity who deny the realities of sacramental grace. But experience appears to shew that their position may be only a transitional one. History illustrates the tendency to Humanitarian declension even in cases where sacramental belief, although imperfect, has been far nearer to the truth than is the bare naturalism of Zwingli[k]. Many English Presbyterian congre-

[g] Eph. v. 30. See Lect. VI, p. 352, note w. [h] Gal. iii. 27.

[i] Communion Service.

[j] Mill, University Sermons, p. 190; Gladstone on Church Principles, p. 185.

[k] Zwingli de Verâ et Falsâ Relig. Op. iii. p. 263. n. A: 'Est ergo sive eucharistia sive synaxis, sive cœna dominica nihil aliud quam commemoratio, quâ ii, qui se Christi morte et sanguine firmiter credunt patri reconciliatos esse, hanc vitalem mortem annunciant, hoc est laudant, gratulantur et prædicant. Jam ergo sequitur, quod qui ad hunc usum aut festivitatem conveniunt mortem domini commemoraturi, hoc est annunciaturi, sese unius corporis esse membra, sese unum panem esse ipso facto testentur . . . . .

gations, founded by men who fell away from the Church in the seventeenth century, were, during the eighteenth, absorbed into Arianism or Socinianism [l]. The pulpit and the chair of Calvin are filled by teachers who have, alas! much more in common with the Racovian Catechism than with the positive elements of the theology of the Institutes [m]. The restless mind of man cannot but at last press a principle to the real limit of its application, even although centuries should intervene between the premiss and the conclusion. If we imagine that the Sacraments are only

Qui ergo cum Christianis commeat, quum mortem domini annuntiant, qui simul symbolicum panem aut carnem edit, is nimirum posteà secundum Christi præscriptum vivere debet, nam experimentum dedit aliis, quod Christo fidat.' Here God does and gives nothing; the ceremony described is not a 'means of grace' but only and simply an act of man, a human ceremonial action, expressive of certain ideas and convictions, shared by those who take part in it. It is substantially the same account as that which is given in the formal documents of early Socinianism. (Cat. Rac. qu. 334, 335, 337.) It would be an extreme injustice to Calvin to identify his belief on the subject with these unspiritual errors. Calvin even says: 'Quicquid ad exprimendam veram *substantialemque* corporis ac sanguinis Domini communicationem, quæ sub sacris cœnæ symbolis fidelibus exhibetur, libenter recipio; atque ita ut *non imaginatione duntaxat aut mentis intelligentiâ percipere, sed ut re ipsa frui in alimentum vitæ æternæ intelligantur.*' Instit. iv. 17, 19. The force of this language was, however, practically destroyed by Calvin's doctrine of Divine decrees, which made sacramental grace wholly dependent upon the sense of election, that is to say, upon the subjective state, upon the feelings, of the believer, instead of upon the promise and word of Christ. Thus it happened that humble minds among Calvinists would naturally, in virtue of their very self-distrust, tend to adopt a Zwinglian estimate of the Eucharist: and, historically speaking, Calvinism has in this matter shewn a consistent disposition to degenerate in a Zwinglian direction. Belief in the reality of Sacramental grace is only secured, when men believe that such grace depends not on themselves but on the promise and words of their Saviour, in other words, that it is objective. And the objectivity of Sacramental grace implies of necessity an Omnipotent Saviour, Whose grace it is. St. Augustine's famous saying, 'Accedit verbum ad elementum, et fit Sacramentum,' is hopelessly unintelligible, unless He who institutes the Sacrament and warrants its abiding efficacy be indeed Divine.

[l] See Bogue and Bennett's History of Dissenters, iii. 240, 319; iv. 319, 383; and the Law Magazine, vol. xv. (May, 1836,) p. 348. In our own country, other Calvinistic communions have in general been happily preserved from such a fall. But the case of English Presbyterianism finds parallels in Geneva, in Holland, in France, and in America. Such loss of truth by others can never give Churchmen *any* 'controversial' satisfaction; the more truth is held by Dissenters, the better both for them, and for the honour of Christ. But the subject may suggest warnings to ourselves.

[m] Laing's Notes of a Traveller, pp. 324-5, quoted in Chr. Rem. July, 1863, p. 247.

[LECT.

picturesque memorials of an absent Christ, we are already in a fair way to believe that the Christ Who is thus commemorated as absent by a barren ceremony is Himself only and purely human. Certainly if Christ were not Divine, the efficacy of Sacraments as channels of graces that flow from His Manhood would be the wildest of fancies. Certainly if Sacraments are not thus channels of His grace, it is difficult to shew that they have any rightful place in a dispensation, from which the dead forms and profitless shadows of the synagogue have been banished, and where all that is authorized is instinct with the power of a heavenly life. The fact that such institutions as the Sacraments are lawful in such a religion as the Gospel, of itself implies their real efficacy: their efficacy points to the Godhead of their Founder. Instead of only reviving the thought of a distant past, they quicken all the powers of the Christian by union with a present and living Saviour; they assure us that Jesus of Nazareth is to us at this moment what He was to His first disciples eighteen centuries ago; they make us know and feel that He is the same yesterday, to-day, and for ever, unchanging in His human tenderness, because Himself the unchanging God. It is the doctrine of Christ's Divinity to which they point, and which in turn irradiates the perpetuity and the reality of their power.

(δ) It is unnecessary for us to dwell more at length upon the light which our Lord's Divinity sheds upon His Priestly office. We know that as His promise and presence make poor human words and simple elements the channels of His mercy, by taking them up into His kingdom and giving them a power which of themselves they have not, so it is His Divinity which makes His Intercession in Heaven so omnipotent a force. He intercedes above, by His very presence; He does not bend as a suppliant before the Sanctity of God; He is a Priest upon His Throne [n]. Nor may we linger over the bearings of His Divinity upon His Kingly office. The fact that He rules with a boundless power, may assure us that, whether willingly or by constraint, yet assuredly in the end, all moral beings shall be put under Him [o]. But you do not question the legitimacy of this obvious inference. And time forbids us to linger upon the

[n] Zech. vi. 13. Christ's perpetual presentation of Himself before the Father is that which constitutes His Intercession. It lasts until the Judgment, as the enduring antitype to the High Priest's presentation of the victim's blood in the Holy of Holies. Heb. viii. 3; ix. 24.

[o] 1 Cor. xv. 25; Heb. ii. 8.

topic, suggestive and interesting as it is. We pass then to consider an objection which will have been taking shape in many minds during the course of the preceding discussion.

III. You admit that the doctrine of Christ's Godhead illuminates the force of other doctrines in the Christian creed, and that it explains the importance attributed to her sacramental ordinances by the Christian Church. But you have the interests of morality at heart; and you are concerned lest this doctrine should not merely fail to stimulate the moral life of men, but should even deprive mankind of a powerful incentive to moral energy. The Humanitarian Christ is, you contend, the most precious treasure in the moral capital of the world. He is the Perfect Man; and men can really copy a life which a brother man has lived. But if Christ's Godhead be insisted on, you contend that His Human Life ceases to be of value as an ethical model for humanity. An example must be in some sense upon a level with those who essay to imitate it. A model being, the conditions of whose existence are absolutely distinct from the conditions which surround his imitators, will be deemed to be beyond the reach of any serious imitation. If then the dogma of Christ's Godhead does illuminate and support other doctrines, this result is, in your judgment, purchased at the cost of practical interests. A merely human saviour would at least be imitable; and he would thus better respond to the immediate moral necessities of man. For man is, after all, the child of common sense; and before he embarks upon a serious enterprise, he desires to be reasonably satisfied that he is not aiming at the impracticable.

1. Now this objection is of an essentially *à priori* character. It contends that, if Christ is God, His Manhood must be out of the reach of human imitation. It does not deny the fact that He has been most closely imitated by those who have believed most entirely in His true Divinity. In fact it seems to leave out of sight two very pertinent considerations.

(*a*) The objector appears to forget, on the one hand, that according to the terms of the Catholic doctrine, our Lord is truly and literally Man, and that it is His Human Nature which is proposed to our imitation. His Divinity does not destroy the reality of His Manhood, by overshadowing or absorbing it. Certainly the Divine attributes of Jesus are beyond our imitation; we can but adore a boundless Intelligence or a resistless Will. But the province of the imitable in the Life of Jesus is not indistinctly traced. As the Friend of publicans and sinners, as the Consoler of those who suffer, and as the Helper of those who want, Jesus Christ is at home among us. We can copy Him, not merely in the outward activities of charity, but in its inward temper; we can copy the tenderness, the meekness, the patience, the courage, which shine forth from His Perfect Manhood. His Human Perfections constitute indeed a faultless Ideal of Beauty, which, as moral artists, we are bound to keep in view. What the true and highest model of a human life is, has been decided for us Christians by the appearance of Jesus Christ in the flesh. Others may endeavour to reopen that question. For us it is settled, and settled irrevocably. Nor are Christ's Human Perfections other than human; they are not, after the manner of Divine attributes, out of our reach; they are not designed only to remind us of what human nature should, but cannot, be. We can approximate to them, even indefinitely. That in our present state of imperfection we should reproduce them in their fulness is indeed impossible; but it is certain that a close imitation of Jesus of Nazareth is at once our duty and our privilege. For God has 'predestinated us to be conformed' by that which we do, not less than by that which we endure, to the Human Image of His Blessed Son, 'that He might be the Firstborn among many brethren [p].'

(β) Nor, on the other hand, may it be forgotten that if we can thus copy our Lord, it is not in the strength of our fallen nature. Vain indeed would be the effort, if in a spirit of Pelagian self-reliance, we should endeavour to reproduce in our own lives the likeness of Christ. Our nature left to itself, enfeebled and depraved, cannot realize the ideal of which it is a wreck, until a higher power has entered into it, and made it what of itself it cannot be. Therefore the power of imitating Jesus comes from Jesus through His Spirit, His Grace, His Presence. Now, as in St. Paul's day, 'Jesus Christ is in us' Christians, 'except we be reprobates [q].' The 'power that worketh in us' is no mere memory of a distant past. It is not natural force of feeling, nor the strength with which self-discipline may brace the will. It is a living, energizing, transforming influence, inseparable from the presence of a 'quickening Spirit [r]' such as is in very deed our glorified Lord. If Christ bids us follow Him, it is because He Himself is the enabling principle of our obedience. If He would have us be like unto Himself, this is because He is willing by His indwelling Presence to reproduce His likeness within us. If it is His Will

[p] Rom. viii. 29. [q] 2 Cor. xiii. 5. [r] 1 Cor. xv. 45.

that we should grow up unto Him in all things Who is the Head, even Christ[s]; this is because His life-giving and life-sustaining power is really distributed throughout the body of His members[t]. Of ourselves we are 'miserable, and poor, and blind, and naked[u].' But we take counsel of Him, and buy of 'His gold tried in the fire;' and forthwith we 'can do all things through Him That strengtheneth' us[v]. It is the Spiritual Presence of Christ in the Church and in Christian souls which makes the systematic imitation of Christ something else than a waste of energy[w]. But if the Christ Whom we imitate be truly human, the Christ Who thus creates and fertilizes moral power within us must be Divine. His Divinity does not disturb the outline of that model which is supplied by His Manhood; while it does furnish us with a stock of inward force, in the absence of which an imitation of the Perfect moral Being would be a fruitless enterprise.

2. Indeed, it is precisely this belief in the Divinity of our Lord which has enriched human life with moral virtues such as civilized paganism could scarcely have appreciated, and which it certainly could not have created. The fruitfulness of this great doctrine in the sphere of morals will be more immediately apparent, if we consider one or two samples of its productiveness.

(*a*) When Greek thought was keenest, and Greek art most triumphantly creative, and Greek political life so organized as to favour in a degree elsewhere unknown among men the play of man's highest natural energies, Greek society was penetrated through and through by an invisible enemy, more fatal in its ravages to thought, to art, to freedom, than the sword of any Persian or Macedonian foe[x]. And already in the age of the early Cæsars, Rome carried in her bosom the secret of her impending decline and fall in the coming centuries. Christian moralists detected and exposed it in terms[y] which are fully borne out by writers devoted to the old pagan society. The life-blood of a race may be drained away less nobly than on the battle-field. Every capacity for high and generous exertion, or for the cheerful endurance of suffering at the bidding of duty, all the stock of moral force on which a country can rely in its hour of trial, may be sapped, destroyed, annihilated by a domestic traitor. So it fared with imperial Rome. The fate of the great empire was not really decided on the Rhine or on the Danube. Before the bar-

[s] Eph. iv. 15. [t] Ibid. i. 23; iv. 16. [u] Rev. iii. 17.
[v] Phil. iv. 13. [w] Eph. iv. 15-24.
[x] Döllinger, Heidenthum und Judenthum, bk. 9. i. 2. p. 684, etc.
[y] Rom. i. 24-32. Cf. Lect. III, p. 142.

barians had as yet begun to muster their savage hordes along the frontiers of ancient civilization, their work had wellnigh been completed, their victory had been won, in the cities, the palaces, nay, in the very temples of the empire. And upon what resources could the old Pagan Society fall back, in its alarm at, and struggle with this formidable foe? It could not depend upon the State. The Emperor was the State by impersonation; and not unfrequently it happened that the Emperor was the public friend and patron of the State's worst enemy. Nor could any reliance be placed upon philosophy. Doubtless philosophy meant well in some of its phases, in some of its representatives. But philosophy is much too feeble a thing to enter the lists successfully with animal passion; and, as a matter of fact, philosophy has more than once been compelled or cajoled into placing her intellectual weapons at the disposal of the sensualist. Nor did religion herself, in her pagan guise, supply the needed element of resistance and cure. Her mysteries were the sanction, her temples the scene, her priests the ministers of the grossest debaucheries: and the misery of a degraded society might have seemed to be complete, when the institutions which were designed to shed some rays of light and love from a higher sphere upon the woes and brutalities of this lower world, did but consecrate and augment the thick moral darkness which made of earth a very hell[z].

Now, that Jesus Christ has breasted this evil, is a matter of historical fact. His victory is chronicled, if not in the actual practice, yet in the conventional standard of modern society. Certainly the evil in question has not been fairly driven beyond the frontiers of Christendom; the tone of our social intercourse, the sympathies of our literature, the proceedings of our law-courts, would remind us from time to time 'that the Canaanite is yet in the land.' But if he is not yet expelled from our borders, at least he is forced to skulk away from the face of a society which still names the Name of Jesus Christ. The most advanced scepticism among us at the present day does not venture with impunity to advocate habits which were treated as matters of course by the friends of Plato: even the licence of our sensuous poetry does not screen such advocacy from earnest and general indignation. This is because, far beyond the circle of His true worshippers, Jesus Christ has created in modern society a public opinion, sternly determined to discountenance and condemn moral mischief, which yet it may be unable wholly to prevent.

[z] Döllinger, Heidenthum und Judenthum, bk. 9. ii. 4. p. 718 sqq.

This public opinion is sometimes tempted to disown its real parentage and its undoubted obligations. Instead of rejoicing to confess itself the pupil of Christ, it imagines schemes of independent morality framed altogether by human thinkers, which may relieve it of its sense of indebtedness to our Lord. But as a matter of fact, all that is thus true and wholesome in the national mind is an intellectual radiation from that actual mass of living purity, wherewith the Healer of men has beautified the lives of millions of Christians. And how has Jesus made men pure? Did He insist upon prudential and hygienic considerations? Did He prove that the laws of the physical world cannot be strained or broken with physical impunity? No. For, at least, He knew human nature well; and experience does not justify the anticipation that scientific demonstrations of the physical consequences of sensual indulgence will be equal to the task of checking the surging impetuosity of passion. Did Christ, then, call men to purity only by the beauty of His Own example? Did He only confront them with a living ideal of purity, so bright and beautiful as to shame them into hatred of animal degradation? Again I say, Jesus Christ knew human nature well. If He had only offered an example of perfect purity, He would but have repeated the work of the ancient Law; He would have given us an ideal, without the capacity of realizing it; He would have at best created a torturing sense of shortcoming and pollution, stimulated by the vision of an unattainable standard of perfection. Therefore He did not merely afford us in a Human form a faultless example of chaste humanity. He did more. He did that which He could only do as being in truth the Almighty God. He made Himself one with our human nature, that He might heal and bless it through its contact with His Divinity. He folded it around His Eternal Person; He made it His own; He made it a power which could quicken and restore us. And then, by the gift of His Spirit, and by sacramental joints and bands, He bound us to it [a]; He bound us through it to Himself; nay, He robed us in it; by it He entered into us, and made our members His own. Henceforth, then, the tabernacle of God is with men [b]; and 'corpus regenerati fit caro Crucifixi.' Henceforth Christian humanity is to be conscious of a Presence within it [c], before which the unclean spirit cannot choose but shrink away discomfited and shamed [d]. The Apostle's argument to the

[a] Col. ii. 19.
[b] Rev. xxi. 3.
[c] Col. i. 27; 2 Cor. xiii. 5.
[d] St. Luke iv. 33.

Corinthian Christians expresses the language of the Christian conscience in presence of impure temptations, to the end of time. 'Know ye not that your bodies are the members of Christ? shall I then take the members of Christ, and make them the members of an harlot? God forbid[e].' From that day to this, the recoil from an ingratitude which a Christian only can exhibit, the dread of an act of sacrilege which a Christian only can commit, the loving recognition of an inward Presence which a Christian only can possess—these have been the controlling, sustaining, hallowing motives which by God's grace have won the victory. But these motives are rooted in a doctrine of Christ's sacramental union with His people, which is the veriest fable unless the indwelling Christ be truly God. The power of these motives to sustain us in purity varies with our hold on the master-truth which they so entirely presuppose. Such motives are strong and effective when our faith in a Divine Christ is strong; they are weak when our faith in His Divinity is weak; they vanish from our moral life, and leave us a prey to our enemy, when the Godhead of Jesus is explicitly denied, and when the language which asserts the true incorporation of an Almighty Saviour with our frail humanity is resolved into the fantastic drapery of an empty metaphor.

(β) If the civilized pagan was impure, he was also proud and self-asserting. He might perhaps deem overt acts of pride an imprudence, on the ground that they were likely to provoke a Nemesis from some spiteful deity. The fates were against continued prosperity; and it was unwise to boast of that which they waited to destroy,—

> 'Invida fatorum series, summisque negatum
> Stare diù, nimioque graves sub pondere lapsus[f].'

But when this prudential consideration did not weigh with him, the pagan gave full scope to the assertion of self in thought, word, and act. The sentiment of pride was not in conflict with his higher conscience, as would be the case with Christians. He indulged it without scruple, nay rather upon principle,—

> 'Secundas fortunas decent superbiæ[g].'

He was utterly unable to see intrinsic evil in it; and it penetrated in a subtle but intense form into the heart of those better ethical systems which, like the later Stoicism, appeared most nearly to rival the moral glories of the Gospel. Pride indeed might seem to have been the misery of paganism rather than its

[e] 1 Cor. vi. 15. [f] Lucan i. 70. [g] Plaut. Stich. ii. 1. 27.

fault. For man cannot detach himself from himself. Man is to himself, under all circumstances, an ever-present subject of thought; but whether this thought is humbly to correspond to the real conditions of his existence, or is to assume the proportions of a turgid and miserable exaggeration, will depend on the question whether man does or does not see constantly and truly That One Being Who alone can reveal to him his true place in the moral and intellectual universe. Paganism was not humble, because to paganism the true God was but a name. The whole life and thought of the pagan world was therefore very naturally based on pride. Its literature, its governments, its religious institutions, its social organization and hierarchy, its doctrines about human life and human duty—all alike were based on the principle of a boundless self-assertion. They were based on that cruel and brutal principle which in the end hands over to the keenest wit and to the strongest arm the sceptre of a tyranny, that knows no bounds, save those of its strongest lust, checked and controlled by the most lively apprehensions of its selfish foresight. Now how did Jesus Christ confront this power of pride thus dominant in the old pagan world? By precept? Undoubtedly. 'The kings of the Gentiles,' He said to His followers, 'exercise lordship over them; and they that exercise authority upon them are called benefactors. But ye shall not be so[h].' 'Whosoever exalteth himself shall be abased; and he that humbleth himself shall be exalted[i].' By example? Let us listen to Him. 'Learn of Me; for I am meek and lowly in heart: and ye shall find rest unto your souls[k].' 'If I your Lord and Master have washed your feet, ye ought to wash one another's feet[l].'

But *why* was His example so cogent? What was it in Jesus Christ which revealed to man the moral beauty and the moral power of the humiliation of self? Was it that being a Man, Who had within His grasp the prizes which are at the command of genius, or the state and luxuries which may be bought by wealth, He put these things from Him? If He was only Man, did He really forego wealth and station? Were they ever—at least on a great scale—within His reach? Even if it be thought that they were, was His renunciation of them a measure of 'that mind which is in Christ Jesus[m],' to which St. Paul directs the gaze of the practical Christian? St. Paul, as we have seen, meant something far higher than the refusal of any earthly

[h] St. Luke xxii. 25. [i] Ibid. xiv. 11. [k] St. Matt. xi. 29. [l] St. John xiii. 14. [m] Phil. ii. 5.

greatness when he drew attention to the self-renunciation of his Lord and Master. 'Being in the form of God, . . . He emptied Himself of His glory, and took on Him the form of a slave[n].' Historically speaking, it is not Christ's renunciation of earthly advantages which has really availed to make Christians humble. The strongest motives to Christian humility are, first, the nearer sight of God's Purity and Blessedness which we attain through communion with His Blessed Son, and next, or rather especially, as the Apostle points out, the real scope and force of Christ's own example. Christ left the glory which He had with the Father before the world was, to become Man. He 'took upon Him our flesh, and suffered death upon the Cross, that all mankind might follow the example of His great humility[o].' Therefore the manifestations of humility in Christendom have varied, on the whole, correspondingly with earnestness of belief in that pre-existent glory from which the Redeemer bent so humbly to the Cross of shame. Certainly, in Jesus this deepest of humiliations was the fruit of His charity for souls; whereas, in us, humble thoughts and deeds are the necessary because the just expression of a true self-knowledge. Yet, nevertheless, the doctrine of Christ's true Godhead, discerned through the voluntary lowliness and sufferings of His Manhood, braces humility, and rebukes pride at the bar of the Christian conscience. Can men really see God put such honour on humility, and be as though they saw it not? Can a creature, who has nothing good in him that he has not received, and whose moral evil is entirely his own, behold the Highest One thus teaching him the truthful attitude of a created life, without emotion, without shame, without practical self-abasement? What place is there for great assertions of self in a man who sincerely believes that he has been saved by the Death of the Incarnate Son of God? Who has the heart to vaunt his own opinion, or to parade his accomplishments, or to take secret pleasure in income or station or intellectual power, when he reflects upon the astonishing grace of our Lord Jesus Christ, Who, when He was rich, for our sakes became poor[p]? It is the Incarnation which has confronted human pride, by revealing God clearly to the conscience of men, but also, and especially, by practically setting the highest possible honour upon extreme self-humiliation. It is the Incarnation which has led men to veil high gifts, and to resign places of

[n] Phil. ii. 6, 7.

[o] Collect for Sunday before Easter.

[p] 2 Cor. viii. 9.

influence, and to forego the advantages of wealth and birth, that they might have some part, however fractionally small, in the moral glories of Bethlehem and Calvary. It is the Incarnation which has thus saved society again and again from the revolutionary or despotic violence of unbridled ambitions, by bringing into the field of political activity the corrective, compensating force of active self-denial. An enthusiasm for withdrawal from the general struggle to aggrandise self has fascinated those worshippers of an Incarnate God, who have learnt from Him the true glory of taking the lowest place at the feast of human life. But the motive for such repression of self is powerful only so far as faith in Christ's Godhead is clear and strong. The culture of humility does not enter into the ordinary schemes of natural ethics; and Humanitarian doctrines are found, as a rule, to accompany intellectual and social self-assertion. It has been true from the first, it is true at this hour, that a sincere faith which recognises in the Son of Mary, laid in His manger and nailed to His Cross, none other than the Only-begotten Son of God, is the strongest incentive to conquer the natural pride of the human heart, and to learn the bearing of a little child [q]—that true note of predestined nobility—in the Kingdom of Heaven.

(γ) Let us take one more illustration of the moral fruitfulness of a faith in the Divinity of our Saviour. There is a grace, to which the world itself does homage, and which those who bend neither heart nor knee before the world's Redeemer admit to be the consequence of His appearance among men.

Heathenism, as being impure and proud, was consistently unloving. For as the one vice eats out the delicacy and heart of all true tenderness, so the other systematically enthrones self upon the ruins of the unselfish affections. Despite the Utopian sketches which have been drawn by the philosophers of the last century, the sentiment of 'humanity' is too feeble a thing to create in us a true love of man as man. Man does not, in his natural state, love his brother man, except it be from motives of interest or blood-relationship. Nay, man regards all who are not thus related to him as forming the great company of his natural rivals and enemies, from whom he has nothing to expect save that which the might or the prudence of self-interest may dictate.

[q] St. Matt. xviii. 3.

τὸ γὰρ οἰκεῖον πιέζει
πάνθ' ὁμῶς· εὐθὺς δ' ἀπήμων κραδία
κᾶδος ἀμφ' ἀλλότριον[r].

Such is the voice of unchristianized nature: man's highest love is the love of self, varied by those subordinate affections which minister to self-love: and society is an agglomeration of self-loving beings, whose ruling instincts are shaped by force or by prudence into a political whole, but who are ever ready, as opportunity may arise, to break forth into the excesses of an unchecked barbarism. Contempt for and cruelty towards the slave, hatred of the political or literary rival, suspicious aversion for the foreigner, disbelief in the reality of human virtue and of human disinterestedness, were recognized ingredients in the temper of pagan times. The science of life consisted in solving a practical equation between the measure of evil which it was desirable to inflict upon others, and the amount of suffering which it might be necessary to endure at their hands. Love of mankind would have seemed folly to a society, the recognised law of whose life was selfishness, and whose vices culminated in a mutual hatred between man and man, class and class, race and race, thinly veiled by the hollow conventionalisms which distinguish Pagan civilization from pure barbarism[s].

How did Jesus Christ reform this social corruption? He gave the New Commandment. 'This is My commandment, that ye love one another, as I have loved you[t].' But was His love merely the love of a holy man for those whose hearts were too dull and earthly to love Him in return? Could such a human love as this have availed to compass a moral revolution, and to change the deepest instincts of mankind? Is it not a fact that Christians have measured the love of Jesus Christ as man measures all love, by observing the degree in which it involves the gift of self? Love is ever the gift of self. It gives that which costs us something, or it is not love. Its spirit may vary in the degree of intensity, but it is ever the same. It is always and everywhere the sacrifice of self. It is the gift of time, or of labour, or of income, or of affection; it is the surrender of reputation and of honour; it is the acceptance of sorrow and of pain for others.

[r] Pind. Nem. i. 82.
[s] Tit. iii. 3: ἦμεν γάρ ποτε καὶ ἡμεῖς ἀνόητοι, ἀπειθεῖς, πλανώμενοι, δουλεύοντες ἐπιθυμίαις καὶ ἡδοναῖς ποικίλαις, ἐν κακίᾳ καὶ φθόνῳ διάγοντες, στυγητοί, μισοῦντες ἀλλήλους.
[t] St. John xv. 12.

The warmth of the spirit of love varies with the felt greatness of the sacrifice which expresses it and which is its life. Therefore the love of the Divine Christ is infinite. 'He loved me,' says an apostle, 'and gave Himself for me [u].' The 'Self' which He gave for man was none other than the Infinite God: the reality of Christ's Godhead is the truth which can alone measure the greatness of His love. The charities of His earthly life are but so many sparks from the central column of flame, which burns in the Self-devotion of the Eternal Son of God. The agonies of His Passion are illuminated each and all with a moral no less than a doctrinal meaning, by the momentous truth that He Who is crucified between two thieves is nevertheless the Lord of Glory. From this faith in the voluntary Self-immolation of the Most Holy, a new power of love has streamed forth into the soul of man [v]. Of this love, before the Incarnation, man not only had no experience; his moral education would not have trained him even to admire it. But the Infinite Being bowing down to Self-chosen humiliation and agony, that, without violating His essential attributes, He might win to Himself the heart of His erring creatures, has provoked an answer of grateful love, first towards Himself, and then for His sake towards His creatures. Thus 'with His Own right Hand, and with His holy Arm, He hath gotten Himself the victory [x]' over the selfishness as over the sins of man. 'We love Him because He first loved us [y].' If human life has been brightened by the thousand courtesies of our Christian civilization; if human pain has been alleviated by the unnumbered activities of Christian charity; if the face of Christendom is beautified by institutions which cheer the earthly existence of millions; these results are due to Christian faith in the Charity of the Redeemer, which is infinite because the Redeemer is Divine. And thus the temples of Christendom, visibly perpetuating the worship of Christ from age to age, are not the only visible witnesses among us to His Divine prerogatives. The hospital, in which the bed of anguish is soothed by the hand of science under the guidance of love; the penitentiary, where the victims of a selfish passion are raised to a new moral life by the care and delicacy of an unmercenary tenderness; the school, which gathers the ragged outcasts of our great cities, rescuing them from the ignorance and vice of which

[u] Gal. ii. 20.

[v] Phil. i. 8, where note ἐν σπλάγχνοις Ἰησοῦ Χριστοῦ, and compare St. Luke i. 78.

[x] Ps. xcviii. 2.

[y] 1 St. John iv. 19.

else they must be the prey;—what is the fountain-head of these blessed and practical results, but the truth of His Divinity, Who has kindled man into charity by giving Himself for man? The moral results of Calvary are what they are, because Christ is God. He Who stooped from heaven to the humiliations of the Cross has opened in the heart of redeemed man a fountain of love and compassion. No distinctions within the vast circle of the human family can narrow or pervert its course; nor can it cease to flow while Christians believe, that Christ crucified for men is the Only-begotten Son of God.

It is therefore an error to suppose that the doctrine of our Lord's Divinity has impoverished the moral life of Christendom 'by removing Christ from the category of imitable beings.' For on the one hand, the doctrine leaves His Humanity altogether intact; on the other, it enhances the force of His example as a model of the graces of humility and love. Thus from age to age this doctrine has in truth fertilized the moral soul of human life, not less than it has guarded and illuminated intellectual truth. How indeed could it be otherwise? 'If God spared not His Own Son, but freely gave Him up for us all, how shall He not with Him also freely give us all things?' Who shall wonder if wisdom and righteousness and sanctification and redemption are given with the gift of the Eternal Son? Who shall wonder if by this gift, a keen, strong sense of the Personality and Life of God, and withal a true estimate of man's true dignity, of his capacity, through grace, for the highest forms of life, are guarded in the sanctuary of human thought? Who shall gainsay it, if along with this gift we inherit a body of revealed and certain truth, reposing on the word of an Infallible Teacher; if we are washed in a stream of cleansing Blood, which flows from an atoning fountain opened on Calvary for the sin and uncleanness of a guilty world; if we are sustained by sacraments which make us really partakers of the Nature of our God; if we are capable of virtues which embellish and elevate humanity, yet which, but for the strength and example of our Lord, might have seemed too plainly unattainable?

For the Divinity of God's Own Son, freely given for us sinners to suffer and to die, is the very heart of our Christian faith. It cannot be denied without tearing out the vitals of a living Christianity. Its roots are struck far back into the prophecy, the typology, the ethics, of the Old Testament. It alone supplies a satisfactory explanation of the moral attitude of Jesus Christ towards His contemporaries. It is the true key to His teaching, to His miracles, to the leading mysteries of His life, to His power of controlling the issues of history. As such, it is put forward by apostles who, differing in much besides, were made one by this faith in His Divinity and in the truths which are bound up with it. It enters into the world of speculative discussion; it is analysed, criticised, denounced, proscribed, betrayed; yet it emerges from the crucible wherein it has been exposed to the action of every intellectual solvent that hostile ingenuity could devise; it has lost nothing from, it has added nothing to, its original significance; it has only been clothed in a symbol which interprets it to new generations, and which lives in the confessions of the grateful Church. Its later history is explained when we remember the basis on which it really rests. The question of Christ's Divinity is the question of the truth or falsehood of Christianity. 'If Christ be not God,' it has been truly said, 'He is not so great as Mohammed.' But Christ's moral relation to Mohammed may safely be left to every unsophisticated conscience; and if the conscience owns in Him the Moral Chief of humanity, it must take Him at His word when He unveils before it His superhuman glory.

But the doctrine of Christ's Divinity does not merely bind us to the historic past, and above all to the first records of Christianity; it is at this hour the strength of the Christian Church. There are forces abroad in the world of thought which, if they could be viewed apart from all that counteracts them, might well make a Christian fear for the future of humanity. It is not merely that the Church is threatened with the loss of possessions secured to her by the reverence of centuries, and of a place of honour which may perhaps have guarded civilization more effectively than it can be shewn to have strengthened religion. The Faith has once triumphed without these gifts of Providence; and, if God wills, she can again dispense with them. But never since the first ages of the Gospel was fundamental Christian truth denied and denounced so largely, and with such passionate animosity, as is the case at this moment in each of the most civilized nations of Europe. It may be that God has in store for His Church greater trials to her faith than she has yet experienced; it may be that along with the revived scorn of the old pagan spirit, the persecuting sword of pagan hatred will yet be unsheathed. Be it so, if so He wills it. The holy city is strong in knowing 'that God is in the midst of her, therefore shall she not be removed; God shall help her, and that right early. The heathen make much ado, and the kingdoms are

[LECT.

moved; but God hath shewed His Voice, and the earth shall melt away.' When the waters of human opinion rage and swell, and the mountains shake at the tempest of the same, our Divine Lord is not unequal to the defence of His Name and His Honour. If the sky seem dark and the winds contrary; if ever and anon the strongest intellectual and social currents of our civilization mass themselves threateningly, as if to overwhelm the holy bark as she rides upon the waves; we know Who is with her, unwearied and vigilant, though He should seem to sleep. His presence forbids despondency; His presence assures us that a cause which has consistently conquered in its day of apparent failure, cannot but calmly abide the issue. 'Although the fig-tree shall not blossom, neither shall fruit be in the vines; the labour of the olive shall fail, and the fields shall yield no meat; the flocks shall be cut off from the fold, and there shall be no herd in the stalls: yet I will rejoice in the Lord, I will joy in the God of my salvation.'

Would that these anxieties might in God's good providence work out a remedy for the wounds of His Church! Would that, in presence of the common foe, and yet more by clinging to the common faith, Christians could learn to understand each other! Surely it might seem that agreement in so stupendous a belief as the Divinity of our Crucified Lord might avail to overshadow, or rather to force on a reconciliation of the differences which divide those who share it. Is it but the indulgence of a fond dream to hope that a heartier, more meditative, more practical grasp of the Divinity of Jesus will one day again unite His children in the bonds of a restored unity? Is it altogether chimerical to expect that Christians who believe Christ to be truly God, will see more clearly what is involved in that faith, and what is inconsistent with it; that they will supply what is wanting or will abandon what is untenable in their creed and practice, so that before men and angels they may openly unite in the adoring confession of their Divine Head? The pulse quickens, and the eyes fill with tears, at the bare thought of this vision of peace, at this distant but blessed prospect of a reunited Christendom. What dark doubts would it not dispel! What deep consolations would it not shed forth on millions of souls! What fascination would not the spectacle of concordant prayer and harmonious action among the servants of Christ exert over the hearts of sinners! With what majestic energy would the reinvigorated Church, 'terrible as an army with banners,' address herself forthwith to the heartier promotion of man's best interests, to the richer development of the Christian life, to more energetic labours for the conversion of the world! But we may not dwell, except in hope and prayer, upon the secrets of Divine Providence. It may be our Lord's purpose to shew to His servants of this generation only His work, and to reserve for their children the vision of His glory. It must be our duty, in view of His revealed Will, and with a simple faith in His Wisdom and His Power, to pray our Lord 'that all they that do confess God's Holy Name, may agree in the truth of His Holy Word, and live in unity and godly love.'

But here we must close this attempt to reassert, against some misapprehensions of modern thought, the great truth which guards the honour of Christ, and which is the most precious feature in the intellectual heritage of Christians. And for you, dear brethren, who by your generous interest or by your warm sympathies have so accompanied and sustained him, what can the preacher more fittingly or more sincerely desire, than that any clearer sight of the Divine Person of our glorious and living Lord which may have been granted you, may be, by Him, blessed to your present sanctification and to your endless peace? If you are intellectually persuaded that in confessing the true Godhead of Jesus you have not followed a cunningly-devised fable, or the crude imagination of a semi-barbarous and distant age, then do not allow yourselves to rest content with this intellectual persuasion. A truth so sublime, so imperious, has other work to do in you besides shaping into theoretic compactness a certain district of your thought about the goodness of God and the wants of man. The Divine Christ of the Gospel and the Church is no mere actor, though He were the greatest, in the great tragedy of human history; He belongs not exclusively or especially to the past; He is 'the Same yesterday, to-day, and for ever.' He is at this moment all that He was eighteen centuries ago, all that He has been to our fathers, all that He will be to our children. He is the Divine and Infallible Teacher, the Healer and Pardoner of sin, the Source of all graces, the Conqueror of Satan and of death—now, as of old, and as in years to come. Now as heretofore, He is 'able to save unto the uttermost them that come unto God by Him;' now, as on the day of His triumph over death, 'He opens the Kingdom of Heaven to all believers;' now, as in the first age of the Church, He it is 'that hath the key of David, that openeth, and no man shutteth; and shutteth, and no man openeth[z].' He is ever the Same; but, as the children of time, whether for good or evil, we move onwards in perpetual change. The hours of life pass, they do not return; they pass, yet they are not forgotten; 'pereunt et imputantur.' But the present is our own; we may resolve, if we will, to live as men who live for the glory of an Incarnate God. Brethren, you shall not repent it, if, when life's burdens press heavily, and especially at that solemn hour when human help must fail, you are able to lean with strong confidence on the arm of an Almighty Saviour. May He in deed and truth be with you, alike in your pilgrimage through this world, and when that brief journey is drawing to its close! May you, sustained by His Presence and aid, so pass through the valley of the shadow of death as to fear no evil, and to find, at the gate of the eternal world, that all the yearnings of faith and hope are to be more than satisfied by the vision of the Divine 'King in His Beauty!'

[z] Rev. iii. 7.

NOTES.

NOTE A, on Lecture I.

The works upon the Life of our Lord alluded to in the text are the following.

1. *Das Leben Jesu, von Dr. F. D. Strauss*, 1835. This work passed through several editions, and in 1864 was followed up by *Das Leben Jesu, für das Deutsche Volk bearbeitet.* Leipsig, Brockhaus.

Strauss' argument is chiefly concerned with the differences between the Evangelists, and with the miraculous features of their narratives. He regards the miracles as 'myths,' that is to say, as pure fictions. His position is, that the speculative ideas about Jesus which were circulating in the first century were dressed up in a traditional form, the substance of which was derived from the Messianic figures of the Old Testament. This violent supposition was really dictated by Strauss' philosophy. Denying the possible existence of miracle, of the supernatural, of the invisible world, and even the existence of a personal living God, Strauss undertakes to explain the Gospel-history as the natural development of germs previously latent in the world of human life and thought. Upon the ground that nothing is absolute, that all is relative, Strauss will not allow that any one man can absolutely have realized the 'idea' of humanity. The sanctity of Jesus was only relative; and, speaking historically, Jesus fell far below the absolute Idea to which the thought of the Apostolical age endeavoured to elevate Him by the 'mythical' additions to His 'Life.' Thus Strauss' criticism is in reality the application of Hegel's doctrine of 'absolute idealism' to the Gospel narratives. 'It is,' observes Dr. Mill, 'far more from a desire of working out on a historical ground the philosophical principles of his master, than from any attachment to mythical theories on their own account, that we are clearly to deduce the destructive process which Strauss has applied to the Life of Jesus.' (Myth. Interpr. p. 11.)

Strauss' later work is addressed not to the learned, but to the German people, with a view to destroying the influence of the Lutheran pastors. He observes in his Preface: 'Wer die Pfaffen aus der Kirche schaffen will, der muss erst das Wunder aus der Religion schaffen.' (Vorrede, p. xix.) With this practical object he sets to work; and although the results at which he arrives are perhaps more succinctly stated than in his earlier book, the real difference between them is not considerable. He makes little use of the critical speculations on the Gospels which have been produced in Protestant and Rationalistic Germany during the last thirty years. Thus he is broadly at issue with the later Tübingen writers on the subject of St. Mark's Gospel; he altogether disputes their favourite theory of its 'originality,' and views it as only a colourless *résumé* of the narratives of St. Matthew and St. Luke. His philosophical theory still, however, controls his religious speculations: Jesus did for religion what Socrates did for philosophy, and Aristotle for science. Although the appearance of Jesus in the world constituted an epoch, He belonged altogether to humanity: He did not rise above it; He *might* even be surpassed. The second book, like the first, is an elaboration of the thesis that 'the idea cannot attain its full development in a single individual of the species;' and to this elaboration there are added some fierce attacks upon the social and religious institutions of Europe, designed more particularly to promote an anti-Christian social revolution in northern Germany.

2. *Das Charakterbild Jesu, ein biblischer Versuch, von Dr. Daniel Schenkel.* 2te Auflage. Wiesbaden, 1864.

Dr. Schenkel begins by insisting upon the 'irrational' character of the Church's doctrine of the Union of two Natures in our Lord's Person. Nothing, he thinks, short of the oppression with which the mediæval Church treated all attempts at free thought can account for the perpetuation of such a dogma. The Reformers, although they proclaimed the principle of free enquiry, yet did not venture honestly to apply it to the traditional doctrine of Christ's Person; primitive Protestantism was afraid of the consequences of its fundamental principle. The orthodox doctrine accordingly outlived the Reformation; but the older Rationalism has established a real claim upon our gratitude by insisting upon the pure Humanity of Christ, although, Dr. Schenkel thinks, it has too entirely stripped Him of His 'Divinity,' that is to say, of the moral beauty to which we may still apply that designation. As for the Christ of Schleiermacher, he is a product of the yearnings and aspirations of that earnest and gifted teacher, but he is not, according to Schenkel, the Jesus of history. Strauss does in the main represent Jesus such as He was in the reality of His historical life; but Strauss' representation is too much tinged with modern colourings; nor are his desolating negations sufficiently counterbalanced by those positive results of this thoroughgoing 'criticism' upon which Dr. Schenkel proposes to dwell. For the future, faith in Christ is to rest on more solid bases than 'auf denen des Aberglaubens, der Priesterherrschaft, und einer mit heiteren oder schreckenden Bildern angefüllten Phantasie.' (p. 11.)

Dr. Schenkel makes the most of the late Tübingen theory of the 'originality,' as it is called, of St. Mark, and of the non-historical character, as he maintains, of the Gospel of St. John; although he deals very 'freely' with the materials, which he reserves as still entitled to historical consideration. Dr. Schenkel does not hold that the Evangelistic account of Christ's miracles is altogether mythical; it has, he thinks, a certain basis of fact. He admits that our Lord may have possessed what may be termed a miraculous gift, even if this should be rightly explained to be only a rare natural endowment. He had a power of calming persons of deranged mind; His assurances of the pardon of their sins, acting beneficially on their nervous system, produced these restorative effects. Dr. Schenkel holds it to be utterly impossible that Jesus could have worked any of the 'miracles of nature;' since this would have proved Him to be truly God. All such narratives as His calming the storm in the lake are therefore part of that 'torrent of legend' with which the historical germ of His real Life has been overlaid by later enthusiasms. The Resurrection, accordingly, is not a fact of history; it is a creation of the imaginative devotion of the first disciples. (See p. 314.) Dr. Schenkel considers the appearances of our Risen Lord to have been only so many glorifications of His character in the hearts of those who believed in Him. To them He was manifested as One who lives eternally, in that He has founded His kingdom on earth by His word and His Spirit.

The main idea of Dr. Schenkel's book is to make the Life of Jesus the text of an attack upon those who are Conservatives in politics and orthodox Lutherans in religion. It is not so much a biography, or even a sketch of character, as a polemical pamphlet. The treatment of our Lord's words and actions, and still more the highly-coloured representation of the Pharisees, are throughout intended to express the writer's view of schools and parties in Lutheran Germany. The Pharisees of course are the orthodox Lutherans; while Jesus Christ is the political demagogue and liberal sceptic. With some few exceptions, the etiquette of history is scrupulously observed; and yet the really historical interest is as small, as the polemical references are continuous and piquant. The woes which Jesus pronounces against the Pharisees are not directed simply against hypocrisy and formalism; 'the curse of Christ,' we are told, 'like the trumpet of the last Judgment, lights for ever upon every church that is based upon tradition and upon the ascendancy of a privileged clergy.' 'Der Weheruf Jesu ist noch nicht verklungen. Er trifft noch heute, wie eine Posaune des Gerichts, jedes auf die Satzungen der Ueberlieferung und auf die Herrschaft eines mit Vorzugsrechten ausgestatteten Klerus gegründete Kirchenthum.' (p. 254.) Perhaps the most singular illustration of profane recklessness in exegesis that can easily be found in modern literature is Dr. Schenkel's explanation of the sin against the Holy Ghost. This sin, he tells us, does not consist, as we may have mistakenly supposed, in a deliberate relapse from grace into impenitence; it is not the sin of worldly or unbelieving persons. It is the sin of orthodoxy; it is a 'Theologisch-hierarchischer Verhärtung und Verstockung;' and those who defend and propagate the ancient faith of Christians, in spite of rationalistic warnings against doing so, are really guilty of it. (Charakt. p. 106.)

Dr. Schenkel has explained himself more elaborately on some points in his pamphlet 'Die Protestantische Freiheit, in ihrem gegenwärtigen Kampfe mit der kirchlichen Reaktion' (Wiesbaden, 1862). He fiercely demands a Humanitarian Christology (p. 153). He laments that even Zwingli's thought was still fettered by the formulæ of Nicæa and Chalcedon (p. 152), nay, he remarks that St. Paul himself has assigned to Christ a rank which led on naturally to the Church-belief in the Divinity of His Person (p. 148). That belief Dr. Schenkel considers to be a shred of heathen superstition which had found its way into the circle of Christian ideas (ibid.); while he sorrowfully protests that the adoration of Jesus, both in the public Services of the

Church and in the Christian consciousness, has superseded that of God the Father. 'Vom fünften Jahrhundert bis zur Reformation (he might have begun four centuries earlier and gone on for three centuries later) wird Jesus Christ durchgängig als der Herrgott verehrt' (p. 149). Indeed, throughout this brochure Dr. Schenkel's positions are simply those of the old Socinianism, resting however upon a Rationalistic method of treatment, which in its more logical phases regards much of what Socinianism itself retains, as the yoke of an intolerable orthodoxy.

3. *Geschichte Christus' und Seiner Zeit, von Heinrich Ewald.* Göttingen, 1857. 2te Ausgabe.

This work is on no account to be placed on the level of those of Strauss or Schenkel, to which in some most vital particulars it is opposed. Indeed, Ewald's defence of St. John's Gospel, and his deeper spirituality of tone, must command a religious interest, which would be of a high order, if only this writer believed in our Lord's Godhead. That this, unhappily, is not the case, will be apparent upon a careful study of the concluding chapter of this volume on 'Die Ewige Verherrlichung,' pp. 496–504,—beautiful as are some of the passages which it contains. His explanation of the titles 'Son of God' and 'Word of God,' p. 502, is altogether inadequate; and his statement that 'nie hat Jesu als der Sohn und das Wort Gottes sich mit der Vater und *Gotte Selbst* (from whom Ewald accordingly distinguishes our Lord) verwechselt oder vermessen sich selbst diesem gleichgestellt,' is simply contradicted by St. John v. and x.

4. *Die Menschliche Entwickelung Jesu Christi, von Th. Keim.* Zürich, 1861. *Die geschichtliche Würde Jesu, von Th. Keim,* Zürich, 1864. *Der geschichtliche Christus, Eine Reihe von Vorträgen mit Quellenbeweis und Chronologie des Lebens Jesu, von Th. Keim.* Zürich, 1866.

Dr. Keim, although rejecting the fourth Gospel, retains too much of the mind of Schleiermacher to be justly associated with Drs. Strauss or Schenkel. Dr. Keim, indeed, sees in our Lord only a Man, but still an eminently mysterious Man of incomparable grandeur of character. He recognises, although inadequately, the startling self-assertion of our Lord; and he differs most emphatically from Strauss, Schenkel, and Renan in recognising the real sinlessness of Jesus. He admits, too, the historical value of our Lord's eschatological discourses; he does not regard His miracles 'of nature' as absolutely impossible; and he heartily believes in the reality of Christ's own Resurrection from the dead. He cannot account for the phenomenon of the Church, if the Resurrection be denied. Altogether he seems to consider that the Life of Jesus as a spiritual, moral, and, in some respects, supernatural fact, is unique; but an intellectual spectre, the assumed invariability of historical laws, as we conceive them, seems to interpose so as to prevent him from drawing the otherwise inevitable inference. Yet for such as he is, let us hope much.

5. *La Vie de Jésus, par E. Renan.* Paris, 1863.

Of this well-known book it may suffice here to say a very few words. Its one and only excellence is its incomparable style. From every other point of view it is deplorable. Historically, it deals most arbitrarily with the data upon which it professes to be based. Thus in the different pictures of Christ's aim and action, during what are termed the second and the third periods of His Ministry, a purely artificial contrast is presented. Theologically, this work proceeds throughout on a really atheistic assumption, disguised beneath the thin veil of a pantheistic phraseology. It assumes that no such being as a personal God exists at all. The 'god' with whom, according to M. Renan, Jesus had such uninterrupted communion, but from whom he is so entirely distinct, is only the 'category of the ideal.' It is, however, when we look at the 'Vie de Jésus' from a moral point of view, that its shortcomings are most apparent in their length and breadth. Its hero is a fanatical impostor, who pretends to be and to do that which he knows to be beyond him, but who nevertheless is held up to our admiration as the ideal of humanity. In place of the Divine and Human Christ of the Gospels, M. Renan presents us with a character devoid of any real majesty, of any tolerable consistency, and even of the constituent elements of moral goodness. If M. Renan himself does not perceive that the object of his enthusiasm is simply an offence to any healthy conscience, this is only an additional proof, if one were needed, of the fatal influence of pantheistic thought upon the most gifted natures. It destroys the sensitiveness of the moral nerve. Enough to say that M. Renan presents us with a Christ who in his Gethsemane was possibly thinking of 'les jeunes filles qui auraient peut-être consenti à l'aimer.' (p. 379.)

It ought perhaps here to be added that M. de Pressensé's work, 'Jésus-Christ, son Temps, sa Vie, son Œuvre,' Paris, 1865, although failing (as might be expected) to do justice to the sacramental side of our Lord's Incarnation and Teaching, is yet on the whole a most noble contribution to the cause of Truth, for which the deep gratitude of all sincere Christians cannot but be due to its accomplished author.

6. *Ecce Homo; a Survey of the Life and Work of Jesus Christ.* London and Cambridge, Macmillan, 1866.

Every one who reads 'Ecce Homo' must heartily admire the generous passion for human improvement which glows throughout the whole volume. And especial acknowledgment is due to the author from Christian believers, for the emphasis with which he has insisted on the following truths:—

Christ's moral sublimity.
Christ's claim of supremacy.
Christ's success in His work.

Incidentally, moreover, he has brought out into their true prominence some portions of the truth, which are lost sight of by popular religionists in England. As an example of this, his earnest recognition of the visibility of the Society founded by Christ may be instanced. But, on the other hand, this writer has carefully avoided all reference to the cardinal question of Christ's Person; and he tells us that he has done this deliberately. (Pref. to 5th Ed. p. xx.) The result however is, that his book is pervaded, as it seems to many of his readers, by an essential flaw. It is not merely that our Lord's claims *cannot* be *morally* estimated apart from a clear estimate of His Person. The author professes to be answering the question, 'What was Christ's object in founding the Society which is called by His Name?' Now to attempt to answer this question, while dismissing all theological consideration of the dignity of Christ's Person, involves the tacit assumption that the due estimate of His Person is not relevant to the appreciation of His Work; in other words, the assumption, that so far as the evidence yielded by the work of Christ goes, the Christology of the Nicene Creed is at least uncertain. The author of 'Ecce Homo' is however either a Humanitarian, or he is a believer in our Lord's Divinity, or he is undecided. If he is a Humanitarian, then the assumption is, as far as it goes, in harmony with his personal convictions; only it should, for various and obvious reasons, have been more plainly stated, since, *inter alia*, it embarrasses his view of our Lord's claims and character with difficulties which he does not recognise. If he believes in Christ's Divinity, then in his forthcoming volume (besides rewriting such chapters as chap. 2, on The Temptation) he will have to enlarge very seriously, or rather altogether to recast, the account which he has actually given of Christ's work. If the writer be himself in doubt as to whether Christ is or is not God, then surely he is not in a position to give any account whatever of Christ's work, which is within the limits of human capacity on one hypothesis, and as utterly transcends them on the other. In short, it is impossible for a man to profess to give a real answer to the question, what Christ intended to accomplish, until he has told us who and what Christ was. That fragment of Christ's work of which we gather an account from history contributes its share to the solution of the question of Christ's Person; but our Lord's Personal Rank is too intimately bound up with the moral justification of His language, and with the real nature and range of His action upon humanity, to bear the adjournment which the author of 'Ecce Homo' has thought advisable.

There are several errors in the volume which might seem to shew that the author is himself unfamiliar with the faith of the Church; as they would not have been natural in a person who believed it, but who was throwing himself for the time being into the mental position of a Humanitarian in order the better to do justice to his arguments. For instance, the author confounds St. John's Baptism with Christ's. He supposes that Nicodemus came to Jesus by night in order to seek a dispensation from being publicly baptised, and so admitted into Christ's Society. He imagines that Christ prayed on the Cross only for the Roman soldiers who actually crucified Him, and not for the Pharisees, against whom (it is a most painful as well as an unwarranted suggestion) He continued to feel fierce indignation. This indeed is an instance of the author's tendency to identify his own imaginations with the motives and feelings of Jesus Christ, where Scripture is either silent or points in an opposite direction. The author is apparently carried away by his earnest indignation against certain forms of selfish and insincere vice, such as Pharisaism; nor is he wholly free from the disposition so to colour the past as to make it express suggestively his own feelings about persons and schools of the present day. The naturalistic tone of his thought is apparent in his formula of 'enthusiasm,' as the modern equivalent to inspiration and the gift of the Holy Spirit; in his general substitution of the conception of anti-social vice for the deeper Scriptural idea of sin; and in his suggestion that Christians may treat the special precepts of Christ with the same 'boldness' with which He treated those of the law of Moses.

Of the practical results of his book it is difficult to form an estimate. In some instances it may lead to the contented substitution of a naturalistic instead of a miraculous Christianity, of philanthropic 'enthusiasm' instead of a supernatural life, of loyalty to a moral reforming hero, instead of religious devotion to a Divine Saviour of the world. But let us also trust that so fearless a recognition of the claims of Christ to be the King and Centre of renewed humanity, may assist other minds to grasp and hold the truth which alone makes those claims, taken as a whole, justifiable; and may recruit the ranks of our Lord's true worshippers from among the many thoughtful but uninstructed persons who have never faced the dilemma which this volume so forcibly, albeit so tacitly, suggests.

* * * *

Since these words were written, the volume under discussion has found an apologist, whose opinion on this, as on any other subject, is a matter of national interest[a]. If the present writer has been guilty of forming and propagating an unjust estimate of a remarkable work, he may at least repair his error by referring his readers to pages, in which genius and orthodoxy have done their best for the Christian honour of 'Ecce Homo.' These pages must indeed of necessity be read with sympathy and admiration, if not with entire assent, by all who do not consider a theological work to have been discredited, when it is asserted to uphold some positive truth. But it may also be a duty to state briefly and respectfully why, after a careful consideration of such a criticism, the present writer is unable to recognise any sufficient reason for withdrawing what he has ventured to say upon the subject. Unquestionably, as Mr. Gladstone urges, it is allowable in principle to teach only a portion of revealed truth, under circumstances which would render a larger measure of instruction likely to perplex and repel the learners. But then such teaching must be loyally consistent with the claims of that portion of the truth, which is, provisionally, left untaught; and this condition does not appear

[a] 'Ecce Homo,' by the Right Hon. W. E. Gladstone. Strahan & Co. London, 1868. [Reprinted from 'Good Words.']

to be satisfied by 'Ecce Homo,' if it be, as we may hope, only a preparation for a second volume which will assert in plain language the Deity of our Adorable Lord. The crucial chapter on the Temptation altogether ignores our Lord's true and Divine Personality; as it also appears to ignore the personal presence of the Tempter. 'What is called Christ's Temptation is the excitement of His Mind which was caused by the nascent consciousness of supernatural power,' p. 12. Such a description fails altogether to do justice to the real issues involved; it might apply with equal propriety to a struggle in the soul of an apostolic man. Even if this chapter does not imply Christ's inward sympathy with outward solicitations to accept a wrong choice, it could never have been written by a person who kept clearly before his mind the truth of our Lord's Divinity.

Mr. Gladstone draws out and insists upon an analogy between the original function of the three Synoptic Evangelists in the first propagation of the Faith, and the present function of 'Ecce Homo.' But this analogy would appear to be disturbed by the following considerations. First, there is nothing in 'Ecce Homo' which corresponds to the great Christological texts in the Synoptists. To these texts Mr. Gladstone has indeed referred, but they do not readily harmonize with his representation of the gradual unveiling of Christ's Person. Indeed they teach a doctrine of Christ's Person which is virtually identical with that of St. John. Are there any passages in 'Ecce Homo' which, like St. Matt. xi. 27, or St. Luke x. 22, place the Christological belief of the writer beyond reach of question? Secondly, the ethical atmosphere of 'Ecce Homo' differs very significantly from that of the Gospels. The Gospels present us with the Scriptural idea of Sin, provoking God's wrath and establishing between God and man a state of enmity: and this idea points very urgently—at least in a moral universe,—to some awful interposition which shall bring relief. But the Biblical idea of sin is a vitally distinct thing from the impoverished modern conception of anti-social vice, in which man and not God is the insulted and offended person, and by which the protection of individual rights and the well-being of society are held to be of more account than the reign of peace and purity within the soul. The idea of sin points to a Divine Redeemer: the idea of anti-social vice points to an improved system of human education. Thirdly, the first and third Evangelists preface their records of the Ministry with an account of the Nativity. That account clearly attributes a Superhuman Personality to Christ; and thus it places the subsequent narrative in a light altogether different from that suggested by the opening chapter of 'Ecce Homo.' And the first verse of St. Mark's Gospel is sufficiently explicit to range him as to this matter, side by side with St. Matthew and St. Luke.

The real needs of our time are more likely to be known to public men who come in contact with minds of every kind than to private clergymen. But it would have appeared to the present writer that an economical treatment of the Faith which might have been possible and natural in the first age of its promulgation, must fail of its effect at the present day. Whether men believe the Gospel or not, its real substance and contents are now fairly before the world; and it is increasingly felt that the question whether Christ is or is not God, is really identical with the question of His moral character. [Since these lines were written the publication of 'Natural Religion,' by the author of 'Ecce Homo' has shewn, among other things, that Mr. Gladstone's estimate of the latter work was too generous. No true religion can be 'adapted' to meet the requirements of hostile thought with entire impunity.]

NOTE B, ON LECTURE II.

The word 'Elohim' is used in the Old Testament—

(1) Of the One True God, as in Deut. iv. 35, 1 Kings xviii. 21, etc., where it has the article; and without the article, Gen. i. 2, xli. 38; Exod. xxxi. 3, xxxv. 31; Numb. xxiv. 2, etc.

(2) Of false gods, as Exod. xii. 12; 2 Chron. xxviii. 23; Josh. xxiv. 15; Judg. vi. 10, etc.

(3) Of judges to whom a person or matter is brought, as representing the Divine Majesty in the theocracy, yet not in the singular, Exod. xxi. 6, xxii. 7, 8, (in Deut. xix. 17 it is said in the like case that the parties 'shall stand before the Lord,' יהוה); and in allusion to the passages in Exodus, Ps. lxxxii. 1, 6, 'Recte Abarbenel observavit, judices et magistratus nusquam vocari אלהים nisi respectu loci judicii, quod ibi Dei judicia exerceant.' (Ges.)

(4) There is no case in which the word appears from the context to be certainly applied, even collectively, to superhuman beings external to the Divine Essence. 'Nullus exstat locus,' says Gesenius, 'in quo haec significatio vel necessaria vel præ cæteris apta sit.' In Ps. lxxxii. 1, the word is explained by verses 2 and 6 of the 'sons of God,' i.e. judges; cf. especially verse 8. Yet in Ps. xcvii. 7, the LXX, Vulg., Syr. translate 'angels'; the Chaldee paraphrases 'the worshippers of idols'; in Ps. cxxxviii. 1, the LXX and Vulg. render 'angels,' the Chald. 'judges,' the Syr. 'kings'; in Ps. viii. 2, the Chald. too renders 'angels,' and is followed by Rashi, Kimchi, and Abenezra (who quotes Elahin, Dan. ii. 11), and others. It is possible that the earlier Jewish writers had a traditional knowledge that אלהים might be taken as בני־אלהים, Job i. 6; ii. 1; xxxviii. 7, and בני־אלים.

(5) But, however this may be, it remains certain that Elohim is nowhere used with the singular of any except Almighty God.

NOTE C, ON LECTURE IV.

On our Lord's Temptation, viewed in its bearing upon His Person.

The history of our Lord's temptation has been compared to an open gateway, through which Socinianism may enter at will to take possession of the Gospel History. This language proceeds upon a mistaken idea of what our Lord's temptation really was.

A. How far could Jesus Christ be 'tempted'? How far could any suggestion of Satan act upon His Manhood?

1. Here we must distinguish between

(α) Direct temptation to moral evil, i.e. an appeal to a capacity of self-will which might be quickened into active disobedience to the Will of God; and

(β) What may be termed indirect temptation; that is, an appeal to instincts *per se* innocent, as belonging to man in his unfallen state, which can make obedience wear the form of a painful effort or sacrifice.

2. Now Jesus Christ, according to the historians of the Temptation, was—

(α) Emmanuel, St. Matt. i. 23. That this word is used by St. Matthew to mean 'God *is* with us,' as a title of Christ, like 'Jehovah nissi,' appears partly from the parallel of Isa. ix. 6, partly from the preceding αὐτός (ver. 22), used with reference to Jesus. Mary's Son is to be Jesus, not as witnessing to a Divine Saviour external to Himself (as was the case when Joshua bore the name), but as being Himself God the Saviour.

(β) Υἱὸς Θεοῦ, St. Luke i. 35. This title is directly connected with our Lord's supernatural Birth, and so, although applied to His Manhood (τὸ γεννώμενον), yet implies a pre-existent superhuman Personality in Him.

3. This Union of the Divine and Human Natures in Christ was not fatal to the full perfection of either. In particular it did not destroy in Christ's Manhood those limitations which belong properly to creaturely existence. A limitation of knowledge in Christ's Human Intelligence would correspond to a limitation of power in His Human Will.

But it was inconsistent with the presence of anything in Christ's Manhood that could contradict however slightly the Essence of the Perfect Moral Being, in other words, the Holiness of God. This would have been the case with falsehood in Christ's Human Intelligence, or with any secret undeveloped propensity to self-will, that is (in a creature), to moral evil, in Christ's Human Will. If the Incarnate Christ could have erred or sinned, the Incarnation, we may dare to say, would have been a phantom.

The connection between Christ's Personal Godhead, and the complete sinlessness of His Manhood was well understood by Christian antiquity. Thus Tertullian: 'Solus homo sine peccato Christus, quia et Deus Christus' (De An. c. 13). Thus in the synodical letter of Dionysius of Alexandria to Paulus of Samosata, it is argued that εἰ μὴ γὰρ ἦν ὁ Χριστὸς αὐτὸς ὁ ὢν Θεὸς Λόγος, οὐκ ἠδύνατο εἶναι ἀναμάρτητος. Οὐδεὶς γὰρ ἀναμάρτητος εἰ μὴ εἷς ὁ Χριστὸς ὡς καὶ ὁ Πατὴρ τοῦ Χριστοῦ, καὶ τὸ Ἅγιον Πνεῦμα (Labbe, Conc. i. p. 855). So St. Augustine, still more explicitly, teaches: 'Ut autem Mediator Dei et hominum homo Christus Jesus non faceret propriam, quæ Deo adversa est, voluntatem, non erat tantùm homo, sed Deus et homo: per quam mirabilem singularemque gratiam humana in illo sine peccato ullo posset esse natura. Propter hoc ergò ait, Descendi de cœlo, non ut faciam voluntatem meam, sed voluntatem ejus qui me misit (Joh. vi. 38): ut ea caussa esset tantæ obedientiæ quæ omninò sinè ullo peccato esset hominis quae gerebat, quià de cœlo descenderat; hoc est, non tantum homo, verùm etiam Deus erat' (Contr. Sermon. Arianor., c. vii. c. 6). Again, 'Ista nativitas profectò gratuita conjunxit in unitate personæ hominem Deo, carnem Verbo. . . . Neque enim metuendum erat, ne isto ineffabili modo in unitatem personæ à Verbo Deo natura humana suscepta, nullum in se motum malæ voluntatis admitteret' (De Correp. et Grat., c. xi. n. 30). Again, he gives as a reason for the Divine Incarnation, 'Ut intelligant homines per eandem gratiam se justificari à peccatis, per quam factum est ut homo Christus *nullum habere posset peccatum*' (Enchir. ad Laur., c. 36, n. 11; compare Ench. c. 40. See also the passages from St. Athanasius and St. Cyril Alex. qu. by Petav., De Incarnat., lib. xi. c. 10, § 6). Theodorus of Mopsuestia was anathematized at the Fifth Œcumenical Council of Constantinople, A.D. 553, for maintaining among other things that our Lord was *ὑπὸ πάθων ψυχῆς καὶ τῶν τῆς σαρκὸς ἐπιθυμιῶν ἐνοχλούμενον, καὶ τῶν χειρόνων κατὰ μικρὸν χωριζόμενον, καὶ οὕτως ἐκ προτροπῆς ἔργων βελτιώθεντα, καὶ ἐκ πολιτείας ἄμωμον καθίσταντα* (Con. Const., ii. can. xii.; Labbe, v. p. 575). The language of Theodorus was felt to ignore the consequences of the Personal Union of the Two Natures: it was practically Nestorianism.

Our Lord's Manhood then, by the unique conditions of its existence, was believed to be wholly exempt from any propensity to, or capacity of, sinful self-will. When, as in the temptation on the mountain, He was beset by solicitations to evil from without, He met them at once in a manner which shewed that no element of His Human Nature in any degree responded to them. For, as St. Athanasius says, He was *δίχα σαρκικῶν θελημάτων καὶ λογισμῶν ἀνθρωπίνων, ἐν εἰκόνι καινότητος* (Contr. Apollinar., lib. ii. c. 10). The sharpest arrows of the tempter struck Him, but, like darts lighting upon a hard polished surface, they glanced aside. Moreover, as it would seem, the Personal Union of the Two Natures in our Lord involved, at least, the sight of the Beatific Vision by our Lord's Humanity: and if we cannot conceive of the blessed as sinning while they worship around the throne, much less can we conceive it in One in Whom 'dwelt all the fulness of the Godhead bodily.' Thus to any direct temptation to evil He was simply inaccessible, to Whom alone the words fully belong, 'I have set God always before Me, for He is on My right Hand, therefore I shall not fall.'

4. But the Personal Union of our Lord's Manhood with His Godhead did not exempt It from simple human instincts, such as, for example, a shrinking from bodily pain. For, 'As Man's Will, so the Will of Christ hath two several kinds of operation; the one natural or necessary, whereby it desireth simply whatsoever is good in itself, and shunneth as generally all things which hurt; the other deliberate, when we therefore embrace things as good, because the age of understanding judgeth them good to that end which we simply desire. . . . These different inclinations of the will considered, the reason is easy how in Christ there might grow desires, seeming but being not in deed opposite, either the one of them unto the other or either of them unto the Will of God' (Hooker, E.P. v. 48, 9; cf. St. John xii. 27). Upon our Lord's Human Will in its inchoate or rudimentary stage of Desire, uninformed by Reason, an approaching trial might so far act, as a temptation, as, for instance, to produce a wish that obedience might be compatible with escape from suffering. But it could not produce, even for one moment, any wish to be free from the law of obedience itself; since such a wish could only exist where the capacity for sinful self-will was not absolutely excluded. The utmost that temptation could do with our Lord, was to enhance the sacrificial character of obedience, by appealing to an innocent human instinct which ran counter to its actual requirements.

B. This statement of the matter will perhaps suggest some questions.

1. Is it altogether consistent with the Scripture language which represents our Lord as κατὰ πάντα τοῖς ἀδελφοῖς ὁμοιωθείς (Heb. ii. 17); as πεπειραμένος κατὰ πάντα καθ' ὁμοιότητα (Heb. iv. 15); as One Who ἔμαθεν ἀφ' ὧν ἔπαθε τὴν ὑπακοὴν (Heb. v. 7)?

Yes. For Holy Scripture qualifies this language by describing Him as χωρὶς ἁμαρτίας (Heb. iv. 15); as ὅσιος, ἄκακος, ἀμίαντος, κεχωρισμένος ἀπὸ τῶν ἁμαρτωλῶν (Heb. vii. 26); and by connecting His manifestation as the Saviour with the entire absence of any sinful element within Himself: ἐκεῖνος ἐφανερώθη, ἵνα τὰς ἁμαρτίας ἡμῶν ἄρῃ, καὶ ἁμαρτία ἐν αὐτῷ οὐκ ἔστι (1 St. John iii. 5). It is clear that Holy Scripture denies the existence, not merely of any sinful thinking or acting, but of any ultimate roots and sources of sin, of any propensities or inclinations, however latent and rudimentary, towards sin, in the Incarnate Christ. When therefore Scripture speaks of His perfect assimilation to us, to our condition, our trials, our experiences, this language must be understood of physical and mental pain in all their forms. It cannot be understood of any moral assimilation; He is, according to Scripture, the absolutely Sinless One; we are, by nature, corrupt.

2. 'Is this account consistent with the exigencies of our Lord's Redemptive Work?' Did He conquer sin for us, when His victory was won under conditions differing from our own?

Certainly. He is not less truly representative of our race, because in Him it has recovered its perfection. His victory is none the less real and precious, because, morally speaking, it was inevitable. Nay, this perfect internal sinlessness, which rendered Christ inaccessible to direct temptation to evil, was itself essential to His redemptive relationship to the human family. It accordingly was deliberately secured to Him by His Virgin-Birth, which cut off the entail of inward corruption. He could not have been the Sinless Victim, offered freely for a sinful world, δίκαιος ὑπὲρ ἀδίκων (1 St. Pet. iii. 18), unless He had been thus superior to the moral infirmities of His brethren.

3. But does not such an account impair the full force of our Lord's example?

Certainly an example is in a sense more powerful when it is set by one who is under exactly the same moral circumstances as ourselves. And, if Christ our Lord had been a sinner, or at any rate had had sinful dispositions within Him, He would so far have been more entirely what we really are; although He would have been unable to redeem us. If, like His apostle, He had beheld 'another law in His members warring against the law of His mind,' He would have come not in 'the likeness of sinful flesh,' but in flesh that was actually sinful, and so exactly like our own. But then He took our nature upon Him, precisely in order to expel sin altogether from it, and thus to shew us of what it was capable, by shewing us Himself. The absence of an absolute identity of moral circumstances between Him and ourselves, is more than compensated by our possession of what else we could not have had, a Perfect Model of Humanity. We gain in the perfection of the Moral Ideal thus placed before us, to say nothing of the perfection of the Mediator between God and Man, more than we can lose in moral vigour, upon discovering that His obedience was wrought out in a Nature unlike our own in the one point of absolute purity. And by His grace, we ourselves are supernaturalized, and 'can do all things.'

4. But does not such an account reflect upon the moral greatness of our Lord? Is not an obedience 'which could not but be,' less noble than an obedience which triumphs over pronounced disinclination to obey? In other words, does not this account practically deny Christ's moral liberty?

No. The highest liberty does not imply the moral capacity of doing wrong. God is the one perfectly free Being; yet God cannot sin. The free movement of a moral being, who has not fallen, is not an oscillation between sin and moral truth; it is a steady adherence to moral truth. To God sin is impossible. To created natures sin is not impossible; but it is always, at first, a violation of the law of their being; they must do violence to themselves in order to sin. So it was in Eden; so it is, in its degree, with the first lie a man tells now. Our Lord's inaccessibility to sin was the proof and glory of His Moral Perfection. 'Nonne de Spiritu Sancto et Virgine Mariâ Dei Filius unicus natus est, non carnis concupiscentiâ sed singulari Dei munere? Numquid metuendum fuit, ne accedente ætate homo ille libero peccaret arbitrio? An ideo in illo non libera voluntas erat; ac non tantò magis erat, quantò magis peccato servire non poterat?' (S. Aug., De Prædestinatione Sanctorum, c. 15, n. 30.)

The real temptation of a sinless Christ is not less precious to us than the temptation of a Christ who could have sinned, would be. It forms a much truer and more perfect contrast to the failure of our first parent. It occupies a chief place in that long series of acts of condescension which begins with the Nativity, and which ends on the Cross. It is a lesson for all times as to the true method of resisting the tempter. Finally, it is the source of that strength whereby all later victories over Satan have been won: Christ, the sinless One, has conquered the enemy in His sin-stained members. 'By Thy Temptation, good Lord, deliver us.'

NOTE D, ON LECTURE IV.

ON 'Moral' explanations of the Unity of the Father and the Son.

Referring to a passage which is often quoted to destroy the dogmatic significance of St. John x. 30, Professor Bright has well observed that 'the comparison in St. John xvii. 21, and the unity of Christians with each other in the Son has sometimes been abused in the interests of heresy.' 'The second unity,' it has been said, 'is simply moral; therefore the first is so.' But the second is *not* simply moral; it is, in its basis, essential, for we are members of His body, of His flesh, and of His bones; it is the mysterious incorporation into His Sacred Manhood which causes the oneness of affections and of will. Thus also in the higher sphere, the Father and the Son are one in purpose, because They are consubstantial. 'Those,' says Olshausen on St. John x. 30, 'who would entertain the hypothesis—at once Arian, Socinian, and Rationalistic—that ἓν εἶναι refers only to unity of will, not of nature, should not forget that *true* unity of will without unity of nature is something inconceivable. Hence, if Christ speaks of unity of will between Himself and His people, this can subsist only so far as such unity of will has been rendered possible to them by a previous communication of His nature' (Eighteen Sermons of St. Leo, p. 132).

NOTE E, ON LECTURE V.

'The Presbyter John' and the Apostle.

Who was the author of the Second and Third Epistles attributed to St. John the Evangelist in the present Canon of the New Testament?

I. The existence of a 'Presbyter John,' a contemporary of the Apostle, depends on the following evidence:—

(i.) Papias in Eus. iii. 39 names him with Aristion separately from St. John, as a disciple of the Lord. Eusebius adds that this confirms the report of (α) two Johns in Asia who had been in close relations with our Lord, (β) two tombs at Ephesus both bearing the name of John.

(ii.) Dionysius of Alexandria, in Eus. vii. 25, ascribes the authorship of the Apocalypse to 'the Presbyter John,' as Eusebius himself was inclined to do. Dionysius repeats the story of the two tombs.

(iii.) According to the 'Apostolical Constitutions' (vii. 47) a second John was made Bishop of Ephesus by the Apostle St. John.

(iv.) St. Jerome (Catal. Script. c. 9 and 18) makes a statement to the same effect: he says that John the Presbyter's tomb is still shewn at Ephesus, although some maintained that both tombs were memorials of St. John the Evangelist.

Dr. Döllinger admits that the Presbyter John lived as a contemporary of the Evangelist, and that his grave could be seen at Ephesus next to St. John's. (First Age of the Church, p. 113, Eng. trans., 2nd edit.)

II. But this admission would not necessarily involve the further admission that the Presbyter John was the author of the Second and Third Epistles ascribed to the Apostle. All that can be advanced in favour of the Presbyter's authorship is stated by Ebrard (Einleitung); the ordinary belief being defended by Lücke, Huther, Wordsworth, Alford and Westcott. Among reasons for it are the following:—

i. *The argument from style.* The differences upon which Ebrard lays such stress may fairly be accounted for by the distinct character and object of the two Epistles; while their general type of language and thought is unmistakeably Johannean. Bretschneider denied that the Apostle had written any one of the three Epistles. Yet he had no doubt of the fact that all three had been written by a single author.

ii. *Church-tradition.*

(α) The great authority, in this matter especially, of St. Irenæus; Hær. i. 16. 3; iii. 16. 8. (See Alford.) Neither St. Irenæus nor Polycrates had ever heard, it would appear, of the Presbyter John, which shews at least that he cannot have been an eminent person in the Church.

(β) That of Clement and Dionysius of Alexandria (see Alford); Aurelius, quoted by St. Cyprian in Conc. Carth.; St. Jerome, cf. Ep. 2 ad Paulinum, Ep. ad Evagrium.

(γ) On the other hand, Origen was doubtful about the authorship as about many other things. (Eus. vi. 25.) The two Epistles are not even mentioned by Tertullian or Theodoret. They were rejected, together with the other Catholic Epistles, by Theodore of Mopsuestia.

(δ) The late reception of the two Epistles into the canon of so many Churches may be accounted for, according to Ebrard, by (1) their private character; (2) the fact that one was addressed to a woman; (3) the amount of matter in them common to the first Epistle (?). The verdict of the Muratorian Fragm. is doubtful. The Peschito probably did not contain either. Eusebius reckons them among the Antilegomena; yet his own opinion appears in Dem. Ev. iii. 5. (See Alford.)

iii. Nothing against the apostolic authorship can be inferred from the title ὁ πρεσβύτερος. St. Paul calls himself ὁ πρεσβύτης (Philem. 9), and St. Peter ὁ συμπρεσβύτερος (1 Pet. v. 1). Probably 'the Presbyter' John did not assume the title until after the death of the Apostle. St. John may have used it in his private correspondence, either to hint at his age, or as a formal title the force of which was at once recognized and admitted. Surely the Presbyter would have added to ὁ πρεσβύτερος, his name Ἰωάννης. An Apostle could afford to omit his name. The authority too, of which the writer of the third Epistle is conscious in his reference to Diotrephes, seems inconsistent with the supposition of a non-apostolical authorship.

NOTE F, ON LECTURE VII.

The worship of Jesus Christ as prescribed by the Authorized Services of the Church of England.

A. In a letter to the Editor of the 'Times,' dated August 9, and published in that journal on September 26, 1866, Dr. Colenso writes as follows:—

'I have drawn attention to the fact that out of 180 collects and prayers contained in the Prayer-book, only *three* or *four* at most are addressed to our Lord, the others being all addressed through Christ to Almighty God. I have said that there are also ejaculations in the Litany and elsewhere addressed to Christ. But I have shewn that the *whole spirit* and the *general practice* of our Liturgy manifestly tend to discourage such worship and prayer, instead of making it the "foundation-stone" of common worship.'

'It appears,' Dr. Colenso further observes, 'that the practice in question is not based on any Scriptural or Apostolical authority, but is the development of a later age, and has very greatly increased within the Church of England during the last century, beyond what (as the Prayer-book shews) was the rule at the time of the Reformation—chiefly, as I believe, through the use of unauthorized hymns.'

1. Now here it is to be observed, first of all, that prayer to our Lord is either right or wrong. If it is right, if Jesus Christ does indeed hear and answer prayer, and prayer to Him is agreeable to the Divine Will, then three or four hundred collects addressed to Him (supposing the use of them not to imply a lack of devotion to the Eternal Father and to the Holy Spirit) are quite as justifiable as three or four. If such prayer is wrong, if Jesus Christ does not hear it, and it is opposed to the real Will of God, then a single ejaculation, a single Christe Eleison, carries with it the whole weight of a wrongful act of worship, and is immoral, as involving a violation of the rights of God.

Dr. Colenso says that prayer to Jesus Christ is 'not based on Scriptural or Apostolical authority, but is the development of a later age.' He does not mean to assert that 'development' is a sufficient justification of a Christian doctrine or practice; since he is assigning a reason for the discouragement which he feels it to be his duty to offer to the practice of prayer to our Lord. But, if his reason be valid, ought it not to make any one such prayer utterly out of the question? It is not easy to understand the principle upon which, after admitting that 'three or four Collects' in the Prayer-book *are* addressed to our Lord, Dr. Colenso adds, 'I am prepared to use the Liturgy of the Church of England as it stands.'

To a clear mind, unembarrassed by the difficulties of an untenable position, this painful inconsistency would be impossible. Either Jesus Christ is God or He is not; there is no third alternative. If He is God, then natural piety makes prayer to Him inevitable: to call Him God is to call Him adorable. If He is not God, then one-tenth part of the worship which the Church of England in her authorized formularies offers to Him is just as idolatrous as a hundred litanies, such as ours, would be. Dr. Colenso would not explain his use of 'Christ, have mercy upon us' as Roman Catholics explain an 'Ora pro nobis.' If one such 'ejaculation' is right, then prayer to our Lord for an hour together is right also. In short, it is not a question of more or fewer prayers to Christ; the question is, Can we rightly worship Him at all?

2. Dr. Colenso maintains that 'the whole spirit and the general practice of our Liturgy manifestly tend to discourage' prayer to our Lord.

What is meant by the 'whole spirit' of our Liturgy? If this expression is intended to describe some sublimated essence, altogether distinct from the actual words of the Prayer-book, it is of course very difficult to say what it may or may not 'tend' to 'discourage.' But if the 'whole spirit' of a document be its intellectual drift and purpose as gathered from its actual words, and from the history of its formation, then we may say that Dr. Colenso's assertion is entirely opposed to the facts of the case.

(*a*) The devotional addresses to our Lord Jesus Christ *alone* in the Church Service are as follows:—

Daily Service, Morning and Evening—	
Verses of the Te Deum	16
'Christ, have mercy upon us'	2
Prayer of St. Chrysostom	2
Litany—	
Invocation, 'O God the Son'	1
'Remember not, Lord'	1
Deprecations	5
Obsecrations	2
'In all time of our tribulation'	1
Petitions	21
'Son of God, we beseech Thee,' etc.	1
'O Lamb of God, That,' etc.	2
'O Christ, hear us'	1
'Christ, have mercy upon us'	1
Preces, 'From our enemies'	10
Prayer of St. Chrysostom	1
Collects—	
Third Sunday in Advent	1
St. Stephen's Day	1
First Sunday in Lent	1
Communion Office—	
Of the three parts of the Gloria in Excelsis	2
Solemnization of Matrimony—	
'Christ, have mercy upon us'	1
Visitation of the Sick—	
'Remember not, Lord'	1
'Christ, have mercy upon us'	1
'O Saviour of the world, Who by Thy Cross'	1

Burial of the Dead—	
'In the midst of life,' etc.	1
'Christ, have mercy upon us'	1
Churching of Women—	
'Christ, have mercy upon us'	1
Commination—	
'Christ, have mercy upon us'	1
Prayers to be used at Sea—	
'O blessed Saviour, That didst save' . . .	1
'Christ, have mercy upon us'	1
'O Christ, hear us'	1
	83

(β) Devotional addresses to our Lord conjointly with the Eternal Father and the Holy Ghost:—

Daily Morning and Evening Services, not including the Psalms—Gloria Patri at least . . .	6
Athanasian Creed—Gloria Patri	1
Litany—	
'O Holy, Blessed, and Glorious Trinity' .	1
Gloria Patri	1
Collect for Trinity Sunday	1
Communion Office—	
Preface for Trinity Sunday	1
Ter Sanctus	1
Matrimony—Gloria Patri	1
Visitation of the Sick—Gloria Patri . . .	1
Burial of the Dead—Gloria Patri at least . .	1
Churching of Women—Gloria Patri	1
Commination—Gloria Patri	1
Psalter—Gloria Patri	171
Prayers to be used at Sea—	
Gloria Patri	4
'God the Father, God the Son,' etc. . . .	1
	193

Besides this, there are at the end of Collects seven ascriptions of Glory, addressed to Christ our Lord with the Father and the Holy Spirit. In one Collect (Ordering of Deacons) such an ascription is addressed to Christ alone.

(γ) It should further be added, that in each of the Ordination Services the whole of that large part of the Litany which is addressed to our Lord is repeated, with the exception of the Prayer of St. Chrysostom; while in the Doxology, twice repeated, at the end of the Veni Creator, Christ is praised with the Father and the Holy Ghost. Nor should the solemn Benedictions in the name of the Three Blessed Persons which occur in the Communion, the Confirmation, and the Marriage Services, be forgotten in estimating the devotional attitude of the Church towards our Lord. For a view of the real amount of change in the Prayer-book which would be necessary in order to expel from it the worship of our Lord, see 'The Book of Common Prayer of the Church of England adapted for general use in other Protestant Churches'; London, William Pickering, 1852. This compilation appears to have been the work of a Socinian, as those Protestant Dissenters who believe in the Godhead of our Lord would regard most of its 'adaptations' as shocking to their dearest convictions.

(δ) Of the Collects for Sundays or Holy-days now addressed to the Father, only two (those for the Fourth Sunday in Advent and Sunday after Ascension) were, in the old Ritual, prayers to Christ. Yet of these, it happens that the former was, in its original form, as it stood in the Sacramentary of Gelasius, addressed to the Father (Muratori, Lit. Rom. i. 680): and the latter was not originally a Collect, but an antiphon for the second vespers of the Ascension, which Ven. Bede sang shortly before his death. Another prayer, beginning 'Hear us,' in the Visitation Office, was a prayer to our Lord until 1661. On the other hand, of the three Collects now addressed to our Lord, that for the First Sunday in Lent dates from 1549, that for the Third Sunday in Advent from 1661, while that for St. Stephen's Day, originally a prayer to the Father, became a prayer to the Son in 1549, and was enlarged and intensified, as such, in 1661. The Office for Use at Sea, containing prayers to Christ, also belongs to 1661.

In order to do justice to the spirit of the Reformers of the sixteenth century on this subject, two facts should be noted:

1. Prayers to our Lord abound in the semi-authorized Primers which were put out at that period. In Edward the Sixth's

Primer of 1553 there are sixteen. In Elizabeth's Primer of 1559 there are twenty-two. In one portion of the Preces Privatæ of 1564 there are twenty-one. In the 'Christian Prayers' of 1578 there are fifty-five.

2. On the other hand, from all of these manuals, as from the public services of the Church, all addresses to any created being were rigorously excluded. And one effect of the expulsion of antiphons and hymns addressed to the Blessed Virgin and other Saints from the Liturgy of the Church of England, has been to throw the praises, prayers, and adorations, which the Church of England publicly addresses to our Lord Jesus Christ, into a sharper prominence than belonged to such prayers in pre-Reformation times, or than belongs to them now in the Church of Rome.

The old Puritanism would have shrunk with horror from the discouragement of prayer to our Lord. Witness the speech of Sir E. Dering in the Long Parliament of 1641, after an order of the House of Commons forbidding men to bow at the Name of Jesus:—

'Was it ever heard before, that any men of any religion, in any age, did ever cut short or abridge any worship, upon any occasion, to their God? Take heed, Sir, and let us all take heed, whither we are going. If Christ be Jesus, if Jesus be God, all reverence, exterior as well as interior, is too little for Him. I hope we are not going up the back stairs to Socinianism!' (Southey, Book of the Church, p. 462.)

* * * * *

B. The worship of Christ our Lord in the Litany has lately been explained by a very popular and accomplished writer[a], upon principles, which, if they could be admitted, would deny to it the significance assigned to it in these Lectures. After commenting on the historical origin of Litany-worship in the fifth century, and on the compilation of our own Litany at the Reformation, Dean Stanley observes that the Litany forms the most remarkable exception to the ordinary practice of the Church, in respect of addressing prayers to God the Father. The Dean then proceeds:—

'It is not perhaps certain that all the petitions are addressed to Christ our Saviour[b]; but, at any rate, a large portion are so

[a] 'The Litany,' by the Dean of Westminster. In 'Good Words' for July, 1868, p. 423.

[b] 'We beseech thee to hear us, O Lord,' is in the older Litanies addressed to God (Martene, iii. 52), and so it would seem to be in some of the petitions

addressed. It stands in this respect almost isolated amidst the rest of the Prayer Book. Now, what is the reason—what is the defence for this? Many excellent persons have at times felt a scruple at such a deviation from the precepts of Scripture and from the practice of ancient Christendom. What are we to say to explain it? The explanation is to be sought in the original circumstances under which the litany was introduced. When the soul is overwhelmed with difficulties and distresses, like those which caused the French Christians in the fifth century to utter their piteous supplications to God—it seems to be placed in a different posture from that of common life. The invisible world is brought much nearer—the language, the feelings of the heart become more impassioned, more vehement, more urgent. The inhabitants, so to speak, of the world of spirits seem to become present to our spirits; the words of common intercourse seem unequal to convey the thoughts which are labouring to express themselves. As in poetry, so in sorrow, and for a similar reason, our ordinary forms of speech are changed. So it was in the two exceptions which occur in the New Testament. When Stephen was in the midst of his enemies, and no help for him left on earth, then "the heavens were opened; and he saw the Son of Man standing on the right hand of God," and thus seeing Him, he addressed his petition straight to Him—"Lord Jesus, receive my spirit,—Lord, lay not this sin to their charge." When St. Paul was deeply oppressed by the thorn in the flesh, then again his Lord appeared to him (we know not how), and then to Him, present to the eye whether of the body or the spirit (as on the road to Damascus), the Apostle addressed the threefold supplication, "Let this depart from me," and the answer, in like manner, to the ear of the body or spirit, was direct—"My grace is sufficient for thee." So is it in the Litany. Those who wrote it, and we who use it, stand for the moment in the place of Stephen and Paul. We knock, as it were, more earnestly at the gates of heaven—we "thrice beseech the Lord"—and the veil is for a moment withdrawn, and the Son of Man is there standing to receive our prayer. In that rude time, when the Litany was first introduced, they who used it would fain have drawn back the veil further still. It was in the Litanies of the Middle Ages that we first find the invocations not only of Christ our

in the English Litany. But perhaps the most natural interpretation is to regard the whole as addressed to Christ." Note by Dean Stanley in 'Good Words.'

Saviour, but of those earthly saints who have departed with Him into that other world. These we have now, with a wise caution, ceased to address. But the feeling which induced men to call upon them is the same in kind as that which runs through this exceptional service; namely, the endeavour, under the pressure of strong emotion and heavy calamity, to bring ourselves more nearly into the presence of the Invisible. Christ and the saints at such times seemed to come out like stars, which in the daylight cannot be seen, but in the darkness of the night were visible. The saints, like falling stars or passing meteors, have again receded into the darkness. We by increased reflection have been brought to feel that of them and of their state we know not enough to justify this invocation of their help. But Christ, the Lord and King of the Saints, still remains—the Bright and Morning Star, more visible than all the rest, more bright and more cheering, as the darkness of the night becomes deeper, as the cold becomes more and more chill.

'We justly acquiesce in the practice of our Reformed Church, which has excluded those lesser mediators. But this one remarkable exception of the Litany in favour of addressing our prayers to the one great Divine Mediator may be surely allowed, if we remember that it is an exception, and understand the grounds on which it is made. In the rest of the Prayer Book we follow the ancient rule, and our Saviour's express command, by addressing our Father only. Here in the Litany, when we express our most urgent needs, we may well deviate from that general rule, and invite the ever-present aid of Jesus Christ, at once the Son of Man and Son of God[c].'

1. Now, first of all, it cannot be admitted that any 'defence' or 'explanation' of the worship of our Lord in the Litany ought to be required by any person who sincerely believes in Christ's Godhead; while as to those who do not believe in it, the Dean's explanation does not touch the real point of their objection. If 'many excellent persons have at times felt a scruple at such a deviation from the precepts of Scripture and from the practice of ancient Christendom,' they ought to have been told that their scruple was based on a misapprehension. As to Scripture, every precept in the Gospel on the subject is in harmony with and governed by the primal law: 'Thou shalt worship the Lord thy God, and Him only shalt thou serve.' This precept is at once positive and negative: it prescribes the

c 'Good Words,' p. 432.

adoration of God, and it excludes the adoration of beings external to the Godhead. The one practical question then is whether Jesus Christ is internal to the Divine Essence, or a created being outside It. If the former, then not merely may we adore Him: we must. If the latter, then no poetry, no feeling, can relax the rule: we dare not. If Christ is God, the Litany does not require an apology. If He is only a creature, it does not admit of one.

And as concerns 'the practice of the ancient Church' the scruple in question is very unnecessary. Certainly, in the greatest public act of Christian worship, the Eucharist, the rule was, as defined at Carthage, to address prayer to the Father. This rule however resulted from the specific belief of the ancient Church respecting the Eucharist, namely, that it was a sacrificial presentation of Christ, once for all sacrificed on Calvary, to the Eternal Father. The rule did not govern ancient Christian practice in respect of non-Eucharistic prayer. The Litanies of the fifth century did but repeat and expand devotions which had long been ancient and popular; such as were the Kyrie Eleison and the Gloria in Excelsis;—both of them containing prayers to Christ our Lord, and both ultimately finding their way into the Eucharistic Service. Prayer to our Lord had long been the natural resource of the Christian soul. Not to repeat examples which have been cited in the text of these lectures, let two be instanced which shew that prayer to Christ did not first become popular in the ancient Church, when, under the pressure of public calamities, Bishop Mamertus instituted Litanies in the diocese of Vienne. Such prayer was already the common and ancient practice of Christendom. A century earlier St. Athanasius is vindicating his loyalty to Constantius: 'I had only to say,' he observes, 'Let us pray for the safety of the most religious Emperor, Constantius Augustus; and all the people immediately cried with one voice, "O Christ, send Thy help to Constantius." And they continued praying for some time.' (Apol. ad Constant. § 10.) Again, St. Augustine is describing a spontaneous burst of fervid prayer from the Christian multitude —They exclaimed, 'Exaudi Christe, Augustino vita:' and he adds—'dictum est sexties decies.' (Ep. 213.) These great fathers would no more have thought that prayer to our Lord had to be justified before well-informed Christians, than they would have hoped to justify it, let us say, to intelligent but unconverted Jews.

2. Dean Stanley's 'explanation' of the worship of our Lord

in the Litany refers it to 'difficulties and distresses like those which caused the French Christians in the fifth century to utter their piteous supplications to God.' He traces it back to the passion, the vehemence, the urgency of a great sorrow; to 'the endeavour, under the pressure of strong emotion and heavy calamity, to bring ourselves more nearly into the presence of the Invisible.' Now there is no doubt that calamities, whether public or private, do very greatly enlarge and intensify the life of prayer in Christian souls. Scripture teaches us, in various ways, that this is one of the providentially-intended results of such calamities; and upon no point is Scripture more in harmony with experience. But sorrow, of itself, does not make the prayers which it multiplies or intensifies either lawful or availing. Sorrow may quicken the instincts of superstition not less than those of revealed truth. Sorrow, as such, is not a revelation; it does not ensure progress in truth; it may bring a Christian more sensibly into God's Presence; it may throw pagan multitudes at the feet of a debasing and odious idol. Whether the practices which it leads us, in our agony, to adopt, are wholesome and defensible, must be determined independently of it. If a practice is indefensible, on grounds of faith or grounds of reason, sorrow cannot consecrate it. If it was in any sense or degree wrong to pray to Jesus Christ, St. Stephen's dying agony, and St. Paul's mental distress under the thorn in the flesh, could not justify their prayers to Him; if they were right in praying to Him then, they were right in praying to Him, as we know St. Paul did pray to Him, at other times. If the prayers to our Lord in the Litany were really a 'deviation from the precepts of Scripture and from the practice of ancient Christendom,' then neither the difficulties and distresses of Southern France in the fifth century, nor the 'extremity of perplexity[d]' which men felt at the convulsions of the Reformation-period, nor any public or private sorrows or emotions of modern times, can avail to justify such a 'deviation.' It is indeed natural for Christians in times of sorrow to appeal in prayer to our Lord's Human sympathies, more earnestly than in the brighter hours of life. But assuredly if such prayers to Christ are wrong, no amount of mental agony can make them right; and whether they are right or wrong is a point to be determined by Christ's having or not having any solid right to receive human adoration, and any real capacity of

[d] 'Good Words,' p. 421.

hearing and answering the cries of His worshippers. If this right and this capacity are once established, the duty of adoring Jesus Christ is placed on a basis which does not admit of our restricting it to times of sorrow. If they are not established, human sorrow cannot really affect the unseen realities, and St. Stephen and St. Paul did but beat the air.

If the Psalter teaches us any one great lesson with respect to sorrow, it is that we should be driven by it to renounce all merely human aids and hopes, and to cling more trustfully, exclusively, perseveringly, to God as the true help and shield and strength of souls. And the Christian Bishop of the fifth century was not, we may be sure, unmindful of the teaching of David, or rather he was not notoriously false to it. The whole Church of his day, as the Church before him, adored Jesus Christ as Very God, and the Litanies of Vienne only elaborated into a new form a devotion which was based not on the panic of certain rural Christians, but on the broad and assured faith of Christendom.

3. But the Dean's expressions respecting the relation of the adoration of our Lord to the cultus of the saints in pre-Reformation times, present the most serious difficulties of this perplexing passage. In times of sorrow, he says, 'Christ and the saints *seemed* to come out like stars, which in the daylight cannot be seen, but in the darkness of the night were visible.' The saints 'have again receded into the darkness.' 'We by increased reflection have been brought to feel that of them and of their state we know not enough to justify this invocation of their help. But Christ, the Lord and King of the Saints, still remains' .... 'We justly acquiesce in the practice of our reformed Church, which has excluded these lesser mediators. But this one *remarkable exception* of the Litany in favour of addressing our prayers to the one great Divine Mediator may be surely allowed, if we remember that it is an *exception*, and understand the grounds on which it is made.'

This language seems to imply that the prayers to our Lord in the Litany are, in principle, identical with the prayers which in mediæval times have been, and in Roman Catholic countries still are, addressed to the saints. There is indeed some confusion in speaking of the retention of prayer to the one great Divine Mediator as constituting a 'remarkable exception' to the proscription of prayers to the saints. For if the Great Mediator is 'Divine,' in the natural sense of being personally God, and not only in the sense in which good men are said to be 'divine,' as possessing in a high, the highest known degree, some moral qualities of God; then the word 'exception' is inapplicable to the case before us. If, on the contrary, Christ is not truly God, then, no doubt, the retention of worship addressed to Him is a 'remarkable exception' to the expulsion of all other 'worship' of the kind from the Prayer-book of the English Church. But it will hardly be contended that the English Reformers retained the old prayers to Christ our Lord, and added new ones of their own, on such a ground as this. Had they done so, they would have been false to a principle to which they professed a devoted loyalty, and by means of which, so to speak, they made their way;—the principle of restricting all prayer to God. They notoriously believed the adoration of Christ to be identical with, inseparable from, the adoration of God; to be guarded, justified, enforced by the first two commandments of the decalogue, just as truly as is the adoration of the Father, and of the Holy Ghost, 'Who with the Father and the Son together, is worshipped and glorified[i].' And, whatever may be said of the language used in popular Roman Catholic devotions to the saints, it is certain that no Roman Catholic divine would for one instant coordinate in word or thought the adoration paid to Jesus, with the 'relative honour' paid to His glorified servants. In short, neither Roman Catholic nor Reformer regarded the adoration of Christ retained in our Prayer-book, as an 'exception' to the general proscription at the Reformation of the cultus of the saints. Had the Reformers done so, they would have had to reconstruct, not the Litany, but the Nicene Creed; they must also have re-written the second Article in a Socinian sense, and altered a clause of the twenty-second. Had the Roman Catholics done so, they would certainly have availed themselves of a vantage ground which would have enabled them to deal with the Reformation as with a manifest revolt against the most fundamental truths of the Christian revelation. Whether the Roman invocations of the saints did or did not in any way wrong the Divine Prerogatives, was a point upon which the Reformers and their opponents differed seriously; but they were perfectly agreed in justifying such language as that of our Litany by referring it to a truth which they held at least with equal earnestness;—the truth that Jesus Christ is God.

If, in Origen's phrase, 'caro Domini honorem Deitatis assu-

[i] Nicene Creed.

mit;' if, as a consequence of the Hypostatic Union, our Lord's Manhood rightly and necessarily shares in the adoration offered to Deity, this is because His Divine Person is ultimately and in reality, the object adored. 'O God the Son, Redeemer of the world, have mercy upon us miserable sinners.' 'O Lamb of God, That takest away the sins of the world, have mercy upon us.' In either case it is Christ's Eternal Person which claims our adoration; that Person, with Which His Manhood is now for ever joined, as an attribute of It. And Christ's Person is adored, for precisely the same reason as that which leads us to adore the Father; nor could such adoration be offered to any created personality whatever, without repudiating altogether the first, the most sacred, prerogative of Deity.

NOTE G, ON LECTURE VII.

Cardinal de Turrecremata's work on the Conception of the Blessed Virgin.

The only copy of this work which I have seen is in the Mazarine Library at Paris, where it is numbered 12144. Its full title is, '*Tractatus de Veritate Conceptionis Beatissimæ Virginis, pro faciendâ relatione coram patribus Concilii Basileensis, Anno Dni. M.CCCC.XXX.VII. Mense Julio. De mandato Sedis Apostolicæ Legatorum, eidem sacro Concilio præsidentium compilatus. Per Reverendum Patrem, Fratrem Joannem de Turrecremata, sacræ Theologiæ professorem, ordinis Prædicatorum, tunc sacri apostolici Palatii Magistrum, Posteà Illustrissimum et Reverendissimum S. R. Ecclesiæ Cardinalem Episcopum Portuensem, nunc primo impressus. Romæ apud Antonium Bladum Asulanum, M.D.XLVII.*'

The book opens with a Preface by '*Frater Albertus Duimius de Catharo, ordinis prædicatorum, Sacræ Theologiæ professor: et in Sapientiâ urbis Romæ, divinæ speculationis interpres,*' addressed '*sinceræ veritatis amatoribus.*' After reviewing, chiefly in the language of Scripture itself, the grounds, nature, and obligations of the Christian faith, he proceeds:—'Est autem præ cæteris a sacris literis admodum aliena et Christi evangelio dissona humana quædam inventio, nostro infelici ævo ita errata, ut posthabitis sacræ scripturæ clarissimis testimoniis, spretis etiam ecclesiæ sanctorumque patrum veterumque ecclesiæ doctorum salutaribus monitis et doctrinis, cujusdam vanæ devotionis prætextu, sanctissimam Dei genetricem virginem, cœli reginam, angelorum atque hominum dominam, propriis quibusdam adinventis laudibus celebrare cupiens, eam non fuisse Adæ peccato obnoxiam, ac perinde Christi sanguinis pretio non indiguisse, ineptiùs dogmatizare præsumpserit, ut hinc liceret aliquibus (qui sacris abuti consuevêre) liberiùs vorare domos viduarum, seducereque corda simplicium longâ oratione orantibus, existimantibusque quæstum esse pietatem. Quorum audacia divus Bernardus abbas, beatæ virgini super omnes devotissimus, acriùs reprehendit dicens: Miramur satis quod visum fuerit hoc tempore quibusdam voluisse mutare colorem ecclesiæ optimum, novam inducendo celebritatem, quam ritus ecclesiæ nescit, non probat ratio, non commendat antiqua traditio. Numquid patribus doctiores aut devotiores sumus? Periculosè præsumimus quicquid ipsorum prudentia præterivit. Virgo regia falso non eget honore veris honorum titulis cumulata, et infulis dignitatum. Non enim indiget Deus nostro mendacio. Hanc autem fore sanctorum patrum et ecclesiæ luminarium doctrinam, quam Augustinus innumeraque antiquorum multitudo prædicavit, quamque posteriores sancti doctrinâ et moribus probatissimi amplexati sunt, quam Thomas Aquinas sustinet, Divusque Bonaventura Minoritani ordinis, S. R. E. Episcopus Cardinalis, fortissimè tueatur, luce clariùs patere poterit, opus hoc Christianâ mente legentibus. Horum autem sequacium tetigit Deus corda, ut veluti fortissimi milites Christi, sacram Scripturam in sui simplicitate et candore tuerentur et conservarent. Inter alios autem, qui ex sacro Prædicatorum ordine (patrum imitati vestigia), huic se militiæ devoverunt, Reverendissimus olim sacri Apostolici Palatii Magister, ac postea (sic exigentibus virtutum meritis) S. R. E. Cardinalis Episcopus Portuensis, D. Joañes de Turrecremata Hispanus, jussu et mandato sedis apostolicæ, præsenti relatione scripta disseruit. Opus quidem ita sincerum et christianæ pietati conveniens, ut nusquam, vel humanæ inventionis tenebræ, vel propriæ opinionis affectus appareant, sed undique evangelicæ veritatis candor splendere videatur. Opus inquam, summè necessarium sed hactenus rarissimum, et id quidem scriptorum inscitiâ innumeris mendis respersum fœdatumque, neglectu penitus habebatur. Quietior namque erat omnium nostrum mens et animus, et hujusmodi quæstionibus oblitis, necessariora fidei dogmata tueri animo insederat, et temporum opportunitas exigebat. Sed immoderatior quorundam audacia, dum apud doctos et verè Theologos minoris se existimationis advertunt, vulgarem debiliumque mentium auram jamdiu sepultis novitatibus affectantes, in Tridentinâ synodo, de hujusmodi humani conceptûs immunitate verbum facere verita non est. Quo factum est ut Reverendus pater frater Bartholomeus Spina Pisanus ordinis prædicatorum, sacræ Theologiæ professor, et sacri apostolici Palatii magister, zelo fidei accensus, opus hoc erroribus expurgari, typisque excussum, in publicum prodire, magno labore curaret. Accessit, (Deo favente) sanctissimi D. N. D. Pauli Papæ Tertii consensus et favor.'

For these reasons, and under these auspices, the work was printed at Rome in 1547. Towards the conclusion of his preface, the editor contrasts the theological aim and spirit of Turrecremata with that of his opponents in such terms as these:—

'Non enim alio tendit ista disparitas, quam ut hinc sacræ scripturæ germana veritas, et ecclesiæ sanctorumque patrum et doctorum adprobata doctrina, laudatissima pietas, et vera religio, illinc autem quædam vulgarium affectata devotio, sacris literis et doctoribus non admodum consona, quinimo (ut quibusdam visum est,) repugnans, et ab aliquâ ecclesiæ consuetudine aliena, defendatur. Hinc Christi universalis redemptio, et super alios omnes Sacræ Humanitatis Ejus excellentiæ prærogativæ, illinc æqualitas virginis sacratissimæ et piæ Dei genetricis, ad Filium Dei Hominem Deum, et à reatu inimicitiæ Dei, et naturali captivitate peccati immunitas, pro pietate defenduntur. Illis, quod vulgaribus, quodque mulierculárum auribus gratum judicaverint pietatem adstruentibus; nobis e contra nil pium, nil devotum, nilque Christianâ celebritate dignum existimantibus, quod non ex sacris literis auctoritatem habere comprobatur.'

The work itself is divided into thirteen parts. The first deals with the principles which are to govern the discussion. In the second, are considered those passages of the Old and New Testament which, as interpreted by the Gloss and by the explanations of the saints, assert that Christ alone was free in His Conception from the taint of original sin. In the third part, Holy Scripture and the Fathers are quoted to shew that all human beings without exception who descend from Adam by way of natural propagation, are conceived in original sin. The fourth part is devoted to a consideration of the attempts of opponents to set aside the inferences drawn from Rom. iii. 22, v. 12; Gal. iii. 22; St. Matt. ix. 13; St. Luke xix. 10; 1 Tim. i. 15, ii. 5; 2 Cor. v. 14. In the fifth part, Scripture, saints, and doctors, are cited to prove that 'the Blessed Virgin Mary did in fact contract original sin.' St. Luke i. 47 is interpreted as implying this. The subject is pursued in the sixth part; passages from St. Leo the Great, St. John of Damascus, St. Gregory, St. Anselm, Hugh of St. Victor, and especially St. Bernard's Letter to the Canons of Lyons, and the deliberate decision in the Summa of St. Thomas Aquinas, whose doctrine had been endorsed by the University of Paris, are passed in review. Lest opposition to the doctrine should be supposed to be only a Dominican peculiarity, an appeal is made to Minorite, Augustinian, Carmelite, Carthusian, and Cistercian theologians. In the seventh part, the weight of ancient authority is pressed against the opinion of the 'modern doctors'; the conduct of the Dominican theologians is justified in detail; and the truth of their doctrine is argued, from an examination of the prerogative glories of our Lord, especially in His Conception, and from the real limits of the 'privileges' commonly ascribed to the Blessed Virgin. The eighth part is an argument from the universality of our Lord's redemption to man's universal need of it; 'omnis redemptus per Christum fuit aliquando peccati servitute captivus:' while, in the ninth, our Lord's titles of Mediator, Reconciler, Healer, Justifier, Sanctifier, Cleanser, Shepherd, and Priest of His people are successively expanded in their relation to the doctrine of the absolute universality of human sin. In the tenth, the author attacks the arguments and authorities which were cited to prove the *à priori* position, that God ought to have preserved the Blessed Virgin from original sin; here too he criticises the Scotist theory of the reason for the Incarnation. In the eleventh he assails in detail the arguments which were adduced to prove that the Blessed Virgin was in point of fact preserved from the taint of original sin; in the twelfth, those which were brought forward to shew that she was thus preserved by a prevenient grace of sanctification. The last part of the work recapitulates the disputed propositions; discusses the opinion that 'pejus sit stare per unum instans in originali peccato quam eternaliter esse damnatum;' meets the allegation of miracles wrought to prove the Immaculate Conception by alleging miracles wrought to disprove it; examines the bearing of the established festival of the Conception on the faith of the Church; and finally insists that between those who asserted and those who denied the Immaculate Conception of the Blessed Virgin there were not less than twenty points of difference.

At the end of the book, Turrecremata subjoins a personal explanation. He states that on presenting himself at Basle, with a view 'ad faciendam relationem mihi injunctam,' he was told by the Cardinal Legate who presided, that the Fathers were so occupied with the questions raised by the arrival of the Greeks, that he could not be heard. He remained at Basle for some months, but to no purpose. Upon the outbreak of the disagreement between the Legates of Eugenius and 'patres aliquos Basileæ residentes,' Turrecremata returned to Rome with his book. He adds with reference to the later proceedings of the Council in the matter of the Immaculate Conception: 'Ex his apertissimè intelliget quisque doctus quod vacua et invalida sit determinatio quam in materiâ præfatâ conceptionis beatissimæ virginis factam quidam aiunt post recessum meum Basileâ. Invalida quidem est veritate, cum facta sit manifestè contra apertissima sanctorum patrum ecclesiæ testimonia, ac contra doctrinam expressam principalium doctorum tam divini juris quam humani, sicut ex præfato opere luce clariùs videri potest.' A further reason for this invalidity he finds in the previous departure of the papal legates and the proclamation of the transference of the Council to Bologna.

Such a work as Turrecremata's has only to be described, and it speaks for itself. Here is an elaborate treatise of between 700 and 800 closely-printed pages; abounding in appeals to authority, the most ancient and the most modern; full of hard, scholastic argument; scarcely less full, at times, of passionate rhetoric. It shrinks from no encounter with the maintainers of the doctrine which it impugns; it traverses, with fearless confidence, and according to the learning and methods of its day, with exhaustive completeness, the whole field of the controversy. Whether it has been really answered or not by the arguments of Bellerini, of Perrone, of Passaglia, is not here the question. Enough to say that in the year of our Lord 1437, it represented the mind of the reigning Pope, the mind too of the Theologian who in his 'Apology for Eugenius IV.' most stoutly maintained the extreme papal claims against the superiority of a General Council, as asserted at Basle. Turrecremata had no tinge of what afterwards became 'Gallicanism'; he was a hearty Ultramontane, and in the confidence of the Pontiff. He, if any one, could speak on behalf of the Western Church, of its learning, of its piety, of its central authority, in the middle of the fifteenth century. And his work against the Immaculate Conception is perhaps the most remarkable of the many documents, which make any real parallel between the claims of the truth asserted at Nicæa, and those of the definition of Dec. 8, 1854, impossible.

A high Roman Catholic authority has said that 'they who ask why the Immaculate Conception has been defined in the nineteenth century, would have asked why the "homoousion" was defined in the fourth [f].' If they had done so, they would have received in the fourth century an answer for which in the nineteenth they must wait in vain. In the fourth century they would have been told that the substantial truth defined at Nicæa had always been believed as a fundamental truth of the Gospel; that those who had denied it had been accounted heretics, from the days of the Apostles downwards; that Arius was accounted a heretic, on first broaching his novel doctrine; that the circumstances of the time demanded for the old unchanging truth the protection of a new definition; but that the definition added, could add, nothing to the faith which had been held in its fulness from the first—the faith that Jesus Christ is God. In the nineteenth century they are told that the definition of the Immaculate Conception had the effect of raising to a certainty of faith that which was, before Dec. 8, 1854, only a matter of pious opinion; that those who, before that date, had denied this opinion were so far from being accounted heretics, that they were expressly protected from censure by the highest authority; that although the newly-defined truth had been taught to the Church by the Apostles themselves and had all along been latent in her mind, yet that her most representative divines and doctors had again and again, with perfect impunity, nay with the highest sanctions, expressly repudiated and condemned it.

It will be said that the same authority speaks at Rome which spoke at Nicæa. Upon that most important question we do not here and now enter. But with a book like Turrecremata's before us, we cannot decline the conclusion that in A.D. 325 and 1854 two entirely different things were done; unless it can be shewn that some hitherto unknown writer of the highest consideration and of unsuspected orthodoxy in the ante-Nicene period maintained against others who defended the Homoousion, and by an appeal to a vast accumulation of authorities, the precise doctrine for which Arius was condemned. That would be a real counterpart to the position of Cardinal Turrecremata in relation to the recent definition of the Immaculate Conception: as it is, the doctrinal and historical 'parallel' upon which some Roman Catholics and many opponents of the Christian Revelation now lay so much stress, is not sufficiently accurate

[f] The Reunion of Christendom, a Pastoral Letter to the Clergy, by Henry Edward, Archbishop of Westminster. London, Longmans, 1866, p. 51.

to justify either of the opposite conclusions which it is put forward in order to recommend.

NOTE H. On Two Criticisms of this Work. [1881.]

After this work had been revised for the second and stereotyped edition, two notices of it, among others, appeared, under the following titles:—*An Examination of Canon Liddon's Bampton Lectures on the Divinity of our Lord and Saviour Jesus Christ, by a Clergyman of the Church of England.* (London, Trübner); and *The Bible and Popular Theology: a Restatement of Truths and Principles, with special reference to recent works of Dr. Liddon, Lord Hatherley, the Right Hon. W. E. Gladstone, and others; by G. Vance Smith, B.A., Ph. D., Minister of St. Saviourgate Chapel, York.* (London, Longmans.)

At the time when these publications came into his hands the Lecturer had made up his mind that his book had taken its final form; and that, if he was to deal with the great subject discussed in it again, this must be done in another work, and on a more comprehensive scale. It is unnecessary to enter on the reasons which have made such a project less and less easy of accomplishment. Suffice it to say, that, another edition of the Bampton Lectures having been asked for, the Lecturer thinks it better no longer to defer a reconsideration of his work, in the light of these and one or two other criticisms which he has had the advantage of consulting.

While the Bampton Lecturer is under an obligation to both his critics in some matters of detail, he is unable to follow them at all generally, and for a reason which makes a full examination of their criticisms superfluous. He and they disagree, not merely or chiefly in questions of detail, but as to first principles. The province of discussion is to shew either that persons who differ ought to agree, or that they cannot hope to agree. They ought to agree, if, while both parties appeal to the same premises, the true force of these premises is, for whatever reason, not apparent to one of the parties; the duty of discussion being to remove obscurities, and so to make agreement logically imperative. But they cannot agree if they are really appealing to different first principles; when this is the case, discussion can only make the inevitable disagreement conscious and pronounced, by clearing away intercepting matter which obscures the true force of the contradiction.

Now our Lord's Divinity is a truth which we must learn from Revelation, if we are to learn it at all. Nature, measured by experience, and interpreted by conscience and reason, has nothing to say to it. The first question then is, whether a Revelation has been really given, and the second where it is to be found. And if it is agreed that God has really spoken in the Jewish and Christian Revelations, and that the Bible tells us what He has said, a further question arises as to the trustworthiness of the record. Unless this trustworthiness is also recognized, it is impossible to discuss the contents of the Revelation with any hope of arriving at solid results. For any statement containing matter which is, for whatever reason, unwelcome to either party, may be at once challenged on *à priori* grounds, and rejected; and disputants may thus find themselves as little in possession of a common premise, as if they had not agreed that a Revelation from God had been made, or recorded at all.

This then is the issue, as between the Lecturer and his present critics. He does, and they do not, believe in the trustworthiness of the Bible. They believe, no doubt, in the trustworthiness of certain parts of it,—such parts of it as are in agreement with opinions which, for independent reasons, they accept. But they do not treat the Bible as a trustworthy whole; they accept or reject its statements at pleasure, or for reasons which appear to them to be sufficient; and, as a consequence, it is not enough for them if a doctrine is contained in the Bible, unless it be contained in those parts of the Bible which they think it right to accept.

The two writers under consideration are indeed unlike each other in more respects than one. The 'Clergyman of the Church of England' appears to be the better scholar; Dr. Vance Smith the more reverent and philosophical mind. Dr. Vance Smith shews his hand, and is intent upon vindicating such portions of truth as he accepts. The 'Clergyman's' attitude is throughout critical; he tells us what he considers to be the real teaching of the New Testament about our Lord's Person, but he does not say that he believes it. Dr. Vance Smith however welcomes him as on the whole a useful ally; he describes the 'Examination etc.' as 'a careful and effective reply to all the principal portions of Dr. Liddon's Lectures, and, so far as may be judged from a cursory perusal of parts, one of the most powerful modern treatises on the Unitarian side of this controversy.'

He adds, 'The marvel attending it is, that the author should announce himself, on his title-page, as a "Clergyman of the Church of England [a]."'

I. The 'Clergyman,' then, holds that 'the Christian perception which Christ's teaching and example have enlightened, must be *free to weed* the records concerning Him [b].' In other words, certain portions of the Gospel narrative, which approve themselves to modern taste, are put forward as a reason for rejecting other and equally authenticated portions. Thus the Baptismal formula, St. Matt. xxviii. 19, 20, is said to be 'a passage too uncertain to be quoted in a controversial work without some attempt to vindicate its genuineness from the very grave doubts which other portions of the New Testament compel us to entertain [c];' and the 'Clergyman' ventures to add that 'the words are not really His [our Lord's], although found in every known MS. and version of the First Gospel [d].' In the same spirit he objects to St. Mark xvi. 15, as belonging to 'that concluding section which every scholar knows to be an extremely questionable fraction of the Second Gospel [e],' although Dean Burgon's work on 'The Last Twelve Verses of the Gospel according to St. Mark' (Oxford, Parker, 1871), contains facts and arguments which might, at the least, have counselled a less peremptory judgment. We are told that the application of Isaiah vii. 14 in St. Matt. i. 22, 23 is 'in no respect decisive [f].' Assuming a contradiction to exist between the Synoptists and St. John, the 'Clergyman' is 'unavoidably conducted to an unfavourable appreciation of the Fourth Gospel's historical fidelity, and is confirmed in the suspicion that the writer made many statements from a speculative and ideal, rather than from a properly historical point of view [g].' 'The Word' is said to be 'a speculative, nebulous title [h],' and the Last Discourse is at least possibly 'a compilation of the Evangelist's from loose and imperfect data [i].' Our Lord's promise in St. John xiv. 26 is 'an anticipatory explanation and apology for the production of matter so distinct from what the common oral tradition and the existing written memoirs embraced [j].' Speaking of the Last Discourse, the 'Clergyman' anticipates a time when 'passages, from which it is next to impossible to elicit any clear consistent sense, will

[a] The Bible and Popular Theology, Pref. p. iv. note.
[b] Examination, p. 77, note.
[c] Ibid. p. 78.
[d] Ibid. p. 243.
[e] Ibid.
[f] Ibid. p. 63.
[g] Ibid. pp. 87, 88.
[h] Ibid. p. 84.
[i] Ibid. p. 214.
[j] Ibid. p. 43.

no longer be pronounced profoundly spiritual and full of beauty[k].' The Epistle to the Hebrews[l] is criticized with contemptuous severity. The 'Clergyman' finds that 'the writer of this Epistle did not think deeply, and knew too little of his theme to treat it consistently[m];' that he made erroneous applications of the Old Testament[n], and that his 'description of Melchizedek (Heb. vii. 3) is singularly fanciful and exaggerated;' although the 'errors into which the writer of the Epistle has fallen' 'do not justify us in pronouncing him altogether speculative, visionary, and unreasonable[o].' The 'Clergyman' protests against the belief that 'every sentence of the Bible is identical with the word of God,' as a 'hobbling crotchet[p];' he has learnt 'to substitute an intelligent loyalty to his Great Master for an indiscriminating adhesion to every scrap of Evangelical testimony respecting Him[q];' he even avows that 'the concurrence of all ancient MSS. would scarcely suffice' to warrant a reading to which he objects on subjective grounds[r].

Dr. Vance Smith, with, as it appears, a stronger interest in the positive worth of the Bible, arrives at a practical estimate of it which does not much differ from that of the 'Clergyman.' The Bampton Lecturer had referred to the unity of Scripture; and for a moment Dr. Vance Smith is attracted towards this truth as 'an interesting and suggestive idea.' But he presently gives a list of books of Holy Scripture between which, as he thinks, 'the only relation existing is simply one of incompatibility, or of marked antagonism; or else again there is no sort of describable relation at all, the one book simply standing apart in absolute independence, and ignoring the existence of the other[s].' If this be an accurate statement, it is natural to enquire on what defensible ground we continue to speak of this collection of books as 'the Bible,' or 'Holy Scripture,' and whether such titles do not suggest a unity of purpose and design, which, as we are now told, does not in fact exist? When Dr. Vance Smith says that, 'in all probability the whole [of the Old Testament] was in great measure the growth or accumulation of successive ages, without much design on the part of any person con-

[k] Examination, p. 44.

[l] Reference has already been made to Biesenthal's recent *Trostschreiben des Apostels Paulus an die Hebräer*, Leipsig, 1878, Einl. iii. 7, for a powerful argument in favour of the Pauline authorship of this Epistle.

[m] Examination, p. 115. [n] Ibid. p. 115. [o] Ibid. p. 116.

[p] Ibid. p. 199. [q] Ibid. p. 202. [r] Ibid. p. 151.

[s] The Bible and Popular Theology, pp. 8, 16, 17.

cerned[t],' and that the Old Testament comes before us 'simply as being the whole of the remaining literature of the nation, written in their ancient language[u],' it is obvious that he differs fundamentally from the Apostolic judgments that 'whatsoever things were written aforetime were written for our learning, that we through patience and comfort of the Scriptures might have hope[v],' and that 'all Scripture,' namely of the Old Testament, 'is given by inspiration of God[w].' Indeed, his theories as to the dates and worth of the Old Testament books[x] seem to be, not seldom, as in the case of Daniel, inconsistent with belief in the inspired writer's literary honesty; and, in the same way, he holds that 'some of the minor Epistles of St. Paul are extremely doubtful, or almost certainly not from the pen of the great Apostle, according to the judgment of the most competent and freeminded modern investigators[y].' He leaves it doubtful whether he fully accepts Baur's estimate of the New Testament in detail and as a whole; but he holds that 'the larger number of the New Testament writings may be said to be of doubtful or unknown authorship[z].'

It is, perhaps, in keeping with Dr. Vance Smith's theory of the date and origin of St. John's Gospel that he observes that 'the peculiar conceptions of the Fourth Evangelist are altogether alien to the others[a].' Here he is naturally embarrassed by our Lord's solemn words which are reported in St. Matt. xi. 27, St. Luke x. 22. 'The verse,' he says, 'in both Evangelists interrupts the strain of the Gospel, and looks strangely out of place, though it would have been perfectly suitable to John[b].' 'A singular verse,' he exclaims, in a later passage, 'which looks as if by some chance it had been transferred from the Fourth Gospel[c].' Yet there it is, in the Synoptists; and, as we may observe, in those two Evangelists who describe our Lord's miraculous Conception and Birth of a Virgin Mother. But, according to Dr. Vance Smith, these portions of the Gospel narrative 'are most probably to be regarded as non-authentic additions to the original form of the two Gospels, although it is nevertheless

[t] The Bible and Popular Theology, p. 6. [u] Ibid. p. 6.
[v] Rom. xv. 4. [w] 2 Tim. iii. 16.
[x] The Bible and Popular Theology, pp. 2, 3. Dr. Vance Smith appears generally to follow Dr. S. Davidson. [y] Ibid. p. 5.
[z] Ibid. pp. 4, 5. In saying that 'nearly the whole of the N. T. belongs to the first century, with the exception of St. John,' Dr. Vance Smith, of course, declines to accept the more advanced Tübingen theory.
[a] Ibid. p. 178. [b] Ibid. p. 109, note. [c] Ibid. p. 178, note.

true that they are found in all existing manuscripts and versions of those Gospels[d].'

After this it is perhaps not surprising to find that our Lord was too ignorant, in the judgment of our critic, to be a safe guide as to the worth of the Old Testament Scriptures. 'There can,' he says, 'be no good reason to think that the knowledge or the ignorance of Christ was not of the same character which belonged to his age and country, or that he did not participate in the prevailing ideas and feelings respecting the ancient Scriptures and the use that might be made of them[e].' Accordingly, Dr. Vance Smith proceeds to infer that Christ 'would accept the statements of the Old Testament in popular senses; would take passages as Messianic because such was their usual acceptation, and because as the son of devout parents, familiar with the sacred books of their people, he had been educated to do so. We may further understand how it was that he could apply passages usually considered Messianic to the incidents of his own career. So to do was in accordance with the common habit of the time, was justified by it, was its inevitable consequence. It was, we may believe, with Jesus Christ much as with a religious man of our own day and nation. Such a person, trained from childhood to believe the popular theology of the time, will necessarily express himself on religious subjects in accordance with his belief, and quote the words of either Testament according to the meaning which he has been taught to put on them, and this he will do with perfect truthfulness and innocence[f].'

If our Divine Master was thus ignorant, both of the real worth and character of the Old Testament and of the use to be made of it, a similar or greater ignorance might naturally be expected in the case of the Apostles. Dr. Vance Smith therefore devotes the fourth and two following chapters of his work to this subject, with the general result of rejecting, as uncritical, the estimate of the Old Testament which Christians are taught to entertain by the writers of the New[g].

[d] The Bible and Popular Theology, pp. 102, 103.

[e] Ibid. p. 63.

[f] Ibid. p. 64.

[g] Dr. Vance Smith's repeated reference to the 'wise men' as quoting the prophet Micah (p. 54), seems to the present writer a less serious kind of mistake than that which underlies such a passage as the following:— 'The "Blood" of "God" may have been a bearable expression to the Bishops and Fathers who assembled at Nicæa. It is most probable that the nineteenth century will increasingly revolt from it, and come at last to see that even the authority of the two oldest manuscripts is insufficient

It is no part of the Lecturer's object to exhibit the opinions of his critics in an invidious light. In our day, assuredly, no writer loses caste by expressing his disbelief in the Divine authority of Holy Scripture. But enough has been said to shew that the Lecturer and his critics, in appealing to the Bible, do not appeal to a common premise: and that their criticism upon his Lectures, in effect, amounts to saying that he has made a mistake in the choice of a subject. In order to convince them, he ought to have discussed, not the Divinity of our Lord as taught in Holy Scripture, but the reasonableness and trustworthiness of Holy Scripture itself; and to do this at all adequately, as matters stand, would take not one but several sets of Bampton Lectures.

II. The 'Clergyman' maintains that the Bampton Lecturer is open to the charge of professing to appeal to Scripture reasonably interpreted, while in reality he is guided by the Creeds and doctrinal teaching of the Catholic Church. 'The Lecturer,' he says, 'proffers his dogma to be tested by the Bible, thoroughly investigated and reasonably understood. To prove his confidence justified and his conclusions sustained by the Bible is the one great end of his carefully compiled, and, from his own side, virtually exhaustive pleadings. If he had not chosen to stand thus on indefensible ground, I should not have ventured to criticise his lectures. Against the evidence for the doctrine of our Lord's Deity regarded as a revelation through the Church, or as resting on ecclesiastical authority, I have said nothing. The Christian Church is as grand a fact in the world's history as is the Bible, and with reference to the doctrine under consideration, the mind of the Church Universal has long displayed a perspicuity, explicitness, and uniformity of expression, of which the Bible is conspicuously destitute [h].'

This criticism is repeated by the 'Clergyman' in other, and sometimes less temperate, language elsewhere [i].

Thus, for example: 'I only contend that in Scripture alone, it [the doctrine of our Lord's Divinity] has no adequate logical basis, and cannot possibly be deduced by methods of rational interpretation. Assume there is in the Church an authority, co-ordinate with, and in some respects superior to, Scripture, and, so far as I am concerned, the controversy is at an end. I

to justify its acceptance' (p. 184). This reading is retained by Westcott and Hort, New Test., Cambr. 1881.

[h] Examination, p. 2.

[i] Ibid. pp. 3, 27.

do not wish to enter upon the question whether the claims of Church authority can be satisfactorily vindicated. Mr. Liddon exposes himself to criticism by not avowing that he interprets from the ground of ecclesiastical light and prerogative, not from the ground of reason. He wants to be thought rational when he is ecclesiastical, but the two conditions are different; the latter is held by many to be the nobler and more enlightened condition, but it is specifically distinct from the former[j].'

Here, perhaps, it might be sufficient to reply that, as might be inferred from what has been already said, the real fault of the Lectures in the 'Clergyman's' eyes is, that they assume that trustworthiness of Scripture which their critic impugns:—'In assuming the Gospels, and more especially the last of them, to furnish verbally correct accounts of Christ's sayings, Mr. Liddon has followed a method which vitiates all his reasonings. With the essentially Protestant and rational criticism by which time-honoured assumptions about the Bible have been besieged and curtailed, he makes only a semblance of grappling[k].'

Again: 'Unless we are content to resign our reason and judgment in deference to some higher authority, a choice between the guidance of the Fourth Gospel and the prior narrations is here forced upon us. From which are we to collect our dogmatic knowledge of Christ's personal rank? The writer of the last Gospel does more than supplement his predecessors: if the orthodox interpretation of his language is right, he corrects them, and takes ground which convicts them not merely of reservation, but of ignorance and blundering on a vital point. For Protestants who hold Scripture to be the Divine and sufficient Rule of Faith, there is no way of escape: they must either esteem the Logos doctrine a misty speculation, or depress other portions of the New Testament, while they exalt what they conceive to be a contribution from St. John[l].'

It may be needless to say that the Lecturer does not accept this account of the relation of St. John to the earlier Evangelists, and for reasons which appear to him to be very sufficient. He quotes this and the preceding passage in order to shew the real character of his difference with the 'Clergyman.' That difference mainly turns, not as the 'Clergyman' suggests, upon the existence and character of the Church's authority in questions of doctrine, but upon the trustworthiness of Scripture as the most authoritative source of our knowledge of doctrine. The 'Clergy-

[j] Examination, p. 118. [k] Ibid. p. 44. [l] Ibid. p. 86.

man' at the same time, but unintentionally, misrepresents the attitude of the Bampton Lecturer towards Church authority. If the Lecturer had learnt from the Church of England that 'Holy Scripture containeth all things necessary to salvation[m],' he had also learnt from her that the Church 'hath authority in controversies of faith[n]'; and, in view of the real history of the formation of the Canon of the New Testament, the last proposition is at least as reasonable and as certain as the first.

To accept the Church's guidance in recognising the contents and the authoritative character of the Canon of Scripture, and then to refuse her any voice whatever in its interpretation, seems to the present writer impossible; and if he has, in his Lectures, appealed to the natural force of Scripture language, this has not been in any spirit of fancied independence of Church authority, but because he sincerely believes that there is no real antithesis between the judgments of that authority in ages when it was still unimpaired by division, and an honest criticism of the Sacred Text. The function of Church authority, as it was understood by such writers as St. Irenæus, was not to add new doctrine to the Apostolic deposit, as the 'Clergyman' apparently supposes, but to shew what the Apostolic deposit really does contain; to take mankind, as it were, by the hand when exploring the vast field of Scripture; to call attention to expressions, or occurrences, or lines of thought which might otherwise escape observation; and thus to furnish the reader, not with additional material, but with a true point of view, and a sympathetic intellectual and moral temper, for discovering those profound unities and truths for the sake of which alone the Church sets value on Scripture at all. The Christian Revelation was in fact committed, not only to the pages of a Sacred Book, but to the guardianship of a Sacred Society; and the second factor can just as little be dispensed with as the first. If the Church may not contradict or exceed the teaching of the Book, the true authority and import of the Book cannot be long upheld apart from that illuminated consciousness of the Church, which originally recognised it as being the Word of God.

This consideration will perhaps explain a feature of the Lectures on which the 'Clergyman' has felt it to be his duty to comment, again and again, with much severity. The Lecturer has called attention very deliberately, not only to the great dogmatic passages in which Our Lord's Divinity is expressly

[m] Art. VI. [n] Art. XX.

taught, but to that much larger number of passages or even paragraphs in which it is so far implied that, while of themselves they do not prove the doctrine, they look, so to speak, towards it, and are read most naturally, if we assume that it is true. The 'Clergyman' often discusses the reference made to such passages in the Lectures, as if the Lecturer had appealed to them as *dicta probantia*, and had thus put a strain on them which, obviously, they cannot bear. Their real place in the argument is supplemental and subsidiary; and if they were not accompanied or rather introduced by explicit statements of another character, they could not be appealed to at all. But, as the Lecturer conceives, their cumulative force is very great, and as the 'Clergyman' truly observes, the Lecturer cannot be 'charged with originating the use [o]' which he has made of them. He has learnt this 'use' from the authority to which alone he owes it that he receives the Bible as the Word of God, in any serious sense, at all; while reflection has not brought with it any distrust either of his teacher or her lessons.

At the same time the writer must not shrink from professing his conviction that, if there were no Church at all to guide him, the natural sense of such passages as Rom. ix. 5, or of Col. i. 15–17, or of St. John i. 1–14, is that our Lord Jesus Christ is of one Substance with the Father, Very and Eternal God. If the 'Clergyman' would consider Philippi's [p] commentary on the first of these passages, or Bishop Lightfoot's [q] on the second, or Professor Westcott's [r] on the third, he would perhaps feel that there is more to be said in favour of this conclusion than he has hitherto been able to admit. But, in the absence of faith in the trustworthiness of Scripture, no critical insight into the real scope of its language would be of much service. According to the 'Clergyman,' the 'really Scriptural position' is, 'that Christ fills, in the scale of being, a place not perfectly defined, but certainly above man, and as certainly beneath God [s].' This, as he elsewhere says, is the Arian Creed; and it is open, as has been urged in these Lectures, to the grave objection that it could not have been held by serious Monotheists, such as were the Apostles of our Lord. But in a note the 'Clergyman' explains that the formula above cited is only tenable 'if every statement

[o] Examination, p. 44.
[p] Comment. on the Romans in loc.
[q] Epistle to the Colossians in loc.
[r] Gospel of St. John (Speaker's Commentary), in loc.
[s] Examination, p. 248.

of Scripture is accepted in its natural rational meaning with unquestioning acquiescence.' He adds 'The Christ of an uncritical Biblical Protestantism is an Arian, superhuman Christ. The Christ of a critical Protestantism is a merely human, but extraordinarily endowed Christ[t].' It is difficult to see why he should, upon the 'Clergyman's' principles, be even as much as this: but the avowal shews that, even after the sense of Scripture has been minimized by negative criticisms to a point which is fatal to all that is most precious in the Christian Creed, the little that remains is after all peremptorily rejected, and we are left with an estimate of the Divine Saviour of the world which might have been gathered not less readily from the Koran than from the New Testament.

Enough, perhaps, has been said to shew that the Lecturer has carefully considered what his critics have had to say about him. He has indeed read them through attentively. And if he does not farther accompany them, they will believe that this is not from any disrespect, but partly because a large book would be needed in order to discuss some far-reaching questions which they severally raise, and partly because, as has been already suggested, a large proportion of his differences with them in detail are due to earlier and deeper differences of principle. But there are some matters of detail which he has been led to reconsider in the light of their criticisms, and it is a pleasure to express his obligation to both of them, but especially to the 'Clergyman,' for corrections which his book thus owes to them, in its present form.

[t] Examination, p. 248, note.

INDEX.

The numerals refer to the Lectures, the figures to the pages.

D.

E.

F.

G.

H.

I.

J.

R.

T.

INDEX OF PASSAGES IN HOLY SCRIPTURE QUOTED OR REFERRED TO.

ST. MARK.

ST. LUKE.

St. John.

Acts.

2 CORINTHIANS.

GALATIANS.

EPHESIANS.

Printed in Great Britain
by Amazon

22657213R00344